The Collected Wor Reeve: The Muggletonian Prophet

Edited by Mike Pettit

Visit us online at www.muggletonianpress.com **and view our entire range of Muggletonian Literature**

A Muggletonian Press Book

ISBN 978-1-907466-00-7

Cover Image: plate 9 from Isaac Frost's "Two Systems of Astrology" published in 1846, depicting Muggletonian cosmology.

Published by:
Muggletonian Press
129 Hebdon Road
London SW17 7NL
England

I would like to make it clear that in editing and publishing this volume I am not seeking to advocate any element of Muggletonian theology. I fully subscribe to historic orthodox Christianity as expressed in the Reformed Confessions of Faith and would plead with all the readers of this work to consider those sacred claims.

From the Heidelberg Catechism

Question 1. What is thy only comfort in life and death?

Answer: That I with body and soul, both in life and death, am not my own, but belong unto my faithful Saviour Jesus Christ; who, with his precious blood, has fully satisfied for all my sins, and delivered me from all the power of the devil; and so preserves me that without the will of my heavenly Father, not a hair can fall from my head; yea, that all things must be subservient to my salvation, and therefore, by his Holy Spirit, He also assures me of eternal life, and makes me sincerely willing and ready, henceforth, to live unto him.

Mike Pettit

Contents

A LETTER TO THE BRETHREN 91

A DIVINE LOOKING-GLASS 95

Introduction

On each of the three mornings of the 3rd, 4th and 5th February 1651 John Reeve heard Jesus speak to him in an audible voice.

The message on the first morning was:

> "I have given thee understanding of my mind in the Scriptures, above all men in the world. Look into thine own body; there thou shalt see the kingdom of heaven, and the kingdom of hell. I have chosen thee my last messenger for a great work, unto this bloody unbelieving world; and I have given thee Lodowick Muggleton to be thy mouth. I have put the two-edged sword of my Spirit into thy mouth, that whoever I pronounce blessed through thy mouth, is blessed to eternity; and whoever I pronounce cursed through thy mouth, is cursed to eternity. If thou dost not obey my voice, and go wherever I send thee, to deliver my message, thy body shall be thy hell, and thy spirit shall be the devil that shall torment thee to eternity."

The message on the second morning was:

> "Go thou unto Lodowick Muggleton, and with him go unto Thomas Turner, and he shall bring you to one John Tane, and do thou deliver my message when thou comest there; and if Lodowick Muggleton deny to go with thee, then do thou from me pronounce him cursed to eternity."

On the third morning the message was:

> "Go thou unto Lodowick Muggleton, and take such a woman along with thee; and then go thou unto one John Robins, a prisoner in New Bridewell, and do thou deliver my message to him when thou comest there."

Muggleton went with Reeve and from that moment they received revelations such that they declared themselves the Two Witnesses as spoken of in the eleventh chapter of the book of Revelation.

The two prophets slowly gathered a following, reserving particular scorn for the Quakers whose abhorrent doctrines they despised. The Muggletonians (as they were eventually to be called) believed:

   i. That the spirit could be separated from the body
  ii. That God was as a man in size and features
 iii. That Heaven was six miles above the earth
 iv. The sun and moon were no bigger than they looked from earth
  v. That Jesus was the man God, who left Moses and Elijah in charge of Heaven when he came to Earth.
 vi. That God takes no immediate notice of man, prayers and religious services being merely superstition.

Reeve's first book "A Transcendent Spiritual Treatise" was published in 1652 followed by "A General Epistle from the Holy Spirit" in 1653, declaring the Commission and instructing all ministers to cease preaching on pain of damnation (as they did not hold a proper commission).

Both the Prophets were jailed for six months in 1654. During this ordeal "A Remonstrance from the Eternal God" was published. Reeve continued his writing and "The Divine Looking-Glass" was published in 1656, shortly afterward Reeve fell sick and suffered a prolonged illness, however even in his ill health he continued to write both books and letters, publishing "Joyful News from Heaven" shortly before his death in 1658. In 1706 Reeves remaining unpublished works were published in the posthumous "Sacred Remains"

On the death of Reeve in 1658 Muggleton inherited the sole leadership of the movement and wrote several books setting out his message ("A True Interpretation of the Eleventh Chapter of the Revelation of Saint John" in 1662 and "A True interpretation of the Revelation of Saint John" in 1665) and in particular disputing with the Quakers ("The Neck of the Quakers Broken" in 1663), debating with both George Fox ("A Looking-Glass for George Fox" in 1668) and William Penn ("An Answer to William Penn" in 1673). Muggleton was especially active in writing letters to his disciples and the movement slowly grew, although its numbers never grew to number more than a few hundred at any one time.

Muggleton developed Muggletonian doctrine ("A True Interpretation of the Witch of Endor" in 1669 that courageously denounced the murderous pursuit of witches). He built on Reeve's proclamation that all ministers of religion were damned by including the three professions in such a verdict and developing a vitriolic hatred of the Scots. Muggleton's leading lieutenant (Clarkson) attempted to take control of the movement but was rebuffed, eventually showing penitence at the end. A more serious revolt by Medgate and his (Scotch) allies was also crushed.

Muggleton was sent to the Stocks in 1676, a very disagreeable experience for someone in their mid 60's, but he continued to tend his flock with little desire to gain new converts, eventually departing this life in 1698 with his posthumous autobiography "The Acts of the Witnesses of the Spirit" being published in 1699. A further volume "An Answer to Isaac Pennington" written in 1669 was finally published in 1719.

The sect continued under the guidance of Muggletons disciples who took steps to republish the prophets writings in the following century with the letters of Muggleton and Reeve, (collected with great care by Alexander Delamaine) being published in 1755 as "A Volume of Spiritual Epistles", further letters being published in "A Stream from the Tree of Life" in 1758. The membership was now largely located in the independent centers of London and Derby. The London Church was revitalised by the migration of the Frosts from Derby to London where the wealth created by their brass foundry bankrolled a huge republishing effort in the mid 19th century, including the publication of the prophets' letters that were as yet still unpublished in a "Supplement to the Book of Letters" in 1831.

The vast efforts put into modernising the Church failed to expand membership and the sect shrank into obscurity. Alexander Gordon (a prominent Unitarian minister and academic) uncovered the sect, writing about them in 1869 and 1870. Gordon also recorded notable Muggletonians as part of his great and notable contribution to the Dictionary of National Biography, the entry for John Reeve being reproduced in this volume. Sporadic further interest was shown in the Church into the early years of the 20th century. The Church's London meeting room was destroyed in the blitz and the movement began to fade away, with the last known Muggletonian passing away in 1979. Luckily this was not before the archives of the Church (which had been rescued from the bombed out ruins of the meeting room) had been located and presented to the British Museum.

It was the hope of the Muggletonians that at the least their doctrines would survive in print; hopefully this volume helps to achieve their aim.

The Muggletonians were not orthodox Christians and cannot claim to be part of the Church of Jesus Christ. While it is true that there is no salvation outside the Church, we all rest on the mercy of God for our salvation through the blood of his son Jesus Christ, a salvation that we do not earn or deserve by either works or doctrine.

This volume includes all the surviving writings of John Reeve, including the works he co-authored with his fellow Prophet, Lodowick Muggleton. The letters authored by Reeve (or in one case recording one of his debates) have also been extracted from their respective collections and are included in this volume.

I am not attempting to make any theological point by isolating Reeve's works from Muggleton's later works and revisions, the separation is merely due to the practicalities of publishing. I intend to reprint the full Muggletonian canon in due course, together with the historical works written either by Muggletonians, by Muggletonian anti-followers, about Muggletonians or against Muggletonians.

Most notably this volume includes:

- The original 1656 text of "A Divine Looking-Glass", making the full original text available for the first time since 1760.

- A copy of the letter issued to the Church by the Frost's in 1853, pleading that Muggleton's 1661 revision of "A Divine Looking-Glass" be the only acceptable text. This letter has never before been published.

- Six full volumes of Reeve's works presented in chapter and verse, as they were published by the Frosts in the nineteenth century together with Reeve's letters extracted from a further three volumes.

The works reproduced in these volumes have been freshly retypeset and while they are not facsimiles they do follow the same style as their source editions. In transcribing these volumes I have not updated the language or spellings, with the exception of replacing the archaic "f" with "s" where appropriate (a written convention that is confusing and unhelpful to the modern eye). I have corrected some egregious spelling mistakes (where there is no question of the spelling merely being archaic), especially where I was able to consult previous editions for confirmation of the original texts. If my text appears to be in error it is most likely that this "error" is a historical one of the original text, I apologise for any errors that I am responsible for and will seek to correct such errors in subsequent editions of this volume.

This volume contains the following works:

THE DICTIONARY OF NATIONAL BIOGRAPHY

This entry for John Reeve in Volume 47, pages 408 and 409 of "The Dictionary of National Biography" (published in 1896) was written by The Rev. Alexander Gordon, the Muggletonian biographer and great confidant of the Muggletonian Church.

It is this link between Gordon and the Church that makes his insights so valuable and unique; he had access to the oral history and traditions of the Church, a history that has now been lost or obscured.

A TRANSCENDENT SPIRITUAL TREATISE

This work was written in 1652 and has since been republished in 1711, 1756, 1822, 1846 and 1857.

It was John Reeve's first work, setting out the revelation as revealed to John Reeve.

A recurring theme is that each of Reeve's insights was a "revelation of the holy spirit". That for fourteen hundred years (that is since the commission of blood under the apostles) there has "not been one true prophet nor minister". These revelations were not up for discussion.

The work sets out the nature of his revelation, the first lesson (following the actual commission) being the nature of hell with the key revelation being that the devil is internal to man.

The work spends time explaining the nature of God, matter, angels the devil and man. The sin of Satan is now the sin living in man, the devil having transformed himself from a being into the sinful nature present in every man. It is spiritual food that keeps the angels pure; this food (of revelation) was kept from Satan.

> "his spirit began proudly to imagine and think high and lofty thoughts concerning his own person and great wisdom of spirit within him"

This is the evil of "reason" that is the root of the seed of Cain. In chapter five Reeve continues to explain the effect on Adam and Eve:

> "being both defiled with the spirit of the serpent-angel of

unclean reason and wicked imagination; and this was the cursed effect of their becoming gods"

Here is the root of the key elements of Muggletonian theology, appearing to be the work of Reeve. At the time Muggleton appears to be only a mouthpiece and did not appear at that time to have been blessed with revelations of the Holy Spirit.

It is also interesting that right from the start the movement was pacifist, very different to the political maneuverings on this very point by the Quakers.

A GENERAL EPISTLE TO MINISTERS

This short work was written in 1653 and has since been republished in 1719, around 1831 and in 1854.

This second publication by the prophets followed "A Transcendent Spiritual Treatise" and sets out the central tenant that there can be no spirit without a body. The work further establishes the credentials of the prophets.

The lack of a proper commission for all other preachers is proclaimed, such un-commissioned ministers being ordered to desist from preaching or teaching. Failure to obey this message of the Holy Spirit was on pain of being cursed and damned, both soul and body, unto all eternity.

A REMONSTRANCE FROM THE ETERNAL GOD

This work was first published in 1653 and has since been republished in 1791, 1831 and 1854.

This work is directed at the government of England and starts by outlining the crimes of Tanee and Robbins. It then makes the claim concerning the two prophets:

> "That we two only are the last men that ever shall speak or write by commission from the true God unto the powers and people whilest the world endureth"

The work then goes on to list the six "spiritual things" that the Lord has sent the prophets to declare (Chapter II v15):

> "The which blessed Spirit Both enable a man to declare to the sensible understanding of men what the person of God is,

and his divine nature; and what the persons of holy angels are, and their natures; and what the person of the devil was before his fall, and what his person is and shall be to eternity; and what condition Adam was created in, and how he came to fall; also, what the glory of heaven is, and the residence of it to eternity; and what hell and eternal death is, and the place of it to eternity."

The work then recaps the previous letter to ministers and the nature and unjustness of the Prophets trial and imprisonment.

A LETTER TO THE BRETHREN

Muggletonianism has always faced a continuing tension between those who regard the equality of the prophets in all matters to be a doctrinal necessity and those who believe that Muggleton's alleged revisions of Reeve's revelation to be open to question.

The only area where Muggleton openly disagreed with Reeve concerned whether God took "immediate notice" of his creation. Muggleton went as far as revising the 1656 first edition of the "Divine Looking-Glass" to excise passages that supported the notion of immediate notice or reflected what was perhaps on reflection an unwise allegiance to Cromwell's Protectorate.

This tension often surfaced when The Divine Looking-Glass was republished, as happened when the ultra-orthodox Frost's realized, with horror, that when publishing their mammoth three volume collected Works in 1832 they had inadvertently included the 1656 text of Divine Looking-Glass rather than Muggleton's 1661 revision.

In a letter of 24th Feb 1853 to the Principal Librarian of the British Museum Joseph Frost requested that the "Letter to the Brethren" which is reproduced in this volume be fastened to the libraries copy of the 1656 text of The Divine Looking-Glass that had been included in their Volume 1 of "The Works".

A DIVINE LOOKING-GLASS

This volume is the major theological work of Muggletonianism, it appears to be mostly the work of John Reeve, restating and reinforcing previous theological positions covering the major tenants of Muggletonianism; namely the physical nature of God, the nature of the angels, the nature of man, the two seeds, the commission and the natures of heaven and hell.

No copies of the original 1656 text have survived, and indeed in the "Acts of The Witnesses" Muggleton records a great dissatisfaction with that edition at chapter 4 verse 27:

> "But the printer being knavish and covetous, quite spoiled it in the press, he hudled it up so close together, for want of more paper, that nobody had any delight to read it through, so that it never yielded the mony it cost to print"

The work was altered slightly by Muggleton for the 1661 printing, chiefly to remove the glowing reference to Cromwell which was no longer wise due to the restoration as well as what some saw as strengthening his own position regarding the vexed question of "immediate notice".

Republications in 1719 and 1760 reprinted the original 1656 edition, although both differ in presentation and in some minor details, while the 1661 revision was finally reprinted in 1846.

The edition reproduced here consists of the 1846 edition (i.e. Muggleton's 1661 revision); however, I have restored those passages and sections excised from the 1760 edition (i.e. the original 1656 text), annotating the text accordingly. This has necessitated some amendments to verse numbers but such alterations have been annotated in the text.

JOYFUL NEWS FROM HEAVEN

This work was written in 1658 and has since been republished in 1706, the 1750's and in 1854.

This 1854 edition includes a forward where Joseph Frost sets out the Muggletonians' support for both the Book of Enoch and The Testament of the Twelve Patriarchs as being canonical.

This work specifically seeks to explain "How the soul dieth in the body" and then goes on to set out at some length the nature of worship and continues with a spirited and extended assault on the Baptists.

Most of the arguments contained in this book are repeated from the previous works; in particular the assault on the Baptists is really an extension of "A General Epistle to Ministers" in claiming that a specific commission is required in order to preach.

This was Reeve's last work, the frail prophet not living to see the entirety of his work in print.

Letters from "A VOLUME OF SPIRITUAL EPISTLES"

This work was first published in1755 and was republished in 1820. The full text of 619 pages was comprised mainly of Muggleton's letters, but five of Reeves letters were also included, which are reproduced here.

Letters from "A STREAM FROM THE TREE OF LIFE"

This work was published in1758, containing seventeen letters. The seven written by Reeve and a further letter recording Reeve's discourse with a merchant are reproduced here.

Letters from "SUPPLEMENT TO THE BOOK OF LETTERS"

This work was published in 1831, The Frosts' preface being self explanatory:

"WITH the authority of the Church we have made diligent search through the Manuscript Records of the Church, and have found the following Letters, not in print in the" Book of Letters." The following Letters may be considered the conclusion of all the Writings of the Prophets REEVE and MUGGLETON both of spiritual matter and temporal advice, as far as the Church is in possession of'

This work contained two of Reeve's letters which are reproduced in this volume.

EXTRACTS FROM "SACRED REMAINS"

This work was originally published in 1706, being reprinted in the same format on one undated further occasion (which can be found in the 1832 publication of "The Works").

A final republication split the work into two sections (Epistles and Extracts), the epistles being published in 1854 and the extracts being published in 1856 with "A General Epistle to Ministers".

This section comprises the "Extracts" taken from the 1854 volume.

EPISTLES FROM "SACRED REMAINS"

This work was originally published in 1706, being reprinted on a further occasion (which can be found in the 1832 publication of "The Works").

A final republication split the work onto two sections (Epistles and Extracts), the epistles being published in 1854 and the extracts being published in 1856.

This section comprises of the "Epistles" taken from the 1854 edition

THE DICTIONARY OF NATIONAL BIOGRAPHY

REEVE, JOHN (1608-1658), sectary, second son of Walter Reeve, gentleman, was born in Wiltshire in 1608. His father, who is described as 'clerk to a deputy of Ireland,' was of a good family which had fallen to decay. With his elder brother, William, he was apprenticed in London to the tailor's trade. He was 'no Latin scholar,' but his handwriting shows that he had received a fair education. Both brothers were originally puritans, and both fell away, about 1645, to the 'ranters.' This was the ruin of William, who neglected his business, became a mere sot, and subsisted on charity. Joint Reeve, under the guidance of John Robins [q.v.], known as 'the ranters' god,' became a universalist. His cousin, Lodowicke Muggleton [q.v.], had been William Reeve's journeyman in 1631, but there seems to have been no great intimacy between Muggleton and John Reeve till about twenty years later. In April 1651 Muggleton believed himself the subject of an inward illumination, opening to him the meaning of scripture. This attracted Reeve, who constantly visited at Muggleton's house in Great Trinity Lane, and wearied him with questions. About the middle of January 1652 Reeve suddenly announced his own experience of similar illumination. His immediate re-solve was 'to meddle no more with religion . . . but to get as good a livelihood as I can in this world, and let God alone with what shall be hereafter.' A fortnight later (3 Feb.) he alleged a call 'by voice of words' from heaven, constituting him the Lord's last messenger,' with Muggleton as his 'mouth.' Next morning a similar voice sent him, with Muggleton, to deal with Thomas Tany [q.v.], the ranter; on the third day the cousins were despatched on a like errand to Robins. This ended the series of communications.

Reeve and Muggleton now presented themselves as the 'two witnesses' (Rev. xi. 3), printed their 'commission book,' obtained a following, and excited odium. Unfriendly critics hooted Reeve with the cry, 'There goes the prophet that damns people;' boys pelted him in St. Paul's Churchyard. A warrant was obtained by Goslin (a clergyman), Ebb (an exciseman), Chandler (a shopkeeper), and two soldiers, charging the witnesses' with blasphemous denial of the Trinity. They were imprisoned from 15 Sept. 1653 till April 1654. In Newgate they fared ill, and were badly used by their fellow-prisoners. Three wild highwaymen tried to hang Reeve. The confinement told upon his health, which was never robust.

In 1656 he visited Maidstone, but left in haste to avoid a threatened arrest. He reached Gravesend, where he took boat when overheated, caught a chill, and fell into a consumption. For two years he lingered in a wasting condition, unable to work, dependent on the earnings of his wife and daughter, and ultimately on the contributions of friends. After his wife's death, on 29 March 1658, he visited Cambridge; returning to London, he lodged with three sisters, Mrs. Frances, Mrs. Roberts, and Mrs. Boner, who kept a semptress's shop in Bishopsgate Street, near Hog Lane end. Ann Adams (afterwards the wife of William Cakebread of Orwell, Cambridgeshire) was 'his handmaid to guide him to other friends' houses.' He died at the latter end of July 1658; 'Frances,' he said,' close up mine eyes, lest mine enemies say I died a staring prophet.' He was buried in Bethlehem new churchyard (in what is now Liverpool Street).

The 'six foundations' of the Muggletonian theology were formulated by Reeve. His most original position is the doctrine of the two seeds' in man, a divine element and a diabolic, one of which obtains the mastery. By this conception, elaborated in a peculiar vein of mysticism, he found a way out of universalism, for 'damnation would be impossible, if all sprang from one root.' Other points of doctrine, common to both, are specified in the article on Muggleton. Reeve, however, retained, while Muggleton rejected, the doctrine of the divine notice of human affairs, and accessibility to prayer. His writings are not without passages of considerable beauty; their tone is much more subdued and suasive than that of Muggleton. The contrast between their respective addresses to Isaac Penington the younger [q.v.] is very marked; Reeve sympathises with quaker tendencies, which Muggleton flouts and scorns. There have always been followers of Reeve (known as Reevites and Reevonians) who have held aloof from the thoroughgoing Muggletonians.

The following works are by Reeve and Muggleton, but chiefly by Reeve. The dates of first editions are given, all quarto, and all except No, 7 without publisher's or printer's name: 1. 'A transcendent Spirituall Treatise,' &c., 1652. 2. 'A General Epistle from the holy Ghost,' &c., 1653. 3. 'A Letter presented unto Alderman Fouke,' &c., 1653. 4. 'A Divine Looking-Glass,' &c., 1656. Posthumous publications, containing letters and papers by Reeve are: 5. 'A Volume of Spiritual Epistles,' &c., 1755. 6. 'A Stream from the Tree of Life,' &c., 1758. 7. 'A Supplement to the Book of Letters,' &c., 1831. The following are by Reeve alone: 8. 'Joyful News from Heaven or the Soul's Mortality proved,' &c., 1658; and a posthumous collection of papers, 9. 'Sacred Remains, or a Divine Appendix,' &c., 1706 (written in 1652-7); another edition 1751.

Another John Reeve, author of 'Spiritual Hymns upon Solomon's Song,' 1693, 12mo, was a general baptist minister at Bessel's Green, Kent.

[Muggleton's Acts of the Witnesses, 1699; The Origin of the Muggletonians, and Ancient and Modern Muggletonians, in Transactions of Liverpool Literary and Philosophical Society, 1869 and 1870; Reeve's Works; manuscript records of the Muggletonian body. For the bibliography of Reeve's writings, see Smith's Bibliotheca Anti-Quakeriana, 1873.]

A. G.

A
TRANSCENDENT
SPIRITUAL TREATISE,

UPON

SEVERAL HEAVENLY DOCTRINES,

FROM

THE HOLY SPIRIT OF THE MAN JESUS, THE ONLY TRUE GOD

SENT UNTO ALL HIS ELECT,

AS

A TOKEN OF HIS ETERNAL LOVE UNTO THEM BY THE HAND OF HIS OWN PROPHET, BEING HIS LAST MESSENGER, AND WITNESS, AND FORERUNNER OF THE VISIBLE APPEARING OF THE DISTINCT PERSONAL GOD IN POWER AND GREAT GLORY, IN THE CLOUDS OF HEAVEN, WITH HIS TEN THOUSANDS OF PERSONAL SAINTS, TO SEPARATE BETWEEN THE ELECT WORLD, AND THE REPROBATE WORLD, TO ALL ETERNITY;

CONTAINING

THOSE SEVERAL HEADS SET DOWN IN THE INDEX
OF THIS WORK.

JOHN REEVE & LODOWICK MUGGLETON,
The two last witnesses and true Prophets

OF

THE MAN JESUS, THE ONLY LORD OH LIFE AND GLORY, BENT BY HIS HOLY SPIRIT TO SEAL THE FOREHEADS OF THE ELECT, AND THE FOREHEADS OF THE REPROBATE, WITH THE ETERNAL SEALS OF LIFE AND DEATH; AND SUDDENLY AFTER WE HAVE DELIVERED THIS DREADFUL MESSAGE, THIS GOD, THE MAN JESUS, WILL VISIBLY APPEAR TO BEAR WITNESS WHETHER HE SENT US OR NOT.

Ye that are the Blessed shall patiently wait for the Truth of this thing.

Fifth Edition

CAREFULLY EXAMINED BY THE ORIGINAL, PRINTED IN CHAPTER FOR THE AUTHOR IN THE YEAR 1652, THEN RESIDENT IN LONDON; AND IS NOW PUT INTO VERSE, 1857.

LONDON:
PRINTED FOR JOSEPH FROST, BY ANDREW T. ROBERTS, HACKNEY ROAD,
OPPOSITE SHOREDITCH CHURCH.

1857.

AN EPISTLE

FROM

THE Holy Spirit of the Lord Jesus Christ, the eternal Father, written by the Lord's two last Witnesses and Prophets that ever shall declare the mind of God, the Man Jesus, that was crucified without the gates of Jerusalem; the Lord Jesus, by us, His poor despised Messengers, hath sent this writing unto the Christian world so called. Wherefore we declare, by virtue of our Commission given unto us by voice of words from the Holy Spirit of the Lord Jesus, from the throne of His glory, to make known His prerogative will and pleasure, both to the elect world and reprobate world, a little before His glorious coming to separate between the two worlds, that whosoever despiseth this writing, whether he be a king or a beggar, by calling it blasphemy, or heresy, or delusion, or a lie, or speaking evil of it in any kind whatsoever; in so doing they have committed that unpardonable sin against the Holy Ghost or Spirit that sent us. Wherefore, in obedience to our Commission from the Lord Jesus Christ, whom they have despised, and not us, we pronounce them cursed, both soul and body, from the presence of the Lord Jesus, elect Men, and Angels, to all eternity.

> JOHN REEVE and LODOWICK MUGGLETON, the Lord's two last true Witnesses and Prophets, spoken of in the Eleventh of Revelation, a little before the coming of Him that sent us, who is the Judge of both quick and dead.

————————

*** *The Printer of this edition was instructed to follow the original edition, printed for the Authors, as closely as possible.*

CONTENTS.

A
TRANSCENDENT
SPIRITUAL TREATISE,
&c.

CHAPTER I.

Of my Commission received by Voice of Words from the Spirit of the Man Jesus in Glory.

FEBRUARY the 3rd, 4th, and 5th, 1651, three mornings together, much about an hour, the Lord Jesus, the only wise God, whose glorious Person is resident above or beyond the stars;

2. I declare from the Spirit of truth, that this Jesus, from the throne of His glory, by voice of words, spake unto me John Reeve, saying: I have given thee understanding of my mind in the Scriptures, above all men in the world.

3. The next words the Lord spake unto me were these, saying: Look into thine own body; there thou shalt see the kingdom of heaven, and the kingdom of hell. The Lord spake unto me twice together.

4. Again, the Lord spake unto me these words, saying: I have chosen thee my last messenger for a great work, unto this bloody unbelieving world; and I have given thee Lodowick Muggleton to be thy mouth.

5. At that very moment the Holy Spirit brought into my mind that Scripture of Aaron given unto Moses.

6. Again, the Lord spake unto me these words, saying: I have put the two-edged sword of my Spirit into thy mouth, that whoever I pronounce blessed through thy mouth, is blessed to eternity; and whoever I pronounce cursed through thy mouth, is cursed to eternity.

7. When I heard these words, my spirit desired the Lord, that I might not be His dreadful messenger: for indeed I thought, upon the delivering of so sad and unexpected a message unto men, I should immediately have been torn in pieces.

8 Again, the Lord spoke unto me these words, saying: If thou dost not obey my voice, and go wherever I send thee, to deliver my message, thy body shall be thy hell, and thy spirit shall be the devil that shall torment thee to eternity.

9. Then for a moment I saw this hell within me, which caused me to answer the Lord these words, saying: Lord, I will go wherever thou sendest me; only be with me.

10. These were the Lord's words, spoken unto me the first morning, and my answer unto

my God; I being as perfectly awaked when He spoke unto me, the Lord is my witness, as I was at the writing hereof

11. Again the next morning the Lord spake unto me, saying, Go thou unto Lodowick Muggleton, and with him go unto Thomas Turner, and he shall bring you to one John Tane, and do thou deliver my message when thou comest there; and if Lodowick Muggleton deny to go with thee, then do thou from me pronounce him cursed to eternity.

12. These words the Lord spoke unto me the second morning and no more.

13. The third and last morning, the Lord spoke unto me these words, saying: Go thou unto Lodowick Muggleton, and take such a woman along with thee; and then go thou unto one John Robins, a prisoner in New Bridewell, and do thou deliver my message to him when thou comest there.

14. These were the Lord's words the third and last morning, and all the words in the commission of the Lord spoken unto me; only this message of the Lord extends in general to the whole world, because the elect Jews and Gentiles are mixed in marriages through all parts of this earth, for whose sakes only we are sent:

15. But as for those natural unbelieving Jews, that deny that God is come in flesh, those Jews shall never come to the faith of Jesus; we are not sent unto these.

16. The Holy Spirit beareth witness in my spirit of the truth of that which I shall write unto you, that the first words that the Lord spake unto me, the words speaking came into my spirit and body, with such an exceeding bright burning glory of God-like majesty, that I did not well know whether I was a mortal man or an immortal God;

17. So glorious are the words of the immortal God, that the tongues of men or angels can never express it;

18. My body also was changed at that time for a season in a most dreadful manner to behold, of which there be many that can bear witness, at this time.

19. Again, for your information that are spiritual, the Lord opened the understanding of my fellow witness, and made him obedient with me in the messages of the Lord, as Aaron's understanding was opened, to make him obedient with Moses in the messages of the Lord at that time.

20. And the Lord hath given him as glorious testimonies by revelation from his Holy Spirit, many a time, of the full assurance of this commission to be from the Lord, as ever the Lord gave to Aaron, to assure him that Moses's commission was from the Lord;

21. Only Moses's commission (he being the Lord's first com-missioner unto men) was mani-fested by natural signs, visibly upon the bodies of men and women;

22. And, on the contrary, we being the Lord's last commissioners, our commission is manifested by spiritual signs upon the invisible spirits of men and women, because our message is all spiritual, concerning men and women's eternal weal or woe in the life to come.

CHAPTER II.

Of the last great deceiving Antichrist, and Man of Sin, that ever shall be.

AGAIN, that you that are A elected unto eternal glory may understand something of this John Robins aforesaid;

2. I declare from the Holy Spirit, that this John Robins was that last great Antichrist. or man of sin, or son of perdition, spoken of by Paul the Apostle in the Thessalonians, who (as it is written) opposeth and exalteth himself above all that is called God; so that he as God, sitteth in the temple of God, showing himself that he is God;

3. This is he that was to appear in this last age, a little before the personal visible coming of the Lord Jesus in the clouds with His ten thousand of saints in power and great glory.

4. To separate between the persons of the true Christians. whose weapons are spiritual faith, that work by love and patience, with all other such-like heavenly virtues, from the persons of all lying hypocrites, who call themselves Christians, but they are indeed far worse than heathens, by killing their neighbours with the sword of steel.

5. Therefore their damnation will be far greater than the heathens in the day of the Lord's vengeance.

6. Again, it would be too tedious to write unto you, wherein this John Robins did appear to be the man of sin as aforesaid;

7. So that the Pope is not the man of sin, as men blindly imagine, for want of the spirit of the Scriptures; but, on the contrary, I declare from the Spirit of the Lord Jesus, that all men that call themselves Christians, and yet make use of the sword of steel, in any case whatsoever, the Pope and those men are both Christians alike;

8. Therefore to be an Antichrist or a man of sin, to oppose God, as beforesaid, I declare from the Holy Spirit that is, when a man doth exalt himself in the place or person of God, and doth set up a worship seemingly far more pure than the simple plain worship of God.

9. And to manage his design he doth show many great lying signs and wonders, as this John Robins did, to the amazement of many deceived by him.

10. It was a spiritual opposing of Jesus, which is the only God, by showing of seeming spiritual lying signs and wonders, as this John Robins did; yea he showed such signs as the popes could never show, nor never shall show:

11. Wherefore, that you that are the elect may no longer

remain in the dark concerning the last great spiritual Antichrist, I declare from the Lord Jesus, that this John Robins did attribute to himself the titles of the only God:

12. First, he called himself Adam Melchisedek; again, he called himself the God and Father of our Lord Jesus Christ:

13. Also, he held forth a Trinity of persons; as, namely, Adam, Abel, and Cain: again, he called himself the first Adam, saying, after he had been five thousand six hundred and odd years in the dust, he was risen from the dead, to deliver his people;

14. Then he said Abel was his son Jesus, the second person of his Trinity; then he called Cain the Holy Ghost, and this was his third person of his Trinity.

15. This Cain, that was the seed of the serpent, or son of the devil, this was his Holy Ghost.

16. I could write very much of his Trinity concerning his wife Eve, so called by him; and of a Jesus he said should be born of her, of his begetting; and of a disciple of his that he called Cain, to make up his counterfeit Trinity, but that it would hinder things of more value.

17. Again, he declared, that he knew all angels, their names and their natures; also, he said, he had a power over all voices; also, he said, that he knew what the spirits of men spake that were in the dust; again, he said, that he was judge both of quick and dead:

18. Again, he said, that the Lord Jesus was a weak and imperfect Saviour, and afraid of death; but he said, that he had no fear of death in him at all; but this Cain hath proved himself an old liar, since his great blasphemy against the Lord Jesus:

19. Again, this John Robins did declare, that he was to gather the Jews in all nations, and to lead them into their own land, unto Jerusalem; with many more such-like things declared by him.

20. As for his lying spiritual signs and wonders, they were these and such-like: unto some that were deceived by him, he did present the form of his person riding upon the wings of the wind, like unto a flame of fire:

21. Also he did present unto some in their beds a great light like unto a flame of fire over all the room, that they have been compelled to hide their faces in their beds, fearing they should be burned; but when they hid their faces in their bed, the light did appear brighter than before:

22. Also he would present unto them half-moons and stars, and sometimes thick darkness, darker than any natural darkness whatsoever.

23. Also he did present his head only in the day time, without a body, to a gentlewoman that I know, in her chamber; also presenting unto her, to deceive her, the forms of strange beasts, as, namely, dragons and such-like.

24. Again, I declare from the Lord, that this John Robins did present the form of his face, looking me in the face in my bed

the most part of a night, insomuch that I cried in my spirit unto the Lord, and the Lord, by his Spirit, revealed this great Antichrist unto me, to my exceeding joy and his everlasting praise.

25. Much more might be spoken of his deceits in this kind; but now I shall declare the manner of his being worshipped as a god by those deceived by him.

26. They prayed unto him, and they fell flat on their faces, and worshipped him, calling him their Lord and their God.

27. Also he gave commandment to some of them, that they should not make mention of any other god, but him only:

28. Also he gave authority unto some of his disciples, both unto men and women, to change their wives and their husbands, telling them that they were not united to their own bone.

29. This cursed Cain changed his own wife first, for an example, and called her name Eve, telling his disciples that she should bring forth his Son Jesus, and it should be caught up into heaven: many of his disciples following of his cursed example to their utter ruin in this life, and that to come.

30. Also he commanded his disciples to abstain from meats and drinks, promising them that they should in a short time be fed with manna from heaven, until many a poor soul was almost starved under his diet, yea, and some were absolutely starved to death, whose bodies could not bear his diet;

31. For those that believed on him indeed, they brought in their whole estates unto him, so that then he had full power over their souls, and bodies, and estates, and he did plague their spirits and bodies at his pleasure in a most dreadful manner, if they were not obedient to his commands, of the which I myself was an eye-witness.

32. I could speak more of this prince of devils in this last age, but I know I have written enough for a spiritual Christian to discern something of this great deceiver in what I have written.

33. When his wickedness was at the full, the Lord Jesus sent me, as beforesaid, unto this John Robins, to declare his wickedness unto him, and immediately to pronounce him cursed in soul and body, from the presence of the Lord Jesus, to all eternity; unto the which I, with my fellow-witness were made obedient.

34. Then about two months after this sentence of the Lord Jesus, this John Robins wrote a recantation of all his seeming great matters declared by him, and sent the writing to General Cromwell, and so obtained his liberty:

35. And when he was out of prison he gave all his disciples about London the slip, and with what silver he had left, that he had cheated from them, Cain-like, instead of building of cities, he went into his own country and repurchased his land;

36. But it was rebought with the innocent blood of many poor innocent souls, in the highest

nature, that ever any man gained such a sum of silver as he did.

CHAPTER III.

Of the Unlawfulness for a Spiritual Christian to war with a Sword of Steel. 21. What was from Eternity.

AGAIN, I declare from the Lord Jesus, that all those that bear the name of Christians and yet make use of the sword of steel to slay men who are the image of God, they are utterly ignorant of the true God, the Man Jesus, and enemies to His Gospel that commands men to love their enemies;

2. Therefore their fleshly reasoning causeth them to forsake the gospel of suffering the cross of Christ, and they apply themselves to the law of Moses, to prove it lawful to kill the gospel of Jesus, instead of yielding obedience to it.

3. Unto you that are chosen to work righteousness, I declare, by revelation from the Holy Spirit, that no spiritual Christian hath anything to do to meddle with any Scripture from the law given by the hand of Moses, to prove it lawful to war with the sword of steel, because it was lawful for the nation of the Jews only, by commission from the Lord, to war against all the heathen Gentiles that rose up against the Jews, because they worshipped the God of Israel, who was contrary to the heathen's idol gods;

4. And this war of the Jews was lawful until God the Father became flesh, to reconcile both Jew and Gentile into that one faith in the body of his flesh, and no longer.

5. Therefore, since God became flesh of our flesh, and bone of our bone, sin only excepted, I declare from the Lord Jesus, that they that are Christians indeed, they are not under the law of Moses, that is, a sword of steel, but they are under grace, or the gospel of Jesus, that is, the sword of the Holy Spirit.

6. That makes all true Christians to understand, that in this world their portion is to suffer all kind of wrong from all men, and to return mercy and forgiveness unto all men, yea, and to forgive those that would kill them, because they know all vengeance is the Lord's, and He will repay it; therefore they dare not rob God of His glory.

7. Again, when the Lord Jesus gave that new law of love unto all his elect believers, where He saith, It was said of old, An eye for an eye, and a tooth for a tooth; but I say unto you, Love your enemies, bless them that curse you, do good to them that hate you.

8. These be those Christians indeed that may be called perfect, as their heavenly Father was perfect; the Lord Jesus, who did all good, and suffered all wrong, yea, and laid down His life for that whole world of His elect, when they were all become His enemies.

9. Again, I declare from the

Lord Jesus, that they that are new born by the Holy Spirit, they are so far from killing or consenting to the killing of any man, offensively or defensively, in their own behalf or in the behalf of any other man, that they are afraid of their own evil thoughts, and much more of evil words or deeds, against God or men;

10. Because they know nothing but pure righteousness, pure love without envy, and pure innocence, shall reign in eternal glory with the only eternal Father, the Lord Jesus.

11. And on the contrary, they know all man-slayers, under what pretence soever, and all covetous, idolaters, drunkards. swearers, liars, sorcerers, whoremongers, and all those that vindicate unrighteousness, through the love of silver, in opposing of that pure law of love that commands all Christians not to do as they are done unto, that is the hypocrite's unrighteousness on the contrary, to do unto all men as you would they should do unto you, this is the righteousness of pure faith, which is the righteousness of God, which makes men to fulfil all righteousness.

12. For want of this, those unrighteous persons beforesaid must all perish to eternity.

13. Again, I declare from the Lord Jesus, that all those that hate to yield obedience to this pure peaceable law of love, proceeding from the pure spirit of the Lord Jesus; I say in the great and notable day of the Lord, by His decree, or by a word speaking from His mouth, they shall every one of them rise out of the dust together, not with the same bodies they died or fell asleep in, because there was somewhat Of God in those bodies whilst they lived, which perisheth with them in death;

14. But the bodies which they shall have shall be in form of their former bodies, but they shall be fiery bodies of spiritual darkness, yea, bodies of all unrighteousness, having all their wicked deeds of their former bodies conveyed into these bodies as fuel to kindle the fire of new sorrows in these bodies of hell and utter darkness, and their spirits in their bodies shall be all fiery devils;

15. So their bodies shall be their kingdom of hell, and their proud spirits, that had pleasure in unrighteousness, shall be the devils that shall be barred in close prisoners within their bodies, from all motioning or thinking of any former comforts, either spiritual or natural, to give them any ease at all, because all time is past;

16. Then, as beforesaid, shall their spirits and bodies burn together like a flame of fire, that is, all as dark as pitch, they never stirring from the place of their resurrection, nor never seeing one another's faces more, much less shall they see the face of God, just men, or angels, to all eternity;

17. And the place of their eternal torment shall be upon this earth, where they acted all their bloodshed and all other unrighteousness.

18. Then shall the sun, moon, and stars, and all other natural lights in this lower creation or world, vanish or go out like the snuff of a candle, giving no more light to eternity:

19. Then shall this fruitful, pleasant earth be like unto dry burning sand, the seas and all rivers or springs of water being dried up for evermore, as if they never had any being.

20. This whole creation being turned into a chaos of confusion, without form, and void of all light or sap, either natural or spiritual, to all eternity, as beforesaid.

21. Again, I declare by revelation from the Holy Spirit, what was from eternity, before any creature was formed, that had any sensible life, either in heaven above or in this earth beneath.

22. There were these two uncreated substances of earth and water, with the uncreated spiritual Person of God the Creator, in whose glorious presence these senseless substances of earth and water were eternally resident, that the Creator might create or form by His infinite wisdom, out of those dead substances, all variety of sensible living creatures in His own time, for the setting forth of His visible glory to eternity.

23. Again, I declare by revelations from the Holy Spirit, that the earth and the water were both dark substances, having no light or sensible life at all in them; but the Person of the Creator was infinitely full of all glorious light and sensible life to Himself, both within and without. Thus it is clear there was death from eternity, only it was not in a sensible form; as well as there was sensible life, light, and glory, in form from eternity.

24. Again, eternal life, or God, was a substantial Form from eternity; but eternal death, or darkness of earth and water, was substance without form, void of all spirit or life; so that life or spirit only is all substantial form, and death or darkness only is all substance without form:

25. So that life and death from eternity are not bare words, as blind hypocrites imagine, but the invisible Creator of all life or spirits was a God of a glorious substance, a spiritual Body, in the form or likeness of a man from all eternity.

26. Again, I declare from the Lord Jesus, that the glorious sensible life or light, in the Person of the Creator, could not possibly be known by men or angels, but by His creating or forming of some creatures to live sensibly in death and darkness, shame and misery, and by His creating other creatures, in opposition, sensibly to live in life and light, joy and glory.

27. Again, the infinite glorious prerogative power of the Creator could not possibly be known to any of His creatures to make a distinction between the glory of eternal life and the misery of eternal death, but by His forming of creatures of the same lump to be vessels of honour and vessels of dishonour to eternity.

28. But, on the contrary, if the Creator, without distinction, had formed His creatures to be all eternally glorious, like Himself, then the glory of His prerogative power of infinite love or mercy, and infinite justice or wrath, and all His infinite new wisdom, increasing or flowing in His glorious Person as a fountain of living waters, must in a manner have been shut prisoner in His own Person, and the creatures must have been all as gods instead of creatures:

29. And so the Creator would have had no glory in His creation at all of the prerogative power of His Godhead.

30. Wherefore I declare, by virtue of my commission from the only wise God and everlasting Father, the Man Jesus in glory, that all those that are made to yield obedience in love to the prerogative power of God are His elect ones, appointed for blessedness to all eternity.

31. But, on the contrary, all those that are offended at the prerogative power of the Creator, and love to dispute against it, are all reprobates, and appointed to be cursed to all eternity.

CHAPTER IV.

Of the Creation beyond the Stars, or of the other Side of the visible created Heavens.

AGAIN, for your information, I declare from the Holy Spirit, that the creation, above or beyond the stars of the holy angels, who are spiritual bodies, in their persons formed like men, and all other creatures that God hath made in the heavens above, of that substance of earth and water aforesaid, that was from all eternity in the presence of His eternal spiritual Person;

2. I declare from the Lord Jesus, that God the Creator hath made that creation in the heavens above as visible to be seen as this creation is seen in this earth beneath.

3. Again, I declare from the Holy Spirit, that the glorious Person of the only wise God and eternal Father, the Lord Jesus, is as visibly seen of the creatures where His Person is resident, as man is visibly seen of the creatures in this earth beneath, where his person resides.

4. As for this creation in the heavens above, it is to set forth the glory of His immortal Person that all the creatures in His presence, visibly beholding the glorious Person of their Creator, both holy angels and other creatures, according to their wisdom or understanding, might give Him the glory of their eternal happiness of this their creation.

5. And, on the contrary, if the Creator were not visibly seen by the eyes of His creatures, then no creatures could possibly know Him, to return any praise or glory unto Him at all, for the happiness of their condition.

6. Therefore it is a cursed lying imagination for any man to think that the glorious Person of God is not as visibly seen of His creatures in the heavens above,

as the person of man, who is the image of God, is visibly seen of the creatures in this earth beneath.

7. Again, you must not think after a fleshly manner, that the creatures above the stars are male and female for natural generation, as they are in this creation beneath the stars:

8. For a woman had never been made but for generation, that the immortal God might have a woman's womb in this world, to clothed Himself with flesh;

9. And that the reprobate angel, which is the devil, might have the womb of a woman to clothe himself with flesh also, to bring forth God's glorious design, between the seed of the woman and the seed of the serpent.

10. Wherefore I declare from. the Holy Spirit, that the holy angels, and all other creatures that are in the presence of God in the creation beyond the stars, are all spiritual male creatures, never increasing in their numbers, not being fleshly, desiring generation;

11. But their spirits or natures, instead of fleshly pleasures in generation, are full of spiritual and heavenly joys, of a more transcendent glorious content within themselves, and visible glorious contents,

12. In their beholding of the glorious Face of God, and the faces of one another, and the glory of that place they enjoy, the which exceeding glory shineth forth through that heavenly kingdom, from the bright burning glorious Person of God

the Creator, the Lord Jesus Christ, who alone hath all the glory of His creation in the heavens above, wherein dwelleth nothing but righteousness in glory.

13. Again, I declare from the Lord Jesus, that no man can understand or know anything of these things, that are invisible unto our natural eyes, but by the spirit of revelation;

14. Therefore it is written, that "faith is the substance of things hoped for, the evidence of things not seen." Again it is written: "Through faith we understand that the worlds were framed by the word of God; so that things which are seen were not made of things which do appear"

15. So that in the letter of the Scripture it is clear, to you that see by the eye of faith, that God hath made or framed two worlds or two creations, which is all one: for you know, to frame a thing, or to make a thing, is all one.

16. Again, unto you it is clear there are spiritual visible things in that world above or beyond the stars, as well as here are natural visible things in this world beneath the stars;

17. Because you may understand, that this world, and the things that are visible therein, were made or created out of that world which is invisible to us who are in mortality, but visible to those who are above in glory;

18. So that now you, that are appointed to enter with spiritual bodies into that glorious creation or world beyond the stars, may

understand a little clearer of your inheritance in that kingdom made without hands, or city eternal in the heavens,

19. Where you shall visibly see with your eyes the face of God, men, angels, and all creatures, in that creation above the stars, as you see the face of man and all other creatures in this creation beneath the stars, with glorious new songs of spiritual and heavenly praises unto a glorious God to all eternity.

20. This proves the truth of these Scriptures, where it is written, "My kingdom is not of this world;" and of this saying, "Lord, remember me when thou comest into thy kingdom;" and of that saying, "In my Father's house, or kingdom, are many mansions;" and of that saying, "For thine is the kingdom, the power, and the glory, for ever;"

21. And of that saying, "The kingdoms of this world are become the kingdoms of our Lord, and of his Christ;" this world was the heavens above;

22. And of that saying, "Nevertheless, we look for a new heaven and a new earth, wherein dwelleth righteousness;" and of that saying, "He hath made us kings and priests unto God, and we shall reign with Him upon the earth."

23. This is that glorious new heaven and new earth, in the presence of God, above or beyond the stars.

24. But blind carnal hypocrites imagine that God's reigning with His elect ones will be upon this bloody earth; because

they have no spiritual eyes, to see or know that new heaven or new earth above or beyond the stars, where nothing but pure righteousness reigneth in glory for everlasting, or world without end. Amen.

CHAPTER V.

1. Of the creating that reprobate Angel Serpent that beguiled Eve, and became a Man.

AGAIN, concerning that serpent beforesaid, so called of the Lord for his subtilty; I declare by revelation from the Holy Spirit, that God created His spiritual Person more glorious than the persons of all the holy angels that are in the presence of God in heaven;

2. Because this mighty angel, by the wisdom and secret counsel of God, was to be as a God, to bring forth his seed or generation of wise and prudent, subtil serpent-men and women, to oppose the Creator and His innocent seed or generation of simple, plain-hearted men and women, that are of the Spirit of faith and pure love, with all other heavenly virtues;

3. For the nature or Spirit of God is faith and love, and all other divine virtues, infinitely living in his glorious Person; the which faith is all power of righteous actings naturally flowing from His pure Spirit, as from a pure over-flowing fountain of living waters;

4. But, on the contrary, the nature or spirit of this God-like

angel, and all the rest of the holy angels in their creation, were pure reason, from whence naturally flows no good at all, but what comes into them continually by revelation from that pure Spirit of faith, in the Person of God their Creator;

5. And this is that spiritual manna that keeps the holy angels' natures or spirits pure in the presence of God;

6. For it is the nature of that pure reason in the holy angels continually to desire the knowledge of that Spirit of wisdom in the Creator that made them, and the overflowings of that new wisdom in the Spirit of the Creator, by the decree of God.

7. It is that spiritual food that keeps the holy angels pure in their glory; or else not one of them could stand upright in the presence of God, not one moment, but they would all become serpent-devils, and fall down into this earth, as that great angel did presently after the Lord withheld the revelation of His glorious wisdom from him;

8. Then this angel, for want of His spiritual food of revelation, that kept his spirit in obedience to his Creator, presently his spirit began proudly to imagine and think high and lofty thoughts concerning his own person, and great wisdom of spirit within him;

9. Wherefore secretly he was lifted up in his spirit to disdain the persons and wisdom of all the holy angels, in. comparison of the glory both of his person and wisdom.

10. Pride being begun in him,

Lucifer-like, he soared higher in his pride, for he thought both his person and his wisdom to be as glorious, if not more glorious, than the Person and wisdom of the Creator;

11. Wherefore, he being very proud of his own wisdom, he imagined that, if he had been the Creator, he would by a word speaking have created angels and all other creatures without earth or water, as God made all things of;

12. For his proud spirit thought he could by a word speaking have created all creatures of nothing at all; therefore he counted his wisdom rather greater, and of a more higher nature, to have formed all things for a greater glory to himself, if he had been the Creator, than the Creator's wisdom in the things or creatures formed by Him.

13. So, imagining his wisdom above the Creator's, he thought himself more fit to reign over the holy angels, and all other creatures, than the Creator.

14. He, being wise in his own conceit, became an absolute fool; for out of nothing comes nothing, and out of nothing comes no form, or nothing can be formed;

15. For to create or make a living form or creature out of senseless matter or substance, of earth or water, by a word speaking, of what nature or form the Creator pleaseth, whether contrary to His own nature and form, or of His own nature and form, this is the power and wisdom of my Creator, the Lord

Jesus;

16. For He, by his infinite glorious wisdom, by a word speaking, did create all living creatures in the two creations or worlds of insensible earth and water, that was without His Person, from all eternity in His presence with him.

17. Because His eternal glorious Person, you know, must have a place of residence; therefore reason itself cannot deny the eternity of earth and waters, and the Person of the Creator, let it imagine never so much, nor never so long.

18. Again, as beforesaid, when the time of this proud and lofty angel's glory was, by the decree of the Creator, expired in the heavens above, to the exceeding joy of all the holy angels, unto whom the Lord revealed his exceeding pride, the Lord then cast down this angelical wise serpent into the earth;

19. Therefore it is written: "Woe be to the inhabiters of the earth, for the devil is come down amongst you."

20. This angel that was cast into the earth is that devil beforesaid; and his nature or spirit of pride and envy, and all other wickedness, being changed, his name or titles are changed according to the uncleanness of his nature.

21. And now, instead of the name of an angel of light, he is called an "angel of darkness," as in Jude.

22. Yea, he is called a serpent, a dragon, a devil, Satan, or an unclean spirit, or that wicked one, suitable to his cursed nature; but the Lord changed not the form or person of this reprobate lost angel at all, but his names or titles only, as beforesaid, according to his nature.

23. Again, I declare by revelation from the Holy Spirit, that that serpent spoken of in the Scripture, that tempted the virgin-wife Eve, he was a spiritual body, in the form of his person like unto a man;

24. Yea, I say from the Lord, that this angel-serpent was more amiable or glorious in the form of his person, to the outward appearance of Eve's eyes, than the person of the man Adam was.

25. Wherefore, by the prerogative power, and secret wisdom and counsel of God, to bring forth His glorious design, it was the outward comeliness of the serpent's person, and his seeming wise and glorious Godlike counsel, by the decree of God became a snare, to deceive and overcome the innocent virgin-wife Eve, as many poor innocent virgins in these days are deceived and overcome by the outward comeliness of men's persons, through their serpent counsels and cursed temptations.

26. Wherefore it is written. "The woman was deceived, and not the man."

27. Again, I declare by revelation from the Holy Spirit, that when this angel-serpent, by his seeming wise God-like counsel, had overcome innocent Eve, as beforesaid, the very

person of this spiritual serpent, reprobate angel, entered into the body or womb of innocent Eve, and there he died, or was changed from his spirituality;

28. And immediately he quickened, in her pure undefiled seed or nature, all serpentine lust of all natural uncleanness; wherefore, she being now naked from her former pure created virginity, presently she is full of natural lust after her innocent husband, that had no desire to a woman at all;

29. Therefore it is written, "And she gave also unto her husband with her, and he did eat;"

30. Then were they both naked from that pure spiritual life of their virgin creation of Godlike content within their own spirits; and in the room thereof they are both full of all natural lusts whatsoever, they being both defiled with the spirit of the serpent-angel of unclean reason and wicked imagination;

31. And this was that cursed effect of their becoming as gods, knowing both good and evil, until they were both born again, by the Spirit of faith, to the full assurance of a more glorious inheritance than that which was lost, through the eternal love of God to His lost image.

32. Again, I declare from the Lord Jesus, that that Cain that was the first-born of Eve, he was the very seed or spirit of that reprobate serpent-angel in the body of Eve, and the first-born child or son of the devil;

33. And so he became, and none but he alone, that Beelze-bub, the prince of devils, and the only father of all those angels of darkness spoken of in the epistle of Jude, that are kept or reserved in chains of darkness, of unbelief; unto the judgment of the great day.

34. Therefore, where it is written of the warfare between Michael and his angels, and the dragon and his angels, that Michael is the Spirit of the Lord Jesus in His angelical believers, whose spiritual weapons are faith, and love, and patience, and such-like, unto the death, because they see a crown of life in yielding obedience to the cross of Christ;

35. The dragon, that is, the spirit of cursed Cain in his persecuting believers, whose carnal weapons are swords, and guns, and all kind of murdering weapons whatsoever, flowing from ignorance, cursed covetousness, and vain-glorious envy, selling their eternal birthright for a mess of pottage, because the Lord Jesus hath no delight in their persons.

36. Again, it is written, "And the great dragon was cast out, that old serpent, called the Devil and Satan, he was cast out into the earth, and his angels were cast out with him."

37. That Cain beforesaid was that serpent-dragon angel; and his angels are that fleshly seed of his, or offspring, or generation of serpent-wise prudent men and women, that mind earthly things.

38. These are those serpent reprobate angels, that go upon the bellies of their spirits, and

lick up the dust of the earth all the days of their lives; that is, their spirits lick up the gold and silver, and put it into a bag, for their generations; and this is the food of their souls, and suchlike, all their days.

39. This is that spirit of unclean reason and wicked imagination that was in Cain, and now is in all his angels, who are the lords of this world, whose spirits wholly thirst after things that perish;

40. And they are never in their proper centre, but when the thoughts of their spirits are feeding upon riches, or honours, or friends, or fleshly delights, or long life, and such-like.

41. This was the food of that serpent Cain that slew his brother Abel, because he was more righteous than he; and this is the food, and no other, of all those serpent angelical men and women, both great and small, that are the very sons and daughters of cursed Cain, hating all spiritual righteousness in all spiritual Abels as he did;

42. Therefore, as beforesaid, cursed together with that serpent reprobate devil, their father Cain, from the presence of the Lord, just men, and angels, to all eternity.

CHAPTER VI.

1. The Eternal Creator clothed Himself with flesh, and so became a pure Man.

AGAIN, for your information, in whose persons the Lord by his Holy Spirit delights to dwell, I declare, by revelation from the Holy Spirit of the Lord Jesus, a little of that wonderful unspeakable mystery of God the Father clothing Himself or manifesting Himself in flesh.

2. It is written: "She was found with child of the Holy Ghost."

3. Again, it is written: "For that which is conceived in her is of the Holy Ghost; and the Word became flesh." And, "Behold, a Virgin shall be with child, and shall bring forth a son, and they shall call his name Emanuel, Which being interpreted is, God with us."

4. Again, it is written: "For unto us a child is born, unto us a son is given; and the government shall be on His shoulders, and His name shall be called Wonderful, Counsellor, the mighty God, the everlasting Father, the Prince of Peace; of the increase of His government and peace there shall be no end."

5. From these Scriptures it is very clear in the bare letter, unto you that see God by the eye of faith, that that holy child Jesus, that was born of the virgin-wife Mary, He is the only God, and alone eternal Father, unto you that have faith in a personal God, or a God of one distinct Person, and no more.

6. Unto you alone, for whom is prepared a crown of immortal glory, I declare, by revelation from the Holy Spirit of the Lord Jesus, that the Holy Ghost beforesaid was the glorious Person of that one only wise God, and everlasting Father, and

Creator of all things, that entered into the Virgin's womb, and died, or changed His immortality or spirituality, in the body or womb of the Virgin;

7. And immediately quickened or conceived Himself of the very nature or seed of the Virgin, a pure natural child or son, in whom, as it is written, "The fulness of the Godhead lived bodily."

8. So that, as the serpent-angel beforesaid entered into the womb of the virgin-wife Eve, and defiled her pure nature or seed throughout, and died in her womb from his spirituality, and quickened in mortality, and brought forth himself the first-born child or son of the devil, and so he became the father of an innumerable company of serpent reprobate devils, of men and women;

9. So, in opposition of that reprobate angel, and prince of devils beforesaid, the glorious Person of the eternal God entered into the womb of the virgin-wife Mary, and died in her womb from His immortality, and purified her nature or seed throughout, that was unclean before, and quickened Himself in pure mortality, and brought forth Himself the first-born Son of God, and the only eternal Father of an innumerable company of elect sons and daughters, purchased by His own precious blood.

10. Thus immortality died and quickened in mortality, and this pure mortality died and quickened in immortality and glory again, in that very same flesh or Person that died, and now reigneth in glory in the highest heavens and the lowest hearts, God alone, blessed to all eternity.

11. Thus eternity became time, and time is become eternity again; for there is nothing but an eternal, immortal God, that is the Creator of all life, that can by His own power live and die, and live again.

12. But, on the contrary, no creature hath any power at all, neither to live nor to die, but by the decree of the Creator alone, the Lord Jesus Christ.

13. Thus, you that see by that single eye of faith may understand in some measure the difference between the seed of the woman and the seed of the serpent;

14. For ever since the angel-serpent, by his wise cursed counsel, took possession of the garden of God, the bodies of our first parents; I declare, from the Holy Spirit, that there is no devil at all without the body of man or woman, but what dwells within the bodies of men and women;

15. So that that devil, so frequently spoken of in the letter of the Scripture, that tempts men and women to all unrighteousness, it is man's spirit of unclean reason, and cursed imagination, that insatiably lusteth after things that perish, until the Holy Spirit of faith enters into the man, and purifies his unclean spirit, and reveals unto his dark understanding spiritual and glorious durable things;

16. And that makes a man

trample this perishing world, and all its vain-glory, under the feet of his spirit, as dung, as it is in comparison of the glory that is to come, in that world above the stars, that remains to all eternity.

CHAPTER VII.

1. The same Subject continued:

AGAIN, it is written: "A woman shall compass a man;" that woman was the Virgin Mary, and that man was God the Father.

2. Again it is written: "A woman clothed with the sun, and the moon under her feet, and upon her head a crown of twelve stars;" this woman was the Virgin Mary beforesaid, and the sun that she was clothed withal was the only-begotten Son of God, the Eternal Father, in the Virgin's womb:

3. And the moon under her feet, that was the worship of the law of Moses; for she, being clothed with the sun, was filled with the revelation of the everlasting gospel of that Son within her, which was of a more transcendent glory than that of the law;

4. And that crown of twelve stars upon her head, that was the twelve Apostles, that sprang from her head, Jesus, to preach the everlasting gospel of truth and peace unto His elect.

5. Thus that saying, that "every seed shall have his own body," is a little more clear unto you that have faith in a personal God, than it was before.

6. You may understand that God the Father was a spiritual Man, from eternity, and that in time His righteous spiritual body brought forth a righteous natural body: that the Father to show forth His infinite love and humility, and to bring forth a new transcendent glory to Himself, might become a son, yea, and a servant, unto His creatures, in the very condition of a creature for a season,

7. That He might exalt His elect creatures into the same condition of the Creator in His glory in the highest heavens to all eternity, when the curtains of this lower heavens are drawn and vanished like smoke, never more to be, time being past.

8. Again, it is written: "He that hath seen me hath seen the Father; and the Father liveth in me, and I live in Him, and I and the Father are one;"

9. The only meaning or mind of the Lord Jesus in those words is this:

10. His Spirit living within His body, that was the Father; and His visible body, that was the Son, both God and Man in one Person, and so but one Personal God, the Man Christ Jesus.

11. He, perfectly knowing Himself to be the only God, said unto the Jews, "Except ye eat my flesh, and drink my blood, you have no life in you:"

12. Again, He said, "Except ye believe that I am he, ye shall die in your sins;"

13. His very mind in those words was this: except they did believe, that that very Person of

His, of flesh, blood, and bone, that spake unto them was the only God and eternal Father, and alone Saviour of all that were to be saved; and that there was no salvation to mankind, but tints spiritually eating of His flesh, and drinking of His blood;

14. Except they did thus own His Person to be their Lord and only Saviour, they must all die in their sins, and perish to all eternity; because there is nothing, but the precious blood of a God can possibly cleanse the spirit of man from the power of sin.

15. Therefore, if the very God-head had not died, that is, if the very soul of Christ, which is the eternal Father, had not died in the body, or with the body, to quiet or satisfy the cry of the guilt of sin in men's spirits, all men would have perished to eternity.

16. Because the spirit of unclean reason, the devil in man, whose nature is all sin, did reign in the very bodies of the elect, as their lord and king; and they were free from the power of righteousness, until the precious blood of a God, by the Holy Spirit of faith, was sprinkled in their consciences, that, by the pure life of spiritual love to God and man, they might break the serpent's head of sin, of reigning any longer in them.

17. But, on the contrary, they that have no faith given them in the precious blood of God to cleanse their spirits from the power of that devil, sin, in them, their sins will be their lord and king, and they must perish together eternally as beforesaid.

18. Again, by this time it is very clear to you that have the faith of Jesus, that the serpent-angel beforesaid was a spiritual body or person in the form of a man, before he entered into the womb of Eve, by that seed or son of his called Cain:

19. Thus every seed or spirit, by the decree of God, brings forth his own body, according to its nature or kind.

20. God the Father, being a spiritual Man from all eternity, in time begot and brought forth Himself a man-child in mortality, of all pure righteousness;

21. Therefore He was called "the express image of the Father," because He was indeed the very Father; and that made Him say, "He thought it no robbery to be equal with God;" and that was the cause that made Him say, that "all power was given unto Him, both in heaven and in earth," because He knew perfectly, that there was no other God but Himself to possess all power.

22. And this made the prophet Isaiah attribute the chief titles, of the "everlasting Father" unto the Son, that was to be made of a woman, or of a virgin; because the prophet knew very well, that the Father and the Son was but one inseparable Person in immortal glory from all eternity; and so he knew they were to become in time one inseparable Person of all purity in mortality.

23. And I with him know, from the same Spirit that revealed it to the prophet long

before God became flesh, that that pure mortality, both spirit and body, that died together, They did both immediately quicken together a new life in death or out of death.

24. And They inseparably, both Father and Son in one Person, did ascend together into that immortal glory that They possessed together from all eternity; and so They now enjoy it again, in one transcendent glorious Person, both God and man, to all eternity.

25. This proves the truth of these sayings: "Glorify me with the same glory I had with Thee before the world was;" and of that saying, "My glory I will not give to another;"

26. And of that saying: "Before Abraham was, I am;" according to that saying of God to Moses, when He bade Moses tell Pharaoh that "I AM sent him;"

27. And of that saying: "He thought it no robbery to be equal with God;" and of that saying: "I am the living bread which came down from heaven; if any man eat of this bread, he shall live for ever;"

28. And of that saying: "This is the bread which cometh down from heaven, that a man may eat thereof and not die;" and of that saying: "For the bread of God is He which cometh down from heaven, and giveth life unto the world;" and of that saying: "I am that bread of life;"

29. Again; "Not that any man hath seen the Father, save He which is of God, He hath seen the Father;" and of that saying: "What, and if ye shall see the Son of Man ascend up where He was before?"

30. And of that full saying, that proves Jesus to be the Father: "He was in the world, and the world was made by Him, and the world knew Him not;"

31. And of that saying: "In the beginning was the Word, and the Word was with God, and the Word was God; the same was in the beginning with God; all things were made by Him, and without Him was not anything made that was made."

32. Whosoever is not stark blind, by this Scripture must needs understand that there is no Creator nor Father but the Man Jesus only, the Lord of life and glory.

33. And where it is said: "Through faith we understand that the worlds were framed by the word of God, so that the things that are (visible or) seen were not made of things that do appear;"

34. And of that saying: "I am Alpha and Omega, I am the First and the Last; and behold, I create all things new;" and of that saying: "I am He that was dead and am alive, and behold, I live for evermore." This was the Man Jesus, that sat upon the throne of the Father.

35. With many other Scriptures too numerous to relate, that prove clearly, to all that are appointed to eternal glory, that the Lord Jesus Christ, that died without the gates of Jerusalem, is the only God, and everlasting Father, and alone Creator of all things that were made, both in heaven and earth.

36. Therefore I declare, from the Holy Spirit of the Lord Jesus that sent us, that whosoever prays in his spirit or tongue unto any other God or spirit but unto my God, the Man Jesus, that sent me, he prays unto a devil of his own imagination, instead of a God;

37. For that Man Jesus, then to come, was David's only God and Saviour; therefore he said, "The Lord said unto my Lord, Sit thou on my right hand until I make thine enemies thy footstool."

38. And this Jesus was all the true prophets' God in the time of the law; and this Jesus was the holy apostles, God, and all the Christians' God, in the time of the apostles' commission, or dispensation, or administration, that lasted about three hundred years;

39. And this glorious Man Jesus is my God alone, and the God of all spiritual Christians in this last age, until He comes in His glory.

CHAPTER VIII.

1. Of Elias the Prophet ascending bodily into Heaven, to represent the Person of God the Father. 5. Moses represented the Person of God the Son. 25. Of the creating of Man, and the nature of the Holy Angels in their Creation. 47. Corruption in Death caused by Sin.

AGAIN, but some may say, if Jesus Christ be the only God and eternal Father, who was that Father that He spake so much of when He was in mortality, where He said "My God, my God, why halt thou forsaken me?" and, "Father, into thy hands I commend my spirit," and such like.

2. To this I answer, by revelation from the Holy Spirit, that Elias, spoken of in the law, that was taken up bodily by a whirlwind into heaven, where the likeness of a chariot and horses of fire appeared to Elisha at his departure;

3. I say from the Lord, that the body or person of that Elias was taken up and glorified in the heavens by the Creator for that very purpose, that he might represent the Person of God the Father for that time or season whilst God the Father went that journey in flesh, as aforesaid.

4. Again it is written: "He shall give his angel's charge over thee;" those angels were Moses and Elias, who being both glorified, they did both represent the Person of the Father in the heavens above the stars, as they did represent the Person of the Son and of the Father when they were in earth beneath the stars.

5. When Moses was upon this earth, he represented the Person of God the Son, that lamb Jesus that was then to come in flesh, in these things:

6. First, Moses was called the meekest man upon the face of the earth.

7. Again, he was a great type of Christ in this, in offering up himself to be blotted out of the book of life for the salvation of Israel, as the Lord Jesus became a curse for his elect Israel.

8. Likewise, Moses was a great sufferer at the hands of Israel with much patience, as the Lord Jesus suffered with all patience at the hands of his own people or nation.

9. Again, Moses was made an angel of the covenant of the law unto all Israel, as the Lord Jesus was made or became an angel of the covenant of grace, or the gospel, unto all the elect Israel;

10. So that whosoever despised the law of Moses was to die a natural death without mercy, as a type of the eternal death of all those that despise the grace or gospel of Jesus;

11. And in this he was a great type of the Lord Jesus, when he said, "God will raise up a prophet unto you like unto me, Him shall you hear."

12. Much more might be spoken of Moses representing the person of God the Son, but I suppose it is sufficient for any moderate man.

13. Again, when Elias was in this world, he did represent the Person of God the Father in these things:

14. First, in a God-like manner, by commanding fire to come down from heaven to destroy his enemies.

15. And it was so again by his commanding, like unto a God, all the priests of Baal, that were the national false priests, to be put to death, for drawing the hearts of Israel from worshipping of the true God;

16. And that was a type of the eternal perishing of all the national priests of Baal in the world at this time who are ministers of the letter only, but call themselves ministers of the Spirit, and yet the Lord Jesus sent them not; these are those croaking frogs that keep the people in darkness, unto whom the people give their silver for nought.

17. Again, Elias, by his asking of Elisha, in a God-like manner, what he should do for him before he was taken up from him, with his granting of Elisha a double portion of his spirit, if Elisha saw his departure from him.

18. Again Elias spake in the authority of the Father, when he told king Ahab to his face, that it was he, and his father's house, that were the troublers of Israel, by their departing from the living God; with more such-like actings of his, after a God-like manner, showing clearly his representing the Person of God the Father when He was upon this earth; which was but a type of his representing the Person of God the Father in the heavens afterwards.

19. But some may say, it seems very strange, the Lord having so many glorious angels in His presence, that He should pass them by, and take up a mortal man, or a sinner into that exceeding glory, of the representing of the Person of God the Father, as beforesaid.

20. To this I answer from the Holy Spirit: All the counsels of my God, the Man Jesus, are quite contrary to man's unclean reason; yea, and contrary to the pure reason of the holy angels also that God alone may have all the glory of the revelation of His

unsearchable counsels of wisdom, from his elect men and angels.

21. Again, I declare, by revelation from the Holy Spirit, that the man Adam, in his creation, was of the very nature or spirit of faith, with all divine virtues of pure love, patience, meekness, and such-like spiritual virtues in his spirit or person, which were the very same divine virtues that lived in the Spirit or Person of God his Creator:

22. Only in the Person of God every spiritual virtue in Him was infinite above all measure; but in the person of the man Adam, although they were the very same heavenly virtues, yet in him they were in measure;

23. Thus man in his spirit was created like unto the Creator, of the very same divine nature; only they differed in this, for the body or Person of God was all spiritual or heavenly, not subject to mortality; but the body or person of the man Adam was natural or earthly, subject to mortality at the pleasure of the Creator;

24. For if the body or person of the man Adam had been spiritual in his creation as his spirit was, then there would have been no difference between the Person of the Creator and the person of the creature:

25. Thus the man Adam was made like unto God, a pure natural person, of all righteousness in mortality, like unto the spiritual Person of God, which is all righteousness in glory.

26. Again, it is written, "The first Adam of the earth, earthly; the second Adam, the Lord from heaven, heavenly."

27. Thus you that see by that single eye of faith, you may know, that God became flesh, or a man, as well as Adam, who was called the image of God, because God was a spiritual Man from eternity, as abundantly beforesaid.

28. Now you must understand the reason why Jesus, the only God, was called the second Adam, was this; because the body or Person of the Lord Jesus was a pure natural body of all righteousness in mortality, just like unto the body or person of the first Adam before his fall;

29. Only Christ, the second Adam, had the spirit of faith in Him above measure, and the first Adam had the spirit of faith in him by measure as beforesaid.

30. Again, the second Adam differed from the first Adam in this, He being made a Man of sorrows, but the first Adam knew no sorrows before his fall.

31. And why did He become a Man of sorrows? It was to redeem the elect seed of the spirit of faith, overcome in His image, the first Adam, by the reprobate angel-serpent, as beforesaid.

32. Again, as for the natures or spirits of the holy angels in their creation, they were pure reason, quite contrary to the nature or Spirit of faith in God their Creator; only in their bodies or persons they were spiritual, or swift of motion, like unto the spiritual Person of God their Creator.

33. But if the nature or spirit

of the holy angels had been of the spirit of pure faith as they were of pure reason, then there would have been no difference between the Person of God their Creator, and the persons of the holy angels in their creation, who are but creatures as well as men;

34. Wherefore not the holy angels, for they are not of the nature of God, as it is written, "He took not upon him the nature of angels, but the seed of Abraham;"

35. But Elias, as beforesaid, by the secret wisdom and counsel and love of God unto man, above angels, was exalted upon the throne of glory for a moment, to represent the Person of God the Father, and he was made the protector of my God, when God became a child;

36. And it was Elias, by virtue of his commission, as a faithful spiritual steward upon the throne of glory, that filled the Lord Jesus with those great revelations of His former glory, that He possessed in the heavens, when He was the immortal Father; and it was Elias that spake those words from heaven, saying, "This is my beloved Son, in whom I am well pleased."

37. Hear him again, when Christ was transfigured upon the mount, that His garment glittered with the glory of his transfiguration.

38. It was the visible glorious appearance of the persons of Moses and Elias talking with Him, that were the instrumental commissioners of that visible glory of the Lord Jesus unto His disciples, who said, "Master, it is good for us to be here;" for that glory was so great, that they would have been building of tabernacles for a continuance in it.

39. Again, I declare, from the Lord, that Elias, by virtue of his commission, did fill elect men and angels also with revelation to keep them in obedience, until the Lord Jesus was upon the throne of His glory again.

40. So that when the Lord Jesus, who was an absolute creature, cried in His agony unto His Father, and when He prayed unto his Father that that cup might pass from Him if it were possible, it being a dreadful cup for His innocent flesh and blood to drink, He being as sensible of pain in His body as we are in our bodies; and when He cried out saying, "My God, my God, why hast thou forsaken me?" and "Father, into thy hands I commend my spirit;"

41. I say again, from the Lord, that Elias, by commission from this Man Jesus, was that Father that He thus cried unto in His mortality, Elias being then in glory.

42. And the chief ground of all those actions, and sufferings, and cryings out of the Lord Jesus, in the condition of a creature, unto a Father, or a Creator, was to fulfil the Scriptures foretold by His Prophets in the time of the law. Therefore He said, "Heaven and earth shall pass away, but my word shall not pass away."

43. Again, but you may say

unto me, did God the third day rise from the dead by His own power, or by the power of His deputy Elias?

44. To which I answer, He by His own decree, and spiritual compact with Elias, and by that Spirit of faith in His innocent body, the which faith died in His pure body and quickened immediately, and brought forth, at the appointed time, that natural innocent body out of the grave, a pure spiritual body, which naturally (at the time appointed) ascended into glory;

45. For it was impossible for God by death to be held in the grave; because, His Person being pure, His pure spirit and death could not remain together, because there was no sympathy, or agreement, or union between them;

46. Yea, they were so contrary, it was impossible for them to be together, except one of them were absolutely extinguished;

47. Wherefore, death being too weak, the Lord Jesus, who is the only God of all created life, brake through death, and hell, and the grave, and through all the sins of His elect, by the shedding of His most precious blood, and so entered into His eternal glory, that all those that have faith in His glorious Person may be delivered at the appointed time from sin, hell, death, and the grave, and enter into eternal glory with Him, when He comes in the clouds of heaven.

48. Again, the reason why men's bodies in death, or after death, do rot or stink in the grave, and come to dust, is, because there was sin in their bodies whilst they lived, the which sin and death had a sympathy, and, as it were, a sweet communion together, whereby death had full power, as lord and king, to keep the spirits and bodies in the dust, until the time appointed of the Lord of life.

49. But, on the contrary, if men had no sin in their natures or bodies, they might live and die, and naturally rise again by their own power, in their own time, as the Lord of life did, whose body was too pure to see corruption.

50. Thus, unto you that have faith in the Lord Jesus, it is not strange that Elias should represent the Person of God the Father, until the Lord Jesus ascended into the right hand of all power and glory of His Father Elias again.

51. Then, when Jesus was set down in the throne of the glory of the Father again, Elias then, as a glorified creature, did return all praise and glory unto the Lord Jesus his Creator; so that now it is the Lord Jesus alone, by His Holy Spirit, that revealeth all spiritual and heavenly wisdom to elect men and angels;

52. Elias having now, with exceeding joy, surrendered up his spiritual and glorious stewardship, of representing the Person of God the Father, unto the right owner, and sole heir of heaven and earth, and all that therein is, the Lord Jesus Christ, the eternal Father, God alone, blessed to all eternity.

53. I know I have spoken enough to the spiritual Christian of this truth.

CHAPTER IX.

1. Of all Priests or Ministers in this World being false, not knowing the true God; therefore not sent by the God of all Truth, the Man Jesus.

AGAIN, I declare, by revelation from the Holy Spirit, that about this fourteen hundred years, there hath not been one true prophet, nor minister, sent with a commission from the Lord Jesus, to declare, or write, or preach, the everlasting gospel of truth and peace unto His elect.

2. Wherefore I declare (by virtue of my commission, received by voice of words from the Lord Jesus) that all the ministry in this world, whether prophetical or ministerial, with all the worship taught by them, whether invisible or visible, to the people, it is all a lie, and an abomination unto the Lord;

3. Both the ministry and their worship are as acceptable unto my God, the Man Jesus, that sent me, as the cutting off of a dog's neck.

4. Now unto you that discern truth from the Lord, I shall give you light into this truth.

5. First I declare, that all the true commissionated prophets of the Lord in the time of the law, from Moses unto John the Baptist, with all the true commissionated apostles and ministers of the Lord Jesus in the gospel, they had every one of them in their commission a power given them, to set life and death before men, or to declare blessing or cursing unto men, which is all one, according to their administrations received from the Lord.

6. Again, I declare, from the Holy Spirit, that the Lord Jesus did purpose within Himself to send His messengers three times to the world, and but three times to this bloody unbelieving world, and no more, for a witness or testimony unto them, and to make known unto His elect, that He alone is the only God and everlasting Father;

7. Wherefore you shall find it written, "There are three bear record in heaven, the Father, the Word, and the Spirit; and these three are one." Again, it is written, "There are three bear witness in earth, the water, the blood, and the spirit; and these three agree in one."

8. Again, I declare from the Holy Spirit, that those three in earth are the Lord's three dispensations, given to His prophets or messengers beforesaid;

9. The water was the commissions of Moses and the prophets under the law; the blood was the commission of the apostles, and those ministers of the gospel chosen by appointment from the Lord; the spirit, which is the third and last witness, by commission from the Lord, are those two witnesses spoken of in Revelations xi. prophesied by John, the beloved disciple of Jesus, that were to come in the last age.

10. Whose message, or ministry, or prophecy is all invisible and spiritual, cutting off or condemning all fleshly formal worshipping of an invisible spiritual personal God, taken up by vain and glorious men from the letter of the Scripture, which were the prophets' and apostles' commissions, because they want a commission from the Lord.

11. Again, I declare from the Holy Spirit, the Lord spake by voice of word unto His three commissioners that He hath sent unto the world.

12. Yea, I know, God the Father spake unto Moses as a man speaks unto his friend, as it is written; and I know that God spake unto the apostles in the Person of the Son, as it is written; because I know the Lord Jesus spake unto me in the Person of the Holy Ghost, or Spirit, as beforesaid.

13. Only, the two former witnesses saw the Person of God in part visibly, but I saw the glory of His Person invisibly or within me, because I am the messenger of the holy invisible Spirit.

14. Again, concerning those three bearing record in heaven beforesaid; the meaning of those words is this:

15. God from heaven, in a threefold name or title, bare witness by signs and wonders unto His three commissioners, according to their several administrations given unto them.

16. Unto Moses and the Prophets, this personal God bare witness in the name or title of the Father.

17. Unto the holy apostles, God bare witness in the name or title of the Son;

18. And unto us, His third last messengers, God beareth witness in the name or title of the Holy Spirit, because our commission is all spiritual, we have to do only with the invisible spirits of men, concerning the eternal estates of men's and women's persons, in the great and notable eternal day of the Lord's account:

19. Therefore, instead of natural signs upon the bodies or persons of men and women, as in the two former commissions of the prophets and the apostles, the Lord Jesus beareth witness that He hath sent us, by spiritual signs or wonders upon the spirits of those that are sealed up, through our mouths, unto eternal life and unto eternal death, as many do bear witness, whose eyes are opened at this day in England, in this great city of London.

20. Again, this is a true testimony unto you that have faith in the Lord Jesus, that He hath sent us by His Holy Spirit, be-cause there is none upon this earth that beareth witness unto that Man Jesus that was crucified at Jerusalem, to be the only God and everlasting Father, but we only;

21. As Moses, the prophets, and the apostles bare witness in their times unto this Jesus, to be the only God, and alone eternal Father.

22. But on the contrary, there is hardly a minister in the world

that confesseth an invisible God; but they preach unto the people, either a God of two persons, or a God of three persons, that is a monster, instead of a one true personal God;

23. Or else they teach the people to worship an infinite Spirit, that is everywhere, without a body or person; but He is fain to borrow His creatures' bodies to live in;

24. That is, a God of words only, without any form or substance, or an infinite Nothing, that never can be comprehended nor apprehended in the least by any formed creature; a cursed, lying, imaginary God, from man's own unclean blind reason, which occasioneth all kind of blood-shed and cruelty to be committed in this wicked world between man and man.

25. For if men understood, indeed, that there is but one only wise God, and that this God is a distinct body or Person, as a man is a distinct body or person, then would men understand, that all those that are led by the voice of the Holy Spirit of God, the Man Jesus, to work righteousness in their bodies, they lived in, they only shall appear with bodies of all righteousness, like unto their God, the Man Jesus, visibly to behold, face to face, the glorious body of the God of all righteousness for everlasting, world without end.

26. Thus it is clear to the understanding of all those that are appointed to know the true God, the Man Jesus, unto life eternal, that there is no true ministry in the world, because they teach not the true God unto the people;

27. Therefore as it is written, they are blind leaders of the blind, therefore they must needs both fall into the ditch. Oh! it is an eternal ditch.

28. These are those merchants of the letter of the Scripture, that make the blind nations their prey; these are those ravening wolves that come in sheep's clothing; these are those dumb dogs in spiritual things, that bark at true prophecy and heavenly revelation, that a man declares by commission from the Lord Jesus;

29. These are those that the apostle Paul complained of in his time, that bewitched the people to turn from the spiritual gospel to the legal form, who began by the apostle in spirit, but were deluded by false hypocrites to be made perfect in the flesh; these are of those hypocrites that were in Christ's time, who, under pretence of long prayers, devour widows' houses;

30. These are those hypocrites that are always teaching of God what He should do for His own glory, when indeed it is their own glory, in lusting after things that perish, they desire when they thus pray, or preach, or prate;

31. These are those bloody hypocrites, and workers of iniquity, that the Lord Jesus will never own, because He never sent them.

CHAPTER X.

1. Of all heathen Magistrates, and their heathen Prophets' false Worship, or Image.

AGAIN, I declare, by revelation from the Holy Spirit, that there is no magistrate in this world, that bears the name of a Christian, that hath any authority or commission from the Lord Jesus to set up any visible form of worship whatsoever, to compel the spirits or consciences of men to bow down to his image that he hath set up for his own glory;

2. Because ever since the Lord Jesus ascended into His glory, He alone is the teacher of all His elect by His Holy Spirit.

3. It is true, that in the time of the law, before God became flesh, there were many magistrates and priests commissionated from the Lord to set up and to declare the true worship of God unto all Israel;

4. And it was death by the command of the Lord, if the people despised to yield obedience unto it, because it was the Lord's worship, and not man's worship, set up by his own lying imagination, that would be a God.

5. But he is a devil, for his creating of a worship to deceive the people without a commission from the Lord, and by taking the prerogative power and glory of God to himself, who will not give His glory to another, as it is written;

6. Therefore in the Revelations, the dragon there spoken of is the imagination of the beast; and the beast is the body of the magistrate, wherein that dragon imagination liveth; and the false prophet there spoken of is the magistrate's priest;

7. And the image of the beast is that false worship set up by the imagination of the magistrate, and the serpent counsel of his false prophet or priest, to deceive themselves, and the people with them;

8. Therefore it is written, "And all that dwell upon the earth shall worship him whose names are not written in the book of life, of the Lamb slain from the foundation of the world;"

9. That is, all reprobates, both rich and poor, shall bow down unto that false, idolatrous worship set up by heathen magistrates and their heathen false prophets, the national priests, who call themselves Christian magistrates and Christian ministers, and are blindly called so by the people also.

10. And yet both of these devils together persecute with the sword of steel all spiritual Christians, under the name or title of blasphemers, seducers, heretics, deceivers of the people, and such-like, because the spiritual Christian cannot bow down unto that carnal, anti-christian, formal worship set up by those carnal magistrates and their carnal ministers beforesaid.

11. Who, being both lovers of the glory of this world, loving to be honoured as gods, for that cursed heathenish idol-worship from their own invention, set up to deceive themselves and those

appointed to damnation with them.

12. Wherefore the dragon magistrate, and the false prophets, his serpent ministers, that committed spiritual fornication together, and all those of their own spirits, shall every one of them, in the day of the Lord's vengeance, burn in their spirits and bodies together as a lake of fire.

13. Those spirits and bodies that they shall appear with in the resurrection, shall be that lake of spiritual fire and brimstone that, by the decree of the Lord Jesus, shall burn together to all eternity;

14. This is that giving them their own blood to drink, who eat up the innocent as bread, and thought they did God good service in shedding of the blood of the lambs of Jesus, as their forefathers did;

15. Then will these Scriptures be fulfilled, "And those mine enemies, that would not that I should reign over them, bring them and slay them before my face;" and, "Go ye cursed into everlasting fire."

16. And the carcases of the rebels shall be cast out, where the worm never dies, and the fire never goes out.

17. And, "Tophet is ordained of old for the king;" that Tophet is the body of man, and that king is the spirit of unclean reason in man.

18. "For behold, the day cometh that shall burn as an oven, and all the proud, yea, and all that do wickedly, shall be stubble;

19. "And the day that cometh shall burn them up, saith the Lord of hosts, and ye shall tread down the wicked, for they shall be ashes under the soles of your feet, in the day that I shall do this, saith the Lord of hosts:

20. "Fill ye up the measures of your fathers, ye serpents, ye generation of vipers; how can ye escape the damnation of hell?

21. "For ye shall have judgment without mercy that hath showed no mercy; but the fearful and unbelieving, and the abominable, and murderers, whoremongers, and sorcerers (or astrologers), and idolaters, and all liars, shall have their part in the lake which burneth with fire and brimstone, which is the second death."

22. Again, the bloody persecutors beforesaid, instead of feeding and clothing the hungry saint, quite contrary, they do not only take away the food and raiment of the Lord Jesus, in His elect innocent lambs, but they crucify the Lord of life afresh, in the shedding of the blood of His believers,

23. Because they yield obedience to the spiritual law of faith and love, or command of the Lord Jesus, either by prophesying, or writing, or speaking the truth by command from the Man Jesus, who is the only spiritual Magistrate and Minister unto all that are appointed unto eternal glory with Him, in that glorious creation of that new heaven and earth above the stars, when this creation beneath the stars is utterly destroyed, and fitted only for

persecuting   dragon-serpent devils to lament, howl, and weep to all eternity upon this earth, where the saints by them were put to grief for a moment.

CHAPTER XI.

1. The same Subject continued.

BUT some may say unto me, Do you not allow of the civil magistrate to govern the rude people?

2. To this I answer: The magistrate is very needful in every inhabited land, for the government of the people in all civil things, to do equal justice between man and man.

3. If such a magistrate could be found, it would be a rare thing.

4. Again, I declare, from the Holy Spirit, although the magistrate be but a heathen ruler, as he is; wherefore Christ saith of this magistrate unto His apostles, "The kings or princes of the Gentiles exercise lordship over them, and they that exercise authority upon them are called benefactors; but ye shall not be so: but he that is greatest among you, let him be as the younger;"

5. Yet I say from the Lord, the magistrate beareth not the sword in vain; but he is a type of the true spiritual Magistrate, that can do nothing but equal justice between the just and unjust, the Lord Jesus Christ.

6. Wherefore all men ought to yield obedience to the civil laws of the magistrate, either by executing of his laws, or by patiently bearing the curse of the law upon their own persons, leaving all vengeance unto God.

7. Or else they rebel against God, and they are in danger of an eternal curse: because the government of this world, and the glory thereof, belongs only unto the wise and prudent heathen magistrates in this earth, who are the very sons of Cain, that old serpent-dragon devil, that slew his righteous brother Abel, that he and his seed that are of his own spirit might be, the lords and rulers of this world for ever.

8. Because Cain thought, and his dark angels think, that there is no world at all, but this only: they have purchased the lordship of this perishing world at a dear rate, for it was the price of the innocent blood of righteous Abel; it is their only heaven.

9. Therefore let us, that have received faith to believe in the glorious Person of the Lord Jesus, by His power patiently suffer the cursed spirit of Cain in his heathen magistrates to shed all our innocent blood, if our God will have it so; that they may fill up the measure of their fathers' sins, from the blood of righteous Abel and the holy prophets, to the precious blood of the Lord Jesus, and the holy apostles;

10. That our blood, that are the two last witnesses and prophets of the Lord Jesus, may make the last persecutors of Christians complete devils, with their father Cain, who was the first bloody persecutor of the

first suffering Christian.

11. Therefore it is written, that "Christ was a Lamb slain from the beginning of the world," He being slain in believing Abel.

12. I say from the Lord, by the power of His Holy Spirit, patiently let us yield up our lives with our God unto those perishing gods beforesaid; because we that suffer with Him are appointed to enter into an eternal kingdom of glory in another world, hid from the wise and prudent rulers of this vanishing world.

13. Therefore it is written, "Which of the rulers have believed in Him?" Again, as it is written, "Why do the heathens so furiously rage together, the kings of the earth stand up, and the rulers take counsel together, against the Lord and against His Anointed," or against His Christ?

14. Again, as it is written by Paul, "Howbeit, we speak wisdom amongst them that are perfect; yet not the wisdom of this world, nor of the princes of this world, that come to nought."

15. Again, it is written, "Which none of the princes of this world knew; for had they known it, they would not have crucified the Lord of glory."

16. Again, that world that we are to reign in, after we have suffered, it was purchased also by blood; but it was the price of the precious, invaluable un-defiled blood of our God, the Man Jesus, who by His Holy Spirit, that sent us only, maketh us willing to taste a little of His cup that He so deeply drank of

17. The servant is not greater than the Master, because we are to sit down with Him upon His eternal throne of glory, to behold His face, in the presence of all His holy angels.

18. Then these Scriptures will be fulfilled: "Blessed are they which are persecuted for righteousness' sake, for theirs is the kingdom of heaven." Again, "Blessed are ye when men shall revile you, and persecute you, and shall say all manner of evil against you falsely, for my sake. Rejoice, and be exceeding glad, for great is your reward in heaven: for so persecuted they the prophets which were before you."

19. Again, "Then shall the righteous shine forth as the sun in the kingdom of their Father."

20. Again, "For the Son of Man shall come in the glory of His Father, with His angels; and then He shall reward every man according to his works."

21. Again, "Then shall the King say unto them on His right hand, Come, ye blessed of my Father; inherit the kingdom prepared for you from the foundation of the world."

22. Again, "Then shall He say unto them on the left hand, Depart from me, ye cursed, into everlasting fire; prepared for the devil and his angels."

CHAPTER XII.

1. Of the Mortality of the Soul, and how and when it became mortal.

AGAIN,   I   declare,   by

revelation from the Holy Spirit, that, since the fall of our first parents, the spirit and body of man are both mortal; and that, by the decree of the Creator, the soul and body of man are both procreated or begot together, and they are both of one nature, and so both but one creature;

2. For it is the invisible spirit that liveth in the seed and nature of man, that by the decree of God creates or begets that form of flesh in the person of a man or woman according to their kind.

3. And thus it is with this whole creation; every seed or spirit naturally, by the wisdom of the Creator, brings forth their own bodies or kind, whether man, beast, fish, or fowl; and all things else that grow naturally bring forth in their season according to their natures.

4. Because the Creator, by His secret counsel and wisdom decreed within His glorious Person, before anything was created or formed by Him, that all things or creatures that should be created or formed by His infinite wisdom should bring forth their own bodies or kind only, and no other, for ever.

5. Therefore, when men's and beast's seeds are unnaturally mixed together, contrary to their kind, the Lord discovers them both, to their destruction, and His glory.

6. Wherefore, I declare, from the Lord Jesus, that it is a cursed imagination in any man to think, when men die, their spirits may go into other forms and bodies, contrary to their own natures or kind, as many a cursed lying atheist prates, that denies the resurrection of men's bodies, through the love of some dark fleshly lust they live in.

7. They are in spiritual darkness, understanding nothing of the power of God, and so erring, not knowing the Scriptures, as it is written, nor the power of God.

8. Therefore it is a common thing for these blind atheists, in their discourse, to say, when men die, their spirits may or do go into a horse, or into a root, or into a flower, with many more such-like cursed expressions.

9. They being more ignorant if it be possible, of the Lord Jesus, through the love of fleshly pleasures, than the brute beasts, therefore they reason against their own reason, and say, this creation or world had never any beginning, nor ever shall have any ending, two cursed lies.

10. Again, they call perishing nature God or Creator, saying, God is all things, and all things is God.

11. Thus these blaspheming devils liken the incorruptible Spirit of God, the Man Jesus, not only unto the unclean spirit and cursed imagination living in the body of corrupt man, but unto the spirits of unclean beasts and creeping things, as those atheists in the time of Paul.

12. These are those who received the truth to prate of it only, but not in the love of it, having pleasure in unrighteousness, therefore given up to strong delusions to believe a lie, that they might all be damned.

13. Then these Scriptures will be fulfilled, "He made all things for His own glory, and the wicked for the day of wrath."

14. Again, "He shall come in flaming fire to render vengeance upon them that know not God, and obey not the Gospel of Jesus Christ."

15. Again, "But these, as natural brute beasts made to be taken and destroyed, speak evil of the things they understand not, and shall utterly perish in their own corruption."

16. Again, "They having eyes full of adultery, and cannot cease from sin, beguiling unstable souls; an heart they have exercised with covetous practices, cursed children which have forsaken the right way and are gone astray, following the way of Balaam the son of Bosor, who loved the wages of unrighteousness."

17. Again, "Raging waves of the sea, foaming out their own shame; wandering stars, to whom is reserved the blackness of darkness for ever."

18. Again, "And also Enoch, the seventh from Adam, prophesied of these, saying, Behold, the Lord cometh with ten thousands of his saints, to execute judgment upon all, and to convince all that are ungodly among them of all their ungodly deeds which they have ungodlily committed, and of all their hard speeches which ungodly sinners have spoken against Him."

CHAPTER XIII.

1. The same Subject continued.

AGAIN, unto you that see by the eye of faith from the Lord, I shall show you that general error amongst men concerning the spirit of man in death.

2. Some say the spirit dieth not at all, but immediately goeth into heaven or into hell; and the body goes to the dust only.

3. Others say, the spirit dieth not, but goeth into another form, either of man, or some other creature, as beforesaid.

4. Others say, or think, all men's spirits go into a hell or purgatory, when they die, for a season.

5. Others blasphemously say, that the spirit of man is God, and that the body only dies and turns to dust.

6. These say also, God is an infinite Spirit, and all spirits came from His Spirit, and so return into His Spirit again.

7. Others think and say, the spirit and body turns to dust for ever.

8. Indeed, almost all men are in darkness, because they walk by thinking only about things of eternity; but about things that perish, they think them hardly ever sure enough unto them.

9. Wherefore, unto you whose bodies are the temples of the Holy Ghost, from the Lord Jesus, I shall declare unto you the truth of this secret.

10. You may know, that the spirit is nothing at all without a body, and a body is nothing at all without a spirit; neither of

them can live, or have a being, without the other.

11. You may know it is the spirit only in the body of man that lives, and speaks, and walks, and works, and eats, and drinks, and dies.

12. For the spirit is a natural fire of reason, which is that life of light, heat, or motion, that as a fire kindleth life and strength through all the flesh or body of man.

13. Only the principal part of the understanding of this natural fire of the spirit of reason liveth in the head of man, because that is the glory of the man; so that the spirit or soul is the man, although it cannot possibly be without the form or body.

14. Wherefore when man dies and returns to his dust, it is that natural spirit of the fire of reason that was the life or spirit of the body that dieth, or is quenched, and goeth out within the body, as a fire goeth out in an oven that is closed.

15. So doth the spirit of man die within his body from all sensible life, heat, or motion, until the visible coming of the Lord of life in the clouds of heaven at the last day.

16. Therefore it is written, "Dust thou art and unto dust thou shalt return."

17. When the Lord spake those words, He did not speak to the flesh, or outward form or body of the man, but He spake to the inward spirit or soul, that understands the words of a spirit.

18. Again, it is written, "In the day thou eatest thereof, thou shalt die the death;" that is, if thou, through disobedience to my command, dost forfeit the image of thy creation, then thou shalt see mortality or death within thy own body, both spiritual and natural, and the fear of eternal death also.

19. Thus it is clear, to you that believe in the Lord Jesus, that the spirit of man dies and returns to dust within the body, because nothing can possibly die, but it must first live;

20. So likewise nothing can possibly quicken or live again, but that which is absolutely dead, or dust, or asleep, void of all notion, heat, light, life, or sense, being utterly annihilated to itself and all other creatures, only being alive in the memory of God, that God alone, the Man Jesus, might have all the glory in the new creating of mankind at the last out of dust, as He had in creating of man at the first out of dust;

21. According to that saying in the Revelation, "Behold, I create all things new," in answer to that creation in Genesis.

22. Thus it is with the grain or body of wheat; except it dies, it never comes to perfection, but abides alone in the dust for ever; but, on the contrary, if the spirit of life, which is in the body of wheat, doth absolutely die within its body, then, by the decree of God, it quickens out of death into a new life immediately, and brings forth a glorious resurrection in due season of many bodies in the same form, like unto that which died, of the

very same nature.

23. Thus it is, by the decree of the Lord Jesus, with the natural spirits of all the elect.

24. First they are dead in sins and trespasses, before they are capable, by the Spirit of truth, to live in righteousness; so likewise the spirits of men and women must be absolutely dead, when they fall asleep in the dust, or else they were never capable to rise again, neither in glory nor in shame.

25. So that, by the decree of God, all life, both spiritual and natural, must first enter into death, that through death, or in death, they may quicken a new life of a glorious increase, both spiritual and natural; so that death in its place is as useful for the Creator's raising of glory to Himself as life is in its place.

26. This proves the truth of these Scriptures, "He poured out His soul unto death." Again, "The soul that sins shall die." Again, "He cried with a loud voice, and gave up the ghost." Again, "In the day thou eatest thereof thou shalt die the death."

27. Again, "His soul was made an offering for sin." Again, "He was put to death in the flesh and quickened in the Spirit."

28. I know I have written enough to satisfy in the proof of this truth all spiritual Christians.

CHAPTER XIV.

1. With what Bodies the Elect shall appear after Death.

AGAIN, it is written, "And those that sleep in Jesus shall rise first;" that is, those that fell asleep in the believing of the visible coming of the glorious Person of the Lord Jesus in the clouds of heaven in power and great glory, their bodies shall be raised first out of the sleep of death.

2. Because they were united by faith unto the Person of their Lord Jesus, who was the first that ever rose from the dead by His own power, who raised life in death or out of death, therefore He was called the first-fruits of the resurrection, or of life from death:

3. Again, you that see by faith may understand, that not the same bodies that died or fell asleep shall appear any more at all than the body of wheat doth as beforesaid, which Saul fitly compareth together in their resurrection where it is written, "But God giveth it a body as it pleaseth Him, and to every seed his own body:"

4. That is, as beforesaid, that grain or body of wheat that died quickened a new life out of death, and brought forth in a glorious manner, in due season, many bodies of the same form of that that died, and yet that body that died appeared no more.

5. So likewise it shall be with all that died in the faith of Jesus, not the same bodies or persons they lived in and died in shall appear again any more, but that spirit of faith mixed with pure love, and all other spiritual virtues, that were in their former bodies, by the which they died

unto the power of sip, and lived unto the power of righteousness:

6. That divine seed of faith sowed in the former body died with the first body, and immediately quickened a new life out of death by the decree of the Lord Jesus.

7. For you know there is no time now unto God, nor unto them that are dead, and so brought forth a spiritual body in its form like unto that in the dust; yea, of a body of pure righteousness, of the same nature of that holy spirit of faith that raised it out of death; yea, a glorious body, brighter than the sun in its strength, and as swift as thought;

8. Yea, bodies of such a bright burning glory, that no persecuting Canaanites can behold and live, because our spirits and bodies, according to our faith, shall be made like unto the glorious body of God, the Man Jesus, the which no man in mortality with his natural eye can behold and live.

9. Then shall all the elect, in the twinkling of an eye, both those that sleep in the dust, and those that are alive at that time, whose bodies also shall be changed like unto those that sleep; then, I say, they shall all ascend together as one body, to meet their head, the Lord Jesus in the air;

10. And with their King they shall enter into His kingdom of eternal glory, where that new heaven and new earth are before-said, there with holy angels to behold the glorious face of the only wise God, and everlasting Father, the Lord Jesus Christ, with new glorious songs and praises unto their Redeemer that was dead, as it is written, to redeem us by His precious blood from eternal death;

11. And now, behold, He liveth for evermore; therefore we eternally live with Him.

CHAPTER XV.

1. How the Bodies and Spirits of the World of Elect Believers shall be like unto the glorious body of God their Redeemer, in His Glory to Eternity.

AGAIN, I declare by revelation from the Holy Spirit, that when the elect are thus glorified, they are absolutely of the very same glorious nature, both in spirit and body, as God is; as God and they were both of one nature in mortality, sin only excepted.

2. Wherefore, as the Spirit of faith and love infinitely, in the glorious Person of God, overfloweth, as a fountain, continually with revelation of new heavenly wisdom, from whence flow new joys and glory to Himself and the holy angels;

3. So shall every believer, according to his degree in glory, be as a well springing up unto everlasting life, of revelation of new wisdom, from whence flow new joys and glory within his own person, like unto his God;

4. Only they shall naturally return the glory and praise unto their fountain, the Lord Jesus, for this their exaltation upon the

glorious throne of His own likeness.

5. For it is the righteous acting and suffering that was in the innocent body of the Lord Jesus when He was in mortality, that by His infinite wisdom is made naturally that glorious fire to kindle new revelation of heavenly wisdom within His body, for the increase of His glory to all eternity as beforesaid.

6 So, likewise, all those righteous actings and sufferings, for truth's sake, that were acted and suffered in our former bodies, by the appointment of our God shall be conveyed into our new spiritual bodies, that are like unto our God, and shall be that glorious fire naturally to kindle revelation of new wisdom, from whence flow glorious new songs and praises unto our Redeemer, the fountain of all our glory, for everlasting, world without end, as abundantly beforesaid.

7. Then shall these Scriptures be fulfilled: "To him that overcometh will I grant to sit with me in my throne, even as I also overcame, and am set down with my Father in His throne."

8. Again, "And he that overcometh and keepeth my works unto the end, to him will I give power over the nations; and he shall rule them with a rod of iron, as the vessels of a potter shall they be broken to shivers, even as I received of my Father; and I will give him the morning star."

9. Again, "Him that overcometh will I make a pillar in the temple of my God, and he shall go no more out; and I will write upon him the name of my God, and the name of the city of my God, which is New Jerusalem, which cometh down out of heaven from my God; and I will write upon him my new name."

10. Again "He that overcometh shall inherit all things; and I will be his God, and he shall be my son."

11. Again, "Henceforth I will not drink of this fruit of the vine until that day I drink it new with you in my Father's kingdom."

12. Again, "And from Jesus Christ, who is the faithful Witness, and the first begotten of the dead, and the Prince of the kings of the earth."

13. Unto Him that hath loved us, and washed us from our sins in His own blood, and hath made us kings and priests unto God and His Father, to Him be glory and dominion, for ever and ever. Amen.

CHAPTER XVI.

1. Of the Difference between the Glory of Elect Men and Angels in Heaven above.

AGAIN, from the Holy Spirit, I shall show you the difference between elect men and angels in glory.

2. The angels' natures or spirits being pure reason, they must always be supplied by revelation from the Spirit of faith in the Person of God, to keep their spirits in pure obedience unto their Creator.

3. But, on the contrary, the

believers' spirits being of the very same divine nature of God, they are but one voice or spirit, speaking all pure obedience within themselves unto their Redeemer.

4. To whom alone be all glory and praise from my spirit, with His elect men and angels, to all eternity.

A GENERAL EPISTLE TO MINISTERS,

BY JOHN REEVE AND LODOWICK MUGGLETON,

THE TWO LAST SPIRITUAL WITNESSES, AND ALONE TRUE
PROPHETS OF THE HOLY SPIRIT, BY COMMISSION FROM THE
TRUE GOD, THAT EVER SHALL WRITE OR SPEAK UNTO
UNBELIEVING MAGISTRATES, MINISTERS, AND PEOPLE, UNTIL
THE ONLY LORD OF LIFE AND GLORY, THE MAN JESUS,
PERSONALLY APPEARETH, IN THE AIR, WITH HIS MIGHTY ANGELS,
TO BEAR WITNESS TO THIS TESTIMONY: EVEN SO, COME, LORD
JESUS.

~~~~~~~~~~~~~~~~~~~~~~~

FIRST PRINTED FOR THE AUTHORS IN THE YEAR OF OUR LORD
1653
THEN RESIDING IN LONDON.

FOURTH EDITION.

~~~~~~~~~~~~~~~~~~~~~~~

LONDON
PRINTED FOR JOSEPH FROST, 17, HALF MOON STREET,
BISHOPSGATE STREET,
BY LUKE JAMES HANSARD, 5, PEMBERTON ROW, GOUGH SQUARE, FLEET STREET.

1854.

CONTENTS.

GENERAL EPISTLE TO MINISTERS.

GENERAL
EPISTLE TO MINISTERS.

WHEREFORE, IF ANY MAN IN THE WORLD SHALL BE LEFT TO DESPISE THIS MINISTRY, FROM THE GREATEST TO THE LEAST, BY CALLING OF IT BLASPHEMY, A DEVIL, DELUSION, OR A LIE; IN SO DOING THEY HAVE COMMITTED THAT UNPARDONABLE SIN AGAINST THE HOLY SPIRIT THAT SENT US: WHEREFORE, FROM THE PRESENCE OF THE LORD JESUS, WE PRONOUNCE THEM CURSED AND DAMNED, SOUL AND BODY, TO ALL ETERNITY.

JOHN REEVE and LODOWICK MUGGLETON, the two last Spiritual Witnesses, and alone true Prophets of the Holy Spirit, by Commission from the true God, that ever shall write or speak unto unbelieving Magistrates, Ministers, and People, until the only Lord of life and glory, the Man Jesus, personally appeareth, in the air, with his mighty Angels, to bear witness to this testimony: even so, come, Lord Jesus.

———————

FROM GREAT TRINITY LANE, AT A CHANDLER'S SHOP, AGAINST ONE Mr. MILLIS, A BROWN BAKER NEAR BOW LANE END, LONDON, 1653, IN THE SECOND YEAR OF OUR COMMISSION, BY VOICE FROM HEAVEN.

~~~~~~~~~~~~~~~~~~~~~

CHAPTER I.

1. Introductory Remarks. 2. The Creator came down personally in a spiritual Form, and conceived Himself of the seed of the Virgin. 3. The Spiritual Person of the Deity was absent from Heaven while the second Man, the Lord, was resident on earth. 4. No Spirit exists without a Body or Form. 5. The Creator, from eternity, was a spiritual Body or Person, in the form of a Man. 6. The Eternal Spiritual Form, Father and Son, was God and Man in one Person.

SIR,—By virtue of my commission, received by voice of words from the Holy Spirit of The only wise God, and everlasting Father, the man Jesus in glory, present I this epistle as an eternal witness between us.

2. FRIEND,—In the account of many, you have appeared as a true minister or preacher of the everlasting Gospel, or God, the man Jesus, and you have lived in glory for a season, through your ministry, taken up by your natural wit from the letter of the scripture, which were other men's words, received by voice

and inspiration from the Lord, you having no commission or revelation from the glorious mouth of the Lord Jesus to preach unto his elect:

3. Wherefore, because my God, the man Jesus, sent you not, you preach unto the people out of the bottomless pit of your own lying imagination, which is the devil, a God of words only, without substantial form, a bodiless God which you call an eternal Spirit, which you imagine was in heaven when the Lord Jesus was personally on this earth, unto whom you suppose the man Jesus prayed; but I declare, by revelation from the Holy Spirit, that you are utterly ignorant of that Father that the Lord Jesus cried unto, in the body of his flesh.

4. For it is hid from the wise and prudent men of this world, that the eternal Creator of all spiritual forms came down from the throne of his glory personally in a spiritual form or likeness of a man, and with his spiritual body or form personally entered into the body or womb of the Virgin Wife Mary, and in her womb uncreated himself from his eternal immortal glory, and in the same moment created or conceived himself of the seed of the Virgin in pure mortality, and in his appointed time became a child, a son, yea, a perfect creature: thus the immortal eternal Creator for a season became an absolute mortal man or creature, sin only excepted.

5. Again, I declare from the Holy Spirit, that in that heaven and earth above or beyond the stars, where the persons of the holy angels are resident, the personal presence of God was wholly absent from them for that season; the second man, the Lord from heaven, was resident on earth.

6. Again, it is hid from your eyes, that there is no spirit without a body or form hath any living being, nor ever had, neither of God the Creator from eternity, nor angels or man created in time.

7. Again, it is hid from your eyes, that from eternity the Creator was a spiritual body or person in the form of a man, having all parts in immortality, as a man hath in mortality, who was created in his spirit within like unto God, and in his form without like unto God also; only his fleshly form was natural and earthly, and God's form was spiritual and heavenly.

8. Again, because you preach without a commission, you understand not that the eternal spiritual form, both Father and Son, was a spiritual God and man in one person or form from all eternity; and so, it being impossible to divide them, unseparably the immortal God, Father and Son, did, as beforesaid, lay down their eternal immortal glory in the Virgin's womb together, and did transmute their spiritual glory both together into pure mortality, of flesh, blood, and bone, and in that body of flesh they did raise unto themselves new transcendent glory from elect men and angels, in revealing unto them the

wonderful spiritual mystery of the whole Godhead clothing itself with flesh, in the person of a man.

9. Therefore it is written, "For in him dwelleth all the fulness of the Godhead bodily;" again, "From his fulness we all receive grace for grace."

10, Again, "He that hath seen me hath seen the Father, and the Father and I are one." Again, "He thought it no robbery to be equal with God."

11. Again He is called "the Creator of the worlds." Again, it is written, "Hereby perceive we the love of God, because he laid down his life for us."

12. Again, "I am he that liveth and was dead, and behold I am alive for evermore, Amen." And, "I have the keys of hell and of death."

13. Again, "These things saith the First and the Last, which was dead and is alive." Again, "To the only wise God our Saviour, be glory and majesty, dominion and power, now and ever. Amen."

14. Thus it is clear, unto all that are instructed by revelation from the Holy Spirit, that there is no Creator nor God, nor ever was, but the man Jesus, that died without the gate, and rose again out of death by his own power; and in that body of flesh and bone he ascended far above all heavens, angels, and men: therefore it is written, "When he ascended on high, he gave gifts unto men."

CHAPTER II.

1. The Creator glorified the body of Elijah in Heaven, and commissioned him to represent the glorious Person of God the Father, while He came in flesh to redeem His Elect. 2. Elijah, with Moses, from the throne of glory, ministered consolation to the Lord then in Mortality. 3. The Man, Jesus, ascended personally to that glory whence He came, and by His Holy Spirit reveals to elect Men and Angels the Mystery of the Eternal Majesty. 4. Those who are the Lord's ambassadors receive the infallible Spirit, to discern between the Elect and the Reprobate, and to know who commit the unpardonable Sin. 5. The Lord speaks to his commissioned Prophets mouth to mouth. 6. Of the third and last Witnesses.

AGAIN, because you have no commission to preach, you understand not that, before the eternal Creator became a pure mortal creature, he glorified the body of his creature, the prophet Elijah, in that heaven and earth without the globe, and gave him a commission to represent the glorious person of God the Creator, whilst God the Father went that sore journey in flesh to redeem his elect ones by faith in his blood.

2. Thus the creature, by the unsearchable wisdom of the Creator, by commission from the Creator, for a season was representatively in the very glory of the Creator; and the Lord Jesus, the only Creator, was in the lowest abasement of a

creature; to show forth his infinite prerogative power, wisdom, and glory, love, and humility unto his elect, that they only may understand, by inspiration from the Holy Spirit, that the immortal Creator became an absolute creature, like unto us, except sin as beforesaid, that we that are his elect creatures, believing in the body or person of God, the Lord Jesus, our Creator, may in the resurrection possess glorious bodies of the same divine nature of our God the Father, and alone Creator, the man Jesus, to all eternity.

3. So that it is not so strange as true, that it was the prophet Elijah that my God, the man Jesus, in mortality, cried unto in all his extremities; and Elijah, as a faithful spiritual steward, with Moses, from the throne of glory did minister consolation unto his Lord and Saviour in mortality, as an immortal God and Father in glory, until the Creator of all life passed through hell by intolerable sufferings for his elect, the whole Godhead being dead and buried for a moment; and by his own power in his decreed time, in that body of flesh wherein his soul died, in death or out of death he quickened a new glorious life, wherein naturally as fire he ascended personally into that place of glory from whence he came, and now it is he alone sitteth on the right hand in the midst of the throne of the Father's immortal majesty, wisdom, power, and glory again.

4. So that the man Jesus being upon the throne, it is he alone, by his Holy Spirit, reveals unto elect men and angels in measure that unutterable wonderful mystery of the eternal Majesty, clothing himself with a garment of flesh to all eternity.

5. Wherefore I declare, by revelation from the Holy Spirit, that whoever in his spirit or tongue offers up prayers or praises unto any eternal Spirit, or God, or Father, but unto that man Jesus that was put to death in the flesh, and quickened in the spirit, he prays unto his own lying imagination, which is the devil, instead of the true God, the man Jesus

6. Again, unto us that are the Lord's spiritual ambassadors is the infallible Spirit given, whereby we are enabled to discern between the elect and the reprobate, and to seal them up unto eternal life and eternal death; and it is really so as sure as there is a Creator.

7. Again, the Holy Spirit, that sent us, enables us to answer all needful spiritual questions of the deep things of God, for the consolation of the elect, and the condemnation of the reprobate; but, of the contrary, because you have no commission to preach, you wanting the infallible Spirit, you know not whether any shall be saved or damned, because you have no assurance of your own salvation, neither do you know when men commit that unpardonable sin against the Holy Spirit.

8. Therefore all men may repent first or last, and find mercy, for ought you know; but the Lord hath given us to know

our own salvation, and of the salvation of some of his chosen ones, his holy name be eternally praised.

9. Again, we know, by that infallible Spirit of the Lord Jesus within us, when men fall under that unpardonable sin against the Holy Spirit; yea, we know of hundreds that are under that unpardonable sin at this time, who must all perish to eternity.

10. Again, you understand not that God hath a mouth to speak unto men as a man hath; and that he speaks to all his commissioned prophets and apostles as a man speaks unto his friend.

11. Thus the Lord spake unto Moses and the holy prophets in the time of the law, who were the Holy Spirit's first witnesses unto men, that the man Jesus, then to come in flesh, was the only God.

12. Again, the man Jesus spake unto his apostles mouth to mouth, who were the Holy Spirit's second witnesses unto the man Jesus, then come in the Flesh to be the only God.

13. Again, the third and last witnesses of the Holy Spirit unto the man Jesus to be the only God, are those two in the Revelation, spoken of by John the beloved disciple, that were to appear in this last age, and are upon the stage of this world at this time in the great city of London, where the elect shall see the great wonders of the Lord:

14. But they are hid from reprobate, hypocritical, Pharisaical, unmerciful men and women, that they may despise the Holy Spirit of the Lord Jesus, in us his last witnesses, that they may fill up the measure of their forefathers' sins, who despised the Holy Spirit in the Lord's two former witnesses, that, in the resurrection, at the great day of the Lord's account, they may be cursed, suffering together in their spirits and bodies, through the absence of that Holy Spirit rejected by them, the vengeance of eternal death, that shall burn as a flame of fiery darkness to all eternity,

CHAPTER III.

1. The Man Jesus hath all parts as a Man hath, but they are glorified. 2. Those only who are the true messengers of Christ can endure his Cross. 3. Conclusion.

AGAIN, I declare, from the Holy Spirit of the Lord Jesus, that my God, the man Jesus, from his throne of glory, spake to me, JOHN REEVE, his third and last witness, three mornings together, voice to voice, or mouth to mouth, by the which I know that God, the man Jesus, spake unto his two former witnesses, according to the scriptures; but you cannot possibly know it, as I do, but think you know it, because my God never spoke unto you as his messenger or minister, nor ever will.

2. Therefore you cannot understand that the eternal God, the man Jesus, hath all parts as a man hath, only all the members of the body of God are glorious, but man's members are

in shame, being defiled with the spirit of unclean reason and wicked imagination,

3. Therefore you cannot possibly preach or declare the true spiritual worship of my God, the man Jesus, because you went before you were sent. You know what is written, "Faith comes by hearing, and hearing by the word of God preached:" and how can he preach except he be sent?

4. Again, you being ignorant of the body of God, you cannot endure the cross of Christ, in suffering shame for his name's sake: but we that are his true messengers, through continued sufferings for his name's sake, are filled, by his blessed Spirit, with full assurance of a crown of immortal glory at his appearing, who, after he had suffered all his days in mortality, at the appointed time entered into his eternal immortal glory.

5. Nay, quite contrary to the true messengers of Christ, your ministry rather brings you in silver and honour from the men of this world, whereby your heart is made fat, and your understanding is darkened through pride from men's good opinions, in darkness like yourself; and so you run on, offering up a lying sacrifice unto an unknown God, and that gives great content to a proud, covetous, vainglorious people of your own spirit, because you know not the Lord Jesus Christ, who requires mercy and not sacrifice, who causes the sun to shine upon the just and the unjust.

6. But how can you that are ignorant of my God, the man Jesus, and the glory of that life to come prepared for the merciful, and are ignorant of that eternal death reserved for all hypocrites who blind their eyes with sacrifice, because they hate mercy;

7. How can you, that seek honour one of another, believe in the man Jesus to be the only God, to yield obedience unto the voice of his Holy Spirit of love and mercy unto all men, which is the only sweet-smelling sacrifice required by the Lord Jesus from all his elect?

8. Again, how can you distil upon men's spirits the glorious, things of eternity, without the spirit of prophecy, which is a spirit of revelation, or inspiration, given only to the true ambassadors of the Lord Jesus?

9. SIR,—Once more to your own particular person, if, after the receipt of this epistle, sent unto you from the Lord of glory to forewarn you before it was too late, you shall either write, prophesy, preach, or teach unto magistrates or people, public or private, than in obedience unto our commission; because you have disobeyed the message of the Holy Spirit, from the presence of the only wise God, the man Jesus, elect men, and angels, we pronounce you cursed and damned, both soul and body, unto all eternity.

A
REMONSTRANCE
FROM THE
ETERNAL GOD:

DECLARING

SEVERAL SPIRITUAL TRANSACTIONS

UNTO THE

PARLIAMENT AND COMMONWEALTH OF ENGLAND;

UNTO

HIS EXCELLENCY THE LORD GENERAL CROMWELL,
THE COUNCILS OF STATE AND OF WAR;

AND TO
ALL THAT LOVE THE SECOND APPEARING OF

THE LORD JESUS,

THE ONLY WISE GOD AND EVERLASTING FATHER, BLESSED FOR EVER.

BY JOHN REEVE & LODOWICK MUGGLETON,

THE TWO LAST WITNESSES AND TRUE PROPHETS, IMPRISONED FOR
THE TESTIMONY OF JESUS CHRIST, IN OLD BRIDEWELL.

FIRST PRINTED FOR THE AUTHORS (THEN RESIDING IN LONDON)
IN
THE YEAR OF OUR LORD, 1653.

FOURTH EDITION.
(COPIED FROM AN ORIGINAL, PRINTED FOR THE AUTHOR.)

LONDON:
PRINTED FOR JOSEPH FROST, 17, HALF MOON STREET,
BISHOPSGATE STREET.

BY LUKE JAMES HANSARD, 5, PEMBERTON ROW, GOUGH SQUARE, FLEET STREET.

1854.

CONTENTS.

A REMONSTRANCE
FROM THE YEAR 1651 TO 1653

CHAPTER I.

1. Of our being sent with a message unto one John Tanee, by command from God. 2. Of our being sent, by command from the Lord, with a message unto one John Robbins. 3. Of our being moved by the Holy Spirit to deliver a message unto some ministers.

RIGHT HONOURABLE AND WELL-BELOVED, —By virtue of a commission which we received by voice of words from Heaven, through the glorious mouth of the Lord Jesus Christ, the only true God and everlasting Father: the Lord, upon pain of eternal death, commanded us to deliver these messages following: —

2. First we were directed to go to one John Tanee, to convince him of errors which was exceeding great, in obedience to which command we accordingly went unto him, who first affirmed that there was never any personal God.

3. Sure he forgot that saying of the Apostle Thomas, who when he had handled the blessed body of the Lord Jesus, he called him his Lord and his God; there are divers other places in holy writ that clearly prove the man Jesus to be the only God.

4. Likewise he affirmed that God could not possibly be confined into the womb of the Virgin. I am sure also that if ever he did read these Scriptures he wanted faith to believe them, where it is written, "Is there anything too hard for God? with God all things are possible."

5. He further said, that could not be a God that suffered death, and after that was closed in a tomb three days and three nights. I am certain he knows nothing of these Scriptures, where it is written, "I am he that was dead and am alive: and, behold, I live for evermore, and have the keys of hell and death."

6. Again, it is written, that "he poured out his soul unto death," and that "believers are redeemed by the blood of God;" that is, by the life, soul, or Spirit of God; because the life, or soul, or spirit lieth in the blood, as it is written.

7. Likewise it was very strange to this John Tanee, that God should die, and by his own power raise himself from death to life, and personally ascend into that place of immortal glory beyond the stars, where the persons of holy angels are resident.

8. Sure I am, this man believeth no place of Scripture that proveth the power of that God, the man Jesus, who said to the Jews, "I have power to lay down my life, and I have power to take it up again."

9. Also it is written, "What and if you shall see the Son of Man ascend from whence he came?" Also, he was seen to ascend up by above an hundred disciples at one time, where it was said by two men in white, "Why stand ye gazing here? The same Jesus which ye see ascend, shall in like

manner come again."

10. So that of this man Jesus, the only Lord of life, which the Scripture throughout bears witness unto, John Tanee knew nothing.

11. But although John Tanee's God, which he professed, be an infinite Spirit, without any personal substance, yet he affirmed that he had a commission from his bodiless God, to lead the nation of Jews unto Jerusalem, to make them the only happy people; but this we know from that God that sent us, that his God and himself, and his designs, must all perish to eternity.

12. For this John Tanee is the last great mystery, Babylon, of that lying notion of the ranters, that ever shall speak or write against that spiritual mystery of the immortal God clothing himself with flesh in the person of a man, sin only excepted.

13. Moreover, we declare from our God, that this John Tanee is the prince and head of that atheistical lie held forth by all filthy sodomitical ranters, which are now in the world.

14. These are those spoken of by the apostle Paul that were to fall away from the faith, utterly denying the Lord Jesus and the holy scriptures, a little before the coming of the great God: these are those cursed children of that dragon devil, Cain, who say light and darkness are both one, good and evil are both one.

15. So likewise, like blaspheming reprobates as they are, they say that God and devil are both one; from which hellish tenet, with greediness they act unrighteousness, sporting themselves in all fleshly filthiness, as the people of Sodom and Gomorrah did, that they may justly be damned in themselves at the great day of the Lord, because they charged God with all their folly, who (as it is written) is of so pure a nature, that he can neither be tempted, nor tempt any man to evil. And so much for all ungodly ranters that despise a personal God, and John Tanee their king.

16. The second message that we were sent withal by command from God, was to one John Robbins, then in the new prison; which was to pronounce a sentence of eternal death upon him for his cruelty towards men, and his blasphemy against the Lord Jesus Christ.

17. For this John Robbins is the last great Antichrist, or man of sin, that was to appear to fulfil that Scripture, spoken of by Paul in 2 Thess. ii. 4, where it is written, "Who opposeth and exalteth himself above all that is called God, or that is worshipped; so that he as God sitteth in the temple of God, shewing himself that he is God."

18. For this John Robbins by many people was honoured as a God, for they fell upon their faces at his feet and worshipped him, calling him their Lord and their God; likewise, he was prayed unto as unto a God.

19. Moreover he gave them a law, commanding them not to mention the name of any other God, but him only; and if they disobeyed his laws, by his witch-

craft power he plagued their spirits and bodies, in the strangest manner that ever was seen, of which we were eye-witnesses.

20. But after the sentence of death from the Lord Jesus, through our mouths, was declared against this prince of devils in this age, he was constrained about the space of two months after to disown his assumed Godhead, through which many were deceived by him.

21. And some brought in their whole estates unto him, believing on him as their God and only Saviour, unto whom he promised to make the prison doors fly open, and safely conduct them through the seas into the city of Jerusalem, and there make them eternally happy.

22. But this cursed design came to a sudden conclusion as is beforesaid, which the magistrates' power could not accomplish though they imprisoned him; yet after he had heard the sentence of death denounced against him, for his taking the glory of God to himself, he spake these words and no more, saying, "It is finished; the Lord's will be done."

23. And so much concerning John Robbins, who was the king and chief head of all the false Christs, and false prophets and prophetesses, and counterfeit Virgin Maries, with all other witchcraft appearances, whether quakers or shakers, or whatsoever they be, that go under the notion of spiritual power from God at this day.

24. After the delivering of these two messages, by virtue of our commission, we were moved by the Spirit of Jesus Christ to deliver a message unto some mi Asters, to make known unto them, that they have no commission from God to preach unto the people, but they have taken up a commission from the letter of the Scripture to preach, and from men only, which some of them confessed to be true.

25. But some of them that were puffed up with fleshly honor and profit through their ministry, would not acknowledge that they had no commission from God to preach, although they could not give a positive answer to any spiritual question, to prove themselves ministers by commission from the Spirit of Jesus Christ.

26. For this we know from the Lord, that the sacred Scriptures were spoken by holy prophets and apostles: as they were inspired by the Holy Spirit, so did they speak.

27. Therefore none can interpret the Holy Scriptures that are so mysterious, according to the mind of God, except he is endued with the infallible Spirit of inspiration, as they were that spake the Scriptures.

28. And he that is endued with that blessed Spirit hath the life and power of the holy Scriptures shining through his spirit and body, having life eternal abiding in him; and he knows that, in the resurrection of the spirits and bodies out of the dust of all mankind at the last day, he shall visibly enjoy a

personal glory in immortality, in that everlasting kingdom of the undefiled heavens and earth above the stars, where the glorious person of God and holy angels are resident.

29. This is that place of blessedness that is utterly hid from the wise and prudent men of this world; but prepared for those men that spake the holy Scriptures, and those only that yield obedience unto the Holy Spirit of Jesus Christ, the only God all their days. And so much concerning that message unto some of the ministers of God, so called.

CHAPTER II.

1. A discovery of the Lord's two last Spiritual Witnesses that ever shall speak or write unto men, by commission from the true God, until time be no more. 2. Of the Roman Gentiles being Lords of the Scriptures, by conquest over the Jews.

THE next thing we shall declare unto you from the Lord is this:—that we two only are the last men that ever shall speak or write by commission from the true God unto the powers and people whilst this world endureth: therefore whoever lives to see an end of us shall suddenly see the dissolution of this vain world, and all the glory thereof; but the day and hour is known only unto Jesus Christ, the everlasting Father.

2. Moreover, this we know also:—that we two are the last men that ever God will give such heavenly understanding of his divine person any more; for we are those two spiritual witnesses prophesied of by John in Rev. xi., who to fulfil the Scriptures were appointed to appear in this blind age, to make known unto the elect a little of that unspeakable spiritual mystery of the immortal God and alone eternal Father, clothing himself with flesh in the person of a man as beforesaid.

3. Likewise we know that the only true God, the man Jesus, upon the throne of glory, (to his everlasting praise be it spoken!) hath by his blessed Spirit revealed unto us more spiritual understanding of that glorious mystery concerning Himself than ever was, is, or shall be revealed unto men, until time be swallowed up into eternity; and, without the knowledge of this mystery in some measure, no man can possibly enjoy any true peace unto his soul.

4. Again, we declare, by voice and inspiration from God, that we are the conclusion of this mystery which God made known at the first unto Adam, in that promise unto him, that "the seed of the woman should break the serpent's head;"

5. Revealing also of it by his blessed Spirit, to his chosen, from hence until Moses and the prophets, who spake much of this mystery to the elect in their times;

6. And from thence to the birth of our Lord and Saviour Jesus Christ, the holy mystery itself, when Jehovah, the everlasting Father, in the time of the

law, became a Son Jesus in the time of the Gospel—yea, and a servant to his elect creatures;

7. And from thence to the commission of the apostles, whose preaching was chiefly of this mystery, because in the knowledge of it only is the assurance of everlasting life.

8. But as for this commission of the apostles, it continued about three hundred years, before it was by the ten persecutions persecuted quite out of the world.

9. Then after the Roman Gentiles, by the sword, to fulfil the words of Christ, had conquered the nation of the Jews, they took possession of the letter of the Scriptures, which is the court without the temple, spoken of by John in Rev. xi.;

10. By which conquest over the Jews they have been lords over the letter of the Scripture unto this day, ordaining ministers of their own to be the interpreters of the Scriptures keeping the people in perpetual bondage, making such merchandise of them, that they have lived like princes by them.

11. Oh, how profitable have these Scriptures been to reprobate preachers!

12. Again, but as for the Spirit of life within the holy temple, God hath reserved it to himself, and he gives it to his elect Jews and Gentiles, from whence they have power within them to obey the letter without them:

13. But the reprobate worshippeth the letter and his own inventions for his God, but he hath no power from the Holy Spirit within the temple to yield obedience to the letter without, so much honoured by his lips:

14. And this is the cause in men, why so many must suffer the vengeance of eternal death, because they take upon them to be the ministers of God and interpreters of the sacred Scriptures, without a commission from God, they being utterly ignorant of his infallible Spirit;

15. The which blessed Spirit Both enable a man to declare to the sensible understanding of men what the person of God is, and his divine nature; and what the persons of holy angels are, and their natures; and what the person of the devil was before his fall, and what his person is and shall be to eternity; and what condition Adam was created in, and how he came to fall; also, what the glory of heaven is, and the residence of it to eternity; and what hell and eternal death is, and the place of it to eternity.

16. Moreover, we declare, from our God, that no man in the world at this time doth clearly understand any one of these six spiritual things, but we two only, whom the Lord hath sent to declare them unto his chosen ones, appointed unto eternal life. And so much for that truth.

17. Then immediately after this there came many people unto us, most of them pretending to know what the Lord had spoken unto us, unto whom we gave a full account, with which many seemed well satisfied; but some of them, being wise in their conceits, did presume to call our commission from Jesus Christ,

blasphemy, and a delusion of the devil, and such like;

18. For the which, in obedience to the command of our God, we did pronounce them eternally damned for their blasphemy against the Holy Spirit that sent us:

19. And after this manner we continued about the space of one whole year and a quarter, declaring the prerogative power and pleasure of our God, in which time many ignorant blasphemers being moved with envy, they brought themselves under an eternal curse. And so much for that truth.

CHAPTER III.

1. Of our being moved by the Holy Spirit to command, in general, all the Ministers about London and Westminster to lay down their preaching, because the Lord Jesus gave them no commission to preach. 2. Of our being sent with a message to all Spiritual Counterfeits about London.

AFTER this we were moved by the Holy Spirit that sent us, to command in general the eminent ministers (in the account of the people) about London and Westminster to lay down their ministry, because there is not a man of them, as beforesaid, hath the spirit of inspiration, to declare unto the people what the true God is, that they may be saved from the wrath to come.

2. Wherefore, for want of the gift of the Holy Spirit, they teach the people a false God, a false heaven, a false devil, and a false hell;

3. And this is the cause that the people remain in darkness, acting all cruelly one towards another, dying in their sins, and so consequently must be eternally damned.

4. For we that are the Lord's messengers, unto whom God hath given the infallible Spirit, do certainly know, that all the priests, ministers, or speakers to the people in the world are false and vain, both deceivers of themselves and of those that love to be deceived by them.

5. Therefore they teach the people an imaginary God, which they call an infinite Spirit, not having any bodily substance.

6. Thus, instead of instructing the people in true understanding of a spiritual personal God, whom to know is life eternal, they teach the people a God of words only.

7. So, likewise, they teach the people an imaginary devil also, persuading them that the devil is an invisible spirit, without a bodily substance, walking or flying to and fro in the air; and they say this imaginary evil spirit or devil is he that tempteth all men to that wickedness committed by them.

8. Thus they teach the people a devil that is not, nor ever was, like unto the rest of their false and lying tenets.

9. As for this truth, which is of a transcendent excellency, in general they are utterly ignorant of it:—that is, that no invisible spirit, neither of God, angels, nor men, can possibly have any living

being, without a body or person, nor never had.

10. Thus the people are kept from the knowledge of the true God, and from the knowledge of the right devil; they not thinking in the least that there is no other devil, since the fall of Adam, but a man's own spirit of unclean reason, and wicked imagination.

11. Therefore it is written, that "all the imaginations of man's heart are evil, and only evil, and continually evil; What is that but the devil that has nothing in it but evil?

12. Again, it is written, "Not that which goeth into the belly defileth a man, but that which cometh out of the man: out of the heart proceed evil thoughts, murders, adulteries, and such like."

13. Again, it is written, "When a man is tempted to evil, he is drawn aside of his own lust."

14. Thus it is clear, to those that see by the eye of faith, that that devil so much spoken of in holy writ is that unsatiable lust, naturally arising from that spirit of unclean reason and wicked imagination dwelling in the body of man, which tempts wicked men to all unrighteousness.

15. Wherefore from the Lord we counsel you to watch that devil within you; and our souls for yours, you shall never be troubled with any invisible devil without you: for indeed there was never any such evil spirit or bodiless devil in the air, as ignorant men have for a long season taught.

16. Again, if men and women were convinced that there are no other devils but their own spirits, until they are born again by the Spirit of Jesus Christ, they would then be afraid to act wickedness one towards another, seeing there is nothing to be eternally damned, but that which acteth unrighteousness; and there is nothing committeth wickedness but men and women.

17. Without all controversy, since the fall of man there are no other devils but men and women only: so, likewise, as aforesaid, they must needs teach a false heaven and a false hell, that know neither God nor devil.

18. Again, as for the persons of holy angels, they know nothing of them, nor what condition Adam was created in, or how he came to lose his first estate: only like children they make mention of a God, and of angels, and of a heaven, and of a devil, and of a hell: but as for the true understanding of these spiritual things and places, they know certainly no more of them than babes.

19. And so much for all false priests, ministers, or speakers in this world, who are ministers of the letter, and by the will of man, but are not ministers of the spirit by the will of God; and must all perish to eternity, who know or hear of the truths of God declared by us, and yet wilfully disobey the commission of the Lord in us.

20. Again, the next thing we shall remonstrate unto you is this:—that there was a necessity that God, to vindicate his own glory, should give unto us, or some other men, a commission to

go forth to the world; because within these twelve years there have been so many in this land that have come in their own names, calling themselves Christs, and prophets, and Virgin Maries, and such like.

21. Upon these several sorts which arose to fulfil the Scriptures, we have pronounced the sentence of eternal death, for their robbing God of his glory, who will not give his glory to another, they assuming the titles of God to themselves; yet they lived like devils, as they are, in all carnal and unnatural lusts.

22. Moreover, although lately there hath appeared so many spiritual counterfeits to fulfil the Scriptures, which say, "You shall know them by their fruits;" yet in general the people are so blind, because their own deeds are evil, that they cannot discern the fruits of these wicked men, whether they be good or evil.

23. Likewise, there are but very few, in comparison of the multitude, that know whether there hath appeared any of these fig-trees whose fruits are leaves only; notwithstanding the lying priests, before their eyes, attain to great estates, through their skilful merchandising of the sacred Scriptures.

24. But know this from the Lord, both powers and people (for you shall know it, either for your weal or woe):—that God hath chosen us two only to be the spiritual teachers of his everlasting gospel, and hath given us power to work all righteousness, and hath given us this great power to pronounce his sentence of eternal death upon all spiritual counterfeits, and deceiving Scripture merchants; and it is irrevocable, as sure as there is a God.

25. Again, if men that counterfeit commissions from kings or states seldom find mercy, what think you then will become of all those that counterfeit commissions from the Lord of heaven and earth, and Creator of all powers?

26. And so much for all spiritual counterfeits, and Scripture's lamb-like wolves, that preach in their own names, or by a commission from man, for want of a commission from the man Jesus, the only wise God, and alone everlasting Father.

CHAPTER IV.

1. Of our being apprehended, and committed to Newgate, for our faith, by the Lord Mayor. 2. Of the injustice of one Alderman Andrews. 3. Of our unjust Trial, and Sentence against us, for our faith in God, by the Recorder Steele, and the London Jury, about the 15th October, 1653.

THEN after we had made it appear to many of the ministers, that they have no commission from God to preach; and the sentence of death being denounced against them, for their despising to obey the message of the Lord; some of them sent their disciples unto us, who being of their own persecuting spirits, they came under the sentence of death also

2. Which occasioned the peo-

ple to come unto us very much for the space of three months following: many, blaspheming against the Holy Spirit that sent us, came under the same curse.

3. Thus we continued, in obedience to our commission, declaring the counsels of God unto men, until about the 12th of September, 1653;

4. At which time some of our persecutors, which were under the sentence, accompanied with the marshalmen, with a warrant took us out of our house, and brought us before Alderman Fouke, then Lord Mayor;

5. Who, after he had examined us, he despised the Holy Spirit and person of the Lord Jesus Christ that sent us, and so came under the sentence of death with our Judas accusers, for his cursed blasphemy against the Lord Jesus Christ, and his blessed Spirit that sent us;

6. And for his unjust committing us to the common gaol of Newgate, to try us by the civil law, who did not nor cannot break any civil law of the Commonwealth of England.

7. This is the first magistrate that brought himself to public shame, besides an eternal curse which he shall not escape in the day of the Lord's vengeance, for his persecuting of the messengers of the Lord Jesus, and for his meddling with that which in the least belongs not to any civil magistrate.

8. For the duty of the magistrate is to be skilful in the civil laws of the land; and if they find any man to wrong one another in word or deed, contrary to those laws, then impartially ought they to execute justice between man and man:

9. But they have no authority to judge us, that are messengers and prophets sent from God, who are kept by the power of God so innocent from the breach of any civil laws of men, that we are made examples in the fulfilling of them to the whole world.

10. Moreover, we declare, from the Lord, that no civil magistrate ought to call any man to account for his faith concerning God, or the sacred Scriptures, because there is not a magistrate in the world at this time that doth clearly understand what the true God is, or the truth of holy writ.

11. Yet this magistrate, to fulfil that prophecy in Rev. xi., concerning his making war with the witnesses, must needs walk in his brother Pilate's steps, who condemned the Lord of all life, although his conscience made him say, "that he saw nothing in him worthy of death or blame!"

12. Wherefore, as sure as Pilate must suffer the vengeance of eternal death, because he preferred his honour among men of more value than a good conscience towards God; so, likewise, this magistrate, Alderman Fouke, for his unjust committing of us to prison, who are the Lord's messengers, by his prerogative will, for his honour's sake (although his conscience told him that we had not broke any of the civil laws of England);

13. Therefore the Lord, by us his messengers, hath set a mark of reprobation upon him, as the Lord marked his father Cain,

which shall remain with him to all eternity. And so much for that reprobate angel, Alderman Fouke, and our anti-Christian accusers.

14. The next thing we shall remonstrate unto you, is concerning one Alderman Andrews, who in his mayoralty persecuted one Captain Norwood for blasphemy, which no magistrate ought to do, as beforesaid:

15. Because the Lord Jesus gave them no commission to be the judge of men's consciences on earth, concerning blasphemy against God and the sacred Scriptures.

16. For you may know, that the civil law instructs no man in the knowledge of a spiritual personal God, nor gives him understanding to interpret holy writ, that he might know what is blasphemy against God:

17. Yet, notwithstanding, this alderman, about the time of our unjust trial for our faith, caused my two daughters (being but young) to come before him, and he put one of them to her oath, that she should confess unto him whatever he should ask of her.

18. Ye powers of England! we appeal unto you whether this alderman acted by your law, or by his own will?

19. Likewise he caused my house to be searched at the same time for books, into which he is not worthy to look.

20. Wherefore, for his blasphemous speeches unto one Mr. Ledder, a New England merchant, against the Holy Spirit that inspired us to write those heavenly books, for the conso-

lation of the blessed; in obedience to our commission that we received by voice of words from heaven, we pronounce him cursed and damned, soul and body, to all eternity.

21. This will be that second reprobate angel's portion in the day of the Lord Jesus, and the portion of all civil magistrates that persecute men for their consciences, who have not broken their civil laws.

22. O ye despisers of true prophecy, and persecutors of innocent men, wonder and perish! for so did your forefathers to the holy prophets and apostles in their time. And so much for that persecutor, Alderman Andrews.

23. The next thing we shall remonstrate unto your honours, will be the unjust practice of the Recorder Steele, and the London jury, at the sessions' time in the Old Bailey, notwithstanding we gave them a clear demonstration from the Lord Jesus, before our trial, that they have no commission from heaven to judge men, or try men for their faith, concerning God and the sacred Scriptures.

24. But, as aforesaid, they ought to be wise and learned in the civil laws of the Commonwealth of England, and to execute equal justice unto all men; and in so doing they may enjoy the righteousness of the law, and live in peace all their days.

25. Is it not a strange thing, that most magistrates cannot be contented with their earthly authority and honour they are invested withal; but, without a commission from God, presump-

tuously they will sit upon his throne, and rob Him of his glory, by taking upon them to judge the prophets of the Lord?

26. And they will be the judges of blasphemy against God; and yet they know not what the true God is, or whether there is any God at all, but perishing nature only?

27. And they will be the judges of the mind of God in the sacred Scriptures; and yet they know not whether those spiritual testaments are the wisdom of the immortal God, or the wisdom of mortal men?

28. Which, if they had faith to believe that holy writ to be the wisdom of Jesus Christ, then would they yield obedience to his blessed Spirit, which teacheth men to suffer persecution for the name of Christ; but not to persecute any man for his faith, but to show mercy to their greatest enemies.

29. But, quite contrary to the everlasting gospel of following peace with all men, and holiness, without which no man shall see the Lord to his comfort, the recorder and the jury did pronounce us to be blasphemers, for our declaring the man Jesus, that died at Jerusalem, and arose from death to life by his own power, to be the only God and everlasting Father.

30. For this glorious truth's sake, which they call blasphemy, they have committed us to Old Bridewell, there to remain six months without bail or mainprise.

31. O ye parliament and powers of England, if there be a man amongst you that hath any light of the Spirit of Jesus Christ within you, you must needs acknowledge this sentence against us to be contrary to all your civil laws, and all your engagements you were pleased to make with your brethren, the free-born people of England!

32. And contrary to all equity and conscience in those men that have any true hope of salvation at the appearing of Jesus Christ, who will suddenly come in flaming fire, with his ten thousands of saints, to recompense vengeance upon the souls and bodies of all persecutors of conscience, both great and small, and upon all men that know not God, nor obey the gospel of Jesus Christ.

33. Wherefore, because the Recorder of London and the jury beforesaid did rob Jesus Christ of his glory, and, like devils, as they are, did condemn the, Lord of life that sent us, by blaspheming against his Holy Spirit, in obedience to the commission we have received from the glorious mouth of the ever-living God, from the presence of the Lord Jesus Christ, elect men, and angels, we pronounce the recorder and the jury cursed and damned, souls and bodies, to all eternity.

34. And so much for our unjust trial, and the just sentence of Jesus Christ upon the third reprobate angel and his brethren, those inferior dark angels who esteemed more of the honour of a man, appointed to perish, than the glory of God and their own eternal salvation.

35. Thus, according to truth, we have given your honours a brief description of the commission of the true God committed to our charge, with a remonstrance of those spiritual transactions we have been carried through by the power of our God, having often been in danger of our lives, by unreasonable men, for his name's sake, because they could not bear this sharp commission which the Lord put upon us the third, fourth, and fifth days of February, 1651.

CHAPTER V.

1. Of our humble requests, in the behalf of the chosen of God, unto all the chief powers of England.

AND now, in the last place, in the name and power of our Lord Jesus Christ that sent us, we shall write a few lines unto all your Honours' serious considerations, by way of recital of your engaging your lives, and liberties, and honours, and all that is dear unto you, unto your brethren, the free people of England, that they should not only enjoy their civil liberties, but the liberty of their consciences also towards God, which is of more value than this whole world.

2. Upon this account your brethren did not only write engagements with you, but they did freely venture their lives, and all that was dear unto them, against the common enemy, for the preservation of your persons and posterities, they not doubting in the least of your faithfulness towards them that were so faithful towards you concerning their liberties, but especially the liberty of their consciences, which belongs not to man to judge, but to God only that knows the heart.

3. You know that the Scripture saith, that Jesus Christ is the only judge both of the quick and dead: therefore we hope you will allow him also to be the alone judge of all men's faith concerning God and the sacred Scriptures:

4. Which, if you grant him this His royal prerogative, then you will come to understand that that magistrate who takes upon him to sentence men for their faith concerning God and the sacred Scriptures, he usurpeth God's throne, and robs him of his glory, and so brings upon himself an eternal curse.

5. Again, we declare, from the Holy Spirit that sent us, that, if you perform your covenant to your brethren, concerning their conscience towards God and the Holy Scriptures, then you shall tread all the common enemies of this nation under your feet both by sea and land for ever.

6. Let all the wise men in the nation gainsay what we have written, you shall find them all liars, if you make trial of this counsel of the Lord's, sent unto you by us his last messengers:

7. For you know that it was the ecclesiastical tyranny of the bishops' courts over men's consciences, which was the chief thing that provoked the religious, conscientious men, more

faithfully than others, courageously to fight your hottest battles, for the liberty of their consciences; many hundreds of them being slain upon this account, leaving their wives and children in a mourning condition behind them.

8. Also you know that the Synod sat about four years in an ecclesiastical manner to prove themselves Jure Divino, but in the end they were all found to be but Jure Humano:—that is, they were manifested not to be the ministers of God, but ordained of men only.

9. Thus this Synod of young bishops, striving to sit in the old bishops' tyrannical chair, being discovered, they were soon dissolved.

10. Wherefore, O ye powers of England, seeing you and the people, for liberty of conscience, did join together as one man, and have conquered all ecclesiastical tyrants and monsters of men, we beseech you let your brethren, the free-born people, enjoy the liberty of their conscience, which they have bought at so dear a rate:

11. And suffer not this ecclesiastical tyranny to reign in the civil magistrate, which you have fought against in those that were established from the king's power in their ecclesiastical tyranny by a law, which, if you do establish again by a law, you can never sit upon the throne in safety, nor enjoy the peace of your consciences, which is of more value than this whole world.

12. For we that are the Lord's messengers, whatever we suffer, we must tell you (whatever cursed men tell you to the contrary), that persecution of conscience is the great sin of rebellion against God, which is as the sin of witchcraft.

13. Wherefore that magistrate who persecutes men for their faith concerning God and the Scriptures, commits that unpardonable sin against the Holy Spirit which can never be repented of, and so consequently must perish eternally, as sure as God is God.

14. Therefore, O ye powers of England! be wise and learned, and quit yourselves like wise councillors, by delivering yourselves from that spiritual Babylonish yoke of persecuting men for their faith; and hearken no more to the cunning Achitophels, and lying Trenchar chaplains, of this perishing world; but hearken to the voice of Jesus Christ within you, who is the only true God, alone minister and councillor, by his Holy Spirit, of all men appointed to salvation.

15. Then may you clearly distinguish between the things that are Caesar's, and the things that are God's.

16. Thus we being confident that, if the Lord Jesus, that sent us, have delight in any of your persons, then after the perusal hereof you will never enjoy any true peace more, until you have set at liberty all the prisoners in your dominions, that suffer purely for their conscience towards God, they not being guilty of the breach of the civil laws of the parliament and commonwealth of England:

17. And in so doing, your Honours' names that are made the instrument thereof shall refresh or heal the wounds of all the chosen of God living in your territories, like unto the balm of Gilead; and you shall be renowned unto the ends of the earth, above all the princes in the world.

18. But, on the contrary, if you are all left to the hardness of your own hearts, as King Pharaoh was, to join with the persecutors of the little ones of Jesus Christ beforesaid, "It had been better for you that you had never been born, or that a millstone were hanged about your necks, and that you were all cast into the midst of the sea."

19. These words of truth were spoken by Him that cannot lie, who hath sent us that are the last messengers to give you notice, whilst you have time, of His sudden appearing to judge both quick and dead. So, desiring our God, if it be his good pleasure, to make your spirits obedient unto this spiritual message of His,

We remain,

Your Honours' to command,

In all righteousness, till death,

JOHN REEVE AND LODOWICK MUGGLETON.

In opposition to all gainsayers in the world, we are made able, from the Spirit of Jesus Christ that sent us, clearly by the sacred Scripture to remonstrate and prove, that the man Jesus, now glorified, was and is the only God and Father from eternity to eternity, and that He is the alone Creator of all things or forms that are made in both worlds: and this Jesus, our blessed Lord and Saviour, hath sent us for this very end and purpose, to pronounce all those that receive this divine truth, the blessed of the Lord to eternity; and all those that despise this saving truth, to declare them from the Lord cursed to eternity.

JOHN REEVE and LODOWICK MUGGLETON.

THE END.

PRINTED BY LIKE JAMES HANSARD, 5, PEMBERTON ROW, GOUGH SQUARE, FLEET STREET.

A LETTER TO THE BRETHREN

This letter read:

Sir

Through you, I receive with pleasure the thanks of the trustees of the British Museum, for the Divine Looking-Glass.

Yet I have another request to make of them, which I hope they will oblige me in

That is, if they will allow the enclosed printed letter to be fastened in front of the Divine Looking-Glass bound in the first volume of Reeve & Muggletons Works, I shall esteem it a great favour.

Feeling that every aughthers work should be kept entire as he leaves it.

I am Sir, with great respect
your obedient humble servant

Joseph Frost

[A written copy of the following was sent to the BRITISH Museum, with the Revised Edition of "THE DIVINE LOOKING GLASS,"— Reprinted in 1846.]

TO THE READER.

BELOVED BRETHREN,

There appears to be a very great error crept in amongst us, in some way or other, which I cannot account for, there being no account or List of the Subscribers, nor record in the Church respecting the re-printing of that Divine Looking-Glass, in the year 1760; nor any thing in the records of the Church to justify any person in mixing and re-printing that again, which the Prophet Muggleton has left out in his Revised Edition, but altogether to the contrary, as may be seen on reference to the Stream, bound in the Third Volume, page 9, in a letter to Walter Bohenan, and in the Acts of the Witnesses, bound in the Third Volume. See Epistle Dedicatory, page 6, and Answer to Nine Assertions in the same book, pages 136 to 152, and for the danger of adding and taking away from the true Prophets, Apostles, and Minis-ters. See the Interpretation of the whole Book of the Revelations, bound in the second volume, page 318. More places might be named, but I suppose there is enough to show the error, which will appear as follow:—

In the year 1836, we presented to the British Museum, the Prophets Reeve and Muggleton's Writings, bound in three volumes with other Books relative thereto. But it appears that the Divine Looking-Glass, bound in the first volume of those Books, is not authorised by the Prophet Muggleton, he being the longest liver, and on whom the commission of the Spirit wholly rested, after the decease of John Reeve, as will appear on references to the places before mentioned.

In a few years after we had presented the Books to the British Museum, we had occasion to re-print the Divine Looking-Glass.

But before we began to print it, we collected all the old Divine Book we could find, with a view to correct any error that might have occured in the press; and, in doing so, we found three different Divines, that is to say, the first Book printed in John Reeve's life time, in the year 1656, and one revised by and printed for Lodowick Muggleton, in the year 1661; which the Prophet Muggleton has recorded as having done so, as may be seen in the Acts of the Witnesses, bound in the Third Volume, page 82, a true copy of which was printed by subscription in the year 1846.

And one printed in the year 1760. In this one appears to be re-printed all that which the Prophet Muggleton left out in his revised edition, which is 99 years after the Prophet Muggleton.

And there appears no authority from him to re-establish or reprint that again which the Prophet Muggleton has left out; but to the contrary, which makes it appear error in those that printed it; and not only so, but they have turned that into chapter and verse; which is not so in the first Book, apparently to make it appear like the second edition, which is in chapter and verse, and not only that, but they have made use of the Preface which the Prophet Muggleton wrote for his second edition, as may be seen on reference to both Books.

This Book (1760) appears under a cloak, which I hope will be thrown off, as I have no doubt it has misled many, seeing by the Preface, they would naturally think they had got a copy of the Second Edition, which it is not.

Now I shall leave it for the Reader to consider and judge for himself, and subscribe myself

Your's truly,
JOSEPH FROST.

17, Half Moon Street, Bishopsgate Street, London, January, 1853.

P.S.—The following is not written in the Divine Looking-Glass, sent to the British Museum, but to the Church generally, thinking it would be well for the believers of the Prophet Muggleton, or The True Muggletonians, to look and see if the same spirit is not striving to divide the Church, as there appeared to be at the time when The Acts of the Witnesses was printed.

I have heard some of the old Believers say that there was a party of that sort, as is spoken of in the Acts, which called themselves Reeveonians, which I have no doubt was the party which re-printed that Divine Looking-Glass in 1760. And the same spirit appears to be now in the Church, endeavouring to establish that Book for the true Muggletonians' Church Book, which cannot be allowed by any who take Muggleton for their guide. Neither can we possibly divide the Prophets, because the Prophet Muggleton says that John Reeve wrote all his points of Doctrine by an Infallible Spirit, which points of Doctrine is retained in his Revised Edition; and what the Prophet Muggleton has done, it appears, must be taken on his bare word, or perish; besides, there would appear a deal of nonsense in any calling themselves Muggletonians, and not to follow the Prophet Muggleton throughout.

And if those Acts which he gave to his true Friends, to publish after his death, be true, which I have no doubt of, they must stand unalterable for ever amongst his true Friends, and will be received as a Legacy, and his Last Will, by the Faithful, who believe that the Commission wholly rested an him after John Reeve's decease.

A Quotation from the Acts, see Epistle Dedicatory, page 6, words as follow: —

"Again, we see by this Book of the Acts, that these two Prophets were jointly chosen of God, and made equal in Power and Authority; for the Prophet Reeve saith, that his fellow Witness had as great power as he had himself; and further saith, that he was The Lord's Last High Priest. If this be granted, then it must follow that there can be no salvation to such as shall reject him or his Writings. Although they pretend to own John Reeve, "Obedience to the Prophet is better than sacrifice." So I conclude,

Yours in the true Faith of REEVE AND MUGGLETON,

JOSEPH FROST.
31st January, 1853.

[Please to place this in your Divine Looking Glass.]

A

DIVINE LOOKING-GLASS

OR,

THE THIRD AND LAST TESTAMENT

OF

OUR LORD JESUS CHRIST,

WHOSE

PERSONAL RESIDENCE IS SEATED ON HIS THRONE OF ETERNAL
GLORY IN ANOTHER WORLD:
BEING

THE COMMISSION OF THE SPIRIT, AGREEING WITH, AND EXPLAINING OF
THE TWO FORMER COMMISSIONS OF THE LAW AND THE GOSPEL,
DIFFERING ONLY IN POINT OF WORSHIP.

SET FORTH FOR THE TRIAL OF ALL SORTS OF SUPPOSED SPIRITUAL
LIGHTS IN THE WORLD, UNTIL THE EVER-LIVING TRUE JESUS, THE ONLY
HIGH AND MIGHTY GOD, PERSONALLY APPEAR IN THE AIR WITH HIS
SAINTS AND ANGELS.

BY

JOHN REEVE & LODOWICK MUGGLETON,

PENMEN HEREOF, AND THE LAST CHOSEN WITNESSES UNTO THAT EVER-BLESSED BODY OF
CHRIST JESUS GLORIFIED, TO BE THE ONLY WISE, VERY TRUE GOD ALONE, EVERLASTING
FATHER, AND CREATOR OF BOTH WORLDS, AND ALL THAT WERE MADE IN THEM.

"EVEN SO COME LORD JESUS, COME QUICKLY, TO TESTIFY AND FULFIL THY OWN PROMISE IN THY RECORDS
OP TRUTH, THAT THY REDEEMED ONES MAY REALLY KNOW THAT THOU HAST SENT US; AND ART THAT
UNCHANGEABLE GOD WHICH CANNOT POSSIBLY LIE, THOUGH MILLIONS OF UNREDEEMED MANKIND
THEREBY SHOULD EVERLASTINGLY PERISH."

Fifth Edition

LONDON:

FIRST PRINTED IN 1656 REVISED BY, AND PRINTED FOR, LODOWICK MUGGLETON, IN 1661;
RE-PRINTED (BY SUBSCRIPTION) IN 1846, BY CATCHPOOL & TRENT, 5, ST. JOHN'S SQUARE,
FROM THE SECOND EDITION REVISED BY THE PROPHET LODOWICK MUGGLETON;

AND MAY BE HAD OF
JOSEPH AND ISAAC FROST, ST. JOHN'S SQUARE, CLERKENWELL; JOSEPH
GANDAR. 18, NORTHAMPTON PARK, ISLINGTON; AND WILLIAM RIDSDALE, LENTON,
NEAR NOTTINGHAM; AND OF BOOKSELLERS.

{Here begins a section that was omitted in Muggleton's 1661 revision}

A
Divine LOOKING-GLASS;
OR
Heavenly Touch-Stone.

Proceeding from the unerring Spirit of an Infinite Majesty, whose Personal Residence is seated on his Throne of bright burning Crowns of Eternal Glory in another World; purchased in this World from his Divine Self only, by Virtue of pouring forth his unvaluable Life Blood unto Death, through the Transmuting of his incomprehensible Glory into a Body of Flesh, sent forth for a Trial of all sorts of supposed Spiritual Lights in this Nation, or World, until the Ever-living True Jesus, that most High, and Mighty God, personally appeareth in the Air with his Saints and Angels, to judge between the Truth of this Epistle, and all Spirits that shall contest with it under Heaven. Even so come Lord Jesus, come quickly, and fulfil thine own Promise in thy Records of Truth, that thy Redeemed Ones may really know, thou art that unchangeable God which cannot possibly Lie, though Millions of Unredeemed Mankind thereby should everlastingly Perish.

Or, An Epistle Written by Inspiration from the fiery glorious Spirit of Jesus Christ, that Immortal Jew, and Spiritual Lion of the Tribe of Judah, who alone is the Lord protector of Heavens, Earth, Angels, and Men. Unto Oliver Cromwell, that Mortal Jew, and Natural Lion of the same Tribe according to the Flesh. Who is stiled Lord protector of England, Scotland, and Ireland, through the secret Decree of this most High and Mighty God. And to his, and the Common-wealth's most eminent Council, and Head Officers in Martial Affairs within his Dominions, as the fore-runner of the sudden, dreadful Appearing of this impartial Judge of Quick and Dead, with his elect Angels, to make an Everlasting Separation between the Persons of Tender-hearted Israelites, and Bowelless Cananites. Even so come Lord Jesus, come quickly. Amen.

Printed in the Year of our Lord, 1656. And re-printed by Subscription in the Year, 1760.

Most Heroic Cromwell, who art exalted unto Temporal Dignity beyond the Foreknowledge of Men or Angels. In the most Holy Name and nature of our Lord Jesus Christ, upon the bended Knees of our Souls, we most humbly beseech thee to peruse this Epistle with thy own Eyes, not trusting any Man about thee to view it before thee, why, because there is something written in the Book which more principally concerns Thee more then all other Men within thy Territories. And in so doing, with Spiritual Delight, by the glorious Power of the Everlasting God. thou may'st in due season become the only Counsellor to thy Council above all Earthly Princes under Heaven, and not only so, but also a faithful Defender and Deliverer of all Suffering people upon a Spiritual Account within thy Dominions, and if so, what Mortal Persecuting Powers can stand before thee, or Serpentine cursed Plots come near Thee or thine for ever?

John Reeve and Lodowick Muggleton, Penmen of this Epistle, and chosen Witnesses unto that ever Blessed Body of Christ Jesus Glorified, to be the only wise, very True God alone, Everlasting Father, and Creator of both Worlds, and all that were made in them in a sober Opposition of Men or Angels.

{Here ends a section that was omitted in Muggleton's 1661 revision}

TO THE
SPIRITUAL DISCERNING READER.

MY beloved spiritual brethren, in whom is rooted and really grounded the saving light of life eternal, I know that the manifold breakings forth of seeming glorious appearances in this age can by no means be hid from your eyes.

Also you know that the true light of life hath almost discovered them all to be nothing else but the very depth of men's serpentine subtleties, cloaked over with the divine titles of the most infinite and holy God, so that men's glittering language now is of no value unto you, unless the Holy Spirit beareth witness unto your spirits, that the Lord hath spoken unto them from heaven; neither can men blind your eyes with their natural miracles, artificial jugglings, sophistical signs and wonders, to cause you ever the sooner for that to receive them as immediately sent forth by the ever-living God.

I say it is not lofty words of imaginary voices, visions, dreams, revelations, variety of languages, declarations of the knowledge of the heights and depths of perishing nature, pretended Jerusalem journeys, supposed seeing of spiritual angels with eyes of natural flesh, and familiar conversing with them, and knowing the names of all the holy angels in glory, and every man's protecting angel in this world, or any such like carnal fancies, can blind your eyes any more which have received from above a distinguishing gift between the things of eternal life and death, not only from its effects, but from its first causes also.

My selected brethren unto a pure light, language, and life, from the very true God, I certainly know, that nothing in this world will satisfy your hungry souls, but a right understanding of spiritual things which are eternal in that world to come; therefore, unto you alone which look not after gilded words, but glorious things, present I this epistle from that Spirit which can neither deceive, nor be deceived, by men or angels.

Wherefore, if any sober man, of a quick comprehension, shall suppose that this writing might have been composed into fewer words than is here inserted, I hope he shall wisely consider that things of such concernment require more words than ordinary, not only for informing and confirming of the simple saints, but also for confounding of the subtle serpents of this age.

Moreover, you that peruse this epistle, which are of an unjudging tender spirit, may also know, that before the eternal Spirit in Christ Jesus became my minister, I was very weak in the knowledge of learned men's opinions, their disputes, or writings, concerning heavenly things which are hid from them, and revealed unto unlearned babes.

Therefore, the chief desire of my soul is, that it may be manifested. unto elect men and angels, whether the substance of this epistle proceeds from mine own carnal spirit, or from the most pure and holy Spirit of God Himself; I mean that one personal glorious majesty of our Lord Jesus Christ, whose divine nature both is and shall be crowns of immortal ravishing excellencies in all his elect, at the great and dreadful day of eternal burning vengeance upon the souls and bodies of all bloody-minded impenitent persecutors that ever were born.

JOHN REEVE.

ANOTHER EPISTLE ANNEXED TO THIS BOOK.

My beloved spiritual brethren, who are or shall come to be really grounded in the true doctrine, which is held forth in the three commissions, namely, the commission of Moses and the prophets; 2. Of Christ Jesus and the Apostles; 3. Of the commission of the Spirit; which commission is now extant in the world, though not accompanied with visible signs and natural miracles as the other two commissions had in their time, when their commission was in being; yet this I am sure, that this commission of the Spirit being the last commission that God will ever send. into this world, while time is no more; therefore it is that this commission of the Spirit hath the only interpretation of the two former commissions: for there is no man in the world at this day, let him be of what sect or opinion soever, that doth truly know any part of the scriptures, but this commission of the Spirit only, notwithstanding they labour so much after the knowledge of them; yet, for want of a commission from God, they have no true understanding of any one principal or true ground of faith; for all that they do of that nature is nothing else but the very strength of reason, and reason can never truly know the deep things of eternity; because there is no man in the world at this day that hath the knowledge of the true God, his form and nature the right devil, his form and nature, but this commission of the Spirit only.

Therefore, when God spake these words unto John Reeve, saying, I have given thee understanding of my mind in the scriptures, above all the men in the world; also God did say at the same time, I have given thee Lodowick Muggleton to be thy mouth; so that according to the words of God, He hath given us two to understand more of his mind in the scriptures, than all the men in the world do at this day, that is, more spiritual knowledge of the scriptures than all the men in world, because God hath chosen us two to be his last commissionated prophets and witnesses of the Spirit, to declare and make known unto the seed of faith those great mysteries which have lain hid in the breast of God ever since the foundation of this world was laid; and in the time of their commission was in some measure made manifest unto the sons of men, by some part of the mystery of God, as those commissions aforesaid, namely, Moses and Jesus.

But now, in this last age, is the commission of the Spirit, which is to finish the mystery of God, according to that saying of John, Rev. x. 7, where it is said, "But in the days of the voice of the seventh angel, when he shall begin to sound, the mystery of God shall be finished, as he hath declared to his servants the prophets."

And now this mystery of God is made manifest in the world by this commission of the Spirit both in our discourse and writings: so that it may be clear to you that are capable to understand, and to comprehend those deep and high mysteries which hath been declared by this commission of the Spirit, both by word of mouth and pen;

wherein we have unfolded the mystery of the true God, and the right devil, with the persons of angels, and their natures, with many other sacred mysteries, which never were revealed unto the sons of men, until this last commission of the Spirit.

And the knowledge of the two seeds is these two keys which doth open or unlock the gates of heaven and of hell; that is, they know what the commission of Moses and the prophets was, and how far a man is freed from the visible worship of his commission which was of the law, which is the gates of hell.

Also we know what the other commission of Jesus and the apostles was, and how far a man is bound to observe the visible worship which was set up in their time, which was then in great force so long as that commission stood: but when God doth give a new commission, the old is made void, as with reference to the visible worship which is set up by a commission; therefore you know that the apostles' commission did wholly thrust out the visible worship which was set up by Moses.

Therefore it was that Christ said unto Peter, "I have given thee the keys of heaven and of hell;" that is, thou shalt be a preacher of the gospel, which is the kingdom of heaven, and so thou shalt open the gates of heaven unto all those that shall believe in thy declaration: also, thou shalt have the true interpretation of the law of Moses, which shall open the gates of hell unto all those persecuting Jews which were under the law of Moses, at that time when the commission of the apostles was in being.

So, likewise, it is with this commission of the Spirit, because this commission of the Spirit doth hold forth no visible nor external outward worship, as the other two commissions did.

But as it is the commission of the Spirit, therefore, there is no outward nor visible worship to be used in it, but that invisible and spiritual worship only, which is to worship God in spirit and truth; which spiritual worship doth consist in the knowledge of the true God, and the right devil, upon which the foundations of the other two commissions both stand upon, which no man in the world at this day doth or can know, but this commission of the Spirit only, and those which come to understand, and to believe the truth of this commission.

Much more might be said in this thing, but it would be too large an epistle; therefore, my counsel and advice unto you that do believe, or shall come to believe in this last spiritual commission, is, that you would seriously read and peruse this book, called A DIVINE LOOKING-GLASS, though it hath been much slighted and disregarded because of the abuse that it did receive in the press, yet there is contained in it the most highest mysteries of all, which have not been revealed since the world began until now.

But I having occasion for to reprint it again, have read it over with much serious deliberation, and finding in it such variety of matter, with such deep profound mysteries, which could not be declared but by the unerring Spirit of God which was given unto John Reeve; so that I hope, that you that have received some light in your understandings concerning the mystery of the true God, and the right devil, upon the knowledge of which doth depend many other heavenly mysteries which is treated upon in this book, which I do desire and shall be glad that you may increase and grow in the knowledge of them, so that you may be satisfied in the full assurance of faith while you are here, and your knowledge perfected in glory hereafter.

BY LODOWICK MUGGLETON.

TO THE READER.

St. John's Square, London, 1846.

BELOVED BRETHREN,

WE having examined and compared this edition with the second edition, printed for the prophet LODOWICK MUGGLETON, in the year 1661, and finding very few errors therein, (the printer having kept as close as possible to the copy,) we think it not worth printing an errata, there being nothing to impede the general meaning of the work; therefore we desire the reader to amend them with his pen.

On research, we found the scripture texts were taken from a Bible and Testament printed in London, by Robert Barker, printer to the King's most excellent Majesty, in the year 1608, which will account for the difference of words used by him, and some of the more modern translators.

This edition being a copy, as near as possible, of the before-mentioned edition, with this exception only, we have added the chapter and verse to several of the scripture texts, (which we found not printed before,) to render reference more easy to those who search to compare spiritual things with spiritual things.

JOSEPH & ISAAC FROST.

CONTENTS.

CHAPTER

Throne of eternal ravishing Glories. 2. A Throne of natural perishing Glories. 3. An invisible spiritual Throne leading to eternity

IX. An exact Scripture Rule, to prove the man Christ glorified to be Father, Son, and Holy Spirit in one distinct Person

X. 1. Of Persecution of Conscience. 2. Of the Sin against the Holy Ghost

XI. 1. Of the true nature of Infiniteness. 2. Wherein it lieth, viz. in the not knowing its beginning or ending. 3. Infiniteness and Finiteness are uncapable of equal glory. 4. Against all true Reason that there should be Three Persons in the Trinity. 5. Christ and the Father one undivided Godhead. 6. Denying Christ to be the only God, is Antichrist. 7. How Prayers are heard

XII. 1. To own or believe any other God but Christ, is a cursed lie. 2. Who are the deceived Persons. 3. Concerning the true knowledge of God. 4. The Deceivers of others under Conflicts of Mind, described by many and various expressions

XIII. 1. Of the Language and Condition of two sorts of Men and Women. 2. The one elected unto Glory, the other rejected unto Shame. 3. The Prophet's Declaration thereupon

XIV. 1. A moderate Discourse concerning Civil Wars in a Kingdom. 2. The People's subjection to the Laws. 3. Wherein several Objections are answered. 4. Many things of very great consequence seasonably declared

XV. 1. Of the Error of Errors in Men, who say that there is no other God or Christ but in this Creation only. 2. Several Objections and Answers concerning the Death of the Soul. 3. The light of Christ in Man is the invisible Image of God which purifieth the Inward Filthiness of the Flesh and Spirit, and presents the certain Truth of an Eternal Life of Glory or Shame. 4. No need of a new Birth if there be a sufficient Light of Christ in Generation to conduct to heaven. 5. Children cannot understand Spiritual or Natural Good or Evil; so need not Christ's spiritual Gifts in the Womb for eternal Happiness. 6. A great Error to believe that the Essence of the Eternal Spirit dwelleth in any Man but in the Lord Jesus only. 7. Two marks of Reprobates

XVI. 1. Of divers Comparisons of the Spirit or Person of Christ, unto the Face of the Natural Sun. 2. No Man or Angel can be capable of the indwelling of God's Essence, but his own Person only

XVII. 1. No Man's Salvation or Damnation lieth in his own Will, but in the Prerogative of God. 2. Divers Absurdities which follow from the Opinion that Christ is only within Men. 3. A Question and Answer concerning a Twofold presence of God in the Creature. 4. If the essential Spirit were united unto Creatures, it could not be Infinite

XVIII. I. A Discourse that the Divine Being is clothed with Flesh and Bone. 2.

differing from his own Nature. 5. Though all Creatures were made by God, yet they came not out of Him but by the Word of his Power. 6. No Creature, spiritual or natural, can be said to be the Image of God, but Man only. 7. It is the Property of Reason to promise obedience to God by his Prophets, but perform none. 8. Why the Angels are called Mighty

XXIX. 1. Of the Creation of Adam. 2. Why God spake in the Plural Number in the making of Man

XXX. 1. How God made Man in his own Image or Likeness. 2. The Soul of Adam was of the same Divine Nature of God. 3. Not of the Nature of the Angels. 4. Of the created Virtues in Adam's Soul, 5. Adam did not know of his Power to stand or fall. 6. The Breath of Life which Adam had received from God, died

XXXI. 1. Of the Seed of the Woman. 2. Of the Seed of the Serpent. 3. How Sin came into Man's Nature. 4. No Angel cast out of Heaven but that one which deceived Eve. 5. No true knowledge of the Scriptures but in the knowledge of the two Seeds. 6. No Speech could proceed from any but from the Angel

XXXII. 1. The Condition of Adam and Eve in their Fall. 2. The Angel called a Serpent. 3. He was more comely in Eve's eyes than Adam. 4 How the fallen Angel became Flesh. 5. How God became Flesh

XXXIII. 1. What Form the Devil was of before he tempted Eve. 2. Spiritual Bodies do not change their Forms, but their Glories. 3. Spirits can take up no Bodies but their own. 4. The forbidden Fruit was not an Apple, or any other Fruit that could be eaten with the Teeth

XXXIV. 1. The Tree of Knowledge of Good and Evil was no Natural Tree. 2. What it was. 3. Whence the Originality of Sin came

XXXV. 1. The Curse was not pronounced upon any natural Beasts, but the fallen Angel

XXXVI. 1. Of the Mind of the Spirit in the word Eating of the Tree of Knowledge of Good and Evil. 2. No true Interpretation of the Scriptures but by immediate Inspiration. 3. Reason not capable of the Mysteries of God; 4. but Faith only. 5. No Devils but Men and Women. 6. No Devil, without man tempteth any, 7. but the seed or lust of his own Spirit

XXXVII. 1. The prerogative Power of God is above all Law. 2. Why God cursed the fallen Angel in the Womb of Eve. 3. The Angel's Nature (after his offence) was not satisfied without being Ruler

XXXVIII. 1. The Bodies of Angels are capable of dissolving into Seed. 2. The Seed of the Serpent only damned. 3. Pure Reason lost the Knowledge of the Creator, and of itself. 4. Cain not the Son of Adam, but of the Serpent. 5. Cain was Brother to Abel, only by the Mother's side. 6. All that Died in the first Adam shall be saved by the second. 7. Those that are not lost in themselves, can never be saved

hid in the Person of God only

AN OCCASIONAL DISCOURSE from the First and Second Verses of the Second Chapter of the DIVINE LOOKING-GLASS; concerning the Prophet REEVE, that Darkness, Death, and Hell, lay secretly hid in the spiritual Earth eternally with God. By the Prophet MUGGLETON, Sept. 28th, 1668

A DIVINE LOOKING-GLASS.

CHAPTER I.

1. From whence all writings proceed. 2. A necessity of extraordinary light to satisfy or silence curious questions. 3. The names of the two last witnesses, and the time of their call. 4. The highest queries concerning the eternal estate of mankind. 5. Of the form and nature of God from all eternity, who continually increaseth in wisdom. 6. The person of God is the object of true faith. 7. No reason in God. 8. The purest reason in man cannot understand the scriptures.

MY beloved brethren, you know that all speakings or writings are either natural or spiritual, and that of necessity they proceed from their several heads of divine inspiration, or human imagination.

2. Moreover, you know also, that a man had need be endued with an extraordinary light to satisfy or silence curious questions concerning things which are eternal.

3. Dear friends, I, John Reeve, being a poor layman (so called), upon a declaration that the Most High from the throne of his glory, spake unto me in the year 1651; you may be sure since that, the propounding of nice questions have not been wanting unto me and my spiritual companion Lodowick Muggleton,

both from the strong and the weak.

4. Amongst the rest, not many months past, a friend of mine being somewhat troubled in mind, was moved to propound these high queries:

"Whether any creature was formed on purpose for eternal sufferings?

Or whether it would not have been as advantageous for the Creator's glory to have formed all creatures for eternal happiness, as otherwise?

Or if any creature was made to be a vessel of wrath, to show forth the prerogative royal of its Creator, wherein is that creature blameworthy of sin or evil, which, through a secret decree, could not possibly avoid it?

Or whence came that sin or evil into the spirits of man or angel, if they were pure in the first creation?"

My Christian brethren, these curious queries will occasion variety of spiritual matter; yea, and it will further me also to treat upon the original of all heavenly secrets. Wherefore, in answer to these difficult queries, I shall write of several things of most highest consequence unto mankind, namely, concerning the glorious Creator Himself, and the original cause that moved the divine majesty to produce any creature sensibly to live in his sight, and of the creation of the true God, and of the imaginary lying creation in the spirit of sinful man, and whence it came. Also of the creation of angels before man, with the materials and manner of it.

5. I confess I have been moved briefly to touch upon most of these things to the public view of many already; but now, through assistance of the unerring Spirit, I shall handle them more fully, in removing many obstructions in the way, and for more clearer satisfaction unto the true spiritual Christian, and confutation of all fleshly lying anti-christians whatsoever.

6. First, by immediate inspiration from the Holy Spirit, I positively affirm against all naturalists under heaven, that there is a Creator.

7. Secondly, with the same confidence I affirm against men or angels, that this our God from all eternity was an untreated spiritual person, in form like a man.

8. Thirdly, from the same spirit I declare, that that blessed god-man Christ Jesus, so exalted throughout the true scriptures, was and is that eternal Creator beforesaid.

9. Fourthly, I declare against all literal-mongers in this world, that this our Creator and gracious Redeemer was only one immortal, undivided, personal god-man from all eternity, and in time, and to all eternity.

10. Fifthly, I declare from the Holy Spirit, that the addition of two persons more unto this our only wise God, blessed for ever, proceeded only from the old serpentine anti-christian devil in carnal men.

11. Moreover, as for those words of Father, Son, and Spirit, or Lord Jesus Christ, or any other divine titles in scriptures, you may know that they are only variety of names to set forth the infinite godhead glory of the Creator's person.

12. Again, I declare from the spirit of truth, that from all eternity the Creator's person was of a sun-shining fiery glory of sensible heavenly motion, light, heat, voice, and speech, and his divine person was swifter than thought.

13. Moreover, all variety of divine excellencies, as a crystal sea, did infinitely reign in his heavenly person: as, namely, pure spiritual faith, his Almighty power, or heavenly love, his ravishing glory, or any other divine virtue that can be named.

14. Thus you that are truly spiritual may undoubtedly know, that from all eternity the Creator possessed his heavenly joys or new glories by Himself alone, when no created being sensibly appeared to behold his, excellent majesty.

15. By true inspiration from the Holy Spirit, I positively affirm, that the principal motion of all variety of heavenly wisdom, joy, or glory, which the Creator foresaw He should eternally possess, naturally sprang in Him from an incomprehensible knowledge of his own endless infiniteness;

16. Or from a perfect understanding of an eternal increase of all manner of glorious excellencies to solace Himself

withal, and elect men and angels that should be created by Him.

17. If the Creator should be an infinite formless Spirit, as some men vainly imagine, my spiritual brethren, you know then that it were impossible for any spirit of man or angel to be made capable of fixing his understanding upon any such spiritual Creator.

18. You know that no man can describe the form of an invisible spirit, whether it be finite or infinite, unless it be covered with a body or person.

19. Moreover, you know also, that no man or angel can be made able in the least to comprehend the nature of any spirit whatsoever that wants a distinct body or person of its own to inhabit in.

20. Therefore you cannot but understand that the Creator of mankind must needs be a substantial glorious person, and not a nonsubstantial formless Spirit as beforesaid.

21. Again, notwithstanding every divine virtue in the Creator's person be infinite, yet by inspiration from his own Spirit I positively affirm, that there was never any kind of reason in Him

22. Whatever the learned men of this world have long imagined concerning pure reason being the divine nature of God, they are utterly dark concerning a true understanding of the Creator's divine nature, or personal glory, in the least.

23. I declare from the true God, that all those men that call pure reason God's divine nature, if they understand no other light

before death seize on them, they shall find their imaginary reason nothing else but a dark tormenting fiery devil of burning envy in their own bodies at the great day, even against the Creator Himself, and his elect men and angels for everlasting.

24. For this I say from the Lord, unto you that are spiritual, the very nature of reason, though it be never so pure, is nothing else but mere desire: therefore you may know, that if the Creator Himself should have any desire in his Spirit, there would be a kind of want in Him.

25. For if his nature be all variety of heavenly satisfaction in itself, as it is, what rational desire can find place in such an infinite fulness of divine glory?

26. Moreover, my spiritual brethren, what is the principal ground of all anti-christian darkness in the spirits of Solomon-like men, in reference to a right understanding of the, Creator, and his divine nature, is it not because they think to apprehend the true God by a false light, which they vainly call pure reason?

27. What is this which worldly men call pure reason Is it any thing else but that proud angelical serpent devil in them, which by its own natural strength continually strives to find out the tree of eternal life, that they may cure themselves of their deadly wounds of soul, arising from all their spiritual and fleshly rebellions against God and man?

28. Again, doth the true understanding of the Creator run in

the line of pure reason, or pure faith in the scriptures?

29. Is there any saying in scripture that God's divine nature is pure reason, or by pure reason we know the true God, or any thing that is spiritual? Indeed I have read scriptures that say, "by faith the apostles knew the worlds were made, and by faith they knew their mortal bodies should be raised immortal bodies, at the great day of the appearing of Christ in his glory;" but, as before said, I never read or heard any spiritual wise man say, that the invisible things of eternity were understood by man's pure reason; no, nor angels, that behold the glorious Creator face to face. It is written, "with thee is the well of life, and in thy light shall we see light." It is also written, that "men were partakers of the divine nature," and that "Abraham believed God, and it was imputed to him for righteousness;" and "by faith men were justified before the Creator, and in their own spirits;" and that "without faith it was impossible to please God." Furthermore it is written, that "faith is the gift of God."

30. In these records, and many more such like, you see the scriptures take no notice of the word pure reason, by which men could know any thing of the true God, or of his heavenly secrets at all.

31. Therefore I would fain know whether those men that call pure reason the divine nature, are fit to interpret scriptures, or to bear the name of gospel ministers? But I will leave them at present to Him that will discover them soon enough to their cost.

CHAPTER II.

1 What the substances of earth and water were from eternity. 2. A great secret revealed concerning death and hell. 3. Concerning the heavens above. 4. Earth and water not eternally glorious. 5. The residence of the Creator. 6. Earth and water uncreated substances.

AGAIN, in the next place, by inspiration from the unerring Spirit, I positively affirm, that the substances of earth and water were from all eternity in the Creator's presence, uncreated, senseless, dark, dead matter, like unto water and dust, that have no kind of life, or light, or virtue in them at all.

2. Also I declare from the Holy Spirit, that darkness, death, or devil and hell lay secretly hid in that earth above this perishing globe, and in the sight of the Creator were eternally naked and bare, both in their root and in their fruit.

3. Again, I declare from the true light of life eternal, that that world or kingdom where the Creator's glorious person is visible, is a place or throne infinite in length, breadth, or height, answerable unto an infinite majesty.

4. Moreover, for your information that are spiritual, from the true God I declare, that in this heavenly city there is no firma-

ment, sun, moon, nor stars: so that you may understand that it is an infinite open place for divine personal ascending or descending at pleasure, only under foot is fixed a spiritual earth and a crystal sea.

5. Furthermore, you that are spiritual may know that it stands to very good sense that an infinite majesty cannot be confined to a finite world or kingdom, as this is; I mean when He possesseth the throne of immortality as at this time, or before He became a body of unspotted flesh.

6. Again, concerning that glorious earth and crystal sea aforesaid, I would not have you to think that I mean it was eternally so, but after, or in the finishing of the creation of angels, and variety of other creatures, the infinite virtue of the Creator's word produced that crystal spirituality in them, that both visible as well as invisible, every thing or creature appointed to abide in the presence of the divine majesty, might be all glory in their kind and measure, answerable to the unmeasurable variety of unspeakable glory in the Creator Himself.

7. My spiritual brethren, you know that it is an opinion of the learned, that those substances, earth and water aforesaid, were not eternal; but they have long imagined that the Creator spake the word, and so they came to be; and after He had given them their being, He formed all things that were made out of them.

8. My beloved brethren, you may know that this must needs be an error, because you know that the word create is to make formless dead matter into sensible living forms.

9. Besides this, you know, as for creating of those elements of water or dust, there is no scripture maketh mention of any such thing, therefore a mere imagination; but more of this in the seventh chapter.

10. Again you know, that from eternity the divine nature of the Creator's Spirit was nothing but immortal fiery glory of life and light. It is written, "God is light, and in him there is no darkness at all:" and it is written in Gen. i. "and darkness was upon the deep."

11. My brethren, if the Creator be all life and light, as you know He is, then, without controversy, the dead earth and dark deep water never proceeded out of his glorious mouth: but if that scripture should be objected where it is said, "I create light, and I create darkness," to that I answer, the mind of the Holy Spirit in those words was this, that He created those souls that were naturally dark, and He created these mortal spirits that were full of immortal light; but, on the contrary, there was not the least meaning in those words, or any other throughout the scriptures, that God created or gave any being or beginning unto dead, dark, senseless earth and water, as aforesaid.

12. Whatever men vainly imagine the Creator to be, if they shall conclude there was nothing eternal but God only, if they acknowledge the Creator to be

some glorious thing which is incomprehensibly infinite, then I would fain learn of those wise men where the glorious Creator was resident when He gave a being to earth and water. If they shall say unto me, that He was uncapable to be in any one place, because He was every where, as to that, I cannot understand which way the Creator should be every where, or any where at all, if He had no place or habitation to abide in, neither finite nor infinite.

13. God being all light, life, joy, and glory in Himself from eternity, is it not against all divine or human light, that is not unreasonable, that ever those dark, dead elements of earth and water should have their original from his glorious spirit, because their natures are so contrary, that it was impossible that they should proceed from one another; for, alas! what is death or darkness? Is it not through the absence of life or light? and is not life, being overcome by death, absolutely become death and darkness, or utter silence for a moment?

14. Again, if light and darkness, or life and death meet together, is there any peace or agreement between them until life be swallowed up by death, or death be swallowed up into life?

15. If this be so, the which no sober man can gainsay, then without controversy earth and water were untreated substances, eternally distinct from the God of glory; because the scripture saith, "and darkness covered the face of the deep."

CHAPTER III.

1. Of the angels. 2. Their form and nature. 3. Out of what they were made. 4. The serpent which tempted Eve. 5. The cause why any creature was formed. 6. Who are partakers of the divine nature. 7. No created being capable of the essence of God to dwell in it.

AGAIN, from the true light of life I affirm, that the angels were the first sensible living beings formed by the Creator.

2. I declare also, that the angelical host were all produced by his word speaking into that dust without or above this visible heavens.

3. Moreover, I positively affirm from the same light, that all the angels in the heavenly throne aforesaid are persons in forms like men, and not bodiless spirits, as the learned have long declared, and the nature of their angelical spirits are pure reason only.

4. From the God of all truth I declare, that that serpent which tempted Eve unto evil was one of those angels of light.

5. Moreover, that serpent angel was more wise or god-like in his creation than all the elect angels of glory; for the most wise God, in this, may be likened to a wise earthly prince, that, for the manifestation of his royal pleasure, exalteth that subject to the highest dignity, which he hath secretly decreed to the highest disgrace.

6. Thus it was with the glorious Creator, who foreknowing that his prerogative royal would compel Him to create this angelical reprobate, in reference to his divine justice, therefore, for the manifestation of his most glorious power unto his elect men and angels, his wisdom saw it most fit to endue him with more piercing rational wisdom and brightness of person than all his angelical companions, because he was decreed to the greatest shame and pain, as aforesaid.

7. And not only so, but also because the elect angels should admire their Creator's wisdom and power, when they should see the outcast condition of the highest created glory, and be filled with new declarations of honour, praise, and glory unto the divine majesty, for his free-electing love towards them through which they were ensured eternally to reign in their created purity.

8. Again, from the true light of life I positively affirm, that there was but only one reprobate angel created at the first, which is fully cleared in this book.

9. Moreover, you spiritual ones may understand that if the most merciful Creator could possibly have known any other way for the manifestation of his divine excellencies unto men and angels, I say you may be confident He would never have created any thing on purpose for eternal suffering.

10. Furthermore, can you possibly imagine or think that the most gracious and wise Creator would ever have suffered the nature of any creature to become rebellious against Himself, for the occasioning of such marvellous transactions in this world, and suffering both of God, angel, and man, if He could have possessed his infinite glory, in the creating of every thing unto eternal pleasures.

11. Again, if dust and water were eternal substances distinct from the Creator, it being dark and dead matter, it could not produce any kind of life at all of itself, but was brought forth into life by another.

12. Wherefore it may be queried by some, what was that which entered into dust, and brought forth angelical bodies to live in the Creator's presence's was it any thing else but that spiritual life or divine nature of God Himself?

13. Unto this curious query from the true light of life I answer, that neither the spirit of angels, nor any other creatures, were formed of the divine nature, but the souls of Adam and Eve only.

14. But they were created of variety of spirits to one another, and to the Creator also; yet they were all purely created and in a sweet harmony with each other, and their Creator also, even so long and no longer than they abode in their created purity.

15. Again, by inspiration from our Lord Jesus Christ, I affirm, that the unsearchable wisdom of the most high God was secretly hid in the infinite power of his word speaking only.

16. So that it was the fore-

knowledge of his own mighty power, which was one of the principal grounds that moved Him to produce any living creature in his presence.

17. Wherefore, before any creature was formed by Him, if He had not perfectly known that of those aforesaid elements of dust or water by his word speaking only, He could create as many several spirits, with bodies suitable to their natures, as He saw good, and yet wholly retain the divine nature of his Spirit to Himself, He would never have formed any creature to have lived in his sight:

18. Because then, you know, there would have been no distinction of natures or names between the creatures themselves and the Creator; nor none of the variety of his infinite wisdom, power, and glory ever seen or known by the creatures;

19. For you that are spiritual may understand, that the Creator's royal will or pleasure was that glorious wheel that moved Him to form any creature at all.

20. Therefore you may also know, that it was impossible for Him to create the spirits of angels and man to be both of the nature of his own Spirit, or neither of them to be of his divine nature, because, as aforesaid, the variety of his wisdom, power, and glory, would have been all lost for want of distinction.

21. Moreover, if angels and man had been both of God's divine nature in their creation, then instead of their being capable to be transmuted into a higher or lower condition at the divine pleasure of the Creator, would they not rather have been unchangeable creators than changeable creatures?

22. Therefore the most wise and holy Creator, that He might prevent all that might impede his divine purpose, He created the bodies of angels spiritual, and their natures rational; and He made the body of the man Adam natural, and his soul spiritual.

23. For if their spirits and bodies had been both of the divine nature, then it would have been impossible for them to be capable of any change of sin or evil, or consent to evil in them, no more than the Creator Himself.

24. Where then had been all the wonderful transactions of his glorious majesty, or what would have been formed but creators only, instead of creatures, as aforesaid?

25. Again, because of our weak comprehension in the deep things of God, I shall speak something by way of imagination only, which is as followeth

26. Suppose the most high God should have created both angels and men all glorious like Himself, and eternally so to remain, yet those created beings could not possibly be the divine essence of his godhead spirit, but only a created light of sensible life, of divine joys proceeding from the eternal Spirit, by virtue of words speaking through his heavenly mouth into those elements beforesaid.

27. Because you may know

that the untreated essence or godhead spirit of an infinite majesty was utterly uncapable to be conveyed into a finite created being, for infiniteness is only capable of its own glorious centre:

28. So that you that are truly spiritual may understand, that after the angels were formed into living bodies, the divine majesty and those created beings were become distinct in their essences for everlasting;

29. That the angels, by apparent sight of their Creator's face, might know themselves to be but creatures, and subject to the divine pleasure of Him that made them.

30. Moreover, from the true light of the Holy One of Israel, I affirm that the elect angels of eternal glory had no certain knowledge of continuing in their created purities, until the Lord had discovered the reprobate angel unto them.

31. It is written, that "he made all things for his own glory, and the wicked for the day of wrath."

32. My beloved spiritual brethren, you know that the heavenly nature of the divine majesty is nothing else but all variety of glorious excellencies.

33. Also you know that the Creator's Spirit being variety of spiritual perfections, He could create nothing against his glory but for his glory only, because that glory of his is Himself, or his all in all, or only pillar upon which He built his everlasting kingdom;

34. Wherefore, if angels or man had been framed in unchangeable conditions, then instead of making known his manifold divine glories to his creatures, He must have created things for his own eternal ruin.

35. For if such a thing could possibly have been, instead of being creatures, as aforesaid, they would all have been creators; and being unchangeable, it could not possibly be avoided, but they must all have shared in, or of the Creator's unchangeable glory also.

36. Moreover, if the Holy One of Israel should be divided into three divine persons, as many men blindly imagine, then you know that being all eternal, they must of necessity be equal in godhead, wisdom, power, and glory: a kingdom thus divided cannot stand.

37. For you that are truly spiritual know, that all the true prophets in the time of the law did never acknowledge any more gods than that Holy One of Israel only; and by inspiration they attributed many holy names unto his divine majesty, for the exaltation of his glorious person above all angels and men.

38. Moreover, you know that in scriptures it is written, that "the Holy One of Israel will not give his glory to another."

39. Therefore, whatever men vainly dream of a Creator, or God, or three persons, or of a bodiless infinite spirit, yet unto us that are heirs of eternal glory, there is but one only wise God, Creator, Redeemer, and alone everlasting Father, which is our Lord Jesus Christ, in one

blessed body of flesh and bone glorified.

CHAPTER IV.

1. Of the angels further. 2. Of the nature of pure reason. 3. Of the divine nature. 4. Wherein they differ. 5. The angels were under the moral law which was written in their natures. 6. The Creator above all law. 7. A necessity of supplying the angels with continual revelations from the Creator. 8. He that was above all law, made Himself under the law, by becoming flesh. 9. Who is antichrist. 10. No joy in God without a form. 11. Death an enemy to all kind of life in God, angels, and men.

BEFORE I treat of the first appearance of sin or evil in the reprobate angel, I shall speak of the creation of angels by a comparison.

2. Suppose a man should speak words unto dry dust or sand distinct from his person, and before he spake unto that senseless chaos, he did perfectly know or believe in himself, that out of that dead dust his very words would produce so many several sensible living bodies in his sight, though those words proceeded from the soul of the man.

3. Yet you may know that they were not the essence of the man's spirit, but only a powerful influence of speech, or words spoken through his mouth, for manifesting the variety of his natural wisdom, power, or glory, over the words which he had spoken.

4. Moreover, you know that a man with great ease might spare a few words without any trouble of mind in reference to what use he saw fit to employ them, they being his own workmanship; can any sober man deny this man's prerogative pleasure with his own? I trow not.

5. This was the Creator's very case in the matter of creation, and who dares to speak against it no spiritual wise man, I am sure; only some lustful persons may dispute against it, though it be contrary to their own reason when it is sober.

6. But deeds of darkness hate the light, and can do no otherwise; and those that live in the light are made to abhor all deeds of darkness or vain disputes against the Creator's royal will, or righteous ways.

7. Thus you which are truly spiritual may understand, that neither the spirits of angels, no, nor of the man Adam himself, was of the divine essence in their creation. It is truth the soul of Adam was of the very nature of the Spirit of God; but it was a created nature, or virtue which brought forth its pure natural body as its house or tabernacle of abode; so that as the body had a beginning of dust, through which it was capable of change,

8. So likewise when that divine soul was covered with an earthly temple, it was capable of mutability, though it proceeded from an immutable glory.

9. But, on the contrary, though the spiritual bodies of angels had beginning also, yet

they were not subject to change, but their spirits not being of the divine nature of Him that made them, was wholly subject to mutability.

10. For the angels' spirits were pure reason, as aforesaid; and what is the nature of the most purest reason Is it any thing else but all pure desires? And what is the original of the most purest or perfect desire that is? Is it not a want of something that is desired, or a kind of unsatisfaction until its desire be satisfied from something that is not inherent in itself

11. Again, my spiritual brethren, is it possible, think you, that there should be the least motion of the most purest desire that is in the nature of that spirit, which is all fulness of divine satisfaction in itself?

12. Or is it possible that that spirit that hath any desire in its nature should enjoy fulness of content in itself?

13. Wherefore, though the holy God created that angelical reason of all pure desire, let no spiritual wise man call it his divine nature.

14. Why? because you know there can be no kind of desire in the nature of that immortal God, that is all variety of glorious satisfaction in itself, as beforesaid.

15. But let him know from the true light of life, that the Creator, by his infinite wisdom or power, from a word speaking unto dust, could create, yea, and did make divers living creatures, and yet not one motion of the natures of those created beings was inherent in his heavenly Spirit.

16. Therefore you that are possessed with that new and true divine birth from the immortal throne, may know that the spirits of elect angels are not in the least of any part of the glorious natures of his Spirit, but only a created rational spirit of all pure desires, which was not only become distinct from his divine nature now it possessed its personal living being in itself;

17. But was also in its non-being, in the foreknowledge of the Creator, eternally distinct from his undesiring nature of all spiritual glories, secretly hid in its own dark senseless elements as beforesaid, only by a powerful word it was commanded to appear and manifest itself in its own creaturely condition.

18. Again, some may say unto me, Were the angels under any law in their creation? From the unerring Spirit of our Lord Jesus Christ to this I answer, All the angels were equally created under one law; the which moral law was written in their angelical natures, motioning in them that all obedience was properly due unto their Creator, which had made them such marvellous creatures.

19. Again, you that are spiritual may know, that no created being was capable to be formed in a lawless condition.

20. Why? because there is nothing uncapable of being made under a law from another, but that divine Being only which was eternally in or from itself.

You may also know, that those very words of creation, or creatures, includes a Creator, and a command of all obedience due unto Him.

21. Also you know, that no creature could acknowledge any kind of obedience to be due unto a God, unless he were guided thereunto by a light or law from Him that formed him.

22. My spiritual brethren, from the divine voice of God Himself I affirm, that the untreated godhead itself is unto the created beings of angels or men either a law of perfect faith and pure burning love in them towards God and man unto life eternal;

23. Or else a fiery law of unbelieving burning envy in them against God, elect men, and angels, unto death eternal.

24. Not that any sin or evil could possibly proceed from the Holy Spirit of the Creator into the nature of the creatures, either in his creating of them, or after they were formed by Him.

25. You know that was impossible, because his divine nature in itself is nothing else but all variety of ravishing purities to Himself, or elect men, or angels.

26. Moreover, you spiritual ones may know that though the spirits of angels were created perfectly pure in their kind and measure; yet if they were not continually supplied with inspirations from that divine glory which gave them their beings, instead of continuing in their angelical brightness, their spirits would become nothing else but a bottomless pit of imaginary confused darkness of aspiring wisdom above the Creator:

27. For the elect angels' spirits being only pure reason, the very nature of them is to desire after the knowledge of that incomprehensible glory which gave them their beings; and it is the variety of his divine excellencies flowing into their desiring natures, which is that heavenly food that is prepared for their eternal preservation.

28. My beloved brethren, if you look into the first epistle of St. Peter, you may see that the elect angels are of a desiring or prying nature into the secret mysteries of our God, when He manifested Himself on this earth in a body of flesh. The words are these: Searching when or what time the Spirit which testified before of Christ, which was in them, should declare the sufferings that should come unto Christ, and the glory that should follow, the which things the angels desire to behold."

29. Furthermore, I am persuaded in my spirit, that the forming of angels was not very long before the creating of Adam and Eve.

30. Because you know that the elect angels were not only made for the personal society of the Creator in his heavenly throne, or kingdom of glory; but they were appointed also for ministering spirits unto the heirs of salvation in this world, according to that in the first of the Hebrews.

31. Moreover, you that are spiritual may undoubtedly know,

that it was utterly unpossible for man or angels to be void of all law in their creation.

32. Because the Creator Himself became subject to his own law, when his divine godhead was transmuted into pure manhood.

33. It is truth that the uncreated eternal God was above all law, and so uncapable of any kind of law before He descended from his infinite glory into the womb of a woman.

34. But that He might be capable of the condition of a servant, for the manifestation of this his infinite wisdom, power, and glory, in a body of flesh unto elect men and angels, therefore He transmuted his unchangeable godhead into the likeness of sinful mortals for a season, that He might become the heavenly pattern of perfect obedience to his own law, in the visible sight of elect men and angels.

35. And that from thence, by virtue of his sufferings at the hands of cursed Canaanites, He might also become a purchaser from Himself of a twofold infinite ravishing glory to Himself, and elect men and angels, the which his spiritual body was uncapable of, until it became suffering flesh, blood, and bone.

36. Therefore whosoever saith that any other body ascended into glory, but that very same body of flesh and bone that suffered death upon the cross, he is an antichrist, and in utter spiritual darkness, let him be the perfectest literalist or naturalist in the whole world.

37. Moreover, you that are truly spiritual do know, that it was utterly impossible that heaven and earth, with all the wonderful works in them, should be from eternity, as godless atheists would vainly imagine, because they cannot attain to know what the Holy One of Israel is by their own natural reason:

38. For, alas! if no mortal man can give a being to one hair of his head, though he be lord of all other creatures under the sun, how should he possibly be from eternity?

39. I hope these overwise men will not say, that men were brought forth by earth, air, water, fire, sun, moon, stars, or any suchlike weak means as those are. Why? because the spirit of man far exceeds all such creatures.

40. You may know that though those creatures have life in them according to their kind; yet man, being a sensible living soul to itself, and being capable in some measure to comprehend the nature of those creatures aforesaid, must of necessity be a more eminent living being than they all.

41. For, alas! you know, though the sun, fire, earth, water, wind, or air, are powerful in their natures, oftentimes destroying mankind; yet when they have done it, they are no way capable in themselves of any sensible joy or sorrow for what was done by them, no more than the stones in the street;

42. Therefore, seeing all these creatures were formed for man's use, and are in measure known

by man, and yet are all uncapable of any sensible knowledge of themselves or of man either; and seeing no man by his natural reason can perceive how any spirit brings forth its own body unto maturity, neither how it by degrees passeth away into its dust or nonbeing again, nor no creatures worth naming, were ever seen by men to have a beginning in any other way but that of generation only.

43. How can any rational wise man possibly imagine or think that man, or any other living forms, should ever appear to be without a glorious Creator to give them their beings at the first?

44. Furthermore, my spiritual brethren, can any of you be so weak, after a sober consideration, to imagine or think that a formless God gave being to all these marvellous living forms?

45. How is it possible for that which hath no distinct form or person of its own, to create any kind of living form at all?

46. What though the Spirit of our blessed Creator and gracious Redeemer be infinite, can it possibly enjoy any kind of sensible life, light, or glory, unless it hath a distinct body or person of its own to possess it in?

47. Again, though many seeming wise men, for want of true divine faith, do imagine the Lord to be a vast Spirit, yet you know that when they are moved to speak of a Creator, they usually say that the eternal Being is an incomprehensible infiniteness of variety of divine glories; as, namely, wisdom, faith, love, patience, meekness, righteousness, with all spiritual excellencies.

48. My spiritual brethren, if the Creator's nature be all variety of divine virtues, and every qualification in Him be infinite, how can those divine glories be sensible of their own being, or incomprehensible blessedness, unless they possess a distinct body of their own to possess that glory in? yea, a transcendent heavenly body, answerable unto an unutterable spiritual glory.

49. For, alas! you know that no finite living being can possibly be capable to possess divine virtues which are infinite, and live.

50. You know that mortality and infinite immortality cannot continue together.

51. Therefore you may understand, that that pure light which shineth in our dark spirits, though it be called the divine nature or spirit of an infinite majesty, yet it is not infinite nor immortal in us:

52. But it is a heavenly light or virtue in us, changed into a condition of pure mortality, that it might instruct a mortal sinful soul concerning immortal things, which are eternal.

53. For you experimental ones know, that if that light of life enjoyed by us were immortal and eternal in us, then it were impossible that we should be capable of any kind of misery or mutability in the least.

54. Therefore you may know also, that the greatest light in sinful man is but an inspired motion into the man's spirit, to

purify the lying imagination or impure reason in the soul of that man, that he may be capable to understand that the Creator hath a purpose to crown him with unchangeable personal glory at the great day.

55. But as for those men which dream of a condition of possessing an unchangeable glory in this being through an essential oneness with an infinite majesty, they are in the depth of spiritual darkness, concerning a right understanding of the Creator of his heavenly ways in man.

56. Moreover, you spiritual ones may know, that though no man hath any light of life in him, but what he hath received from an unchangeable glory, yet because that vessel wherein this light doth shine is a mortal sinner, and must die, therefore the heavenly light is made subject to mortality also.

57. Because the most high God, by his unsearchable wisdom, hath decreed, that all light of life in man shall become dead dust or earth for a moment, that in his appointed season it may quicken again a new and glorious life out of death itself for the manifestation of his infinite wisdom, power, and ravishing glory, unto elect men and angels.

58. Thus you that are truly spiritual may know, that though death be and was that king of fears, and enemy to all kind of life in God, men, and angels, yet, for a further increase of infiniteness of glory in the Creator, and finite glory in elect men and angels, it was his divine pleasure to make it as useful in its kind as life itself.

59. Though this truth will be the judge of me and all men at the last, yet I expect but few to embrace it, through that endless opposition in man.

CHAPTER V.

1. The cause of the angel's fall; and the fruit thereof. 2. The condition of the elect angels. 3. The spiritual nature of the fallen angel remained, and what names are given to him. 4. An objection, and the answer concerning two vessels. 5. Of the fallen angel and Adam. 6. No distinction between God and the creature, but by names and natures. 7. Election and reprobation proved by divers scriptures.

IN the next place, I shall write of the occasion of the downfal of the angelical reprobate, from that height of his created glory which he possessed above all the elect angels: my beloved brethren in the pure truth, you know that light of the Holy Spirit in the Creator breathing itself into my ignorant soul, hath abundantly remonstrated the distinction between the natures of God and angels aforesaid.

2. Moreover, you may remember I told you, that the spirits of angels were pure reason in their creation; and furthermore you know, it is clearly proved that the nature of the highest reason that ever was, or possibly can be, is nothing else but mere desire.

3. Wherefore, though the Cre-

ator gave it its rational being, yet unto you spiritual ones I made it appear, that in his glorious Spirit not one motion of reason was inherent.

4. Because where any desire is, though it be never so pure, it is a want of something desired.

5. Therefore you know that an infinite fulness of divine perfections in its own spirit cannot possibly have any kind of want in it, therefore uncapable of any kind of desire in the least.

6. Because what it hath a mind to do concerning itself, or any thing it hath made, you know it can do it to the utmost and who can let it, or shall dare to say, in the day of his eternal account, why hast thou made one vessel for eternal glory, and another vessel for everlasting shame?

7. Wherefore, my Christian friends, you may know that the continuance of the glory of the angelical reprobate being expired, the Creator only withheld the inspiration of his divine glory from him; and immediately, for want of that spiritual meat to satisfy his desiring nature, his god-like created purity became nothing else but imaginary impurities of secret aspiring desires above the Creator.

8. So that his former pure reason was then become nothing but a loathsome sink of unclean reasoning concerning the true knowledge of the Creator's being the Creator, and the creatures being but creatures; and instead of honouring the Creator for his unsearchable wisdom, of forming out of a little dead dust such an innumerable host of elect angels for his majesty's personal society.

9. At the blind bar of his lying imagination secretly he arranged all the wisdom of the infinite God in creation, and condemned it as weakness itself, in comparison of his imaginary wisdom if he had been the Creator.

10. Again, his angelical spirit being wholly out of all creaturely order, and being lifted up with the wisdom of his spirit, and glory of his person, he beheld both the wisdom and persons of all the elect angels as simple uncomely creatures, in comparison of him or his wisdom.

11. Moreover, conceiving himself most fit for divine rule, and beholding himself and the Creator together, he imagined his personal wisdom more capable of a divine throne than He which sat thereon.

12. Furthermore, he began to imagine a new creation of his own, for he thought if he had been the Creator, by a word speaking he could have formed more glorious creatures than those angels were, without any dust or any other matter whatsoever:

13. Or if he must have had some materials to form things withal, he imagined by his word speaking or thinking only, he could have produced matter of a more excellent nature for creation than a little dry dust, out of which he conceited he could have created creatures all glorious, and yet have retained his divine glory within himself

distinct from them all.

14. Furthermore he imagined, that he could have created as many spirits as he saw fit, without any bodies at all;

15. Or if he saw good, he could have formed spiritual bodies that might be transformed into any other nature or form after he had created them, and not to continue only in one nature and form always:

16. For he thought it want of wisdom or power in a Creator, yea, and a veiling of his infinite glory over the things which he had made, if they might not be transmuted into any condition whatsoever, at his pleasure that formed them.

17. Wherefore in the midst of these and such like creative confusions, his irrational wisdom of imaginary impossibilities, so elevated his outcast spirit that secretly he utterly abhorred that the Creator, or any other creatures, should remain in being, unless he only might bear rule over them all.

18. Wherefore, when the secret pride and envy of this angelical reprobate was at that height of unthroning the Creator, or else a dissolution of all, then the most wise God revealed his spiritual cruelties unto his holy angels; and, answerable unto what he would have done for a Creator's throne, in the visible sight of his elect angels, He condemned him to be cast out of his personal presence, and heavenly throne or kingdom, for everlasting;

19. And immediately, like unto lightning, he was thrown down into this perishing world, where his desired kingdom of god-like government was prepared for him and his lineal angels in another way:

20. And so having left their first estate, they are reserved in everlasting chains of darkness or unbelief, until the judgment of the great day, then to give an eternal account of their devilish government over God's elect righteous Abels on this earth, which was so exalted by Him in the highest heavens beforesaid.

21. My beloved spiritual brethren, you may know that then, and not till then, all the elect angels in glory were filled with variety of new spiritual praises in their mouths, of honour, power, praises, glory, majesty, wisdom, counsel, dominion, faith, love, mercy, patience, peace, meekness, justice, righteousness, or any divine excellency that can be named to their glorious Creator, for his electing free love unto them, eternally to abide in their created purity, to behold his glorious face.

22. And for his wonderful wisdom in creating such angelical perfection, unto an everlasting rejection of desperate burning envy in utter shame.

23. Moreover, you which expect crowns of immortal glory may know, that in the downfal of the angelical reprobate, his spiritual form remained.

24. But the nature of his spirit was only changed as beforesaid, and so after our first parents were deceived by him,

answerable unto his filthy nature of impure reason or lying imagination.

25. In scripture records you know, the Lord is pleased to call him by such like titles as these: namely, devil, a dragon, an enemy, a wicked one, a murderer, a liar, a thief, an envious man, an hypocrite, a Lucifer, a Beelzebub, or a prince of the air, or Satan, or reprobate, and such like.

26. O ye blessed ones of the most high God! with astonishing admiration it behoveth you not to slight, but seriously to ponder God's wonderful wisdom in the creating of angels and man: why? because in it is hid all spiritual secrets which are appointed to be revealed to elect men and angels unto eternity.

27. Again, I humbly beseech you which have really been possessed with that spiritual new birth of our Lord Jesus Christ in glory, is there any light, or life, or love, or any kind of divine excellency in the glorious Spirit of our Creator?

28. Again, had He any power over Himself, or over any creature which He had formed, either to fill them with glimpses of his most excellent glory, or wholly to retain them to Himself?

29. If you grant Him this his royal prerogative, the which no spiritual one can possibly deny, then without all controversy, unless the most wise and holy Creator had formed two vessels of several spirits to remain only for a season in their created purity,

30. And at the decreed time leave them both to their own created strength, and so withholding that heavenly manna of divine inspiration from them both, by which they stood, that in order to their change they might unite their spirits and bodies unlawfully together, for producing of two several generations of mankind on this earth, for the manifestation of his ravishing glories unto the one, and retaining the heavenly splendour of his divine excellencies wholly from the other, for the demonstration of his divine justice, will, or pleasure;

31. Would not all his heavenly wisdom, divine power, or ravishing glory, have been veiled from men and angels? And must they not either have been all creators, or creatures like unto senseless stocks or stones to all eternity, in reference of any knowledge of the various wisdom, power, and glory of the Creator, as abundantly before said?

32. Again, in that pure distinguishing spirit of all divine truth, I humbly beseech you which are delivered from the power of all natural, notional, or literal witchcraft, and in the room thereof are endued with a good measure of spiritual understanding in the things of eternity, can there possibly be any distinction between the unchangeable Creator and changeable creatures, without variety of distinct natures and names, to manifest the difference between them?

33. As, namely, since the outcast condition of the angelical reprobate, and fallen estate of

the man Adam.

34. Can there now be any Creator or God at all, unless there be a devil or devils also?

35. Or can there be any light in life, and no darkness in death?

36. Or can there be any eternal immortal glory for some men, and no eternal shame and misery for other?

37. Again, can any man, from any kind of faith or truth, possibly imagine or think, that any one of these can be without the other?

38. Doth not the one give an absolute being unto the other? Can any man therefore think that if one of them should be dissolved, that the other could continue to be?

39. Thus you which enjoy that true distinguishing light of eternal life in you, may clearly see that immortal heaven or glory Must of necessity be essentially distinct from hell or shame, or else there can be no perfect heaven or glory at all; and hell or misery must be essentially distinct from heaven or glory, or else there can be no certain hell or misery at all.

40. Moreover, the glorious person of the divine majesty Himself, must of necessity be essentially distinct from men, angels, heaven, earth, and all in them, or else it were impossible that there should be any God or angels, men or devils, heaven or hell, or anything else besides, but accidental things, proceeding from those four elements of earth, air, water, and fire, as all filthy Atheists vainly and blindly imagine.

41. But my beloved spiritual brethren, you have not so learned Christ, or received the truth of the ever-living Jesus into your innocent souls, to abide in any such foolish darkness.

42. Wherefore for your confirmation chiefly is this epistle written, that you may be enabled to discern the lying notions, and fleshly voluntary will-worship in man, contending against the secret decrees of the Holy One of Israel.

43. Furthermore, because many of the elect of God are as yet in bonds, by the exceeding subtilty of many silver-soul merchants of this perishing world, therefore I shall endeavour to confirm what is written from a cloud of unerring witnesses, my spiritual brethren, the former true prophets and apostles of our Lord Jesus Christ; wherefore it was said by our God, which is Christ Jesus the Lord, that "heaven and earth shall pass away, but his words shall not pass away."

44. Again it is written, that "he made all things for his own glory, and the wicked for the day of wrath." Also it is written, that "Jacob was loved, and Esau was hated, before they had done good or evil, that the purpose of God might remain according to election;" for he saith to Moses, "I will have mercy on whom I will have mercy, and will have compassion on whom I will have compassion; so then it is not in him that willeth, nor in him that runneth, but in God that

showeth mercy." Further it is written, "but, O man, who art thou which pleadest against God? Shall the thing formed say to him that formed it, why hast thou made me thus? Hath not the potter power over the clay, to make of the same lump one vessel to honour, and another to dishonour? What if God would, to show his wrath, and to make his power known, suffer with long patience, the vessels of wrath prepared to destruction, and that he might declare the riches of his glory upon the vessels of mercy, which he hath prepared unto glory," Rom. ix. And in Rom. viii. it is thus written, "also we know that all things work together for the best unto them that love God, even to them that are called of his purpose; for those which he knew before he also predestinated to be made like to the image of his Son: moreover, whom he predestinated, them also he called, and whom he called, them also he justified; and whom he justified, them also he glorified." Again in the first epistle of Peter, it is thus written, "wherefore also it is contained in the scripture, behold, I lay in Sion a chief corner-stone, elect and precious, and he that believeth therein, shall not be ashamed: unto you therefore which believe, it is precious; but unto them that be disobedient, the stone which the builders disallowed, the same is made the head of the corner, and a stone to stumble at, and a rock of offence, even to them which stumble at the word, being

disobedient, unto the which thing they were even ordained: but ye are a chosen generation, a royal priesthood, an only nation, a people set at liberty that ye should show forth the virtues of him that hath called you out of darkness into his marvellous light." Moreover, in the epistle of Jude are these words: "for there are certain men crept in, which were before of old ordained to this condemnation; ungodly men they are, which turn the grace of God into wantonness, and deny God the only Lord, and our Lord Jesus Christ: they are the raging waves of the sea, foaming out their own shame; they are wandering stars, to whom is reserved the blackness of darkness for ever." Again, "for if God spared not the angels that had sinned, but cast them down to hell, and delivered them into chains of darkness, to be kept unto damnation, what will become of all those angelical fleshly hypocrites which bless themselves in their unrighteousnes, and cursedly contend for it, even against the holy God, elect men, and angels, and their own consciences, which will become their eternal chief accountant in the great day."

45. Again, as a conclusion unto what is written aforesaid, I shall write something concerning the scriptures themselves.

46. My spiritual brethren, can you possibly think that those men as yet have received the spiritual truth of the true God: which idolize the visible records, and worship them instead of that

holy Spirit in our Lord Jesus Christ which spake them?

47. Again, did ever any man attain to a true understanding of that Holy One of Israel, by any endeavour whatsoever, from the bare letter of the scripture?

48. It is written, "the letter killeth, but the Spirit giveth life." Again it is written, that "the scriptures are sufficient to make the man of God wise unto salvation."

49. My brethren, can any man be a godly man, or a man of God, unless he hath the spiritual light of life eternal, to enable him to understand the mind of God in the records, and so believe unto immortality?

CHAPTER VI.

1. Of the scripture records. 2. Of the ignorance of men that deify or vilify them. 3. The prophet's prayer in the conclusion.

IS there any testimony in scriptures that ever any man of God received the true faith of the spiritual Jesus in him from the letter of the scriptures, or could possible know whether those literal records proceeded from the wisdom of God, or from the wisdom of prudent men only, unless he were inspired from that Spirit which spake them? In the third of the Galatians it is thus written: "O foolish Galatians, who hath bewitched you, that ye should not obey the truth? This only would I learn of you, received ye the Spirit by the works of the law, or by the hearing of faith preached? Are ye so foolish, that after ye have begun in the Spirit, ye would now be made perfect by the flesh?"

2. My spiritual brethren, is it not a work of the flesh in man, which studies day and night in the letter of the scripture, to find out the Spirit of God in the letter?

3. Is it not a work of the flesh in man, which labours to reconcile scriptures of seeming contradiction, without a divine gift of the Spirit?

4. Is not that man in the depth of spiritual darkness, which persuaded his hearers that the scriptures are easy and plain in the very letter of them unto that man's reason that is laborious to version, was a very able man in know them?

5. Are not the scriptures all matters of faith, and very mysterious for the most part, how then can any man comprehend spiritual mysteries, which are eternal, by his natural perishing reason?

6. Is not the most piercingest reason in man only natural? And can that which is natural comprehend that which is spiritual?

7. Are they not as contrary as fire and water, or as light and darkness? How then can any man, by his natural reason, understand any thing that is spiritual? It is written, "but the natural man perceiveth not the things of God, because they are spiritually discerned; but he that is spiritual discerneth all things, yet he himself is judged of no

man." Again it is written, "now we have received not the spirit of the world, but the Spirit which is of God, that we might know the things that are given to us of God, which things also we speak, not in the words which man's wisdom teaches, but which the Holy Ghost teaches, comparing spiritual things with spiritual."

8. My beloved brethren, you may see that the apostles came not to understand spiritual things by their study in the writings of Moses and his prophets, but by a gift from the Holy Ghost they were enabled in a great measure to comprehend the invisible things of God which they should enjoy in the resurrection of the just.

9. Moreover, you know that the apostle Paul, before his conversion, was a very able man in the letter of Moses and the prophets, yea, and according to the letter, blameless in his conversation; yet for all that, in zeal towards an unknown God, he persecuted the spirit of that letter through ignorance of that second man, which was the Lord from heaven.

10. It is truth, that when the apostles preached the spiritual things of eternity, they alluded unto Moses and the true prophets, because some of those mysteries were fore-prophesied of by them; but yet you may see that they were not instructed in those heavenly things by virtue of their prophetical letter but, as beforesaid, by inspiration from the Holy Spirit only.

11. Thus you that are spiritual may clearly see, that no man, by his natural reason and study in

the letter of the scripture, can ever be established in the truth of those glorious things, unto which the letter beareth record, unless he hath received a spiritual gift from that glorious God that moved holy men of old to speak and write those records of truth.

12. Therefore you may be confident, that those men which ignorantly call the letter *Spirit,* as yet they are not acquainted with those spiritual teachings of the things of God, which many of his elect do enjoy, that cannot read one letter in the Bible: his divine secrets are treasured up for the simple, and the subtle learned rationalists are sent empty away.

13. My beloved spiritual brethren in the glorious things of eternity, though men seemingly appear never so innocent in their way, is it probable, think you, that those men are immediately moved to speak unto the people by the Spirit of God, that slight all the scripture records as a thing of nought?

14. I humbly beseech you that are sober, can any man, of what tongue or language soever, speak or write a better or as good a language as the scriptures are, and not speak scripture words, or prove it was not the glorious God that moved the holy men of old to speak or write these scripture records?

15. Again, if the most desperatest man living, which saith in his heart there is no God, shall

commit murder or the like, and should escape the vengeance of man's laws for a season, yet he cannot possibly prevent the voice of that spiritual law within, crying for vengeance from that law without him, answerable to that within him.

16. Moreover, though natural wise men, as a nose of wax, produce those records to bear testimony unto all error whatsoever, yet you that are spiritual may know that the scriptures themselves are words of pure truth, not having the least error in them; but error proceeds only from that serpentine devil in men, which take upon them to interpret the scriptures without a spiritual gift.

17. Can any man that hath the spiritual power of the scriptures in him, be offended with those records which are witnesses of his innocent life, in the faces of those carnal hypocrites which, for love of silver or honour, prate of them only, but secretly hate all obedience to them.

18. Are not the literal records a demonstration of the mind of the Holy Spirit unto the chosen of God, which have the light of life in some measure to comprehend them?

19. Moreover, are not the teachings of the blessed Spirit more abundantly consolate to him, if those heavenly breathings in him be harmonious with the commands of our Lord Jesus Christ without him?

20. Can any man, therefore, which expects that eternal glory unto which these scriptures above all the writings in the world bear record, possibly despise the letter, and yet love that Spirit from whence it came?

21. Again, give me leave to make one comparison, in reference to this matter: suppose two friends that loved each other as their own souls, had their personal residence in several kingdoms, and one of them, as a testimony of his real love before he passed away, left behind him a book containing variety of sweet expressions of friendship unto the other, until he come again; if that man, in the absence of his friend, should burn that book to ashes, instead of embracing it, is that any sign of love in him to his friend afar off?

22. Wherefore can any sober man imagine or think, from any ground of truth, that the eternal Spirit of the true Jesus, upon any account, did ever command any man to burn those records which are a remonstrance of the wonderful spiritual transactions of the most high and holy God since the world began, yea, and before this world was?

23. O Lord God, of heavenly order, and not of earthly confusion, even for the glory of thy dreadful Name's sake, deliver thy redeemed ones not only from exalting the literal scriptures above the Holy Spirit which spake them, but also from disputing against the mysteriousness of them;

24. Then no kind of natural witchcrafts, which bear the name of spiritual power, shall have dominion over them for

ever; but they shall patiently wait for their change by a peaceable death; or being swallowed up of life, through the appearing of our only God and Saviour in the air, with his mighty angels, to reward every man according to his works.

25. Even so come, Lord Jesus, come quickly, and make it manifest in the sight of men and angels, whether thou hast sent us, as we have declared, or no.

CHAPTER VII.

1. Of the creation of the firmament, sun, moon, and stars. 2. Of the earth in the deep waters. 3. The meaning of the word create. 4. Why the deep waters are eternal. 5. By what the firmament was formed. 6. How the sun, moon, and stars came. 7. Of the distinct and fixed bodies of the sun, moon, and stars. 8. The sun and moon of contrary natures.

SEEING a right understanding of the mysteries of the true creation or redemption, or any spiritual truth whatsoever, consists only in the knowledge of Him which gave them their beings, therefore by divine assistance in the next place I shall treat again of that glorious Being concerning whom there is and hath been in this world such innumerable dark disputes.

2. My beloved brethren in the truth, you may remember that unto any sober man's understanding it is cleared already, that earth and water were an eternal chaos of confused matter, essentially distinct from the Creator.

3. Also you may remember, that out of those elements I have told you by inspiration from an unerring Spirit, that the divine majesty hath created all things that were made, into that heavenly order they appear to be, whether for a time or for eternity.

4. Moreover it is clear also, that without those eternal materials, was nothing made that was made, neither possibly could be, only that serpentine devil in the learned men of this world, have long imagined a confused creation of more seeming wisdom, power, and glory, than that of the Creator, as abundantly beforesaid.

5. Again, concerning the word create, make or form, I shall write a little of the sense of it.

6. My beloved brethren, the very true meaning of that word create is to compose confused dead matter into complete living forms; or that word create is light and life, producing dark dead dust or water, into sensible living beings; or it is a powerful word proceeding from a glorious form of sensible light and life, into a chaos of confused formless matter of senseless darkness and death, and from thence producing variety of sensible living bodies, according to their kind, for the demonstration of the Creator's infinite wisdom, power, and glory, in creation unto some of these living forms.

7. Again, seeing unlearned spiritual men wrest the scripture

to their own destruction, therefore for our more clearer understanding of the true Creator, in order thereunto, I shall speak somewhat of the visible heavens, and the lights formed in them for man's natural comfort, next unto the Creator's glory.

8. My beloved spiritual brethren, you know concerning the deep waters throughout the scripture records, no man can find one word or tittle in reference to its beginning, therefore of necessity it must be eternal.

9. Likewise you know, that the waters covered the earth before the creation; wherefore the earth being as it is in the deep waters, of necessity must needs be one essence eternally with those deep waters aforesaid.

10. Therefore though it be said, "in the beginning God created the heavens and the earth, and the earth was without form and void, and darkness was upon the deep, and the Spirit of God moved upon the waters,"

11. My spiritual brethren, you cannot be deceived by literal interpretations, as to think that the deep waters might be eternal, but that lump of hid earth within those waters had a beginning by the word of the Lord:

12. No, you know that is against all sober sense or reason itself; for if that earth which was within the water proceeded from the word of the Lord, then the dark deep water must of necessity have its beginning also at that time the earth received

its being, because in the lump they were essentially one.

13. Wherefore whatever man in darkness have dreamed, as to say that God created all things of nothing, or that God created that confused chaos of water and earth, it is so far from having any truth in it, that it is all one as if they should say, there is no Creator at all, but earth and water, and such like stuff as they are.

14. Again, by inspiration from an unerring Spirit, I positively affirm against men or angels, that the earth and the deep water were eternally one chaos of confused matter distinct from the ever-living God.

15. And whereas it is said, "in the beginning God created the heaven and the earth," that is, out of that matter of water and earth that were formless and void, God did by a word speaking create a formidable world, as a place of convenient residence for mortals to inhabit in.

16. I also declare from the Holy Spirit, that God created no light nor darkness at all without bodies;

17. Wherefore, concerning those words, "then God said, let there be light, and there was light;" that is, the Spirit of God being all light, moving or speaking into the deep dark waters, his word caused a light to appear throughout those waters, to make a distinction between light and that utter darkness that was both in the deep water and the earth, inclosed as a prisoner in the womb of darkness:

18. So that the Lord called this created light day; not only because it was all darkness before, or that He did not purpose to form a more eminent natural light than that was; but, as aforesaid, an ordinary created light is worthy to be called day, as well as ordinary darkness is called night.

19. Or you may know, that the very word light signifieth day, as the word darkness signifieth night.

20. Likewise you know, that darkness was not darkness without its body; therefore you may know, that light can be no light, unless it be in a body also.

21. It is not the word light, nor the word darkness, is, or possibly can be any thing at all, unless they be in distinct bodies, that they might become absolute beings of light, or beings of darkness.

22. It is written, "again God said, let there be a firmament in the midst of the waters, and let it separate the waters from the waters."

23. My spiritual brethren, I declare from the Holy Spirit, that this visible firmament called heaven, was formed by the powerful word of the Creator, out of those very waters in which it is now fixed, to keep them asunder.

24. Moreover, it is written, "and God said, let there be lights in the firmament of the heaven to give light upon the earth, and it was so. God then made two great lights, the greater light to rule the day, and the lesser light to rule the night. He made also the stars, and God set them in the firmament of heaven, to shine upon the earth."

25. My spiritual brethren, whatsoever hath been written formerly from men's imaginations concerning the vastness of the bodies of the sun, moon, and stars, it arose in them from their utter darkness of that glorious Creator, from whence all true light proceeds.

26. Wherefore, from that light by whom no man ever was deceived, in some measure I shall demonstrate why the Lord called the sun and moon two great lights, and of that matter of which they were made.

27. My spiritual brethren, though the sun, moon, and stars transcend each other in glory; yet you may know that they were all created of that element of water, and are distinct bodies of light fixed in the heavenly firmament.

28. I do not mean that they are so fixed as to be uncapable of motion; but of the contrary, from the Lord I affirm, that the firmament itself is not capable of motion; but by the word of the Lord that formed it, it is made unmoveable until the day of its dissolution, and those bodies of sun, moon, and stars, motions in that firmamental heaven in their seasons, to fulfil that word of government in them.

29. For you that are spiritual may know, that the firmament of heaven, and those rulers of sun, moon, and stars, set in them, as to govern both the day and the night, may be compared to a prince, with his nobles, throne, and other inferior rulers.

30. For you know that his kingdom whereon they have their living being is unmoveable; but the governors do the work unto which they are appointed.

31. My brethren, you may understand also, that the firmamental body above us, or below us, if you think it so, for its appointed season, is as firmly fixed as the earth we tread on; and as things in power are motional on this earth, so likewise those created lights are only motional in that heavenly body aforesaid.

32. Again it is said, that "God set them in the firmament of heaven to shine upon the earth."

33. My brethren, hearken no more unto vain astronomers, or star-gazers, concerning the bulk of the sun, moon, and stars; for I positively affirm from that God that made them, that the compass of their bodies are not much bigger than they appear to our natural sight.

34. "O empty vain liars! how long have you been suffered to deceive the people with your monstrous imaginary bodies of sun, moon, and stars, which are not? and of your great knowledge concerning them; your things are too big to be good or true, and the time of your serpentine sophistry is almost finished.

35. Again, I declare from the Holy Spirit, that the bodies of the sun, moon, and stars are all distinct beings from each other, and possess their own created light alone, neither borrowing nor lending their light to one another, whatever hath been imagined to the contrary, concerning new moons or eclipses.

36. Again, you know the scriptures do not say that the sun and moon are two great bodies, but two great lights only: neither doth the scripture say, that the bodies of the global earth and heavenly firmament, are covered with the vastness of the sun, moon, or stars, or that they inclose any other bodies within their own bodies, or that any other bodies are fixed in them:

37. But on the contrary the scripture saith, that "the sun and moon were set in the firmament of heaven, to shine upon the earth: wherefore it is as clear as the light, that that which is fixed is of a less bulk than that wherein it is inclosed.

38. Yet you know that the greater bulk may receive its principal light from that lesser body within its circumference, as a rich diamond in a ring, or a candle or torch in the night in a wide room or the like.

39. My spiritual brethren, you may understand that the glory of the most high God consists not in bulk of things, but in the exceeding brightness of them.

40. Nay, moreover, you cannot but know that the infinite wisdom of the divine majesty doth the more abundantly appear in an extraordinary light shining from a very little body.

41. My brethren, it is not the bulk of the sun or moon which causeth so great a light; but, as aforesaid, it is the transcendent brightness of their created purities which displayeth those

beams of light through the visible heaven and earth.

42. Whatever hath or shall be said to the contrary, from the Lord I positively affirm, that the bodies of the sun, moon, and stars are all fixed beings, only in one firmament.

43. Moreover, from the Lord of glory I declare, that this visible heaven is all the firmaments that ever was formed by the Creator.

44. Furthermore, though the bodies of the sun and moon were both formed out of that element of water; yet they were made as contrary in their natures as fire and water.

45. Because you know their government were over contrary beings, the one to rule the day, and the other to rule the night; so that as the sun is a fiery glorious light for consolation unto the natural things of the day, so likewise the moon is a qualifying cold watery light, answerable to the watery things of the night:

46. Wherefore, though the body of the sun is of a more eminent brightness than that of the moon, yet they being of contrary natures, it is against all sober reason that the one should receive any light from the other in the least.

47. Again, you know that when the bodies of the sun and moon seem close together, instead of any agreement between them, there is such a fiery contest, as if they would absolutely destroy each other. And what think you is the just occasion of it? Is it not the difference of their natures?

48. Can fire and water, or light and darkness agree, if they be united together? Is there any rest unto either of them until one of them is dissolved?

49. My beloved friends in the pure truth, whatever men have long declared concerning the eclipse of the sun, through the near appearance of the moon, you may understand, that the true occasion of the sun eclipsed, whether in part or whole, is according to their appearing at a further or nearer distance unto each other;

50. For, as beforesaid, the nature of the one being fiery, hot, and dry, and the nature of the other being watery, cold, and moist, if the most high God had not decreed the time of their contest, when they are nearly conjoined, there would be no communion between them until one of them were utterly dissolved.

51. Again, is it not as clear as the light itself unto us, that the true occasion of all variance between created beings, whether sensible or insensible, ariseth only from a difference of natures or spirits in them?

52. Moreover, when any kind of natures are suitable to each other, is there not a sweet harmony between them?

53. Wherefore, if the moon received her light from the sun, as natural wise men have long imagined, is it not against all sense or reason that there should be no union between them, but at a distance?

54. Doth it not rather agree with all true sense, that if the one received her light from the other, that the more nearer they

are in bodily appearance, the more greater harmony would ensue, and occasion the lesser light rather to shine more clearly than darken each other's brightness?

55. I think that William Lilly, and his learned brethren in astrologian figures, dare not say, that either the sun or the moon were ever at variance with their own selves; or that the eclipses of the sun or moon proceedeth from any harmony between that which occasioneth the eclipse, and the thing so eclipsed.

56. Well, then, if they acknowledge this rational truth, without controversy, when the light of the sun is eclipsed from us, it is through its near conjunction with the natural light or ruler of things of the night.

57. And when the light of the moon is eclipsed from us, though it be in the night, or early in the morning, it is through her near conjunction with the natural light or ruler of the day, or a planetary fire answerable to his nature.

58. My beloved spiritual brethren, as for the time and effect of eclipses, I leave them unto the figurative merchants of a sun, moon, and stars, which they rightly understand not; because no man can truly know them, but by inspiration from Him that made them.

CHAPTER VIII.

1. Of the heavens. 2. How many were created. 3. No more but three.

1. A throne of eternal ravishing glories. 2. A throne of natural perishing glories. 3. An invisible spiritual throne leading to eternity.

AGAIN, if there was but one heavenly firmament created in all, some men may say unto me, What is the meaning of that third heaven in the scriptures?

2. From that light which cannot lie, to this I answer, The Spirit of God speaketh of a third heaven in scripture, that some men might be capable to declare unto his redeemed ones how many heavens there are, and where those heavens are, and what those heavens are.

3. My spiritual brethren, which have ears to hear, hearken unto the pure light of life eternal. There are three created heavens spoken of in scripture records, and no more, no, nor never was any more, whatever vain men have imagined.

4. The first is that third heaven of visible and invisible ravishing glories which are eternal; this is that vast kingdom where the persons of the mighty angels and glorified bodies of Moses and Elias do now inhabit, beholding the face of that most excellent majesty, whose divine nature unto his elect is crowns of unutterable excellencies.

5. This is that habitation, third heaven, throne, or kingdom of ravishing glory above the starry heaven, spoken of so frequently in scripture records, which is needless to nominate unto you which are spiritual.

6. But lest some vain-glorious men should say, Where is the

word of God for what I speak? seeing the letter is their God whom they adore, instead of the Holy Spirit which spake them, therefore, to stop their carnal mouths, if it may be, I shall write down two or three scripture records: "Heaven is my throne, and earth is my footstool," Acts vii.; "O God, thy throne is for ever and ever," Heb. i.; "that we have such an high priest, that sitteth at the right hand of the throne of the majesty in the heavens," Heb. viii.

7. The second heaven which the Lord created, was not a spiritual, but a natural, therefore of necessity it must fade away.

8. This heaven is this visible firmament, adorned with majestical lights above us, and a fixed earth beneath us, beautified in its seasons with variety of delights, which is nature's only desired heaven, through the secret decree of the most wise God, to manifest the variety of his most infinite wisdom unto elect men and angels, in the creating of such natural glory to perish, and the angelical merciless rulers thereof, after they have enjoyed their momentary glory.

9. Give me leave to cite two or three scriptures, as a visible testimony to this second heaven also: it is written, "in the beginning God created the heaven and the earth."

10. My beloved spiritual brethren, you know that there could not be any beginning unto the Creator, therefore it may be understood that saying did include that immortal throne above, and this mortal world beneath, as having a beginning, was spoken for the capacity unto men or angels, which knew their being was from another, and understood also their continuance in those several heavens for a time or for eternity.

11. In the first of the Hebrews it is thus written, "and thou, Lord, in the beginning hast established the earth, and the heavens are the works of thine hands; they shall perish, but thou dost remain, and they shall wax old as doth a garment."

12. Again, the third and last created heaven is that within the bodies of men, or the first man Adam, the which spiritual creation being in natural bodies, and within this perishing globe, it is made capable through its union with changeable nature to enter into mortality, that by the most secret decree of the most high God, after a moment's tasting of silent death, as He Himself did, it may quicken again through death itself, spiritual bodies full of divine glories, that as one man naturally as a flame of fire, all the elect may (as swift as thought) ascend to meet their Lord in the air, and with his divine person of bright burning glory, enter into that prepared throne of eternal pleasure.

13. This created or inspired light in man you know hath variety of scripture expressions for the setting forth its excellencies that it shall enjoy in the life to come; as, namely, "the kingdom of heaven is within you. Christ in you the hope of glory.

Know you not that the Spirit of Christ is in you, except ye be reprobates? It is a true saying, for if we be created together with him, we also shall live together with him," 2 Tim. ii. "Thus God created the man in his image, in the image of God created he him; he created them male and female," Gen. i.

14. Thus briefly I have touched upon the three created heavens nominated in the literal records, unto an invisible, yet visible infinite Being of all finite beings, blessed for ever, viz. a throne of eternal ravishing glories: secondly, a throne of natural perishing glories: lastly, an invisible spiritual throne, leading them to eternity.

15. From that spiritual majesty by whom was formed the heavens aforesaid, and all in them, I positively affirm against all mortals that ever were or shall be, that though men have written or shall speak of more worlds than what is forewritten, those additional heavens proceeded from their own imaginary confused reason, and not from that Holy Spirit of all heavenly order.

CHAPTER IX.

1. An exact scripture rule to prove the man Christ glorified, to be Father, Son, and Holy Spirit in one distinct person.

MY beloved brethren, which desire a right understanding of spiritual things in scripture records, take special notice of this one thing, and you cannot be deceived by all the wisdom or subtilty of men.

2. I say again from the Lord, take good notice of those scriptures which speak positively concerning God, or the highest heavens, or angels, or eternal life, or eternal death, or of a natural heaven, and all mortal things within its orb. Why? because you may know that all privative scriptures, though never so eminent or numerous, wholly depend upon positive scriptures.

3. My dear brethren, for whom my soul is in continual travel until the pure truth be rooted in you, some of you being weak of comprehension, I shall write variety of expressions for explaining my meaning in this weighty thing.

4. Again, I say those scripture sayings which are positive, though never so few in number, yet they, as gods, command all other scripture sayings to bow down unto them, upon what account soever they are spoken, whether spiritual or natural, to continue for a time or for eternity.

5. Therefore seeing all privative scriptures are of none effect, but in reference unto those which are positive, are not those seeming wise men spiritually dark as pitch, which exalt the privative scriptures above the positive, because of the number of them?

6. My beloved brethren, you may know the privative scriptures can have no being without the positive; but it seemeth possible that the

positive might have been without the privative, as the glorious Creator was eternally alone, before any creaturely beings appeared in his sight.

7. Again, all positive sayings in scriptures may be compared unto the inward motion of a clock or dial; and all privative sayings in scriptures may be compared unto the outward wheel or hand, that always motions from, or points to, the inward cause of its outward motions.

8. My spiritual friends, if you diligently observe this golden rule, as sure as the Lord liveth, and as sure as you are living creatures, you shall find it that spiritual touchstone, which will not only discover all vainglorious opinions of literal or notional wise men, but it will also further you in the true understanding of the mind of God in the scripture, above all men which are ignorant of this rule, or enemies to this advice.

9. For the strengthening of the weak, in the next place I shall prove by many positive scriptures, that the man Christ Jesus glorified, is the Holy One of Israel only, or is both Father, Son, and Spirit in one distinct person, God and man blessed for ever and ever.

10. In the first of St. John's Gospel it is thus written: "In the beginning was that Word, and that Word was with God, and that Word was God, and that word was made flesh, and dwelt among us, and we saw the glory thereof, as the only begotten Son of the Father, full of grace and truth."

11. My brethren, though the one pure Being hath variety of expressions in holy writ, to set forth the infinite glory of his divine majesty, yet yeti may see in these very literal records themselves, that those holy names of Word, or God, or Father, beareth but one sense only.

12. Furthermore, this divine word God, or glorious Father, was made, begotten, or changed into flesh.

13. Again, you may by the true light of life in you, clearly see from the first words of the text, that Christ and the Father were but one essential glory before they became flesh: behold the one divinity in trinity of expressions only: "In the beginning was that Word, and that Word was with God, and that Word was God."

14. If that Word was God, that was in the beginning with God, and that God from everlasting was that spiritual Word, Christ being that divine God, or God that divine Word, "which in the beginning created heaven and earth," Gen. i., "and in the beginning or fulness of time became flesh," then without controversy He is the alone everlasting Father and Creator of both worlds, and the only Redeemer of his chosen ones out of their natural darkness, into this mysterious light of a right understanding of one divine personal majesty, in variety of expressions only.

15. Again, this positive scripture in this first of John, doth open many other sayings of

Christ and his apostles, as, namely, those in the eighth of John, where it is thus written: "And if I also judge, my judgment is true, for I am not alone, but I and the Father that sent me. Then said Jesus unto them, When ye have lifted up the Son of man, then shall ye know that I am he, and that I do nothing of myself; but as the Father hath taught me, so I speak these things; for he that sent me is with me: the Father hath not left me alone: because I do always those things that please him." Again, it is written in the tenth of John, "I and my Father are one."

16. The next positive scriptures bearing record unto the one personal divine Being, is in 1 Cor. xv. 47; the words are these: "The first man is of the earth earthy: the second man is the Lord from heaven." And in Rom. ix. 5, it is thus written: "Of whom are the fathers, and of whom concerning the flesh, Christ came, who is God over all, blessed for ever. Amen." Again, in 1 Tim. iii. the last, it is thus written: "And without controversy great is the mystery of godliness;" which is, "God is manifested in the flesh, justified in the Spirit, seen of angels, preached unto the Gentiles, believed on in the world, and received up into glory;" Col. ii. 9, "For in him dwelleth all the fulness of the godhead bodily."

17. Again, in John xiv. 9, it is thus written: "Jesus said unto him, I have been so long time with you, and hast thou not known me, Philip? he that hath seen me hath seen my Father; how then sayest thou, Show us thy Father" And in Matt. iv. 7, are these words: "Jesus said unto him, It is written again, Thou shalt not tempt the Lord thy God:" and in ver. 10, "Then said Jesus unto him, Avoid Satan: for it is written, Thou shalt worship the Lord thy God, and him only shalt thou serve:" and in Matt. i. 23, are these words: "Behold, a virgin shall be with child, and shall bear a son, and they shall call his name Emmanuel, which is by interpretation, God with us." John i. 10, "He was in the world, and the world was made by him, and the world knew him not." Col. i. 16, 17, "For by him were all things created which are in heaven, and which are in earth, things visible and invisible, whether they be thrones, or dominions, or principalities, or powers: all things were created by him, and for him and he is before all things, and in him all things consist." Col. ii. 3, "In whom are hid all the treasures of wisdom and knowledge." John i. 16, "And of his fulness have all we received, and grace for grace." Isa. ix. 6, "For unto us a child is born, and unto us a son is given: and he shall call his name Wonderful, Counsellor, The mighty God, The everlasting Father, The Prince of Peace." 2 Thess. ii. 16, "Now the same Jesus Christ, our Lord and our God, even the Father which hath loved us, and hath given us everlasting consolation, and good hope through grace." Philip ii 5-7, 20, 21, "Let the same mind be in you that was even in Christ

Jesus: who, being in the form of God, thought it no robbery to be equal with God; but he made himself of no reputation, and took on him the form of a servant, and was made like unto men, and was found in shape as man. But our conversation is in heaven, from whence also we look for the Saviour, even the Lord Jesus Christ, who shall change our vile bodies, that it may be fashioned like unto his glorious body, according to the working whereby he is able even to subdue all things unto himself." 2 Thess. i. 7-9, "And to you which are troubled, rest with us: when the Lord Jesus shall show himself from heaven with his mighty angels in flaming fire, rendering vengeance unto them that do not know God, and which obey not unto the gospel of our Lord Jesus Christ, which shall be punished with everlasting perdition from the presence of the Lord, and from the glory of his power." 1 Thess. iv. 16, 17, "For the Lord himself shall descend from heaven with a shout, and with the voice of the archangel, and with the trumpet of God: and the dead in Christ shall rise first: then shall we which live and remain, be caught up with them also in the clouds, to meet the Lord in the air: and so shall we be ever with the Lord." 1 Tim. iv. 10, "For therefore we labour and are rebuked, because we trust in the living God, which is the Saviour of all men, especially of those that believe." 1 John v. 19, 20, " We know that we are of God, and the whole world lieth in wickedness; but we know that the Son of God is come, and hath given us a mind to know him which is true, and we are in him that is true, that is, in his Son Jesus Christ; this same is very God, and eternal life." Jude 24, 25, "Now unto him that is able to keep you that ye fall not, and to present you faultless before the presence of his glory with joy, that is, to God only wise, our Saviour, be glory and majesty, and dominion and power, both now and for ever. Amen."

18. Remember the golden positive rule, and none can deceive you concerning the one glorious personal god-man blessed for ever: 1 Tim. i. 15-17, "This is a true saying, and by all means worthy to be received, that Christ Jesus came into the world to save sinners, of whom I am chief. Notwithstanding for this cause was I received to mercy, that Jesus Christ should first show on me all long-suffering, unto the example of them which shall in time to come believe in him unto eternal life. Now unto the King everlasting, immortal, invisible, unto God only wise, be honour and glory, for ever and ever. Amen."

19. My spiritual brethren, if you take good notice of this place of scripture, you may plainly see that the apostle Paul owneth no other God, Father, or eternal Spirit, but that one personal majesty of our Lord Jesus Christ in immortality: Eph. iv. 5-10, "There is one Lord, one faith, one baptism, one God and Father of all, which is above all, and

through all, and in you all. But unto every one of us is given grace, according to the measure of the gift of Christ. Wherefore he saith, When he ascended up on high, he led captivity captive, and gave gifts unto men. Now in that he ascended, what is it but that he also descended first, into the lowest parts of the earth? He that descended is even the same that ascended far above all heavens, that he might fill all things."

20. My beloved spiritual brethren, which are appointed unto an immortal personal glory, you may see that the Lord Jesus Christ is that Holy One of Israel which first descended from his throne of infinite godhead glory, into the lower parts of the virgin earth, and so became a body of pure flesh of her seed, and by virtue of his divine power in that very body of flesh and bone, He descended into the lowest part of the earth, death, hell, or the grave, for a moment; not only for improving the power of his godhead life entering into death, and in that very body of flesh quickening and reviving a new and glorious life again; and as a flame of fire naturally ascending and immortalizing that body of flesh and bone with a Father's throne of transcendent excellencies, but also for destroying of the power of sin, and fear of eternal death in all his new-born elect trees unto eternal life.

CHAPTER X.

1. Of persecution of conscience.
2. Of the sin against the Holy Ghost.

MY beloved brethren, by immediate inspiration from that Holy One of Israel, in the next place I shall clearly demonstrate unto the heirs of glory the confused darkness of two or three sorts of men, concerning the knowledge of the only very true God, the which confusion riseth in them through their misunderstanding of the true grounds of certain scriptures, as, namely, these: "God is a Spirit," John v. 24; and "a spirit hath not flesh and bones as you see me have," Luke xxiv 39. "But more especially these trinitary expressions, "baptizing them in the Name of the Father, and of the Son, and of the Holy Ghost," Matt. Xxviii.

19. "For there are three which bear record in heaven, the Father, the Word, and the Holy Ghost, and these three are one," 1 John v. 7.

2. The first sort of deceived persons, past or present, which affirm the Holy One of Israel to consist of three persons, were Athanasiun, Socinus, alias John Biddle, and their literal adherents.

3. My brethren, I do not say they can help this their darkness, or blame them for this their error; for, alas! poor, simple, or over-wise men, to their imaginary understandings it is a pure truth, and those which are contrary-minded to them, in darkness.

4. Therefore, whoever are left

to persecute their persons for their judgment's sake only, it would have been better for those men that they had never been born, if they acknowledge a Christ.

5. Take this for an infallible rule, those that persecute a man for an error in judgment concerning his God, will as soon persecute him for the truth of Christ as for a lie.

6. Let no persecutor flatter himself that he may repent and find mercy as well as Paul, because Paul acknowledged no Jesus at all when he persecuted his saints; therefore you know how he pleads God's mercy towards him, in that he did it ignorantly.

7. Moreover, how deeply did he pledge that cup of persecution upon his own body for the truth's sake all his days, which instrumentally for Christ's sake he had caused others to drink?

8. Again, before I go forward concerning the point in hand, it will be necessary for me to show you who those persecutors are, which commit that unpardonable sin against the Holy Ghost.

9. My spiritual brethren, if a Turk do persecute a man that professeth himself to be a Christian, for despising of his Mahomet, or if a man called a Christian should persecute an infidel for despising the Lord Jesus Christ, this persecuting each other is pardonable, though not justifiable in their consciences, when they shall understand the truth of leaving all vengeance in spiritual things unto God Himself.

10. But on the contrary, suppose two men shall acknowledge that the man Christ Jesus glorified is the Son of God spoken of in the scriptures, both of them affirming that all their hopes of eternal salvation only depends upon Him; if these men, for difference in judgment only concerning this Jesus, shall persecute each other before a magistrate, or the like, there remains no more sacrifice for that sin;

11. For that is the unpardonable sin against the Holy Spirit, because they persecuted each other for his sake, which they both confessed to be their God and Saviour, even to their own knowledge.

12. And in so doing they condemned their own faith, and to the utmost of their power they crucified the Lord of glory afresh, and put Him to an open shame, even before his filthy scoffing enemies.

13. Again, if a man shall come in the holy name of our Lord Jesus Christ, and shall declare many heavenly secrets which he hath received from the throne of glory:

14. If men which confess the same Jesus, because the things declared are contrary to their ways, and hard sayings to their comprehensions, shall therefore condemn them as delusions and blasphemies, and the Spirit which spake them to be of the devil, in so doing they have fallen under that sin of eternal condemnation, because, as

aforesaid, they have crucified the Lord of glory afresh, and put Him to an open shame, and have judged themselves unworthy of everlasting life, and have denied their own faith and hope in Him, through their despising that Holy Spirit which seals men up unto the day of redemption.

15. My beloved brethren, though any one beloved Dalilah reigning in men unto the death, tendeth to eternal condemnation, yet there are no actual sins whatsoever but are pardonable, unless men commit them upon the account aforesaid.

16. My spiritual brethren, there is a vast difference between the heirs of glory and the vessels of shame concerning this sin.

17. The Holy Spirit of Christ Jesus hath endued his elect with such a measure of light, though most of them know it not, that by virtue of that holy fire, they are not only preserved from that condemning evil, but are rather fearful they have or shall commit it.

18. But on the contrary, the desperate reprobate is so far from any kind of fear in him concerning the committing of that castaway sin, that, when occasion is offered, he glorieth in it as the acceptable sacrifice unto his God, and yet knows it not.

19. Thus briefly I have touched upon the unpardonable sin against the Holy Spirit of our Lord Jesus Christ, whose very saying only makes a sin pardonable or unpardonable, because He is truth itself, and

cannot possibly lie: "Verily I say unto you, All sins shall be forgiven unto the children of men, and blasphemies wherewith they blaspheme; but he that blasphemeth against the Holy Ghost shall never have forgiveness, but is culpable of eternal damnation, because they said he had an unclean spirit," Mark iii. 28-30. You blessed ones, know who it was that spake those words.

CHAPTER XI.

1. Of the true nature of infiniteness. 2. Wherein it lieth, viz. in the not knowing its beginning or ending. 3. Infiniteness and finiteness are uncapable of equal glory. 4. Against all true reason that there should be three persons in the Trinity. 5. Christ and the Father one undivided godhead. 6. Denying Christ to be the only God, is antichrist. 7. How prayers are heard.

IN the next place, from the Holy One of Israel I shall demonstrate the absurdity of that error of trinity of persons in the unity of godhead.

2. My beloved spiritual brethren, if the divine majesty should contain of three distinct persons in coequal godhead glory, and each person be uncreated and eternal of itself, then instead of those names of Father, Son, and Holy Ghost, they would of necessity be three fathers only.

3. Because you know that if the person of a Son or Holy Ghost were created or begotten,

or proceeded from a father, then it is contrary to all sober sense or reason, that the persons of Son and Holy Ghost should either be coequal with the Father, or eternal of themselves.

4. Moreover, if the persons of Son and Holy Ghost proceeded from the Father, then they are but finite created glories, and in degree lower than the Father.

5. You that are spiritual know, that that which received its beginning from another could not possibly be made equal with that which was eternal itself.

6. Uncreated incomprehensible infiniteness was capable to transmute itself into a lower condition for its own transcendent advantage in the spirits of his elect; but it was utterly impossible for Him to create infinite incomprehensible beings, to become coequal in godhead, wisdom, power, and glory with Himself.

7. For uncreated glory is so unutterably infinite, that it is uncapable to comprehend the height, length, breadth, or depth of its own eternal excellencies.

8. If this saying seem strange unto any man, as to cause him to think it ridiculous, or dishonourable to the Creator's glory, unto that man I positively affirm from the spirit of truth, that it is so far from any kind of dishonour unto the divine majesty, that on the contrary all the variety of spiritual joys or heavenly pleasures for himself, or elect men and angels, consists only in his perfect understanding, that he cannot possibly know any beginning or ending of his glorious excellencies.

9. To know the beginning or ending of itself, you know causeth nothing but sorrows rather than joys.

10. So likewise on the contrary, not to know any beginning or ending of itself, must needs occasion nothing else but ravishing everlasting joys.

11. Thus you which are spiritual may clearly see the fallacy of the three persons and one God, spoken of in Athanasius's Creed; you know that infiniteness and finiteness are uncapable of equal glory.

12. Also you know that if there should have been three persons eternally of themselves, there could not possibly have been any Son or Holy Ghost at all: because a Son or Holy Ghost proceeds from a Father, and not, as beforesaid, from themselves.

13. Moreover, you may understand that if it stood to any true faith or sober reason, that there were three persons eternally of themselves, yet they of necessity must be three Fathers only, and so agreeing together, two of those Fathers must be transmuted into a Son and Holy Ghost by the other Father, or from themselves, to make up this confused Trinity, proceeding from the literal mongers of this vain-glorious perishing world, or conscientious noncommissioned men, which would compel words to become persons, having no positive records to prove any such three persons throughout the whole scriptures, but the

contrary altogether. "My glory I will not give to another," saith the Holy One of Israel: Jehovah, our everliving Jesus, God only wise, blessed for ever and ever, honoured only from his elect men and angels.

14. My spiritual brethren, you know that the Lord Jesus Christ hath not only the godhead titles in scripture records, but also all the glory from men and angels was attributed unto Him in the body of his flesh: "And let all the angels of God worship him," Heb.i. To worship, honour, magnify, or adore man or angel, is not that giving glory to Him, or glorying in Him?

15. Doth not all such kind of divine worship, honour, or glory, belong only to the Creator? And doth not the Holy One of Israel positively say, that He will not give his glory to another What sober sensible man that hath any spiritual light in him, dares say that Christ and the Father are not one undivided personal being, seeing all glory in heaven and earth was given unto Him only?

16. Again, seeing God hath said, that He will not give his glory to another, and yet all his glory was given unto that man Christ, do not those trinitary literal mongers call the divine majesty a liar to his face, which deny Christ Jesus the Lord of glory to be that "everlasting Father?"

17. Doth not the Father give all glory to the Son in scriptures, as well as the Son gives all glory to the Father? Who art thou, then, that dividest them into three personal beings, presumptuously taking upon thee to share the infinite glory of the Holy One of Israel, seeing his glory He will not, no, nor cannot, give to any other distinct person?

18. And what art thou, then, but that antichrist and utter enemy unto thine own soul, and a deceiver of those which are deceived by thy literal wit, which saith, that Christ was only an extraordinary messenger sent forth by the most high God to do his will; or that Christ was only a God, and not the God; or that Christ only had the titles of the divine majesty put upon Him for a season, that He might become a fit mediator between God and man, but there was another Father above Him that sent Him, abiding in the highest heavens, unto which He was fain to cry out for help in his need.

19. My spiritual brethren, if men so acute in the letter can attain to understand this one thing in scripture record, then those sayings of Christ, or Son, and such like, will be no stumbling-block in their way concerning Christ's Father. You know that the Lord Jehovah saith, "Because there was none greater than himself, he swore by himself," concerning something that was in his mind to bring to pass: the thing is this, that God of glory that was compelled to swear by Himself for the exaltation of his own greatness in men and angels, because there was none beside Himself, therefore He glorifieth Himself alone.

20. Again, because none

could humble or exalt Him but Himself, therefore He alone first exalts Himself by an oath, that He might be the more admired at of all that know Him; after that He abaseth Himself a little lower than his angelical creatures in respect of death, that by virtue of his infinite humility in flesh, his glorious godhead might in that personal manhood exalt itself in a new and wonderful way, far above all gods, heavens, angels, and men.

21. Wherefore concerning the scripture saying, "The Lord said unto my Lord, Sit thou at my right hand until I make thine enemies thy footstool," that is, the everlasting Father speaking to Himself in a twofold condition, or God the great Jehovah in the height of his glory exalting Himself over all opposition in his creatures, in the lowest appearance of a creature Himself.

22. Again the Lord saith, "He will set his king upon his holy hill of Sion:" and God saith, "O God, thy throne is for ever and ever; wherefore God, even thy God, hath anointed thee with the oil of gladness above thy fellows."

23. My beloved brethren, is there any more than one God and king of glory perpetually sitting in the midst of the throne of the highest heavens?

24. Is there any more than one God and king, spiritually sitting upon his throne of Sion, or souls of his redeemed ones?

25. Is not this one God in his throne above, and in his throne beneath, Christ Jesus our Lord?

26. If this be granted, which none can deny but filthy atheists, over-wise literalists, or very weak saints, I would fain know from any man under what kind of trinity soever, who that God and king was, unto which God said, "I will set my king upon my holy hill of Sion. O God, thy throne is for ever and ever?"

27. If there be but one God and king of Sion's glory alone, then there cannot be a God, and God or a king, and a king of eternal glory: if this be not good sense, let me be reproved with better.

28. Again, hath God any other king to exalt upon Sion's holy hill but Himself; or to sit on the right hand of all majesty, wisdom, power, and glory, in the personal presence of his mighty angels, Moses and Elias, but Himself?

29. Who then is that most high and mighty God and king of Sion's glory, or that spiritual all in all, or that Alpha and Omega, or that Father, Son, and Holy Spirit, but our Lord Jesus Christ in immortal glory itself?

30. Thus you that have any true light of life eternal in you, may clearly see that the Holy One of Israel which swore by Himself, to Himself, for his own further exaltation, by the same rule He may change his glorious condition into flesh, and having humbled Himself to Himself, He may cause his humanity to speak, pray, or cry, unto his divinity within Him, or unto his own spiritual charge committed unto his angels without Him, for a further manifestation of his

unsearchable wisdom, power, and incomprehensible glory in shame and weakness, as well as in power and glory, as aforesaid.

31. Is any thing hard or impossible for an infinite Creator to do, when his glory moves Him to do it?

32. Again, did not his infinite power, wisdom, and glory more abundantly appear in the lowest abasing Himself in the visible sight of elect men and angels? Why then should it seem strange to any sober wise man, that the everlasting Father should be clothed with flesh and bone, as with a garment?

33. Or that Christ Jesus should be both God and man in one distinct body glorified, there is none but Christ, none but Christ; no other God but that man Christ Jesus our Lord, if men or angels should gainsay it.

34. Though this may seem strange unto many at present, yet they only are eternally blessed that are not offended with this saving truth, but are made obedient unto this crucified and glorified Jesus.

{Here begins a section that was omitted in Muggleton's 1661 revision}

35. Again, If it should seem strange unto any Man, that the Creator should cause such Variety of Expressions in Scriptures, in reference to one Divine Person only, if that man be an earthly Prince sitting on his Throne; I would faine know of that Princely Father, if he knew sufficient Power in himself for advancing of his Glory in the Spirits of his Subjects; whether he would not for a Season disrobe himself of all his Princely Greatness, and abase himself in the lowest Appearance of a Subject, and serve his Subjects.

36. Yea, and suffer himself to be exceedingly abused of the Basest of them for his Glory's Sake, and Prerogative Pleasure over those Vassals when he is set on his Throne.

37. Again, moreover, for the Improving of thy Kingly Power, And advancing thy princely Glory, wouldst thou not stoop to the lowest Way that could be imagined, for so mighty a Prince to bow unto? as namely, wouldst thou not commit the Government of thy Throne unto some of thy Princely Favourites: and furnish them with Gifts that should make them as fit in Measure for that Throne, as Faithful as thou art to thy own self?

38. After that, wouldst thou not enter into one of thy Virgin's Womb, and transmute thy Fatherly Glory into a Condition of Sonship; and so have a Beginning from thine own self, in a New and wonderful Way of seeming Weakness unto thy Luciferian Subjects, that were ignorant of thy Princely Wisdom and Transcendent Humility?

39. Furthermore, thou being now in the appearance of a Subject thy self, wouldst thou not yield all Childlike Obedience unto thine own representative Power in thy Favourites Persons, as a perfect Pattern of all Righteousness to thy beloved

obedient Subjects whom thou delightest to Honour?

40. And for an everlasting Terror unto those non-favourable Subjects, whose Pride and Envy caused them utterly to abhor that Prince and his Laws that should so abase himself to his own Subjects:

41. Again, Suppose thou vast the sole Emperor of this whole World, and didst possess of thy Body only one Son and Heir, and being both alive at once, thou shouldst set thy Son on thy Throne and bequeath all thy princely Titles unto him; and command all thy Subjects to honour him as their only Lord and King for ever:

42. What art thou then, when thy Throne, Titles, and Honour, is invested upon the Person of another? Are thou any more unto that Prince, and his People, than a Round O, or an absolute Nothing?

{Here ends a section that was omitted in Muggleton's 1661 revision}

CHAPTER XII.

1. To own or believe any other. God but Christ, is a cursed lie. 2. Who are the deceived persons. 3. Concerning the true knowledge of God. 4. The deceivers of others under conflicts of mind, described by many and various expressions.

ALL the divine titles of the Holy One of Israel, made over to the second man, the Lord from heaven; and is not the Father's throne invested upon his person? And is not all spiritual honour, praise, and glory, commanded to be attributed unto Him by men and angels?

2. And is it not all the fulness of the godhead dwelling in Him bodily; and from his fulness only do we not all receive, and grace for grace, if we have any grace at all ruling in us?

3. And is He not the Redeemer of his beloved people with his own blood? And is He not the judge of quick and dead? And was not all things made by Him, and for Him? And was there any thing made that was made without Him? And was He not before all things And do not all things consist in Him? And are not all things upheld by that almighty word of his Holy Spirit only?

4. Seeing these are undeniable words of truth itself, do not all those men that own any other God, or Father, or Creator, above, before, or besides our Lord Jesus Christ, deny the Holy One of Israel, and imagine a cursed lie, and bow down to that cursed idol of their own invented words only, utterly denying that honour and glory due unto Jesus Christ, the Creator Himself?

5. "Who is a liar but he that denieth that Jesus is that Christ, the same is that antichrist that denieth the Father and the Son. Whosoever denieth the Son, the same hath not the Father: he that hath the Son, hath life; and he that hath not the Son of God, hath not life: he that believeth in the Son of God, hath the witness

in himself: he that believes not God, hath made him a liar; because he believed not the record, that God witnessed of his Son, and this is the record, that God hath given unto us eternal life, and this life is in his Son. But ye have anointment from that holy one, and know all things." These literal words of truth are in the epistle 1 John ii. 22, 23; v. 10; ii. 20. "All things are given unto me of my Father, and no man knoweth the Son, but the Father; neither knoweth any man the Father, but the Son, and he to whom the Son will reveal him," Matthew xi. 27.

6. Some deceived persons ignorantly hold forth a false God, or trinity, which say, that the infinite majesty is a vast bodiless Spirit; also they call their God by a twofold name or spirits, a Spirit Father and a Spirit Son, and these spirits they say are in their spirits, and so these three spirits being one essence, make up their imaginary trinity in unity.

7. These are those which affirm that there is no other God, or Father, or Creator, but what is invisibly living in the creation, or in the creatures only; and if you soberly ask them whether there be a Creator, and concerning the true knowledge of any such Creator, you shall receive such like answers as this is:

8. The Creator is an infinite, incomprehensible Spirit, essentially filling all things and places; or they will say, that a creature is utterly uncapable of any knowledge of the Creator Himself, but within the creatures only; or else they will tell you, that not to know the Creator is the greatest knowledge of a Creator.

9. Again, you shall have such confusion as this from some of these high-flown atheists, the Creator is all things; and yet He is nothing at all, and is every where, and yet He is no where at all.

10. If a man shall reply and say, nothing is nothing: but if you grant a Creator, He must be something as well as his creatures, or else there can be no Creator at all.

11. Further, if a man shall say the Creator must of necessity be some glorious thing, which is infinite in itself, and distinct from all creatures, as well as the creatures are distinct from one another, or else you utterly deny a Creator.

12. Then these men will say, What is your Creator you pretend to know, and where is his residence? did you ever see Him? or such like.

13. If a man shall reply that the Creator is an incomprehensible glorious person in the form of a man, and that by virtue of his brightness He fills heaven and earth, angels and men, spiritually or naturally; only his ever-blessed person is resident on a throne of infinite glory, in but one place at once, as the person of man is in this world.

14. Then these men are ready to vilify such a Creator as a simple weak thing; or else they will say, this is to confine an unknown infiniteness into a creaturely substance, and such

a God of a bodily appearance any way like unto themselves in the least, they utterly abhor; but, as before said, a wonderful God, which is uncapable of ever being seen or known by the creatures, such a non-sensible, infinite nothing, all vain-glorious men delight to own; who love darkness rather than light, because their deeds are evil.

15. Another sort there are of these men which appear more angelical than the rest; these are those which are full of expressions of heavenly ruptures, through a supposed union with a Father and Son within them only, and various songs, which they call spiritual breakings forth in them; unto which hymns or natural songs, mixed with many spiritual expressions in metre, or otherwise, they bow down their souls, and ignorantly say, "It is the Father breathing forth those fleshly ballads through their mouths." Moreover, if these notional flashes shall see any of their own fancies lying under a wounded spirit, and through some extraordinary guilt crying out, they have that fire of hell burning in them, and are those devils which are under eternal damnation already.

16. Further, though their condition be like unto Cain, through the eternal absence of the Spirit of God speaking peace unto their outcast condition; yet, when these notional flashes shall come to visit their friend in this his horrid unutterable pain and shame, they will speak such like empty speeches as these:

"Come, come, it is very good for you, that you should be thus afflicted, it is a token of the Father's love unto you, He will bring all men and women into your condition, more or less, that the glory of his mercy might shine over all." Or else they will say, "It is the Father's love in darkness appearing unto you, if you could but see it." Further, they will say unto their hopeless friend, "Wherefore do you thus torment your own soul? There is but one pure Being, and all our spirits came forth from this Father of spirits, and in the end we shall all be swallowed up into the eternal Being again: wherefore, then, do you talk so much of eternal damnation, or call yourself a devil, making such lamentation for your sins, as if you could possibly be divided from your Father's love, or cast out of his glorious presence, I boldly affirm unto you it is no such matter; for there are no such devils, or damnation, or sins at all, but in the esteem of men deceived so to think by their fellow-creatures, which ignorantly laud one over another, from some blind opinion in them; wherefore our counsel is, that you would hearken no more unto vain thoughts or motions, or imaginations within you, or words from any creature without you, as to become so weak or foolish to trouble or torment yourself, seeing there is nothing in us but God only in variety of appearance. Furthermore, do you not know, that He is all in all: what, then, is there besides

Himself? Comfort up your despairing self therefore, and understand that it is the Spirit of the Father only appearing in you, sometimes in light and love, and sometimes in death, darkness, or seeming wrath or envy, in the end you shall find that all visibilities are but mere forms, shapes, or shadows; and that all invisible operations of seeming contrariety, was the Father only, who is the first and the last, and there is none beside Him.

17. Again, if a more grosser sort of these trinitary mongers, or rather fleshly atheists, shall come to visit their friend in the condition beforesaid, they will endeavour to comfort them or sooth them up with these and such like expressions: "Friend, what is the matter with thee? Or what is there that should cause thee to be so full of fears, or trouble of mind? Thou fearest where no fear is, thou art like unto a child or fool that is frighted with their own shadows, or else thou art mad, and wantest a surgeon to let thee blood, that the devil, damnation, sins, or cyphers, may fly from thee." Further, they will say unto their wrathful friend, "Let not that called sin in the least trouble thee, but rather let it be thy glory. Because there is none in such bondage as those that are so nice or scrupulous concerning sin. Sin, what is sin or sins in us? Are they any thing else but so many several stars or angels in us Art thou not worse than mad, therefore, to be troubled with the variety of thy Father's

brightness appearing in thee, though in seeming darkness?

18. Again, if none of these or such like cursed speeches take effect with their despairing friend, then out of atheistical madness they will say unto one another, "That he is an ass and a fool for making such a noise, and to trouble his friends as he doth, when he will he may help it with ease; sure it is somewhat doubtful that he dissembles with himself for some bye-end, to bring his friends into public shame amongst their religious adversaries?"

19. My beloved spiritual brethren, this is the end of such comforters, and their hellish counsel unto their friend under present wrath. O will not Job's comforters rise up in judgment, and condemn all such wretched counsellors as these are, at the visible appearing of our Lord Jesus Christ with his mighty angels?

20. Another sort of empty comforters will say unto this their despairing friend, "Brother, how is it with you? Do you earnestly pray unto the Lord to forgive you your great transgressions committed against Him Or are you heartily sorry for all your evils? Or are you willing to be prayed for when the saints shall meet together? Or shall we set a day apart of fasting and humiliation before the Lord for you? Or are you not guilty of some secret sins lying heavy upon your conscience, because you do not disclose them, through which the prayers of the saints are not answered?

Certainly your sins are not so great, but if you confess them and forsake them, they are pardonable: cry, therefore, mightily unto the Lord day and night, we also will do the like, that your wounded spirit may be healed; but it may be you have committed some horrible wickedness, that God will not suffer you to be in peace, though you cry never so much or long unto Him, until you are made to desire his saints to lay open your rebellions before him in public or private, zealously fasting and crying unto Him with a loud and bitter voice, that this sort of soul-despairing sins, or devils, may be cast out of you: or it may be you have committed some secret action of murder, buggery, or such like; and, therefore, the Lord will neither answer our prayers or your own, or ever suffer you to be in peace more, until you are cut off by the hand of the magistrate; therefore, that you may be delivered from the wrath of God upon you, and die in peace, our counsel is that you will hide none of your rebellions committed against the Lord or man.

{Here begins a section that was omitted in Muggleton's 1661 revision}

21. Again, my Beloved Brethren, these last Sort of Literal Comforters are those Speakers and People, which for the most Part combine together as one Man, and in their solemn Meetings of imaginary Worship, under pretence of their Duty towards God, and tender Compassion unto the Souls of Men instead of counselling one another to desire the Holy Spirit's Assistance, of following Peace with all Men to the utmost, and Forgiveness unto their supposed Enemies, as our Lord Jesus Christ and his Saints did unto their blood Persecutors for Righteousness Sake; they spend a great Part of their precious Time, in the discovering of the Unfaithfullness of Civil Magistrates, but especially of the chief Magistrate of these three Nations in present Power.

22. So that their Holy Meetings so called tend principally to the involving of the three Nations into Blood, Fire, Famine, Pestilence, and what not? when all Sorts of Men have a Sword of Steel in their Hand again,

23. Again, suppose the Head Magistrate, called the Lord Protector, be guilty of many unjust Acts of Breach of Covenants in general or in particular; of the which his own Light of Conscience often puts him in Remembrance:

24. My Spiritual Brethren, can you possibly imagine or think that those Speakers or People have any Spiritual Light ruling in them; which are not only full of scurrilous and bitter Language against the Head Magistrate, in reference to his former Evils; but are also ready, if they had Opportunity to unthrone him, and kill him, to cure him of his Maladies; or rather satisfy their own bloody

Madness, with which they think God would be well pleased?

25. But some Men may be offended with what I have here written, and say unto me, that they are very willing to yield Obedience unto the just Commands of a Head Magistrate, lawfully chosen by a free Parliament; but that Man which with us engaged against Monarchical Government, ruleth more rigorously in the same Way, therefore he appeareth unto us as a Tyrannical Usurper, over a free-born People, rather than a lawful Magistrate.

26. Whoever thou art that thus reasoneth, To thee I answer by Way of Query, Didst not thou account Old Charles Stuart thy lawful Head Governour, and didst thou not swear to be obedient to him and his Heirs in all their just Commands?

27. And yet for all this, didst thou not war against him and his Council, as Tyrants over the People, thro' monopolizing, and the like? And when they were overcome, didst thou not consent to their cutting off as Tyrants and Traytors, or justify it when it was put in Execution? Deny it if thou canst.

28. And now is thy Friend Cromwell, with whom thou didst engage thy self, and all that was near and dear unto thee against Tyranny, become the greatest Tyrant of all, because he possesseth the highest Place of Government without thy Consent?

29. Was Charles a Tyrant? And is Oliver a Tyrant? And art thou a good Christian, because thou wouldst cut both their Throats?

30. Again, you that have sided with the Protector, and his Head Officers against the common Enemy, (so termed), if this present Power by Consent of any Parliament had established your Opinions as the purest Christian Religion in Europe, thro' the three Nations, that from your Roman See you might subject Mens Persons and Estates, whose Consciences could not bow down to your Idol:

31. Is it not to be suspected, that your Zeal would have been as fiery hot as any Men in this World, for the Protector's Government as the most fittest man alive?

32. Again, are not all Civil Powers whatsoever established by the secret Decree of the most High God?

33. And is it not he that setteth Kings upon their Thrones, and pulleth them down again, and setteth up their Subjects in their Stead, to bring about his unsearchable Wisdom of Mercy, or Judgment, towards a Nation?

34. Again, is there any Rule in the Letter of the New Testament to warrant any Spiritual Christian to resist the Civil Magistrate, with the Sword of Steel? Nay, doth it not altogether command the contrary?

35. Likewise, notwithstanding these Sleepers also defile the Flesh, and despise Government which are bold, and stand in their own Conceit, and fear not to speak evil of them that are in Dignity, the 2d Chap. And 10th

verse of the 2d Epistle of Peter. If it should be objected, these were filthy Sodomites that resisted both Spiritual and Temporal Dignities: To that I answer, If thou countest thy self a Spiritual Christian, and yet resists the Temporal Power, art thou not liable to the greater Condemnation, because thou rebellist against greater Light?

36. Then said Jesus unto him, Put up thy Sword in his Place, for all that take the Sword, shall perish with the Sword, Mat. xxvith. and 52d verse; Ye stiff-necked bloody minded Rebels against your own Native Magistrates, behold the Example and Words of the Lord of Lords, and King of Kings himself: And if there be any Light left in you, you may see, that he was so far from allowing any Resistance against the Temporal Magistrate under what Pretence soever, that he layeth it down as an absolute Rule unto all Spiritual Christians, that he that killeth with the Sword, shall perish with the Sword:

37. Wherefore, by an immediate Commission from the God of all Truth, I pronounce Woe, Woe, Woe, yea everlasting Woe unto all the Speakers, or people, which pretend Love unto our Lord Jesus Christ, and yet provoke the People to kill their Magistrates, and butcher one another with a Sword of Steel.

{Here ends a section that was omitted in Muggleton's 1661 revision}

CHAPTER XIII.

1. Of the language and conditions of two sorts of men and women. 2. The one elected unto glory, the other rejected unto shame. 3. The prophets declaration thereupon.

IN the next place I shall speak of two sorts of men and women, the one elected unto glory, the other rejected unto shame; or which have committed the unpardonable sin against the Holy Spirit through reprobation, and which have not through election, yet both of them may continue under despair to their lives' end; for the manifestation of the prerogative will or pleasure of the Creator over his creatures: and who art thou that dares dispute against it?

2. My spiritual brethren, if an elect vessel hath been left to commit adultery, buggery, murder, or such like, and lieth under despair; and if he hath not fallen under these serpentine stinging evils, but is wounded in spirit, through a continual fear of being overcome through temptation, to commit it one time or other:

3. Or suppose he is full of blasphemous thoughts against the Creator, through which there is a continual fear in him of eternal damnation; yet there is so much light of life in him, secretly upholding his bleeding spirit, that if you discourse with him concerning his condition, he will usually utter these or such like words:

"I know God is able to pass by

all my rebellions against him, but I fear He will not:" or he will say, "Do you think that if God did purpose to show mercy unto me, or had ever any thoughts of love unto my poor soul, that He would suffer me to do those detestable evils against nature itself, besides my inward dreadful temptations against Himself?" Again they will say: "I cannot believe that ever any of the beloved of the Lord were ever under any such strange temptations or desperate thoughts against the Lord, or against myself, my wife, my children, or relations, as I am." Again they will say, "When I find any motion of deep sorrow in me for all my rebellions, and a full resolution by the power of the Lord to forsake them, and a desire to love the Lord in hope of his mercy, or to praise Him for his preserving me under all past dangers, then immediately I am subject to the most firiest temptations of all; therefore, what hopes can there be for such a one as I am? I fear hopes or desires concerning me is but vain; sure my condition is as bad, if not worse, than Cain, Balsam, Judas, or any such like."

4. Notwithstanding these and such like hopeless expressions, yet if they find a man that experimentally understands the sadness of their condition, they are apt to desire that man to intreat the Lord for them.

5. Again, whatever befals them, they have this property abiding in them, that if you speak of the Creator, you shall never hear them speak evil of his most glorious person, nor endure to hear any one blaspheme his holy name; but, on the contrary, in the very depth of their despairings, they will speak honourably of the Holy One of Israel, and justify Him in all his proceedings towards them or any other of his creatures.

6. The truth is, this is that repentance or godly sorrow in them, proceeding from the Holy Spirit, and that most acceptable spiritual sacrifice that can be offered up unto Him, if the wounded spirit did but know it.

7. An elect vessel under fear of the wrath to come, hath this property in it also, that it is both ready and willing, if it be persuaded that the Lord will speak peace through the mouth of any man or woman unto its poor soul, even to walk unto the ends of the earth, to hear the voice of the Lord in that creature.

8. Another true testimony in a chosen vessel is this, notwithstanding his present hopelessness of mercy in reference to his former rebellions, yet his soul, through the secret love of God by his own light in him, is not only fearful of further temptation unto evil; but it doth also abhor all kind of iniquity whatsoever, upon the account of its contrariety against the divine majesty, and is full of longing after perfection, whether it be through life or death.

9. Again, another infallible testimony of an experimental wounded spirit is this, if out of

bitterness of spirit they open their sorrows unto their supposed or real friends, they will oftentimes say these or such like words:

"O wretched creature that I am, sure never any one rebelled against such light as I have done: I have been so ravished sometimes with the presence of the divine glory shining into my poor soul, that I thought I had been unmoveable for ever; and yet in a little season, through the remembrance of former iniquities committed against so glorious a majesty, or new temptations against so gracious a Father, I am so full of burning horror, of confused darkness, as if never any true light of life had appeared in me."

10. Again, through a strong desire of knowing of the secret purpose of the Creator towards them, they will say:

"O that I never had been born, or that I had been a toad, or any other created being, but a man; or that that God which gave me a being would finish my intolerable sorrows through my everlasting dissolution: or if I must perish, O that I were in it, that I might know what I must trust unto, for I think I should find more ease than now I do: or if it be thy pleasure neither to let me know it, nor know it not, O give me strength to bear it, and leave me under the hottest wrath that thy fury can administer unto me."

11. These and such like bitter lamentations are the elect beloved of the most high God subject unto, which are left under a despairing condition upon what account soever. A man may bear any natural sufferings whatsoever, because he knoweth they will have an end; but a wounded spirit who can bear, not knowing any end thereof?

12. It is Thou, O Lord Jesus Christ, which wounds the souls of thy redeemed ones, through thy spiritual absence; and it is Thou alone must heal them with thy glorious presence.

13. It is not in the power of men or angels, if they could weep rivers of blood, or could submit for a season to bear the same wrath in their own spirits, that can move Thee in the least to release that wounded soul whom Thou lovest as thine own self, until the fixed time thereof, which is only known to thyself, that Thou alone mayest have the glory of all thy love trials.

{Here begins a section that was omitted in Muggleton's 1661 revision}

14. Again, in the next Place, according to former Thoughts, I shall write of the Language of a despairing Reprobate, which after great literal or notional Light, is not only fallen under the Guilt of many natural and unnatural Evils, but is also guilty of despising the holy Spirit of all divine Purity, either because it did not prevent him from his Uncleanness, or because it will not justify him in his Filthiness.

15. Again, if a Friend shall visit him and inquire him of his

Condition, instead of receiving any Hopes concerning Deliverance from his present unspeakable Misery, you shall hear him utter these or such like Words: My Sins are greater than can be forgiven, what are God, Men, or Angels unto me seeing I am eternally damned; or else he will say, I did not care if they were eternally cut off, or in my Condition, so that I were delivered:

16. Again, he doth not only abhor all Expressions of Hope concerning a spiritual Deliverance, but he also hateth to hear the very Name of God, Mercy, Salvation, or the like.

17. Again, instead of a Spiritual yielding unto the divine Pleasure of the Creator, through a longing after his glorious Presence, his dark Spirit is full of all secret Envy and blasphemous Cursings against his holy Spirit; yea, it is become so natural unto him, through the absenting of Motions of the Holy Spirit, that nothing is so suitable unto him as the language of fiery Wrath, or burning Death, or Blackness of utter Darkness, or cursed Devil, Hell and Damnation, and such like doleful Expressions as these are:

18. So that instead of having any desire of having Hopes of Mercy from its Creator, it rather is pleased with a language of condemning its God of Unjustice or merciless Cruelty.

19. Again, all the Love or Mercy remaining in such an outcast Condition as this, is but hypocritical Hellishness at the best;

20. for in the midst of his unspeakable Torment, if he seemeth unwilling that his familiar Friends should possess the like Misery, it is because he thinks it will increase his own Torments.

21. Again, a Man in this desperate Condition is full of Torment, at the visible Sight of any living Creature whatsoever, with bloody Thoughts or Desires to it; especially if he thinks that that Creature possesseth any kind of Joy or Peace in it self in the least.

22. Again, a despairing Reprobate is very ready to hear an experimental Man, that can speak of a more dreadful Damnation, answerable to his present Condition; but if any man speaks unto him that is ignorant of his Condition, it doth so enrage him that he would tear him in Pieces if he could.

23. Again, you shall seldom or never hear a despairing Castaway complain of Cold; truly he hath small Cause for it; Why, because his Spirit being close Prisoner in the Flesh, it burneth oftentimes more terrible through the whole Man than natural Fire, through want not only of cooling divine Motions from above, but also for want of motioning forth upon natural Comfort beneath as formerly.

{Here ends a section that was omitted in Muggleton's 1661 revision}

24*. O empty vain man, who,

---

* This verse was originally

ever you are, which measure the unsearchable wisdom of the Holy One of Israel by your own lying imaginations, and by your blind reason think to persuade the unchangeable God with goodly words to walk out of his own way.

25. And because your vain spirits are upon any occasion subject to change, you think the unchangeable God is like unto yourselves, and may change, also; and so either for silver or honour, or both, you combine together as one man to public or private meetings, to cheat one another with flattering speeches, and call it the pure worship of God, being ready to condemn all that come not to it, as ungodly men or heretics, though in their dealings between man and man they are seven times more righteous than yourselves; and in obedience unto the Lord Jesus Christ, are subject to all civil authority for conscience sake; by suffering under them, leaving all vengeance unto the Lord, who hath said, "Vengeance is mine, and I will repay it."

CHAPTER XIV.

1. A moderate discourse concerning civil wars in a kingdom. 2. The people's subjection to the laws. 3. Wherein several objections are answered. 4. Many things of very great consequence seasonably declared.

number 14 in the 1846 edition, the chapter ending at verse 15 in that edition

IN the next place, give me leave

{Here begins a section that was omitted in Muggleton's 1661 revision}

to reason a little in a Divine Balance between the present Civil Magistrates, and all Men whatsoever which have engaged with them, or against them in the late unnatural Wars: But before I begin

{Here ends a section that was omitted in Muggleton's 1661 revision}

to take notice of this, that I do not count those men truly rational which say there is no God, but nature only.

2. Or which say, that God is only an incomprehensible, formless Spirit:

3. Neither do I account them spiritual or rational, which confess an infinite Being of beings, and yet deny the creature to be a creature, and the Creator to be the Creator. My meaning is this, which make no difference between the glorious Creator and the poor empty creature, but affirm the divine majesty of glorious purities to have his abode in all impure spirits.

4. Though God is the life of all sensible or insensible living beings by the virtue of creation, yet I positively affirm against men or angels, that neither heaven, earth, angels, nor men, are capable of the indwelling essence of his Holy Spirit, but his own

person only.

5. Again, I do not account those men truly spiritual or rational as yet, which pretend to know themselves to be personal living beings, and yet deny the personal God of all infinite glories.

6. Moreover, though men speak like oracles, and seemingly appear to be innocent as doves, yet if they say there is no God but within this world only; or if they confess a God upon the throne of his glory in another world, if they say He is three persons in coequal godhead glory, or in degree one above another; or their spirits are in one personal majesty, or any such like confusion concerning the one personal being of our Lord Jesus Christ:

7. From his unerring Spirit I declare, that none of these are the men that I account spiritual or rational grounded men, whatever good thoughts they have of themselves, or one of another; wherefore, if there be any sober rational man in the world, come, let us reason together.

8. What though thou and this present civil powers, to your own thinking, and full resolution of equal good to the three nations, did engage together against the former powers, as enemies to the common good, and did purpose by God's assistance to establish such a government for the people's good, that the like could not be paralleled in the world; whatever you intended by covenants or engagements, I would fain know whether you are any more than creatures? and if you grant me that rational truth, then, in the next place, I would know whether any man hath sufficient power in himself to continue one minute in his resolution, though never so solemnly engaged?

9. Again, if it should be replied, thus reasoning, all covenants made in the presence of God, or between man and man, are of none effect; no, that doth not follow, for the moral or civil law is very good in itself, and was added for transgressors; but whosoever hath the true love of God in him, that man hath no need of man's law to be his rule, but he is a law unto himself, and lives above all laws of mortal men, and yet is obedient to all laws.

10. Again, I declare from the God of all truth, that no rational wise man, unless God Himself by infallible grounds had declared it to him, dares enter into covenants or vows, to make a people more happier than they are, by a sword of steel.

11. I confess that civil laws, are just and good in themselves, and according to equity all men are alike liable to the law, but this I would fain know from any sober man in this world, if he were guilty of the law in what kind soever, whether he would not rather live than be put to death?

12. Or if he were troubled with guilt of innocent blood, and breach of oath with faithful friends, would he not say in his spirit being in a place of power, what advantage will my life be unto the dead wronged by me, for want of power from above to

have prevented it?

13. Or what profit would my blood be unto the living friends of him that is dead? My life cannot possibly yield any true peace to the living any more than the dead; therefore O let me live, that I may do what good I can, seeing what is past cannot possibly be recalled.

{Here begins a section that was omitted in Muggleton's 1661 revision}

14. Again, if it be objected, if those in present Power did that Good I speak of, there was something in it, but we find quite the contrary, therefore suppose Things which are not: To this I answer, Be thou a Cavalier, or otherwise, I dare boldly affirm, that the Occasion of your present Sorrows of Death, or such like, ariseth from your Endeavours to cut off the Civil Powers now in Being.

15. Again, would you not do all that lay in your Power, if you were in their Stead, for your own Preservation? Would you gently yield up the Throne unto any one when you are settled in it by Love, or by Force, because he shall pretend Birthright unto it? Is it Birthright or excellent Endowments preserves any prince upon his Throne, or enlargeth his Dominions without carnal Weapons?

16. Again, if Kings preserve their Crowns, or purchase Kingdoms by Policy, Silver, and Swords of Steel, are not those Men as worthy of Thrones that win them with the same Weapons?

{Here ends a section that was omitted in Muggleton's 1661 revision}

17*. Again, if magistrates act any unjust things in their places, is any man sure that another power should act better? Do not men that seem to be very sober, just, and wise, oftentimes secretly act most unjustly of all, when exalted into high places?

18. But some may say unto me, if we had had that we sought for, we should have taken such a course, that no unjust magistrate should have continued long in his place, without being called to an account.

19. To this I answer, truly my friend, the heart of man is so desperately wicked, and places of authority so full of fleshly snares, that men are apt to act unjustly, if they die for it at the year's end.

20. Is there not a law of death without mercy against murder, and was there almost ever murders committed more than now? Where then is the power in the law to prevent it?

21. Is there not a law of death also against those which are taken in adultery, or such like uncleannesses? And is there not more adultery or such like committed than in former ages, when there was no law of putting

---

* This verse was originally number 14 in the 1846 edition, the numbers for the following verses increasing sequentially

men to death? Where then is the power of the law to prevent natural or unnatural lusts?

22. Is there not a law of death against robbing on the highway, breaking up of houses, and such like And was there in many ages such house-breaking and highway robbing as now there is, even by many men of very good estates? Where then is the power of the law to make an unjust man to do that which is right unto his neighbour?

23. Again, as beforesaid, the heart of man by nature is exceeding full of pride, envy, lust, and such like wickedness, that they are apt to commit it so much the more if men speak against it or make laws to prevent it. If men think this strange, or question the truth of it, if they know their own heart, and that God that preserves men from these evils, they would then know this to be as true as God is truth.

24. If it be so, some men may say, what need there then be any law at all?

25. For a just man there is no need of any law as aforesaid; but for a godless, the moral law of Moses and the civil law of magistrates are very useful in several respects; "for where there is no law," as the scripture saith, "there is no transgression:" but devils clothed with flesh, blood, and bone do want a whip, and is there any so fit to scourge them withal as their own laws Wherefore the laws of God and man are useful to convince and condemn the wicked, but not to convert them.

26. Again, you know the civil law is also useful to defend an upright man from the violence of a wicked man, it being instituted for that very end, that, as beforesaid, he may be justly condemned in his own conscience by his own law, for acting cruelty upon him that was always ready to do him good.

27. Though I thus write in the true defence of the civil law, with the obedience due unto it, sure I am that a merciful man, instead of taking advantage of the law for the imprisoning or the cutting off the most wickedest of men, if it be possible he will rather overcome him by love. O that all the chosen of God knew but the power of love, patience, mercy, or forgiveness to men that are averse unto all good!

28. If you which are offended with the civil magistrate did but understand what equal good soever was intended by your combinations together; or if your intended good of rest and peace had been attained unto through your establishing silver laws in a golden balance, by loadstone magistrates of your own choosing, instead of such a glorious happiness as you have imagined as beforesaid, through the desperate wickedness of the men of this age, is it not more probable the quite contrary would have ensued?

29. I pray you what were the acts of the Sodomites when they became all magistrates through an equal general ease, from a mighty fulness of bread, and such like? If you have any spiritual faith in you to believe

the record, read the first chapter to the Romans, and there you may see the effects of this your natural wisdom of general happiness to the creation or nations.

{Here begins a section that was omitted in Muggleton's 1661 revision}

30. Again, Thou that art offended with Oliver Cromwell, for his accepting the Title of a Lord Protector, and governing the People in a Kingly Manner in a more imperious Way in thy Judgment than the former Powers did, if thou hadst had his Opportunity is it not very probable, if thou hadst been an Atheist before, that for the attaining so honourable a Place thou wouldst have become such a Christian, that notwithstanding thy former Covenants thou wouldst have concluded, that the God of Heaven saw this Way of Government most fit for the General Good of the People.

31. Furthermore, and having obtained the Throne, is it not to be suspected, that instead of the intended Good unto the Nations, that thy imperious Hand would have been more heavy than his whole Body that now ruleth?

32. Again, but it may be objected by some, that contrary to Magna Charta, John Lilbourn is under Restraint; notwithstanding he was freed in open Court, by an honest Jury of Twelve Men of England:

33. To this I answer, Might he not have his Liberty if he could

but acknowledge the present Government, or would engage himself not to war against it nor to provoke the People by Writing, or otherways to rebel against it?

34. Thou that lookest upon such Things as these as unreasonable and intolerable to be born, wouldst thou not do the very same Things, if thou wart the Lord Protector, for thy own Preservation? And not only so but also for preventing of a new unnatural bloody War, which irrational seeming wise Men would provoke the People unto, upon the Account of Breach of Vows and Covenants.

35. Notwithstanding generally they are guilty of the same, and know not what they shall do, if they were tried to the Purpose.

36. Again, seeing Oliver Cromwell is become the Head Magistrate of these three Nations in such a Way which was contrary to his own Thoughts in my Judgment, at that Time when he solemnly engaged the contrary, wouldst thou be counted a sober rational Man to set the Nations together by the Ears?

37. Again, to make the Remedy worse than the Disease, that thou mightest under Pretence of Justice and Good unto the People, execute thy Wrath upon the Head Magistrate for that which he could not possibly avoid, through the secret Decree of the most High God.

38. Whatsoever men shall imagine to the contrary, thy Reason tells thee, thou wouldst not be so dealt withall, if his

Case were thine: Therefore art thou not unreasonable, if weighed in the equal Ballance of sober Reason itself?

39. Again, if thou really believest there is a Creator, what needest thou trouble thy self about Oliver Cromwell, his Council, or Head Officers, in reference to Things that perish?

40. Who can tell for what End the protector of Heaven and Earth hath so highly exalted him?

41. Again, if thou hast but a little Patience, and shalt see the Lord Jehovah make Use of Oliver Cromwell to be an Instrument of Acts of General Good beyond thy Expectation, though in a Kingly Way, wilt thou not then be ashamed of all thy Reasoning, in Reference to his Ruin?

42. Again, if on the contrary, he should be an Instrument of Cruelty above others before him, and so in a short Time be removed by the Creator himself, will it grieve thee then, that thou wast not guilty of his Blood?

43. Again, doth any Men in the World possess such a kind of continual Peace, as those men which are tender of the Lives of the worst of Men? Who are thou then that wouldst be counted a sober Rational Man, and yet wouldst do that to another which by no Means wouldst have done to thy self?

{Here ends a section that was omitted in Muggleton's 1661 revision}

44*. Again, because of the endlessness of man's reasoning against that innocent peace of conscience, and joy in the Holy Spirit full of glory, belonging unto all those that are made obedient to this heavenly rule; therefore I shall write a little further concerning this needful point.

45. If this golden rule be general, and without obedience to it no man can enjoy true peace, some men may say unto me, are the magistrates excluded from obedience to it because they are law-makers?

45†. From the Holy Spirit of our Lord Jesus Christ, to this I answer, it is impossible for any civil magistrate to be obedient to this rule, because you know then that he could not execute justice upon any man upon what account so ever.

46. Again, whether a magistrate be a just or unjust person, yet you may know, that upon a civil account, he represents the person or place of the righteous judge of quick and dead; wherefore according to his obedience or disobedience unto his commands, he shall be rewarded in this world or that to come; therefore know, that since the God of glory clothed Himself with flesh and bone in the form of a man, to kill or consent to murder the head magistrate, it is as if

---

* This verse was originally number 27 in the 1846 edition, the numbers for the following verses increasing sequentially
† This duplicated verse number arises in the 1760 edition

thou hadst murdered the king of glory Himself.

47. Though nothing comes to pass by chance or fortune, but by the providential decree of the most high God, yet no man can be cleared in his conscience from the guilt of innocent blood all his days, if secretly or openly he shall consent to kill the ruler of the nation, without an immediate command by voice of words from the God of heaven and earth.

48. Suppose the former governors of these nations were guilty of much innocent blood, and ruin of families, by their spiritual courts, so called, and through their imaginary wisdom, Lucifer-like, sat in the throne of God, commanding men to worship their inventions, triumphing over all tender consciences which. could not bow down to their Egyptian calves; and yet what spiritual or sober rational man can blame those men for their wilful bloody-mindedness, seeing a blind fiery zeal moved them to it, in reference to the worship of their God?

49. If any of them through covetousness of silver or honour amongst earthly princes, did only pretend a divine worship, and through secret envy to those which could not obey their commands, did ruin men to the utmost of their power, through those jesuitical counsellors who were atheistical, can any sober man imagine or think that those men were not oftentimes convinced of hypocritical irrationality, besides a secret fear of eternal vengeance, notwithstanding all their fleshly glory, through which they were strengthened in their spirits to flatter themselves up with vain hope that there was no God at all; or if there was any God, to cheat themselves with a conceit that it was irrational cruelty for a man to think that the Creator could be so unmerciful as to create man for eternal damnation, in reference to momentary infirmities which their frail natures could by no means prevent.

50. Again, if thou which thus reasonest didst truly understand that thou hast no power in thyself to withstand these natural evils beforesaid, thou couldest not possibly then commit them; but this is hid from thine eyes by the secret wisdom of the most high God, that thou mightest clear his divine justice, in reference to thy former cruelties, with everlasting thoughts that thou mightest have done otherwise when thou wast in thy earthly pomp if thou wouldest.

51. If the God of glory should neither recompence men in this life nor in that come, for all their wilful vain-glorious bloody cruelties, which they think they could prevent if they would, then indeed these seeming wise men may justly say, if there be a God, He is so far from any spiritual equity, that He falleth short of all rational equity whatsoever.

{Here begins a section that was omitted in Muggleton's 1661 revision}

52. Again, this sort of Spiritual bloody Persecution of long continuance, being come to the height, whoever thou art, that are offended with the present Power because they have not established such a Government as was by many imagined,

53. It is because of thy rational Atheism, or spiritual Weakness in the wonderful Transactions of the most high God in this present Age.

54. Again, whatsoever Oliver Cromwell, his Council and Adherents are Guilty of, it is best known to God, and the Light of their own Conscience.

55. But this I positively affirm, by an immediate Commission from the Holy Spirit, that the God of Glory, that Spiritual Lion of the Tribe of Judah, hath exalted Oliver Cromwell a Lion of the same Tribe according to the Flesh, into the Throne of Charles Stuart; that the Yoke of Jesuitical Persecution, for Conscience sake, may be utterly taken off the Necks of his People in these three Nations.

56. And that all those Powers which endeavour to exalt the Roman See of Charles's Seed upon his Throne again, may be cut off as Spiritual Rebels against the Everlasting God, and his glorious Apearances in the Spirits of his Redeemed Ones out of Darkness into his marvellous Light.

57. I say again, by full Assurance from the Everlasting Emanuel, that whatever Oliver Cromwell hath been suffered to act for attaining the Lordship of Three Crowns or Kingdoms, or whatever Depths of Counsel shall proceed from him and his fellow Counsellors, for enlarging their princely Territories.

58. Yet because he denies Throning himself as a Spiritual God in the Consciences of his fellow Mortals upon what account soever; though all the princes of the Earth Band together against him, which are guilty of Spiritual Tyranny, they shall Prosper as those that fought against Joshuah or Judah.

59. Again, whoever thou art which art offended at the present Government, under what Pretence soever, if Health, Wealth, Honour, Friendship with Mortals, or long Life be thy esteemed chief Good, or if thou confess an Eternal Being of all timely Beings, besides their perishing Delights; yet if thou say'st there is no other God but what is within thee, be thou never so seemingly Pure at present, it shall be manifested one Day in the Presence of God, Elect men, and Angels; and in thine own Conscience, that thou art so far from any Spiritual purity, that thou never truly knewest what Rational Purity was, nor where it is.

60. Again, seeing all Created Beings thro' their Finiteness, are naturally Subject to Change, or to be changed in their Resolutions, and that nothing comes to pass by Man's Will, nor Angel's Wills, but by the Will of the Unchangeable God of all Infinite Power, Wisdom, and

Glory.

61. who then is that Spiritual or Rational wise Man, but he that is made truly to understand, that to contend with a Sword of Steel against a Head-Magistrate exalted upon the Throne, thro' so many marvellous Difficulties as this present Power hath been possessed withal; is to Call in question the Wisdom and Power of God in all the Transactions of Foreign or Civil Wars since this World began.

62. Thus thou which art Spiritually Rational may'st know, that it is neither Chance, nor Fortune, nor natural Endowments, nor deep Subtility, nor Valour, not Silver, not carnal Weapons, nor any Power in Men, nor Angels, is the Cause of exalting Oliver Cromwell in a Place of so great Concernment.

63. But the mighty God of Jacob hath brought it to pass, to manifest his Prerogative will on Earth, as it is in Heaven; that his Natural Wonders may be as visible unto Men in this World, as his Spiritual Wonders are visible, I say unto Angels, Moses and Elias, in that World to come.

64. Therefore whoever thou art, after the Knowledge or Perusal of this Epistle, whether Emperour, King, or Beggar, that shall be left to thy own fleshly Wisdom to endeavour the Ruin of this present Power of England, Scotland, and Ireland; thou shalt be possessed with Fear of natural Destruction in this Life, and with a secret Fear of eternal Damnation in the life to come.

65. And now as an eternal Memento of Glory, or Shame in this Life, and that to come, from the Spirit of the Divine Majesty himself, suffer me to speak a few Words unto thee, which possesseth the Title of a Lord Protector's Highness:

66. If thou hast Ears to hear, I humbly beseech thee with a meek and patient Spirit deeply to consider what I shall say.

67. If thou shalt be left unto thy own Natural Wisdom, only to pretend Liberty of Conscience, and Temporal Equity between Man and Man, that Alexander like thou mightest conquer the whole World, and through great Victories shalt say in thy Heart, There is no other God, or Glory, but what thou injoyest already: Then after the Divine Majesty hath delivered his innocent people by thy hand out of their Spiritual and Natural Tyranny in many places; as sure as the Lord liveth, thou mayest justly expect that he will discover thy exceeding Hypocrasy in the Sight of Men and Angels.

68. Remember what befel Herod, when the People said, it was the Voice of God, and not of Man.

69. Though I am made thus to write, there is a Secret hope in me of better Things concerning thee.

70. Again, if thou hast any true Light in thee, concerning an Eternal Glory in the Life to come, thou knowest then that Truth cannot flatter; but it will be a righteous Judge in all our Consciences in the great and dreadful Day of our Lord Jesus Christ.

71. Lastly, Be it known unto thee, most noble Cromwell, though this Epistle was written by the hand of a poor sinful Man, if it be not owned by the Eternal Spirit, as proceeding from the Divine Majesty himself, then I neither can desire, hope, or expect from the Lord any Mercy upon my Soul and Body to all Eternity.

72. So much concerning a Rational Discourse in a Divine Ballance between the present Civil Powers, and those which ingaged with them or against them, in the late unnatural Wars. O Blessed are all Spiritual Warriors, for their Crowns are Immortal and Eternal.

73. Again, If thou shalt peruse this Epistle, and in thy Heart shalt say, these are but Words only, and many in these Days of Liberty of Conscience have declared strong Expressions, with pretended Commissions from the Lord Jehovah, and have appeared with lying Signs and Wonders to confirm them, thro' which many have been deceived and utterly ruined both in Body, Mind and Estate, and whether thou art one of this Sort, Time will make manifest:

74. To this thy supposed reasoning, from the Lord Jesus, I answer, if thou Oliver Cromwell dost as really understand and believe with thy Heart that there is a Creator, as thou confessest it with thy Tongue, then by this infallible Rule thou shalt one Day believe the Truth of this Epistle from all imaginary Voices, Visions, Revelations, Dreams, or high-flown Fancies whatsoever in this confused Age.

75. Mark what I say, both thou and thy Council, yea and all Men which truly confess a Personal Divine Majesty; Whether I live or die, if the God of eternal Glory from his immortal Throne, do not own this Writing, and utterly disown those Men and their Writings which are left to despise it, then it was not from the Spirit of the true God, but meer imaginary Flashes from mine own Spirit.

{Here ends a section that was omitted in Muggleton's 1661 revision}

76*. Another infallible demonstration of the truth of this writing is this, that though many writings extant are more acute in form of words, yet throughout this book thou shalt find no point absolutely contradicting itself, nor one another.

77. Again, another testimony of the truth of this writing is this, that it discovereth the vanity of all formal or irrational opinion in man concerning God, worship, angels, devil, sin, heaven, or hell.

78. By this infallible rule also thou mayest know, that this epistle proceeded from a spirit infinitely above all kind of reasoning in man or angels, because it alloweth no man, upon. what pretence soever, to

---

* This verse was originally number 36 in the 1846 edition, the numbers for the following verses increasing sequentially

murder one another, or to sit in God's throne to cut off the head magistrate, or to rebel against him with a sword of steel, or to speak evil of him, or desire evil unto him.

79. Moreover, though this book was penned by the hand of a sinful man, yet by this undeniable argument thou mayest know it proceeded from that Spirit that cannot be deceived; because it denies all power in man or angel, as to be capable to act spiritual or natural good to one another, or to resist spiritual or natural evil without a continued light proceeding from a spiritual body, too infinitely glorious to be essentially united to heaven, earth, angels, or men; yet this wonderful God is now for everlasting abiding in a body of flesh and bone; therefore not a bone of Him was suffered to be broken upon the tree or corrupted in the grave, only his godhead natural life was left in this world for an everlasting consolation unto those that shall attain to believe that it was the unvaluable life-blood of the only wise God Himself, that was freely poured out unto death for the redemption from the power of sin and fear of eternal death, and for a dreadful witness at the great day against those men that shall be left to their own unbelieving spirit, to vilify the glorious God for abasing Himself into the likeness of sinful mortals.

CHAPTER XV.

1. Of the error of errors in men, who say that there is no other God or Christ but in this creation only. 2. Several objections and answers concerning the death of the soul. 3. The light of Christ in man is the invisible image of God which purifieth the inward filthiness of the flesh and spirit, and presents the certain truth of an eternal life of glory or shame. 4. No need of a new birth if there be a sufficient light of Christ in generation to conduct to heaven. 5. Children cannot understand spiritual or natural good or evil; so need not Christ's spiritual gifts in the womb for eternal happiness. 6. A great error to believe that the essence of the eternal Spirit dwelleth in any man but in the Lord Jesus only. 7. Two marks of reprobates.

YOU that are truly spiritual may know, that there are many thousands of atheistical-minded men and women at this instant, which are possessed with a spirit reprobated unto all inward and outward purity, out of which there is no redemption, whatever men shall vainly imagine to the contrary; only their decreed time of eternal damnation in the sight of elect men and angels is fixed: these are those which say, "All things comes naturally of themselves:" also they will say, "There is no beginning of any thing at all, but from all eternity all things were as you see, and so shall continue to all eternity."

2. There are many of these men, which appear in temples of stone or elsewhere, as

experimental speakers of the everlasting gospel, and are more acute in a seeming glorious language than most men.

3. Usually they will talk of one pure being within all men only; also if they branch forth this their pretended God unto their deceived hearers, you shall hear them utter these or such like expressions: "Brethren, be not so carnally minded as to think of a God in the form of a man sitting in a heaven above the stars, but mind that spiritual God in the invisible heaven of your hearts," Again they will say, "That Spirit of the Father within you is that God of love, beauty, virtue, with all variety of glorious perfections whatsoever, if you were but once acquainted with it; wherefore, if fears of eternal damnation seize upon you, they are apt to say it ariseth from your ignorant conceivings of a God and a heaven at a distance." Again, for managing of this their sophistry, that their deceit might not be perceived, they will treat upon these and such like scriptures, "Christ in you the hope of glory: know ye not that Christ is in you except ye be reprobates? As He is, so are we in this present world: the kingdom of heaven is within you: at that day shall ye know that I am in my Father, and you in me, and I in you: that they all may be one, as thou, O Father, art in me, and I in thee: even that they may be also one in us: he that is born of God sinneth not."

4. Thus they wrest these literal scriptures to hide their fleshy glory and subtle hypocrisy, that their eternal vengeance may exceed all men's in this age at the visible appearing of our Lord Jesus Christ with his mighty angels.

5. You that are endued with a gift of spiritual distinguishing between perishing glittering words and glorious things which are eternal, if you observe these sorts of golden sophisters, you shall find that whatever scripture they treat upon, they carry it in an allegorical notional mystery of nothing but mere empty words only: as, for example, if they speak of the persons of Cain and Abel, or of the persons of the bond-woman and her son, and the free-woman and her son, they will bid you look within you, and you may see them all there in seeming contrariety only.

6. Again, if you observe these men, you shall seldom or ever hear them speak of any thing after this life: but they will tell you of a death and resurrection of man in this life, but as concerning this mortal soul and body of our's entering into the grave or death, and quickening again a new and glorious life, by raising this mortal body into a glorified condition, in the visible sight of itself, and presence of a personal God, elect men, and angels, in a kingdom of eternal glory, these are riddles or uncertain things at a great distance.

7. It is not a God or Christ, or throne of eternal glory above the stars, which no mortal man can make visible unto men's eyes, that will clothe men in plush-

jackets, and feed their bodies with dainty delicacies; no, no, the infallible truth concerning a bodily resurrection of a purified spirit unto eternal glory, and a personal appearing of an impurified soul unto everlasting shame, will yield no such peacock's feathers nor Dives dishes as those are: the apostles and those of the same faith with them, will one day personally appear again to bear record unto this truth.

8. My brethren, what difference is there between those men which glory of a God, Christ, heaven, word, ordinances, and salvation without them, and are ignorant of the teachings of the Holy Spirit within them; and those men which glory of all these heavenly things within them, and yet are ignorant of that glorious personal majesty and throne of immortality without them?

9. Are not these men those hypocritical Pharisees, and atheistical Sadducees, which endeavour to cover their nakedness with inward and outward leaves of rational words only?

10. Do not all men which confess a Creator conclude that his Spirit is infinite, immortal, unchangeable, and eternal?

11. Doth not every man possess a distinct living spirit in his own body?

12. Is not every man a sinner, and subject to all manner of loathsome diseases of mortality?

13. Wherefore if this one pure Spirit of God Himself was dwelling in the body of any mortal man whatsoever, is it possible, think you, that that man could be desirous after carnal copulation, or subject unto any kind of putrefaction whatsoever?

14. Who art thou, then, poor vain perishing clay, which boasteth of possessing of a most holy immortal spirit within thee, and yet canst not enjoy any life of peace in the least without a continual supply of fleshly carnalities without thee?

15. Again, art thou capable of possessing an infinite eternal Spirit, which are but a finite piece of fading dust?

16. Art thou so vain in thy imagination, as to think that such a changeable piece of confusion as thou art, can possibly be capable to bear about thee that bright burning glorious Spirit of the unchangeable God, whose glory is above all heavens, at whose power of a word speaking, all kind of lights within this creation are immediately subject to enter into silent darkness, as if they had never had any being?

17. Again, is not the glorious body of Jesus Christ, in the throne of the Father, the eternal Son of God?

18. And is not all the divine godhead of the everlasting Father living and reigning in Him bodily?

19. And is this Spirit any more than one spirit united unto, that one body of glorious flesh and bone of our Lord Jesus Christ?

20. And is not all the treasures of wisdom hid in this Jesus only, and is it not from his

fulness that we all receive grace for grace?

21. If we have any true light at all ruling in us, if this be truth, which none can deny but notional atheists or bloody-minded formalists, what art thou then but that outcast angelical reprobate which Both not only divide the godhead Spirit of Christ Jesus our Lord, but impudently affirmest, that thou and all of thy opinion do possess the very godhead Spirit within you?

22. And not only so, but like a devil incarnate, as thou art, thou cursedst those that discovereth this thy horrible blasphemy.

23. Again, thou which earliest thy. God about thee wherever thou art, when thou hast breathed out thy sinful soul, and all thy light or life, into silent dust or death, where then is thy inward God and self become?

24. But it may be thou wilt reply and say, thy soul is immortal and cannot die: to this lying conceit of thine I answer by way of query,

25. Dost thou indeed believe any truth in scripture records?

26. If thou reply thou dost, then my query is this, whether thou thinkest that the soul of Christ, when He was in a body of flesh on this earth, were not as immortal as any other man's is, or rather immortal alone, and all others mortal besides Him?

27. Well, then, if I prove that the soul of Christ died and was buried, canst thou then be convinced that thy sinful soul is mortal, and must die also?

28. In the fifty-third of Isaiah it is written, "He poured out his soul unto death." Again, it is written, that "his soul was heavy unto death." Again, it is written, that "his soul was made an offering for sin." Again, in the first of Revelation it is written, "I am he that was dead and am alive, and, behold, I live for evermore." Again, it is written in St. John, "I lay down my life of myself, no man takes it from me: I have power to lay it down, and power to take it again: Christ therefore died, and rose again, and revived, that he might be Lord both of the dead and the quick." In the second of the Acts of the Apostles it is written, "Thou wilt not leave my soul in the grave, nor suffer thy holy one to see corruption."

29. Behold, is it not as clear as the light in these scripture records, that the pure soul of Christ Himself died and was buried in the grave for a moment? and dost thou think thy sinful soul is immortal, and shall escape death?

30. Again, thou canst not be so sottish as to think that the Spirit of Christ was buried alive in the grave; neither canst thou possibly prove by these scriptures, that his soul was not buried with his body in the grave: how then canst thou, or darest thou, say that thy polluted soul is immortal, and cannot die?

31. Again, did that spotless soul that was uncapable of the least motion of folly, enter into death; and dost thou think that thy soul shall scape death, which naturally is become so full

of folly, that it is utterly uncapable in itself of all kind of purity whatsoever?

32. If no sinful man be capable of the indwelling of the Spirit of God, some men may say unto me, what is that Spirit, light, or life of Christ, spoken of in the scriptures, which all men are made partakers of, except they be reprobates?

33. From a divine gift of the eternal Spirit, to this I answer, the elect of God being endued with the virtues, fruits, or effects of the most Holy Spirit, these heavenly graces or motions in the mind, proceeding from the glorious Spirit of our Lord Jesus Christ, are called by the divine titles of God Himself; because they are of the very same nature, operating the very same effects of immortal glory in the end of the world as it did upon Christ Himself.

34. Again, you know it is written in scripture, " The fruits of the Spirit is love, peace, gentleness, goodness, faith, long-suffering, brotherly kindness, and such like, against which there is no law." Also it is written, that "men were made partakers of the divine nature, and that Christ did live in men's hearts by faith:" and that Christ said, "He was the vine, and his apostles or believers were the branches, and his Father or Spirit was the husbandman." Again, it is written, "Let the same mind be in you that was even in Christ Jesus." Likewise it is written, "There were diversity of gifts or operations of the Spirit of God in men."

35. My spiritual brethren, which wait for a crown that fadeth not away, if you compare scriptures with scriptures you may see then that no sinful mortal did or possibly could possess the indwelling essence of the Spirit of God Himself, but only the inshining motions, operations, voices, virtues, fruits, or effects of that most glorious Spirit.

36. Again it is written, that "Christ is the light that lighteth every man that cometh into the world;" and why so? truly because there is no other Father, Spirit, Creator, or God at all but Christ Jesus alone, to give light unto men or angels; that is, all men which are enlightened with the true light that leadeth unto life eternal, receive it only from the glorious Spirit of our Lord Jesus Christ.

37. Again, though it is said that "Christ is the light of the world, or that he giveth light unto every man that cometh into the world;" yet it doth not therefore follow, that all men are partakers of the light of Christ in them unto life eternal.

38. Furthermore, I confess there is so much light of Christ in the most wickedest of men to convince them of sin, but not to restrain them or convert them from evil.

39. Again, there is a twofold light of Christ in men: the one is literal, and the other is spiritual.

40. Now you that are truly enlightened from above may understand, that there is naturally so much light of Christ's law written in every sensible man's

spirit to convince him of good and evil; and to cause him oftentimes to confess the truth, and to wish that he could love it, or do it, or that he might die the death of the righteous like unto Baalam.

41. But though this legal light of Christ in men be never so great in measure, yet no man was ever capable by it to be made inwardly obedient unto the Spirit of Christ our Lord Jesus.

42. Therefore, whoever thou art which sayest that all men have so much light in them as will make them happy if they will, thou knowest not as yet what it is to possess that spiritual new birth of true light unto life eternal.

43. That light of Christ which doth not only convince a man of inward rebellions, and convert him from the ruling power of them, may also be called by a twofold name, either a created light or a renewed light.

44. This light of Christ in man is that invisible image of God, which doth not only purify the inward filthiness of flesh and spirit, but doth also in some measure present unto the understanding the certain truth of an eternal personal glory or everlasting shame of a life to come.

45. Again, you know that it is written, that "except a man be born again, he cannot enter into the kingdom of heaven." Also it is written, "From his fulness we all receive, and grace for grace."

46. My spiritual brethren, if a man's understanding is not capable to comprehend any thing of the invisible and visible things of the kingdom of glory, except the eternal Spirit of Christ Jesus convey a new and shining light into him, what then think you will become of those men which say, "there is so much light of Christ planted in every man's spirit that is sufficient to make him eternally happy, if he will but hearken unto it?"

47. If all men which are begotten and brought forth by the spirits of sinful parents, were naturally endued in the womb with such a measure of the light of Christ in them, that will safely conduct them into the kingdom of glory if they will, what need then would there be of any new birth at all from the Lord Jesus Christ? or what man would want any further light from the Holy Spirit of the only ever-living God?

48. Again it is written, "When Christ ascended on high, that he led captivity captive, and gave gifts unto men."

49. My spiritual brethren, you know that by nature we are all under a tyrannical yoke of spiritual darkness, and all manner of fleshly uncleanliness whatsoever:

50. Also you know that innocent infants, though defiled in their natures through generation, yet they are neither capable to understand spiritual or natural good or evil; therefore they have no need of Christ's spiritual gifts in the womb, for to ensure themselves of their own eternal happiness.

51. Again, if the Lord Jesus Christ alone is the light and life

of men; and if all men that are saved must of necessity receive a new light unto their dark souls from his divine Spirit, then, without controversy, those men as yet are utterly ignorant of the new and true birth of the ever-living Jesus, which say every man hath so much light of Christ in them, that is sufficient to salvation if they will.

52. Again, if every man have the Spirit of Christ living in his conscience, as many men vainly imagine, what then is become of the spiritual body, or that Jesus that ascended into the throne of his glory in the visible sight of men and angels?

53. Or what man hath any need of his spiritual gifts or heavenly graces at all, if his Christ and he was conceived and born together from the womb of his mother?

54. When the apostle said, "For in him dwelleth all the fulness of the godhead bodily, and from his fulness we all receive, and grace for grace," I would fain know from any man whatsoever, whether that God or Christ were in them when they spake or wrote those words?

55. Again, if that godhead Spirit of Christ Jesus our Lord had been within them when they uttered those speeches, I suppose it had been more proper for them to have said, "for in us dwelleth all the fulness of the godhead bodily." If the apostles had always possessed the Spirit of God or Christ within them, then they uttered but vain words when they spake of receiving of grace or truth from a personal Christ without them.

56. Again, if Christ or his Spirit had been within the apostles when they spake of his divine glory or godhead fulness of grace and truth, would it not have been more proper for them to have said, from that God or Christ within us we are filled with all manner of spiritual consolations or heavenly perfections whatsoever?

57. If Christ or his Spirit were within men when they uttered those words, all faith or hope in reference to eternal glory was vain and of no effect: why because if men have their God or Christ within them only, they are no more under the teachings of another spirit, but are as glorious already as, ever they are like to be: but what saith the scripture, "If our hopes were in this life only, we were of all men most miserable." Again concerning these words, "Christ in you the hope of glory:" or know ye not that the Spirit of Christ is in you, except ye be reprobates?

58. My beloved brethren, what need any man hope for glory, if he hath the Spirit of glory resting upon him already?

59. Again, I hope no man will say that he hath a Christ in him that hopes after glory, or stands in need of any glorification whatsoever: well, then, the mind of the Spirit of Christ in those words was this, that except your understanding be enlightened from the eternal Spirit of a glorified Christ in that heavenly throne above the stars, ye are but reprobates.

60. Or thus: except you are filled with the gifts of graces of that glorious god-man Christ Jesus, who is ascended far above all heavens, angels, or men, know ye not that you are but in the state of reprobation?

61. Or as if the apostle should have said, know ye not that you are but mere reprobates, if ye glory of a God or Christ within you, and deny the godhead person of that Lord Jesus Christ that was crucified upon a tree without you?

62. Again, whoever thou art which glorieth of a spiritual union with a God or Christ within thee, and despisest a personal glorified Christ of flesh and bone without thee, yea, and distinct from thee in another world, I say from his eternal Spirit thou art but a reprobate.

63. Whoever thou art which boasteth of a God and a Christ, and his ordinances, and of a glory to come without thee in the highest heavens; if thou shalt be left to the pride and envy of thy formal spirit, to condemn the invisible teaching of the Lord Jesus Christ in his innocent people, because they are contrary to thy opinion, I say from the ever-living Emanuel, that thou art also but a reprobate.

CHAPTER XVI.

1. Of divers comparisons of the Spirit or person of Christ, unto the face of the natural sun. 2. No man or angel can be capable of the indwelling of God's essence, but his own person only.

THE Spirit or person of Christ may fitly be compared unto the face of the natural sun in divers respects: you may know that the natural spirit of the sun, by virtue of the decreed word of the Lord, is so exceeding fiery glorious, that no created thing that hath natural life in it, is capable of its indwelling brightness, but its own body or face only.

2. So likewise that infinite Spirit abiding within the glorious body or face of our Lord Jesus Christ, is so unspeakable fiery glorious, that no created spirit of man or angel is able to bear the indwelling essence of it, but its own body or face only.

3. Again you know that all natural things of the day are preserved only by virtue of that inward light, life, beauty, or glory in them which shineth through the body or face of the sun only.

4. So likewise all spiritual light, life, beauty, joy, or glory within the spirits of elect men and angels, shineth only through the glorious heavenly mouth of Christ Jesus our Lord.

5. Again, though both sensible and insensible creatures are preserved in their well-beings, by virtue of a measurable light and heat proceeding from the sun, you may know that if the essence of the sun were on this earth, it would not only put out the fire, but also immediately consume all things to ashes or dry sand.

6. So likewise, though the spiritual well-beings of elect men and angels are only preserved by

virtue of a measurable light and life proceeding from that bright shining spirit, through the face of Christ Jesus our Lord, yet if the essence of his Spirit were within the spirits of any created beings, it would consume them immediately to powder.

7. Again, though all created beings under the sun are enlivened and continued by virtue of its light and heat, through which, according to their kind, they are full of joy, yet if the sun should absent itself a little too long, all his former light would. vanish like smoke, and the creature would both languish and perish, for want of a new supply from its presence: so likewise it is with elect men and angels, for though that in-shining light and life be of the very same nature of God Himself, yet if his spirit should wholly retain its glorious brightness within his own body, all its former light or life would either be subject to be defiled as Adam's was, or else it would perish for want of the renewing presence of his glorious spirit.

8. Again, through that consolation flowing from the inshining light of the sun, you know in all sensible or rational creatures, there is a desire to behold that bright shining face from whence their joys proceed.

9. So likewise through that spiritual joy and hopes of glory flowing from the inspiring light of the Son of God, there is a strong desire in those that enjoy this light, to behold that glorious face from whence it proceeded.

10. Again, if the sun had not a distinct body or face to give forth his light into the creation, you 'know there could be no sunshine at all:

11. So likewise you may also know, that if the God of glory had not a person or immortal face to display the sunbeams of his heavenly glory into elect men and angels, there could be no God at all.

12. Therefore you that are truly spiritual may know, that all that light, life, or glory shining in the spirits of elect men or angels, doth not proceed from a God or Christ within them, but from an eternal Spirit of a God or a Christ without them, too transcendent glorious to be possessed by heaven, earth, angels, or men as beforesaid.

13. Again, though the natural life of created beings, by the decree of the most high God, he continued by virtue of the inshining light of the sun, yet you may know that whatever joy the creatures are possessed thereby, it doth neither add nor diminish unto the glory of the sun in the least:

14. So, likewise, though the spiritual light of elect men and angels be everlastingly continued by virtue of the inshining light of the eternal Spirit, yet you may also understand, that what joy or glory soever the creatures are possessed withal, that it doth neither add nor diminish the Creator's glory in the least: therefore you which are truly spiritual may understand, that if any man or angel could be possessed with the indwelling essence of the eternal Spirit, it

could not possibly be avoided, but he must become infinite, immortal, unchangeable, and eternal, even as the Creator Himself is.

15. Again, whether creatures are possessed with joy or sorrow, life or death, by an extraordinary light proceeding from the sun, yet you may know that according to his understanding he glories in himself equally in reference unto what was effected by him; so, likewise, whether creatures are possessed with spiritual joy or sorrow, eternal life or death, by a more than ordinary presence or absence of the eternal Spirit, yet you may also understand that the most glorious God equally rejoiceth in Himself in relation unto what was produced.

16. Again, though the nature of the sun through its created brightness, is so exceedingly glorious that it is utterly uncapable of natural pollution from any creatures within its orb, yet you know that things which are not by virtue of his power, in measure qualified with a suitable capacity to receive his inshining light, are rather hardened or destroyed by his appearance, than any way comforted or revived in the least: witness the fire or any thing else of an adamantine nature.

17. So likewise it is with the Son of God, the everlasting Creator; for though his eternal Spirit in its own nature is so infinitely pure, that if it be his divine pleasure it destroyeth all impurity immediately, and wholly converts a polluted creature into its own divine likeness; you may also know, that if the spirits of men or angels by his power be not in some measure qualified to receive his glorious incomes, instead of dissolving their spirits into a soft and. sweet pleasantness, it hardens their legal spirits with envy against the Creator like unto brass or the nether millstone, according to that of Paul, where he said, "they were a sweet savour unto God of life unto life in them that are saved, and of death unto death in them that perish."

CHAPTER XVII.

1. No man's salvation or damnation lieth in his own will, but in the prerogative of God. 2. Divers absurdities which follow from the opinion that Christ is only within men. 3. A question and answer concerning a twofold presence of God in the creature. 4. If the essential Spirit were united unto creatures, it could not be infinite.

THIS I would gladly have men 1 and women to understand which were elected unto glory, that the eternal salvation or damnation of created beings lieth not in the will, power, or desire of men or angels, or in any divine light received from the Holy Spirit that made them, but only within the glorious breast of the divine majesty Himself:

2. That neither elect men nor angels may glory in themselves, or render praise, honour, power, wisdom, or salvation unto any spiritual light, joy, or glory what-

soever: why? because that is but the sunbeams of life eternal shining in them; but as most due is by virtue of that light, they may return all praise and glory unto that infinite majesty upon the throne of glory without them.

3. Wherefore you know it is written, that "It is not in him that willeth, or in him that runneth, but in God that showeth mercy." Also it is written, "To will is present, but how to perform I know not." Also it is written, "Every branch that beareth not fruit in me, he taketh away; and every one that beareth fruit he purgeth, that it may bring forth more fruit." Now ye are clean through the word which I have spoken unto you. The words that I speak unto you are spirit and life.

4. I would fain know of any man whether the Spirit of Christ were not in his own body when He spake those words unto his apostles or disciples.

5. If it be granted it was, which none can deny but reprobates, then that light of Christ in men or angels cannot be the essential Spirit of the Lord Jesus Christ, but a spiritual word proceeding through his mouth from the throne of his infinite glory, as it did formerly on this earth the footstool of his divine majesty.

6. If there should be no other spiritual God or Christ but what dwelleth in the spirits of men or angels, then of necessity this must follow, that every man and angel is a God or Christ to himself.

7. It is not to be wondered at that many thousands should be so easily persuaded of attaining to a perfection in this mortality, if they be possessed with the God of heaven and earth.

8. If there be no other God or Creator but within men only, I would fain know for what end men so mightily contend with one another about a God or worship due unto Him.

9. Or why they vex one another by writings or speakings, unless they are hurried on for silver, or an everlasting name.

10. If there be no other God or Christ but within men's consciences only, is it not one of the maddest things in the world for men to talk of rebellion against the divine majesty, or of any cruelty acted between man and man whatsoever?

11. Is not the divine nature of the Spirit of our Lord Jesus Christ all wisdom, power, glory, love, meekness, patience, long-suffering, justice, righteousness, yea, salvation itself; or condemnation to whom it pleaseth, for manifesting the glory of its power?

12. Sure I am that none can, will, or dare deny this truth, but reprobates: wherefore if the very Spirit of God were living within the spirits of men, could there possibly then be any thing else but a godlike harmony between them?

13. Is not the eternal Spirit of Christ Jesus in itself a glorious order? and is not every man living at variance within himself, and so at the best is but a

disorderly piece of contradiction or confusion in himself?

14. If this be truth, which none can deny but vain-glorious castaways, how then think you it possible that any mortal man, that is but polluted dust, should be capable of the indwelling essence of the Spirit of God? or if he enjoyed the eternal Spirit, what could be in him but a glorious harmony?

15. If no created being is cable of the' indwelling essence of the Spirit of our Lord Jesus Christ, because of its incomprehensible glory, but its own body only, some men may say unto me, if the Spirit of God be infinite, what person, place, or creatures, can be excluded of its invisible presence, from that light of life eternal?

16. To this I answer, there is a twofold invisible presence of God in all sensible or insensible beings that have any light or virtue in them.

17. There is a natural presence of God by virtue of creation, which shall perish, and come to confusion, for everlasting:

18. Also there is a spiritual presence of God in elect mankind. by virtue of redemption, which gloriously increaseth and continueth to all eternity.

19. Again, whatever natural wise men imagine or think from the Spirit of all truth itself, I declare that all created natural light, life, or joy, both visible and invisible, shall become utter darkness, and a chaos of everlasting confusion; because,

though it made not itself, it is as contrary to the nature of that Spirit that made it, as light and darkness, or life and death.

20. Whoever thou art unto whom this seemeth strange, if thou wast in nature as wise as Solomon, yet if thou hast no distinction in thee, between this natural perishing God of time, and that spiritual flourishing God of eternity, as yet thou art in utter darkness concerning any heavenly thing whatsoever.

21. Though all natural or spiritual light do virtually flow from the divine Spirit of Christ Jesus our Lord, yet if that eternal Spirit were not a glorious being distinct from all created beings, it could not possibly be infinite.

22. Why? because you may understand that infinite life doth not consist in bigness or bulk of things, but in its exceeding brightness of wisdom, power, and glory in itself, in that it can contain its infinite brightness within its own person only, or let forth his in-shining glory by degrees in the spirit of elect men or angels, as it pleaseth Him.

23. Though all light or life in men or angels proceed from the natural or divine presence of the one Holy Spirit of God Himself, yet if that eternal Spirit were essentially united unto those creatures, it could not possibly then be infinite.

24. To be essentially dwelling within all living things, is not infiniteness, but finiteness; but, as beforesaid, to be a glorious being in itself, in the bigness of man, and essentially distinct from heavens, earth, angels, and men,

and yet from so small a compass, though at never so great a distance, all created beings in heaven or in earth to be virtually filled with his divine or natural presence in their measures, according to the pleasure of his good-will, by a word speaking, in this is all infiniteness indeed.

25. If there were no God or Creator at all but what doth live in created beings, then it is possible that all beings, and their indwelling God, may eternally vanish together; because there is that in them which is more natural to provoke them all to murder one another, and kill themselves, than the good of one another: for, alas I you know that it is both a common and easy thing oftentimes with small means for men to destroy themselves or one another. And is it not, by the same rule, as easy totally to cut off all the creation at once?

26. If this be truth, which no sober man can deny, what then would become of men and their Christ, if this total dissolution at once should fall upon them?

27. If the Spirit of the most high God be so infinitely vast, boundless, or that it is both the light and life of all spiritual or natural things or places whatsoever, as is abundantly declared, some unsatisfied men in this point may say unto me, that to confine this incomprehensible Spirit of the omnipresent God of heaven and earth, into one single person and place at once, like unto a poor mortal man, seems unto us an imprisoning of infiniteness into a narrow compass, instead of declaring its incomprehensible glory, from a divine gift of life eternal. To this I answer,

28. Is it not rather an imprisoning of the ever-living God, and robbing him wholly of his infinite glory, for any man to divide his most blessed majesty into distinct persons, or to divide his godhead Spirit into all spirits of men and angels, leaving no throne or person for the divine glory to be in, but his created beings only.

29. Instead of honouring that Spirit within the glorious person of Christ Jesus our Lord, doth not those men that affirm the in. dwelling of that infinite Spirit in the whole creation, not only share the divine glory and godhead titles of the eternal Spirit amongst the lying creatures, but also wholly deny any other Creator, or eternal Spirit, within or without men, but perishing nature only, whatever they pretend to the contrary?

30. What dishonour or disadvantage is it unto an. infinite Spirit, to possess his ravishing glories to Himself within a distinct body of his own? Nay, is it not altogether advantageous unto his divine majesty that it should be sot and that it can be no other ways? for, alas! you know that it stands to good sense or reason, that if the God of glory were only an invisible Spirit dwelling within the creation, He could not then possess any new joys or ravishing glories to Himself, but

the whole creation of men or angels must be partakers with Him, as soon as He.

31. Therefore you that are truly spiritual may know, that those men that talk of a God or a Christ living in men's consciences only, and cannot endure to hear of a distinct personal God upon the throne of his glory in the heavens above the stars,

32. Whatever godlike shape they appear in, as yet they are but freewill redemptionists or refined naturalists at the best: and all their speakings, though mixed with many words of truth, tend to nothing else but meritorious popery from themselves, and tyrannical prelacy over one another.

CHAPTER XVIII.

1. A discourse that the Divine Being is clothed with flesh and bone. 2. How God knows all things in the world. 3. Of the manner of God's taking upon Him human nature. 4. What the form of God was before He became flesh. 5. No spirit can enjoy happiness or misery without a body.

IS not heaven, earth, angels, and men, as they are created beings, subject to change, or to be changed?

2. Doth not all men that acknowledge a Creator, conclude that his Spirit is infinite, unchangeable, immortal, and eternal, as beforesaid?

3. Wherefore if this infinite or boundless Spirit of the eternal majesty were dwelling within the spirits of men or angels, could it possibly be avoided, but every thing then would become infinite, unchangeable, immortal, and eternal in itself, as He is?

4. Doth not the scriptures call the glorious Spirit of the ever-living God by titles, a consuming fire, and everlasting burnings?

5. O all ye Luciferian despisers of a glorious God, in the person of a man, wonder and perish, at a miracle of all miracles that shall be declared unto the general view of men in this place:

6. Wherefore, behold, ye elect and precious jewels of divine glory, though the eternal Spirit of your Creator and Redeemer be of so fiery glorious a nature, that neither fire, air, earth, water, sun, moon, stars, heavens, earth, angels, men, nor any thing else, is capable of the indwelling of it one moment, without being consumed to ashes, dust, sand, or powder, yet this infinite bright burning Spirit is contained within a single person of flesh and bone glorified:

7. Yea, and is so united unto it, that all its divine pleasures naturally floweth from its essential owness to all eternity:

8. Insomuch that from that unerring Spirit I positively declare, against men or angels, that this fiery glorious Spirit cannot possibly possess any sensible living being, out of that blessed body of flesh and bone in glory, no more than the mortal soul of a man can live without its natural body of flesh, blood, and bone in shame.

9. Though the heavenly body of the eternal majesty be very flesh and bone itself, yet I would gladly have you that are spiritual to understand, that through the indwelling of its godhead Spirit, it is so fiery glorious, that neither men nor angels can behold his face and live, unless their spirits be strengthened by virtue of its inshining excellency.

10. Though the glorious body of the ever-living God be very flesh and bone, yet you may understand, that it is clearer than crystal, brighter than the sun, swifter than thought, yea, and infinitely more softer than down, and sweeter than roses.

11. You may also know, that the visible sight of so glorious a face, is that which will eternally ravish the spirits of men and angels.

12. You may also understand, that though the body of Christ glorified be very flesh and bone of a burning, bright, swift, soft, sweet nature, beyond all expressions of men or angels, yet it is of an immortal, fiery, glorious softness or sweetness, and not of a mortal fiery nature mixed together, as the most softest or sweetest of pleasures in this world are.

13. Though the infinite Spirit of the unchangeable God, is clothed with his eternal Son beforesaid, which was too pure to be subjected by sin, wrath, death, hell, or the grave; yet you that are truly enlightened from on high may know, that by virtue of his wisdom or transcendent glory, He perfectly seeth through heavens, earth, angels, and men at once, and knoweth all motions, thoughts, desires, words, or actions in all things whatsoever, without charging his spiritual memory in the least.

14. Therefore it is written, that "the eyes of the Lord pass to and fro through the earth, beholding the just and the unjust; and the Lord knoweth that the heart of man is vain, and his imaginations are evil, and only evil, and continually evil: and all evil things that are done now in secret with delight, shall be revealed upon the house-top or head of men's understandings," soon enough, and with sorrow, pain, and shame enough, whatever is thought or said to the contrary.

15. If the Spirit of the divine majesty be so infinitely glorious that no created being is capable of the indwelling of its divine godhead, some men may say unto me, had not that man Christ, called the Son of God, his being on the woman's part from the loins of Mary his mother, as well as other children? If this be truth, which the scriptures clearly demonstrated, how then could that child Jesus be capable of the indwelling of an infinite Spirit any more than any other child whatsoever?

16. Unto this curious query, from the unerring Spirit, I answer, though that child Christ Jesus had beginning of the seed of his virgin mother, as all children have, yet He was that Holy One of Israel, which from eternity was a spiritual body in form like a man; therefore, when He entered into the virgin's

womb, He laid down his infinite spiritual glory by virtue of his godhead power, that He might be capable to transmute, create, or conceive Himself of the virgin's seed, into a condition of pure flesh, blood, and bone, in a new and wonderful way, for an everlasting astonishment unto elect men and angels:

17. Wherefore the Virgin Mary, his mother, was forewarned by the angel of his glorious and gracious purpose, that her soul might be prepared for that marvellous incoming of her only God and Saviour, to become the Redeemer of his elect people from the power of sin and fear of eternal death.

18. It is written, "Great is the mystery of godliness, which is, God was manifested in the flesh, justified in the Spirit, seen of angels, preached unto the Gentiles, believed on in the world, received up to glory," 1 Tim. iii. 16. Again, it is written, "Who being in the form of God, thought it no robbery to be equal with God; but he made himself of no reputation, and took on him the form of a servant" Phil. ii. 6, 7.

19. Is there any more than one God? And was not Christ the form of this invisible God before He became the person of a man? And did not that spiritual form of Christ Jesus enter into the virgin's, womb, and become a pure natural form?

20. Moreover, was not Christ and his Father only one uncreated heavenly person from all eternity?

21. Though I undoubtedly affirm that Christ Jesus eternally was the divine form of the invisible God, yet I would not have any man imagine or think that I go about to prove the Creator to be a body of flesh, blood, and bone from eternity.

22. Neither would I willingly have any of the blessed of the Lord to be so grossly ignorant as to think that the glorious Creator could possibly be a spiritual living substance, without a body or person.

23. If Christ Jesus and the Father from all eternity were but one distinct person, some men may say unto me, what might the form of his uncreated majesty be before He became flesh, from the light of life eternal:

24. To this I answer, his divine form did not consist of natural earth, air, water, or fire in the least; but it was a bright burning fiery glory of uncompounded purities, continually satisfying itself with variety of divine excellencies.

25. Though the spiritual person of the Holy One of Israel was from eternity so transcendently glorious, that no elements could possibly contain Him without being immediately consumed to ashes; yet He was absolutely, from the crown of his glorious head to the soles of his divine feet, in form like unto the first man Adam.

26. You that possess the heavenly truth in you may know the divine form of Jesus Christ, the everlasting Father, was of so pure, thin, or light nature, that, as beforesaid, it was swifter than

thought, clearer than crystal, infinitely more glorious than the sun, purer than the purest gold or any thing more precious:

27. So that when the eternal Spirit moved Him to enter into the virgin's womb, it being swifter than thought, and its body being of its own nature, He was in her womb before she was aware of it; only by a wonderful change in her soul, she felt Him converting his godhead glory into flesh, blood, and bone according to his promise by the angel Gabriel; this was that wonderful mystery of God the everlasting Father, which manifested Himself in a body of flesh, at which most men and women stumble and perish.

28. Is any thing impossible for God to do when his divine glory moves Him to it?

29. Moreover, is not the infinite power, wisdom, or glory of the ever-living God, most of all seen by men or angels, in the lowest abasing himself?

30. Do not all men which confess a Creator, conclude that his Holy Spirit is infinitely full of all divine qualifications whatsoever, and is the incomprehensible Spirit of the Holy One of Israel any thing at all without its glorious virtues?

31. Is it possible, think you, that this eternal Spirit could be sensible of its heavenly glories, without a distinct body of its own to enjoy them in? If this be truth, the which none can gainsay but senseless sots or simple saints, then without controversy, Christ Jesus and the Father was eternally but only one spiritual body, in form like a man.

32. Is there any created being, whether sensible or insensible, either in heaven or in earth, that possesseth any kind of spiritual or natural motion, heat, light, life, joy, or glory in the least, without a distinct body of its own, suitable to its present condition?

33. Hath the most wise Creator so ordered every living being, that all the joy they possess is in their own bodies, chiefly distinct from one another, and that each other's joy is nothing at all to one another, unless they be both sensible of the same.

34. Can any sober man be so senseless as to imagine or think that the glorious Creator of all spiritual and natural order can possibly be any thing at all, without a distinct body of his own, as abundantly beforesaid?

35. Are not all finite creatures a mere chaos of senseless matter until they are formed into distinct beings of themselves, and have names given them by God and man according to their natures? And are they any thing at all until they become living spirits in complete bodies of their own, as aforesaid?

36. This being known to be as true as truth itself, can it possibly be that He that gave beings to all things, should not be something that is infinite also; or a distinct glorious body, having variety of holy names attributed to Him according to his divine nature, for the exaltation of his infinite ma-

jestical person above all heavens, angels, and men?

CHAPTER XIX.

1. Of the true spiritual trinity in unity. 2. Of the one personal divine majesty. 3. No scripture mentioneth God to be three persons, only one God and one person. 4. Why God calleth Himself by a threefold name.

IN the next place I shall treat I of that divine trinity in unity of the Holy One of Israel.

2. You may remember I have already elsewhere, in this epistle, clearly demonstrated the horrible fallacy and absurdity of that old error of three distinct persons or spirits, and but one God, from these words; "For there are three that bear record in heaven, the Father, Son, and Holy Ghost; and these three are one," 1 John v. 7.

3. My spiritual and literal brethren also that have any desire in you to know the truth, take special notice of this thing, there is not one positive record in scripture that affirmeth the God of heaven and earth to consist of three persons.

4. Was not the eternal Jehovah called the Holy One of Israel in the law?

5. Was not the eternal Jesus called the Holy One in the saints' time of the gospel?

6. Is not Jesus called a consuming fire in the gospel, as well as Jehovah in the law?

7. Hath not Jesus attributed unto Him the titles of a Creator, ancient of days, everlasting Father, mighty God, or Redeemer, and such like, as well as Jehovah?

8. Was not all divine honour, glory, praise, might, or dominion by men and angels, in as full a manner ascribed unto Jesus as Jehovah?

9. Doth not the scripture say, that the Holy One of Israel will not give his glory to another? And yet you know Christ Jesus had all glory from men and angels given unto Him; who then is that eternal Jehovah but the everlasting Jesus? And who is that eternal Jesus but the everlasting Jehovah?

10. Before the eternal Jehovah became Jesus in flesh, was not his invisible Spirit the everlasting Father?

11. Was not that fiery glorious body wherein God the Father had his heavenly habitation, that eternal Son of God?

12. Was not the Holy Ghost that almighty word that proceeded through his heavenly mouth, when his Holy Spirit moved Him to speak?

13. Is not this trinity in unity, or unity in trinity, more agreeable to the Holy One of Israel than any other trinity whatsoever, unto all men which acknowledge but one eternal Being?

14. What difference is there between the holy names of Father, Son, and Spirit, and Lord Jesus Christ? Was it any thing else but one and the same godhead person in a threefold condition appearing unto men?

15. Again, if need be, will not the names of Father and Lord

bear one sense? The names of Son and Jesus signify one thing; and may not the titles of Christ and Spirit be of one signification also?

16. Doth not the word Lord signify divine protection? And doth not the word Father bear the same sense?

17. Doth not the word Jesus signify a Saviour? And doth not the word Son bear the same sense? And doth not the word Christ signify chrystal clearness or anointing? And doth not the word Holy Ghost bear the same sense?

18. If this be truth, which none can gainsay but men as yet under spiritual darkness, what difference is there then between the word Father, Son, and Holy Spirit, and Lord Jesus Christ? Are they not only names, words, or titles in relation to the only wise, immortal, invisible, distinct glorious god-man, blessed for ever and ever in Himself, and honoured only of men and angels, unto whom He is made manifest.

19. Though the eternal Jehovah had variety of divine titles for the exaltation of his infinite majesty, under the legal or ceremonial worship of Moses and the prophets, was He ever owned by any more than one name of glorious God or Holy One of Israel?

20. If He had contained of three divine persons or spirits in co-equal godhead glory, can any man be so senseless to think that He would have hid it from Moses and Aaron, Abraham, David, and all those prophets,

with whom He was so familiar in divine appearances or wonderful miracles.

21. If the most high and mighty Jehovah was but only one spiritual person in the time of Moses and the prophets, which none can gainsay but men in Egyptian darkness, are not those men at present utterly ignorant of the only wise God, which endeavour by literal violence to persuade themselves and others, that the Holy One of Israel is three persons, because He is called by a threefold name in the New Testament?

22. You know in scripture a man is called soul, body, and spirit, though he be but one person.

23. Also you may know, that men in highest places are called by a threefold title, as, namely, king's excellent majesty, or the like.

24. Though they attribute to themselves never so many honourable titles, to manifest their earthly greatness, that they might be dreadful in the spirits of earthly-minded people, yet you know they are but one person only:

25. So, likewise, though the eternal Jehovah be called by a threefold name of Father, Son, Spirit, or Lord Jesus Christ; or though He hath never so many divine titles attributed to Him for exaltation of his infinite majesty within the spirits of his redeemed ones, yet you may know that He can be no more than one glorious being only.

26. You that are truly spiritual may know why the God

of glory called Himself by a threefold name, because no man by human learning should, by the letter of the scripture, truly know what the Holy One of Israel is or was, that God alone might have all the praise or glory in revealing Himself unto mankind.

27. Christ Jesus, the Holy One of Israel, called Himself by a threefold name, in reference to a threefold manner of appearance to his elect Israelites?

28. In his first appearance unto Moses and the prophets, He was pleased to manifest Himself by the divine titles of Jehovah, the mighty God of Jacob, the Holy One of Israel, and such like.

29. When the God of glory abased Himself in flesh in the form of a servant, answerable unto that second appearance unto his chosen ones, you know He called Himself Jesus the Son of God, the Son of man, the Saviour, and such like.

30. Jesus Christ, the Holy One of Israel, being ascended into the throne of his former glory, now in his third and last appearance, He is pleased to call Himself by the names of Holy Ghost or Spirit, because of his immediate spiritual teaching of his redeemed ones.

31. Or thus: the only God may be understood a spiritual lion in the days of Moses and the prophets; a divine lamb in the days of Christ and the apostles; a heavenly dove in these our days of confused darkness.

32. Or thus: the Holy One of Israel may be described the eternal Jehovah in the law, the eternal Jesus in the gospel, the eternal Spirit in this age.

33. And yet but one only distinct personal majesty, even from eternity to eternity.

34. Though the Lord of life and glory commanded his apostles to baptize those of the faith in the name of the Father, Son, and Holy Ghost, yet you know their miracles were done by the name of the Lord Jesus Christ.

35. Whatever any literal monger shall object, you that are spiritual may know that the Lord Jesus Christ, and Father, Son, and Spirit, beareth but one sense.

36. Jesus Christ, the Holy One of Israel, called Himself by a threefold name of Father, Son, and Spirit, in relation unto his threefold witness on earth, in the words following, which are these: "And there are three which bear witness in the earth, the Spirit, and the water, and the blood, and these three agree in one," 1 John v. 8.

CHAPTER XX.

1. No title of honour ever attributed but to a person. 2. Who it was that Christ prayed unto in the days of his flesh. 3. The Creator distinct from all his creatures. 4. Of God's oath concerning his transmutation into pure flesh and bone.

MY spiritual brethren, because all true and lasting peace wholly depends upon a right understanding of the only wise God, and because most of the heirs of glory are not clear in their understandings concerning his personal majesty, though much hath been declared to that purpose in this epistle already, I shall write distinctly concerning the Creator and his immediate commissionated messengers or ambassadors, from these two threefold scripture records.

2. You know that in scripture records, as beforesaid, a man is called by a threefold name of soul, body, and spirit, as if he contained of three distinct essences; yet you know that in the originality of nature, he is but one distinct personal being.

3. So likewise, though the only wise God in scripture records be called by a threefold name of Father, Son, and Spirit, or Lord Jesus Christ, as if He contained of three distinct essences; yet you which are spiritual may know, that He is but only one distinct glorious person, in form like a man.

4. If an earthly monarch did not possess a distinct body, could there be ascribed any honourable titles of emperor, king, or such like, unto him at all?

5. If the eternal majesty were not a distinct person, what holy names could be attributed unto Him in the least?

6. Is it names, words, or titles makes a king to be, or gives being to an emperor, without a natural person?

7. Is it divine words, names, or titles make a God to be, or gives being to a divine majesty, without a spiritual person?

8. You know that all the honourable titles in this world to be vain, and of none effect, if there were not the person of a man to ascribe them unto.

9. You may know that all honourable titles concerning a divine majesty would also be of none effect, if there were not a spiritual person to attribute them unto, or unless they were a signification of the divine nature and form of a something that is infinite.

10. It is as clear as the purest light itself unto you that are experimentally spiritual, that it is not names, words, or titles proves God or man to be any living beings at all, except they be distinct persons, to manifest their honourable names, as proceeding from comprehensible somethings, and not from incomprehensible nothings.

11. If the God of glory in scripture records should be called not only by three divine titles, but by threescore thousand holy names also, yet all the men in this world, or angels in that world to come, can never prove Him to be an infinite Spirit without a body, or prove Him to be any more than only one distinct glorious person also.

12. You heavenly ones may also know, that the divine majesty is called in scripture records by three divine titles, that as beforesaid, that the most learned, prudent men in this world might never attain to a right understanding of the very true God and the spiritual mysteries of his everlasting kingdom, by all their rational study in the scripture records, or any other ways: and that was the very cause that the Lord Jesus

Christ said unto his own spiritual power, represented by angelical Moses and Elias, "I thank thee, Father, that thou hast hid these things from the wise and prudent, and hast revealed them to babes and sucklings," Matt. xi. 25.

13. Concerning that threefold title of Father, Son, and Holy Ghost, instead of three persons, as of long time by blind guides have been imagined, doth it not rather stand to better sense, that the word Father hath reference unto the godhead Spirit, eternally united unto Christ Jesus our Lord.

14. And that the word Son hath relation unto the glorious body of the ever-living Emanuel, which is visibly seen by elect angels, Moses and Elias.

15. And that word Holy Ghost hath reference unto a divine word of light, life, or power, proceeding from the invisible Father, through the glorious mouth of the visible Son, into the invisible spirits of elect mankind, to the enlightening of their dark understandings, and purifying of their fleshy minds.

16. Thus you which are truly enlightened from above may clearly see what that threefold heavenly record signifieth, of that only distinct personal majesty of the Lord Jesus Christ, God alone, blessed for ever and ever. Amen.

17. It is also as clear to you that are spiritual as the light itself, that the Holy One of Israel could not possibly be three distinct persons or spirits in one godhead being, or any such like confused deities.

18. You know that wheresoever the scriptures exactly make mention of the Holy One of Israel, it attributes all honour, praise, and glory unto Him, always in the singular number, as unto one distinct personal majesty or glorious Being, and not in the plural number of three distinct persons or spirits in one body, as hath been long imagined by deceivers of the whole Christian world so called, which are in bondage to their confused God, and invented formalities.

19. You know that in the conclusion of many several things the scriptures run in such a line as this: "To the only wise God, or unto God only wise, or though there be that are called many Gods, or many Lords, yet unto us there is but one God, or the Holy One of Israel," and such like.

20. You know because there is none above a king, or head magistrate, in his own kingdom, or equal with him upon an extraordinary occasion, he will swear by himself or by the faith or word of a king.

21. Thus it was with that Holy One of Israel, because there was none above Him, or beside Him, or equal with Him in heaven or earth, He swore by Himself concerning the transmutation of his uncreated glory and everlasting spiritual priesthood, into a pure body of flesh, blood, and bone.

22. Before the God of glory was descended into the virgin's womb, you know He had many holy names attributed unto Him;

wherefore you may also know, from all eternity He was a distinct divine person, and not an infinite formless Spirit, as most men blindly imagine.

23. You spiritual ones may also know, before He was clothed with flesh, it is not the holy names of Creator, infinite Spirit, Jehovah, ancient of days, mighty God, Lord of hosts, Redeemer, Holy One of Israel, king of glory, or everlasting Father, or any glorious expressions that can be uttered by the tongues of men or angels, that can prove any God at all, except He was a divine person, distinct from heavens, earth, waters, angels, men, and all things else.

24. That the one personal infinite majesty may remain in the heavenly centre of his own uncreated glory, and all beings that He hath formed to live in his sight, may continue in their own creaturely stations for an everlasting distinction between the glorious Creator and poor changeable creatures.

25. Thus by a free gift received from the Holy Spirit of our Lord Jesus Christ upon the throne of glory, in simplicity of spirit and plainness of speech, in a small measure I have declared the mind of the Holy One of Israel in those literal expressions: "for there are three which bear record in heaven, the Father, the Word, and the Holy Ghost, and these three are one."

CHAPTER XXI.

Of a threefold record of natural witnesses, proceeding from the blessed person of Christ at his death.

I SHALL write a little of a threefold record in that most pure natural body of Christ, when He was on this earth, in relation unto the threefold record of his spiritual body, in the invisible heavens beforesaid: in the fifty-third of Isaiah it is written, "He poured forth (or out) his soul unto death:" and in the nineteenth chapter by St. John you may find it thus written, "But one of the soldiers with a spear pierced his side, and forthwith came there blood and water:" here you that are spiritually discerning may clearly see a threefold record of natural witnesses, proceeding from that blessed person of our only God and Saviour, at his voluntary death:

2. As, namely, blood, water, and Spirit, wherefore his most precious soul pouring forth itself unto death, that was the witness of the death of the everlasting Father in flesh.

3. The issuing forth of the unvaluable blood, that was the witness of the death of the eternal Son in flesh.

4. The flowing forth of the water that was the witness of the death of the eternal Spirit in flesh on earth.

5. These sayings are not only hard, but intolerable to be borne by cursed Canaanites, which understand nothing truly of the power of an infinite majesty:

6. Nevertheless unto you which are made to understand the deep and hidden mysteries of

the most wise and powerful Creator, doth not this answer these scripture sayings?

7. "I and the Father are one; and from Jesus Christ, which is that faithful witness, and that first-begotten of the dead, and that prince of the kings of the earth, unto Him that loved us, and washed us from our sins in his own blood, will pour clean water upon them and they shall be clean; he died in the flesh, and quickened in the Spirit."

8. Thus you that are truly enlightened from on high may see a little into that wonderful mystery of the only wise God, manifesting Himself in earth, answerable unto his threefold record in the heavens beforesaid.

9. Three glorious words, names, titles, or distinctions, in reference unto one divine person only, in a threefold manifestation of his spiritual glory unto elect men and angels.

CHAPTER XXII.

1. Of the three witnesses on earth, 2. Of spirit, water, and blood. 3. The three records on earth are the three commissions. 4. What the commissions are.

SEEING all spiritual power and wisdom in heaven above, or in earth beneath, is no where to be found, nor never was, but only within the divine ark or spiritual person of our Lord Jesus Christ;

2. In the next place, by his own light in some measure, I shall remonstrate unto you that

are capable, what is the meaning of those three witnesses of water, blood, and Spirit in earth, which agree in one, unto which the foregoing words have relation of Father, Son, and Spirit, which are but one.

3. My spiritual brethren, are not those three witnesses in earth the commissionated messengers, which by voice or words, through the glorious mouth of God Himself, were sent forth unto an unbelieving bloody worldly-minded people, for a witness unto them to this purpose at the unexpected dreadful day of the Lord Jesus Christ?

4. Doth not that water witness in earth signify Moses and the true prophets under the law, in reference unto the holy name of God the everlasting Father?

5. Doth not the witness of the blood in earth signify Jesus and the chosen apostles, in relation of that heavenly name of God the eternal Son?

6. Doth not that witness of Holy Ghost in earth signify those two witnesses in the eleventh of the Revelations?

7. As water, blood, and Spirit, mixed together, are in a sweet harmony in the body of a man in perfect health, and through a defect of either of them the body could not subsist:

8. So likewise it is with those witnesses of God in earth, called spirit, water, and blood; for these three sweetly unite, bearing witness unto but one only wise, distinct, personal God glorified.

9. Therefore they agree in one

heavenly harmony, and cannot possibly be one without the other, not only because they proceeded from one glorious Spirit, but also because they three only, by the secret wisdom of the eternal majesty, were chosen to bear witness in earth before men and angels, unto that threefold record in heaven of Father, Son, and Holy Ghost aforesaid.

10. But some men may say unto me, the law and gospel being witnessed unto by the prophets and apostles already, what need is there of this third witness of the Spirit in earth, or what doth it bear record unto?

11. From a divine gift to this I answer, in many respects there is as much use of the witness of the Spirit in this atheistical age, as of the two former witnesses of water and blood.

12. To fulfil the scriptures which saith, "Heaven and earth shall pass away, but his word shall not pass away; or not one tittle of his word shall be unfulfilled."

13. How should Christ Jesus, the Lord of glory, be known to be the only God of truth, if there were not at one time or another a third witness in earth to fulfil the scripture, "For there are three that bear witness in earth."

14. Another necessity of this third witness of the Spirit is this, because you may know that there hath not been above these thousand years a commissionated messenger sent forth by the eternal Spirit, to bear witness unto that truth, which the two former witnesses

sealed, too, with their blood.

15. Another necessity of the witness of the Spirit is this, because of late, and at present, so many several antichristian spirits are come forth into the world in their own names, and from the power of their own strong imaginations, and cunning cursed observations, have acted many visible lying signs and wonders upon their own bodies, and other ways, to the ruining of many a poor deceived soul, in body, mind, and personal estate, all of them pretending when those fleshly fits comes upon them, that it is the power of the eternal Spirit immediately moving them.

CHAPTER XXIII.

1. Of several empty opinions concerning the two witnesses in the eleventh of the Revelation. 2. What they are. 3. No true witness without a voice from heaven. 4. Who are the two last spiritual witnesses.

IN the next place I shall write I somewhat of men's empty opinions concerning the two witnesses in the Revelation, for your better understanding of the insuing truth; some men have imagined them to be the Spirit of Christ, and the flesh of Christ.

2. Now you may know that cannot be, because the Spirit and body of Christ were both glorified together in the highest heavens, long before John prophesied of the two witnesses standing before the God of the whole earth, amongst the sons of

men.

3. Others there are that would have them to be the literal law and gospel: now you that are spiritual may also know that cannot be the witnesses here spoken of, because without a true interpreter the scripture in itself is but a killing letter.

4. You know that the invisible truth of the scriptures proceed only from a true light received from the spiritual person of Christ Jesus our Lord, in the throne of immortal glory.

5. You know that from the bare records it is impossible to attain to the knowledge of the only very true God, or the spiritual mysteries of his everlasting kingdom; and that was the very cause of these and such like scripture sayings, "I thank thee, Father, that thou hast hid these things from the wise and prudent, and hast revealed them to babes: make the heart of this people fat, which have eyes, and see not; ears, and hear not; hearts, and understand not:" and why so? to fulfil the word of the Lord spoken through the mouths of his prophets in the time of the law.

6. If the two witnesses here spoken of were the letter of the scripture, what need then would there be of the invisible teachings of the Spirit.

7. For the most part doth not the ministers and people set up the letter of the scriptures and offer divine worship unto them, as the children of Israel worshipped their golden calves?

8. The two witnesses cannot be meant the literal scriptures, because it is said, "If any man will hurt them, fire proceeds out of their mouths and devoureth their enemies: and if any hurt them in this manner, they must be killed"

9. Now you may know that at this very present, there are many thousands in these three nations, that do not only count the scriptures mere inventions of wise men, to keep the simple in awe under their rulers; but if it were not for fear of men, if they could have their wills, they would burn all the scriptures in the world to ashes, and instead of fearing any fiery vengeance following them, their unbelieving seared spirits would greatly rejoice at it as a most noble or profitable act to the whole world, for preventing all literal contestations concerning a God, or glory, or misery to come.

10. Some men would imagine these witnesses to be the magistrates and the ministers.

11. Now you may know that cannot be, because both magistrates and ministers are either chosen by one another or by the voice of the people, instead of being chosen by the voice of God Himself, or a true prophet sent forth by his eternal Spirit for that purpose.

12. It is written, that "The witnesses had a powerful gift of prophecy:" now you know that since God became flesh, instead of the magistrates or ministers owning themselves to be commissioned witnesses or prophets of the divine majesty, for the most part, if men have appeared upon that account,

they have persecuted them by imprisonments, stripes, banishment, or death itself.

13. Again it is written, "The witnesses were clothed in sackcloth," therefore they cannot be the magistrates or the ministers; because you know that for the most part they are rather clothed in satin or other costly garments than sackcloth or mean apparel; wherefore seeing all magistrates with their ministers are chosen by men only through the secret decree of the most high God, and it being apparent that instead of honouring the Lord of life and glory, or showing mercy unto his prophets, for the most part they seek the honour of one another and persecute his messengers, and rejoice in feasting one another through the fastings of others.

14. It is as clear as the light unto any man whose heart is not stone blind, that they are none of the witnesses prophesied of by St. John in the eleventh of the Revelation.

15. Another sort of atheistical people there are that would imagine themselves to imply the two witnesses there spoken of, saying, "The two witnesses are within them, or every man's soul and body are those two witnesses," and such like:

16. Now you may know that this is so far from any spiritual truth, that there is no sense or reason in it: why? though a man be called soul, body, and Spirit, yet he being but one person only, you know he can be no more than one witness upon what account soever.

17. Again, the invisible witness of men's consciences concerns men's own particular only between God and man, or between man and man, and God only wise perfectly seeth that witness always, and not men; therefore that cannot be the witnesses here spoken of, because you know that the witnesses or prophets of the Lord were always visible whilst they had a being in this world.

18. Thus it is as clear as the light, that none of all these are those two witnesses spoken of by St. John, but mere imaginary fancies of men's own brains, for want of a divine light in them to distinguish between the true witnesses, sent forth by the Creator Himself, and the false ones that went before they were sent.

19. Again it is written, "But I will give power unto my two witnesses, and they shall prophecy: "my spiritual brethren, you may know that when John spake those words, that the two witnesses were to come into the world, to bear testimony unto the truth of the two past witnesses of the Lord, because the text saith," But I will give power unto my two witnesses, and they shall prophecy."

20. And you know, according to the truth of unerring scriptures, the two former witnesses had power given them from the Lord, and they did prophecy in their times:

21. So that you may understand, that the Lord did purpose to raise two men in this atheistical age, out of the very ashes of the two former

witnesses, not only for discovery of all lying appearances in his name, as they did in their times, but also for a more clearer manifestation of the deep things of God, than ever was since this world began.

22. You that are spiritual may know, that since the Lord's two former witnesses fell asleep in the dust of the earth, not a man have powerfully appeared to bear witness unto one distinct personal Creator, as they did, until we came forth in the latter end of the year 1651, in the name of the Lord Jesus Christ, by voice of words spoken unto me, by his eternal Spirit three mornings together, to the hearing of the ear as a man speaks to his friend.

23. Again, the scriptures call them by the name of two witnesses only; wherefore if any man addeth to their number, or despiseth them because they appear not like a God, to bring fire down from heaven, or turn water into blood, or such like natural plagues, or miracles as hath been acted already, if there be any truth in the scriptures, can that man escape the plagues of God in the life to come threatened in such a case?

24. Again, you know it is said, "The Lord gave power unto the two witnesses to prophecy:" is not this answerable unto the word of the Lord, when He said unto me, that "He had given me understanding above all the men in the world, and that he had chosen me as his last messenger for a great work unto this bloody unbelieving world, and had given

me Lodowick Muggleton to be my mouth."

25. You know that the witnesses are said to be "two olive trees and two candlesticks, standing before the God of the whole earth:" my beloved spiritual brethren, hath not the glorious God of heaven and earth, both by speaking and writing, manifested through our earthly candlesticks or mortal mouths, more divine oil or golden truth than in any men in the world besides?

26. Again, you know it is said, "The witnesses were clothed with sackcloth:" I humbly beseech you that have truly tasted of the glory of eternity, did any men upon the face of the earth, since the time of the apostles, upon an account as sent forth from the eternal Spirit, suffer persecution for bearing witness unto the man Christ Jesus glorified, to be the only wise God and alone everlasting Father, but we two only?

27. Again, you know it is written, "If any man will hurt them, fire proceedeth out of their mouth and devoureth their enemies:" my spiritual friends, is not this answerable unto the word of the Lord, when He said unto me, "I have put the two-edged sword of my Spirit into thy mouth, that whoever I pronounce blessed through thy mouth, is blessed to eternity; and whoever I pronounce cursed through thy mouth, is cursed to eternity?

28. Whoever thou art that shall see these passages and be offended with me because of them, be it known unto thee and

all men else, that I, of all men, neither do nor can expect any mercy from the glorious God to all eternity, if the Creator Himself did not speak those very words unto me by voice from heaven as aforesaid.

29. Though at present atheistial men shall laugh to scorn what we speak or write in the name of the Lord Jesus; yet they being words of truth by an immediate commission from the eternal Spirit, you that are heirs of immortal crowns may know in that unexpected day of the Lord's general account, they will become an invisible fire within the spirits and bodies of those that heard them, of eternal bright, burning, ravishing glories, or everlasting fiery shame in eternal death.

30. What power is attributed unto the two witnesses in the eleventh of the Revelation, you may know that it is spiritual and invisible; why, because as beforesaid, it being the third and last witness in earth of the eternal Spirit, its declarative plagues upon the spirits and bodies of persecutors were spiritual, answerable unto the natural plagues that were executed by the two former witnesses, upon the spirits and bodies of those that persecuted them for their commission's sake.

CHAPTER XXIV.

1. Of the witnesses' trials and persecutions, after the publishing of their commission. 2. The prophet's interpretation of some verses in the eleventh of the Revelation. 3. An objection against the true witnesses answered.

YOU that are experimentally spiritual may understand, that the true light of Christ in his beloved apostle Saint John, hath in those two Revelation-witnesses concluded in one, both the true prophets in the law and chosen apostles in the gospel, and the two last commissionated witnesses of the invisible Spirit, in this spiritual conceited age:

2. Why because they jointly as one man, against all gainsayers in the world, do bear witness unto that man Christ Jesus, clothed with flesh and bone in glory, to be the only wise, very true God, and alone everlasting Father and Creator of both worlds, angels, and men.

3. Again, you know it is written, that "When the witnesses have finished their testimony, the beast out of the bottomless pit shall make war against them, and overcome them, and kill them:" behold as that bottomless pit, beastly imagination within the spirits of the Canaanitish Pharaohs and Herods, was stirred up unto cruel persecution upon the two former witnesses for their testimony's sake;

4. So likewise a little after that testimonial truth of the same nature was published by us, the Holy Spirit's two last witnesses, in a book intituled, "A Transcendent Spiritual Treatise;" I humbly beseech you that were the moderate eye-witnesses thereof, through the instigation of the people,

5. Did not the spirit of persecution appear in the head magistrate of this city of London, when he committed us unto the common gaol of Newgate (so called) in September, 1653. Notwithstanding no man did accuse us in the least of the breach of any civil law of England?

6. The next sessions following, in the Old Bailey, were we not arraigned at the bar like thieves or murderers, before Alderman Foulke, then lord mayor of London, the Recorder Steel, and some other magistrates?

7. And did not the magistrates beforesaid, in open court, condemn us as blasphemers against God, because we did bear witness unto the man Christ Jesus glorified, to be the only wise God, and alone everlasting Father, by virtue of a commission we received from his eternal Spirit?

8. Upon the account aforesaid, were we not kept close prisoners in the house of correction, called Old Bridewell, six months, without bail or mainprize?

9. I appeal unto any man that heard our trial, that hath any true hope of eternal salvation by that Jesus Christ that was nailed to a tree, without the gates of Jerusalem, whether any thing was laid to our charge by our accusers, the lord mayor, and the witnesses, upon any civil or natural account in the least?

10. It is truth, because of some speeches spoken unto the lord mayor first, and afterwards to the whole bench and jury, by

the power of the Lord Jesus Christ in us, in reference unto our commission and innocence of spirit, whether it was to gain the magistrates' favour, or whether they knew of it, the Lord knoweth. Some said, whipping was too good for us: others said, hanging was too good for us, burning of us was most fit:

11. But where was the man that had so much love of truth, or natural pity in him, as to say, but what evil have they done? Was there any such man upon the bench, or in the jury, or among the officers, or amongst all those men that heard our trial? If there were, it was in secret.

12. I remember it is written, when our Lord Jesus was accused before Pilate, for a deceiver of the people, blasphemy, and such like, notwithstanding he was vehemently accused by the chief priest and rulers;

13. Yet Pilate oftentimes said, "But what evil had he done? I find no fault in him;" so likewise, though we are but poor sinful dust and ashes, and, in comparison of our Lord Jesus Christ, not worthy in the least to make mention of his most holy name;

14. I am fully persuaded in my soul, if Pilate had sat in the judgment-seat with the recorder, he would have asked the lord mayor and our accusers what evil we had committed, or what law we had broken, before he had passed sentence upon us.

15. Whatever men's thoughts and opinions are concerning the

Recorder Steel, I appeal unto God, elect men, and angels, and to his own conscience, whether he came not short of Pilate, when he sat in the judgment-seat concerning us? If this be truth, which none can deny that heard our trial, if truth be their guide, I hope he doth not think much of Pilate's being his elder brother, but will also grant him the pre-eminence in the day of the Lord's eternal account.

16. Some of you that heard our trial may remember that the recorder did examine us chiefly, if not wholly, concerning Christ's Father, or what that Father was, that in his agonies He cried or prayed unto?

17. If you have not forgot it through distance of time, you may remember our answer was to this purpose:

18. That that Father which our Lord Jesus Christ made mention of in all his extremities, was his own representative spiritual power or charge, which He had committed unto angelical Moses and Elias in glory, whilst He went that sore journey in flesh for the redemption of his elect lost Israelites: it is written, "He shall give his angels charge concerning thee," that He and thee was but only one divine Being, let men and angels disprove what I have written concerning this thing if they can, that I may be ashamed and confounded of my great confidence in that which is not.

19. So much concerning our trial for our bearing testimony unto Jesus Christ to be the only true God, and alone everlasting Father, before the powers of this perishing world.

20. For a more clear manifestation of the commissionated witnesses of the eternal Spirit unto the heirs of immortal glory, I shall write somewhat of the mind of Christ from John's words in the beginning of the eleventh chapter; the first words are these, "Then was given me a reed like unto a rod, and the angel stood by, saying, Rise and measure the temple of God, and the altar, and them that worship therein: but the court which is without the temple, leave out and measure it not, for it is given unto the Gentiles, and the holy city shall they tread under foot forty and two months."

21. My divine friends, you may understand that that reed, like unto a rod possessed by John, was a free gift of inspiration which he received from a glorified Christ in the high heavens by his angel, whereby, like unto a skilful land-measurer, his understanding was enabled to comprehend the spiritual signification of the temple of God, and the altar, and them that worship therein.

22. You may also understand that the temple, and them that did worship therein, did signify God's spiritual house, or tabernacle of elect Jews and Gentiles, which make but one complete body for Christ Jesus their head to reign in, by his heavenly light.

23. That altar spoken of by John, did signify the glorious body or tabernacle of the eternal Spirit, unto which divine altar or godhead person those spiritual

worshippers were virtually united by a received light from that infinite majesty: through which invisible intercourse sometimes their souls were full of spiritual joy, through that inward seal of godlike glory which they were to enjoy in the life to come.

24. You may understand that that unmeasured court without the temple, did signify the visible scriptures.

25. You know that when sacrifices or ordinances were in force at Jerusalem, there was the inward temple and outward porch or court joining to the temple.

26. You also know the court without the temple was a common place for all people to meet in, but none might enter into the inward temple in the time of their worship but the chief priests, or those that were confessors of the true God, and approved of by those teachers of the law.

27. Likewise you may understand, that the outward court or scripture, which is common to all men, that was left unmeasured or cast out, did signify all the outcast unbelieving Jews and Gentiles: and the inward temple or spirit of the scriptures did signify all the elect believing Jews and Gentiles, in that glorious altar beforesaid.

28. Again, you know that the court of the temple was an outward ornament or witness unto the beauty or glory within the temple:

29. So, likewise, the court of the visible scriptures is an ornament or testimony unto that eternal Spirit of all truth within the temple, body, or tabernacle of the ever-living God: and, virtually, in a great measure living in the temples or bodies of his elect, that are enabled to give a true distinction between the things of eternal life and eternal death.

30. Again, you know it is said, that "The unmeasured court without the temple was given to the Gentiles, and that they should tread the holy city under foot two and forty months."

31. You spiritual ones may know that the mind of the Holy Spirit in those words was this: that to fulfil the prophecy of Christ concerning the destruction of the Jews, their temple and city of Jerusalem by the Romans through conquest, they should possess the literal records, written by the prophetical and apostolical Jews, and not only worship it instead of the eternal Spirit, but also by cruel persecution for above thirteen hundred years, were to tyrannize over the holy city of spiritual Jews and Gentiles that could not bow down unto their inventions.

32. You that are spiritual may know that the Roman Gentiles here spoken of by John, are those people which men call cavaliers, whose princely race sprang first from the loins of king Herod, that bloody persecutor of the Lord of glory, and so streamed into the line of the tyrannical Roman empire or popedom.

33. From this papal power, whatever apostolical or Christian style they attribute to themselves through all the Christian world so called, they have banded together as one man, to tread underfoot, as beforesaid, that chosen city of heavenly-minded Jews and Gentiles.

34. Because their innocent souls could not forsake that ever-living altar manifested unto them, and bow down to their Egyptian calves set up as a snare unto the people, chiefly for fleshly gain and perishing glory from men of their own spirits.

35. Also you that are spiritual take special notice of this, that these two witnesses or prophets spoken of in the eleventh of the Revelation, did not appear unto men until the gentile power of persecuting bishops were extinguished in this land.

36. But it may be objected by some that one Bull and Varnum, and others long before them, have pretended to be these two witnesses, and yet it came to nothing.

37. To this I answer, by way of query, can any man make it appear from any record since the apostles' time, that in any land or nation, two men did ever bear witness in all opposition of all men or angels unto the man Jesus Christ glorified, to be the only God, everlasting Father, and Creator of both worlds, angels and men?

38. Again, amongst all the pretended prophets in the world, doth any of them bear witness unto one personal majesty, distinct from heavens, earth, angels, and men?

39. Nay, of the contrary, do they not all rather disown such a God as a weak or carnal thing, and as one man like unto Baal's four hundred priests, and the false prophets, and priests in all ages, imagine the Creator to be an infinite formless Spirit?

40. If any man should moderately inquire of the pretended prophets or spiritual lights in this age, concerning the knowledge of the Creator or a glory to come, is there any answer to be had from them but this or such like: "the Creator is an infinite, invisible, unchangeable, eternal Spirit:" or else they will say, "the Creator is all wisdom, love, purity, riches, beauty, joy, righteousness, justice, or divine excellencies; He fills heaven and earth; He is the all in all, and there is nothing besides Him:" or else they will say, "the more ye desire the knowledge of the Creator, the less you will know of Him, because He is infinite:" or they will bid you "mind that God or Christ within you, and trouble not yourself about incomprehensible infiniteness:" thus these false prophets of cursed Cain, make a wonderment of an infinite Creator of nothing, but mere words only.

41. Thou which art puffed up with such a Creator as this is, shalt one day know to thy eternal sorrow and shame, what it is to despise a personal God infinitely full of all glorious perfection.

42. When this personal

majesty shall show his infinite power upon thee, through the retaining of his inshining light from thy Luciferian spirit, and shall leave thee and thy inward God in an unspeakable condition of eternal shame and confusion of soul and body, then shalt thou know that thou didst hear of a personal God infinitely too glorious for heavens, earth, angels, or men, to be capable of the indwelling essence of his eternal Spirit.

CHAPTER XXV.

1. Of the sinful soul of man. 2. Of its mortality. 3. All souls that are generated are mortal. 4. If men's souls were immortal they could not be capable of diseases.

CAN the soul of man be any thing at all but dust without their bodies, or can their bodies be any thing at all but dry, dead, cold dust, also without their spirits?

2. Doth not the rational soul or spirit of man lie secretly hid in his seed like unto a spark of fire, and can this seed of man have any living being without its body?

3. Can the soul and body of man be therefore any more than one distinct living or dying essence?

4. When a woman conceives life in her womb through mixtures of seeds, by virtue of the decreed word of the Lord spoken at the first creation of nature, is not that life the very soul or spirit of the child?

5. Doth not that soul or spirit in the womb by degrees congeal together into rational fire, blood, and water, and so in due time become a complete body of flesh, blood, and bone?

6. If men and women together beget and conceive the soul and body of the child by an instinct in nature, which none can gainsay but senseless sots or conceited wise men, which through an ambition of tongues or languages, have studied beyond all sober sense, reason, or wit,

7. Is it then possible, think you, that the soul of a man should be immortal, and the body wherein it liveth be mortal?

8. Doth it not stand to very good sense that being both conceived into life in the womb together, and both born together into the world, and both living together upon the earth their appointed time, and being both polluted together with sin, that they should also both die together, and turn to their dust or nonbeing again, until the general bodily resurrection of all mankind that are dead asleep in the dust of the earth, when time is no more, either unto eternal glory or everlasting shame.

9. Again, it is written in the forty-sixth chapter of Genesis, "All the souls that came with Jacob into Egypt, which came out of his loins, beside Jacob's wives, were in the whole three-score and six souls."

10. In the tenth of Deuteronomy and the last verse, it is written, "Thy fathers went down into Egypt with seventy

persons:" here you see the scriptures are plain for proving the souls proceeding out of the loins of man as well as the bodies.

11. Also you see that a man in scripture is called soul, and sometimes is called body or soul, body and spirit, and yet you know he is but one living essence or substance.

12. If all souls and bodies since the fall of Adam by natural generation proceed from the loins of one another, as it is proved clearly by spiritual sense, reason, and scripture, how can poor vain perishing dust imagine that his sinful soul is immortal and cannot die?

13. Is it not natural for an immortal spirit to be united only unto an immortal body? and is it not natural for a mortal soul to be united only unto a mortal body?

14. Is it not against all sober sense or reason that the body of man could be subject to any kind of diseases or distempers in the least, if his soul were immortal and could not die?

15. Is it not the very nature of immortality immediately to swallow up all into life, or to transmute that body wherein it liveth from all manner of corruption into his own uncorrupted glory?

16. Is it not the nature of a sinful soul to become subject to die through the defilement of its first created purity?

17. Is there any undefiled soul now living upon the face of the earth, and is not immortality all spotless purity as aforesaid, how then thinkest thou it possible that the sinful souls of men are immortal already and cannot die?

18. It is written, "The soul that sins shall die;" also it is written, "In the day thou eatest thereof, thou shalt die the death." I confess that the souls of Adam and Eve were not capable of any kind of death, until they were both defiled with the sinful nature of the angelical serpent:

19. But as soon as ever they had eaten of that cursed serpentine tree of knowledge of good and evil, their souls and bodies were free from all their former pure life:

20. In the room thereof were subject to all kind of impure death whatsoever, and did not know but that they were both cut off from the divine presence of the eternal Spirit.

21. Until the God of glory Himself graciously promised them to become flesh, blood, and bone, of the virgin seed, to redeem their sinful souls and bodies again out of all kind of death, into an unchangeable immortal glory, at his personal appearing with his mighty angels.

22. Again, the Lord hath said in divers places of scripture, that "The souls of men shall be cut off from the land of the living, and that the soul that sins shall die, and that the pure soul of Christ himself was poured forth unto death, and that the soul of Christ should not be left in the grave, nor that his blessed body should see corruption;" and the Lord hath said, that "Adam and

Eve were but dust, and to dust they should return again." And yet thou, contrary to all prophetical or apostolical scripture, and against all sober sense or reason in its right mind, ignorantly or impudently affirmest, that "The sinful soul of man is already immortal, and cannot die, or be put to death."

23. Again, from this thy nonsensical imagination, dost thou not call all the scriptures lies, and the eternal majesty from whence they proceeded, a liar to his face? And dost thou not call all sober sense and reason a mere lie also?

24. I know it is a common thing for men to say they have in them a good spirit and a bad spirit; it is confessed that every man in his fallen spirit hath remaining a little light or motion of the Spirit of God in him.

25. Yet take notice of this, though he hath a twofold motion in him to justify all the righteous proceedings of the Creator in his conscience at the last day, yet he hath but one Spirit or soul in him.

26. Indeed the apostles saith, "The flesh lusteth against the Spirit, and the Spirit against the flesh, and these two are contrary:" Gal. v. 17, that which the apostle calls the Spirit in this place of scripture was a divine light of life, received into the dark understanding, by virtue of a word speaking from the eternal Spirit of a glorified Christ, but not the essence of the Holy Spirit.

27. And that which he calls the flesh, was man's own spirit, which consists of nothing but confused lying imagination, or cursed carnal reasoning against that heavenly light aforesaid.

28. Again, you that are spiritual do know, that all men that do expect a glory to come in the invisible heavens, do confess that the Spirit of the divine majesty is infinite, unchangeable, immortal, and eternal.

29. If the Creator's person is of an incomprehensible brightness, which none can gainsay but angelical carnalities, how then thinkest thou it possible for men or angels to be capable of the indwelling essence of the eternal Spirit?

30. Though every man as aforesaid have little or much of the spiritual motions of God abiding in his soul, yet take notice of this, when he inspireth any light into sinful spirits, that very light itself being distinct from the infinite Spirit, and essentially one with mortality, is made capable, not only to live, but also to die together, that it through death might be capable by the decree of that Spirit from whence it was produced, to quicken and revive that mortality again into the glorious likeness of the eternal majesty itself from whence it came.

CHAPTER XXVI.

1. Of the nature and place of the reprobates torment. 2. The last witnesses' great confidence concerning the end of the world. 3. Without a tongue no speech can be

made by God, angels, or men. 4.
God is visibly seen by spiritual
bodies as kings are by their
subjects.

TAKE notice of this also, that
in what soul soever this inshining light hath appeared, though
he be preserved from despising a
personal God, if before he taste
of death he doth not attain to
understand this glorified Jesus
to be the only wise very true
God, upon the sight of so clear a
discovery as this is, then this
will be his portion, all the light at
his death shall vanish and come
to nothing, and in the day of the
Lord's account, by virtue of his
decree, that Luciferian
serpentine spirit which abhorred
the simple plain truth because it
discovereth its carnal deceits,
shall quicken and bring forth a
body spiritually as dark as pitch,
and naturally as heavy as lead, a
body of thick darkness, or
blackness of darkness, according
to holy writ.

2. Again, it will be a body
whose invisible spirit shall be a
fire of such a dark envious
nature, that it shall burn more
intolerably fierce than any fire in
this world whatsoever, through
which it shall be tormented, as if
it were nothing else but a
carcase or pillar of unsavoury
burning brimstone.

3. In that very place where it
doth appear upon this earth, it
shall either stand, sit, kneel, or
lie along, neither seeing its own
dreadful person nor no man's
else.

4. And the main ground of all
his unspeakable sorrow will
arise from hence, because its

spirit is barred close prisoner in
its own body, from all kind of
former thoughts, or motioning
forth upon any spiritual comforts
whatsoever, through the total
absenting, inshining presence of
the Lord Jesus Christ, the
everlasting Father.

5. Again, all thy former pride,
envy, covetousness, lying, lust,
and hypocrisy, which thou with
delight didst act towards thy innocent brother's ruin, shall then
be acted against thine own self;
it will be the eternity of thy condition that will increase thy sorrows and shame: O it will be in
vain then to wish thou hadst
never been born, or anything
else.

6. Whoever thou art that shalt
out of thy atheistical soul laugh
these words to scorn, and say,
"these are but mere fancies of
my own brain," know this from
the Lord of glory, when this
whole world and all the beauty
and natural glory thereof, as,
namely, the firmament, sun,
moon, and stars, are become
nothing but burning dust or dry
sand, and an utter chaos of
everlasting confused darkness,
then thou shalt remember thy
despising things thou knewest
not.

7. Is not this answerable to
Christ's own words, where He
saith, "If that light in thee be
darkness, how great will that
darkness be?" Again, "The Son of
man shall send forth his angels,
and they gather out of his kingdom all things that offend, and
them that do iniquity, and shall
cast them into a furnace of fire,
there shall be weeping and

gnashing of teeth," Matt. xiii. Take notice of this record of scripture, and you shall find that He said, "These things should be done at the end of the world." Again, " And when the Son of man cometh in his glory, and all the holy angels with him, then shall he sit on the throne of his glory, and before him shall be gathered all nations, and he shall separate them one from another, as a shepherd separateth the sheep from the goats: and he shall set the sheep on his right hand, and the goats on his left; then shall the king say to them on his right hand, Come ye blessed of my Father, take the inheritance of the king-dom prepared for you from the foundation of the world. Then shall he say to them on the left hand, Depart from me ye cursed into everlasting fire which is pre-pared for the devil and his angels," Matt. xxv.

8. Here ye may see that the Lord Jesus doth not speak of cursing or burning up of sin in all men, and eternal salvation unto all men's persons, but make as clear a distinction as there is between sheep and goats, of an eternal separation of two distinct generations.

9. The one personal nation to enter into that most blessed estate or kingdom of the right hand of eternal ravishing glory, with Christ and his holy angels, and the other personal generation to be cast out into the left hand of the fiery burning kingdom of everlasting utter darkness, with that devil Cain and his cursed generation, being

thereunto appointed from the foundation of the world.

10. Again, whatever men shall imagine or think to the contrary, this was the very mind of Christ in those words of his, concerning blessing elect Israelites to eternity, and cursing Canaanitish reprobates for everlasting.

11. Who shall dare open his mouth in that day to say, Why hast thou made me thus As sure as the Lord liveth, and as certain as thou art a living soul and body, this very thing will come to pass in a short season, though men or angels should gainsay it.

12. The Lord Jesus Christ neither can nor will be found a liar in this nor any thing else, for all the cursed whimsies of men in this age or any other age, though the persons of ten hundred thousand times ten millions of men and women should suffer the vengeance of eternal fiery death in utter darkness. O poor vain despiser of a personal God, what a cursed condition art thou in and knowest it not?

13. In the next place I shall speak again concerning the Cre-ator's being an infinite personal majesty, unto which the visible forms of men and angels bear record as unto an incomprehen-sible glory, from whence all their comprehensible things had their beings.

14. Was there not an untreated eternal majesty alone, when no creatures, whether men or angels, appeared in a sensible living being?

15. Again, seeing there was

from eternity a distinct glory, is it not of necessity that this ever-living being should be a glorious something?

16. Is it not both lawful and expedient also for a man according to sobriety, to declare unto his spiritual and natural brethren, what this glorious God was and is, that man being sent forth by the eternal Spirit for that very end or purpose?

17. Doth not all men which confess a Creator conclude positively there is but one God, and no more?

18. If this one God was an infinite distinct spiritual substance before any created being appeared to themselves, is it not of an absolute necessity that He should abide in his own divine centre, and so continue a distinct glorious being to all eternity, for an everlasting distinction between the unchangeable Creator and the changeable creatures?

19. Do not all men which acknowledge this distinct glorious being, conclude Him to be an infinite, eternal, unchangeable Spirit, and do they not conclude this incomprehensible Spirit to be an eternal godhead being in itself, and so of necessity must He not be a distinct glorious Being, from all things and places?

20. If there be a Creator, and if this glorious Creator be an infinite distinct something, too transcendently divine to be essentially united unto heavens, earth, angels, or men, which none can deny but conceited notionalists or literal hypocrites, are not those men as yet utterly ignorant of the Holy One of Israel, which imagine the Creator to be an infinite formless Spirit essentially united unto the whole creation, utterly hating that God that is a distinct glorious Being to Himself?

21. Again, if the eternal Being be an infinite Spirit, can that glorious Spirit be any thing at all without it be endued with variety of divine qualifications?

22. Is not that infinite Spirit and its glorious properties but only one essence or godhead substance?

23. Is not every virtue in the eternal Spirit infinite?

24. Is that eternal Spirit and its heavenly virtues any thing else but immortal crowns of bright burning glories?

25. Can this infinite spiritual glory be sensible of its divine excellencies, or be a perfect blessedness, except He hath a distinct body suitable unto his eternal Spirit, to enjoy his divine pleasures to Himself, and at his pleasure to distribute by measure into the elect spirits of men and angels, the inshining glimpses of this incomprehensible glory?

26. Though the eternal Spirit be that invisible God that by the power of its almighty word hath created all things either for a time or for eternity, into that glorious order they now appear to be, yet you that are spiritual may know that without a body, face, or tongue, his glorious Spirit could not possibly have spoken any distinct words at all, no more than the spirits of men or angels can speak distinct

words without a body, face, or tongue of their own.

27. Though all power, wisdom, and glory proceeds only from an invisible eternal Spirit, yet you may know that it cannot be a perfect glory except it be clothed with a majestical person, as a visible ornament for men and angels, to behold face to face in the high heavens, no more than the invisible spirits of earthly monarchs could be complete without natural bodies or persons, for their subjects beholding them face to face.

28. Thus you that are truly spiritual may know, that though there was nothing created by any bodily labour or painful study of the glorious Creator,

29. Yet without a distinct heavenly body there was nothing made that was made, neither possibly could be, whatever is or shall be imagined to the contrary.

30. So much at present concerning that one personal majesty or incomprehensible Being of all beings which are subject to change, or to be changed at his divine pleasure.

31. O blessed only are all you that have the faith of this one glorious personal God abiding in you.

CHAPTER XXVII.

1. A more full discourse of the two witnesses. 2. No true messenger or witness without a voice from God to the hearing of the ear. 3. The three commissions agree all in truth. 4. Differing only in point of worship. 5. There was not, nor can there be, assurance of eternal happiness but in the belief of a commission. 6. God owneth no worship in this commission but what is spiritual. 7. The difference between true and false commissioners.

IN the next place I shall treat again concerning the witnesses according to former intention: you may remember where I ceased I challenged the whole world, whether since the primitive times any men upon the account of bearing record unto the man Christ Jesus in glory to be the only wise God, Creator, Redeemer, and everlasting Father, appeared as the two Revelation witnesses?

2. Again, until the Roman bishops' persecuting tyranny was expired in this land, you may know the two Revelation witnesses or prophets never appeared:

3. For according unto scripture order, you that are of a spiritual comprehension may know, that we are those two commissionated witnesses or prophets of the Holy Spirit of the Lord Jesus Christ, because as beforesaid,

4. According to the prophecy by St. John, we exactly appeared when the Roman bishops' times were expired, of treading under foot the holy city or people of the Lord Jesus Christ in this land.

5. Some men may object and say, why are the witnesses of the Spirit but two in number, and the former witnesses of so great a number? Unto this objection from the Lord I answer by way of

query, doth not the glorious wisdom of the eternal Spirit most of all appear in the smallest number of things for the acting of a wonderful work?

6. Is it not most advantageous unto the Creator's glory to prevent men or angels from knowing his witnesses or their number, either by miracles or without miracles, until his pleasure is to reveal them?

7. You know that God's worship formerly was not only invisible but visible also, and to continue for a long season, therefore there required a great number of spiritual speakers unto the elect.

8. But the worship of God being now only spiritual or invisible, thou mayest know that a witness or two is sufficient, the day of the Lord being near at hand to proclaim his glorious coming by speaking or writing unto the ends of the earth.

9. Again, is not a witness or two sufficient to discover the vanity of all vain-glorious fleshly formalities amongst the sons of men, seeing the Lord is at hand to make an eternal separation between the blessed Israelites and the cursed Canaanites?

10. Doth not these three witnesses in earth only agree in one divine body of all truth in this respect, because they received their commission by voice of words to the hearing of the visible as well as invisible ear, through the glorious mouth of a personal majesty?

11. Wherefore can any man upon this earth, that counts himself, or is accounted by others, to be a true prophet, apostle, minister, preacher, teacher, bishop, shepherd, priest, ambassador, or witness from the God of heaven and earth, without a voice of distinct words to the hearing of the ear from the ever-living God?

12. Or can he possess any true joy or peace of conscience in his prophetical declarations, without such an immediate commission from the true God as beforesaid.

13. Again, though spirit, blood, and water, by the wisdom of God, sweetly agree within the body of a healthful man, yet you know that they are of contrary natures to one another;

14. For the soul or spirit of man is an absolute mortal fire within the blood and the water, which by virtue of its fiery nature qualifieth the blood and the water according to their capacities;

15. Through which they are so sweetly composed, that unanimously they give natural life and strength through the whole man, insomuch that the one cannot live without the other, though they are of contrary natures.

16. Thus through the secret decree of the divine majesty, there is a marvellous trinitary mystery within the natural body of man.

17. But very few men understand it, for want of the prophetical spirit of David in them, who cried out with exceeding admiration of the Creator's wisdom, saying, "I am fearfully and wonderfully made!"

18. So likewise you may know, it is with these three commissionated witnesses of the divine majesty in earth:

19. For though all three proceeded from one and the same spirit of truth, and all bear record unto only one distinct personal god-man glorified, yet; in the manner of their declarations concerning the worshipping of the Holy One of Israel, they differ, and are as contrary as fire, blood, and water, which are without the body of men.

20. But in the spirituality of their administrations concerning invisible worshipping of the Lord Jesus Christ, they harmoniously agree as one soul, like unto spirit, blood, and water, within man's body as aforesaid.

21. If any man should ask, why the Holy One of. Israel hath put such a vast difference between the administrations of his three witnesses in earth, to this, from the Holy Spirit, I answer by way of query, is it not to blind the eyes of the-wise and prudent men of this world, that from their strength of reason in scripture records, they may war against the pure light of life within the witnesses of the God of all saving truth?

22. That they may remain in their rational darkness of unbelief wherein they were born, and so everlastingly perish for want of that new and true birth of the fiery glorious Spirit of our Lord Jesus Christ.

23. Is it not also that God alone may receive all the honour, power, praise, and glory, from his redeemed ones, in the revealing his true witnesses or prophets unto them by his eternal Spirit, through which they attain to the right understanding of the very true God, and the glorious things of eternity, declared by his own chosen messengers?

24. And so are made to receive those divine truths in the purity of them, by loving of them above the gain or glory of this conceited perishing world?

25. Moreover, do they not thereby enjoy an invisible seal of an assurance of the eternal immortality of their persons at the visible appearing of the divine majesty of the Son of man?

26. That most infinite glorious God, with all his mighty angels, Moses and Elias, at that dreadful day when all time shall vanish immediately, and eternity only seize upon all mankind in their several persons.

27. Again, if water, blood and fire, without the body of man, be mixed together, being of contrary conditions or natures, you know they cease not contending until they have conquered one another.

28. Also you know blood is too strong for water, and fire too powerful for blood; so likewise you may know it is with the three commissionated witnesses of God in earth, Moses, the apostles, and two last witnesses.

29. Though they unanimously agree in bearing record unto only one distinct personal God of all saving truth, as spirit, water, and blood sweetly accord within the healthful body of a mortal

man as aforesaid,

30. Yet you may know that in their visible worship they are at warfare with each other, until they have obtained victory one over another.

31. That the present immediate spiritual wisdom of the divine majesty might bear rule in the consciences of the chosen jewels of immortal crowns, and not that which is past.

32. Wherefore, when that gospel administration of blood appeared, you know that the apostolical commissioners thereof did, with all their power, preach against all mosaical observations of Jewish circumcision, new moons, or abstinence from meat, drinks, or any kind of sabbatical ceremonies whatsoever, to be vain and of none effect, and contrary to the Spirit of Christ.

33. Thus you that are enlightened from on high may see that that spiritual wine of the everlasting gospel, in the chosen of God, transmuted all watery ceremonies into its own spiritual substance, even as water being mingled with blood is converted into its own nature.

34. Moreover, since the appearing of the two last witnesses of the eternal Spirit, you may know that all apostolical ordinances imitated by men called ministers of the gospel, are counterfeit apostles, which take upon them to preach, pray, baptize with water, break bread, lay on hands, or any such like, without a commission from on high.

35. Whether for silver, or honour, or a name amongst men, under pretence of conscience unto a God which they truly understand not nor desire to know.

36. From the true God, I say again, you that are spiritual may know that these idol shepherds, and their imaginary formalities, are now become vain and contrary to the heavenly breathings or incomes of the glorious Spirit of our Lord Jesus Christ, god-man glorified.

37. Thus in. what soul soever this divine worship of the true God powerfully appeareth, it immediately transmutes all apostolical formalities into invisible spiritualities of glorious joys,

38. By virtue of an heavenly intercourse between the divine Spirit and the poor soul that is acquainted with his heavenly voice or still motions.

39. Again, if divers men appear as witnesses or prophets immediately sent forth by a powerful commission from the ever-living God, are there not certain divine seals to distinguish between those ambassadors which are infallible and them that are but fallible?

40. My elect brethren, is it not the property of a commissionated witness of Christ Jesus at the first appearance of God unto him, to desire the most high that He would pass him by, and make choice of any other to be his ambassador unto his people?

41. Furthermore, in the manner of his spiritual declarations unto the most wisest natural men, doth he not

appear not only seemingly quite contrary unto the Lord's former witnesses, but also as the most blasphemous, simple, base fellows that ever appeared in the name of the Lord?

42. But of the contrary, for the most part in men that are deceived, is there not a strong desire in their fleshly spirits to be a spiritual witness of the Lord?

43. And upon that account will not the least appearance within them or without them, stir up their spirits to go or run before they were sent?

44. Moreover, for want of a true commission by voice of words from the God of heaven and earth, do they not declare marvellous natural things that shall suddenly come to pass, or spiritual voices of power within them, with many lying signs and wonders suitable unto the nature of man?

45. Through which the most wisest rational men are not only outwitted by them, but subject to become one with them.

46. Furthermore, for want of spiritual declaration to witness in the consciences of the people of pure light, language, and life, that they are from the unerring Spirit, do they not deceive their own intoxicated spirits by taking upon them to act over anew the former actions of the true prophets or witnesses, or high priests of the Holy One of Israel?

47. Doth not this demonstrate those to be the commissionated witnesses of the unerring Spirit, that are endued with a divine gift to write a volume as large as the Bible, and as pure a language as that is, with as much variety of matter, without looking in any writing whatsoever, or having any real contradiction in it?

48. Again, if men are endued with a divine gift to remonstrate the real grounds of the invisible things of eternal glory and shame, appointed for two worlds of people when time is no more, is not this a clear manifestation unto the elect Israelites that those men are the immediate witnesses or prophets of the eternal Spirit?

49. But on the contrary, if men pretend to be prophets, high priests, or kings of Israel, by an immediate power from the eternal Jehovah, and yet are ignorant of the invisible things of eternity,

50. Is not this a clear manifestation unto all that have any divine light in them, that such men are but spiritual counterfeits?

51. If men by a divine gift unto those that have any light of life eternal, shall make an undeniable discovery of all sorts of spiritual counterfeits in the world, is not that a real evidence of the infallibility of their commission from the Holy One of Israel?

52. On the contrary, if men are so far from a true discovery of all spiritual counterfeits that they can show no sensible divine grounds of their own commission from above, is not that a clear manifestation unto all that are truly enlightened, that they are persons under spiritual deceits?

53. If all sober men in

general, upon the perusal of this epistle, shall in their consciences be convinced, that concerning the invisible things of eternity, this is the clearest discovery that ever their eyes beheld, and yet but very few of them shall dare to own the penman thereof, for fear of losing their present enjoyments of fleshly honour, profit, or pleasure amongst men.

54. Is not this a clear demonstration unto the chosen of God, that this book was penned by the infallible witness of the eternal Spirit, in the glorified person of our Lord Jesus Christ;

55. Whom men durst not own when He was on this earth for fear of being excommunicated out of their vain-glorious synagogues, or because of many hard sayings unto man's reason, spoken through his gracious and unerring mouth.

56. So much at present concerning the chosen witnesses, prophets, and apostles, sent forth by the eternal Spirit unto the sons of men, to bear record unto the man Christ Jesus, the Lord from heaven, the only wise God and alone everlasting Father, against all gainsayers that ever were, are, or shall be, from these scripture words: "And there are three which bear witness in the earth, the Spirit, the water, and the blood, and these three agree in one."

57. Crowns of eternal glory are prepared for those men and women, which are not only preserved from despising things that seem strange unto them, but are also made with patience to wait upon the Holy Spirit for his discovery of them.

CHAPTER XXVIII.

1. No reason in angel or men can be satisfied in itself without revelation from the Creator. 2. God created reason. 3. Yet it was not of his own nature. 4. Infiniteness is to create persons and things differing from his own nature. 5. Though all creatures were made by God, yet they came not out of Him but by the word of his power. 6. No creature, spiritual or natural, can be said to be the image of God, but man only. 7. It is the property of reason to promise obedience to God by his prophets, but perform none. 8. Why the angels are called mighty.

AGAIN, because of the endlessness of that serpentine reason in man, continually warring against the innocent dove of plain truth, proceeding from the eternal Spirit of a glorified Christ,

2. Therefore I shall write again concerning the vast difference between the nature of angelical reason and the nature of divine satisfaction in itself, utterly unknown to men or angels, until it be his pleasure to impart the in-shining glimpses thereof into their shallow comprehensions.

3. Though the spirits of the mighty angels are pure reason, yet you that are spiritually quick may know, that their undefiled reason would immediately become all rebellious imagination against the Creator's glory, if it were not continually

supplied with inspirations from his eternal Spirit.

4. Is the nature of the most piercing reason that is, any thing else but mere desire?

5. Where any desire abideth, is there not a want of something desired? And where any thing is wanting, can that Spirit be fully satisfied in itself?

6. Again, seeing the pure spirits of the mighty angels are but rational, and the most excellentest reason that is, but mere desire, and desire a want of inward satisfaction, and where such satisfaction is wanting in itself, there can be no true peace enjoyed, or continuance one moment in its present purity.

7. What spiritual power is there in the most piercing reason that can be?

8. Is it any thing else but a mere desire that it might be partaker with the glorious purity of that Spirit that gave its sensible being?

9. Hath it any power at all to desire after wisdom, love, or any kind of divine excellency in the least from its own rational nature? If this be truth, which no spiritual or sober rational man can deny, are not those men under deep darkness which say, "The divine nature of God himself is pure reason only?"

10. If the most purest reason in its own' nature be nothing else but unsatisfactory desire, is it possible, think you, that Spirit should have one thought or motion of reason inherent in his nature, whose divine virtues are all transcendent satisfaction in itself?

11. Some men may say unto me, "Could the divine majesty create a rational living Spirit, and yet have none of that life or rational nature living in himself?"

12. You may remember I have written upon this point already in the creation of angels; yet, for a further convincing or confounding of that Luciferian reasoning in the learned men of this world, against the infinite power, wisdom, or glory of the Creator, I shall speak somewhat from the Lord Jesus in answer to this curious query.

13. You may know that all things are possible and very easy for an infinite Spirit to bring to pass, when his glory moves Him to do it.

14. You may also know, that though the eternal Spirit be infinite, yet it hath no power to do any thing at all, except his glory moves Him to it, or against its own glory.

15. I confess it is not only contrary to reason, but far above all reason's reach, truly to understand the mysteries of the creation, or redemption of the mighty Jehovah, or everlasting Jesus.

16. What is the height or depth of the purest rational comprehension in men or angels, concerning the glorious things of eternity? Is it any thing else but either strength of memory, or excellency of speech, or swiftness of understanding, in comprehending all words whatsoever, whether they are uttered according to acuteness of sense or no? But for a true

understanding of those heavenly things signified by those divine words, it knoweth nothing at all in the least.

17. You know it is written, "With thee is a well of life, and in thy light shall we see light." Here you see that David did not attribute the sight of that light of the well of life unto his rational comprehension, but unto the divine light which he received from the well of life eternal:

18. So likewise you may understand, that the holy angels themselves do not comprehend that inspired light of life in them by their own rational purity, but by virtue of the glorious incomes themselves, proceeding from the divine nature of the eternal Spirit.

19. So that you that are spiritual may clearly see, that neither men nor angels are capable to comprehend divine truths by any rational comprehension whatsoever:

20. But only by virtue of divine words or motions received from the Spirit of an infinite majesty of all glorious truths which are eternal.

21. If the divine majesty could not, by the power of his word speaking, into some substance distinct from Him, as well create sensible and insensible living beings of variety of natures, contrary to his own heavenly nature, as produce sensible beings of his own divine nature, how could He possibly then be infinite?

22. If the most high God should have inherent in his own Spirit somewhat of every nature that He hath created, how could He then be all variety of nothing but infinite purity in Himself?

23. Or how could there be any spiritual Creator at all, but perishing nature only, as over-wise men blindly imagine?

24. I would gladly have you that are spiritual minded to understand this divine secret, though every thing that have life had its original from the Creator, yet all spirits, whose natures are opposite to the divine glory, were without Him, and not within Him, and so were eternally distinct from his most pure Spirit.

25. From eternity He perfectly foresaw all those spirits alive in their own elements, though they were nothing but senseless confused matter in themselves; and when his divine pleasure moved Him to make them appear into distinct living beings, you may know that it was none of his divine nature, but a powerful word only, commanding those spirits to come forth out of secret death or darkness, and manifest themselves according to their several properties, into distinct living beings, in the visible sight of themselves, and elect men and angels, as manifestations of his eternal decree.

26. Wherefore you know, in the forming of the man Adam it is recorded that God said, "Let us make man in our image;" but you never read or heard that any other creatures were made in the image or likeness of God besides him.

27. You know it is written, that "Christ took not on him the

nature of angels, but the seed of Abraham." Why did not the Creator take on Him the "nature of angels, but the seed of Abraham?" You that are spiritual may know, it was because the one was created or renewed into his own image or spiritual likeness, and the other was in his nature quite contrary to the divine majesty.

28. If the angel's spirits had been of the divine nature, how could it be said that Christ took not on Him the angelical nature.

29. But it may be objected, that those words were spoken in relation to Christ's fleshly part. To that I answer, was not Christ both God and man in one person? And was not his divine Spirit and natural flesh one bodily essence, after his godhead was transmuted into pure manhood?

30. Though the unchangeable glory of the Creator was wholly transmuted into a body of flesh, blood, and bone, that sinful mortals might behold their God face to face, and live;

31. Yet you may know that the nature of his Spirit, in respect of its divine purity, neither was, nor possibly could be, changed, but only his infiniteness was laid down in flesh for a season, for the fulfilling of scripture prophecies.

32. Again, if Christ took not on Him that angelical nature of pure reason, what then, think you, will become of all rational wise men, which understand nothing but what is visible unto the eyes of carnal flesh?

33. If the eternal Spirit of the Creator hath no angelical reason in his divine nature, some men may say unto me, how will you answer that scripture where the Creator saith unto the Jews, "Come, let us reason together?"

34. As to that, you may know, when that scripture was spoken, that the Lord did not talk with the nation of the Jews in his own person, but in the persons of his true prophets, which were sent to convince those stony-hearted Jews, by declaring the glorious God and his spiritual truths unto them, in the balance of their own reason.

35. You know it is written that the Israelitish Jews cried out, "Let not God speak to us any more, lest we die;" and it was granted unto them, that He would not speak unto them any more in his own person, as they desired;" therefore you may know, that the Lord's reasoning with the Jews was only by his prophets, which were rational men, like unto themselves.

36. If the Creator Himself seemeth to reason with any man, is it any other ways but to confound the wisdom of unclean reason in man, by way of query, and such like, as Christ, the only God, often did to the Jews, in the days of his flesh?

37. You know it is written, that "Christ wept over Jerusalem, and the Jewish nation, saying, How often would I have gathered you together, as a hen gathereth her chickens under her wings, and ye would not:" behold, as He was a man, He wept over the unbelief of their bloody-minded spirits, but as He

was a God, He rejoiced at their damnation, in relation unto his eternal decree.

38. Is not this answerable unto those sayings of his, where He calleth them "serpents, and generation of vipers, and children of the devil?" and "How should ye escape the damnation of hell?" and such like.

39. Again, concerning those words, "Ye would not," you that are spiritual may know, that the divine will or pleasure of God in his prophets did spiritually contend with the carnal spirits of the legal Jews, answerable to their cursed imagination, of having power in their own rational wills to do whatsoever He should command them.

40. If the nature of the most purest reason be nothing but unsatisfactory weakness, some men may say unto me, why then doth the scriptures call them Christ's mighty angels? From the true light of life eternal, to this I answer, by a comparison, if men are chosen by the greatest monarch in the world for his society, that they may be always ready to obey his will in whatsoever he shall command them, when they have received a commission from his own mouth, to execute vengeance upon rebels, their towns, cities, or castles, in his dominions, you know they appear mighty or dreadful unto all his people, as the king himself that sent them:

41. So likewise you may know it is not in reference unto the purity of the angels' natures, that they are called mighty angels, but because they were created not only to stand in the personal presence of an infinite majesty, to behold his bright burning glory face to face, but also to be ready to receive commissions from Him to execute vengeance upon the persons, goods, towns, or castles, of Canaanitish rebels, that are left to despise his spiritual government, or glorious truths, declared through the mouths of his chosen messengers.

42. Again, though those men that stand in the presence of the world's monarch, are looked upon as the most mighty nobles on this earth, yet you know that the sight of them is not very dreadful to behold, until men know they have received a commission of life and death from their mighty Lord and master.

43. So likewise, though the holy angels are called. mighty, because they stand in the personal presence of the most infinite majesty of heaven and earth, yet you may know that the sight of them are not very dreadful to behold, until they have received a commission of life and death from their most mighty Lord of heaven and earth.

44. Again, you know that the servants of the most eminent prince are not only looked upon as honourable and mighty persons, because they stand in the presence of so powerful a prince, but also because they inherit a temporal kingdom of such. exceeding vastness, with variety of honour, beauty, riches, or pleasures.

45. So likewise you may also know, that the persons of angels are not only called holy or mighty, because they stand in the visible presence of so infinite a majesty, but also because they inherit a kingdom of such infinite vastness and unspeakable fulness of all variety of ravishing honours, beauties, riches, or pleasures which are eternal.

46. Again, you know that the servants of an earthly monarch, for the magnifying of their Lord and master, in the spirit of his subjects, are clothed not only with ornaments decked with silver, gold, precious stones, or the like, but their bodies also are anointed with precious odours, and fed with the finest delicacies.

47. So likewise, for exalting of the transcendent glory of the infinite God in the spirits of his obedient subjects, you may know that the persons of the elect angels doth not only shine brighter than gold, or any precious stones whatsoever, but their bodies also are anointed with divine odours, and their spirits are fed with glorious delicacies, by virtue of a continual inshining brightness, proceeding from the eternal Spirit that made them.

48. So much at present between the divine nature of the eternal Spirit of undesiring satisfactory fulness in its own personal majesty, and the rational spirits of unsatisfactory desires, dwelling in the spiritual bodies of the elect angels, and why they are called mighty angels.

CHAPTER XXIX.

1. Of the creation of Adam. 2. Why God spake in the plural number in the making of man.

IN the next place I shall treat of the created purity of the first man and woman that ever were made, that the heirs of immortal crowns may the more clearer understand my ensuing discourse. In the first and second chapters of Genesis it is thus written: "Furthermore God said, Let us make man in our image, according to our likeness, and let them rule over the fish of the sea, and over the fowl of the heaven, and over the beasts, and over all the earth, and over every thing that creepeth and moveth on the earth; thus God created the man in his image, in the image of God created he him: he created them male and female. The Lord God also made the man of the dust of the ground, and breathed into his nostrils the breath of life, and the man became a living soul."

2. My beloved spiritual brethren, I do not question your satisfaction concerning the Holy One of Israel, being but only one eternal personal majesty, because not only the ridiculousness of three persons in the Deity is so fully discovered already in this epistle, but because the true ground why the God of glory calleth Himself by a threefold title of Father, Son, and Holy Spirit, is clearly manifested also.

3. Before I write concerning what that image of God in man's creation was, give me leave to reason a little upon those words, "Let us make man in our own likeness."

4. If thou which art so literally acute or exact, do but soberly mind the first and last words of the three scripture texts together, thou canst not possibly but be convinced of thy trinitary error.

5. Concerning those first words, "Furthermore God said," hath not those sayings relation unto the singular number only.

6. Moreover, though God spake in the plural number, "Let us make man in our image, according to our likeness," it doth not therefore follow that the Holy One of Israel can possibly consist of three personal beings in coequal glory, as men vainly imagine.

7. Again, thou which little thinkest that university tongues keep thee under spiritual darkness, whether was it most proper for the glorious Creator to say, "Let us make man in our image, according to our likeness," or to say, "I will make man in my image, according to my likeness."

8. Is not the word us in creation more emphatical, or spiritual order, than the word I in creation?

9. What is thy natural wisdom but rational exactness, whether words bear a good sense, sound, or language, and from thence to imagine the Holy One of Israel to be three personal beings, because He was compelled to speak words in the plural number, in reference unto the glory of his wisdom or counsel, concerning the creating of man in his image or likeness?

10. Again, as in the foregoing words the creation of man was spoken in the plural number of trinitary expressions, "Let us make man in our image, according to our likeness;" so likewise in the following words you may see the plural number converted wholly into the singular number of one divine glorious Being, in those sayings, "Thus God created the man in his image, in the image of God created he him: he created them male and female."

11. Doth not these trinitary expressions themselves, unto all men that have any spiritual light in them, clearly discover the confused darkness of any kind of personal trinity whatsoever?

12. Can three persons in equal power, wisdom, and glory, possibly be but one God?

13. Is not three in number absolutely three? How then, or by what diabolical logic, canst thou make three beings appear to be but one divine essence?

14. Three distinct persons, as beforesaid, cannot possibly be less in number than three gods, unless two of them in number be removed, that there may remain but one personal God alone, that none may share with the Holy One of Israel in his infinite wisdom, power, and glory: if this be not good sense, let men or angels reprove me with better.

15. I have better thoughts of thee, than that thou shouldest

imagine the Creator to be three persons, united together in one divine bulk or being, and to think that He, by his infinite power, might disunite his divine trinity, and send two of them forth for a season unto the sons of men as He saw occasion, and so to return unto the divine essence.

16. I confess these and many such like gross absurdities concerning the Creator, every man is subject unto, until his understanding be enlightened from on high by the Holy One of Israel Himself.

17. Because millions of people lie under deep darkness in many nations, concerning the right understanding of the trinity of the only true God in unity, through the deceit of antiquity of custom, proceeding from the orthodox ministers of the gospel, so called, therefore I am compelled to use many words in this most needful point.

18. If through a sober and meek perusal of this epistle, thou attain to know there is an eternal Being of beings, and truly to understand this glorious Creator to be but one personal majesty, thou wilt then, as clear as the light itself, not only see the miserable confused darkness of those men that say, "There is no God but in men's consciences only," or that say, "There is no God at all but perishing nature:" but thou wilt also see all men that are ignorant of this one personal majesty, which come forth in the name of the Lord, but mere deceived persons, though they speak like oracles or angels.

19. Again, because many upright souls, for want of clear distinction in them of the invisible God of eternal glories, are subject to continual doubts of being deceived through the variety of pretended appearances in his most holy name; therefore in the next place I shall write in a comparative way upon those sayings, " Let us make man in our image, according to our likeness."

20. If a mighty earthly prince have secret thoughts of acting a thing of concernment, in relation to his honour, you know with advice of his privy councillors, it is usual for him to say, "It is our royal pleasure to do such a thing, or we think fit so to do; or let us do such a thing, or we rejoice in your welfare as our own," and such like.

21. So likewise, when the king of glory was moved to create a thing of concernment, from his spiritual privy council, it was most requisite for Him to say, "Let us make man in our image, after our likeness."

22. Again, if he intendeth to do some ordinary thing by virtue of his royal pleasure, in reference to his honour, you know not taking advice of his privy council, he speaketh in the singular number altogether; as, namely, "I will such a thing to be, or let it be so," and such like:

23. So likewise, when the king of glory created things for his honour, that were not of his divine image or likeness, those creatures being at a distance, and of lower concernment, to

him you know he spake altogether in the singular number only, as if he had not formed them from his unsearchable counsel, as, namely, "Let such a thing be, or let it be so," or the like.

24. Again, if a king for his highest honour from his most eminent counsellors, having no heir, is moved to set his royal stamp upon a man, as to be called by the name of the blood royal, and to be the next man in the kingdom to the king, you know the thing being of so near concernment unto him, he thinks he can never speak too much, or home enough in the thing, for the taking upon the spirits of his subjects; therefore he will say, "Let us make such a man our heir, or it is our royal pleasure to make that man our kinsman, and ruler over our whole kingdom, next to ourself," and the like:

25. So likewise, as beforesaid, the creating of man being of the highest and nearest concernment unto the king of glory, that his wonderful wisdom and love in the thing might operate not only upon spiritual men, but also in the mighty angels themselves, the glorious Creator with a fulness of speech from the depth of his invisible counsel said, "Let us make man in our image, or in our likeness," because until man was made He had formed nothing in his own likeness, but the contrary altogether, as abundantly beforesaid.

26. Again, you that are renewed from on high with the image of Christ, may know, that one chief ground that moved the divine majesty to say, "Let us make man in our image," it was because He did eternally purpose to become a spotless man of flesh, blood, and bone Himself:

27. So that the word us had relation unto a twofold condition of that spiritual man the king of glory Himself, therefore they were spoken in the plural number, "Let us make man in our own image," and such like.

28. Another ground why the divine majesty said, "Let us make man in our image," was this, because the glorious Creator Himself from eternity was a spiritual person in the likeness of the man Adam.

29. The chiefest ground of all why the divine majesty said, "Let us make man in our own image," was this, because the infinite majesty and the man Adam was to be of so near a union both spiritually and naturally;

30. Therefore the God of eternal glory was compelled to disrobe Himself of his infiniteness by transmuting of it into flesh on this earth, that from his divine self He might purchase for elect mankind in that body of his flesh, personal crowns of god-like glory in the highest heavens, with Himself and his mighty angels;

31. Heaven descended into earth, that earth might be made capable to ascend into heaven.

32. God Himself became very man, except sin on earth, that very man himself might become the very God in the high heavens, and that elect

mankind, except sin, may be all like God Himself in the heavens also in their several divine measures, at the personal appearing of our Lord Jesus Christ in the clouds of heaven, with all his holy angels.

33. Was not this one end also why the Holy One of Israel spake in the plural number, saying, "Let us make man in our image," that the learned men of this world should not only blind their own eyes, but also become that scarlet whore that sits upon many waters, making the nations continually drunk with their spiritual witchcraft of trinitary merchandising lies, that they may be justly condemned in their own consciences in that day when our Lord Jesus Christ shall say unto them, "Depart from me ye workers of iniquity, I know ye not, or I sent you not; ye preached in my name only for silver and honour among men, and ye persecuted my prophets to the death, because they discovered your learned deceits unto my people; from your own subtle imaginations you made laws to stop all men's mouths as blasphemers, heretics, seducers, deceivers of the people, or disturbers of the civil peace," and such like: that you only might usurp lordship over all men's consciences, persons, and estates, "that could not bow down to your idolatrous inventions; you laid snares to entrap all those that you suspected might impede your vain-glorious decrees; you lived in secret lusts and pleasures upon the ruins of my innocent people, and flattered the ignorant, what pains you took in studying after spiritual things for their souls' health; you made use of my holy name only as a cloak to hide all your subtleties from the deceived people; you blinded their understandings with your sabbatical ceremonies of long prayers, and lifting up your eyes and hands towards heaven, as if you had been purity itself, notwithstanding your hearts were full of covetousness, and your feet swift to shed innocent blood; you offered up your bloody fasts and feasts unto me for a sacrifice of acceptation of your doings, as if I were like unto yourselves, to be persuaded by goodly words to justify all your unrighteousness; you pretended my glory in all your imaginary formalities, but it was your own honour principally you sought from the people, and death unto you to lose it; earthly riches, honour, beauty, unsatiable pleasures, long life, and such like, were your only joys; you have had this your desired paradise already, and my poor people have suffered their hell in your heaven, and now must you suffer your eternal pain and shame, and they must possess everlasting joy and glory."

34. So much, at present, why the God of glory spake in the plural number: in the next place I shall in some measure show what that image of God, in the creating of man, doth signify.

CHAPTER XXX.

1. How God made man in his own image or likeness. 2. The soul of Adam was of the same divine nature of God. 3. Not of the nature of the angels. 4. Of the created virtues in Adam's soul. 5. Adam did not know of his power to stand or fall. 6. The breath of life which Adam had received from God, died.

THE scripture declareth what condition man was formed in, in these words; "Thus God created the man in his image, in the image of God created he him."

2. After the man was completely made in the similitude of his Creator, the scripture tells you then what substance he was created of, in those words, "The Lord God also made the man of dust of the ground, and breathed into his nostrils the breath of life, and the man was a living soul."

3. You that are spiritual may know in the creating of man, that the Lord God spake the word only into the dust of the earth, and immediately the virtue of that word brought forth a living man of pure flesh, blood, and bone, like unto God Himself; as near as possibly could be.

4. It was not the visibility of their persons that differ in the least, but the glory of them only.

5. The one was an infinite spiritual body in all parts perfectly holy, and the other was a finite natural body of perfect innocency, resembling that divine form, as aforesaid.

6. You know I have abundantly showed the impossibility of the least motion of reason to be inherent in the nature of God; therefore I would have you to understand, though Adam's body being made of dust, and appointed for generation, was but natural, yet his soul was not rational, but supernatural, or divine: why? because it was formed according to the invisible glory of the eternal Spirit.

7. Therefore you may understand, that if the soul of Adam had been rational in its creation, then it could not have been divine, but of an angelical desiring nature, only of unsatisfaction in itself.

8. Again, you spiritual ones may understand, that that divine soul in Adam, which was created after the likeness of the eternal Spirit, did consist of several heavenly properties in its measure, answerable unto those divine qualifications in the glorious Creator, above all measure.

9. What were those created virtues in Adam's soul? It was an invisible spiritual light and life, called wisdom, faith, love, righteousness, meekness, patience, and such like.

10. Though his soul could be nothing at all without its several properties, and though those qualifications were all in a heavenly harmony, yet this I would have you take notice of, that joy of soul that Adam did possess, arose in him from one divine voice only, called the spirit of faith, which was all satisfaction in himself with his present condition, not having the least thought of any happiness beyond what he enjoyed already.

11. As the divine nature of the eternal Spirit was variety of infinite satisfaction in itself, so likewise the soul of Adam being composed of the very same qualifications, was variety of heavenly satisfaction in itself also, according to its measure.

12. If the nature of Adam's soul had been rational in his creation, then through want of divine satisfaction in itself, it would always have been desiring after something that he wanted, like unto the elect angels and us, which have two contrary voices in one soul.

13. You may know, that the created nature of the soul of Adam could not possibly have any reason in it; why because the very nature of reason is seriously to consider, whether things be good or right that are propounded unto its understanding or no.

14. But of the contrary, that spirit which without the least consideration perfectly knoweth the excellency of a thing, as soon as ever it is presented unto it, as Adam's did, must needs be divine as God's is, and so superrational, though clothed with pure nature only.

15. Again, though the soul of Adam through the divine purity of its nature was immortal, and uncapable of the least motion of any kind of rebellion against the glorious Spirit of its Creator, yet because his body was natural, and had its beginning of dust, and so was subject to change, or to be changed from its present condition, his immortal soul having its being in a piece of clay, was become subject through temptation to be transmuted from its present created glory also.

16. For this I would gladly have you to understand, though the soul of Adam was of a divine nature, yet, because it was a created nature distinct to itself, it was become a son, a subject, a servant unto its divine God, and capable of transmutation through deep temptation into a sinful condition, through which both soul and body might not only be subject to natural death, but also full of fears of an eternal death, or casting out of the spiritual presence of the divine majesty.

17. To bring forth his heavenly design of a more transcendent eternal glory, that He had prepared through sufferings to be enjoyed by his divine image at the last day with Himself face to face.

18. You that are spiritually quick may know, that the body of Adam was not created natural only, because he was appointed for generation, but also because if his body had been immortal in its creation, as well as his soul, he would not only then have been uncapable of natural generation, but also he would have been uncapable of any kind of transmutation whatsoever, unless he gave consent unto it Himself.

19. And where then had the prerogative power, infinite wisdom, and transcendent glory of the Creator, ever been seen, or known by man or angels, as beforesaid?

20. Again, though Adam's soul was of the divine nature in its creation, yet I would have you to understand that he knew not whether he should stand or fall from his present estate or no.

21. Neither did he know what power he was endued withal in his created purity, as many men vainly imagine:

22. If he had known that he had power in his own will to preserve himself in his present condition, he not knowing as aforesaid, any glory above what he had enjoyed, you may be sure if he could have kept himself in that blessed estate, he would never have lost it for want of making use of all the power that was in him to have resisted a temptation unto rebellion; in which he knew there was a threatening of the loss of that created glory he enjoyed, as beforesaid.

23. Again though the soul of Adam was of the divine nature in its creation, yet because it was one essence with a body that was taken out of dust, therefore it was both probable and capable to be brought into a condition of entering into dead dust for a moment, to fulfil those scripture sayings, "For in the day thou eatest thereof thou shalt die the death; in the sweat of thy face shalt thou eat bread till thou return to the earth, for out of it wast thou taken, because thou art dust, and to dust thou shalt return"

24. Was the body of Adam any thing but dead dust before its living soul was infused?

25. Was the soul of Adam ever spoken of as a sensible living being, before it became one essence with his body of flesh, blood, and bone, formed out of the dust as an house or tabernacle for its comfortable subsistence and sensible understanding of its own living being?

26. Seeing the body of Adam was nothing but a lump of dead, cold, senseless dust, before his soul entered into it, and composed it into a complete living man; by virtue of a spiritual word spoken through the glorious mouth of the Creator: dost thou think it possible that either of them could enjoy any sensible living being without the other?

27. You know the scripture saith, "The Lord God also made the man of the dust of the ground, and breathed into his nostrils the breath of life, and the man became a living soul:" though the body of Adam was formed of dust, you see all the life it enjoyed was from its soul only, "and the man became a living soul."

28. When the Lord said, "For in the day thou eatest thereof thou shalt die the death," was it not the very soul of Adam, as well as his body, that was threatened with death itself?

29. Nay, was there any thing could live in the body of Adam but the soul? what then could be capable of dying, but the soul only?

30. Again, canst thou be so senseless as to think that ever the body of Adam could have turned to dust, if his soul had

not died within his body, and like a spark of fire in an oven that is closed from all kind of air?

31. So likewise thou mayest understand, that the immortal soul of Adam became mortal as soon as ever it was polluted with sin, and when it came to taste of death, according to the word of the Lord, through the stoppage of the breath of life, proceeding from the invisible soul, that fiery spark was quenched with silent sleep of death, as life or light that is smothered, and did not fly in the air, as men vainly imagine.

32. Again, it is said, "The man became a living soul;" now you know that every man's sinful soul is the life of its natural body, yet it may be a dark, dead soul in spiritual matters, while it is alive in natural; but, as beforesaid, the spirit of Adam was called a living soul, in relation unto the living virtue, beauty, or invisible glory of its creation.

33. I confess that it was impossible for the soul of Adam of ever being capable of death; if it had been always preserved from being polluted with sin.

34. Moreover, as soon as ever it was but touched with sin, in that very sin was death itself.

35. Whoever thou art that shalt say that the pure soul of Adam was not defiled with sin itself, whatever light thou pretendest to know, thou art utterly ignorant as yet of the spirit of the scriptures.

36. If according to the divine truth of scriptures, thou art made to confess that the pure soul of Adam was overcome of sin, and therewith all defiled through his whole man, though men or angels should gainsay it, thou mayest be fully assured that both the soul and body of Adam are in the dust of the earth dead asleep, void of all life, light, motion, heat, or any thing appearing unto life, until that second man, Adam, the Lord from heaven, by the mighty power of his word, doth or shall raise him again, and all mankind that are asleep with him in the dust, at the last day.

37. Again, though the body of the man Adam being formed of dust, was absolutely natural, through its appointment for generation, yet I would have you that are spiritual to understand this secret, that until Eve lusted after Adam, through her being first defiled with the angelical serpent, the soul of Adam being divine, and free from all kind of rationality, could not possibly have any desire in it after carnal copulation with his wife.

38. You may know that carnal pleasures were too low for a spiritual soul, whose nature was variety of divine satisfaction in itself.

39. Though the woman Eve, through the permission of God, was first guilty of the transgression of lust, and so tempted her innocent husband to lie with her, to cover her folly, if it had been possible, yet because her soul was of the divine nature in its creation, as Adam's was, you may know that that carnal desire in her towards

her husband, proceeded not from her own divine purity, but from the rational nature of the unclean serpent within her, as I shall clearly demonstrate when I come to treat of the manner of her being overcome by the subtlety of that angelical serpent.

40. Thus, though the bodies of Adam and Eve were both natural, and so were capable of lust to bring forth generations, yet you may know, that the secret wisdom of God saw it most fit, that neither Adam nor Eve should be first capable to know what it was to desire after carnal copulation from their own divine spirits, but from that serpentine unclean spirit, that entered into the body of Eve.

41. So much at present why God said, "Let us make man in our image, according to our likeness," and what that image of God was in the creating of man.

CHAPTER XXXI.

1. Of the seed of the woman. 2. Of the seed of the serpent. 3. How sin came into man's nature. 4. No angel cast out of heaven but that one which deceived Eve. 5. No true knowledge of the scriptures but in the knowledge of the two seeds. 6. No speech could proceed from any but from the angel.

IN the next place I shall write of the angelical serpent, and of the manner of his beguiling of innocent Eve.

2. In the twelfth chapter of Revelation, verse 9, it is thus written: "And the great dragon, that old serpent called the devil and Satan, was cast out, which deceiveth all the world, he was cast out into the earth, and his angels were cast out with him." Seeing the scriptures make mention of an old serpent dragon devil and his angels, some men may say unto me, was there many angels cast from heaven into the earth together, or but one only? and, if there were but one or many, where are those angels now become?

3. From a divine gift received from the unerring Spirit, to this I answer, as there was but one man Adam cast out of his heavenly paradise of created purity of soul and body, and all his generation were cast out of their spiritual peace with him,

4. So likewise there was but one angelical serpent cast from his created rational purity, and that was that serpent devil which deceived Eve.

5. The angels which were cast out with him, were of his seed or generation, through his union with the entrails of Eve, as I shall make manifest in the ensuing discourse.

6. My beloved spiritual brethren, because my soul desireth your perfection as my own,

7. Therefore would I gladly have you possessed with an infallible understanding between Michael and his angels, and the dragon and his angels; or between the seed of the woman, and the seed of the serpent; why because in the knowledge of these two distinct seeds, sons, or generations, depends a general

understanding of the spirit of the scriptures.

8. Wherefore, in the second chapter of Genesis, verse 17, you shall find it is thus written: "But of the tree of knowledge of good and evil thou shalt not eat of it, for in the day that thou eatest thereof thou shalt die the death."

9. If you look in the third chapter of Genesis, verses 4-6, with a spiritual eye, then you may clearly see what that tree of knowledge of good and evil did signify; the words are these, "Then the serpent said to the woman, ye shall not die at all, but God doth know that when ye shall eat thereof, your eyes shall be opened, and ye shall be as gods, knowing good and evil. So the woman seeing that the tree was good for meat, and that it was pleasant to the eyes, and a tree to be desired to make one wise, took of the fruit thereof, and did eat, and gave also to her husband with her, and he did eat."

10. My elect spiritual brethren, you know it is a general opinion amongst learned men, that the serpent which appeared unto Eve was one of the beasts of the field, which the Lord God had made.

11. And that the devil was an invisible spirit, which entered into the body of the serpent, and spake those subtle speeches through his mouth;

12. And so caused the woman to eat of the fruit of a natural tree, which the Lord God had forbidden, and tempting her husband to eat of that fruit with her, it operated that venemous

evil in them and all mankind.

13. Behold the gross darkness abiding in the spirits of the learned men of this perishing world.

14. You know that the scriptures are generally expressed in natural terms for the manifestation of spiritual things, to the weak comprehension of sinful mortals;

15. And natural wise men would persuade men to understand them exactly in the letter, because they measure the glorious things of eternity, by their rational learning only, as beforesaid.

16. In scripture records you know that Christ is called a lion, a lamb, a stone, a door, a way, a vine, a green tree, and such like expressions, in reference unto spiritual meanings.

17. Also you know that evil-minded men are sometimes called by the names of devils, dragons, vipers, serpents, fruitless trees, and such like, according to that of John the Baptist, when he said, "Now the axe is laid unto the root of the tree, every tree therefore that bringeth not forth good fruit, is hewn down and cast into the fire," Matt. iii. 10.

18. So likewise you that are spiritual may know, that that angelical reprobate by whom Eve was deceived, was called a dragon, an old serpent, the devil, and Satan, a deceiver or "the tree of knowledge of good and evil," and such like names suitable unto his cursed nature.

19. But the very truth is this, that serpent that tempted Eve

was that angelical dragon devil beforesaid, which the Lord God from the highest heavens cast down to the lowest earth.

20. And it was his seeming divine wisdom, and angelical person, that bewitched Eve's innocent soul to hearken unto him, and her eyes to dote upon him:

21. For you know that Eve had three considerations in her before she was overcome to consent unto the serpent's language;

22. First, "The tree was good for meat." Secondly, "It was pleasant to the eyes." And thirdly, "It was a tree to be desired to make one wise."

CHAPTER XXXII.

1. The condition of Adam and Eve in their fall. 2. The angel called a serpent. 3. He was more comely in Eve's eyes than Adam. 4. How the fallen angel became flesh. 5. How God became flesh.

BEFORE I write of the three secrets hid in the angelical temptation, I shall speak a little of the dispensation of the secret wisdom of God td his chosen ones.

2. You that are spiritual may know, that in the divine will of the infinite majesty is a twofold operation, which is this: "When his wisdom seeth fit to reveal a divine secret to his elect, then his Holy Spirit is all active, and when he seeth fit to obscure it from them, then his divine Spirit is all passive."

3. For the manifestation of his infinite power and wisdom, you know, that He can create light out of darkness, and life out of death, with a glorious advantage:

4. You know that if the glorious Creator, for trial of his creature, should leave the most experimental man that is to his own inspired light, and suffer him to be tempted unto that evil of adultery or murder, and overcome thereby, he must of necessity lose that former joy and peace of the divine light, or love of God in him;

5. And in the room thereof, both See and feel nothing but spiritual darkness, with a secret fear of eternal death,

6. Until the light of life appears again, with a new assurance of a glorious deliverance from that sinful darkness and fearful death, as aforesaid.

7. Truly, whatever men shall imagine to the contrary, as sure as there is a God, this was the condition both of Eve and Adam also, when they were deified with unlawful lust one towards another, by subtle temptation of that serpent's counsel, called "The tree of knowledge of good and evil."

8. Again, though it is said, "It was a tree to be desired to make one wise," yet you may know that the soul of Eve was not of a desiring nature after wisdom in her creation, because she was all divine satisfaction in herself:

9. Therefore that desire of tasting of the fruit of a tree to make her wise as gods, to know both good and evil, proceeded

only from the rational nature of the unsatisfied spirit of the angelical serpent.

10. For this I would have you to understand, at that time Eve was tempted to evil by the serpent, she was wholly left to her own strength;

11. And it was the seeming glory of his angelical language that overtopped her present light, and begot that desire in her understanding, through which her soul was moved with a powerful desire to make trial of his serpentine counsel, and to taste of his spiritual meat so highly exalted by him:

12. Because to her received new thoughts, she had not heard so glorious a language before.

13. Again, "The tree was pleasant for sight;" truly before that glittering serpent appeared, Eve wanted no satisfaction in beholding the man Adam,

14. But she looking a little too long upon the comeliness of his form, through his infused witchcraft, her soul was ravished with the sight of his angelical person.

15. Again, "It was a tree whose fruit was to be desired to make one wise as gods, to know both good and evil." My beloved spiritual brethren, the pretended meaning of the serpent in those words was this; if she did but taste of the fruit of that tree, it was so full of divine virtue, that she should not only be like unto God, but she should be as God to herself;

16. Also to know all that was to be known, whether good or evil, within her own soul; but the truth is, his secret intent was this, that when she had tasted of that forbidden fruit, she should with him both know and feel in her own spirit the difference between light and darkness, life and death, love and envy, peace and war, good and evil, or God and devil.

17. Since Eve, the natural mother of all mankind, was overcome by lust, through the subtlety of the serpent, hath not many a poor innocent virgin, or virgin-wife, been deceived in like manner through the comeliness of men's persons, and their serpentine languages, by persuading them that they loved them above their own lives, and of giving them such content they know not of, or if they deny them, it will be their death.

18. Moreover, by telling them all men are but one man, and all women are but one woman, and therefore it was pure liberty to be free unto all; and that they are in the greatest bondage which are united to one only,

19. I say, hath not these and such like cursed counsels occasioned many an innocent soul to betray their virginity, or virgin-bed, unto their perpetual sorrow, and shame afterwards?

20. Truly, my Christian friends, this was the virgin-wife Eve's very case, though it may seem strange at the first unto many that shall read this epistle:

21. You know the scripture saith, that "She seeing the tree to be good for meat, and pleasant to the eyes, and a tree to be desired to make one wise, took of the fruit thereof, and did

eat;" that is, when the innocent soul of Eve was overpowered with the serpent's subtle language, as beforesaid, her spirit did consent unto him to come in unto her, and take full possession of her to be her God and guide, instead of her Creator.

22. Truly, in this case, the virgin Eve's condition may fitly be compared unto the Virgin Mary.

23. You know after the angel had told her that without knowing of man she should be with child, through the power of the most high overshadowing of her; how easily was she intreated, not only to have it so, but also how exceedingly did her soul rejoice with the very tidings thereof?

24. If men look with a spiritual eye between their angelical salutations, they may see more seeming glorious enjoyments in the unclean angel's greeting of Eve, than in the holy angel's saluting of Mary.

25. Though men or angels should gainsay it, from the spirit of truth itself, I shall declare the very sense of this secret in plainness of speech, which was this:

26. As soon as ever Eve's soul, through the permissive power of God, was overcome to consent to the serpent's cursed counsel, his angelical person entered into her womb through her secret parts;

27. And being united to her soul and body, his serpentine nature dissolved itself into her pure seed, and defiled her throughout, and so became essentially one with her, through which, naturally, she conceived a serpent dragon devil into a man-child of flesh, blood, and bone, and brought forth her first-begotten son of the devil, yea, the very dragon servant devil himself, and called his name, according to his nature, Cain, or cursed, though ignorantly she said she had received a man from the Lord.

28. So likewise of the contrary, the womb of the virgin-wife Mary was honoured with the only wise angelical God Himself;

29. Through which her polluted nature was not only cleansed, whilst He was in her womb;

30. But also, by virtue of the divine power, she was enabled to conceive his glorious majesty of her seed into an holy babe of unspotted flesh, blood, and bone, and in his season to bring forth her first-begotten Son of God:

31. Yea, the true God and everlasting Father Himself, and call his name, according to his nature, Emmanuel, Jesus, or blessed.

32. So that you which are inwardly baptized with the true knowledge of the Holy One of Israel, may see in some measure what is meant by the two scripture seeds, the angelical devil first became a man-child, and the angelical God afterwards became a man-child.

33. Thus the most Holy God abased Himself in the very womb of a woman, that He might first or last destroy, the power of that serpentine reason, or lying imagination, in all his elect Israel-

ites.

CHAPTER XXXIII.

1. What form the devil was of before he tempted Eve. 2. Spiritual bodies do not change their forms, but their glories. 3. Spirits can take up no bodies but their own. 4. The forbidden fruit was not an apple, or any other fruit that could be eaten with the teeth.

IT is written, "But God giveth it a body as it pleaseth him, even to every seed his own body," 1 Cor. xv. 38.

2. My spiritual friends, according to the truth of the letter, you may see, that by the decreed word of the Creator, every seed or spirit naturally bringeth forth its own body or likeness in its season.

3. Thus it was with the serpent-angel when he tempted Eve; he was not a homely beast, as men vainly imagine from their beastly reason;

4. But he was a spiritual body, and appeared unto Eve in form like unto a glorious God or man.

5. For this I would have you to understand, whose souls are fixed upon a substantial glory to come, though the spiritual bodies of God or angels be transmuted into natural bodies, or though the mortal bodies of men be changed into immortality, yet the form of their persons are never altered, but the beauty or glory of them only.

6. But some men may say unto me, is any thing hard for the Lord? or can He not appear in any form, or transmute his creature into any shape whatsoever, after He hath formed him?

7. To this I answer, from the truth itself, the Creator can do whatsoever his divine wisdom seeth fit.

8. Now in his wisdom He foresaw that his infinite power and wonderful glory would most apparently be seen by elect men and angels, in a comely ordering the things that He should make.

9. So that all creatures from eternity appeared most amiable in his eyes, that in time were to bring forth their own bodies, according to their kind.

10. Wherefore, when any monster is born, you may know it is either through unnatural mixing of seeds together, or it is some judgment answerable to some wicked act; or else it is a forerunner of some strange or dreadful thing that is to fall upon the heads of monstrous minded men or women., which abhor the very name of a personal majesty,

11. For our God is the God of all spiritual and natural order, and not of magical confusion.

12. This truth will be an eternal witness in the consciences of all Canaanitish lying devils, which say, "When the body of man turns to its dust, the soul is swallowed up into the eternal ocean, or else it appeareth in some other form, as, namely, a horse, or an ass, or a dog, or a root, or a flower," or such like.

13. My beloved spiritual bre-

thren, from whence, think you, proceedeth this, and all such like errors 1 truly only from some secret lusts men are in bondage unto, which are as dear to them as their very lives:

14. Therefore they are afraid of appearing again in the bodies of men, lest they should reap the fruit of all their former filthiness. "Blessed are the purified spirits, for they shall see their God eternally face to face."

15. Again, it is written, that "She gave also to her husband with her, and he did eat:" that is, being full of natural lust from that serpent within her, she by her angelical speeches did entice her husband to lie with her, and so he was defiled also with her.

16. But it may be objected, that the woman was made for that very end for procreation of mankind; therefore it seemeth something strange that natural lust should be that sin of eating the forbidden fruit, or tree of knowledge of good and evil.

17. To this I answer, it is truth the woman was formed for that very end, and in her seed was the very law of generation:

18. But she was defiled in spirit and body by another, to her own knowledge, before she was capable to know what it was to desire her own husband;

19. And the truth is, as aforesaid, she immediately desired him to hide her known rebellion against her Creator.

20. Besides all this, knowing herself first in the transgression, her conscience told her ' that she ought not to have ensnared her innocent husband, to hide her folly:

21. But to have waited for the issue of her own doings; I mean the birth of that serpentine cursed Cain in her womb, before she had desired the lawful knowledge of her own husband.

22. Again, if you that are sober do but seriously ponder it in your spirits, you cannot be so weak as to think that the law of eternal life and death depended upon the eating of an apple from a natural tree;

23. For you know that the Lord "caused the earth to bring forth all variety of fruit to be eaten by the mouth," principally as a superfluity of delight to the taste of man only:

24. Therefore how can sober men imagine or think, that the souls and bodies of all mankind should be so venomed through the eating of an apple?

25. As sure as the Lord liveth, it was such a devilish apple that was eaten by Eve, that it hath and will bring forth many millions of serpent dragon-devils, in forms of men and women, unto eternal condemnation.

26. Again, you know it is written, that Christ said unto his apostles, "Perceive ye not yet that whatsoever entereth into the mouth goeth into the belly, and is cast into the draught; but those things which proceed out of the mouth come from the heart, for out of the heart cometh evil thoughts, murders, adulteries, fornications, thefts, false testimonies, slanders; these are the things which defile the mans," Matt. xv.

27. My spiritual brethren, I

hope ere this you see that it was not a natural apple eaten by Eve's mouth, and so passing through the belly into the draught, that defiled her whole man.

28. For if our God and only Saviour be all truth, as He is, and cannot possibly lie, then "that which is eaten by the mouth of man goeth into his belly, and is cast into the draught without defiling his soul:" so that without controversy, that fruit or apple taken and eaten, or received by Eve and Adam, through which they were wholly defiled, shamed, and fearfully tormented, never came into their mouths or teeth, as literal wise men vainly imagine;

29. But, as beforesaid, it was a spiritual eating of the serpent angel in the innocent mouth of Eve's soul, by her unlawful lusting after her innocent husband, that knew nothing of the thing, that he might cover her iniquity, or when she was called to an account, help to bear her burden.

30. Again, it is written, "The kingdom of heaven consists not in meats and drinks;" also it is written, "Whatsoever is sold in the shambles, eat, making no question for conscience sake." Furthermore it is written, "There is nothing unclean in itself, but as it is so esteemed, for the earth is the Lord's, and the fulness thereof;" in these and many such like scripture sayings, is it not as clear as the light itself, that whatsoever was made might freely be eaten, so that it were moderately taken?

31. So likewise, whatsoever was created at the first for man's eating with his mouth, was absolutely pure and very good for that end it was made; but of the contrary, that fruit or tree of knowledge of good and evil, eaten of by Eve, was not only full of tormenting spiritual venom to her former peace of soul, but it caused her very body also to be subject unto all manner of mortal diseases;

32. Besides a secret fear of eternal death, which was worst of all, until the voice of God, in the garden of her soul, quieted her wounded spirit, with a gracious promise of a glorious deliverance, through his appearance in a body of flesh, in that saying, "The seed of the woman shall break the serpent's head."

CHAPTER XXXIV.

1. The tree of knowledge of good and evil was no natural tree. 2. What it was. 3. Whence the originality of sin came.

IN the first chapter of Genesis I it is thus written: "And God said, Behold, I have given unto you every herb bearing seed, which is upon all the earth, and every tree wherein is the fruit of a tree bearing seed, that shall be to you for meat: and God saw all that he had made, and, lo, it was very good."

2. If thou which readest this point dost but view this place of scripture with sobriety of spirit,

thou canst not then be but convinced of the gross absurdity of the learned men of this world, that have long imagined the tree of knowledge of good and evil to be a natural tree bearing apples or such like fruit.

3. Again, "If every green herb upon all the earth, and every tree wherein is the fruit of a tree bearing seed," were given unto Adam and Eve for their food, according to what is here written, and that God that gave it them saw all that He had made to be very good, how then can any sober man possibly imagine or think, that the tree of knowledge of good and evil could be of this creation, though it appeared unto Eve upon this earth, seeing all the trees that God had made in this earth, was very good in his sight as aforesaid?

4. This I would fain know from the learned, whether this earth was capable of any curse, or any natural thing that grew in it, before Eve had eaten of the forbidden fruit?

5. If the earth was blessed, and all that was created in it, until Eve had rebelled against the Creator, then without controversy, whatever venomous creatures, trees, or herbs there are, or any thing else that is hurtful to the nature of man, upon the account of eating with the mouth, they had no being in this creation until Eve had transgressed.

6. Therefore that tree of life in the midst of the garden, and the tree of knowledge of good and evil, could not possibly be trees bearing natural apples, as hath been long imagined.

7. But they were trees of higher concernment than of eating their fruit with the mouth, and casting of it into the draught.

8. Do not all men that have any true light in them, look upon the tree of life, from the beginning of Genesis unto the end of the Revelation, to be nothing else but the spiritual person of that Lord Jesus Christ, who is the only ever-living God from whence floweth all living waters into the garden of Eden, who are the spiritual trees of eternal glory?

9. Do not those men that are of a sound judgment in the things of eternity, look upon that tree of knowledge of good and evil, to be the outcast unclean person of that serpent dragon devil, which, through essential union with Eve, became that murdering, lying, cursed Cain, through which the spirits of the elect Israelites are all defiled, as well as the Canaanitish reprobate trees of eternal death, until they are watered anew from the glorious tree of life eternal, as beforesaid?

10. But, alas, in this confused age of seeming lofty light, instead of a true understanding of the spiritual trees of eternal life, and the carnal trees of eternal death, spoken of in scripture records, do not many atheistical-minded men in these our days, endeavour with all their might to convert the glorious truths of the ever-living Jesus into nothing but brain fancies of notional

lying vanities

11. Is it not become a second nature unto them for silver or honour, to deceive their own souls, by flattering their poor deceived brethren, lying under the power of many filthy lusts, that all their sins shall be burnt up, but their souls shall be swallowed up into the eternal Being?

12. Suppose the forbidden fruit had been a natural apple, the Creator's nature being all purity itself, and the soul of Eve being of his divine image, if the forbidden tree was pure in its nature also before it was touched by Eve, whence then came that sin upon the spirit of Eve, seeing all things that was made in this creation was very good at the first, as is clearly proved by the scripture records already?

13. This I am sure of, that no man that is sober neither will, nor dare say, that that evil proceeded from the Creator's forbidding her to touch the tree or its fruit; neither could that sin possibly proceed from the soul of Eve, because it was of the divine nature in its creation.

14. And if that tree and its fruit eaten of by Eve were of this creation, how could there possibly be any evil in its nature either, seeing every thing and tree that was formed in this world, was made very good at the first in the pure eyes of the Creator, as abundantly beforesaid.

15. But some men may say unto me, though the eternal Spirit of the divine majesty was uncapable of the least motion of evil, through the infinite purity of its spiritual nature, yet sin being but a defect of nature, may it not originally rise out of the soul of Eve, though it was purely created, and for want of a Creator's infinite power in itself for its own preservation?

16. From the light of life eternal to this I answer, as for the originality of sin, it is both granted and clearly demonstrated already, in that secret of the creation of angels beforesaid, that the root of all evil sprung from the nature of the unsatisfied angelical reprobate, through the absenting of the Creator's inspiring glorious excellencies to him:

17. But, on the contrary, it is against all spiritual or rational truth that is sober, that the least motion of evil could possibly have its original from the divine spirits of Eve or Adam;

18. Therefore much less out of any kind of apple-tree, or any other wooden trees, herbs, or plants, which were made for man's natural comfort or delight only;

19. For this I would have you to understand, though the souls of Adam and Eve were but finite created beings, yet because they were of the same nature of Him that made them, their spirits were as free from all kind of desire after wisdom or any thing else, as the Creator Himself; for, as beforesaid, where any desire is, there is a want, and the least want that is must needs be a defect or weakness in nature, which being not immediately satisfied, it is subject to become nothing but evil.

20. Wherefore from a divine gift received from on high, I affirm against men or angels, that that first desire of sin in the soul of Eve, proceeded not from the nature of her own spirit, but from the unclean spirit of the unsatisfied serpent's language spoken into her.

21. For you that are spiritually quick may know, that there appeared no kind of desire or lust in the soul of Eve towards Adam, until she had tasted of the forbidden fruit; and if that fruit had been an apple, is it not very strange that Adam should be ignorant of it until his wife had found it out, seeing all the trees in the garden which the Lord God had made, were very good, and given them for food?

22. Moreover, whoever thou art, after the perusal of this truth, shalt call this nonsense, blasphemy, heresy, lies, and such like, because it discovereth thy darkness, is it not a clear testimony in thy own conscience, that thou art one of the cursed brood of the old serpent devil beforesaid, which art not able to endure the light, because by it thy deeds are manifested to be evil?

23. Again, though I know I have written sufficiently concerning this truth already, unto all that are of a quick comprehension, yet, for the satisfying of the lambs of Christ, and for a further convincing of all gainsaying wolves, I shall go on to the utmost in the further clearing of this truth of so high concernment unto mankind.

CHAPTER XXXV.

The curse was not pronounced upon any natural beasts, but the fallen angel.

WHEREFORE in the third chapter of Genesis you may find it thus written: "Then the Lord God said to the serpent, because thou hast done this, thou art cursed above all cattle, and above every beast of the field; upon thy belly shalt thou go, and dust thou shalt eat all the days of thy life; I will also put enmity between thee and the woman, and between thy seed and her seed; he shall break thy head, and thou shalt bruise his heel." My spiritual brethren, can any of you, upon mature consideration, possibly imagine that that serpent was a natural beast that was pronounced cursed by the Lord, for some evil deed done unto innocent Eve

2. If it were an evil spirit that spake through the serpent's mouth, can any sober man think that the most wise Creator would have pronounced a curse upon the brute beast and his seed, if the evil that was done to Eve proceeded only from the devil within the body of that serpent?

3. Can you find in any place of scripture, that ever the Lord charged any evil spirit or devil with that deed done unto Eve, but that serpent that spake unto her?

4. Therefore, whatever men vainly dream of apples pulled from wooden-trees, or of a natural serpent, or of an evil spirit in the body of an ignorant

beast, or any such like imaginary stuff concerning the deceiving of Eve, yet you that are truly enlightened from on high may know, that that serpent by whom Eve was beguiled, was that angelical reprobate cast down from the kingdom of glory beforesaid, into this perishing world.

5. Moreover, you may understand also, that the serpent angel deceived Eve upon a spiritual account, and not upon a natural account: because you know that she was ignorant of that poor and low thing of lusting after a man, until she had obeyed that serpent's voice;

6. Therefore, when the Creator denounced that curse upon the serpent and his seed, that angelical serpent was within the womb of Eve, and not without her.

7. And the Lord called him a serpent, only because of his exceeding subtlety to deceive.

8. Concerning the serpent's going upon his belly, and eating dust all the days of his life, if that had been a natural serpent so threatened by the Creator, was he not as well as if he had enjoyed legs to go, and the choicest of things to eat, seeing the one was become as natural to him as the other?

9. Of what concernment was that to the woman for a natural serpent to be cursed by the Lord? Doth any man or woman heed serpents upon that account, or any other whatsoever?

10. Moreover, suppose that curse had been denounced against an evil spirit distinct from the soul and body of Eve, what hurt would that have been unto Eve or Adam, or their generation?

11. Or who regards a curse upon any devil in the least, so that he himself be not that evil spirit or devil so cursed?

12. Concerning the enmity put between the woman and the serpent, and their seed, I would fain know from any sober man, whether there might not be as much enmity between Eve and a she-bear as a natural serpent?

13. Is it not believed by all men that are possessed with the true light, that that Christ Jesus, recorded in holy writ to be the Son of God according to the Spirit, and the Son of man according to the flesh, was that heavenly seed of the woman here spoken of?

14. Moreover, was not this Jesus conceived of the virgin's seed into flesh, blood, and bone, by the eternal Spirit? and was He not pronounced blessed when He was in the virgin's womb?

15. Furthermore, are not all his spiritual seed of elect mankind pronounced blessed with Him also, as the offspring of the most high God, and heirs of immortal crowns of eternal glory?

16. Doth not the scripture records throughout make a distinction between two seeds or generations of mankind?

17. And do they not attribute names unto them according to their several natures?

18. Moreover, doth not the scriptures make mention of a

day of judgment, both for the dead and the quick? And doth it not frequently speak of an eternal personal glory, and its habitation prepared for some, called by the titles of "elect and precious jewels, chosen ones, sons of gods, saints, the blessed of the Lord," and such like?

19. Doth not the scriptures also speak of an everlasting shame of personal fiery death in utter darkness, ordained for others, and their place of residence?

20. And doth it not ascribe titles unto them according to their natures; as, namely, "devils, dragons, serpents, vipers, sons of Belial, cursed children," and such like?

21. Again, if the Lord Jesus Christ was that angelical God which became that blessed Son of the virgin, promised to Adam and Eve after their transgression, the which none can deny after so clear a demonstration of the scripture seeds as this is, except they be reprobate; then, without controversy, that serpent which was cursed for his evil deed was not without her, but within her, when he received that sentence by the mouth of the Lord; and that seed or first-born of Eve, called Cain, was that cursed serpent-angel himself clothed with flesh, blood, and bone, in the form of a man:

22. Who not being able to endure the sight of righteous Abel, that blessed seed, or Son of God, answerable unto that curse of enmity denounced against him in the womb of Eve, his spirit was restless until he had manifested himself to be that old serpent, murdering, lying devil, and the father of all Canaanitish murdering-minded men and women, so frequently spoken of in scriptures, "Not as Cain, which was of that wicked one, and slew his brother," 1 John iii. 12. "He that soweth the good seed is the Son of man, and the field is the world, and the good seed are the children of the kingdom, and the tares are the children of that wicked one, and the enemy that soweth them is the devil," Matt. xiii. 37.

CHAPTER XXXVI.

1. Of the mind of the Spirit in the word eating of the tree of knowledge of good and evil. 2. No true interpretation of the scriptures but by immediate inspiration. 3. Reason not capable of the mysteries of God, 4. But faith only. 5. No devils but men and women. 6. No devil, without man tempteth any, 7. But the seed or lust of his own spirit.

WHAT is the mind of the Spirit by that word, "eating of the tree of knowledge of good and evil?" From the light of life eternal to this I answer, the most wise Creator called it eating, for several respects:

2. First, you may be sure that the Lord God called it eating, that neither men or angels should know his secrets until it was his divine pleasure, that He might receive the praise and glory alone from all those that He should reveal them unto.

3. The Spirit of God called it eating, because of the civility of that speech: for the scripture-language is much like to a modest pure virgin, who is loath to have her secret parts mentioned in the least, though they are as usefully in their kind, and as honourable, being undefiled, as any part of the body.

4. And why are they honourable? Because the only Lord of all life and glory hath honoured them Himself by his blessed birth.

5. Moreover, you know, if a spiritual or natural thing be propounded to the understanding of a. man or woman, of which they have had no experience, their spirit feeds upon it, and considers the pleasure of it as much as possible may be, before they consent to taste of it with the whole man.

6. So likewise in the word eating, you may know that the meaning of the Spirit of God was this, that the soul of Eve should beware of hearkening unto any other voice that was contrary unto that divine image, or voice of the Spirit of God within her; so that if she should hear the voice of a stranger, she should not give way in the least unto that voice, lest she should be overcome therewith.

7. Again, if the Spirit of God, instead of saying unto Eve, "Thou shalt not eat thereof," should have said, "Thou shalt not spiritually or naturally lust after any God or angel, but be content with what I have appointed for thee;" then,

indeed, there would have been no need of any interpretation upon the words, but, as beforesaid, the wisdom of God saw it most fit to act otherwise.

8. Therefore, whatever the learned men of this world dream of finding out the invisible things of eternity, by searching into the scripture records, and comparing them together, the divine majesty hath locked up all the principal secrets of the scriptures in his own spiritual breast, that He, by an immediate inspiration, may dispose of them into the spirits of elect men and angels, most advantageous for his own glory and their consolation.

9. Therefore the sacred scriptures run not in the line of reason, but in the line of faith, inspiration, or revelation, according to those sayings in the Hebrews and other records.

10. By faith, the divine work of creation, and wonderful mystery of redemption, was and is known with the immortal eternal glory and everlasting shame of men's persons in the end of the world.

11. But of the contrary, you shall never read in any place of scripture, that any man knew the things of eternal glory in the least, by any kind of rational comprehension whatsoever.

12. I confess the natural reason of man is a very good handmaid, if it be well qualified with the spiritual dame of divine faith, for illustrating of the things of God unto weak comprehensions:

13. But as for truly understanding the invisible things of

God by the highest reason that ever was in man or angel, it is utterly impossible, as abundantly beforesaid.

14. Why, because though the spirits of reason were never so pure, yet you may know its nature is but desire only after the knowledge of the divine nature of that Spirit from whence it had its living being.

15. But of the contrary, spiritual truth or faith, being of the very divine nature of God Himself, in what soul soever that heavenly seed is sown, it springeth up in that spirit with variety of glorious consolations, in reference unto life eternal, by virtue of an intercourse with the eternal Spirit from whence it came.

16. Moreover, I confess that a man that is endued with a Solomon-like gift of natural reason, may be able to comprehend all words, whether they are spoken in a good form, sense, or language, or no; and to be mighty in disputes about the glorious things of eternity.

17. But as for his real understanding whether there were any such eternal things or no, he hath no certain knowledge of that at all, but his bare thoughts only, which, equally weighed in that balance, it may be true, or it may be false; and all this is for want of an infallibility of truth itself.

18. Therefore, though the divine things of the eternal majesty be nothing else but spiritual purity of infallible truth in themselves, yet, unto that rational wise man, they are nothing but nonsensical blasphemy or lying tales, till his reason is confounded in him by a true and heavenly faith.

19. Again, if there should be any evil angels or devils living in the air, and a devil amongst them, called Beelzebub, the prince of devils, what need any man trouble himself with the least fear of eternal death, whatsoever wickedness is committed by him; because, if a man is tempted to evil by any devil but what is in his own nature only, that evil spirit is to be eternally damned, and the man to be set free.

20. Nay, moreover, if sin or evil issued not from man's unclean reason, or lying imagination within him, is it possible, think you, that any man should be so tormented as some men are, with an inward burning, through a secret fear of eternal sufferings rising in them from the guilt of former evils, committed against the light of conscience?

21. Furthermore, seeing all men which live after the flesh must die or perish, and that man's own lust is that imaginary devil from whence proceeds all sin or evil, without controversy, though men or angels should gainsay it, there are now no other evil spirits, angels, or devils, but unmerciful men and women only.

22. Again, if envy, pride, covetousness, hypocrisy, lust, and such like, be the devil in man, are not men and women those devils that are under the power of those evils? I would fain know,

from the learned men of this world, whether there any other evil angels or devils besides mankind, that lust after women, or silver, or honour, or revenge, or any kind of evil whatsoever.

23. Truly, if those supposed wise men, which talk so much of the subtlety of the prince of the air, that rules in the children of disobedience, could possibly know that their own imaginary reason was that evil spirit, or prince of all their airy disputes concerning God, angels, devils, heaven, hell, eternal glory, or shame to come, which they know not of, according to truth,

24. Then, instead of their rejoicing in the approbation of many men, in relation unto their natural gifts, their own spirits would immediately become the principle of all those howling, groaning, serpent-devils spoken of in holy writ, even in the sight of elect men and angels in this mortal life.

25. Again, is it not against all spiritual or rational sense that any man, angel, or devil, should suffer eternal damnation for the sins of another, or for another's tempting him to sin or evil.

26. Moreover, doth it not stand to very good sense, that that creature that is left to himself, to be tempted unto sin or evil, and overcome thereby, and remains under the power of it to his life's end, should eternally suffer at the great day for his own sins, and not for another's iniquity?

27. Wherefore, is it not now one of the vainest things in the world, for any man to think that

there is any other evil spirit, angel, or devil, that tempts him to any motion, imagination, thought, desire, word, or action of rebellion, against God or man, but that lying, proud, envious devil, living in his whole man, as beforesaid.

28. Therefore let no man that professeth spiritual light or life in him, for very shame say that God can be tempted, or tempt any man unto sin or evil; neither let him say that any evil spirit, angel, or devil in the air, or earth, or in the water, or in the fire, tempts him to commit any sin or evil, but that airy, watery, fiery, fleshly devil, dwelling only in his own body.

29. I say let him know that that is the prince of the air, which, through the absenting virtue of the Holy Spirit, begets those legions of devils or lusts in the soul of man.

30. And it is the true light of the Lord Jesus Christ, in all his new-born ones, that crushes those cockatrice eggs before they become serpent devils; to sting the whole man with fears of eternal death.

31. Those devils which, by the powerful word of the Lord Jesus, were cast out of Mary Magdalene, or any other creature spoken of in holy writ, were only all manner of filthy diseases, or fiery distempers in man, that hurried him about any desperate wickedness whatsoever, oftentimes increasing so powerfully, that it did not only occasion him to rend his own body and break iron chains,

32. But also he is ready to

tear any one in pieces, until the Lord of glory shine into his distempered soul with that golden grace of true faith, through which that imaginary devil is chained up, whereby all his fleshly goods were spoiled of ever having power in him as formerly; and being now in his right mind, at the glorious feet of the true Jesus, through his own pure light leading him into heavenly raptures, in reference unto his eternal glory, at his visible appearing in the clouds with all his mighty angels.

CHAPTER XXXVII.

1. The prerogative power of God is above all law. 2. Why God cursed the fallen angel in the womb of Eve. 3. The angel's nature (after his offence) was not satisfied without being ruler.

SOME men may say unto me, if it should be granted that that serpent by whom Eve was beguiled was none of the trees of this creation, nor an evil spirit in the body of a natural serpent, as hath been long imagined by the learned ministers of men, but was an absolute serpent devil, as is abundantly declared by you, and that it entered into Eve, and in her womb was pronounced cursed, by the Creator, and so naturally brought forth himself a cursed Cain of her seed; what was this unto Eve? or why should she suffer any kind of punishment for being overcome by an enemy that was too mighty for her?

2. From the light of life eternal to this I answer, concerning the enemy being too potent for her, that was hid from her eyes by the unsearchable wisdom of the Creator.

3. For you that are spiritual may know that the soul of Eve was not only purely created in its kind, like unto angels or other creatures, but it was also of the very same nature of his most glorious Spirit that formed it, so that she could not be ignorant in the least, that all obedience was most due unto her Creator's command.

4. Moreover, you may know also, that the Creator, by the virtue of his royal will for manifesting of his glorious power, might give his creature a spiritual law of light and life in itself, and yet reserve to Himself the prerogative power of it.

5. Furthermore, you know the glorious Creator might present unto the view of his image a serpent-devil, for the trial of his workmanship, and might, upon pain of death, forbid his creature of having to do with that tree, or of hearkening unto it in the least.

6. Also you know, the Creator might leave the divine image unto its, own present strength, through which it might, by a subtle enemy, be tempted and overcome to commit evil with it, against its Creator's law, and yet its sin be upon his own head.

7. Why? not only because it rebelled against its own divine light, but principally because there was no law to bind an infinite majesty to protect it in

its created purity.

8. My beloved moderate brethren, if men could forbear reasoning against the Creator's prerogative power, wonderful wisdom, or ways which are past finding out, then would they enjoy true and lasting peace in their own souls, through deliverance from that conscience-condemning evil, of rash judging things they know not, but this grace of patience is prepared only for the blessed Israelites, and not for scoffing Ishmaelites.

9. Again, if the angelical serpent was in the body of Eve when he received his curse, some men may say unto me, was he capable of understanding of a sentence denounced against him, being in the womb of Eve, and changed from his former condition, as abundantly declared by you?

10. Or why should the serpent and his generation undergo an eternal curse, and Eve and her generation suffer but a temporal curse, seeing she rebelled against greater light than he?

11. Or if that angelical serpent was not cursed before Eve had actually rebelled with him, was not Eve as liable to an eternal curse as he, seeing they both transgressed against an infinite glory?

12. From the light of life eternal to this I answer, that curse denounced by the Creator upon the serpent in the womb of Eve, was not for his satisfaction in the least, but is to convince Eve's deceived thoughts of possessing such godlike happiness promised to her, if she obeyed his counsel, as aforesaid;

13. Also it was to convince her in due time of that error of doting upon her first-born, as a blessing received from the Lord, for when she should see the fruits of her heir, instead of her rejoicing in him as at his birth, her soul would not only loath his company, but would also cast him out of her presence, lest he should murder her, as he did his righteous brother, for her former love and tender compassion towards him.

14. Moreover, that curse against the angelical serpent and his seed, was spoken unto her for her divine satisfaction afterwards, when the light of redemption should shine in her deceived soul, and show her that her first-born son was that angelical serpent cursed in her womb by the Creator;

15. And that his generation of men and women were cursed in his loins also, that she might the more abundantly magnify the free grace of God's electing love towards her deceived soul;

16. That having had so near a union and communion with that angelical reprobate, she was not eternally cursed with him also.

17. Furthermore, notwithstanding the soul of Eve rebelled against a greater light than the serpent did, yet you that are spiritual may know, that she was utterly uncapable of an eternal curse upon her person for these considerations:

18. First, because her soul proceeded from the heavenly na-

ture of the eternal majesty himself.

19. Secondly, because that consent unto evil in her proceeded not from her own nature, but the unclean spirit of the serpent speaking into her innocent soul, as aforesaid.

20. Again, you may know that the serpent was called "the tree of knowledge of good and evil," before Eve was tempted unto evil; therefore, though he had been a tree in his first estate, which had known nothing but good, before Eve or Adam had any sensible being, yet, being fallen from his created purity, he was now become a tree of sin or evil only:

21. Therefore he was a rejected or cursed outcast-tree from the glorious presence of life eternal, before his visible appearing unto Eve:

22. So that though Eve through temptation was overcome to know both good and evil with that cursed serpent, yet she had some relenting light of life in her after her rebellion, which occasioned a secret shame and confusion of soul in her, for her rebellion against the Creator.

23. Therefore she was capable of being made a good tree again; yea, and a tree bringing forth fruit of a more transcendent glory than she was capable of before her fall.

24. But of the contrary, that serpent tree was so far from any kind of relentation of sin, or rebellion against the Creator, before or after he tempted Eve, that instead of being capable of reproof of sin or evil, whereby he

might be restored from his most wretched estate, he did utterly abhor both God and man, unless he might be their counsellor, and ruler over them for everlasting, as beforesaid.

25. This eminent truth of the two scripture seeds, or trees of eternal life and death, is plainly proved in the seventh chapter of St. Matthew, ver.18, where it was said by Christ, the only God Himself, "A good tree cannot bring forth evil fruit, neither can a corrupt tree bring forth good fruit; therefore by their fruits ye shall know them:"

26. So that you which are spiritual may know, that according to the truth of holy writ, though men or angels should gainsay it, the serpent angelical tree being reprobate unto all manner of evil, he and his seed of Canaanitish men and women were not only cursed in the womb of Eve, but also before this world was.

27. But of the contrary, innocent Eve being a good tree in her creation, through her proceeding from the divine nature of the tree of eternal glory itself, though she was overcome by that wicked one as beforesaid, yet she and Adam, or any of their seed, could not possibly eternally perish, because they were trees elected to bring forth good fruit unto everlasting life and glory, long before this world was, as abundantly before-said.

CHAPTER XXXVIII.

1. The bodies of angels are

capable of dissolving into seed. 2. The seed of the serpent only damned. 3. Pure reason lost the knowledge of the Creator, and of itself. 4. Cain not the son of Adam, but of the serpent. 5. Cain was brother to Abel, only by the mother's side. 6. All that died in the first Adam shall be saved by the second. 7. Those that are not lost in themselves, can never be saved.

IF the angelical serpent was of as large a compass as the person of a man, some men may say unto me, how could he enter into the womb of Eve through so narrow a passage as is declared by you? Truly this query is much like that in the third chapter, 4th verse, of St. John, where it saith, "Can a man be born which is old? can he enter into his mother's womb again, and be born?

2. My spiritual friends, as our Lord answered Nicodemus unto his fleshly question, so likewise from his own light in like manner I shall make answer unto this; though the body of the angelical serpent in its length and breadth was as a man is, yet you may know it was not of a gross substance as man's, is;

3. But it was a spiritual body, created in another world;

4. For though the bodies of the mighty angels are in forms like men, yet you may know that they shine like unto the sun, or a flame of fire, being formed in a region of a more higher nature than this:

5. Therefore they are of motion as swift as thought, and of a pure thin or bright fiery nature, so that with great ease they pierce through a narrow passage at the divine pleasure of the Creator:

6. So likewise it was with that serpent tree of knowledge of good and evil, for though his created purity was become all manner of imaginary impurities through his outcast condition, yet you may know that his form was of a more fiery brightness than that of Adam's, or else Eve could not possibly have been deceived by him, as aforesaid.

7. Also his body being spiritual, though his nature was carnal, there was no let to hinder his descending into her womb, to bring forth the Creator's secret purpose of two generations, coming through the loins of one woman, to make an everlasting distinction between the transcendent glory of respection and shame of rejection.

8. Though the angelical serpent descended into the womb of Eve, yet you may know that his ascending nature was utterly lost, in that, instead of his ascending upward into that habitation of ravishing glory from whence he was cast, he was ignorant of it, and of that God and his mighty angels, as if he had never known them in the least;

9. For he imagined his serpentine subtlety to be the only wisdom then in being, and this world to be the only heaven.

10. My beloved brethren in the eternal truth, whatever carnal-minded men vainly dream of a general redemption by Christ, as sure as the Lord liveth there is a serpentine generation of

cursed men and women, which glory in all manner of fleshly sporting themselves about a Creator, or in possessing of a perfection in this mortality, which with their father Cain are utterly ignorant of the true God, his everlasting kingdom, elect angels, immortal personal glory or misery, or any spiritual thing in the least.

11. Doth not the scriptures throughout make mention of two distinct seeds, sons, or generations of mankind?

12. Can Cain and Abel both therefore proceed from Adam's loins, or be of his begetting upon the body of Eve?

13. It is written in the third of Luke, and the last verse, concerning Christ, that "He was the son of Enoch, the son of Seth, the son of Adam, the son of God." If Christ Jesus, the eternal Son of God according to the spirit, was the very son of Adam according to the flesh, can any sober man possibly think that there should be any relation of spirit or flesh between Christ and Cain?

14. Or that the ever-living God, upon any account whatsoever, should be brother unto a cursed serpent?

15. Though righteous Abel was Cain's brother, yet their brotherhood came by the mother's side only, and not the father, though Eve was made out of Adam's side.

16. You know that righteous Abel did represent the glorious person of all righteousness and truth itself, who was that holy and innocent lamb spiritually slain from the beginning of the world in Abel, by the heart and hand of murdering lying Cain.

17. Moreover, is not this answerable unto that of Christ and his brethren? You know their brotherhood was by the mother's side only, and not by the father.

18. Thus if your eyes be opened, you may see in contrariety, a harmony between the seed of the woman and the seed of the serpent.

19. Again, because of the great opposition that may rise up against this glorious truth, through the exceeding pride and unbelief in the heart of most men, give me leave to cite a few scriptures. In the third chapter of the first epistle of John, you may find it thus written, "Not as Cain, which was of that wicked one, and slew his brother." In the thirteenth chapter of Matthew it is thus written, "He that soweth the good seed is the Son of man, and the field is the world, and the good seed are the chidren of the kingdom, and the tares are the children of the wicked one, and the enemy that soweth them is the devil."

20. Moreover, in the 8th chapter of St. John, ver. 44, Christ Jesus, the only God of truth, speaketh thus: "Ye are of your father the devil, and the lusts of your father ye will do: he hath been a murderer from the beginning, and abode not in the truth, because there is no truth in him; when he speaketh a lie, then speaketh he of his own, for he is a liar, and the father thereof"

21. My spiritual and rational

friends which are sober, was not Cain the first murdering lying man that ever was born of a woman? Seeing no true Christian can gainsay it, was not cursed Cain from the beginning that murdering devil and father of lies spoken of by Christ aforesaid?

22. In answer unto those carnal Jews which boasted themselves to be of Abraham's seed, and were not those lustful murdering-minded Jews or Gentiles which our Lord branded with titles of "serpents, vipers, children of the devil," and such like; filthy Canaanites which proceeded out of the spirit of cursed Cain, that old serpent dragon devil, and father of all the damned in this world, and not from the spirit of Abraham, though they might proceed from his loins according to the flesh, through mixtures of seeds in marriages: "The sons of God saw the daughters of men to be fair, and they took of them to be their wives."

23. Though the blessed Israelites and cursed Canaanites are mixed together by carnal copulation since the prince of devils became flesh, yet you that are spiritual may know, that the Lord Jesus that made them both, knew how to separate them for all their close union, and to call them by names answerable to their own natures.

24. I confess that " all that died in the first Adam, shall be made alive in that second Adam, the Lord from heaven;" but what was that whole world that was lost in the first Adam, and found again in the second Adam?

25. If with a spiritual eye you shall look from the first of Genesis unto the last of the Revelation, then you may clearly see what that whole world is which are appointed unto immortal crowns of eternal glory by our Lord Jesus Christ: behold, are they not called "a chosen generation, a royal priesthood, a redeemed people, adopted sons of God, heirs, or coheirs with Christ, blessed children, or the lost sheep of Israel," and such like?

26. Did not the glorious Creator and blessed Redeemer Himself make a clear distinction between two worlds or generations, when He said, "I pray not for the world, but for them that thou hast given me out of the world?"

27. Can you that are sober imagine or think, that there is any spiritual salvation for those men or women, which the Saviour of the world excludes in his petition?

28. Moreover, it is written, that the apostle said, "We know that we are of God, and the whole world lieth in wickedness, or the devil," 1 John v. 19.

29. Behold, ye redeemed ones of the most high God, is it not as clear as light itself, that there is two distinct whole worlds, according to that saying, "then all Israel shall be saved?"

30. A redeemed world of elect lost Israelites, and an unredeemed world of unlost Canaanitish reprobates, that were never truly lost in themselves, and therefore never capable of being found in Christ,

according to that in the epistle of Jude, where it is thus written, "For there are certain men crept in, which were of old ordained to condemnation; ungodly men they are, which turn the grace of God into wantonness, and deny God the only Lord, and our Lord Jesus Christ; woe unto them, for they have followed the way of Cain, and are cast away by the deceit of Balaam's wages, and perish in the gainsaying of Core."

31. Thus is it not clear unto all men that have any faith in them, in the truth of the scripture, that there is two distinct whole worlds to distinguish between the divine glory of election, and everlasting shame of rejection?

32. A cursed Cain, and a blessed Abel, from the beginning of the world unto the end thereof, a subtle serpent, and a simple saint, a scoffing carnal Ishmael, and a spiritual Isaac, a bloody-minded Esau, and a merciful-minded Jacob, a persecuting Saul, and a prophetical David, a treacherous Judas, and a gracious and glorious Jesus, a blessed Seth born in the stead of righteous Abel, whom cursed Cain slew to bring forth the generation of the just, that the Lord of eternal glory might, according to the flesh as well as the Spirit, spring from a spiritual line of his own light of life eternal;

33. And not from a rational or carnal line of eternal death in chains of utter darkness, which if it had power according to its cursed desire, it would destroy God, elect men and angels, hea-ven and earth, and all in them, and itself also, rather than be subject to any, or might not only itself bear rule over all.

34. Seeing the God of eternal glory Himself sprang from the loins of Adam, according, to the flesh, is it not the greatest darkness that can be imagined, for any man to think that Cain and Judas were of the seed of Adam, as well as Abel and Jesus?

35. Do not those men that teach this error out of ignorance, justify Cain and Judas, and condemn Abel and Jesus?

36. From this gross mistake do they not strengthen men in all their rebellions against God and man, what seeming glorious language soever proceed through their mouth?

37. Again, if Cain and Judas, Abel and Jesus, sprang both from the loins of the first man Adam, according to the flesh, or any other account whatsoever, is it not one of the vainest lip-labours under heaven, for men to speak or write concerning the invisible things of eternity, unless it be for a heap of silver or deceitful honour among men that perish?

38. All solid sober men do certainly know, that it is impossible that any man should suffer eternal misery, if all mankind by generation sprang from one root only.

39. What is the reason, think you, that the wise naturalists in disputes, are able to silence the most learned speakers under heaven, in their own supposed spiritual matters? Is it not because those ministers are

uncapable to give a true distinction between the originals of eternal life and death, or the seed of the woman and the seed of the serpent?

40. If men that speak their experiences to one another, as received from the Holy One of Israel, are ignorant of this point, is not that the occasion of all national brain fancies or airy opinions, even amongst the most purest appearances in this present age?

41. Is it not from hence that men of a rational piercing wit are able to counterfeit outlandish chronicles in a methodical manner concerning the strange acts of kings and emperors, many thousand years before the first man Adam had any sensible being, or invent histories so accurately concerning knights, ladies, giants, and such like, that no man by his natural reason can know whether they are feigned or unfeigned?

42. Can any sober man imagine or think those men that want the aforesaid spiritual gift, were ever moved or called by that glorious Spirit to be a public or private speaker, or interpreter of holy writ, or a messenger, or ambassador to his brethren of invisible spiritual excellencies, appointed visibly to be seen to eternity?

43. If Cain and Abel were both begotten by Adam, upon the body of Eve, as almost all men vainly imagine from one bare scripture record, which they understand not, I would fain know of that man that is offended with me concerning this point, why

Cain was nominated in holy writ to be of that wicked one aforesaid, and branded as an "outcast, fugitive, or vagabond, and cursed from the divine presence of the Creator, and cast out of the natural presence of his parents for ever," and condemned with Balaam and Core as a perishing castaway?

44. This I am sure of, that no spiritual or rational man, that is sober, dares say, that either Adam or Eve was that wicked one from whence the cursed spirit of Cain sprang?

45. Why? because there is no such opprobrious names attributed unto them throughout the sacred scriptures.

46. Moreover, you may know, that that wicked one from whence Cain's spirit proceeded, could not possibly have any relation unto Adam or Eve, though Cain was conceived in her womb, and born of her body:

47. Why? because there was an absolute curse denounced upon the angelical serpent, and his seed in her womb, as aforesaid, without any after promise in holy writ for ever being redeemed by the Creator.

48. But on the contrary you know, there was a gracious promise by the Creator Himself, of the redemption of Adam and Eve after their fallen estate, with their whole generation of righteous Abels, Seths, or Abrahams, in that glorious hidden saying, "The seed of the woman shall break the serpent's head;" and that in the fifth of the Romans, where it is thus written:" Likewise then as by the

offence of one, the fault came on all men to condemnation, so by the justifying of one, the benefit abounded toward all men to the justification of life."

49. If you that are spiritually sober, compare this scripture of seeming general redemption unto other scriptures, concerning Cain and his generation, as abundantly aforesaid, you may understand, that the apostle spake only of a restoration of the elect Israelites, or Adamites, and not of the line or generation of Canaanitish reprobates.

50. If you look in the genealogy of Adam unto Jesus, the second Adam, you shall find no Cain there made mention of in the least.

CHAPTER XXXIX.

1. No condemnation but to persons of maturity. 2. No children damned, though they be of the seed of the serpent. 3. He that killeth a prophet, or a righteous man, would kill the Creator if he could. 4. No salvation by the power of man's own will, 5. but by the power of God.

IF two distinct generations at have proceeded through the body of one woman, the one elected unto eternal personal glory in the high heavens, and the other rejected unto everlasting shame, in this perishing world at the end thereof, which we can no ways disprove;

2. Wherefore our desire is to know, whether all the posterity

of Cain are rejected, seeing the whole generation of Adam are elected, is as at length declared by you, from that divine gift I received by voice of words from the ever-living Jesus.

3. To this I answer, that eternal election, or rejection, spoken of in holy writ, had relation only to persons of understanding, and not unto children that were uncapable of any distinction between light and darkness, or good and evil;

4. For you that are well acquainted with the scriptures do know, that throughout the whole Bible there is not one saying in the least that maketh mention of condemnation of children, but the contrary altogether.

5. You may know, that that curse denounced against Cain and his seed, ran in the line of persons of maturity, and not of minority; though it is said, that "God loved Jacob, and hated Esau, before they had done good or evil."

6. You may know that that word was spoken in reference to their being in the persons of men, in the sight of the Creator, and concerning the difference of their spirits, and the effects that would thereby ensue;

7. You know it is said, "there were two nations in Rebecca's womb at the birth of Esau and Jacob;" now you know that could not possibly be, except they lived to the age of men to fulfil that truth.

8. You know it is written, that the Lord of glory commanded his apostles to "suffer little children to come unto him, and forbid

them not, and took them in his arms and blessed them, saying, Of such is the kingdom of heaven."

9. My beloved spiritual friends, if God only wise hath said, that his heavenly kingdom consists of little children, or innocent childlike men and women, are not those men more like unto cursed serpents than blessed saints, which, contrary unto all spiritual, literal, or rational truth, impudently affirm that little children may be eternally damned by original sin?

10. If all the seed of Cain that die in their childhood, shall find mercy in the resurrection of the just, some men may say unto me, shall the saved children of Cain and Adam, being of two contrary natures, appear in the same kind or measure of glory, in the day of the Lord's vengeance upon ungodly men?

11. From the light of life eternal to this I answer, as they differed in their natures in this life, so shall they differ in the manner and measure of their glory in that life to come:

12. The saved children of the angelical serpent will enter into that rational glory, out of which their reprobate father was cast.

13. But of the contrary, the spiritual seed of Adam shall enter into that glory from which he fell, in a more transcendent god. like condition to all eternity;

14. But not in a paradisical separated place of glory in this creation, as some men vainly imagine; but in that glorious new heaven and earth without, or above this vanishing starry heaven, according to the truth of holy writ.

15. Thus the most wise and holy God of all spiritual and natural order, restoreth his spiritual and rational images into their first created conditions, upon a more firm foundation of possessing everlasting life and glory together, purchased at a dear rate from his divine self, by his own most precious blood, or godhead life, according to that saying by the apostle Paul "Christ therefore died and rose again, and revived, that he might be Lord both of the dead and the quick;" and of that saying in the twentieth chapter of the Acts of the Apostles:" Whereof the Holy Ghost hath made you overseers to feed the church of God, which he hath purchased with that, his own blood."

16. Again, if you look in the fourth chapter of Genesis, third verse, with a spiritual eye, you may clearly see that God's eternal election or rejection of men runs in a line of personal understanding, and not in a line of innocent children, or natural fools; the words are these: "And in process of time it came to pass, that Cain brought an oblation unto the Lord of the fruit of the ground; and Abel also himself brought of the first fruit of his sheep, and of the fat of them, and the Lord had respect unto Abel, and to his offering, but unto Cain and his offering he had no regard."

17. Ye that are redeemed from the power of all inward

filthiness, I beseech you, what occasioned the respection or disrespection between Cain and Abel, in the pure eyes of the Creator?

18. Surely not their offerings, for you know that God heeds no man's person for his sacrifice sake in the least, but for the glory of his own namesake only;

19. Yet you know that Cain had as much wisdom from his own reason to present an acceptable sacrifice unto the Lord, as Abel;

20. Yet it was the Creator's eternal free love unto Abel, which caused both his person and sacrifice to find such sweet acceptation with the Lord, that the divine love of God in Abel might be seen in the fatness of his sacrifice;

21. In that you may know he was made to offer up himself a living sacrifice of invisible and visible obedience unto the Creator, as a seal of his being chosen to life eternal.

22. Yet you may know, it is not any kind of sacrifice, worship, righteousness, or desire in man or angel, that can possibly move the divine majesty to accept of it, or his person in the least; but it is his eternal free love in his own season, which operates in him all heavenly mindedness, or love to God or man.

23. But of the contrary you may know, that the original cause of all manner of fearful darkness, and fiery shame in Cain, proceeded only from the non-election of his person;

24. This was his condition when he was marked with the invisible seal, of rejecting both his person and sacrifice, from those words, "Wherefore Cain was exceeding wrath, and his countenance fell down."

25. My beloved Christian friends, what moved Cain to be so full of wrath, or with whom was he so fiery hot?

26. Truly, as beforesaid, his furious anger arose in him from a sensibleness of his outcast condition, and because he could not come at the Creator Himself; therefore his purpose was to avenge himself upon his favourite, even innocent Abel.

27. The scripture gives you the reason thereof, because his "own works were evil, and his brother's good:"

28. Thus you that are endued with that light that cannot be disproved, may see as clear as the light itself, that "it is not in him that willeth, not in him that runneth, but in God alone that showeth mercy."

29. What, then, think you, in the day of the Lord's vengeance will become of those free-will-mongers, or oracle-grace merchants, which cursedly teach their deceived fleshly brethren that a man may be in a condition of salvation to-day, and to-morrow be cast away?

30. Truly, my spiritual friends, if eternal election and rejection depend upon the acceptation of man's will, until he be born again with a distinguishing light from the divine will of the Creator, every man living would choose eternal death instead of life, such power

or purity is in the choicest of men's wills, until the divine majesty present an immortal crown of glory unto their blind born spirits;

31. Then, indeed, and not till then, man's soul, that was averse to all spiritual good, by that divine light is made willing to choose the better part;

32. Because then he certainly knows that there is an eternal life and glory for some, and an everlasting death and shame for others.

33. Therefore you that are truly spiritual cannot but know that though men speak a language like unto angels, or the divine majesty Himself, as the angelic serpent seemed to do in the beguiling of Eve, yet it is utterly impossible they should possess any true understanding of the spiritual things of the ever-living Jehovah or Jesus, until their souls are firmly established with an undoubtable assurance of their own personal glory in a world to come.

34. So much at present concerning the tree of knowledge of good and evil, or seed of the woman and seed of the serpent. O, blessed and happy are those men and women in themselves already, that enjoy this distinguishing light of life eternal in the purity thereof.

CHAPTER XL.

1. Concerning Christ's coming to judgment. 2. The vanity of that opinion that believes Christ's personal reign upon this earth.

BECAUSE of many opinions of Christ, and the ignorance of most men, concerning his coming to judge both the quick and dead, therefore, in the next place I shall treat of his most needful point from certain sayings of Himself, in the seventeenth chapter of Luke, 24th verse. The words are these: "For as the lightning that lightneth out of the one part under heaven, shineth unto the other part under heaven, so shall the Son of man be in his day; and as it was in the days of Noah, so shall it be in the days of the Son of man; they eat, they drink, they married wives and gave in marriage, unto the day that Noah went into the ark, and the flood came and destroyed them all; likewise, also, it was in the days of Lot, they eat, they drank, they bought, they sold, they planted, they built; but in the day that Lot went out of Sodom, it rained fire and brimstone from heaven, and destroyed them all." After these ensamples, shall it be in the day when the Son of man is revealed?

2. My beloved spiritual brethren, you know there is a twofold appearing of Christ unto the sons of men; the one spiritual, and seen only by the invisible eye in the soul; and the other is personal, and seen only by the visible eye of the body.

3. Also you know, Christ being the divine rock of all ages, He hath spiritually manifested Himself unto his blessed Abels from the beginning of the world

till now; but as for his visible appearing in a body of flesh, whereby men might be able to behold the face of their God in the similitude of a man and live, you know that He did but once so appear only for a few years.

4. Again, in the twenty-fifth chapter of Matthew, it is written thus: "And when the Son of man cometh in his glory, and all the holy angels with him, then shall he sit upon the throne of his glory, and before him shall be gathered all nations, and he shall separate them one from another, as a shepherd separateth the sheep from the goats."

5. It is also written in the second of Thessalonians, 1st chapter, 7th verse, thus: "When the Lord Jesus shall show himself from heaven with his mighty angels in flaming ire, rendering vengeance unto them that know not God, and that obey not the gospel of our Lord Jesus Christ."

6. If you that are spiritually sober do but compare these three places of scripture together, then you may clearly see what Christ meant by that day of his personal appearing.

7. After his suffering and glorification, He shall appear like lightning from one part under heaven to the other; He shall appear in his glory with all his holy angels.

8. Behold, ye blessed of the most high God, what kind of appearing of Christ in his glory like lightning, or a flame of fire, is this? is it not the visible appearing of his fiery glorious person, with the glittering persons of his mighty angels under the whole heavens, or in the air

9. If it be not so, how shall all nations be gathered together before Him, that He may make an eternal separation between them, according as He hath spoken?

10. It hath been long imagined by men of rare parts, in the account of many people, that before the general judgment day, Christ would come again personally to reign a thousand years on this earth with his saints;

11. And their opinion is grounded partly upon the twentieth chapter of the Revelation, which was long since fulfilled, as I shall demonstrate in due season.

12. But first I shall prove by scripture record, the failing of this opinion in the third chapter of the Acts, 19th verse, it is thus written: "When the time of refreshing shall come from the Lord, and he shall send Jesus Christ, which before was preached unto you, whom the heaven must contain until the time that all things be fulfilled, which the prophets have foretold since the beginning of the world;" what think you, then, of Christ's personal reign on this earth a thousand years with his saints? is it not point blank against the truth of this plain testimony of holy writ?

13. In the fourteenth chapter by Saint John, you may find it thus written; "Let not your heart be troubled; ye believe in God,

believe also in me: in my father's house are many dwelling-places; if it were not so, I would have told you; I go to prepare a place for you; and if I go to prepare a place for you, I will come again and receive you unto myself, that where I am, there may ye be also."

14. In this place of scripture you see that Christ did not speak in the least to his apostles of his coming again personally to reign upon this earth a thousand years:

15. But of the contrary, He told. his heavy-hearted disciples that He was going to prepare a place for them, or He was going into the highest heavens, or prepared place of eternal glory, appointed for them with Himself, after they had suffered with Him on earth; and He would come again in his glory with his holy angels, and receive them into his father's house, or heavenly kingdom, where He now is, that they might with his mighty angels, Moses and Elias, everlastingly behold his bright burning glory, even face to face.

16. What is this personal reign of Christ with his saints, a thousand years, that supposed wise men have so much talked of?

17. Is it any thing else but a temporal heaven at the best, if spiritually examined?

18. Moreover, is it not a very unlikely matter that the infinite divine majesty should come again personally to remain upon this bloody earth a thousand years with his saints, having suffered here already, and ascended

upon the throne or right hand of transcendent glories, yea, far above all heavens, as it is written, that "he might fill all things."

19. Furthermore, do not all personal reign-mongers confess, that Christ was God and man in one person, and that that most blessed body of his is now glorified in the highest heavens?

20. Do you not also pretend to believe, that the divine person of this god-man glorified, is infinite, immortal, unchangeable, and eternal?

21. Moreover, if there be any such divine light, or heavenly faith in your persons, I would fain know whether you think it possible that this mortal world, or men, can bear the presence of a divine majesty, whose body is become a consuming fire of immortal everlasting burnings; without its being immediately consumed to ashes, or transmuted into his own glorious likeness?

22. O that all the elect did but know how suddenly this personal God will appear in his glory to consume this whole world!

23. Again, if you look in the 11th chapter of the Hebrews, ver. 13, you may find it thus written: "All these died in faith, and received not the promises; but saw them afar off, and believed them, and received them thankfully, and confessed that they were strangers and pilgrims on the earth, for they that say such things declare plainly that they seek a country; and if they had been mindful of

that country from whence they came out, they had leisure to have returned, but now they desire a better, that is an heavenly; wherefore God is not ashamed of them, to be called their God, for he hath prepared for them a city:" here you may see that Abraham himself was so far from expecting a personal reign of Christ on this earth, though he believed that his seed should enjoy the promises of God, both temporal and spiritual, in their appointed seasons;

24. Therefore he only minded a personal ascending into the heavenly city of eternal glory, prepared for him and his elect seed, at the resurrection of the just;

25. So that Abraham looked upon the promises of God, that they were to enjoy in this world only, as types or shadows of that heavenly city or kingdom, with its ravishing excellencies, as aforesaid.

26. Moreover, if that glorious God of Abraham, Isaac, and Jacob, had intended a personal reign on this earth a thousand years with his saints, after his glorification in the highest heavens, can any sober man be so weak as to think He would have hid it from Abraham, whom He was pleased to call the father of the faithful, and friend of God? You know what is written, "shall I hide this thing from Abraham?"

27. Furthermore, if the Lord in life or death had revealed any such thing unto Abraham, the thing being of so great concern-

ment, can you possibly think that He would have hid it from his generation to come? You may be sure if there had been any such thing to be accomplished, He would have declared it to after ages.

28. Seeing neither Abraham, nor any of the patriarchs or prophets, knew of Christ's personal reign on this earth with his saints, but spake as to the contrary altogether, what sufficient ground hath any man in this world to expect such a thing?

29. But how can it be otherwise, when men take upon them to interpret the mysteries of the scriptures, without an immediate commission from the eternal Spirit?

30. Again, the scripture saith, that "The day of Christ's appearing shall be like unto that of Noah and Lot;" now you know in the day that Noah entered into the ark, the flood came, and by degrees destroyed them all.

31. Also in that day Lot departed out of Sodom, it rained fire and brimstone from heaven; and destroyed them all.

32. If the whole world, was drowned with water immediately after Noah entered into the ark, and Sodom and Gomorrah was consumed by fire suddenly after Lot departed out of the city, and the day of Christ's coming shall be in like manner, without controversy, instead of his personal reign on this earth with his saints, at his next appearing, immediately after all his blessed Noahs and Lots are ascended into the ark of his immortal

glory, this firmamental created heaven and the lights thereof shall be all on fire;

33. And shall descend upon the face of the whole earth, and burn all the fruits and glory thereof unto ashes; but it shall not be so favourable as to consume the bloody-minded men therein.

34. If the Lord of glory had purposed to come personally to reign a thousand years amongst his saints, before the general day of judgment, is any man so weak as to think He would have hid it from his chosen apostles, whom He had promised to set upon twelve thrones, to judge the twelve tribes of Israel, when He appeared again in his glory?

35. Is there any one place in holy writ that expressly speaketh of Christ's personal reign in this world?

36. If there be no express record for any such thing, as I am sure there is not, doth not those men that hold forth such an opinion as this, imitate little children or fools, that rejoice in rattles or counters, instead of gold or precious stones?

37. Thou that art confident of Christ's personal reign on this earth, suppose such a thing should come to pass in thy days, and thou shouldest be one of those saints, what condition dost thou think thy body shall be in?

38. Dost thou think it shall live upon carnal things, or shall it be immortalized and live upon spiritual things only?

39. Or if thou thinkest thy soul shall be in a divine condition, and thy body shall feed upon natural things, as now it doth, and shall be in perfect health, and free from diseases;

40. I say, if thou halt imagined such an estate as this is, I would fain know of thee what condition thou thinkest that Christ will appear in?

41. Dost thou think that He will descend from the throne of his glory upon this earth, amongst the sons of men, again to eat and drink of carnal things with them, as formerly?

42. Or dost thou think that He will appear amongst them in a glorious condition, to make them more happy in things that perish than now they are?

43. If Christ should personally reign with his saints, what union or communion could they enjoy with Him, more than now they do, unless He was in a capacity of eating and drinking with them? or else they were delivered from feeding upon natural things themselves, through their transmutation into his own glorious likeness?

44. It is written in the twenty-sixth chapter by St. Matthew, 29th verse, "I say unto you, that I will not drink henceforth of this fruit of the vine, until that day when I shall drink it new with you in my Father's kingdom."

45. Here you that are spiritual may see, that Christ was so far from encouraging his apostles to expect his coming to taste of the fruit of the natural vine, in a personal reign with his saints, that He layeth it down as a positive rule, that "He would drink no more of the natural vine in this earth, until he drank it in a new

and spiritual way with them in his Father's kingdom."

46. Where then is thy imaginary personal reign of Christ on this earth with his saints a thousand years?

CHAPTER XLI.

1. The vanity of believing in a God that hath no form; 2. and of them who say the Creator is an incomprehensible Spirit; 3. or that there is no God but nature only; 4. or who say that God's Spirit and their spirits are but one spirit.

ANOTHER sort of deceived men there are, that through strong delusions from their natural comprehensions, have imagined a mighty spiritual appearance in themselves, from a bodiless God or Christ, that never was.

2. This sort of men are those, which from a cursed conceit do not only despite a glorious God, in the person of a man, but they also talk of great signs and wonders, which they expect shall come to pass by inward voices or visions, from their imaginary bodiless God, as beforesaid.

3. Moreover, being bewitched to the purpose, though they pretend a great spiritual light in them, they can make a hard shift to fool themselves from the literal records, as to think that the Holy One of Israel had commissionated another high priest, or king of the Jews, besides Himself.

4. Though this counterfeit high priest, or king of seven nations, I mean John Tanee, pretends a natural glorious deliverance suddenly unto the Jews in many nations

5. Truly those that understand nothing above a paradisical temporal glory, are not to be blamed in the least, for their bountifulness towards his perishing tenets, in reference to his Jerusalem's conceits.

6. John Tanee, thou mayest remember about three years and six months past, I told thee of thy deceived condition, concerning thy carnal Jerusalem journey with John Robins, also by an immediate voice from on high.

7. Furthermore, if thy high priesthood, kingship, and Jerusalem temporal glory, do not vanish like smoke, as John Robins did, even when thou thinkest thyself most sure in the thing, then the Lord God sent not me to thee.

8. Again, when thou art ashamed and confounded in thyself, from all thy lying voices or visions declared unto saints and serpents, in the name of the great Jehovah, then thou shalt know with sorrow and shame enough, that it was the Lord that sent me unto thee, to declare thy fleshly error.

9. I do not say thou canst help it; it is through the permissive power of the Lord, for some secret end, only known to Himself, that thou, or any man else, should break forth into such strange appearance of darkness, yet seeming glorious lights, when thou art found too light in the balance of divine truth;

10. Is it not thy natural or allegorical whimsies that can blind the elect, nor pacify the judge of life and death within thee and without thee?

11. Again, there is a third sort of deceived persons, which with great confidence have declared, that Christ should spiritually reign over the nations in king Charles's seed; and of this sort one Arice Evans in Blackfriars, was looked upon as a great prophet by many of the royal party.

12. Moreover, from this their foolish conceit, they had many pretty whimsies, and dark sentences, to blind men's apprehensions, like unto John Tanee and John Robins; which took much upon the spirits both of the subtle and simple also for a season.

13. Furthermore, their understandings being utterly dark, concerning the spiritual or personal appearing of the Lord Jesus Christ in his glory,

14. It is usual for them concerning Charles the Second, as to join Christ and him in one, calling him the white pearl, that should make the nations in a sweet harmony of divine unity, through his glorious ruling over them: also they said, that he should not attain to the throne of his father by any carnal weapons, but he should be brought into this land, and set upon the throne by an immediate power of the eternal Spirit of God Himself

15. Again, this carnal cavalier prophet pretended the knowledge of certain scriptures by voices or visions, in reference to the reign of Charles the Second; and John Tanee like,

sought to confirm it by natural observations:

16. And truly I do not blame the people that were deceived by them, because they wanted a true distinction in themselves between those things which are divine and human.

17. Moreover, when all pretended high priests, prophets, or apostles in this land, are clearly discovered by an unerring light of life eternal, I make no question of the subtlety of their serpentine spirits to blind their own eyes and those that were deceived by them.

18. I know they can say, if they be deceived, the Lord hath deceived them; or they can say, we had a mysterious language given us by Jehovah to confound all literal or notional appearances in this confused age, and men understood us in a carnal sense only;

19. Or if they have often fixed a time concerning things that should come to pass, and nothing comes of it, they can also say, as the prophet Jonas understood not the Lord's time and mind concerning the destruction of the Ninevites,

20. So likewise this thing, in the way of our fleshly expectation, was hid from our eyes; but the mighty Jehovah in his season will bring it to pass in a spiritual manner, beyond the comprehension of men or angels.

21. Moreover, if none of these excuses will blind their eyes, which expected wonderful things from them, then because they are not able to bear the shame of being found liars in the name of

the Lord, they will say, all men are liars, or there is not a true prophet upon the face of the earth;

22. Or else they will say, "There is but only one pure Being, invisibly ruling in the whole creation, and this spiritual power manifesteth itself in various manners of seeming contradictions for the confounding of all men's understandings that would find out its secrets;" but in the end, when it hath fooled men to the purpose, it will appear in a glorious harmony, to the content of all.

23. Furthermore, for the blinding of their own eyes, and those of their own spirits, that they may both fall together in a deep ditch of eternal destruction, they will, or may say, "If there be a Creator, he is an incomprehensible Spirit, and all our spirits proceeded out of his Spirit, and when our bodies die, our spirits return into his Spirit again."

24. From this cursed error they may or will say, that "God can as soon destroy himself, as any soul that he hath made, with an eternal condemnation."

25. Moreover, if this grand fleshly deceit prove also but a broken cistern, then as aforesaid, they may, or will say, "There is no God but nature only;" your most wise men in nature know this to be truth, but they are compelled to nominate a God to the people, to keep the rude multitude in obedience to their governors and government.

26. Knowing if they should not confess a Creator besides nature, all their pretended divine voices, or visions, would appear but mere fleshly lies.

27. Therefore for strengthening themselves in their atheistical error to prevent discovery, they may, or will say, "There is no world but this only, and this world had never any beginning, nor will never have any ending: men may talk of a Creator, and a day of judgment for silver and honour, or to keep children or fools in awe, but wise men know as aforesaid, that one generation passeth away, and another cometh in its room, and so it will be for everlasting."

28. Thus you that are truly spiritual do, or may know, that the spirit of every man naturally, is so cursedly proud, that rather than men should find him a liar in the name of the Lord of hosts, even against his own rational light, he is apt to say, "There is no other God, or shame, or world to come," but the elements of air, water, earth, and fire, of this perishing world, though these and such like sandy foundations, are the pillars of cursed Canaanites; yet I know that you blessed ones have not so learned Christ.

29. The fourth and last sort of deceived men, are so far from acknowledging Christ's personal reign with his saints in any kind whatsoever, that they blasphemously affirm they are all Gods or Christs themselves:

30. These are those which say, that God is a Spirit, and that his Spirit, and their spirits, are but one spirit only.

31. Moreover, to strengthen

themselves in this their serpentine sophistry, they can tell you from the records, that "Christ is the head of his church, and his saints are his body."

32. Also this sort of men pretend such a union with the divine majesty, that they do not only attribute to themselves his holy names or titles, but, Lucifer-like, they will tell the simple and fearful soul, that they are set down in the throne of glory with Christ already.

33. Furthermore, though this sort of saints in their own account are all kings, priests, and prophets unto God, yet if you should ask them a saber question concerning any spiritual thing after death, they are so dead drunk with their notional witchcrafts, that they count all men in darkness that see not themselves in the throne of immortal glory already, as aforesaid.

34. Again, they also seem to be full of hymns, or spiritual songs, in reference to the present glory they enjoy with the eternal Spirit, when the Lord knoweth they acknowledge no divine majesty or God at all, but those imaginary Siren songs, and their own natural blind-born spirits, from whence they proceeded.

35. This sort of seeming glorious saints do imagine their spirits so divine, that they think it impossible it should ever see death, but they, like unto children or fools, conceit their bodies turn to dust for ever, but their souls ascend into an unknown spiritual glory.

36. Therefore, if a man speaks of a personal God, or a personal glory in a life to come, they will tell him he troubles himself about a simple carnal God and glory that is not;

37. But if he knew what it was to be possessed with divine light, life, or glory in his own soul, as they do, he would no more trouble himself in the least concerning a God or glory to come at a distance.

38. There are some among these of a more purer sort, which speak many sweet truths, and according to their light, they live in them; only, poor hearts, as yet they are ignorant of the fountain of glory, from whence their spiritual streams proceed.

39. Moreover, though they cannot close with a personal God, and personal glory of the elect in another durable world, and a personal shame of reprobates in this world to all eternity, yet the secret love of God preserves their merciful spirits from that error of the wicked, I mean from despising things that are hid from them.

40. Therefore I make no question but in due season, they shall be revealed to them unto their everlasting joy and glory in the highest heavens, as aforesaid.

41. Furthermore, though these elect vessels at present understand no other God but what is within them, yet they are afraid to call themselves God, or Christ, or Creator, or the like, lest there should be a divine majesty to own those titles Himself.

42. Again, all those simple-

hearted souls, which are appointed to eternal glory, are not so riveted in their present light, but if a more clear manifestation appear, their spirits are both ready and willing to embrace it;

43. But of the contrary, all cursed Canaanites are fully resolved to remain where they are, though never so glorious a light should appear.

44. Moreover, those that are the blessed of the Lord, are very tender of condemning any men, of- what appearance or opinion soever, if they see never so little of the pure light of life eternal appearing in them;

45. But of the contrary, the unmerciful reprobate condemns all men as in a bottomless pit that are contrary unto his fleshly opinion.

46. Furthermore, the blessed of the Lord are made willing to yield all spiritual obedience unto the unknown God, till they know Him, and show mercy unto all, though he perish; this is a Job-like spirit, who said, "though thou kill me, yet will I trust in thee:"

47. But of the contrary, the hypocritical Canaanites love to make a glittering show before men, but as for any inward purity of spirit towards God, and mercy unto all men, they are so far from any such principle, that they count it a delusion in them that enjoy it.

48. Many of the blessed of the Lord do know, that all the desires of men or angels cannot prevail with the divine majesty, to persuade Him to set the seal of his love upon any man's person, until He is graciously moved unto it of his own pleasure, according to those sayings of holy writ, "I am found of them that sought me not, and before they call, I will answer, when they were in their blood I said unto them, live;" and of that notable saying in the fifteenth chapter of the prophet Jeremiah, 1st verse, "Then said the Lord unto me, though Moses and Samuel stood before me, yet mine affection could not be toward this people; cast them out of my sight, and let them depart."

49. But of the contrary, the formal hypocrite is so dark in this divine secret, that he thinks himself the blessed of the Lord for his much babbling, and counts those men cursed that are not of the same mind with him.

50. My beloved spiritual friends, though I have branched these men into four several heads, yet in the main they are all of one spirit; my meaning is this, they are all ignorant of the glorious God being in the person of a man.

CHAPTER XLII.

1. A further discourse concerning the error of Christ's personal reign. 2. The interpretation of the three last verses in the 12th of the Revelations, 3. concerning the dragon and the woman. 4. Of the binding of the old serpent dragon for a thousand years. 5. When they expired. 6. Of the worship of the beast. 7. Of Satan's being loosed out of prison. 8. Who they are that be in the deepest prisons of raging darkness.

IN the next place, according to promise, I shall write somewhat upon the twentieth chapter of the Revelation by Saint John, because that error of Christ's personal reign a thousand years with his saints on this earth, is partly grounded from this chapter.

2. My beloved brethren in the eternal truth, you know that this book of the Apocalypse is too mysterious to be understood by the achitophels of this perishing world.

3. Also you know, that God's way is to chose the base things of this world to confound the most honourable things thereof, that no flesh may glory in his presence.

4. Moreover you know, that if the Most High endues a man with a divine gift, to demonstrate his eternal secrets to his brethren, He preserveth the soul of that man from giving the glory of that heavenly power to his own net. My meaning is this, that man doth not give any praise or glory to any God, or Christ, or light within him, but he is made, as is due, to return all honour, praise, or glory, unto an infinite majesty, or spiritual fountain of glories without him, from whence alone all divine light, as crystal streams, floweth into the spirits of elect man and angels.

5. But to come to the matter in, hand: "And I saw an angel come down from heaven."

Brethren, what angel was that which John saw come down from heaven? Truly it was no other but that angelical personal God, our Lord Jesus Christ Himself, with whom John was more conversant than all the apostles, in divine secrets.

6. Again, having the key of the bottomless pit, and a great chain in his hand, that is, this angelical Jesus alone had all divine power of heaven and earth in his own Spirit, over the bottomless pit, lying imaginations of devils incarnate, or cursed men.

7. Moreover, the everlasting gospel, or truth, which proceeded through his heavenly mouth for the consolation of his saints, and confounding of the serpents, that was the great chain in his hand.

8. Furthermore it is written, Rev. xx. 2, "And he took the dragon, the old serpent, which is the devil and Satan, and he bound him a thousand years, and cast him into a bottomless pit, and he shut him up, and sealed the door upon him, that he should deceive the people no more, till the thousand years were fulfilled." My spiritual friends, what was that old serpent dragon devil which was bound a thousand years by the spiritual power of Christ? It was an imaginary bottomless pit, devil within the body of man, that persecuted the truth of Christ in his own person, apostles, and saints.

9. Again, you that are spiritual may know, that the serpent-devil that was bound or

shut up as in a prison, or in a dungeon of darkness, for a thousand years, was the cursed spirit of murdering Cain raging against Christ and his seed, in the person of king Herod and his seed, or seven sons, in the ten persecutions.

10. In the twelfth chapter of the Revelations it is thus written: "And there appeared another wonder in heaven; for, behold, a great red dragon, having seven heads and ten horns, and seven crowns upon his head." Also in the thirteenth chapter it is thus written: "And I saw a beast rise out of the sea, having seven heads and ten horns, and upon his horns were ten crowns." This red dragon and beast that rose out of the sea, was that Herod and his seven sons in the ten persecutions, as aforesaid.

11. Again, for your clearer understanding in the thing, give me leave to speak of the three last verses of this twelfth chapter. The words are these: "And the serpent cast out of his mouth water after the woman, like a flood, that he might cause her to be carried away of the flood." My spiritual friends, you may know that this serpent was bloody Herod, and the woman was the Virgin Mary, that brought forth the Lord of life, and the flood was the men of war that was sent forth to persecute the virgin, and murder her Son and our Saviour; but the earth helped the woman, and the earth opened her mouth, and swallowed up the flood which the dragon had cast out of his mouth.

12. My spiritual friends, you may know that the innocent children that were murdered by bloody Herod's men of war, was that earth that opened her mouth and swallowed up that flood of persecution that was intended to be poured forth upon the blessed babe or God of eternal glory.

13. Again, then the dragon was wrath with the woman, and went and made war with the remnant of her seed, which keep the commandments of God, and have the testimony of Jesus Christ. My spiritual brethren, you may also know, because Herod could not come at the holy babe and its mother in its infancy, therefore his cursed spirit in his seed or sons, did persecute the Lord of glory, and his apostles and believers, to the death afterwards; if you look with a spiritual eye in the second of Matthew, and the Acts, upon king Herod, his seed, council of priests, scribes, and men of war, then you may see this to be the very mind of the Holy Spirit in these mysterious records.

14. Again, when the earthly powers, through the glorious appearance of the everlasting gospel, are sealed up unto bloody-mindedness, against the messengers of that divine truth, to fulfil the secret decree of the most high God, then are their spirits shut close prisoners in their own bodies, as in a dungeon of spiritual darkness, through which, instead of enjoying any sweet peace, that soul is full of raging madness; and not knowing which way to

turn itself, it thinks to get out of its condition by acting all manner of cruelties to the utmost of its power.

15. My spiritual friends, you may know that this was the spiritual binding of that old serpent dragon devil in king Herod, and his Herodian spirits, for a thousand years; the which thousand years were expired when the ten persecutions ceased, which was the ten horns of that savage beast, aforesaid.

16. For you that are spiritual know, that no man can possibly find out the truth of holy writ of the most perfectest account in the world, because the wisdom of God hath reserved the seasons of all divine secrets in his own heavenly breast, that men or angels may know them, when his glory seeth it most fit.

17. Wherefore all time observation in reference to a right understanding of any thing that is spiritual, is utterly confounded in that scripture saying, "For a thousand years is as one day with the Lord, and a day is as a thousand years," 2 Peter iii. 8.

18. Moreover, when the glorious truths of the divine majesty were poured forth upon the face of the nations, as it was in the primitive times, through the spiritual ministry of the ever-living God, you may know whilst that commissionated spiritual power remained in being, the nations could not be deceived with the hypocritical formalities of the persecuting powers and priests of this perishing world.

19. This was that shutting up of the serpent dragon devil in the evil powers aforesaid, from deceiving the nations any more, until the thousand years of their ten bloody persecutions of the saints was fulfilled.

20. Again it is written, verse 4, "And I saw seats, and they sat upon them, and judgment was given unto them; and I saw the souls of them that were beheaded for the witness of Jesus, and for the word of God, and which did not worship the beast, neither his image, neither had taken his mark upon their foreheads, and they lived and reigned with Christ a thousand years." My spiritual friends, what judgment seats were those which John saw, and who were them that sat thereon in judgment?

21. Those seats of judgment were the accusing consciences of the bloody persecutors aforesaid; and the preaching or publishing of the glorious truths of our Lord Jesus Christ, through the commissionated mouths of the chosen apostles, ministers, or saints, was that judge of life and death reigning in the consciences of the aforesaid spiritual tyrants. "Do ye not know that the saints shall judge the world? Know ye not that we shall judge the angels?" 1 Cor. vi. 2.

22. My spiritual friends, whatever men shall imagine of these literal records, as sure as the Lord liveth, those angels spoken of by the apostle Paul, were the tyrannical magistrates, and their bloody-minded, covetous priests, which committed spiritual wickedness

together in high places.

23. Again, you chosen ones may know, though the bodies of the saints suffer imprisonment or death for the truth of Christ, yet their spirits are in pure peace, and at perfect liberty in life and death.

24, But of the contrary, though the persons of the cruel persecutors be at perfect liberty in their temporal heaven, yet their spirits are close prisoners in their own bodies, and void of all heavenly peace whatsoever, through that envy in them against all divine purity.

25. And that blood spilt upon the earth by them for the testimony of Christ, that was the shutting up of the door of all true hope from them, and sealing up their bloody spirits unto an eternal vengeance at the great day of our Lord Jesus Christ, with his mighty angels.

26. Again, seeing John by a divine light saw the souls of them that were put to death for bearing witness to the word of God, or spiritual truth of Jesus, reigning with Christ over the raging spirits of their bloody persecutors, that thousand years time of the ten persecutions aforesaid, my spiritual brethren, what was that worship of the beast, and receiving his mark in their foreheads and hands, which they were preserved from in the thousand years' reign, or time of their fiery trials, for the name of our Lord Jesus Christ? That is, they were delivered from that idolatrous worship, proceeding from the beastly imagination of their spiritual

bloody tyrants, as aforesaid, not daring in the least to handle any carnal weapons in defence of their cursed inventions, what sufferings soever they endured.

27. This I would gladly have you to understand, that the commissionated witnesses of the Lord of glory, are for the most part appointed unto the greatest trials at the hands of Canaanitish devils, or perishing gods of this vain-glorious world, because of the reward of that transcendent glary which the Lord Jesus hath prepared for them with Himself above ordinary saints, with his holy angels, face to face.

28. Again, it is written, Rev. xx. 5, "But the rest of the dead men shall not live again until the thousand years be finished. This is the first resurrection; blessed and holy is he that hath part in the first resurrection, for on such the second death hath no power, but they shall be the priests of God and of Christ, and shall reign with him a thousand years, and when the thousand years are expired, Satan shall be loosed out of his prison." My spiritual brethren, who were those dead men that lived not again until the thousand years were finished? You know in holy writ it is said, "Ye that were dead in sins and trespasses, hath he quickened."

29. So likewise you may also know, that those dead men there spoken of, were the remainder of the saints and chosen witnesses of the eternal Spirit that were to appear in these last days, to bear record unto that glorious truth

which the prophets, apostolical ministers, and saints, sealed too with their blood, as abundantly beforesaid.

30. Again, you know it is written, verse 7th, that "Satan shall be loosed out of his prison for a little season, when the thousand years are expired, to deceive the people which are in the four quarters of the earth, even Gog and Magog, to gather them together to battle, whose number is as the sand of the sea, and they went up in the plain of the earth, and they compassed the tents of the saints about, and the beloved city; but fire came down from God out of heaven and devoured them."

31. Again you may remember that from an unerring Spirit that sent me to declare divine secrets that I have already demonstrated unto you what that Satan is, and that prison of his thousand years abode.

32. It remains now that I should write somewhat concerning his being loosed out of his prison, that you may the better understand the truth in relation to the dead men as aforesaid.

33. Moreover, you that have been well acquainted with spiritual conditions, cannot but know that no men in the world are in such a deep prison of raging darkness, as those men that tyrannize over the consciences of innocent souls, which cannot bow down to their imaginary divine ordinances.

34. Furthermore, you may also know, that when the magistrate and his pretended prophets were prevented from persecuting men's persons, in reference to their consciences towards God, then, and not till then, was Satan loosed out of his prison.

35. This was that loosing of Satan for a little season out of his unspeakable prison in the temporal powers, when the innocent professors of Christ had freedom of conscience in reference to their faith in the Lord of glory, through which the Christians were multiplied again in the earth.

36. Again, you may know that it was but a very little season since Christ was glorified, that the saints possessed any such spiritual freedom in any kingdom under heaven.

37. Therefore the persecuting spirits of satanical prelates in the civil powers have had but a very little season of resting from shedding the blood of God's innocent people in the whole world:

38. Moreover, though the name of Christ was almost extinguished from the face of the earth in the thousand years spiritual reign of the saints, and raging of the serpents, as aforesaid, yet you may know in that season of liberty of Christian conscience, that the saints were mightily increased again in the world.

39. Furthermore, you may also know, that those saints are the dead men that lived not again until these last times of the invisible teachings of the divine majesty Himself. Wherefore you spiritual ones

may also know, that the Gog and Magog, that are gone forth to battle in the plains of the earth, compassing the tents of the saints, and the holy city, are those heathenish magistrates, and their bloody priests, that proceeded from cursed Cain, through the loins of king Herod, and his priests and scribes, as beforesaid; so that the dead men that lived not again until the thousand years were fulfilled, are those saints and holy city of God, which at this time, and to the end of all time, do suffer cruel persecution for the testimony of a good conscience in all the nations of the world.

40. My beloved brethren, this is that spiritual reign of the first resurrection with Christ on this earth, appointed in some measure for all men to drink, which are delivered from that second death, which is treasured up for all bloody minded tyrants whatsoever.

41. Thus you that are sober may clearly see, that it was not a visible personal reign of Christ a thousand years with his saints on this earth, that John aimed at, as many men have long imagined, but it was a spiritual reign, or suffering with Him for his truth's sake upon earth, that when He appeareth in his glory with all his holy angels, then to reign with him in his throne to all eternity in the third heavens.

42. Now, brethren, I shall go on to prove his personal coining in glory, according to the intent of his most holy Spirit from his own words.

CHAPTER. XLIII.

1. Of the personal glory of Christ's coming to judgment. 2. No man hath so much faith as a grain of mustard seed, but Christ only. 3. Of spirits finite and infinite.

MY beloved brethren, in the unerring Spirit you may know, there is a twofold appearing of Christ's glory in his chosen ones; as the glory of the sun excels the glory of the moon, so these two glories transcend each other.

2. Moreover, you know the moon appears in the brightness of her glory at one time, and at another time she appears altogether like unto darkness or shame:

3. So likewise it is with Christ's appearing in glory to men's souls in this life; sometimes by virtue of the incomes of his eternal Spirit, the soul of man for a moment is transmuted into the glorious likeness of the divine majesty Himself;

4. But at another time you know, when none of these spiritual lightnings appear, through some fleshly guilt, the poor soul seems to be full of fearful darkness, horror, and shame, as if it had never seen any light or life at all.

5. So that you see all the glory of Christ's appearing unto the spirits of men in this life, is but a changeable moon-like glory at the best;

6. Therefore it can be but a spiritual type of this personal appealing of Christ in his judgment-seat glory, with all his

mighty angels.

7. Again, you know the sun is no way subject to change in the least, but, giant-like, runs his course in four and twenty hours through the whole heavens, and in one place or other appears, in his glory unto the end of all time:

8. So likewise you may know it is with this personal appearing of Christ in his glory with his holy angels, for in that day of his appearing, the persons of his redeemed ones shall be nothing else but sunshine, like divine glories in themselves, and so run their heavenly course even to all eternity.

9. Whoever thou art that is ignorant of this personal glory of Christ's coming in the clouds, or air, with his elect angels, to make an eternal separation between the persons of the blessed Israelites and cursed Canaanites, though thou art full of seeming glorious expressions concerning a God or Christ living in men's consciences, yet thou canst never be firmly established, until thou knowest that personal God, or Christ, sitting in the throne of his infinite glory in the high heavens without thee, from whence alone all inward light or life proceeds.

10. I confess if a man become an innocent merciful spirit, he may be able to speak such a language from a supposed God or Christ in men's consciences only, that may confound the seeming holiness of all church fellowships in the world.

11. But what advantage is this to himself, or his hearers, except when he is confounded; in the room thereof he doth not only declare the effects of Christ's truth in the minds of men, but is able to demonstrate in some measure the personal appearing of Christ in his glory in the world to come.

12. If the visible appearing of a glorified God or Chest in the person of a man be such a choke-pear unto thee, or seem low or carnal, because the national priests confess such a like thing;

13. I would fain know of thee by sober speaking or writing, where thy God or Christ is become, when thy soul, and all thy light, or life, for a moment is become silent death, or darkness, with thy body of dust?

14. Moreover, if thou understandest not a personal God or Christ, too transcendent glorious for heavens, earth, angels, or men, to be capable of the indwelling of his eternal Spirit, what is thy inward God or Christ thou discoursest so much about, but pleasant words or perishing nature only?

15. Furthermore, if thou knowest this wonderful secret concerning what a spirit is, then wouldest thou certainly know how impossible a thing it is, for any spirit whatsoever, to possess a living being without a distinct body of his own.

16. Again of what bigness dost thou think a spirit is, whether it be finite or infinite? Give me leave to write a little of this strange thing from those sayings of Christ to his disciples in the seventeenth chapter by St. Matthew, 20th verse; the words

are these, "For verily I say unto you, for if ye have faith as much as is a grain of mustard seed, ye shall say unto this mountain, remove hence to yonder place, and it shall remove: and nothing shall be unpossible unto you." Behold, is not a grain of mustard seed a very little I and yet you see Christ saith nothing should be unpossible unto that man that hath such a quantity of spiritual faith in Him.

17. Again, it is written, "with God nothing shall be unpossible:" who then is capable to possess so much faith in Him as will contain the quantity of a mustard seed, but Christ Jesus the God of glory Himself, unto whom all things are possible, that He is moved unto by that seed of faith, which is the eternal Spirit of his glorified person?

18. Moreover, if a spirit be in its quantity but as a grain of mustard seed, or a spark of fire, how then is it possible for the Spirit of God, men, or angels, to possess any sensible light, life, joy, or glory, but in their own bodies only?

19. Furthermore, if this description of a spirit seem strange, be it known unto thee, the Lord hath made me to declare it, for the confounding of that cursed error of God's essentially being in all things.

20. Again, if the eternal Spirit should consist of so great a bulk, how then can there be any God at all, but nature only?

21. Or how can it possibly be an infinite Spirit, when it is not distinct to itself, but is compelled to have its being in finite things only? this unknown bodiless God is much like unto the star-gazer's monstrous sun and moon aforesaid.

22. Is not this infiniteness indeed for all the spirits of elect men and angels, to be filled with variety of divine glories, with one word speaking from so small a fiery glory as this is?

23. Whoever thou art that shall be left to despise this little spark of immortal crowns, which essentially reigneth in the man Christ Jesus alone, it is because there is no true light of life in thee.

CHAPTER XLIV.

1. Of the great white throne which John saw, Revelation xx. 2. A mark of a reprobate to desire miracles, to make him believe the truth of a commission.

IN the twentieth chapter of the 1 Revelation, 11th verse, it is thus written: "And I saw a great white throne, and one that sat on it, from whose face fled away both earth and heaven, and their place was no more found;" my spiritual brethren, though men's earthly mindedness, and heavenly conceitedness, will fly away, and be no more found, when the true light of life eternal is throned in their spirits, yet from the unerring Spirit I positively affirm, that this place of holy writ had reference only unto Christ's personal appearing in his glory with his mighty angels, to make an eternal separation between the just and unjust.

2. My Christian friends, why did John call it a great white throne, which he spiritually saw? It was because of the glorious brightness of the judge's face, or person, and his angelical attendance, and also because it was the dreadful general appearance of mankind, to receive their eternal dooms.

3. You know when Christ was transfigured upon the mount, through which his face shone, and his garments glittered, the text saith, that "Moses and Elias appeared to him in glory:"

4. So likewise you may know, that John called it a great white throne, as beforesaid, because of the transcendent brightness of Christ's person.

5. What heaven and earth was that which fled away from his glorious face? Whatever men imagine to the contrary, you that are spiritual may know, that it was the dissolution of that heaven and earth that had a beginning, as if it had never had any being; I mean this visible firmamental heaven and earth, and all light or life in them.

6. Therefore where John saith, "their place was no more found," that was spoken in reference unto their former natural brightness, virtue, beauty, power, or glory, being translated into a chaos of everlasting confusion.

7. Again, besides the glorious brightness of Christ's person, and his angelical host, give me leave to write a little more of that great white throne which John saw.

8. You that are truly spiritual cannot be so grossly ignorant as to think, that Christ hath no other throne to inhabit in but his people's spirits, and this natural world only: why? because that error ariseth out of the atheistical hearts of fleshly men, that hath no faith in the truth of holy writ.

9. Moreover, if men's spirits be but rationally sober, though at present they be never so atheistical, they may be convinced that there is another world besides this, which is of a higher nature, compassing this globe round about, and yet it is not global as this is, only there is no elementary firmament, sun, moon, nor stars in it, but it is an open place, city, throne, or kingdom, of infinite vastness in length, breadth, or height, answerable to the person of an infinite majesty.

10. Also it is a throne of exceeding whiteness, or sun-like brightness, suitable unto the transcendent brightness of the king's person that sits thereon, and his glorious companions.

11. Though the joy and glory of an earthly prince consists chiefly in the greatness of his person, power, vast territories, and honourable subjects for his safety, yet for all this, you know, that his palaces are decked with embroidered ornaments of gold, silver, precious stones, and such like, for the further setting forth the mortal glory of his princely majesty:

12. So likewise it is with the divine majesty, for though the variety of his infinite godhead joy

and glory, principally is within his own person, and princely power over so innumerable a company of kingly companions;

13. Yet you may also know, that He hath a great throne, or palace, for the further setting forth of his visible glory, decked with ornaments of spiritual brightness, or immortal glittering whiteness, as beforesaid.

14. Do not all men that acknowledge a Creator, whether they understand Him to be a spirit or a person, confess Him to be boundless, immortal, unchangeable, and eternal?

15. You know this global world is not boundless in length, height, breadth, or compass, but it is surrounded with a firmamental heaven, as with a brazen wall, to keep it within its own station.

16. Moreover, if the eternal majesty be infinite or boundless, as He is, I would fain know of any man how it is possible for a glorified infinite Spirit, or person to be contained in a finite bounded world?

17. Though the doves of divine glory are compelled for a season to live among the tyrannical serpents of this perishing world, yet I would have you to understand that if an infinite, or boundless God, with his mighty angels, should have no other throne to solace themselves in but this, then instead of spiritual liberty, they would all be in natural bondage;

18. If you ask me the reason of it, you may know, that the glorified person of God, or Christ, is of a motion swifter than thought, and the persons of Moses, Elias, and the mighty angels, are of motion as swift as thought;

19. Therefore no inclosed place can contain them, but they must of necessity inhabit a throne, or kingdom of infinite vastness, for ascending or descending at the divine pleasure, according to their motional swiftness.

20. Again, you spiritual ones may undoubtedly know, that there is such a throne as I speak of. Why? because this world cannot possibly contain our thoughts, but they nimbly pierce through the heavens, and in a weak measure they comprehend an infinite or boundless God, and a throne or kingdom of an infinite circumference.

21. If our bodies were answerable to our thoughts, this world could not possibly contain them, but they would ascend through the natural heavens, to see whether there were such a vast kingdom of eternal glory, as they had apprehended.

22. I know all fleshly atheistical-minded men are apt to say unto me, if they could see this infinite personal God, and glorious white throne, I talk so much of then they could believe it.

23. O, how fain would finite carnal eyes behold infinite spiritual glories!

24. Moreover, they may say unto me, didst thou ever see this infinite majesty, and throne of glory, thyself? If thou didst, where are thy miracles to confirm it? or why dost thou not

make us believe it by thy spirituality? or why doth not this infinite majesty bear witness that He sent thee, as. He did, to his former prophets and apostles? or when will He do it, that we may see and believe, and own thee for the truth's sake?

25. Whoever thou art that thus called in question the glorious truths of eternity, under pretence of my weakness, in reference unto miracles, that thou mightest believe;

26. Little dost thou think instead of contending with me, thy sinful brother, according to the flesh, that it is that old serpent devil in thee, that arraigns the glorious God that made thee at the blind bar of thy carnal reason, and by it condemns Him, and his heavenly truths, because thy unbelieving desires are not satisfied.

27. Again, did not the Lord of glory Himself call those Jews that required a sign, "an adulterous and wicked generation?"

28. Moreover, when the Lord of life, by the mighty power of his word only, wrought wonderful miracles in their sights, instead of believing on Him ever the sooner for that, the sign-mongering Jews cursedly say, that He cast out devils through Beelzebub, the prince of devils.

29. Furthermore, if thou shouldest upbraid me for want of the gift of tongues or languages, yet I render praise unto the God of glory by his own light in my poor soul; thou canst not upbraid me for want of a spirit of prophesy, though thou at present shalt slight it;

30. And what if I could speak all languages, would it advantage any sign-monger in the world, but to his further condemnation only?

31. What saith the scripture concerning this thing? "Wherefore strange tongues are for a sign, not to them that believe, but to them that believe not; but prophesying serveth not for them that believe not, but for them which believe," 1 Cor. xiv. 22.

32. Moreover, did not the Lord of glory Himself say, that "John the Baptist was the greatest prophet under the law that was born of woman?" and yet thou never readest of any miracles or tongues possessed by him.

33. The Christian dove waits for a spiritual sign within him, that he may believe the glorious truths of the ever-living God without him; but the carnal serpent requires a natural sign without him, to make him believe the spiritual truths of an invisible God in the high heavens.

34. Again, if there should be no other appearing of a God or Christ but in men's consciences, as thousands vainly imagine in this drunken age, what did Christ mean by these and such like sayings, in St. Matthew, xxv. 31? "And when the Son of man cometh in his glory, and all the holy angels with him, then shall he sit upon the throne of his glory, and before him shall be gathered all nations, and he shall separate them one from another, as a shepherd separateth the sheep from the

goats; and he shall, set the sheep on his right hand, and the goats on the left: then shall the king say to them on his, right hand, Come, ye blessed of my Father, take the inheritance of the kingdom prepared for you from the foundation of the world; for I was an hungry, and ye gave me meat; I thirsted; and ye gave me drink," and such like "then shall he say to them on his left hand, Depart from me, ye cursed, into everlasting fire, which prepared for the devil and his angels; for I was an hungry, and ye gave me no meat; I thirsted, and ye gave me no drink. And these shall go into everlasting pain, and the righteous into life eternal."

35. Again, thou that vainly boasts of a spiritual God or Christ, appearing in glory within thee only, darest thou say that these scriptures are fulfilled?

36. Moreover, canst thou say that thou hast this king on his throne of glory, with his holy angels, and all the nations of the world, within thee?

37. Furthermore, is the devil and his angels, and eternal blessedness and cursedness, within thee also?

38. My beloved friends in the Lord of life, if there were not a generation of cursed men, that glory of a God, or Christ, within them, that are not only full of these and such like discourses, but are also given up unto all filthiness, I could not have mentioned this thing, wherefore there are many of these serpents that creep into houses, telling poor deceived men, and silly women, laden with many lusts, that the resurrection of the dead is past already, since Christ in his glory is risen in them?

39. Moreover, if their captivated friends should seem to scruple at any kind of fleshly community held forth by them, then these wandering stars will say unto them, what poor low things are these that you are troubled withal? What, are you in Egypt still? Is there any more than one pure Being? And is not this pure Being within you all? And is it not He that speaks and acts all in you? Seeing there is but one power, what do ye scruple at? Are ye as little children or fools yet? Do ye not see that there is no union, or true communion in the world among those people that hold, two powers?

40. Furthermore, lest their deceived friends, by whom they possess Balaam's wages, should, fail them, then these cursed captives will tell them, that "their bodies are fleshly forms that turn to dust from whence they came, and shall appear no more; therefore not to be minded in the least in reference to sin, so that ye fall not under the civil law, or oppress nature, but, your, souls are immortal, and cannot die, but ascends into its glory from whence it came: wherefore, since ye have attained to such liberty, that all men are in foolish bondage which know it not, let us eat and drink and be merry, whilst we enjoy these vanishing forms, yet let us solace ourselves with all delights, even as our divine rights."

41. O, thou king of all kings, for the glory of thy great namesake, discover these serpents with their carnal wiles, that all thy simple-hearted people may be delivered out of their satanical snares, and brought into that pure light and liberty of thy own likeness, by one heavenly glance from thy eternal Spirit.

CHAPTER XLV.

1. The Creator's withholding of his divine assistance, was the cause of the fall of our first parents. 2. The ground of all spiritual or natural curses. 3. Noah's ark assimilated to heaven. 4. Of the resurrection.

YOU that are full of the light of life may know, that whilst Adam and Eve continued in the purity of their creation, this whole earth and all things made therein, were as pure in their kind and measure, as that vast kingdom of glory, and all that therein is.

2. Moreover, as soon as ever their pure natures were defiled with the serpentine nature of fiery lust, you know the whole earth, and all things therein, had a curse upon them in one kind or another.

3. Furthermore, you may know that this curse did in some measure extend unto the very souls and bodies of all creatures, with the whole world throughout.

4. Some men may say unto me, seeing the divine nature is all purity itself, what was that curse upon the whole creation 1 or whence came it, seeing they were uncapable of sin or evil in the least? From the unerring Spirit to this I answer, it was not an infusion of any curse or evil into the natures of any thing by the Creator, but it was a withholding the motions of its first created blessedness, through which naturally, it became barren or cursed in itself, this was the fruit of unlawful lust.

5. Moreover, that you may clearly understand wherein the blessing or cursing of the Lord consists, you may know that when He wholly denies the heavenly motion of his holy Spirit unto a man, immediately that soul becomes nothing but cursed envy against all spiritual or natural purity whatsoever:

6. So, likewise, when He denies the natural motions of his blessed Spirit unto any thing that He hath made, it becomes subject to all kind of putrefaction whatsoever: this was that cursing of the Jews' natural blessings, and hardening of Pharaoh's heart, by the Lord spoken of in holy writ.

7. Thus you that are sober may clearly see the ground of all spiritual or natural cursings in the whole creation; for though it was pronounced through the spiritual mouth of the Creator Himself; yet it could not possibly proceed from that word of the Lord's speaking, because of the glorious purity of his divine nature; but that curse rose out of the natures of the creatures themselves, for want of the

motions of the Spirit of God in them, as beforesaid.

8. Again, you that are spiritual know, that immediately after the Lord said, "An end of all flesh was come before him," when Noah and his family, and the creation, were entered into the ark, the whole world of lustful men and women, and the glory thereof, were destroyed by water: now you know all that was in the ark was secured from the raging waters through their ascending above the waters.

9. Moreover, you may know that the ark, and those creatures therein, were not only preserved for the increase of a new world, but they were also a figure of a world to come.

10. Furthermore, the ark itself had relation unto that kingdom of glory in the high heavens, which is too sublime to be overtopped by any natural water or fire whatsoever.

11. The person of Noah, who was made a preacher of truth and righteousness to the unbelieving world, did represent the person of that spiritual preacher of all truth and righteousness in the heavenly ark beforesaid.

12. Furthermore, the other persons and creatures in the ark had reference unto the salvation of the elect of God, and the whole creation that are in being at the personal appearing of Christ in his glory, with his mighty angels.

13. The drowning of the whole world of ungodly men, and the rest of the creation, had relation unto the eternal condemnation of all reprobate men in this world;

14. The burning up of their natural delights, wherewith they sport themselves in excess of riot and drunkenness, little thinking of that eternal vengeance coming upon them.

15. Again, righteous Noah represented the divine judge of ungodly men in this, because he entered into the ark, and by virtue of a great light in him, he was made to sit as a judge in the consciences of wicked men, when the waters rose upon them, in the remembrance of their laughing him to scorn about his ark, and knowing his security in the ark, and their present destruction by water, having no ark of refuge to deliver them.

16. Moreover, as they sported themselves in fleshly filthiness, and vain-glorious mirth about him, his ark, pure language, and life,

17. So likewise, as a mighty prince in his chariot tramples rebellious subjects with delight under his horses heels, he rode in his ark as in a chariot, triumphing in the Lord for his own deliverance, and their destruction under the feet of his ark, as a just recompence of their unrighteous deeds, and despising the Lord and his truth, which he had declared to them for a long season.

18. As sure as the Lord liveth, thus it will be very suddenly with this lustful bloody world, that sport themselves about the resurrection of the dead and judgment day, saying, "It is past

already," or, "There will never be any such thing;" for that righteous Noah, the king of glory will open the firmament of heaven, and stand in the air with his mighty angels, surrounding his person, and by the power of his word speaking, as he raised Lazarus out of the grave;

19. So, likewise, I affirm against men or angels, the very same person, and no other, which did that deed, is that God that will by his word. speaking command all his righteous Noahs, both dead and alive, bodily to ascend into that holy ark of eternal glory in the high heavens, and when they are safely arrived with the whole creation, which according to their kind, groaned longed for deliverance; then, as beforesaid, that mighty God, the man Jesus in glory, with a flood of fire will burn all the beauty or glory of this world to ashes, leaving all cursed Canaanites, bodies and spirits, burning together like fire and brimstone upon this earth, in utter darkness, answerable unto their former burning lusts in their natural conditions.

20. Moreover, those men and women that glory of a God or Christ within them, and whatever filthiness they act, charge the most holy Spirit with it; I say from the Lord Jesus Christ, though they escape the vengeance of men by their satanical subtleties, yet in the remembrance of their despisings of a glory or misery to come, in that day the divine vengeance shall burn more fiery hot in their souls and bodies than all other men whatsoever.

21. Then those that are ascended into the ark of eternal glory with the Son of man, and his holy angels, shall sing that new song of all honour, power, praise and glory, unto the Lamb that sits in the midst of the throne for ever and ever, not only because they are delivered from the eternal vengeance,

22. But, also, because the most wise and holy God hath rewarded those filthy despisers of his glorious truths, according to what they did, and would have done unto Christ, and his redeemed ones.

23. O, blessed are those men and women that are not offended with these plain truths.

CHAPTER XLVI.

1. The last commissionated prophet come into the world. 2. No calling of the natural Jews to the profession of the true Jesus. 3. Two sorts of Jews. 4. Some remarkable signs of the approaching of the day of judgment.

IF there be such a dreadful day of Christ's personal appearing in his glory with his mighty angels, some men may say unto me, may it not be a long season, are there not many prophecies yet to be fulfilled, before his coming, as the calling of the Jews, and the sign of the Son of man in heaven, and such like?

2. From an unerring Spirit, to this I answer, as John the Baptist was the last prophet

under the law, and the forerunner of the sudden appearing of Christ Jesus the Lord in a body of flesh,

3. So, likewise, I positively affirm against all gainsayers under heaven, that I, John Reeve, am the last commissionated prophet that ever shall declare divine secrets, according to the foundation of truth, until the Lord Jesus Christ appear on his throne of glory, visibly to be seen by all his elect, face to face.

4. But of the contrary, in that day of our God and king of glorious crowns appearing, none of those cursed men and women, which blasphemously said, that God hath no person at all, shall ever be able to behold his face, and live; but according to holy writ, they shall cry to the mountains, hills, or rocks, to hide them from the wrath of his bright burning body, or face, that sits upon the throne.

5. Concerning a general visible calling of the Jews in all nations, to the acknowledgment of Christ being come in the flesh, I say from the eternal Spirit that sent me, that there will never be any such thing in the world; indeed, the ministerial artists have of a long season imagined an outward call of the Jews, to their vain-glorious seeming holiness, but the most wise and holy God intends no such thing.

6. Wherefore to confound their carnal wisdom, his glorious pure pose is to call home to Himself those Jews and Gentiles, elected to everlasting life by the invisible teaching of his most holy Spirit.

7. You that are sober may come to understand that there is two sorts of Jews, there is a mosaical Jew, and an apostolical Jew.

8. Moreover you may know, that those men called Independents, Anabaptists, Presbyterians, are the literal apostolical Jews.

9. And those men that observe Saturday for their sabbath, are those mosaical legal Jews, which utterly deny that Christ is yet come in the flesh, but ignorantly expect his appearing in a fleshly glorious manner, to reign over them in the throne of David his father.

10. Moreover, these sabbatical Saturday Jews, John Tanee-like, do imagine when their fleshly Christ appears to reign over them, that He will gather them out of all nations wherein they are scattered, and conduct them into the inheritance of their fathers, that promised land of Canaan; and there they make account with their imaginary king to live in a temporal glorious condition for a long season; and as they have been servants and slaves to all nations wherein they were scattered, so likewise, as a reward of their servitude, they fully expect that all nations shall bow down to them, and bring in their riches and glory unto them, as their vassals for ever.

11. You that are spiritual may know, that these unbelieving mosaical Jews, which expect a carnal Christ to reign over them, were those Jews which, at the death of Christ, said, "His blood be upon us and our children;"

and, truly, you know his blood was upon them and their children to some purpose, in the destruction of Jerusalem, and unto this day, yea, and so it will be to the end of the world.

12. For the Lord Jesus will never spiritually gather the seed of those Jews, which rated a bloody Barabbas above the Lord of life Himself.

13. Moreover, those Jews which were afraid of having any hand in the death of Christ, were the fathers of those spiritual Jews in all nations, that are mixed in marriages with the Gentiles, whose merciful innocent spirits are delivered from all tyranny over men's consciences.

14. Furthermore, those Independent, Anabaptist, Presbyterian men, which hold it lawful, just, and good, to persecute men in their persons and estates upon a spiritual account, I say from the eternal Spirit, that they are for the most part the offspring of those bloody-minded Jews that crucified the Lord of glory upon the account of blasphemy, as aforesaid.

15. O blessed are all unpersecuting merciful-minded men and women only!

16. All innocent, merciful, Independent, Anabaptist, Presbyterian men or women, that are preserved from a persecuting mind of divine things which seem difficult, from the eternal Spirit I declare, those are part of God's spiritual wheat, which are mixed with the chaffy Jews and Gentiles, which are the offspring of cursed Cain, whom the Lord shall burn with unquenchable fire, when He cometh in his glory with his angels, to receive his spiritual wheat into his heavenly barn as aforesaid.

17. Thus you that are spiritually enlightened from on high, may clearly see, that the calling of the elect Jews in all nations unto the knowledge of the divine majesty, and his heavenly truths, was not meant an outward calling of them from a mosaical legality, unto an apostolical literality, as many men have vainly imagined; but it was an inward calling of them by the motions of the eternal Spirit, to the right understanding of the one personal majesty on the throne of glory, and his heavenly truths.

18. Again, concerning the sign of the Son of man in heaven, in the twenty-fourth of Matthew and the 30th verse, it is thus written: "And then shall appear the sign of the Son of man in heaven, and then shall all the kindred of the earth mourn, and they shall see the Son of man come in the clouds of heaven with power and great glory;" this sign of the Son of man was that substance, or very Son of man himself, and the glory of his personal appearing in the clouds of heaven with his glittering angels, caused such a fiery brightness, not only in the visible heavens above, but the whole earth beneath also appeareth like a flame of fire, or burning lightning, insomuch that all the kindreds of the earth, which never expected that dreadful day, because their

persons were not transmuted into the divine likeness of the Son of man.

19. Therefore their unbelieving earthly spirits did quake and tremble, lament and howl, like dogs, for very fear of the foresaid sign of the Son of man should rend them to pieces, and burn them and their inward God, or Christ, to powder; I mean all those which gloried of a God or Christ within them only, and cursedly despised this personal God on his glorious throne without them.

20. Thus you in whose persons the king of glory reigneth, by the heavenly incomes of his eternal brightness, may in some measure see what is meant by the sign of the Son of man in heaven, when He appeareth in his glory with his holy angels.

21. As the immortalized spirits and bodies are filled with astonishing ravishments with the very sight of the Son of man in his glorious throne aforesaid,

22. So likewise the carnal spirits and bodies of all hypocrites, which gloried in a Christ, ordinances, and salvation without them, and despised the invisible breathings of his holy Spirit in his innocent people, as delusion, blasphemy, and such like, shall be full of unspeakable burning, pain and shame, through their inability of bearing the fiery brightness of the Son of man, that most high and mighty God, with his elect men and angels, as abundantly beforesaid.

23. Moreover, you know it is said, Luke xvii. 26, "As it was in the days of Noah, and in the days of Lot, so it shall be in the day when the Son of man is revealed."

24. Furthermore you know the scripture saith, "They were eating and drinking, and marrying of wives, and planting, and building unto the day that Noah entered into the ark; but in the day that Lot went out of Sodom, it rained fire and brimstone, and destroyed them all."

25. Again, you know the whole old world and Sodomites, a little before their final dissolution, were not only possessed with all variety of natural comforts; but they were also given up to all manner of unnatural filthiness, and so continued to the day of their total destruction.

26. Moreover, you know it is recorded of the men of Sodom, that "they were haters of God, and turned the truth of God unto a lie, and worshipped and served the creature, forsaking the Creator which is blessed for evermore. Amen."

27. Furthermore, "While the meat of the unsatiable Jews were in their mouths, you know there was a plague brake out among them." These final dissolutions you know were not only invisible, but visible also.

28. Moreover, if the personal appearing of Christ in his glory shall be like unto that of Noah and Lot, and the final dissolution of the old world, and that of Sodom and Gomorrah, when it was in the midst of the height of all their fleshly filthiness, and

exceeding fulness of bread, which included all good things, and in their more than ordinary planting, building, putting the evil day far from them; is it not thus in these our days also? was there ever more glorying in all manner of sodomitical, unnatural filthiness, than now there is?

29. Did men ever deify carnal creatures as now they do?

30. Moreover, was there ever such a babbling about a God, or Christ, in men's consciences only, as now there is? notwithstanding many of those cursed serpents vilify the very name of a personal God in a throne of glory above the stars, more than the greatest thieving, whoring, murderer, in the land?

31. Furthermore, was there ever such talk of pure love without envy upon a spiritual account, as in these our days, and instead of mercy towards one another, since the world began, under pretence of conscience, and an art of lamb-like words, do not men like roaring lions lie lurking in every quarter, seeking whom they may devour?

32. Again, notwithstanding such varieties of breaking forth in declaring the sudden appearing of the Lord of hosts, to recompence vengeance upon all sorts of bloody-minded covetous men whatsoever; can any man living ever remember such purchasing, such building, such planting, and plenty of all natural comforts, as now there is?

33. Moreover, was there in any man's memory such changes in government, and marvellous transactions in them as in these our days?

34. Furthermore, was there ever such variety of witchcraft, voices, visions, signs, and wonders acted, as in these our days, from a pretended spiritual God, Christ, or power within men only?

35. Besides all this, hath not the God of glory, by poor and contemptible means, discovered the serpentine subtleties of the honourable artificial priests and astrologian sorcerers in this age and land, more than ever He did since the apostles times? And hath there not been many signs in the heavens, and in the earth, and in the creatures, in a marvellous manner, since our civil dissensions with many bloody massacres at home and abroad? And doth these things presage nothing, or did they come to pass by chance or fortune only?

36. O ye hypocritical-minded sign-mongers, and cursed despisers of the Son of God, who is the Lord your Maker; remember what effect those wonderful signs in Egypt took upon Pharaoh, his counsellors, and people! and what effect Eliah the prophet's signs took upon Ahab, Jezabel, and her four hundred idolatrous priests; besides your forefathers, that murdered the Lord of glory, his prophets, apostles, and innocent people, for the truth's sake only, though they had the gift of tongues and miracles; by calling all their miracles languages, or spiritual

truths, delusions, to deceive the people against the very light of their own consciences, through a secret fear of losing their gain and glory among men that perish.

CHAPTER XLVII.

1. Further signs of the approaching day of Christ's coming to judgment. 2. The prophet writes by inspiration, 3. and giveth the interpretation of several scriptures tending thereunto.

AS the old world and Sodom were blinded by abundance of prosperity, and plenty of all things to the very day of their final overthrow, so, likewise, whatever men shall declare to the contrary, it shall be with this bloody-minded world, until the Son of man come in his glory. If you ask me the reason, the main ground of it is this, because the God of glory, that cannot possibly lie, hath said, that the day of his appearing shall be like unto that of Noah and Lot.

2. Moreover, another reason of it is this, not only to prevent man's wisdom to be prepared for the day of his glorious and dreadful appearing, but also to catch those men with their own craft that counted them children or fools that expected any such thing.

3. Furthermore, another reason is this, for the deeper condemnation of all those men that heard the declarations of this personal appearing in his glory, but laughed it to scorn, or put the evil day far from them, because of the present fleshly gain and glory they lived in.

4. Again, you know that it is written, that "in the day Lot departed out of Sodom, it rained fire and brimstone, and destroyed them all;" behold, what a dreadful and sudden desolation fire maketh in a mortal world, even within a day's compass!

5. So, likewise, it shall be when the Son of man appears in his glory; for within the compass of a day, or twelve hours, after man's account, the heavens without the body of man shall be melted with fervent heat, and instead of the former and latter showers of water to nourish the earth, and rejoice man's heart, as a flood of fire and brimstone, it shall pour itself upon the whole world, and burn all the beauty, virtue, or glory thereof to dust or powder, as beforesaid.

6. I write not against the truths of the scriptures, but by inspiration from the Holy Spirit, I bear record to the mind of God in them, in opposition of all pretended spiritual lights under heaven:

7. Wherefore, as an eternal witness against all sorts of men that wrest the scriptures to their own hurt, give me leave to recite that threefold testimony of Peter, as a seal to this glorious truth, that shall burn like fire and brimstone in them that despise it: the words are these: "But the heavens and earth which are now, are kept by the same word in store, and reserved unto fire against the day of condemnation,

and of the destruction of ungodly men; but the day of the Lord will come as a thief in the night, in the which the heavens shall pass away with a noise, and the elements shall melt with heat, and the earth with the works that are therein, shall be burnt up, looking for and hasting unto the coming of that day of God, by the which the heavens being on fire, shall be dissolved, and the elements shall melt with heat; a threefold cord is not easily broken," 2 Peter 10-12.

8. If any hypocrite shall go about by his serpentine sophistry, to tell you that are spiritually weak, those sayings of Peter had relation to the burning up of the carnal heavens and earth in men, through the glorious appearing of the eternal Spirit, you may with ease confute those notional cheats, if you look back upon the ground of Peter's sayings: the words are these; "Knowing this first, that there shall come in the last days scoffers, walking after their own lusts, and saying, where is the promise of his coming, for since the fathers fell asleep, all things continue as they were from the beginning of the creation; for this they willingly are ignorant of, that by the word of God the heavens were of old, and the earth standing out of the water and in the water, whereby the world then was overflowed with water, perished," 2 Peter 4-7.

9. Thus you that have never so little truth of the true Jesus in you, may clearly see, that the apostle Peter, in this threefold language, had not the least thought in him concerning heavens and earth being burnt up within men, but the burning up of the heavens and earth, and the beauty, virtue, or glory thereof without man, which were the fruits of man's handy works; why? because you see the apostle grounds his matter upon the drowning of an outward earthly world.

10. Moreover, you may also know, that it was a burning up of a visible heaven and earth, and the glory thereof, meant by Peter; why? because the apostles tells you, that "There shall come in the last days scoffers, walking after their own lusts, and saying, where is the promise of his coming?"

11. Furthermore, if it had been an invisible burning up the fleshly heavens in men only, what lustful man in the world would have scoffed at such a doctrine, which did encourage him in his lusts, rather than discourage him in the least?

12. If you ask me the reason, my ground is this, because by lustful serpents like himself, he was persuaded that Christ will burn up men's lusts, and save all their souls at the last, and who can find fault with such a burning doctrine? or what bloody minded man or woman in the world, would not embrace a messenger of such tidings as this is?

13. Again, you may know I have written the truth by this token; why? because men that are guilty of almost all manner of lusts, can go into Lombard-street

to hear men speak much concerning the glorious incoming of a spiritual Christ, to burn up all their fleshly or heavenly conceitedness, that they may see nothing in them but God only triumphing on his throne; I say these, or such like expressions, the most filthiest of men can hear with delight:

14. Moreover, if you that speak in Lombard-street, or elsewhere, should once attain to the foundation of all spiritual speaking, and should be able knowingly to tell men of the sudden appearing of the Son of man in glory with his angels, to burn this visible world to ashes, and to cause the spirits and bodies of men that glory in filthiness, to burn as fire and brimstone together to eternity, in utter darkness; I am confident very few filthy persons would be able to hear you speak twice together, and then you would soon have a thin congregation, and be as much affected as men are with us, for what we speak in the name of the Lord.

15. What is the ground, think you, of so many dreadful fires this year in this city, and other parts, above the memory of man? I know, with astrologian sophisters, you may impute it to planets, plots, or peoples' want of care; but of the contrary, I believe you serpent sign-mongers will find these fires came not merely by natural causes, but by a divine power as a forerunner of the eternal burning this world, and all the natural, glory therein to dust, powder, or dry sand, as aforesaid.

16. Moreover, you know it is written, "Blessed and holy is he that hath part in the first resurrection, for on such the second death hath no power," Rev. xx. 6.

17. Also it is written, "But our conversation is in heaven, from whence also we look for the Saviour, even the Lord Jesus Christ, who shall change our vile body, that it may be fashioned like unto his glorious body, according to the working whereby he is able even to subdue all things to himself," Phil. iii. 20, 21.

18. Further, it is written, "When Christ, which is our life, shall appear, then shall ye also appear with him in glory," Col. iii. 4.

19. My beloved friends, who are possessed with a pure light, language, and life, I am undoubtably persuaded in my soul, that for a little season I have both tasted and seen, within my spirit, a greater measure of the eternal glory and shame to come, than any creature now living in this world;

20. Yet for all this, and the continual supply which I receive from that fountain of glories, I know that the most eminent appearances in these bodies of clay, are but mere shadows in comparison of that glory and shame, which many men shall possess "when the Son of man shall appear in his glory with his mighty angels."

21. If a man lie under the power of any lust, how can that man be thought to have his part in the first resurrection, because he that hath part in this first re-

surrection, is both blessed and holy?

22. Moreover, doth not a first resurrection include a second resurrection? how then can that man be thought to have part in this first resurrection, which vainly boasts that he is possessed with the second resurrection of glory with a Christ already?

23. Furthermore, you see that the apostle never boasted that he was glorified with Christ already, neither did he expect any glory, but rather continual shame until Christ did personally appear to change his vile body into the likeness of his glorious body. Again, you know it is written, "If we suffer with him, then shall we also reign with him "

24. Moreover, did Christ reign on the throne of his glory with his angels, Moses and Elias, till He had suffered under a thorny crown of unutterable cruelties unto death itself, and was risen from the dead?

25. And art thou so bewitched as to think scorn to drink of thy Lord and Master's cup, but, Lucifer-like, to exalt thyself above thy Creator, by conceiting thyself in a throne of glory with Christ already?

26. Moreover, be thou never so seemingly holy, or charitable, or a great sufferer, in reference to thy inward God or Christ, yet if thou art left to the pride of thine own spirit, to despise the Spirit of the Son of man glorified in the highest heavens, thou and all that is within thee, will eternally perish.

27. So much doth the man

Jesus in glory heed thee, and all of thy blasphemous lofty spirit: "He that denies me before men, him will I deny before my Father, which is in heaven, and his holy angels."

CHAPTER XLVIII.

1. Of the first resurrection, 2. and what it is by several questions and answers.

IN the next place give me leave to write a little of the new birth, or first resurrection from a glorified Christ.

2. What is this first resurrection, that whoever hath part in it is blessed and holy, and the second death hath no power? Truly it is the enjoyment of a divine light in the understanding which a man hath received by inspiration from the Spirit of a personal Christ on a throne of glory in the third heavens.

3. How shall a man truly know whether he hath this light in him or no, or when he received it? He that hath this light of Christ in him, his very thoughts, desires, and affections, are by the power of it wholly bent upon all spiritual and natural purity whatsoever.

4. So that the scriptures impute justice, righteousness, holiness, or perfection unto that man only which hath this light in him, because he is principally guided by a light which he hath received from the glorious God of all divine perfections without him.

5. Moreover, this light of

Christ sometimes is known by a glorious voice to the hearing of the ear, through which a man is so full of inward joy, glory, or majesty in himself, that he knows not for that present whether he be in the condition of a God or a man; this I certainly know, yet I believe few of the saints themselves have tasted of this condition.

6. Furthermore, this light of Christ conveys itself so secretly into the understandings of most of his redeemed ones, by a low voice of his most holy Spirit, that oftentimes they know not the time thereof; only after this light of life hath once appeared, the soul is so delighted with it, that it thinks it can never have too much of it, or hardly enough of it; therefore, like a woman in travail, it is full of hungering or thirsting after the knowledge of that fountain of glories from whence its light and joy proceeded.

7. Again, he that hath this light of Christ in him, is not only full of longings after more of it, but his soul is also full of that new song of praise, honour, power, and glory unto the infinite unknown God, until he doth in some measure truly know Him.

8. Moreover, he that hath this new and true light, is not rash in judging divine things he knows not, but by virtue of that light of life, he is preserved with a meek and patient spirit to wait the Lord's leisure for manifesting the truth thereof.

9. Furthermore, he that hath received this white stone, or new name of Christ to the purpose, sees all the speakings or writings of non-commissionated men but mere literal or notional emptiness, in comparison of that joy or glory that he possesseth from the invisible motions of the divine majesty Himself.

10. Again, by virtue of this light, he is made able to discern whether men's speakings or writings proceed from a literal, notional, or spiritual Christ, or no.

11. Moreover, he that hath this light of Christ thus grounded in him, doth not lie doting upon men's invisible God, Christ, spirit, light, life, love, joy, beauty, virtue, power, or glory, of mere words only; but nothing will satisfy his new-born hungry spirit but a divine embracing of a personal God of spiritual substance, yea, too transcendently glorious for men or angels to be capable of the indwelling of his eternal Spirit, but of the inshining virtues or motions only.

12. So much at present concerning the first resurrection or new birth, from a personal substantial God or Christ on the throne of eternity in the high heavens, in opposition of a supposed new birth from a notional inward Christ, or literal outward Christ only.

CHAPTER XLIX.

1. Concerning God's becoming a child. 2. None live, and move, and have their being in God, but the seed of faith. 3. No creature capable to be essentially one with God.

AGAIN, it is written, "In him we live, and move, and have our being:" also it is written, "Blessed are the dead which die in the Lord." What did the apostle mean by living in the Lord, and dying in the Lord? or, how can a man be said to live in the Lord, and to die in the Lord also?

2. My spiritual friends, though all men have their life or being in the Creator, or in his power by virtue of creation, yet none but the elect do spiritually live, move, or have any being in Him: and that is by virtue of redemption only, and that was the occasion of the prophet's saying, "For unto us a child is born, unto us a Son is given:" now you know that the prophet spoke them words long before the birth of that glorious babe, and yet you see that all his joy or glory, in reference to a life to come, was fixed only in the person of that child.

3. Thus the prophet, by virtue of the true Jesus in him, did spiritually live and move, and had his being in the Lord of hosts, in a full assurance that God, the everlasting Father, and Creator of both worlds, and all in them, would become a little child for the redemption of his elect from eternal death, by pouring forth of his most precious life. It is written, "Who hath believed our report, or unto whom is the arm of the Lord revealed?"

4. Thus you may see that those men which wanted the light of life in them, to receive that prophetical report, concerning the God of glory's coming by the outstretched arm of his eternal Spirit in a body of flesh, to redeem the elect world to Himself, were utterly ignorant of the prophet's spiritual living, moving, or being in the Lord.

5. So likewise this was the apostle Paul's meaning also, when he said, "For in him we live, and move, and have our being," according to that saying of his, "For the life which I now live is by the faith of the Son of God, which gave himself for me:" also you know, it is written to this effect, that "some men did live without God in the world;" so that you may understand that reprobate men are accounted by the spirit of the scriptures to live and to die in the devil, and to rise again very devils in souls and bodies to all eternity.

6. The chosen of God are guided by the true light or love of Christ, and by virtue of that light they are accounted to live and to die in the Lord, and to rise again in the Lord, both soul and body, because of their God-like condition, even to all eternity.

7. Thus you that are filled with the light of the true Jesus may clearly see, though a natural man by virtue of creation may be said to live in or by the power of the Lord, yet upon a spiritual account in reference to redemption, he may be an absolute devil in himself, and so wholly live in the dark power.

8. Moreover, though it is said that "the saints live and die in the Lord," yet I would not have you think that the spirits of the saints and the Spirit of the Lord are so united, that they are but

one essential life or spirit; no, that was none of the apostle's intent in those words; but, as beforesaid, his meaning was, that those men which were possessed with the true light of life eternal, by a continual intercourse with the God of glory from whence that light proceeded, they were virtually united unto the eternal Spirit.

9. Though the chosen of God are virtually united to the eternal Spirit of a glorified Christ, yet how can it be said they die in the Lord? or what is meant by their dying in the Lord? Truly most of the elect of God themselves are dark in this thing; it is a sealed book unto them; the Lord alone must open it.

10. My beloved brethren, as there is two lives of the elect in the Lord, a life of grace and a life of glory, proceeding from one and the same spirit, only differing much in degree; so, likewise, you may know there may be said to be two deaths or dyings of the saints in the Lord also.

11. Moreover, you know by virtue of the light of Christ in the new-born of God, they become dead to all their former inward filthiness of flesh and spirit, as, namely, they are dead to covetousness, envy, pride, lust, yea, and all excess of vain-glorious delights among men that perish: so likewise they are dead to all their formal righteousness, or hypocritical holiness, to be seen of men.

12. Moreover, they are dead to all carnal Christs in men whatsoever, whether they be literal, natural, or notional Christs of empty words only, arising only from that blind-born devil of man's imaginary reasons.

13. Furthermore, there is such a self-denying spirit in all experimental true-born Christians from the high heavens, that they abhor to put confidence in any God, Christ, light, or life, or to give glory unto any thing that is in sinful man or angels in the least;

14. Because they certainly know that there is not one motion or thought of any spiritual light or truth in man or angel, but what he received from an infinite glorious majesty, whose personal presence is in a world where never any actual rebellions was committed against his holy Spirit.

15. Thus, in a small measure, through divine assistance, I have showed you what is the first dying in the Lord, in reference to the first resurrection from carnal darkness, to the true light of life in Christ Jesus, God-man blessed for ever and ever, Amen. Now give me leave to write a little of the second and last dying in the Lord, because of the eternal personal glory that will immediately follow it.

CHAPTER L.

1. Of the second and last dying in the Lord. 2. What it is. 3. Eternal life is hid in the person of God only.

I KNOW the general cheat of the priests concerning this secret, for they tell the ignorant people, that the body only dies, and the soul ascends to a place of blessedness, or descends to a place of cursedness until the day of judgment, and they say then the soul assumes the body again, and so receives the sentence of eternal life and death, and so enters into heaven to the Lord, or hell with the devil and his angels, which they say are bodiless spirits.

2. If the blind lead the blind, how can they escape falling into a ditch? This opinion of theirs is like unto most of their matters, but I will pass them by, and come to the thing in hand.

3. You that are spiritual may know, that to die in the Lord, is when a man's spirit dies in a frill assurance of the resurrection of his spirit and body again out of the dust of the earth, by the spiritual power of the Lord Jesus Christ at the last day.

4. Furthermore, he that dies in the Lord, though all that is in him turns to dust for a moment, yet, before he entered into the silent sleep of death, he knew who would raise him to life and glory again at the end of time.

5. You know it is written, "When Christ which is our life shall appear, then shall ye also appear with him in glory;" now you may know that the apostle meant a personal glory that was eternal with Christ in his personal presence, and not a particular spiritual glory in the elect, which was hid, and instead of love occasioned a general hatred and persecution of men, as a delusion unto them, and the like.

6. Moreover, you know, though the apostle Paul was ravished with more glorious incomes of the love of Christ, than the rest of his brethren, yet he had many sorrowful afflictions mixed with those heavenly raptures:

7. Therefore you may know, if you are an heir of glory, that this appearing of Christ in glory to his suffering innocent people, was meant such a like glory as He now possesseth Himself in a throne of eternity, where is neither hunger, nor thirst, nor affliction of sickness, nor death, nor need of any sun, moon, or stars, or any kind of natural comforts for everlasting.

8. Furthermore, though a man be full of the glorious incomes of the eternal Spirit, yet you may know that his life is hid in that fountain of spiritual enjoyments in the new heavens and earth above this whole globe, why? because, if a man's life, or glory, were hid in that light within them, then he would not only be full of unmoveable consolations, but he would also increase in himself with such God-like wisdom, power, and glory, that no envious man would be able to behold his face and live.

9. Though the light of Christ in his new born ones, occasion much joy and peace of conscience and power, to suffer persecution for his name's sake; yet you may know, that the glory of that light might well be said to be hid with God in Christ, because the quickening power of his spiritual light in men or

angels, remains only in his own person, which is the fountain or sea of all heavenly glories, as aforesaid; "Without me, said Christ, ye can do nothing; ye are not sufficient to think a good thought," John xv. 5.

10. You may know that it is the glory of Christ's glory, which compels Him to keep the prerogative power of all his light, or life, in elect men and angels to Himself, that they may have no confidence in the strength of that light which is within them, but that they may cast down the crowns of their spiritual confidences at the divine feet of his heavenly majesty, as thee only author, protector, and finisher of their eternal blessedness.

11. So, likewise, it is with the elect also when they die in the Lord, for though the light of Christ was given them as a seal of his eternal love, that they might glory only in the Lamb, and be enabled to wear his crown of thorns to their lives' end, as a preparative unto glorious crowns at his appearing; yet I would have you for whom these thorns and crowns are prepared, to understand, because the life of all light, or glory, you possess, are hid in the divine breast, or book of life with Christ in God;

12. Therefore, when your soul comes to die, all your spiritual motions must enter into death also, until time be no more; because the power, wisdom, and glory of Christ, Will be seen in this thing above all his former works.

13. Again, He being the only light and life of men, will not this be a crown of glory to his infinite power? seeing the spirits of mankind are mixed together in the sea and earth in a marvellous manner, yet, by a word speaking, He shall call his elect by name, as He did Lazarus, and they shall hear his voice, and come forth of their graves as one man, with distinct persons all glorious, yet very flesh and bone, and with those elect then living, whose bodies shall be transmuted into glory also, ascend as swift as thought to meet their God in the air, and sit in thrones of judgment with Him over all the angels of darkness, remaining in this destroyed world for everlasting.

14. Moreover, if that error of men's bodies dying only, and not their souls, could possible be true, then no man could die, or be put to death at all; because the life of man's body is his spirit, and but one spirit only, though there is a double motion in it of contrary natures and effects by the secret decree of the Lord, for the manifestation of his eternal wisdom, power, and glory over the elect and reprobate.

15. Thus you that are spiritual may see what is meant by the saints living and dying in the Lord, and concerning the place of refuge where their lives are hid both in life and in death; is not this truth answerable to those sayings of Christ Himself in John? "The words that I speak unto you are spirit and life," vi. 63; "I am the resurrection and the life: he that believeth in me, though he were dead, yet shall

he live," xi. 25; "And he that sat upon the throne, said, Behold, I make all things new," Revelation xxi. 5; "And I will raise him up at the last day," John vi. 44. Again, "Jesus said unto her, said I not unto thee, that if thou didst believe thou shouldest see the glory of God?" John xi. 40. You know this was spoken by Christ, that God of all power, wisdom, and glory, at his raising Lazarus from death to life.

16. Therefore you may know also, that the greatest glory of all will redound to his infinite majesty; He shall shortly come in his glory with his mighty angels, to call forth the living dead, to glorious blessedness, in the great white throne, with Himself, Moses, Elias, and his angels; and to call forth the dead living, into shameful cursedness of souls and bodies in utter darkness, burning together to eternity on this earth, where they possessed all their former glory, and acted their unrighteousness against Christ and his redeemed ones; then will this scripture be fulfilled: "And they shall hear a great voice from heaven, saying unto them, Come up hither; and they shall ascend up to heaven in a cloud, and their enemies shall see them," Rev. xi. 12, and these scriptures.

CHAPTER LI.

1. Eternal damnation is a living death, and a dying life. 2. Three books will be opened at the last judgment. 3. Signifying the three commissions of the law, the gospel, and the Spirit. 4. The heathens are judged by the law of their consciences, having not had the scriptures. 5. The prophets heavenly conclusion.

AGAIN, "But fire came down from God out of heaven, and devoured them." Moreover, "And the devil that deceived them was cast into a lake of fire and brimstone, where that beast and false prophet is, and shall be tormented even day and night for evermore; and I saw the dead, both great and small, stand before God, and the books were opened, and another book was opened, which is the book of life: and the dead were judged of those things which were written in the books, according to their works: and death and hell were cast into the lake of fire burning with brimstone," xix. 20; "And whosoever was not found written in the book of life, was cast into the lake of fire," xx. 15: my brethren in the spirit and in the flesh also, which are sober, you see when Christ cometh in his glory with his angels, the books must be opened, which are three in number; the book of the administration of the law must be opened in the consciences of them that were under the law, and made a profession of obedience unto it, but hated to perform it; and they will have work enough with that fiery law, and all their former filthiness of flesh and spirit, to sit in judgment on those burning brimstone souls, and bodies of flesh and bone, to all eternity.

2. The second book of the administration of the gospel will

be opened also in the consciences of those that made a profession thereof, and hated obedience to it, and that literal fiery judge, and their former unrighteousness, will neither want work to sit in judgment on those fleshly bodies of burning brimstone, even world without end.

3. Moreover, the third book of the administration of the eternal Spirit, which is the book of life, shall be opened also in the consciences of all pretended lights in these last days, and those whose names were not found written in that book of life, as commissionated messengers of the eternal Spirit, to bear witness unto a personal Jesus in the high heavens, but published a lying Jesus in the lower heavens of their carnal spirits only, that pretended God or Christ with all their lies spoken in the name of the Lord, and blasphemy against his majesty's person, shall burn more fiery hot than any other opinion among men, even to all eternity, as aforesaid; all is not spiritual gold that glitters.

4. Again give me leave to speak of one sort more, whose natural conscience must be opened also:

5. This sort of men are those called heathens, which never had the books of the scriptures among them; I say, from the true God, that these men, and all the naturalists in the world~ according to their rebellions against their rational judge, unto which they acknowledged all obedience of righteousness between man and man was due; this God of their own reason only, with all their rebellions against it, shall be that dreadful judge sitting in their fleshly consciences with an echo of everlasting torments in utter darkness.

6. Thus, in some measure, I have been made to declare unto my spiritual, yea, and fleshly brethren also, the sudden, glorious, and dreadful appearing of the most high and mighty Godman, sitting on the throne of his glory with his elect angels, to judge both the quick and dead, according to his own sayings in holy writ.

7. And now, as a conclusion unto this epistle, I shall speak a few words to all that may peruse it, in the name and power of our Lord Jesus, by whose most blessed Spirit I was inspiringly moved to write it.

8. My beloved brethren, that hath the least hopes in you of a glory to come, I confess, through unusualness Of such a language, many sayings in this book may seem to your reason very absurd at the first;

9. But if the light of life eternal qualify you with a meek and patient spirit, they may be as plain and easy to your understanding at the last, as the Lord hath made them to me, his poor despised messenger.

10. I know if I were an university man, possessing perishing wealth or honour among princes, your rational spirits would be as subject to err on the right hand, as now they are on the left.

11. O forget not that the wisdom of God seeth it most advantageous for his glory, to choose base and despised things to confound the honourable and eloquent things of this vain glorious world.

12. Again, if some men should say unto me, that I have written many sayings without book, concerning the creation of angels, and such like, I would fain know of them, whether Moses had any books by him when he wrote of the creation of this world, and the things therein.

13. Though the holy prophets, Christ and the apostles, alluded sometimes to the former prophetical writings to convince gainsayers, yet you know they spake by inspiration of the eternal Spirit only; according to that saying in holy writ, "All scriptures were given by inspiration, and holy men of old spake as they were moved by the Holy Ghost."

14. Moreover, if you should ask me how shall you know whether I write by true inspiration or no? as to that, if you had the spirit of the scriptures, no man could deceive you.

15. Furthermore, unless you have a light in you that can clearly convince me of error in my epistle, in questioning the truth of my writings, you also question the truth of holy writ.

16. If I should write nothing but what is exactly set down in the scriptures, I should then write nothing at all, because they are other men's works, and you have them already; besides many eloquent men do play upon the harp of those records very harmoniously unto your carnal ears, which godliness of theirs is very gainful unto many of them, as you well know.

17. If I should write nothing but what is recorded in holy writ, there would be no need of any other witness to prove me a liar but my book only, and so I should be bound together in a bundle of literal tares, and burnt with unquenchable fire, at the appearing of the Son of man in his glory with his mighty angels, because I have declared myself sent forth by voice from the Lord of glory Himself, to demonstrate some secrets to his chosen one, that hath not been revealed since the world began.

18. And now I desire no other witness to bear record in the consciences of men to this epistle, whether it be truth or no, but the ever-living Jehovah, or eternal spiritual Jesus Himself, with all his holy angels. Even so, come Lord Jesus, come quickly. Amen, Amen.

JOHN REEVE and LODOWICK MUGGLETON, the two last immediate commissionated witnesses, or prophets, by the eternal Spirit of the man Jesus, glorified in the throne of eternity, which is far above all Gods, heavens, angels, and men.

THE END.

AN

OCCASIONAL DISCOURSE

FROM THE,

FIRST AND SECOND VERSES OF THE SECOND CHAPTER

OF THE

DIVINE LOOKING-GLASS;

CONCERNING

THE PROPHET REEVE

THAT

DARKNESS, DEATH, AND HELL LAY SECRETLY HID IN THE SPIRITUAL
EARTH ETERNALLY WITH GOD.

BY

THE PROPHET MUGGLETON,

SEPTEMBER 28, ANNO DOMINI 1668.

AN OCCASIONAL DISCOURSE,
&c.

THE heaven of glory, that is now God's throne, with the substance of earth and water, was eternally uncreated in the presence of God, who was alone by Himself before any created being appeared in his sight; then his glorious wisdom moved Him by a word speaking to that spiritual earth above this global world, to create an innumerable company of glorious spiritual angels, whose form and image was the same as God's, only differing in their natures; the angel's, nature being pure reason, and God's nature divine faith. And there was no impure thing in his sight; only He created one angel more glorious than the rest. After this, the glorious wisdom of God moved Him to create this mortal visible world of earth and water, which were eternal substances, but dark, dead, and senseless: and of this visible mortal earth, the glorious wise God created Adam and Eve in his own image, and breathed into them the breath of life: that breath of the ever-living God made their souls spiritual and immortal, and would. have so continued: but now, behold, what the wisdom of God moved Him to: He first tries what his creature, that holy angel, would do, or what would become of him if He did withdraw his revelation from him, and leave him to himself: not that God had eternally decreed this, but as his glorious wisdom moved him to this or that: for if God knew what was past, present, and to come, there was an end of his wisdom, and so would not be infinite; but this makes Him infinite, that his wisdom is eternally increasing. Now, when God did withhold his revelation from this glorious angel, his pure reason in creation became impure, and aspired to be above the Creator; which, when God saw and knew, those vilifying thoughts that continually sprang in him, He cast him down from heaven like lightning. From that very moment good and evil was visible in this creation; which was the tree of knowledge of good and evil, which stood before Adam and Eve. Here sin entered into the world: therefore, the glorious God. having found, by the trial of his first creature, how it became with him, his wisdom saw it good to leave man, of his own nature, to himself: only, He first gave man a law, that if he hearkened to the subtlety of that reprobate fallen spiritual glorious angel, by eating or believing in him, he should die the death; that is, that immortal soul he were created in, while he stood in obedience to God, could not fall: but he should by disobedience become mortal. Now the subtlety of this glorious angel was too powerful for Eve, (Adam was not in the least concerned in Eve's temptation,) but being overcome by the serpent angel, he having power, presently enters her womb: for the nature of spiritual bodies can transmute itself into as small a place as it pleaseth; and this angel pollutes her, makes her defiled, fills her pure innocent soul with lustful thoughts and desires towards her husband. There this immortal reprobate angel lays down his immortality, in becoming seed; and had or could Eve have lived without the embraces of her husband, she would, in her appointed time, brought forth Cain, the offspring and only begotten Son of that reprobate angel, the father of all the devils in the world: but she could not forbear, but tempt poor innocent Adam, who is overcome by hearkening to Eve's words, and so becomes polluted too; then at that very time death entered into the world, and not before. Now, as concerning hell, God comes and says, "I will put enmity between the two seeds, the seed of the woman, and the seed of the serpent." There was in Cain part of the woman's seed (which was God's nature) as well as the serpent's: likewise, in Abel, there was two seeds: but here lies the difference; in Cain, the seed of his father, the reprobate angel was predominate, and lord over that spark of the seed of the woman; whereas, in Abel, whom Adam begot, though both seeds were in him, yet the seed of faith being God's divine nature, was predominate, and did so captivate the seed of reason in him, that his sacrifice was acceptable before God, when Cain's was refused, which made him slay his brother Abel. Now, mark, the seed of reason, which is the seed of the serpent, or the reprobate angel, or the devil, should bruise the heel of the seed of the woman, or the seed of faith: but "the seed of the woman shall break the serpent's head." Now, when the glorious God did fulfil his promise, and saw it most fit to transmute his glorious immortality into a mortal human condition of flesh, blood, and bone, by entering into the virgin's womb, who, in time, shedding his most precious blood, hath overcome sin, death, and hell; which hell, as yet, hath no being: although the heaven of glory, which will be the reward of the elect seed, be in being, and ever was: yet the place of torment will appear but in time, when God will call all to judgment.

By LODOWICK MUGGLETON.

THE END.

JOYFUL NEWS FROM HEAVEN:

OR,

THE LAST INTELLIGENCE

FROM

OUR GLORIFIED JESUS ABOVE THE STARS,

WHEREIN IS INFALLIBLY RECORDED

HOW THAT THE SOUL DIETH IN THE BODY:

ALSO IS DISCOVERED,

I. WHAT THAT IS WHICH SLEEPS IN THE DUST.
II. THE NATURE OF ITS REST.
III. THE MANNER OF ITS WAKING.

IV. THE MYSTERY OF THE DISPUTE BETWEEN CHRIST AND THE WOMAN OF SAMARIA, AS TOUCHING THE TRUE POINT OF WORSHIP, CLEARLY OPENED

WHEREIN YOU HAVE, DRAWN UP,

A DIVINE CHARGE AGAINST THE TEACHERS OF THE BAPTISTS;

WITH ALL OTHER TEACHERS, PUBLIC AND PRIVATE, FOR COUNTER-FEITING THE COMMISSION OF

THE MAN JESUS,

BEING THEREIN CONVICTED OF SPIRITUAL HIGH TREASON AGAINST CHRIST, THE GREAT COMMISSIONER OF HEAVEN AND EARTH.

WITH A TRUE DESCRIPTION OF THE KINGDOM OF GLORY, PREPARED ONLY FOR

THE SEED OF ADAM, THAT BLESSED SEED OF FAITH;

AND TRUE RELATION **OF THE KINGDOM OF DARKNESS, PREPARED FOR THE CURSED SEED OF CAIN,**

WORLD WITHOUT *END.*

WRITTEN BY JOHN REEVE AND LODOWICK MUGGLETON.

THE LAST COMMISSIONATED WITNESSES AND PROPHETS OF THAT ONLY HIGH,
IMMORTAL, GLORIOUS GOD, CHRIST JESUS.
FIRST PRINTED FOR THE AUTHOR, IN THE YEAR OF OUR LORD,
1658,
THEN RESIDING IN LONDON.
THIRD EDITION.
London:
PRINTED FOR JOSEPH FROST, 17, HALF MOON STREKT, BISHOPSGATE STREET,
BY LUKE JAMES HANSARD, 5, PEMBERTON ROW, GOUGH SQUARE, FLEET STREET.

1854.

TO THE READER,

17, Half Moon Street, Bishopsgate Street,
London.

BELOVED BRETHREN,—

IN reprinting and putting this excellent treatise on the "SOUL'S MORTALITY" into chapter and verse, great care has been taken to give a correct copy of the original, printed for the Author in the year, 1658.

The printer of this edition having been very careful, there appears no occasion for an errata.

It may be worth observing, that this treatise on the "SOUL'S MORTALITY" appears to agree with our forefathers from the beginning of the world.

As may be seen by the book of Enoch, taken from the Ethiopic bible (the eunuch whom Philip addressed in the chariot was a man of Ethiopia, *Acts* viii. 26, so that there was true faith in Ethiopia enough to preserve the sacred writings), and translated by Richard Lawrence, Archbishop of Cashel (which is sold by J. H. Parker, Oxford, and J. G. Rivington, London). Although this is called an Apocryphal production, yet it does not exactly follow that it is not a true copy of the book of Enoch, the son of Adam. I believe those who understand Hebrew may trace the roots of the language back to the Hebrew, which was the first language spoken, according to that scripture, *Genesis* xi. 5: "And the whole earth was of one language and of one speech," till the Lord confounded their language at the building of the tower of Babel, verse 9. All the covenants of God were made with the Hebrews, and would naturally be written in that language. It is written, "Salvation is of the Jews;" God himself was a Jew, and came in the tribes of Levi and Judah. The visions and prophecies of Enoch appear to be in accordance with the teaching and writings of the prophets and apostles, being directed to the righteous and unrighteous, and pointing to the mortality of the soul, and the resurrection at the last day. Enoch wrote of things from the beginning and prophesies of things to the end of the world;—that is, of Adam and Eve, the Tree of Life, the Tree of Knowledge of Good and Evil, the Garden of Paradise, of Cain and Abel, and of many others whose names are handed down, and with whom he appears to have been very conversant. He also prophesies of the Incarnation of God, who will go forth from his habitation, the Holy and Mighty One, chapter i. 3, and so on to chapter xlvi., where he declares that this Mighty One, the Ancient of Days, the Lord of Spirits, will take on him a body of flesh, whom he calls the Son of Man, because the Lord of Spirits had chosen him, in which body of flesh the Father would do many wonderful things (as may be seen in those parables of Enoch), whom afterwards he calls the Son of Woman, before whom all shall appear at the last day, and in whom the Father dwells; who will give judgment, both to the righteous and unrighteous, through the mouth of his chosen Son. Visions and prophecies cannot be understood now any more than they could be then, but only seen darkly as in a glass, without direct revelations from God, or those persons chosen by him to reveal them; as may be seen by the revelator or angel who taught Enoch, the prophets, apostles, and ministers of the Spirit, through whom we have received the mysteries, revelations, and interpretations, or golden oil, spoken of by Enoch and the rest of the prophets, as *Zechariah* iv. 12, which, through the golden pipes, or prophets, empty the golden oil out of themselves into the vessels of gold, or believers. You may see, after the apostles had received their commission from God, that on whom they laid their hands, they received the Holy Ghost. Also you may see that this grace or golden oil is not to be bought, *Acts* viii. 18, where Simon offered money for that power: but Peter said, "Thy money perish with thee; the gifts of God may not be purchased with money." Also in the parable of the five foolish virgins, *Matthew* xxv., who were shut out, with the servant who had but one talent of reason, without any oil, or faith in the bridegroom or master. It will appear that the book of Enoch was written before the flood or drowning of the old world, because Enoch prophesies of the Deluge, and of Noah and his family being chosen as a foundation for a new world. Enoch wrote books for his son Methuselah, and for those who should come after in the latter days, page 164, which were given to Noah, and Noah handed them to his family, and so on to Abraham, Isaac, Jacob, and the twelve patriarchs.

As may be seen by the book of the Testaments of the Twelve Patriarchs, sons of Jacob, translated out of Greek into Latin by Robert Grotshead, Bishop of Lincoln, Englished and printed for the Company of Stationers, London, in the year 1693; since reprinted by James Frost, Brick-lane, Whitechapel, London, of which I have a few copies; so that any desirous may have one for 1s. 6d. The book of Enoch, and Testaments of the Twelve Patriarchs, not being generally known, is the reason I have given the address where they may be had; but I have none of the books of Enoch for sale. From the book of the Twelve Patriarchs it appears that the book of Enoch was well known to them; for seven out of them say that they have real, in the book of Enoch, of things that should come upon their children in the latter days: the seven are Simeon, Levi, Judah, Zabulon, Dan, Nephtalim, and Benjamin. These testaments bear witness, with Enoch, that the same God will appear on earth in a body of flesh in the tribes of Levi and Judah; in Levi as prince of priests, and in Judah as king of kings, being God and man in one person. They also treat of the soul's mortality, and of its death and resurrection at the last day, saying that God would come eating and drinking with man as man, and be put to death far the redemption of Israel.

I have quoted a few sayings from the seven (which are as follow), to inform or enlighten the reader.

SIMEON.—Page 26: "And now, my children, let your hearts be meek before the Lord, and walk right before man; so shall ye find favour both with God and man; and beware that ye fall not into whoredom." Page 27: "For I have seen in Enoch's writings that you and your children shall be corrupted with whoredom, and do Levi wrong by the sword; but they shall not prevail against Levi, because he shall fight the Lord's battles, and take also your tents, and very few shall be divided in Levi and Judah." Page 28: "Then shall Sem be glorified, when the great Lord God of Israel appeareth upon earth as a man; for the Lord will set up of Levi the prince of priests, and of Judah king of kings, God and man."

LEVI.—Page 34: "Chosen a minister till God visits all nations in the bowels of the mercy of his Son for ever; nevertheless thy sons shall lay their hands upon him to crucify him." Page 40: "I am clear from all the wickedness and sin which you shall commit to the end of the world." Page 41: "Ye shall work wickedness against the Saviour of the world, so that Jerusalem shall not continue by reason of your naughtiness; nevertheless the house which the Lord shall choose shall be called Jerusalem, as the book of Enoch the righteous containeth." Page 44: "And truly, my children, I know by the writings of Enoch that in the end ye shall do wickedly, laying hands most spitefully upon the Lord; howbeit our father Israel is clear from the wickedness of the high priest, which shall lay hands upon the Saviour of the world. Furthermore, I know by the book of Enoch that ye shall go astray, and defile the priesthood, stain the sacrifices, destroy the law, despise the sayings of the prophets, and in the end ye shall kill Him out of hand, as ye think, not knowing that he shall rise again." Page 49: "And stay the threatening sword against Adam, and feed the lambs with the fruit of life."

JUDAH.—Page 66: "And Abraham, the father of my fathers, blessed me to fight for Israel, and so did Isaac bless me likewise; and I know that the kingdom shall stand by me: but I have read in the book of Enoch the righteous that ye shall work wickedness in the latter days." Paige 70: "And my kingdom shall be knit up in strangers till the Saviour of Israel come, and he shall maintain my kingdom in peace for ever." Page 72: "This is the offspring of the most high God, and the well-spring of life to all flesh: they that are buried in sorrow shall rise in joy."

ZABULON.—Pages 84 and 85: "Of Joseph being sold to the Ishmaelites for money, with which they bought shoes for themselves, their wives, and their children, saying, Let us not eat it, because it is the price of our brother's blood, but let us tread and trample it under our feet, because he said he should reign over us, and we shall see what his dreams will come unto. Therefore in the sceptre of Enoch's law it is written of him that would not raise up seed to his brother, I have loosed Joseph's shoe; for when we came out of Egypt the young men unbuckled Joseph's shoes at the gate; and so we worshipped Joseph as if it had been Pharaoh." Page 90: "I know by the writings of my fathers that in the last days ye shall depart from the Lord, and be divided in Israel, following two kings." Page 91: "Working all abominations, and worshipping all manner of idols; after this shall God himself rise up unto you, the light of righteousness, and ye shall see God in the shape of man."

DAN.—Page 98: "For I am sure that in the latter days ye shall depart from the Lord, and walk in naughtiness, working the abominations of the Gentiles, and haunting wicked woman in all lewdness, by the working of deceitful spirits in you; for I have read in Enoch that Satan is your prince, and that all the spirits of fornication and pride shall ply themselves in laying snares for the children of Dan; but the Lord's saving health shall spring up unto you out of the tribes of Judah and Levi." Page 92: "He shall deliver the imprisoned souls of the saints from Belial, and turn your unbelieving hearts to the Lord, and give everlasting peace to such as call upon Him. The saints shall rest in Him, and the righteous shall rejoice in the New Jerusalem which shall glorify God for ever. The Holy One of Israel shall reign over you in lowliness and poverty; and he that believeth in Him, shall certainly reign in heaven."

NEPHTALIM.—Page 106: "Neither break you God's law in the order of your doing: the Gentiles, by going astray, and by forsaking the Lord, have changed their order, and followed stocks and stones and spirits of error, but do ye not so, my children: know ye not that your only one God is the Lord of all creatures, for He is the Maker of them; they whom God cursed in the flood, making the earth desolate and fruitless for their sakes." Page 107: "My children, I say these things because I have read in the holy writings of Enoch, that you also shall depart from the Lord, and walk in all the wickedness of Sodom, till in the mercy of the Lord come a Man that poureth out mercy and righteousness upon all men both far and near. Be helpful to Levi and Judah, for by Judah's sceptre shall God appear, and dwell among men upon earth, to save the flock of Israel."

BENJAMIN.—Page 151: "My children, love the God of heaven, and obey his commandments: follow that good and holy man Joseph, for in Joseph shall the prophecy of heaven be resembled to the full concerning the Lamb of God and Saviour of the world, that the unspotted shall be delivered from the wicked doers, and he that is without sin shall die for sinners in the blood of his testament, to the salvation both of the Gentiles and Israel." Page 155: "A good mind hath not two tongues, one to bless with, and another to curse with; one to slander with, and another to honour with," &c. Page 156: "But all the works of Belial are double, and utterly void of simplicity." Page 158: "I perceive by the sayings of the righteous Enoch, that there shall be evil deeds among you; for you shall defile yourselves with the fornication of Sodom. Nevertheless the Lord's temple shall be made in our portion, for the Lord himself shall take the kingdom upon him, and the twelve tribes shall be gathered together there. He shall enter into the first temple, and there the Lord shall suffer wrong and be despised, and be lifted up unto a piece of timber." Page 159: "And the vail of the temple shall be rent asunder, and the Spirit of the Lord shall come down upon the Gentiles poured out like fire; and rising up from the grave, he shall ascend from earth to heaven. He shall remember how basely he hath been treated on earth, and how glorious he is in heaven. Keep the Lord's commandments, till he reveal his saving health unto all nations." Page 160: "Then shall ye see Enoch, Noah, Shem, Abraham, Isaac and Jacob, sitting at his right hand with joyfulness. Then shall we rise also, every of us to his own sceptre, worshipping the King of heaven. Then shall He judge all nations, as many as believed not in him, when he appeared on earth."

All the twelve patriarchs, with Enoch, are of one faith and one mind in reference to the one personal God. Although I have only quoted from the seven which mention the book of Enoch, yet they all bear one and the same evidence with the prophets and apostles, which the reader may see and compare with the Bible and Testament, and witnesses of the Spirit.

Moses declares, by commission from God, that God created man in His own image and likeness, in the image of God he created him, male and female created he them, and breathed into them the breath of life, and they became living souls; and he gave them a law, and commanded them not to eat of the tree of knowledge of good and evil, saying, "Thou shalt not eat of it, for in the day thou eatest thereof thou shalt surely die." (It is written the soul that sins shall die—it is not written the body, but the soul.) That tree was the tree of eternal death, which through their disobedience they became united with, and so were taken captive by death. The tree of knowledge, being transmuted into flesh, appeared in Cain, he being the destroyer who killed his brother Abel. Therefore it is Written, "Death reigned over all life from Adam," *Rom.* vi. 14. The tree of life, to fulfil his promise to Adam of breaking the serpent's head, being transmuted into flesh, appeared in Christ, to redeem all life lost through Adam's fall. Adam, being only a created nature, could not stand against that which is an eternal nature, for nothing less than eternal life could conquer eternal death. Therefore it is written, "O death, I will be thy death. O grave, I will be thy victory." This God in Christ was Melchizedek, king of

Salem, priest of the Most High God, who brought forth bread and wine, and blessed Abraham, *Gen.* xiv. 18, and *Paul's Epistle to the Hebrews,* chapter vii., and when the Jews said to Christ, "Art thou greater than our Father Abraham?" Jesus said "Verily, verily, I say unto you, before Abraham was I am," *St. John,* chapter viii. He was the same "I am" that sent Moses to Pharaoh. Moses, prophesying, says, "From among your brethren God shall raise up a prophet like unto me, him shall you hear." See Moses in his prayer and supplications, and breaking bread with his hands, and with his eyes looking up to heaven. It is not to be supposed that he was noticing the bread then in his hand, which was but a type or shadow of the true bread; but that he was looking for God corning down to take a body of flesh, and to die for the redemption of the house of Israel, as may be seen, *St. John,* chapter vi. 51: "I am that living bread which came down from heaven," which Isaiah speaks of, chapter xliv. 6: "The Redeemer, I am the first and the last; besides me there is no God." Answerable to those commandments in *Exodus,* chapter xx. "Thou shalt have no other gods but me." "Thou shalt not make any graven image or likeness, nor bow down thyself to them nor serve them." "Thou shalt not commit spiritual whoredom or adultery, in worshipping of false gods which are images or idols, vain thoughts or idle imaginations; but. Him only shalt thou serve." So *Isaiah,* chapter ix. 6, "For unto us a child is born, unto us a Son is given, and the government shall be upon his shoulder, and his name shall be called Wonderful, Counsellor, the Mighty God, the everlasting Father, the Prince of Peace."

In the New Testament the apostles declare that God, who is called Christ, was then come in flesh (which was foretold by Enoch, the twelve patriarchs, Moses and the prophets), and was born of the Virgin Mary in Bethlehem of Judea, who was also called Jesus the Son of God, in respect of his spiritual body being changed into a body of flesh: but his eternal spirit was never less than God. He was transmuted into a body of flesh, but his spirit was not changed as his body was. Therefore it is written, "God was made manifest in the flesh, which is Emmanuel, God with us," in which body He wrought all those wonderful works, when, by speaking a word only, he cured all diseases; cast out devils; caused the lame to walk, the blind to *see,* the deaf to hear, the dumb to speak; healed the sick and lunatics; walked on the sea and rebuked the wind; raised the dead, and performed many other miracles and wonderful things, more than can be named, of which the apostles were witnesses, as may be seen more abundantly in their writings, miracles which no mortal can do, without first receiving power from Him. Also he was a Counsellor, in preaching the everlasting gospel of peace himself, and through his prophets and apostles to all nations; he being Melchizedek, king of peace and prince of priests. The Mighty God, in the he took on him a body of flesh, and suffered death on the cross, and rose again by his own power, which no created nature could do. The everlasting Father, in that he will raise all those who had faith in him. The Prince of Peace, in that they shall ascend with him into his everlasting kingdom, where he will reign over them in perpetual peace and great glory, world without end. That Son Isaiah prophesies of, is the same God that John bears witness of, *John i:* "In the beginning was the word, and the word was with God, and the word was God. The same was in the beginning with God. All things were made by him, and without him was not anything made that was made." Verse 14: "The word was made flesh, and dwelt amongst us, as the only-begotten Son of the Father, full of grace and truth," *Colossians* ii. 9: "For in Him dwelleth all the fulness of the Godhead bodily." See the genealogy of Christ, *Luke* iii.: who called himself the Son of David according to the flesh. But in spirit he was David's Lord, who was the son of Jacob, son of Isaac, son of Abraham, son of Noah, son of Enoch, son of Adam, son of God (seeing the book of Enoch and the book of the twelve patriarchs have been discovered, why they have not been joined and bound with the Bible and Testament I cannot tell, seeing that they appear to have more evidence in their favour, than either the books of the Apocrypha, or the writings of Solomon); "for I, Jesus, say unto you, that many shall come from the east and west, and shall sit down with Abraham, Isaac, and Jacob, in the kingdom of heaven;" *Matthew* viii. 11: who said, "I am not come to destroy, but to fulfil the law and the prophets." Thus the Creator, the Father of Spirits, the great I am, who said, "Heaven and earth shall pass away, but my word shall not pass away," is the Redeemer, "the first and the last, he that was dead and is alive, and behold, he lives for ever. Amen."

In the third and last Testament of our Lord and Saviour Jesus Christ, by JOHN REEVE and LODOWICK MUGGLETON (spoken of in the eleventh chapter of the *Revelations of Saint John the Divine),* who were to appear in the latter days, it is declared that God spake to them by voice of words to the hearing of the ear in the same manner as he spake to Moses, the prophets, and the apostles; and that he gave them a commission to interpret the Scriptures, and to make known his prerogative power, will, and pleasure, before he appears at the great day of judgment. They also declare that the words spoken to them became revelation, which was the spirit of life from God which entered into the dead bodies of the prophets and apostles, giving the true interpretation of all the chief mysterious sayings, visions, revelations, and prophecies. It made the scriptures to stand upon their feet, to the amazement of many, and fear fell upon them, and the remnant gave glory to the God of heaven. Again they declare that, as John the Baptist was the forerunner of the birth of Christ, in like manner they are the forerunners of Christ appearing in glory with His ten thousands of saints and angels at the last day of judgment, to separate between the righteous and unrighteous, who will give every one a reward according to his works; and that they are the conclusion and true interpreters of all the inspirations of the holy prophets that shall ever appear by commission from God to the end of the world. They also speak of the book of Enoch and the book of the twelve Patriarchs, as may be seen in the answer to William Penn, chapter 9, page 32. So that it may be seen that there is a spiritual line of truth drawn from the true God, through the righteous fathers, down to the present day; and that the prophets are all joined hand in hand, making but one chain of evidence from the beginning, which is Adam, Enoch, Noah, Abraham, Isaac, Jacob, the twelve Patriarchs, Moses and the Prophets, Christ and the Apostles, and Reeve and Muggleton, with those in the genealogy of Christ not here named; they all uniting in the faith of a one personal God. I have printed a list of REEVE and MUGGLETON'S books, which will give the reader more information of these heavenly secrets than I can; knowing that secrets belong to God, but when revealed they belong to man, and are set before all nations, without persecution, with reference to His Divine justice, so that they may choose or refuse: because the people of all nations must appear before him at the last day. These, I think, should not be kept back, they being directed or sent in general to the whole world.

Thus, I have endeavoured to point out the strait and narrow path which must be kept, by faith in the true prophets, while in our pilgrimage we pass through the dark wilderness of many opinions towards the new Jerusalem, which was four-square when Christ was nailed to the cross (his divine hands, when spread abroad, being made equal with his glorious head and feet), who receiveth no worship through idols or images, but only through the spirit of true faith in his person.

Yours in the faith

Of a one Personal God,

JOSEPH FROST.

February, 1854.

CONTENTS.

THE SOUL'S SLEEPING IN THE DUST.
(The Manner of the Soul's Waking,)

 I. The Sleep spoken of by St. Paul, as quoted, is that of the Soul. 2. If the Soul does not Sleep with the Body, there can be no Resurrection

 II. The Soul is not capable of sensible waking, without its Body. 2. The Soul must sleep in the earth before it can become immortal

 III. The Seed of Man dies in generation. 2. The Soul is not already. 3. Neither natural nor spiritual Life can be possessed, but through Death

TRUE WORSHIP DISCOVERED.
('The Mystery of the Dispute between Christ and the Woman of Samaria, as touching the True Point of Worship, clearly opened)

 I. The Soul of Christ was God abiding in His Person. 2. The Worship of the Saints is an inward Stillness, by which their Souls are made willing to hearken to the Voice or Motions of the Holy Spirit. 3. None can worship God, until they are enlightened by the Spirit of God

 II. The Worship of God is not an external act, but an internal devotion. 2. Christ's Body, after his Resurrection, was a spiritual Body of Flesh and Bones

NO SPIRIT WITHOUT A BODY.

 I. All Bodies, natural and spiritual, are visible; all Spirits, invisible. 2. The Apostles, through fear, supposed that a Spirit could be visible

 II. Spirits are not merely invisible to, but they are incomprehensible by, mortal men. 2. But the Soul is capable of hearing and understanding the Voice and Motions of the Holy Spirit

THE BAPTIST'S MISSION COUNTERFEITED.
(A Divine Charge against the Teachers of the Baptists.)

 I. The Worship of the Baptists is founded on the letter of the

Scriptures and their own lying Reason. 2. All true Christians are now under the Ministry of the Holy Spirit. 3. No Man, since the Apostles, has been commissioned to administer divine Ordinances. 4. The Scriptures were written by men who were moved by the Spirit of God. 6. The Baptists have no divine authority for their mission

II. There is no evidence in the New Testament to authorise the Mission of the Baptists. 2. The Characteristics of Love and Envy contrasted

III. The difference between the Call of the Apostles and the assumed Mission of the Baptists. 2. The Baptists are not commissioned by the Spirit of Christ. 3. The Case of John Chandler instanced. 4. The Commission of the Apostles was authenticated by apostolical gifts

IV. Men dare not receive any in the place of the Apostles unless by the concurrent testimony of the Holy Spirit. 2. Christ is present with His Apostles, that is, with those who worship Him in spirit with the Apostles, to the end of the world. 3. This presence of Christ is spiritual

V. The Scriptures account those men but Vagabonds, and Workers of Iniquity, who presume to minister in divine things without a Commission from Christ. 2. The sons of Sceva were not in the Scripture called Vagabonds, and Exorcists, until they assumed the Authority of an Apostle. 3. There are two sorts of vagabonds: (1.) Natural, i.e., those who resist the Civil Power; aid (2.) Spiritual, i.e., those who, without authority, aspire to the Gospel Ministry

VI. Christ endued His Apostles with spiritual Power. 2. The Ministry of the Baptists is not accompanied by any manifestations of such divine power. 3. The Baptists preach by Commission from an earthly Power

A TRUE DESCRIPTION OF HEAVEN AND HELL.

I. The Kingdom of Glory is not in a global condition, as this world is, but boundless; 2. Full of all variety of Soul-Delights; and, 3. Full of Glory suitable for the glorified Bodies of Christ and the Elect. 4. There are two sorts of spiritual Bodies appointed for eternal burnings: (1.) The one hash a Spirit of Love; (2.) The other, a Spirit of Envy. 5. Difference between the pleasures of the carnal, and the joys of the spiritual, Body. 6. The Glory of the spiritual Body described.

II. On the Kingdom of Darkness, wherein wicked men shall be tormented, (1.) By the memory of the crimes they have committed, and of the good things they have enjoyed; (2.) By the remembrance that they have despised the glorious Truths of Eternity; and (3.) By the Divine Wrath in their souls re-kindling envy towards God and His redeemed ones. 2. The scene of their former pleasures shall be the place of their torment. 3. Conclusion

THE SOUL'S MORTALITY PROVED AGAINST ALL GAINSAYERS.

(WHAT THAT IS WHICH SLEEPS IN THE DUST.)

CHAPTER I.

1. The divine Power of our Lord, (1.) To enter into Death, and (2.) To quicken Life out of Death. 2. Christ raised the Soul and Body of Lazarus. 3. The Soul of David is not ascended into Heaven. 4. God able to destroy Body and Soul.

YOU have a spiritual epistle full of divine consolation and information of judgment, unto those only which in any measure are enabled truly to comprehend it.

2. In John the 10th, there saith Christ, "I lay down my life that I might take it again. No man taketh it from me, I lay it down of myself. I have power to lay it down, and power to take it again."

3. My beloved brethren, in the latter words of this text is comprehended all the wisdom, power, and glory of Infiniteness itself.

4. First of all, here our Lord doth as it were present unto your spiritual view a two-fold comprehension of his God-head power: First, a divine power to enter into death; Secondly, being dead, a power to quicken life out of death, or silent darkness itself.

5. Moreover, because many of the blessed ones are not fully satisfied concerning Christ's soul dying with his body, therefore I shall write somewhat from his own words, spoken upon that account.

6. In John the 12th, it is thus written, "Except the wheat corn fall into the ground and die, it abideth alone; but if it die, it bringeth forth much fruit,

7. Dear friends, oh, what a fit resemblance is there between the spiritual Prince of Glory, and the natural prince of grain, if it be rightly understood!

8. Furthermore, you know that, except the wheat corn wholly dies, in the heart of the earth, instead of an increase of thirty, sixty, or an hundred fold, for want of dying it appears no more in the least: so, likewise, had not Christ's divine life been wholly dead and buried, in the heart of the grave, with the body of his flesh, what spiritual advantage of a glorious increase to himself, through the spirits of elect men and angels, could have been attained to in the least?

9. Again, you know that the flower is the life of the wheat corn, and that, yea, that life hath its being throughout the whole grain, making but only one bodily living and dying life, that it may be capable to produce a multitude of living bodies into its own likeness; so likewise you may also know, that the soul was the pure life of Christ's

flesh; and that, yea, that divine life had its being throughout the whole man, making but one only living and dying essence, that it might be capable to produce many bodies in his own spiritual likeness, out of the sleep of death, by the glorious power of his word speaking only, when with his saints and angels He shall visibly appear into eternal judgment,

10. Moreover, doth not the spirit of the wheat corn naturally die, and in the same body it died in, even through death itself, quicken into variety of life again, by virtue of a creative word only, without any additional power from the Creator in the least; so that it enjoys its appointed refreshings in the season thereof?

11. It is written, "The last Adam was made a quickening spirit (the second man is the Lord from heaven)." Why then should it seem hard or strange unto a spiritual christian, that the soul of Christ should naturally die within his body, and through death itself produce all variety of divine life again, without any additional power in the least (seeing He alone became that all-quickening spiritual God- man), from whence, as from an everlasting fountain, floweth all spiritual and natural light, even through heavens, earth, waters, men, angels, and all creatures possessing virtue in them.

12. Furthermore, though all the life of the wheat corn by degrees wholly dieth from its present life, yet no mortal man can possibly know, in how short a time it is quickened into life again; so likewise it was with the life of Christ Jesus the Lord; for although his divine soul wholly died with his natural body, yet, because its divine nature was of an all-quickening infinite virtue, and of motion swifter than thought, therefore there can be no expression of time between dying and living again: observing of time belongs only unto that life which is sensible of its own dying; but as for that eternal life which was in Christ Jesus, which passed through death swifter than thought, and those souls that are senseless of all motion, light, or life, in the dust of the earth, what time is there to them in the least?

13. Again, in the next place, for a further insight into this supernatural mystery of Christ's God-head passing through death into a new and glorious life, even naturally, as the most purest grain, I shall write something as concerning Lazarus, and something in relation to David.

14. In the 11th chapter of Saint John, it is thus written: "Then said Jesus unto them plainly, Lazarus is dead; then when Jesus came, He found that lie had lain in the grave four days already."

15. Now, if it should be still imagined, by some that are of a weak faith, that the soul of Lazarus died not at all, but was living in a paradisaical estate elsewhere, whilst his body remained in the grave; then I would gladly know, if known, where that paradise was, or is?

16. Moreover, if, for want of the knowledge of any such place, thou reply and say, his soul for that season was ascended into the highest heavens; then I would also know, whether it he not contrary to all sober sense or reason in man, that a soul once immortalized should descend into a condition of mortality again?

17. Furthermore, seeing, according to truth and sobriety of spirit, there was no paradise nor heaven to be found for the soul of Lazarus, whilst his body remained in the grave, where then should his soul enter, but with his body only?

18. Christ said that his words were spirit and life, and that He was the resurrection and the life. Since the soul of man was therefore polluted, through carnal generation, thou mayest know that man's spirit and body is but only one undivided living and dying essence; and the infinite virtue of Christ's word only, was that God which revived the soul and body of Lazarus out of the grave of death into this natural life again, for the manifestation of the glory of his Godhead power in the spirits of his redeemed ones; that they, in some measure, may know, to the praise of his unsearchable wisdom and power, who it is that quickeneth souls out of the death of sin into the life of grace, and out of the grave of death into the life of glory at the last day.

19. Again, in the 2nd chapter of the Acts of the Apostles, it is thus written: "Men and brethren, I may boldly speak unto you of the patriarch David, that he is both dead and buried, and his sepulchre remaineth with us unto this day; for David is not ascended into heaven." What thinkest thou, is not the soul of man the ascending part, light, or life of the body? What then was that which died, and was buried, and ascended not into heaven? Was it not David's whole man, both soul and body, that saw corruption?

20. If as yet thou art not clearly convinced of the soul's mortality, when the body of David had neither motion, life, light, nor breath, in it, I would fain know where his soul was, seeing the apostle said, "For David is not ascended into heaven."

21. Moreover, when David's not ascending into heaven was mentioned by the apostle, if his soul had been capable of a sensible heaven or paradise, until the end of the world, without his body, would not the prophets, or the apostles, have declared it one time or another, it being a thing of so great concernment? Is there any more than one true peace, or soul-paradise to be enjoyed in this life? And canst thou imagine, or think, that there should be two distinct heavens, or paradisaical conditions, to be enjoyed in the life to come?

22. Furthermore, is the body of man capable of any good or evil in the least, unless it be moved thereunto by its soul? And is it not the spirit or soul only which comprehends all spiritual or natural things

whatsoever? What, then, was that which, instead of ascending into life, heaven, or glory, descended into death or dust, but the very soul of David, as well as his body?

23. Thus you which are of a spiritual comprehension may clearly see, that, wheresoever the Scriptures make mention of ascending, descending, living, or dying of man, they always point at the soul of the man, though the body sometimes be first mentioned.

24. Again, it is written: "And fear ye not them which kill the body, but are not able to kill the soul; but rather fear Him which is able to destroy both body and soul in hell."

25. Almost all men are at a great loss, through the variety and seeming contrariety of Scripture-sayings. Now, you know that the Scriptures bear but a two-fold sense in them, and no more; that is to say, history and mystery, natural or spiritual. No man, therefore, is capable truly to comprehend Scripture mysteries or secrets, unless he possesseth the invisible life or power of them in his own soul.

26. Moreover, unless a man be endued with a divine gift in some spiritual depths above all other men, did the Lord of glory, think you, commission that man to interpret heavenly mysteries to his brethren? I trow not. For I certainly know that those that are sent of God by an immediate call or voice from on high, are endued with an infallible knowledge of God's secret counsels above all other men in this world.

27. You that are swift in spiritual comprehensions, consider what I shall here write, and the Lord give you understanding of the truth of it.

28. There is a two-fold life and death in all mankind, either a natural, or a spiritual. A man may be in perfect health upon a natural account, and sick unto death upon a spiritual account, at one and the same time; so likewise of the contrary, a man may be mortally wounded upon a natural account, and spiritually healed upon an immortal account, at one and the same time also.

29. When all the spiritual light or life in the elect enters into silent death with the mortal soul, in the twinkling of an eye it quickens again into everlasting glory; so likewise of the contrary, when all the spiritual darkness that dwells in the reprobate shall enter into a natural death with their mortal souls, it shall quicken again in a moment into an eternal spiritual death, or shame.

30. Hence you may know, that the mind of Christ in those words was this, Fear ye not them which, by divine sufferance, may kill both soul and body by a natural death; but rather fear Him that hath an absolute power in himself, to slay both soul and body with an eternal death, by raising men's souls and bodies again out of the dust of the earth, into an undying glorious life, or shameful everliving death; in the name of the Lord, I say,

fear Him.

CHAPTER II.

1. The Soul must be capable of a temporal Death before it can be made capable of an eternal Death. 2. Sin is a Defect of Nature, the Effect of which is Death. 3. The Wisdom of Solomon was carnal, not spiritual.

AGAIN, if the soul of man be not capable of a temporal death, as most men vainly imagine how then can it be made capable of an eternal death? Surely, if it be not capable of the lesser, it cannot possibly be made capable of the greater.

2. I say, therefore, that those men which know not the temporal and eternal dying of the souls of reprobate men, cannot understand the spiritual and eternal living of the souls of just men made perfect.

3. Moreover, is not sin or evil a defect or weakness of nature? And is the effect of this defect anything else but death itself? Yea, all kind of death for a moment, even to all mankind.

4. 'Tis confessed, that if the spirit or soul of the first man, Adam, had been so powerfully pure in its creation, that it could not have been defiled by sin or evil, no kind of death then could have had any power over him in the least; but when once sin entered into his undefiled soul, with it nothing else but all kinds of death unavoidably entered also.

5. It is not written that the body, but the soul, that sins shall die, be put to death, or cut off from the land of the living; wherefore, if any man's soul be so perfect, that it cannot be touched with the least motion of sin or evil against God and man, it is impossible then of any capacity of dying in the least; so likewise, if there be no such man living, as I am very certain there is not, it is as impossible also for any sinful soul to escape all kind of dying in the least, as aforesaid.

6. Furthermore, is there any more than one spirit or soul in a man? And do not all rational men, that are sober, confess a change of this present life? And is not that life to come on the other side of death?

7. How, then, can any living soul enter into that life to come, or be changed from what it is already in the least, but by passing through the black jaws of death's kingdom?

8. Not that I look upon death to be dreadful alike unto all men; for I am confident, that a full assurance of an enjoyment of the glory to come, destroys the sting of sin, which occasioneth the fear of eternal death where it prevaileth, by making the natural dying of the soul as falling into a sweet sleep, unto that spirit possessed with such an enjoyment.

9. Again, there is a saying of Solomon, that is taken for as pure a truth as any in holy writ, that is a mere stumbling-block to most men, through which their understandings are so blinded, that they have no

patience to hear anything that is contradictory to the ancient opinion of learned men in those words; which is this: "Then shall the dust return to the earth as it was, and the spirit to God that gave it."

10. Though Solomon was endued with natural wisdom, from whence he uttered many divine sentences, to the excelling of all worldly princes that ever should come after him; yet I dare boldly affirm, against all men in this world, that those words of his proceeded, not from the spiritual knowledge of God in him, but from his own carnal reason.

11. Why? Because that in another chapter of the same book he saith: "For that which befalleth the sons of men befalleth beasts; even one thing befalleth them; as the one dieth, so dieth the other; they have all one breath; so that a man hath no preeminence above a beast."

12. Now, if a man at his death hath no preeminence above a beast, why should not the spirit of the beast return to God that gave it, as well as the spirit of the man? But if man's spirit dieth not with its body, but ascendeth into heaven, and the spirit of the beast, with its body, descendeth into the earth, and perisheth; then, as aforesaid, surely a man at his death hath a preeminence far above a beast.

13. Moreover, concerning the spirit of man and beast being alike in death upon a natural account, is unto my understanding as pure a truth as can be uttered; yet I know that, many times, worldly Solomons understand not the true sense of their own sayings. Many men there are which are mighty in natural wisdom of words, but concerning a real comprehension of spiritual things, they are even as weakness itself; so likewise of the contrary, many men there are which appear weak in natural expressions, but are very powerful in spiritual comprehensions: for the wisdom which is from on high consists not in glittering words, but in a right understanding of glorious things only.

14. Furthermore, since man's nature was polluted with sin or evil, there is no distinction or pre-eminence in death between the man and the beast; for man is become natural as the beast, and, wanting natural food, continueth no more than the beast; and so being subject to natural infirmities or wants, as the beast is, he entereth, both spirit and body, into the dust of the earth with the beast, until the Lord of all life and glory, according to man's faith in his infinite power, doth grant those men a pre-eminence above the beast, by quickening their spirits and bodies again, out of the grave of death into everlasting life, when the beast remains in the dust for ever, for want of the knowledge of spiritual things.

15. This pre-eminence of man's natural dying and spiritual living again above the beast, which the ever-living God hath revealed in me, I do not remember is mentioned in any of the writings of Solomon. True wis-

dom is holy, or pure innocency; this is the light or life of heavenly glory in man.

16. Now for this, Solomon himself wanted true wisdom, even in his old age, according to that in the First of Kings; for it came to pass, when Solomon was old, that his wives turned away his heart after other gods, and his heart was not perfect with the Lord his God, as was the heart of David his father.

17. Again, in the Second Epistle of Saint Peter, it is thus written: "Knowing this first, that no prophecy of the Scripture is of any private interpretation: for the prophecy came not in old times by the will of man, but holy men of God spake as they were moved by the Holy Spirit."

18. And in the last Chapter of Saint Luke, Christ spake thus: " And He said unto them, These are the words which I spake unto you, while I was yet with you, that all things must be fulfilled which were written in the Law of Moses, and in the Prophets, and in the Psalms, concerning me."

19. You know the glory of the sun discovereth the smallest mote; so, likewise, when truth appears in its spiritual brightness, it discovers every motion of carnal darkness in man.

20. Solomon, indeed, was a very wise man, but I never read that he was a holy or prophetical man; therefore, it doth not appear to me, that he was a penman of holy writ.

21. Moreover, when Christ, the only God, repeated the foresaid Scriptures unto his Apostles, which he came in flesh to fulfil, he waveth the writings of Solomon. When Christ also said, "A greater than Solomon is here;" he spake it in reference to Solomon's wisdom, so adored by vain-glorious worldly men. 'Tis as if Christ should have said, A wisdom of a more eminent and glorious concernment presents itself to your view; but, because it appears not decked with Solomon's natural jewels, therefore rejected by you.

22. Furthermore, if the wisdom of Solomon, and the wisdom of Christ, had been of one nature, would the kings of the earth, think you, have embraced the one, and despised the other? Also, if Solomon's wisdom had been spiritual, or prophetical, in relation to his God becoming a body of flesh, I verily believe that both Christ and his Apostles would have alluded to his writings above all other men.

23. Furthermore, why did Christ say that the Queen of Sheba should rise up in judgment against that generation, and condemn it? Because she went from the utmost parts of the earth to hear the wisdom of Solomon, which was but natural; and behold they despised to go over the door-threshold to hear the wisdom of God in Him, which was spiritual.

24. Again, you may know that the wisdom of Solomon was but natural. Why? Because the greatest despisers in this world of the Lord Jesus, and his heavenly wisdom, do embrace the wisdom of Solomon, even as eternal life itself.

25. For, although Solomon was endued with such a large measure of wisdom, as to find out any difficult cause, and to give righteous judgment concerning it, and to speak a language above all other princes, and to find out the secrets of nature above all other men, yet you may know his wisdom was but earthly.

26. Why? Because his spirit was overcome by heathenish women, to forget the living God, and to worship the dead idols of men's imagination, who were made to own the wisdom of Solomon far above their own, until he was deceived by the carnal beauties of his natural wives.

27. Moreover, you may know that heavenly wisdom shows a man the vanity of all things, though he be always temperate in all things: wherefore, if the wisdom of Solomon had been spiritual, he might also have known the vanity of all things, without an excess, union, or communion with them; for though a man (through old age) become never so weak in his body, yet whilst his natural sense or reason remaineth, if his wisdom be spiritual, it will appear more stronger in him to withstand all carnal temptations, than in his youth; not only because youth lusteth after carnal pleasures, but also because divine wisdom is of an eternal growing nature, according to that in the last of Malachi, where it is thus written: '"But unto you that fear my name, shall the Son of Righteousness arise with healing in his wings; and ye shall go forth, and grow up as calves of the stall."

28. Wherefore, if the wisdom of Solomon had been of that spiritual perfection or sincerity of soul towards the Creator, as his father David's was, then he would have been more spiritual, obedient to the God of all spiritual and temporal gifts, than ever David was.

29. Why? Because the Lord bid Solomon ask what he should give him, and granted him his desire, and more than he desired; the which thing was never offered unto David, but the contrary altogether, as in that by choosing which punishment the Lord should lay upon him in his eternal estate in the least: but I only distinguish between the Creator's natural gifts and his spiritual gifts, to show the transcendent excellence of the one above the other, and to discover the vanity and atheistical madness of men's spirits in all ages, in exalting the natural wisdom of a sinful Solomon above the spiritual wisdom of a glorious God, or Christ, from whence alone all good and perfect gifts proceed.

CHAPTER III.

1. The Soul is not separated from the Body in Death. 2. The living Body hath life in every part, and in Death all parts die. 3. The Soul must die before it can enjoy Immortality. 4. The Soul is incapable of Life apart from the Body. 5. Two Sparks or

Seed in Man.

AGAIN, in the next place, I shall return to the point in hand. When the body of man dieth, and returns to its dust, most men do vainly imagine that the cause of it is by the departing of the breathing soul out of the body.

2. Now there is as great a mistake among wise men about the soul's separating itself or being separated from its body in death, as in any one thing in this world: wherefore, if those that shall view this writing are preserved from despising the wisdom of God in a vessel of no account among the sons of Solomon, they may come to understand such secrets as are utterly hid from them.

3. Give me leave to write somewhat of the natural living of the soul in the body of man, for our better understanding of its natural dying in or with the body.

4. So long as man's mortal spirit hath egress and regress, freely, to motion and breath through its body, it liveth; but when the soul comes to die, it is shut close prisoner in its body from all kind of motion or breathing to and fro, as formerly.

5. Moreover, though the motional part of the soul swiftly sends forth its thoughts, to wander into the heights and depths of all things, that it might comprehend all that may be known, yet I would have you know that the sensible life of it centres only in its own body: so that, though the nature of the soul be all kind of living motion, yet it is so essentially one with its body, being both produced together by natural generation, that it is utterly incapable of any kind of life without it.

6. Thus the soul is fixed to the body, as the sun is fixed to the firmament; and as the sun is swift of course, and naturally motioneth through the whole heavens and the earth, yet continueth in its firmamental body, so, likewise, the soul also, being swift in its course, and in peace, naturally motioneth into the heavens above, or into the earth beneath, solacing itself with several contemplations; yet it continueth in its own elementary body only so long as it hath any living being.

7. Some men, being more nice than wise, would fain have a man present a soul into their hand, like unto a bird, that they may comprehend it by visible sight; but men endued with true wisdom, make no such foolish queries.

8. Why? Because they know it is contrary to the very nature of a spirit or soul to be visible, but invisible only; and they also know that the outward eye seeth no more than the hand or the foot, were it not for its invisible life or soul that looketh through the bale of the eye.

9. Thus you that are spiritual may see, that there is no kind of visible light or sight in the least, but the original of it is always invisible.

10. Furthermore, there are many thousands of people do vainly imagine, that there is such an essential oneness be-

tween the Spirit of God, and their own spirit, that, instead of knowing themselves to be but mortal creatures, and must die, they grossly flatter themselves with a foolish conceit, that they are in an immortal state already, and cannot see death.

11. Hence it is, that many of these men are wholly given up to live beneath the very brute beasts, oftentimes destroying their own bodies by unnatural actions; and not only so, but from hence also, they act all manner of cruelty one towards another; for what do these men commonly say of the body of man? Oh! say they, it is but a natural form, or case of clay, that returns to its earthly centre for ever, from whence it came; but, say they, there is a pure spirit in it, which is the life of God, that cannot die, but returns into the spiritual centre of eternity from whence it came.

12. Again, though the princely part of the soul remain in the head and heart of the man, yet, you know, if the body be perfect, it hath life in every part of it.

13. Now, if the body be under some extreme pain, is not all the light or life in man sensible of it? Yea, doth it not participate of that very misery, by being restless throughout, until the extremity of its pains be over?

14. If it be so, as I am certain it is, what then is there in man that can possibly escape death, when the body returns to its dust?

15. For if men were rightly informed, or were made willing to understand the truth when they hear it, they would know then, that there is no spiritual light, life, or divine nature abiding in them, that is capable of eternal life or glory in the least, but by an entering first into a natural death.

16. Why? Because, as before-said, there is no kind of light or life within, that is or can be sensible of the knowledge of God, men, angels, themselves, or any else, but within their own bodies only.

17. Moreover, though the Creator influentially liveth in all the spirits of his redeemed ones, yet you may know, that neither men nor angels are capable of retaining his Godhead spirit, but that ever-blessed body of our Lord Jesus Christ; and because it is infinite, therefore you shall find it written in the Philippians thus: "For in him dwelleth all the fulness of the Godhead bodily."

18. Wherefore, seeing Creator-fulness, or divine infinite-ness, centres itself only in the man Christ Jesus glorified, why should sinful souls dream of enjoying of an eternal immortality with the Lord of Glory in his heavenly kingdom, before they have tasted of mortal death, as He did?

19. Oh, how fain would helpless souls enter into the Creator's throne before the season thereof, or in a new-found way of their own imagining, which the divine Majesty knew not of! For had He known any other way to glorify himself in the salvation of his elect, but by dying, he would gladly have embraced the Apostle Peter's counsel, when he

said unto him, Master, spare thyself.

20. Furthermore, though it be said, that the heavens, nor the heaven of heavens, cannot contain the Lord, yet you may know, that those words were not spoken in relation to his divine quantity, but in reference to his glorious quality only; for it being the nature of his spirit eternally to increase in all manner of spiritual excellencies, the virtue, power, or glory of them, naturally spreadeth itself through all heavens, angels, and men, as it pleaseth Him.

21. Here, you that have eyes may see, that there is a vast difference between men's understandings, concerning the everliving infinite Creator, and everdying finite creatures: hence you may know also, that as the soul and body of man is but one distinct living, or rather dying, form, till the all-quickening power of life raise him from the grave of dead dust, into a personal life of everlasting glory again; so likewise the spiritual soul and body of the man Christ Jesus, now sitting upon the throne of his glory, is that one distinct ever-living God-man, even blessed unto all eternity.

22. Again, though many men imagine they have two spirits in them, distinct from one another, because of a two-fold contradiction in man, yet you may know, they are so united in man's body, that they make but one absolute spirit, soul, or life, and no more.

23. What are these two distinct spirits in the body of man so much spoken of? Are they any thing else, but as it were two sparks of fire, talking unto each other in a still or low voice, so that no creature can truly know what they talk of in the least, but the Creator only?—Now, when these fiery sparks are moved, to declare themselves by voice of words, to the hearing of others, are they not compelled to do it, through one fleshly tongue only?

24. Moreover, though these fiery sparks are of two distinct natures, the one rational, and the other spiritual, yet you here see that, without a tongue of flesh, neither of them can vocally utter words, no more than the stones in the street.

25. Moreover, seeing that divine spark in man, which is as an ascending, glorious property, hath no other way to utter words, but through a tongue of flesh, no more than the natural spark, and is also glad when it can receive more heavenly light into its natural body, to solace itself withal: what sober man living therefore can imagine, or think, where this divine spark can be capable to enjoy any light or life, sensible voice, or speech, but in its own body only it then possesseth, until with its natural body it enters into death, and quickens again into a spiritual body of everlasting life an d glory, like unto God himself, seated on a throne of eternal infiniteness.

26. Furthermore, is this divine light in man's mortal soul any thing else but a mere witness of things, to be enjoyed in

another life, that a man is incapable of, to enjoy in this body in the least? Now, when thou enjoyest this witness of God within thee, is there not an eternal infinite witness at the same time, living in its own glorious centre without thee?

27. Now, if there be an eternal spiritual witness living without thee that is infinite, as without all controversy there is; then, though that witness which is within thee, be of the very same nature, it must needs enter into death, unless thou canst prove that witness which is within thee to be as infinite as that which is without thee; the which I am very certain thou canst not.

28. Why? Because in the midst of thy natural or spiritual life, sudden death may seize upon thee throughout, and thou not know from whence it came, what thou roast, nor where thou art, even in a moment, no more than the dust under thy feet.

CHAPTER IV.

1. The Soul cannot enter Heaven without its Body. 2. Man came from, and must return to, dust. 3. The Souls and Bodies of Mankind are generated from one another. 4. Man has no power to prevent bodily Sorrows or relieve natural Afflictions. 5. Scripture Perfections consist in those of (1.) Grace, attainable in this life; and (2.) Glory, attainable in the Life to come.

AGAIN, if thou didst foreknow, that thy spirit or soul is incapable of dying, why then wilt thou suffer thyself to be overtaken with sudden death? Or, why art thou so foolish to suffer thyself to be overtopt by death, or any kind of misery in the least? Nay, how is it possible for an infinite Majesty itself to compel a creature to suffer any kind of death at all, if that person is possessed with an ever-living spirit?

2. Moreover, seeing it is as clear as the purest light, that no man living would suffer any kind of pain in the least, if he could possibly avoid it; and yet many innocent souls do exceedingly suffer, both upon a natural and spiritual account also: why then should men that are zealous for a God, exalt themselves into his eternal throne, knowing themselves at best to be but perishing vanities, whilst they remain in these bodies of clay?

3. Furthermore, if men were truly acquainted with the spirit of the scriptures, they would know then, that it is contrary to all sober sense or reason whatsoever, that the spirit, soul, or life of mankind, should be capable to enter into a living paradise, heaven, or glory, without its body.

4. Why? Because, according to the truth of holy writ, neither the prophet Elijah, no, nor the Lord of Glory himself, ascended into the kingdom of everlasting glory, without their bodies.

5. Again, what is the ground of men's ignorance of the mortality of their souls? Is it not for want of a knowledge of their non-being, or beginning?

6. For if men knew their sin-

ful souls and bodies had their beginning together from man's nature, which is but dust; then would they also know, they must wholly return into their dust again, and so have an end until the last day.

7. Moreover, you know, that before a creature appears into a bodily form, it is incapable of any sensible light or life in the least, either to itself, or to any other man; so likewise you may know it is impossible, that that creature should be sensible of any light or life, when its body returns to its earth, no more than it was before it became a living form, as beforesaid.

8. Furthermore, though in the beginning, out of an eternal chaos of confused matter, God created all things that were made into life and form by virtue of his word speaking only; yet you may know that, since the nature or soul of man was polluted with sin or evil, not only beasts, fowls, fishes, and all created things, produce one another into a formable life only by natural generation, but the sinful souls and bodies of mankind also are generated one from another.

9. Hence you may understand this much; that is to say, that the soul of man, in its conception, proceeds not by infusion from the spirit of God, no more than the spirit of the beast, whatsoever men vainly have imagined to the contrary.

10. In the law of Moses, you may find it thus written: " the souls that came with Jacob into Egypt, which came out of his loins, were three-score and six," according to the truth of holy writ.

11. Whence is it, then, that natural wise men, contrary to all sober sense or reason, should imagine or think that mortal bodies should be possessed with immortal spirits or souls, which cannot die: nay, is it not for want of a real understanding of the immortal Creator, that men are so ignorant of their own mortality?

12. Again: if the spirit of the Creator, and the spirit of the creature, should be so essentially united that they are become but one ever-living life, as many atheistical men in this age do vainly imagine, what difference would there be then between the glorious Creator and the vanishing creatures?

13. Nay, what effects hath this cursed opinion brought forth among thousands of men and women, within these twenty years, but a glorying in carnal community or unnatural filthiness one towards another, in an utter defiance of any other God but perishing nature only.

14. Hence also it is, that these men and women, or rather devils incarnate, say unto one another, that there is no other God but their own invisible spirits, which never dies, but passeth out of one form into another, from one generation to another, even to all eternity.

15. Moreover, if you would gladly be preserved from the error of wicked men, know then that, as the soul and body of man is but one living person,

distinct from all other creatures, so likewise the spirit and body of our Lord Jesus Christ is both God and man, in one majestical person, distinct from men or angels, as beforesaid.

16. Furthermore, if the blessed Creator be a glorified person, in form like a man, distinct from all things and places, as 'tis clear He is, how is it possible, then, for the spirit of the Creator, and the soul of the creature, to be but one essential life, seeing they are two distinct persons?

17. For if the soul of man, and the spirit of God, are but one living life, whence is it, then, that the souls of some men, yea, oftentimes of men of rare natural parts, not only in their life-time, through spiritual or rational agonies, do curse and blaspheme the Creator, but in their death, also, oftentimes cry out, they are eternally damned, not enduring to hear the name of the most holy God made mention of in the least?

18. Finally, if men's spirits or souls be so divine that they are not capable of dying, or of being put to death, I wonder that they make no use of their immortal power, either by preventing of natural pain, diseases, or death to their persons, seeing no man hates his own flesh, but loves it and cherisheth it; or else by resisting whatsoever is not pleasant to them.

19. Again: if men have no power in them to prevent bodily sorrows, or to relieve their natural afflictions, when they stand in most need of help, why then should any sober man imagine, or think, that such helpless souls as we are should be immortal and cannot die?

20. But some men may say unto me, if the souls or spirits of mankind in general be in a mortal or imperfect condition, and must die, what perfection is that spoken of by Christ and his apostles in holy writ, "Be ye perfect, as your heavenly Father is perfect," and such-like, from a divine gift given me to reveal secrets?

21. To this I answer, there is a two-fold spiritual perfection belonging to the redeemed of the Lord; as, namely, there is a perfection of grace attainable unto in this life, and there is a perfection of glory, which is only attainable in the life to come.

22. Moreover, though the natural body of an elect vessel may be capable to enjoy never so much divine light, life, or perfection in him for consolation and satisfaction to its own soul, and for a further confirmation unto those that shall possess the same light in them; yet you may know it is a glorified body only that is capable of a full enjoyment of divine glories, which are eternal in the life to come.

23. I would have no man therefore imagine, or think, that I dream of enjoying of such a perfection in this body, as to the rooting out of all sin or evil in man whatsoever, as many men would vainly imagine; but the perfection I treat of is this; that is to say, when a soul is possessed with such a measure of the light of life eternal in him,

that it is thereby enabled to stand still, and to see the salvation of God in its own soul, flowing from a fountain of personal glories without him, and not from a formless Christ, or God, within men only, as many men, in these our days, both ignorantly and impudently affirm.

24. Furthermore, you may know, that a principal degree of the perfection here treated of is this; that is to say, when the glory of eternal life, and the shame of everlasting death, are in their proper natures so really made known to a soul, that in relation to profit or pleasure, inward temptations, or outward persecutions for conscience-sake, it is unmoveable like unto God himself.

25. Again, a man may be said to be perfect in a measure, according to the scripture, when he shall knowingly glory in his God, that accounts him worthy to wear a crown of thorns in this life, as a heavenly pledge of a crown of glory in the life to come, as proceeding from the eternity of his free love.

26. Another scripture-perfection in this life is this: when a soul enjoys such a heavenly wisdom in him, as not to give judgment upon any spiritual thing that is spoken, until the thing spoken of be so clear in his understanding, that he has no occasion of after-repentance in himself for ever.

27. Another degree of scripture-perfection is this, when a soul possesseth such a measure of divine love both to God and man, that the hope of eternal glory destroyeth all fear of everlasting vengeance in him; it may be said to enjoy perfection in it, according to the Scriptures.

28. Moreover, when a man certainly knows that he hath received an immediate commission from the living God, to declare divine secrets, and also knoweth that the principal end of all his speakings or writings proceeds only from a spirit of pure love in him to his elect brethren; such a soul as this hath attained to scripture-perfection, as aforesaid.

29. Furthermore, that soul which from infallible grounds is enabled truly to distinguish between the knowledge of the state of grace in this life, and the state of glory in that life to come, from the light of life eternal; I pronounce such a man as this perfect, according to the sayings of holy writ.

30. But if a man shall pretend to comprehend a spiritual perfection in this life and a glorious perfection in that life to come, from no other God, nor Christ, but what is within him only; I say, that such a man as this, through gross ignorance, doth in effect say, there is no other God besides himself, or perishing nature only, whatsoever he shall pretend to the contrary, by glittering words or actions.

CHAPTER V.

1. Scripture Perfections are advantageous in Life, Death, and the

Life to come. 2. Men who are ignorant of the Soul's Mortality, cannot discern spiritual Truth. 3. The natural Body is one of dying Corruption; the spiritual Body, one of incorruptible Glory. 4. The Sleep of Mankind is twofold (1.) of Life, (2.) of Death. 5. On the Soul of Samuel conversing with the Lord by a Vision in Sleep.

AGAIN, if man's soul be mortal, and must die with its body, and so become silent dust till the end of all time, the query may be by some, Of what concernment is this scripture-perfection to any man in this life?

2. To this I answer, To that man which enjoys it, it will be very advantageous, both in life and in death, and in that life to come: in this life, because by it the man is strengthened, patiently and peaceably to endure all kind of afflictions and persecutions for righteousness' sake whatsoever: in death, because it makes the soul willing to die, from a perfect assurance of being raised again out of its dead dust, into a never-dying glorious life at the last day, by the all-powerful word of an ever-living Jesus, that most high and mighty God now sat down in the midst of his eternal throne:

3. In the life to come, because, the more perfect we are in the understanding of divine mysteries in this life, the more God-like glorious shall we be in the life to come for everlasting; for according to the measure of grace and knowledge of God attained to in this mortal body, so shall the measure of glory be in our immortal bodies, which we shall enjoy in the life to come.

4. Moreover, this scripture-perfection is of great concernment for a spiritual confirmation to all those that shall enjoy the same light, unto life eternal.

5. Besides all this, it is of concernment also, because it will be a dreadful witness in the souls and bodies of all those which were left to despise this excellent truth of the soul's mortality, when it presented itself unto them with such an open face as is here inserted.

6. Again, whilst men remain ignorant of the soul's mortality, how can they know the principal ground of any spiritual truth?

7. When a wise and skilful husbandman soweth his seed in the earth, whether it be that of wheat or any other grain, doth he not first look for a dissolution of its present life, before he expects it capable to quicken itself into a more profitable living being?

8. Moreover, seeing Christ and his apostles make use of the wheat-corn principally or only for the setting forth of the soul's mortality, as you may find it written in the 12th of Saint John, and in the 15th chapter of the First Epistle to the Corinthians.

9. What is it, then, but the depths of carnal ignorance, that most men lie under, foolishly to conceive their souls to be immortal in mortal bodies? For if men (in the least) did understand the nature of the immortal spirit, they would then easily know the mortality of their own spirits.

10. What is the nature of an immortal spirit? The nature of it is a fiery spiritual glory; insomuch that, in what body soever it inhabiteth, it immediately consumes it to ashes, or rather makes it to shine more glorious than the sun in his strength. "And his face shone like the sun in his strength."— Rev. i. "And when Christ, which is our life, shall appear, then shall we also appear with him in glory."

11. Furthermore, you know the scriptures make mention of two distinct bodies, and of their several habitations; as, namely, an earthly and a heavenly, a natural and a spiritual, or a mortal and an immortal. As for the natural body, is it not of this side of death; and is not the spiritual or glorified body on the other side of death?

12. Finally, as a spiritual body suits only with an immortal spirit, so likewise a natural body suits only with a mortal soul. Unless thy body, therefore, were immortal, why shouldest thou imagine thy soul immortal? What is the reason that any kind of bodies should be incapable of mortality? Is it not through the immortality of its spirit? So likewise what is the cause of man's body being mortal, but the mortality of its spirit?

13. Again: is a natural body anything else but a lump of dying corruption, though it be never so complete in form and perfect health? So likewise of the contrary is a spiritual body anything else but a perfect lump of incorruptible glory?

14. It is granted that, if the soul of man were so spiritual that it could preserve its body in perfect life and health without natural food, there would need no more dispute concerning this point; but, seeing not only the body, but the soul also, is in a languishing condition, when no natural food is to be had, why then should any wise man count me a fool, for a sober reasoning forth the mortality of the soul, seeing, according to the truth of holy writ, it is both natural and sinful?

15. Moreover, though the scriptures make mention of a natural and of a spiritual body, yet I never read of any essential oneness between them in the least, neither in relation to their natures nor places; but, of the contrary, according to spiritual truth, I find a vast disproportion between them; for, as man's natural body is utterly incapable to enter into the kingdom of eternal glory but only through death, so likewise no spiritual body, in the throne of eternity, is capable to live in a natural way, unless it be changed or it change itself by a kind of dying from its eternal spirituality.

16. It is written: " Behold, I shew you a secret thing; we shall not all sleep, but we shall all be changed in a moment, in the twinkling of an eye."

17. My beloved spiritual brethren, how suitable is this secret thing spoken of by the apostle Paul, to the mystery in hand, if the Lord Jesus will be pleased to clear it up to your understandings!

18. Again: in the next place I shall treat of the word "sleeping." There is a two-fold sleep in all mankind; there is a sleep of life, and a sleep of death.

19. First, I shall write of the sleep of life, for our better understanding of the sleep of death. I speak to sober men.

20. When a poor creature is almost weary of his life for want of rest, what is that in him that desireth after sleep for relief to the whole man? Is it his body or his soul?

21. If it be his soul, as none can deny that are spiritually wise, it is not the body, then, but the soul only that is capable of desiring after sleep.

22. You know the soul is the sensible life of the body; and, whilst that life sensibly operateth in the body, no man can possibly sleep in the least; but, of the contrary, when a man falls into a sweet and silent sleep, it is through the departing of the sensible life out of his memory for that season; so that, though the body of man cannot subsist unless it enjoys some rest through sleep, yet you may know that the original cause of waking or sleeping proceeds only from the sensibleness or insensibleness of the soul.

23. Moreover, if it be the soul only that desires after sleep, some men may say unto me, When the soul of Samuel conversed with the Lord by a vision in his sleep, was it not sensible of what it received from the Lord, seeing he delivered his sayings so exactly to old Ely? How then can it be properly said, that the soul of Samuel was asleep at that time, when it talked with the Lord?

24. To this suitable query, take this following answer:— A man's soul may be in a deep sleep upon a natural account, and yet may be perfectly awake upon a spiritual account, at one and the same time.

25. Give me leave to write a little of mine own experience, which I have received from the Lord.

26. It is impossible for any man, by his sense or reason, to be capable at the first hand to comprehend anything that is spiritual: nay, it is that deadly enemy that is ever warring against the pure truth, in all the elect of God: yet millions of souls there are which, through deep darkness, do adore this hell-hound as their only God, to their eternal condemnation, through the secret decree of an infinite wisdom.

27. Furthermore, if there were never so little of the divine light in all mankind, as some men vainly imagine there is, I say from the Lord, it was impossible then for any man to perish upon a spiritual account in this life, or in that to come.

28. Hence you that are spiritual may comprehend this secret, that is to say, though all mankind, through mixture of seeds, are generated by carnal copulation, yet there is a certain number of them that are only capable of receiving of the light and life of the glory to come; wherefore, though a man outwardly appear never so pure in

expressions, and just in his actions, yet if he shall own no other God, Christ, or glory to come, but what is within him only, or what he is capable to enjoy in this present body, all the light that this man as yet possesseth is nothing else but the depth of carnal darkness. "If the light that is in thee be darkness, how great is that darkness," saith Christ.

29. Again, in answer to this of Samuel, I shall endeavour all plainness of speech; yet I am doubtful it will remain as a paradox, to almost all men that shall see it.

30. When the vision appeared unto Samuel, all that was in him was fast asleep; now that which awoke in Samuel, to enjoy communion with the Lord, was not his natural sense or reason in the least, but it was a spiritual light in him, which formerly he received from that visional glory then appearing to him, or in him; hence the saints may come to understand this secret, that all heavenly visions and revelations belong only to the Lord's redeemed ones.

31. Moreover, though a man be perfectly awake, yet, if he be unsensible of his own thoughts for that season, he may be looked upon as fast asleep; so likewise it is when a spiritual vision appears to a man: for, whether the man's soul be asleep or awake, the glory of the vision converts all the natural senses into a kind of senselessness for a season, that it may communicate its divine pleasure to that which is only capable to comprehend it, as beforesaid.

32. Furthermore, I am so far from denying a sober use of reason in its proper place, that I acknowledge it an admirable instrument for illustrating the things of God to rational men, so that it be truly seasoned with the heavenly visions of everlasting life.

33. But of the contrary, from an unerring spirit, I confidently affirm, that the things of God are not capable to be comprehended by the most purest reason in the angels themselves, but by a light of a more transcendent excellency, secretly flowing into their rational spirits from an incomprehensible glory.

THE VANITY OF DREAMS.
(THE NATURE OF THE SOUL'S REST.)

CHAPTER I.

1. In the time of the Law the Lord often appeared in Dreams and Visions to his Prophets; but, 2.

Dreams are of no value to us. 3. Though the Body is strengthened by Sleep, the Soul only is capable of Sleep.

AGAIN, in the next place, I shall write a little of dreams in sleep: I shall not speak much of it, because the occasions of dreaming may be as numerous as the dreams themselves.

2. Some there are that put such confidence in their dreams, because sometimes, or often, they partly prove true, that, through a fantastical opinion of the truth of their dreams, they vainly adore them as a divine oracle.

3. Indeed, in the time of the law, dreaming of marvellous things was of great concernment, not only because the Lord himself did often appear in dreams and visions of the night to his prophets, but also because some of his servants had the gift of a true interpretation of them in their times, concerning things to come; as namely, Joseph, Daniel, and others; but it is not so now: therefore dreams are of no value unto us, as to put the least confidence in them.

4. Why? Because we know that, instead of dreams or visions in the night, or prelatical charms, God himself is the alone teacher of his elect only, by the immediate inspirations of his most Holy Spirit.

5. Moreover, what dreams soever appears to men in sleep, occasions no marvel to me in the least.

6. Why? Because I know that the spirit of man (both sleeping and waking) is nothing else but all kind of imaginary lying dreams, and carnal wonders, unless it be truly sensible of what it saith and Both.

7. If the soul of man be but as a perishing dream, unless it be established with a right understanding, in some measure, of glorious things which are eternal, how then can any man truly say that his soul, and all that is in him, is not fast asleep, when a dream, whether true or false, shall so take away the use of his senses;

8. So that, while the dream is in force, another man that is awake may wound him, or kill him, and he know nothing of it, for want of the use of his senses?

9. Thus, you that are spiritual may clearly see that, though the body of man is in part strengthened through natural sleep, and without it cannot continue, yet it is the soul only that is capable of sleep, or desire after it, for the comfort of the whole man.

10. But, passing by natural sleeping or dreaming in this body of flesh, I shall come to the true intent of the apostle's saying, "We shall not all sleep," &c.

OF THE SOUL'S SLEEPING IN THE DUST.

(THE MANNER OF THE SOUL'S WAKING.)

CHAPTER I.

1. The Sleep spoken of by St. Paul, as quoted, is that of the Soul. 2. If the Soul does not sleep with the Body, there can be no Resurrection.

AGAIN, what was this sleep that all must not taste of, spoken of by Paul?

2. Truly it was nothing else but the sleep of the soul under death's power in the grave, or a silent sleeping of the soul and body together, in the dust of the earth, till the end of all time, according to that in the last chapter of Daniel, where you may find it thus written: "And many of them that sleep in the dust of the earth shall awake, some to everlasting life, and some to shame and perpetual contempt."

3. In the 4th chapter of the first epistle to the Thessalonians, it is thus written: "I would not, brethren, have you ignorant concerning them which are asleep; for if we believe that Jesus is dead, and is risen, even so them which sleep in Jesus will God bring with him."

4. "For this say we unto you by the word of the Lord, that we, which live and are remaining in the coming of the Lord, shall not prevent them which sleep; and the dead in Christ shall rise first."

5. You know there is a saying, "Them that were dead in sins and trespasses hath he quickened." Was it their bodies, or was it their souls, that was under the deadly power of sin or evil, when Christ, by his spirit, quickened it from the death of sin to the life of righteousness?

6. So likewise, if men's souls be not dead asleep with their bodies in the dust of the earth, there is nothing capable to be raised at the last day, by the all-quickening word of an ever-living God.

7. If the soul did not sleep in the grave with its body, there could be no resurrection of any kind of body at all.

8. Why? Because as the soul in its life-time was only capable in its own body to hear the voice of the Son of God and live, so likewise it is the soul, under death, that is only capable to hear the voice of an infinite Majesty, saying unto the souls of the elect that sleep in their graves, Come forth with bodies all glorious, like unto myself, and enter, with me and my mighty angels, into my everlasting kingdom.

9. Then shall his voice also command the souls of the reprobate to come forth with bodies suitable to their wicked spirits; black and dark bodies; yea, bodies of nothing but shame and confusion of face; bodies of burning envy, wrath, and fury against themselves, because of their everlasting separation from all spiritual and temporal conso-

lations whatsoever.

CHAPTER II.

1. The Soul is not capable of sensible waking, without its body. 2. The Soul must sleep in the earth before it can become immortal.

AGAIN, you that are spiritual know, that the body of man is no way capable of rest or sleep without its soul, no more than the soul is capable of sensible waking without its body; so likewise it is with a man at his death: it is not his body but his soul only, that is capable of the sleep of death; for if men could for ever enjoy their natural life in this body, without any pain or sorrow, no man living would or could desire to change his present condition.

2. Hence you may know, that as pain or sorrow, upon a spiritual account, is death to the peace of the mind, so likewise the extremity of natural grief or pain is that which is the death of the soul.

3. Moreover, if men could understand by what means their natural life was preserved, the natural dying of the soul, in or with the body, would no longer seem strange unto them; for man's life is continually preserved by the death of all that he eats and drinks; wherefore, when the natural life is almost spent for want of rest, the soul is glad to enter into a dead sleep, for the prolonging or the reviving of a new life: so likewise it is with man's soul and body in death, in

reference to the glory to come; for, except the soul of man be capable to enter into a natural death with its body, it is impossible it should ever be capable to be quickened into a life that is eternal.

4. Thus you that have divine eyes may see, that there is as absolute a necessity that the soul of man should sleep with its body in the dust of the earth, that it might be in a capacity of becoming an ever-living glorious body, as it is for a mortal soul to enter into a dead sleep with its body, for the prolonging or renewing its natural life again, as aforesaid.

5. Furthermore, when the soul and body of a man is so fast asleep, that it is insensible of it self, and of all things else, what is it for that season to itself, or any thing else, but a mere lump of dead earth?

6. So that, whether a man sleeps or wakes, lives or dies, his soul and body is so essentially one through natural procreation, that it is as impossible to divide them in death, as to separate them in life; but as they had a beginning together in a creaturely way, so likewise, being but a creature, they must end together in death, for the manifestation of the glorious power of an infinite Majesty, when He shall re-create out of dead dust many millions of souls and bodies, some for eternal blessedness, and other some for everlasting cursedness, by the virtue of a word speaking through his mouth, as beforesaid.

CHAPTER III.

1. The Seed of Man dies in Ge-neration. 2. The Soul is not already immortal. 3. Neither natural nor spiritual Life can be possessed, but through Death.

AGAIN, all men that under-stand generation through carnal copulation do or may understand this following secret; that is to say, though the life or soul of a man lieth secretly hid in their seeds, and, being united together, they become but one life, yet, in the time of conception, the living seed is compelled to die before it can be capable to conceive a babe into life.

2. Both male and female have tasted inwardly of this death and life that I here treat of; in conceiving of their children, only the mystery of the thing is hid from them.

3. Moreover, if all spiritual life in man is begotten through the death of sin, and all mortal life is begotten through the death of nature, how then can any sober man be so weak as to imagine, or think, that his sinful soul is already immortal, and cannot die?

4. Nay, I dare boldly say, that there is nothing that a man eats or drinks for his comfort, that is capable to nourish his natural life, till the life or virtue of that which he hath eaten or drunken first die within him, and so quicken again into living nourishment.

5. Wherefore, if a man, through an incurable disease, is in a languishing condition, then know the true cause why those things ministered to him, though they be suitable to his grief; and never so excellent, take none effect; it is because the pollution of his blood prevents the dying of those living virtues ministered to him.

6. Furthermore, to conclude this point; when a mortal crea-ture is near unto death, you know that which is given to him for his consolation, for want of dying in him, is either vomited up again, or passeth through him, doing no good nor hurt in the least.

7. Thus you that have eyes may see there is no possibility of possessing any natural or spiritual life, but through death.

TRUE WORSHIP DISCOVERED.

(THE MYSTERY OF THE DISPUTE BETWEEN CHRIST AND THE WOMAN OF SAMARIA AS TOUCHING THE TRUE POINT OF WORSHIP, CLEARLY OPENED.)

CHAPTER I.

1. The Soul of Christ was God abiding in His Person. 2. The Worship of the Saints is an inward Stillness, by which their Souls are made willing to hearken to the Voice or Motions of the Holy Spirit. 3. None can worship God, until they are enlightened by the Spirit of God.

AGAIN, in the next place, I shall treat a little of the worship of God from Christ's own words to the woman of Samaria, in the fourth chapter by St. John; where he saith, "Ye worship that which ye know not, we worship that which we know; for salvation is of the Jews: but the hour cometh, and now is, when the true worshippers shall worship the Father in spirit and in truth; for the Father requireth such to worship him. God is a spirit, and they that worship him must worship him in spirit and in truth."

2. In these words Christ did inform the woman of Samaria, that his invisible soul was that God or spirit abiding only in his person, by the which spiritual union sometimes the true believer is filled with joy unspeakable, and full of glory.

3. Moreover, when Christ and the Samaritan woman talked together, if you take notice of the chief ground of their discourse, you shall find it was about the true worship of the true God, from these word: "Our fathers worshipped in this mountain, and ye say in Jerusalem men ought to worship."

4. Therefore, when Christ said, "God is a spirit, and they that worship him must worship him in spirit and truth," he gave the Samaritan woman to understand, that all visible worship from men's tongues, eyes, and hands, was to be done away, that the invisible worship of the invisible God may take place in the hearts of his people for ever.

5. Furthermore, Christ gave her to understand also, that the worship required by him from his saints was an inward stillness, by which their souls were made willing to hearken to the voice or motions of his most Holy Spirit, speaking in them variety of heavenly pleasures, concerning the glory of eternity; so that, as fire purifieth the dross in the gold, Christ, by the virtue of his Godhead spirit, purifieth the whole man from all filthiness of flesh and spirit, flowing from man's unclean rea-

son and evil imagination, which is the Prince of the Air, always ruling in the children of disobedience.

6. Again, this spiritual worshipping of God in Christ is so powerful in some, both in their language and practice, that it makes their very faces dreadful to all glittering tongue-hypocrites whatsoever that know them; even such honour belongs to all living, loving saints.

7. This spiritual communion with God in Christ doth also give a man power to slight the deceitful riches and frothy honor of this perishing world, as dung, in comparison of that most excellent glory that it hath tasted of.

8. Moreover, Christ gave the Samaritan woman to understand, that none can spiritually worship him till the light or virtue of his Spirit first enters into them; therefore he saith, "He was found of them that sought him not."

9. And when they were in their blood, and no eye pitied them, he said unto them, Live; and behold, they lived in his sight; so that, when an elect vessel hath wearied himself out with long seeking after his God, in the visible worships of men, and so is lost in all his worship, then, and not till then, the glory of Christ's free love moves his Godhead spirit to pity that helpless soul, by revealing himself unto him, and writing the spiritual law of his eternal love in his heart, whereby he finds his soul changed from carnal envy into an entire love of all things that are most excellent, with a readiness of mind to suffer all kind of wrong, and render good for evil, for Christ's sake; in obedience to his holy commands, who was a perfect pattern of all manner of righteous obedience to the death, as a forerunner for his renewed ones, to walk in the same steps by his power all their days.

CHAPTER II.

1. The worship of God is not an external act, but an internal devotion. 2. Christ's Body, after his Resurrection, was a spiritual Body of Flesh and Bones.

AGAIN, this spiritual worshipping of the true God fills a soul with divine longings after a visible, as well as an invisible, sight of that glorious person, even face to face; from whence all their heavenly enjoyments, and real assurance of more transcendent excellencies, proceed.

2. Thus it is clear to the heirs of glorious crowns, that are of a discerning spirit, that that worship at Jerusalem, and elsewhere, treated of by Christ, to the Samaritan woman, was to be done away, that a more spiritual might take place; so that all-visible worshipping of an invisible spiritual God, is now but as a golden calf of men's own imaginations, and no more accepted of by Christ than the cutting off of a dog's neck.

3. Thus, from an unerring light in some measure, I have

remonstrated to the elect what is the very true God, and his spiritual worship accepted of him.

4. It is not outward praying, preaching, fasting, or thanksgiving, to be seen of men; but it is an inward, spiritual, silent praying and praising, fasting and feasting upon the glorious things of eternity, which are only seen by divine eyes.

5. God is a spirit, or rather a spiritual person; and they that worship him must worship him in spirit and in truth.

6. Again, in the sixth chapter by St. Mark, it is thus written: "And when they saw him walking upon the sea, they supposed it had been a spirit, and cried out; for they all saw him, and were sore afraid.

7. "But anon he talked with them, and said unto them, Be ye of good comfort. It is I; be not afraid."

8. And in the last chapter by St. Luke are these sayings: "And as they spake these things, Jesus himself stood in the midst of them, and said unto them, Peace be unto you; but they were abashed and afraid, supposing that they had seen a spirit. Then said he unto them, Why are ye troubled? and wherefore do doubts arise in your hearts? Behold mine hands and my feet; for it is I myself: handle me, and see: for a spirit hath not flesh and bones, as ye see me have."

9. My spiritual brethren, these sayings of Christ seem to contradict the truth of all that I have written, concerning God being a spiritual body or person, in form like a man.

10. And many men, for want of the spirit of the scriptures, do imagine that Christ's Father is an infinite Spirit distinct from him, and that it is utterly uncapable to make its abode in so narrow a compass as the person of Christ, if he be in the form of a man; but they imagine him to be of so vast a quantity, that he encloseth or covereth all things and places, through his spiritual bulk or bigness: this is blind reason's imaginary god, that is no God.

11. Wherefore, by divine assistance, I shall endeavour to remove this stumbling-block of long continuance by a clear and full demonstration, why Christ, in answer to his apostles, said, "A spirit hath not flesh and bones, as ye see me have."

12. You know, when Christ walked upon the sea, they supposed they saw a spirit, and cried out for fear: so likewise when Christ was risen from the grave, and was in the midst of them, the doors being shut, the same supposition rose in them again; so that you know they were afraid, supposing they had seen a spirit.

13. Wherefore, to convince them of their carnal suppositions, the Lord Jesus bids them handle his hands and his feet, and see, that they might know that now he was become a spiritual body of flesh and bones; and that now he was quickened into a divine estate, both soul and body, as he had foretold them before he died in the flesh, and quickened himself again in

the spirit,

NO SPIRIT WITHOUT A BODY,

CHAPTER I.

1. All Bodies, natural and spiritual, are visible; all Spirits, invisible. 2. The Apostles, through fear, supposed that a Spirit could be visible.

AGAIN, the apostles themselves, as well as others, were dark in many things till Christ was glorified; and that was the cause of their supposing that spirits might live without bodies, and be seen by natural eyes.

2. The doors being shut, as aforesaid, and Christ being in the midst of them, they not knowing which way he should come in, that was one cause of their sudden fear of supposing they had seen a spirit; wherefore, for removing of their groundless suppositions, and settling their fearful spirits upon a right understanding of flesh and spirit, the Lord Jesus said unto them, "For a spirit hath not flesh and bones, as ye see me have."

3. Moreover, Christ did not say, that a spirit could live without its body, no more than a body can live without its soul: he gave them to understand also, that as all bodies, both natural and spiritual, are visible, so likewise all spirits, whether of God,

men, or angels, are always invisible, and not to be seen by out ward sight, neither possibly cart be.

4. Therefore, Christ would not have them to suppose things that are not, but to understand things that are; and that would for time to come prevent all carnal fears in them, arising from vain suppositions.

5. Again, seeing Christ both times appeared in a body of flesh and bone, what ground had the apostles to suppose him to be a formless spirit?

6. If it should be imagined by some, that a spirit may live without a body, and take upon it what shape it will, to fright ignorant men withal;

7. To this I answer, If Christ had either time appeared before them in a ghostly form or shape, they had then just cause to be affrighted: but, seeing he appeared both times in that body, with whom they had been so long conversant withal, what ground in the least had they therefore to suppose they had seen a spirit?

8. It is truth, his walking upon the sea might much amaze them, through the unusualness of such a sight: but to see Him die, and buried out of sight, and in a moment to appear again in the midst of his friends, when the doors were made fast; this

must needs cause an astonishment to those that had never seen or known any such thing before.

9. Therefore the apostles, through fear, did suppose things that are not, nor possibly can be, by imagining a spirit might be seen by eyes of flesh. "Feel me, and handle me," saith Christ; "for a spirit hath not flesh and bones, as ye see me have."

CHAPTER II.

1. Spirits are not merely invisible to, but they are incomprehensible by, mortal men. 2. But the Soul is capable of hearing and understanding the Voice and Motions of the Holy Spirit.

AGAIN, Christ did inform his apostles, that a spirit could not possibly be seen by visible eyes.

2. Why? Because the nature of it is always to be invisible, and can be no otherways; but also, because there is no visible light or sight in the persons of God, men, or angels, but what proceeds from their invisible spirits.

3. Christ did also inform them, that that invisible spirit, in the body of his flesh and bone, was that God-head power or glory by virtue of which, to fulfil his own will, he could with that body pierce through doors, ascend, or descend, swifter than thought, into the height and depth of all things and places.

4. Moreover, he did also inform them, that a spirit was not only invisible, and not to be seen with visible eyes of flesh; but also, that in reference to its inward quantity or form, it was incomprehensible, therefore, it was utterly uncapable visibly to be seen or handled; for the invisible spirit is that only which sees, handles, or comprehends all visible things, whether they be natural or spiritual.

5. Thus you which are not stone-blind may know, that it is not only impossible for mortal men to see a spirit with natural eyes; but it is also as impossible for any kind of spirit, whether it be of God himself, men, or angels, to be capable of any light or life without distinct bodies of their own to manifest it in, no more than a body is capable of any light or life, without a living spirit to manifest itself in.

6. Again, Christ did inform his apostles, that the invisible eye in the soul, though a man have no natural sight or hearing, is as capable of hearing and understanding the voice or motions of his Holy Spirit, as those that enjoy their natural sight and hearing; yea, and oftentimes better also.

7. Why? Because the outward seeing and hearing is rather a hindrance than a furtherance to the inward whisperings of Christ's spirit in man's soul, concerning the glorious things of eternity.

8. Moreover, you that are skilful in natural music, whether it be instrument or voice, do know, that the lower the sound is, the more sweet is its harmony to the natural ear: so likewise you that are most skilful in

divine music do know, that the still or silent motions of Christ's spirit make the most glorious harmony in your invisible souls.

9. But on the contrary, though a man possess his bodily sight and hearing never so perfect, yet if his invisible spirit be uncapable to distinguish between the true sound of natural or spiritual music, he is like unto a deaf adder that cannot hear, though the natural or spiritual charmer charms never so wisely.

10. For, alas! what music is it to tell a carnal heart of possessing the glory of an immortal crown, full of eternal excellencies? It is all one, as if the most rarest natural music should be sounded in the ears of a man that is so foolish, that he is void of all sense or reason, like the brute beast, or deaf adder, as beforesaid.

11. "Feel me and handle me," saith Christ to his apostles, "for a spirit hath not flesh and bone, as ye see me have."

THE BAPTIST'S MISSION COUNTERFEITED

(A DIVINE CHARGE AGAINST THE TEACHERS OF THE BAPTISTS.)

CHAPTER I.

1 The Warship of the Baptists is founded on the letter of the Scriptures and their own lying Reason. 2. All true Christians are now under the Ministry of the Holy Spirit. 3. No Man, since the Apostles, has been commissioned to administer Divine Ordinances. 4. The Scriptures were written by Men who were moved by the Spirit of God. 5. The Baptists have no Divine Authority for their Mission.

AGAIN, in the next place (by divine assistance) I shall demonstrate the vanity of the ministry of the Baptists, for want of a commission from the Lord for what they ignorantly do.

2. I need not tell you the foundation upon which they build their worship, because it is upon the letter of the scripture, and their own lying reason, which is the devil in them.

3. If all visible worshipping of an invisible spiritual God is now become vain and of none effect, the Baptists may say unto me, What is the meaning of those scripture-sayings, that enjoin men to worship God in his holy ordinances to the end of the world?

4. To this I answer, All true Christians are now under the ministry of the Holy Spirit, and therefore are no more bound in conscience to apostolical worship than the saints were bound in conscience to Mosaical worship, when they were under the doctrines of Christ.

5. If you think it strange, I shall give infallible grounds for the proof of it to all spiritual discerning men.

6. My first ground is this:

Since the apostles' worship ceased, which was in or at the end of the ten persecutions, not a man hath been commissioned by the Spirit of God to administer divine ordinances to his people.

7. From an unerring light, I say again, That above these thousand years there hath not been a man sent forth to prophesy or preach the gospel of the kingdom, by a spiritual commission from Christ, or any one appointed for that end by Christ.

8. But it may be, thou that lowest the pre-eminence among the people, as to be looked upon as an apostle, or minister of the gospel, wilt endeavour to prove thy commission by the scriptures.

9. Now thou canst not deny but the scriptures were men's writings, which the Holy Spirit immediately moved them to speak, as an outward witness of things past, present, and to come, to all generations, in relation to spiritual things, which are eternal.

10. How then canst thou possibly become a minister of divine ordinances, by authority from another man's words or writings, unless, without their letter, thou went immediately moved to speak by the gift of the Holy Spirit as they were?

11. Moreover, though the Scriptures in themselves are true and just to all those that spiritually discern them, having the life and power of them in their own souls, yet there is nothing but death in them to a carnal spirit.

12. " The letter killeth, but the spirit giveth life:" and can a dead or killing letter give thee power to become a spiritual minister of Christ's ordinances to his elect people? I trow not.

13. Oh, deceive not thine own soul with thy counterfeit, if it be possible!

14. Again, if thou shalt still imagine thyself fit to minister gospel ordinances to the people, because thy natural parts have blinded them to make choice of thee for such an end; then I would fain know of thee whether thou art endued with a ministerial power?

15. Doth Christ immediately pour forth the gift of his Spirit upon them thou baptizest? Or cure the sick when thou prayest over them?

16. Or doth He own thee in casting out of devils, devilish diseases, or distempers incident to man's nature, by thy word, praying, preaching, or any gospel ordinance so called by thee?

17. Or doth He own thee, by raising the dead, curing the lame, or in anything appertaining to a minister of the Spirit?

18. Moreover, in holy writ I find thirteen apostles, and no more; and these were chosen, by Christ's spiritual power, for a great and glorious work among the saints. But who made thee an apostle, or minister of the gospel, to gather the people together into church-fellowship, and minister apostolic ordinances to them, and gave thee no power naturally nor spiritually belonging to a messenger of Christ?

19. Furthermore, because you have usurped the place of a minister of the Spirit from another man's letter, what effects doth it bring forth when you are in the place of authority, persecuting of men for their faith in their God by sword, imprisonment, confiscating of estates, banishment, and death itself?

20. These, and such-like, are the effects that proceed from your ministry, in whom is included all ministrations which confess Christ.

21. Again, if thou wouldst gladly escape the vengeance to come prepared for gospel-counterfeits, suffer me to demonstrate a true minister from one that is false; which I shall do by way of comparison.

22. Suppose a king, or head magistrate, makes choice of a man to be his ambassador to a foreign prince; you know he gives that man a commission of express words in writing, sealed up with his own signet.

23. But of the contrary, if any of his subjects should pretend ambassadorship, without the aforesaid commission, you know then that he is judged as guilty of high treason against the king's person and laws, and so is put to death as a traitor.

24. So likewise it is when the King of Glory makes use of a man as his spiritual ambassador to a prince, or to his innocent people: either He speaks to that man from his own glorious mouth, or by the mouth of a messenger chosen for that end or purpose.

25. Wherefore, if any man shall go forth as a minister of the gospel ordinances to the people, without the aforesaid commission, the Holy Scriptures them, selves, in such a case, judge that man guilty of spiritual high treason against Christ.

26. I say again from that God that sent me, whoever thou art that ministerest apostolical ordinances in the name of Christ, without a commission from his Holy Spirit, though some good may redound to some of the hearers; yet in the great day Christ will charge it upon thee as a work of iniquity: or else why doth Christ say that he will say, "Depart from me, ye that work iniquity, I know ye not;" to those that shall say, "Lord, have we not prayed in thy name, and cast out devils in thy name, and in thy name done many wondrous works?"

CHAPTER II.

1. There is no evidence in the New Testament to authorize the Mission of the Baptists. 2. The Characteristics of Love and Envy contrasted.

AGAIN, if a man was so fitted through natural parts, of memory, eloquence, courage, graceful speech, faithfulness, or any natural excellency that can be named, to become an ambassador to a king or protector; yet you know all this is of no value in the least, as to give him an interest of ambassadorship, without an approbation from the prince or protector himself; so likewise it is upon a spiritual account.

2. Suppose thou wast endued with the greatest measure of true light that can be enjoyed by a creature, through which thou shouldest become mighty in the spirit of the scriptures, and excellent in all divine qualifications; all this is of no value in the least to empower thee to become a minister of the gospel, without an approbation from the King of Glory himself, as beforesaid.

3. Moreover, if thou art possessed with natural wisdom, riches, and honour, there is not one title in the New Testament to prove thee a minister of Christ, since God became flesh.

4. Wherefore, in the name of the Lord Jesus, I pronounce Wo! Wo! unto all ministerial counterfeits! But most dreadful woes against those men who know the Lord Jesus sent them not to minister apostolical ordinances to his people, yet go on in their deceit, against the checks of their own consciences, for silver and honour, which perish.

5. Again, the true apostles, or ministers of the gospel, did not premeditate before - hand what they should say to the people; but they declared the mysteries of the kingdom, by an immediate moving of the Holy Spirit, without any real contradiction in their sayings in the least.

6. But of the contrary, either thou studiest, upon their letter, what thou shalt say to the people, that thou mayest please their itching ears with a form of glittering words only;

7. Or else, if thou speakest an hour or two without premeditation, oh, how full of contradiction and confusion it would be found, if it were examined by a discerning spirit!

8. Moreover, to uphold thy borrowed ministry, it may be thou wilt reply and say, that thou art no hireling, but livest upon thine own labour, and that thou speakest thine own experience freely to the people.

9. I shall answer thee in the words of Samuel to Saul: "What meaneth, then, the bleating of the sheep, and the lowing of the oxen in mine ears?

10. I mean your sacramental gatherings thirty, forty, or fifty times in a year; besides your members' monthly or quarterly liberalities?

11. It may be thou wilt reply, and say, it is all free offerings to the Lord, for the relieving of poor church members, and for a stock to help young beginners in their callings. I say, if you be impartially charitable to one another, it is well;

I am sure you have very little or no compassion at all to any other people, though they be more righteous and just than yourselves.

12. Furthermore, is it not your Popish bulls, rather than spiritual truth, that squeezes most of the people's gratuities out of them? I mean by frighting their souls with fear of eternal damnation, if they be not obedient to your gospel ordinances, or rather imaginary formalities of your own inventions.

13. Again, how can you have the face of a minister of the gospel, and can kill and slay mankind with a sword of steel?

14. In the true ministry of Christ I find the contrary altogether: "Our weapons are not carnal, but spiritual," saith Paul; and Christ, who is the only God, teaches his to slay not but with love.

15. These are the effects of the gospel of his kingdom, which is not of this world; for then the princes would embrace it, who now are at variance with it, because it maketh war against their natural wisdom and earthly glory.

16. Moreover, I shall write a little between faith and reason's kingdoms, or between spiritual love and carnal envy.

17. "Love your enemies," saith Christ; "and if he smite thee on the one cheek, give him the other." And when one of his disciples asked Him whether he must forgive his brother seven times, " Yea," saith Christ, "if he acknowledge his fault, forgive him seventy-seven times." What is that but even always?

18. Love lieth down at envy's feet to be killed of him, and slayeth envy by its patience and meekness.

19. Love doth all things in a beautiful and comely manner: love is of so pure and holy a nature that it cannot possibly do any impure or unholy thing; but, if it be moved to manifest itself according to its divine property, it naturally produceth all heavenly excellencies in elect men and angels.

20. Love is generous and pitiful; but envy is covetous and cruel. Love delights to be servant to all; but envy loves to be lord over all.

21. Love is not violent, but leaves all men to their own conscience in point of divine worship; but envy, desiring the pre-eminence in church and state, is always lying in wait to ensnare innocent love, because it cannot bow down to its carnal commands; and, because it cannot take away its spiritual peace, it will avenge itself upon its natural peace.

22. But, instead of rending men's persons or estates, love is that divine balsam which cureth all diseases that envy makes.

23. It cures a wounded spirit, and rejoiceth a broken heart, and reviveth a dying soul: it relieveth natural wounds made by envy's weapons.

24. Love clotheth the naked, feedeth the hungry, visiteth the sick, in prison and out of prison.

25. Love enjoys itself no longer than it is doing good to others. God-man, Christ Jesus glorified, is the fountain of all divine love, peace, joy, or any glorious excellency that can be named.

CHAPTER III.

1. The difference between the Call of the Apostles and the assumed Mission of the Baptists. 2. The Baptists are not commissioned by the Spirit of Christ. 3. The Case of John Chandler instanced. 4. The Commission of the Apostles was authenticated by apostolical Gifts.

AGAIN, love doth not move men to desire after the office of a minister, or to be a parliament man, because of the great weight attending such places, to discharge a good conscience in them to God and man.

2. If the Lord Jesus should say to a man, I have chosen thee for a greater work, love in such a case makes a man to consider his inability and unworthiness of such an office, and to desire the Lord to pass him by and choose another, because of the exceeding unbelief and perverseness of men's spirits, especially if a man shall say, the Lord hath spoken to him.

3. I can bear witness to the truth of this thing with Moses and Paul, though men or angels should gainsay it.

4. Moreover, I do not say all men have such strugglings in them, when Christ makes choice of them for apostles or ministers of the gospel.

5. For Matthew, Mark, Luke, Peter, and the rest of the apostles, seemed easily to be entreated to leave all, and follow Christ; yet no man knows what inward strivings they had, to forsake their parents, and all that was near and dear unto them, to follow a persecuted Christ, or man of sorrows.

6. Furthermore, sometimes, when God makes choice of a man to be his messenger to the sons of men, his voice in such a case is so powerful in him who is chosen, that it swallows up all reasoning in him; and then, indeed, there remains no cause of striving in the least.

7. The apostles being many, and encouraged with Christ's personal presence, that was ready and willing to die for them, must needs be willing to follow Him in the same steps.

8. But, of the contrary, when a man is chosen alone, having only but one companion given unto him, and is compelled to declare the strangest and most terrible message against despisers of their message ever declared as I and my fellow-witness were in this age; in such a case, reason may play its part, before it be made willing to lie down to the pleasure of the Most High.

9. Again, envy which floweth from reason is that which Both not only strongly desire the pre-eminence in Church and State, but, if it cannot attain to its desires in a legal way, then, Simon Magus like, it will give large gifts to attain them.

10. Suppose you, who are the chief ministers of the people called Baptists, do exactly imitate the apostles' worship, according to the letter of the scripture; yet, if you are not stone blind, you must needs know that you have no commission from the Spirit of Christ to administer apostolical ordinances to this generation or any other (if there should be another), whilst the world endures.

11. Why? Because you do certainly know that you did never hear the glorious voice of Christ say unto you these following words: "Go, preach the gospel to all nations, baptizing

them in the name of the Father, and the Son, and the Holy Spirit, teaching them to observe all things whatsoever I have commanded you; and lo, I am with you alway, until the end of the world."—Matt. xxviii.

12. You do certainly know, also, that God did neither send angel, prophet, apostle, nor saint, to commissionate you to minister gospel-ordinances to his people, as beforesaid.

13. Is it not a wonderful thing, therefore, that you should go on with such a high hand, in meddling with holy things, which concern you not?

14. Remember John Chandler, who I heard confess with his own mouth that he was eternally damned, for baptizing people without authority from God; that was one of his sins that lay upon his conscience.

15. Furthermore, if you that are the ministers of the Baptists do imagine or think that the scripture, in Matt. xxviii., makes much for you; if you be sober, I shall show you, from the spirit of Christ, the contrary altogether. Christ, himself, in those words, spake to his chosen apostles, saying, "Go preach to all nations."

16. And to fulfil his promise unto them, He gave them power to work miracles, and tongues to speak unto every man, in his own language, the wonderful things of God; as you may see in the second of the Acts of the Apostles.

17. Wherefore, unless you be endued from on high with such apostolical gifts, how can you be their successors in the least? "Teaching them to observe all things whatsoever I have commanded you."

18. How can you apply this saying to maintain your way, knowing in your consciences that Christ never spake unto you, nor commanded you to teach men to observe any of his commands at all? I say again, from an unerring light, that you never saw his face, nor have heard his glorious voice.

19. How, then, can you truly teach his spiritual commands to his redeemed ones? or convince gainsayers? "And lo, I am with you alway to the end of the world."

20. What do these words of Christ concern you in the least, seeing they were not spoke unto you? I confess, as many of you, and all other opinions, as shall enjoy the spiritual power of these words, in their lives and conversations, are concerned in this matter.

21. Thus, Christ may be said to own the ministry of his apostles to the end of the world.

22. But, of the contrary, the Lord Jesus had not the least thought in him, fifteen hundred years after the decease of his apostles, to commissionate opinionated men, to officiate their ministry over again, as blind Baptists would have it.

23. If I am rude in speech, bear with my weakness: "ye suffer fools gladly."

CHAPTER IV.

1. Men dare not receive any in the place of the Apostles unless by the concurrent testimony of the Holy Spirit. 2. Christ is present with his Apostles—that is, with those who worship him in spirit with the Apostles—to the end of the world. 3. This presence of Christ is spiritual.

AGAIN, what was the mind of Christ in saying, " Lo, I am with you alway, to the end of the world"?

2. From those words, we may understand thus much: As Christ failed not to own Moses in his legal worship, upon the spirits of the Jewish nation, whilst that ministration remained; so, likewise, whilst his apostolical worship was to remain, He would not fail to own it, by his spiritual presence in the hearts of his elect that were under those visible ordinances.

3. But you may reply and say, that Christ in these words did intend that his saints should enjoy the ministry of gospel-ordinances to the end of the world.

4. From the Lord, to this I answer: Unless the people that make choice of you for their ministers have an infallible spirit to know you are commissionated by Christ to supply the apostles' room, the which they dare not say they have; the pope, and you and all other ministers, are Peter's successors alike.

5. Moreover, there is a twofold end of the world—a particular and a general. When a man dieth, it may be properly said that he and this world are at an end to each other.

6. Why? Because his time is past for ever living in this world again: so, likewise, it was with legal and gospel administrations.

7. Whilst the chosen ministrators remained, there was power and life in them over men's spirits: but when they died, and were put to death, for bearing witness to the truth of their ordinances, this world and their worship might truly be said to be at an end to each other for ever.

8. Why? Because the true administrators and administrations ceased both together, when they had fulfilled all that was appointed for them to do by the Lord.

9. Again, though all visible worship is now become of no value in the eyes of the Lord; yet it may be truly and properly said, that Christ is with his apostles alway to the end of the world, in all those that worship him in spirit and truth.

10. I do not mean those that spend their time in Baptistical ceremonies, seeing neither circumcision nor uncircumcision availeth anything, but a new creature; but, as beforesaid, I mean those sober silent saints, whose language and practice speaketh forth the spirit and power of the scriptures in them, in the sight of God and man all their days.

11. Finally, these silent saints I speak of are possessed with such a pure love to Christ in them, that, according to their talents, their hearts and hands are continually open to all that is

good, and locked up and barred against all known evil whatsoever.

12. These are those that love the very dust of the true prophets and apostles, because they certainly know the day will come, when Christ will personally appear again to raise or new create out of dead dust those prophets and apostles, with themselves, into transcendent personal glories, like unto his own glorious body, even to all eternity. "Behold, saith he that was dead, and is alive for evermore, I create all things new."

13. Again, this promise of Christ's being with his apostles alway to the end of the world, was spoken principally upon a spiritual account.

14. Wherefore, when Christ, in any age, manifests his glorious presence in the spirits of the saints, through their believing in the scriptures, then He may be said to own his apostles, because they were the penmen thereof.

15. Moreover, these words of Christ had relation also to his two last witnesses which he hath sent in this blind age, by voice of words from his own glorious mouth, to declare unto his elect, spiritual secrets of his eternal kingdom, that were hid from all mortals in this world, as the true forerunners of his sudden, glorious, and dreadful appearing with his saints and angels, to eternal judgment.

16. Moreover, the records of the two Testaments is God's commission-book, wherein those intended by him to minister holy things have their names written, and Christ their king's name abundantly also, who sealed their commissions often from his own holy mouth, after he had sealed it with his own precious blood.

17. But those whose names are not to be found in the commission-book beforesaid, though they may be approved of by men, yet Christ and his apostles account them but thieves and liars, and deceivers of the people, like priest, like people; if the blind lead the blind, they must needs both fall into the ditch of eternal condemnation.

18. Furthermore, what though Christ said to his chosen ones, "Go preach and baptize all nations;" what is that to you Baptists, when he spake to his apostles? Did he speak to you or to them?

19. Seeing the case is so plain, I would not have you to deceive your own souls with blank commissions, but deal plainly with yourselves and your hearers, by telling them that you are not ministers of the spirit, but of the letter only.

20. Finally, you shall or may know, that neither the scriptures themselves, nor natural nor spiritual gifts, nor the saints, are any way in the least a sufficient ground to empower men to become ministrators of gospel-ordinances, without a spiritual commission from Christ, as abundantly beforesaid.

CHAPTER V.

1. The Scriptures account those Men but Vagabonds, and Workers of Iniquity, who presume to minister in Divine things without a Commission from Christ. 2. The Sons of Sceva were not in the Scripture called Vagabonds and Exorcists, until they assumed the Authority of an Apostle. 3. There are two sorts of Vagabonds: (1.) Natural, i.e., those who resist the Civil Power; anti (2.) Spiritual, i.e., those who, without authority, aspire to the Gospel Ministry.

AGAIN, suppose a Presbyterian, Independent, Separate, Episcopacy, Ranter, Quaker, or Baptist, or any opinionated man whatsoever, should have heard Christ say unto Peter, "And I will give unto thee the keys of the kingdom of heaven, and whatsoever thou shalt bind on earth, shall be bound in heaven; whatsoever thou shalt loose on earth, shall be loosed in heaven," Matt. xvi.; or should have heard Christ say to his apostles, "Go, preach the gospel to all nations:"

2. I say, if it were possible for such a man to perform the office of an apostle exactly, yet the Lord Jesus would have utterly disowned him upon that account, because He spake not to him, nor gave him a commission to preach and baptize in his name.

3. But, of the contrary, that man, for going without a commission from Christ, might rather justly expect to drink of the same cup of those apostolical counterfeits, in the xixth of the Acts of the Apostles.

4. The words are these: "Then certain of the vagabond Jews, exorcists, took upon them to call over them which had evil spirits, in the name of the Lord Jesus, saying, We adjure you by Jesus, whom Paul preacheth. And there were seven sons of one Sceva, a Jew, and chief of the priests, which did so: and the evil spirit answered and said, Jesus I know, and Paul I know, but who are ye? And the man in whom the evil spirit was leapt on them, and overcame them, and prevailed against them, so that they fled out of the house naked and wounded."

5. Moreover, what was it, think you, but vagabondism and exorcism, for those seven sons of Sceva to take upon them the power of an apostle, without a commission from Christ, as Paul had?

6. Surely those men were not looked upon as vagabonds by the people, being sons of the chief priests; but rather, I suppose, were in honour among the people, as their father was, till they were discovered, by taking on them Paul's commission.

7. Thus you may see that the scriptures account men but vagabonds, and workers of iniquity, that take upon them to be ministers of divine things without a commission from Christ.

8. Again, I do not find, in scripture, that the sons of Sceva were called vagabonds, and exorcists, till they took on them the authority of an apostle, and were made naked and wounded

for their impudence.

9. Indeed, if they had forsook their father's house, and got their livings in astrological way, or magic way, or any such like vagabondism art, when they might have lived at home in honour like the sons of a lord bishop, then they would have discovered themselves to the people as men of a vagabond mind, before they were discovered by the Lord.

10. Moreover, if a sophistical priest, astrological star-gazer, or any other unlawful artist, should enjoy a stately house and land of his own, though his conscience tells him he gained it by flattering, lying, and dissembling; yet, instead of such a Man being counted a vagabond, it is more probable men would choose him for a country justice of peace, oftentimes to punish innocent men, instead of a vagabond, if they are not able to get them houses to live in through deceit, as they have done.

11. Furthermore, there are two sorts of vagabonds, a natural, and a spiritual.

12. The natural vagabond against the civil power, is that man that enjoys his health, strength, limbs, and liberty, but cannot endure any kind of lawful labour, and so through idleness hath no certain dwelling to put his head in; but, in a beggarly or thieving way, goes from place to place to get his living, having no conscience in him who suffers, so that he can but get it to maintain his way of idleness: so, likewise, it is with a spiritual vagabond, according to holy writ.

13. That man that hath a good calling, enjoying his health, limbs, and liberty, and sufficiency of food and raiment, and is not therewith content, but, being of a loose and idle mind, through covetousness or secret pride aspireth to be a gospel-minister, and in a beggarly or thieving way runneth from scripture to scripture, adjuring by Jesus whom Paul preached, as if he were Paul, notwithstanding he understands not truly what Paul's Jesus is, no more than those vagabond sons of Sceva, the chief priest, as beforesaid.

14. Again, if a temporal vagabond escapes the lash of the law, he grows impudently confident in his way; so, likewise, it is with a spiritual vagabond: because the lash of divine justice falleth not upon him immediately in his ministry, he groweth impudently confident, that God is well pleased with what he cloth.

15. But it may be thou that art a minister to the Baptists may still reply and say, that thou preachest the word of God, and ministereth his gospel-ordinances, according to the truth of holy writ, and art blameless in thy life and conversation; and therefore thou mayest think the comparison of the seven sons of Sceva belongs not to thee in the least.

16. To this I answer, were not Corah, Dathan, and Abiram, sons of Levi, who in their places did minister to the people as well as Moses?

17. But their rebellion against

God consisted in their lusting after the priesthood of Moses, as the sons of Sceva did after the ministry of Paul.

18. Wherefore, though thou shouldest be as fit to minister legal and evangelical ordinances as Moses and Paul, yet it was as lawful for Corah, Dathan, and Abiram to minister them, as foil thee; yea, and more lawful also, because the sons of Levi in course were to officiate the priestly office, for the which they had the tenths of the people's goods allowed by the Lord.

19. The fire of the Lord consumed Aaron's two sons, for offering up to the Lord strange fire in their censers.

20. And what is all thy Baptistical worship, but the offering up of strange fire of thine own carnal reason, and lying imagination, which the Lord Jesus neither commanded thee to officiate, nor required at thy hands?

21. Wherefore, though many of you in temporals flourish all your days, as sure as the Lord Jesus liveth, who, with his own life and grace, hath redeemed my lost soul from the power of sin, and fear of eternal death, though you escape a temporal vengeance, yet few or none of you will escape the eternal fiery vengeance in the dreadful day of our Lord Jesus Christ.

CHAPTER VI.

1. Christ endued His Apostles with Spiritual Power. 2. The Ministry of the Baptists is not accompanied by any manifestations of such Divine Power. 3. The Baptists preach by commission from an Earthly Power.

AGAIN, what were those heavenly keys of Christ committed to Peter, and ministry of reconciliation committed to Paul?

2. Those keys and ministry bear but one and the same sense only, though they differ in terms; and the true sense of those sayings is this: that is to say, that Christ, by virtue of his word-speaking only, did endue the apostles with such a spiritual power, that their ministry did unlock and break open the prison-doors of darkness, in the elect lost Israelites, "that the King of Glory may enter in," and seal them up with his free love unto everlasting life.

3. But, of the contrary, there was a power in their ministry, also, to lock up and bar the persecuting spirits of merciless reprobates, with the seals of eternal wrath and death, till the judgment of the great day.

4. This is that "binding and loosing of men's souls on earth and in heaven; and binding of kings in chains of darkness, and nobles in fetters of death; and that sweet savour unto God of life unto life in them that are saved, and of death unto death in them that perish," according to the words of Paul.

5. Moreover, is there any of this power in thy ministry, that "what thou bindest or loosest on earth, is bound or loosed in heaven"?

6. Or doth thy ministry "bind kings in chains of darkness, and

nobles in fetters of death"? Or darest thou say, that thy ministry "is a sweet savour unto God of life unto life in them that are saved, or of death unto death in them that perish?"

7. Nay, thy ministry is of so weak a discerning, that thou darest not positively say, that any one of thy hearers shall be saved or damned: how it should be any otherwise, let wise men judge, seeing thou knowest not what shall become of thyself in the day of judgment.

8. It is written: "Faith comes by hearing, and hearing by the word of God preached;" and how can he preach, unless he be sent?

9. Because there is not a man of you sent to preach, it is impossible for you truly to demonstrate the true God, or right devil, heaven or hell, the true faith, or anything concerning the life to come, to the people, seeing it is as clear as the light that ye are none of Christ's ministers.

10. What is it that provokes you, and those that are gone before you, upon the same account to seek the pre-eminence in church and state, but silver and honour among princes or princes' companions, ease, and such like?

11. For when ye become honourable, though ye speak oftentimes like children or fools, your words are taken as gospel by the simple, or winked at by the wise, for your greatness' sake. Many of you, by your gospel-ministry, have become great, but never any of you have become good.

12. Again, by this you may know you are none of Christ's ministers, because you preach by commission of the earthly powers. Wherefore, if they silence you, your honour is lost, and you become dumb, like unto Cordwell.

13. As the false priests, by the powers, were exalted into Moses' chair; so, likewise, by the same power, you have exalted yourselves into the apostolical chair.

14. They sit in Moses' chair, saith Christ; do as they say, but not as they do; for they say, and do not. Oh! is it not so among you all?

15. Many of you can pretend fairly, and speak goodly words, which your memories have borrowed from the scriptures, which belong not unto you, because you have not the spiritual interpretation of them in the least; no, nor the life and power of them in your conversations and daily practice between man and man.

16. Moreover, instead of having the spirit of an apostle in you, are you not rather like unto rebellious Corah, Dathan, and Abiram, or rather the seven sons of Sceva, the chief priest, as abundantly beforesaid, who cried out, "all the Lord's people were holy," when they were in the height of their wickedness, and joined together as one man, to supplant Moses of the priesthood.

17. So, likewise, when, by rebellion against the spirit of Christ, you are become counterfeit ministers of the gospel, do

not many of you in effect say, All men may be holy if they will, when you say, Christ died for all, and all men may be saved if they will; or else you justify none to be truly holy or spiritual men, but those that are in church-fellowship with yourselves.

18. To conclude, what shall I say unto you to persuade you from belying the Lord any longer to the people, by being willing to be accounted ministers of the Spirit, when you do or may know you are but ministers of the letter, and by the wills of men only?

19. But it may be you that are rivetted in your way, and confident in the truth of your worship, will both hate me, and laugh me to scorn, when I am in my grave, for counselling you to forsake your ministerial function, by which some of you have attained to be companions with the great men of the earth, as beforesaid.

20. You may all have time enough to repent it when it is too late, when a flood of fire and brimstone from the Lord shall burn up all your spiritual confidences into a sea of everlasting vengeance upon or within your souls and bodies, as it did unto Sodom and Gomorrah, and the inhabitants thereof.

21. So much concerning the fallacy of the ministry of the Baptists.

A TRUE DESCRIPTION OF HEAVEN AND HELL.

CHAPTER I.

1. The Kingdom of Glory is not in a global condition, as this world is, but boundless; 2. Full of all variety of Soul-Delights; and, 3. Full of Glory, suitable for the glorified Bodies of Christ and the Elect. 4. There are two sorts of Spiritual Bodies appointed for eternal burnings: (1.) The one hath a Spirit of Love; (2.) The other, a Spirit of Envy. 5. Difference between the Pleasures of the Carnal, and the Joys of the Spiritual, Body. 6. The Glory of the Spiritual Body described.

AGAIN, in the next place, I shall treat a little of the spiritual glory of that world which is to come.

2. You know the scriptures have many eminent titles for the setting forth of this kingdom, as namely, "Heaven is my throne." "Nevertheless, we look for new heavens, and a new earth, wherein dwelleth righteousness." "In my father's kingdom are many mansions," and such like.

3. Moreover, you must not imagine the kingdom of glory to be in a global condition, as this world is; no, it is no such matter.

4. But, of the contrary, it is a kingdom of an infinite vastness, in height, length, or breadth, suitable to an infinite glorious Majesty. Furthermore, the world to come is a boundless kingdom,

that lieth all open, that the persons of our God, elect men and angels, may, as we use to say, have free egress and regress for divine pleasure, to ascend or descend as high or as low as they think good, to all eternity.

5. Again, as this world, and the things thereof, are all natural; so, likewise, that world, and the things therein, are all spiritual.

6. Now as Pilate said unto Christ, "What is truth?" so likewise almost all men may say unto me, what is this spiritual world you treat of? Or what man living is capable of the knowledge of it in the least, seeing he was never in it to see it?

7. From an unerring spirit, to this I answer, Though the most excellent glory thereof, in reference to the eternity of it, be incomprehensible, it doth not therefore follow, that no man is capable to comprehend it at all.

8. If it were so, how then could such a simple man as I was, speak or write more distinctly concerning God, the glory and misery to come, than all the ministerial Gamaliels of this present world?

9. Moreover, though no man with mortal eyes is capable visibly to behold the invisible throne I here treat of, yet, from an infallible light which I have received from the Divine Majesty residing therein, give me leave to write something of it, for the provoking of your spirits to a deep affection towards it, far above this world, and the vanishing glory thereof.

10. This world I treat of is full of all variety of new soul-delights, or spiritual ravishing glories, which are eternal.

11. Furthermore, it is a kingdom brighter than the sun, clearer than crystal, purer than gold, softer than down, sweeter than roses: it is a kingdom full of divine music, and crowns of glory decked with immortality.

12. It is a kingdom of divine songs, which none can learn but those that are redeemed from the love of this perishing world.

13. Again, the scriptures liken the Creator to the "Sun in his strength," "a consuming fire," and "everlasting burnings." Truly, the comparison is very suitable to the person of Christ glorified, resident in this kingdom I here treat of.

14. It is a body of such a bright, burning, spiritual glory, that, at his next appearing, the sun, moon, stars, and all natural and artificial lights in this world, will enter into eternal night, through the glory of his infinite brightness: so, likewise, is the kingdom I here write of, suitable unto Him.

15. For the heavens and the earth therein are like unto a flame of glorious fire; and the seas that are therein, being embodied with such an earth as this is, are so pure and clear, like unto crystal, burning glass, or any thing that is purified by fire.

16. The bodies also of the elect are all of a fiery, glorious nature, suitable unto their glorious God, and this his kingdom of fiery, glorious delights, as abundantly beforesaid.

17. Again, there are two sorts of spiritual bodies appointed for eternal burnings the one hath a spirit of all love and such like in it, from whence proceeds nothing but light and life, with variety of fiery, glorious pleasures, which are eternal; but the other body hath a spirit full of all envy and such like, out of which proceedeth nothing but darkness and death, with much fiery shame and pain.

18. Moreover, this God-like spirit of love I here treat of, it is a glorious love-fire, which is more pleasant than can be uttered by the tongues of men or angels.

19. It is a pure, clear, bright, gentle, soft, sweet, and joyful fire. It is a spiritual love-fire, as beforesaid; therefore it must needs be brighter than the sun, clearer than crystal, purer than refined gold, softer than down, sweeter than roses; yea, and more pleasanter to the whole man, than honey is to the natural taste; yea, it is a lovely fire, full of glorious joys, and godly majesty, Which once I had a short taste of in my soul.

20. Moreover, though a man enjoys his perfect health and liberty, yet worldly men do not count him happy, unless he be a wise man, that liveth in honour among the wise and honourable of this world, and except he possesseth all manner of delicacies for the belly and the back; plenty of jewels of gold, silver, and precious stones, to delight the eye; all sorts of harmonious melodies to please the ear; with fragrant smells to please the nose, and a virtuous and comely woman to take delight in, and such like natural contents.

21. Wherefore it may be queried by some, whether there be any other delights besides what I have already declared, in that glorious kingdom aforesaid?

22. To this I answer, There is no excellency in this world for the rejoicing of the natural body, but there is the same excellency in that world to come for the rejoicing of the spiritual body.

23. Now, there is a vast difference between the joys of the natural body, and the delights of the spiritual body.

24. For the joys of this natural life proceed principally from things which are without the body; but the joys of that spiritual life flow principally from things which are within the body.

25. Furthermore, I would have you to understand that, in the resurrection of the body, there is neither marrying of wives, nor giving in marriage; but, as Christ said, "They shall be as the angels of God in heaven:" so, likewise, as a spiritual body hath no desire after anything belonging to nature's kingdom, neither hath a natural body any desire after the things appertaining to this heavenly kingdom.

26. Finally, though glorified bodies are uncapable of any satisfaction from natural food and raiment, yet, without spiritual food and raiment, they cannot subsist: for their blessed bodies, as a robe of divine righteousness, is that heavenly garment wherewith their

innocent spirits are arrayed; and the food, wherewith their souls are eternally nourished, is a never-failing fountain, arising out of their own spirit.

27. Again, suppose a natural body were all over covered with the glittering jewels of this world, yet the glory of it would appear but as the light of a candle to the sun, in comparison of the glorious garment wherewith the spiritual body is covered.

28. Moreover, for our better understanding, give me leave to name some particular fuel, from whence this spiritual fire in a glorified body is continually kindled: it either feeds upon the righteousness and sufferings of Christ for it in the days of his flesh, or else it is nourished with the remembrance of the grace and persecutions which for Christ, and his truth's sake, it suffered in its natural body when it lived upon this earth.

29. Furthermore, every spiritual motion, thought, desire, word, or deed, which the saints enjoyed in their natural bodies, shall, by the infinite power of our Lord (Jesus, be made one with their spiritual bodies in the highest heavens: then, as beforesaid, they shall perfectly remember all their former heavenly motions, desires, thoughts, words, and deeds, which the faith and love of Christ operated in them in the days of their flesh; and from thence shall their divine souls be sensibly fed with Godlike new joys, wisdom, power, and glory, even to all eternity.

30. Finally, the remembrance of the saints' heavenly communion with each other in their natural bodies, will also occasion glorious food in their spiritual bodies; for if the heirs of this heavenly kingdom, through the translation of their bodies, shall be enabled to behold their glorious God face to face, and in their measures as perfectly know him as they are known of him, as I am certain they shall, then you that most mind eternal excellencies may be as confident of the knowledge of each other's persons and qualifications, upon a spiritual account, in this glorious kingdom, as abundantly beforesaid.

31. To conclude, they shall cast their crowns of everlasting praises and new songs at the blessed feet of Christ Jesus, their only God; because, according to his divine justice, answerable to all the cruelties of the mighty men of the earth, done to himself and his saints, his vengeance has seized upon their souls and bodies for everlasting.

32. So much concerning the glory which is to come, which Christ and his redeemed ones are to enjoy together in his eternal throne or kingdom, according to his own word.

CHAPTER II.

1. On the Kingdom of Darkness, wherein wicked Men shall be tormented, (1.) By the memory of the Crimes they have committed, and of the good things they have enjoyed; (2.) By the remembrance that they have despised the glorious Truths of Eternity; and, (3.) By the Divine Wrath in their souls re-kindling envy towards God and his redeemed ones. 2. The Scene of their former Pleasures shall be the place of their Torment. 3. Conclusion.

AGAIN, in the last place, I shall treat a little of spiritual dark bodies, and the kingdom of darkness appertaining to them.

2. This world wherein we live shall be eternally in as dark a condition as the land of Egypt was for three days and three nights, insomuch as the Egyptians saw not one another's faces, nor stirred from the place they were in; for that time the darkness was upon them they gnawed their tongues for pain, as you may find it in the Revelation by St. John.

3. So, likewise, shall these spiritual dark bodies I here write of gnaw their tongues for pain, because they cannot see one another's dreadful faces, nor stir hand nor foot from the place they are in for everlasting: their own spirits shall be their devil, and their own bodies shall be their hell, wherein they shall be tormented for evermore, with the angelical devils of this present world.

4. Moreover, all their wicked thoughts, desires, words, and actions, shall perfectly be brought into their memories, and that shall be the fuel that shall kindle the fire of the Lord's ven-geance in them, insomuch that they shall be tormented with new sorrows, pain, and shame, continually: the remembrance of the good things they formerly enjoyed shall add to their torment also.

5. This is not all; but there is a thing worse than all this, which is this: their despising the glorious truths of eternity, delivered by the tongue and pen of the Lord's two last witnesses: this shall burn in their souls and bodies more fiery hot than all the rest of their wickedness whatsoever; I mean in those that knew them or their writings.

6. Furthermore, the remem-brance of their envy towards God, and his redeemed ones, shall kindle the wrath of God in them afresh; and so it shall burn in them like unto fire and brimstone, hotter and hotter for evermore. This will cause that weeping, and wailing and gnash-ing of teeth, spoken of by Christ in the 24th chapter of St. Mat-thew.

7. Again, where the reprobates enjoyed all their pleasures and honour, there shall be the place of their torment and shame; for our God is a God of order, and not of confusion.

8. Moreover, the remembrance of their communion together in fleshly wickedness, or any other carnal delights, shall add also to their torment and shame; but this will be that which will revive their sorrows continually:

9. Oh, the eternity, the eter-nity, of the condition they are in!

10. This will come to pass, as sure as there is a God, upon all men that live in unrighteousness, at the next

appearing of our Lord Jesus Christ, with his mighty angels.

11. So much concerning the kingdom of darkness, and the devils that are eternally to be tormented therein, with the conclusion of this book, by

JOHN REEVE
AND
LODOWICK MUGGLETON.

THE END.

LUKE JAMES HANSARD, PRINTER, 5, PEMBERTON ROW, GOUGH SQUARE, FLEET STREET.

(John Reeve's Letters from)

A

VOLUME

OF

SPIRITUAL EPISTLES

COLLECTED BY THE GREAT PAINS OF

ALEXANDER DELAMAINE, THE ELDER

A true Believer of God's last Commission of the Spirit.

INTENDED

At first only for his own spiritual Solace; but finding they increased to so great a Volume, he leaves it to his Posterity, that Ages to come may rejoice in the comfortable View of so blessed and heavenly a Treasure.

TRANSCRIBED FROM

ALEXANDER DELAMAINE's ORIGINAL COPY
By TOBIAH TERRY,

A true Believer of the like precious Faith in the true God the Man Christ Jesus, which most holy Faith the reprobate World despises.

PRINTED, BY SUBSCRIPTION, IN THE YEAR 1755.
RE-PRINTED, BY SUBSCRIPTION, IN THE YEAR 1820,
BY W. SMITH, KING STREET, LONG ACRE.

AN EPISTLE TO THE RECORDER STEEL,

OCTOBER 28, 1653.

───────────

S I R,

YOU may remember at the Sessions in the Old Bailey, on October 14, and 15, we had a trial before your honour; and, sir, you may remember we gave your honour notice before our trial, that you had no commission from God to be the judges of matters of faith concerning God; for you must understand that all spiritual power wholly resides in God's person, or in the person of God, until his pleasure is to communicate it unto his creatures; whose pleasure it was to make choice of us two only to be the judges of blasphemy against the Holy Spirit; because no man: clearly knew the Lord until we were commissionated by voice of words from heaven, to declare what the true God is; yet notwithstanding, your honour, with the jury, gave sentence against us as blasphemers, because we declared Jesus Christ to be the only God and everlasting Father; and that there was no other God in heaven or in earth but the man Jesus only.

Sir, we must tell you, that we cannot break the civil law, but we are made examples in fulfilling of it to the whole world: wherefore whosoever tries us by the law of the land, it is allowed as if he tried his God by the civil law as the Jews did, because we cannot break your law, but fulfil it as aforesaid. Let your honour judge whether the sentence of eternal death upon our accusers be not just; for we did them no wrong in word or in deed.

They came to our houses, and spake evil things they knew not, as most men do; and we, in obedience to the commission of God, returned their blasphemy upon their own heads, which provoked them with a warrant to bring us before the lord mayor; who, joining with our blasphemous persecutors, he came under the sentence of eternal death with them.

Is it not a marvellous thing, that you that are magistrates should want the spirit of discerning to judge between the law of the Scriptures, and the law of the land? Do you not understand that the civil law instructs no man in the knowledge of God; therefore you that are invested with authority from men to judge all manner of accounts concerning the breach of the civil law, you ought not to take upon you to judge prophets, who cannot desire to break your law: for, by the power of Him that sent us, we cannot wrong any man in his person or estate, although they would kill us; yet amongst you there is sentence given against us to remain six months in prison, for declaring the Man Jesus to be the only God and everlasting Father; which you think is blasphemy. Wherefore once more from the Lord Jesus, we forewarn you, before it be too late, forthwith to declare unto us, the Lord's messengers, that you disown the verdict to be blasphemy that the jury brought in against us; which if you disobey, then in obedience unto the commission of the Lord Jesus, with those gentlemen of the jury that are guilty of that unjust sentence, from the presence of the Lord Jesus Christ, elect men and angels, we pronounce you cursed and damned, soul and body, to all eternity.

JOHN REEVE, and
LODOWICKE MUGGLETON,

The Two last Witnesses and Prophets, and only Ministers of the everlasting Gospel, by Commission of the Holy Spirit of the Lord Jesus Christ, God alone, blessed to all Eternity.

A Letter presented unto Alderman, Fouke, Lord Mayor of London, from the two Witnesses and Prisoners of Jesus Christ, in Newgate, as an eternal Witness unto him; with a Declaration unto the Recorder Steel, and the Lord Chief Justice Rowles, with the whole Bench and Jury; and in general, unto all Civil Magistrates and Juries in the World: John Reeve, and Lodowicke Muggleton, the two last spiritual Witnesses, and true Prophets, and only Ministers of the everlasting Gospel, by Commission from the Holy Spirit of the true God, the Lord Jesus Christ, God and Man, in one Person, blessed to all Eternity.

BY virtue of our commission, received by voice of words, from the glorious mouth of the only true God upon the throne of Glory, the Lord Jesus Christ, we shall make manifest unto men, what the foundation is of the power of the civil magistrate, and that he ought not to meddle with spiritual things, which God hath reserved himself, not allowing any man to touch them upon pain of eternal death, but those only by him anointed for that purpose: first, we declare that the Scriptures were given by inspiration of the Holy Spirit; therefore, except the magistrates were inspired with the same spirit as those that speak the Scriptures, they ought not to judge any man by them, but ought rather to yield obedience themselves unto holy Writ, or they must perish to eternity. Again, we declare from the Holy Spirit, that since God became flesh, no civil magistrate hath any authority from above to be the judge of any man's faith, because it is a spiritual invisible gift from God, that gives a man assurance of everlasting life; but the magistrate's authority is to judge the civil laws of the land, which is grounded only upon reason; but the things of eternity are from God, who is from eternity to eternity, therefore faith is the evidence of things hoped for, and reason is judge of things that are visible: as for you that are skilful in the law of reason, as soon as you hear an action to be a breach of the law, you understand presently what punishment belongs to the fact; therefore the Apostle saith, The magistrate is the minister of God for good to them that do well, and a terror to the evil doer. Again, we declare from the Lord, that no magistrate, by his power from the law of reason, ought to usurp the law of faith into his authority, because the law of reason is utterly ignorant of the law of faith, the one being carnal, and the other being spiritual; therefore, what magistrate soever takes upon him to be the judge of us, who are the messengers of faith in the true God, they are enemies to the Lord Jesus Christ, and shall surely perish to eternity. Again, from the Lord Jesus we forewarn you that are magistrates, before it is too late, that you tread not. in the lord mayor's steps, presumptuously to take upon you to judge this commission of the two-edged sword of God put into our mouths, which, if you are left so to do, it will cut you in sunder from the presence of our God to all eternity; for our God is a consuming fire, who did pronounce us cursed to eternity, had we not obeyed his voice; therefore we perfectly know whoever is left, great or small, to speak evil of this commission, which God hath put into us, by calling it blasphemy, delusion, a devil, or lie; in so doing, they have sinned against the Holy Ghost, and must perish, soul and body, from the presence of our God, elect men and angels, to all eternity; for God hath chosen us two only, and hath put the two-edged sword of the Spirit into our mouths, as before-said, that whom we are made to pronounce blessed, are blessed to eternity, and whom we are made to pronounce cursed, are cursed to eternity; and this power no mortal can take out of our hands, neither will our God any more give such power unto men whilst the world endures. Therefore, you that are judges of this earth, be wise and learned, and meddle with those things which you know in this world only, and call not your God to account at your bar; for whoever arraigneth a prophet at his judgment-seat, it is all one as arraigning his God, for a prophet cometh in the name and power of his God; therefore he that despiseth the prophet, despiseth him that sent him. Again, we declare from the Lord Jesus, if any magistrate pretends to be a preacher of the Gospel, he having no commission from our God so to do; if he preach any more after we forbid him, then we have full power to pronounce the sentence of eternal death upon him, and it is so unrevocable. Again, we declare from the Lord Jesus, that the cause why so many magistrates and ministers must suffer the vengeance of eternal death, is, because with one consent they fight against the true messengers of God, with the temporal law invested upon them by men. Again, woe would have been unto us, if we had come in our own name; but we know that God sent us, as sure as he sent Moses, the prophets, and the apostles; and that great authority, as to be judges of blasphemy against the Holy Ghost, we only are invested withal: Wherefore, you magistrates that are not yet under this sentence of eternal death from the Lord Jesus, our counsel is, if you desire blessedness in the life to come, that you would not meddle to be the judges of Spiritual things, knowing you have no commission from the Lord. Remember the counsel of Caiaphas, the high priest, if it be possible and prevent the lord mayor's eternal curse.

The Prophet Reeve's Epistle to his Friend, discovering the dark Light of the Quakers written in the Year 1654, September 20.

Loving Friend,

CALLING to mind the letter thou readest to me, which was sent thee out of the country, I am moved to present these lines to the view of thy ponderous spirit; for as Words of truth, flowing from a real foundation, drew forth humility and love to God and man, from that soul that hath received an hearing ear, so. likewise thou mayest know the glittering Words proceeding from Man's carnal wisdom, is that which hath occasioned many men to be exalted above measure, and to imagine himself so essentially united to the Divine Glory, that at length that man hath been so bewitched through the adorations of men and women in deep darkness, with high conceits of his own spiritual wisdom, that he hath been willing to deny his creaturely condition and to embrace the holy-titles and honour of an infinite Creator. Yea, and to say in his heart and tongue also, that there is no spiritual God or personal glory in the least, but what, is in man only, not withstanding, as sure as the Lord Jesus liveth, both he and all that is in him must turn into silent death and dust for a moment; yea, and would so remain unto all eternity, if there were not a distinct personal Majesty living without man to raise him again to everlasting sensible glory or shame, according to the royal pleasure of that God, that neither will nor can give his glory to another.

My dear Friend,

Be not deceived with men's crafty words, who have no true spiritual distinction in them; for if any mortal man have dwelling in him the eternal Spirit, all the motions, thoughts, words and actions of that man must needs be as pure, holy and powerful as God himself, because thou knowest they proceed from a pure, holy, and glorious spirit. But, of the contrary, if thou perceivest a measure of light only abiding in thee, which thou in mercy hast received from an everlasting Jesus without thee, then thou often seest darkness in thee as well as light; for light entered not into sinners to make them spiritual gods one over another, but shined into them to discover their natural enmity, continually warring against a God of eternal love towards them; and not only so, but to prevent also their former darkness from tyrannizing in them for ever, yea, and to consolate their elect brethren by their spiritual experiences.

Wherefore, from a divine gift which I have freely received from an unerring Spirit, I say unto thee, that those men which labour to persuade their hearers, that if they diligently harken to the light that is in them, they may attain to such a power, as to be dead in this body from all kind of inward darkness, sin, or evil, have uttered the falsest doctrine that ever was declared to men. Moreover, if the light of life eternal be thy guide, thou must needs know then, it was neither the justifying light of Christ within man, no, nor the spirit of Christ without man, that moved those men to speak or write to the people; but it was their own lying imagination which hurried them about to beget proselytes to themselves in the man Christ Jesus's stead, who alone is God over all, blessed for ever and ever. Amen.

He that is born of God sinneth not; that is, he is not left to his own heart, to commit the unpardonable sin of unbelief in the true God, in despising the spirit of Christ Jesus, to be the only Lord God of his salvation. He that believeth shall be saved. but he that believeth not is condemned already; not because he hath not believed in a God, or Christ that is within him, but because he hath not believed in a personal God or Christ that is without him, whose Divine Majesty is crowned with such immortal, bright, burning glory, that if he did not veil his fiery nature within his own blessed body, the glory of it is so transcendently infinite, that he in a moment would consume all created beings to powder. He that committed that sin of calling God a liar, which is the sin of not believing in our Lord Jesus Christ as aforesaid, or he that maketh glorious pretences of unfeigned love to Christ and his tender-hearted people, and yet secretly lieth under the power of carnal filthiness; such a man is not only of his father the devil, (cursed Cain) but he also is a very devil himself. He that saith he hath no sin in him, is a liar, and the truth is not in him; that is, he that saith Christ is so powerfully risen in him, that all motions, thought and desire of sin against God or man, is perfectly done away, that man is an horrible liar, and a deadly enemy to all humble and broken hearted saints; for their natural rebellious warring against the light within them, and the Lord of Glory without them. Oh! my precious friend, for whom my soul spiritually travelleth, till thou art firmly established with glorious things which are eternal, not with empty notions proceeding from an imaginary God or Christ within men, only which with Syrenian songs is very pleasing to the carnal ear, which may delude some undiscerning spirits for a season, nor with pharisaical looks, sighs and groans, to be seen of men, which is nothing else but the effects of men's crafty words and gestures proceeding from man's fleshly wisdom, which is abominable in the sight of our God, who is the Lord Jesus Christ in the eternal heavens above the stars.

My beloved Friend,

Give me leave a little to reason with thee, about things of the greatest concernment: what excellent truths above other men hast thou heard from the chief speakers of the Quakers? didst thou ever hear them speak to the purpose? or speak at all of any God or Christ, but what is in man only? or didst thou ever hear them speak of a bodily glory and misery to come sensibly to be enjoyed by the saints in the highest heavens, and to be endured by the serpents in this world at the day of eternal accounts? or dost thou see the image or likeness of the true Jesus in that ministry? the true and living Jesus rejected not the company of publicans and sinners, even when his light appeared not in them; but on the contrary, do they not rashly condemn those men that soberly oppose them, and shun the company of those that are not of their opinion, as serpents; much like unto those hypocrites of old, who said, Stand farther off, for we are more holy than you. Moreover, in all their speakings and writings to the people, do they not make a grand idol of the word Light, and occasion men to worship it as their only God; as if mere words were to be adored without a person, or worshipped within the bodies of sinful man as a God or as if those that enjoy true light in them, have such a measure of God in them, that they stand in no need of any God without them in the least.

My dear Friend.

Thou knowest men of unstable spirits, child-like or rather fool-like, are easily taken with every wind of doctrine; but if thou hast a spirit of true discerning in thee, thou wilt be made thoroughly then to try the spirits and doctrines of men, whether they be of God or no, before thou embrace them; having been in the fire of the devil already, I hope thou hast gained experience. Wherefore, for thy clearer sight concerning of the fallacy of all speakers, which say the Lord Jehovah, or Jesus, sent them, I shall give some discovering characters; he that saith the everlasting spiritual God or Father became not a perfect man of unspotted flesh, blood, and bone, was never moved by the spirit of God or Christ, to preach or speak to the people; or he that saith, that spirit which is dwelling in the glorious body of Christ Jesus, is not the alone everlasting Father, God and Man in one distinct person glorified, is none of Christ's messenger; or he that saith God is not in the form of a man, but is an infinite spirit essentially abiding in all creatures, that man is a liar, and the truth is not in him; or he that saith Christ's godhead died not in the flesh, and did not quicken and raise his manhood to life again, and in that body of flesh and bone, did not ascend into a kingdom of glory in another world, the deep things of

God is utterly hid from that man; or he that saith all mankind proceeded from the loins of the first man Adam, is ignorant of the two Scripture seeds (namely) the seed of the woman, and the seed of the serpent, therefore he is none of Christ's sending; or he that saith mens souls do not die with their bodies, and sleep together in the dust of the earth, till the Lord Jesus, by the mighty power of his word speaking only, do raise them unto life again at the last day, that man is in deep darkness, not knowing the Scriptures, or the power of God; or he that says mens bodies only perish (and not the souls) will be saved at the last, that man is a liar, and the truth is not in him.

Dear Friend,

Thus far was I moved to write unto thee, as an eternal witness between us, when the secrets of all hearts shall be opened. If thou seest good, thou mayst present this epistle to the view of those men called Quakers; not that I can expect a good issue from any of them, unless God hath endowed them with hearing ears, unjudging, meek and patient spirits.

Thine in all eternal excellencies,

JOHN REEVE.

September 20, 1654.

An Epistle of John Reeve to Christopher Hill.

IN the eternal true Iesus, my soul salutes you all: I have received your love-tokens, which is a vessel of cyder and a sixpence: my joy in the Lord is encreased by your communion with each other. I trust to the praise of his glory, his light and love shall abound in you more and more, for the strengthening you in the inward man, and confounding all gainsayers in your outward conversations: neither I nor my wife are in perfect health; especially my wife, who is very ill, and has been so about six weeks: so hoping of your welfare to his infinite grace, I commend you, and remain your friend and brother in Christ Jesus. Our elder brother.

JOHN REEVE.

P.S. Brother Christopher, if my mother comes up, pray tell her she need not trouble herself about any more goods at present, but a bolster and a little more covering for the bed; and as for that you sent for, you shall have it next week, God willing.

An Epistle of John Reeve to Christopher Hill, dated London, July 17, 1757.

Loving Friend in pure truth,

I RECEIVED the six shillings and the hat, and the eighteen-pence you sent me as a token. I am not a little joyed for our brother Martyn's likelihood of recovery, with your wife's safe delivery. But my chiefest rejoycing for you all is, your reality to the things you have received from our ever-loving Father, which is the living Jesus in a bodily form; this is a riddle to your elect brethren, even through the whole world, unless it be to a few. Oh! blessed are you that you are of that number, unto whom it is in some measure unfolded; for by this means you are delivered from all carnal bonds of outward forms, and are sate down in peace through inward enjoyments, which none can take from you.

Brother, I shall be careful in what your mother-in-law requireth. Thus not naming any more, but my tender love to all you that enjoys this truth, I commit you to the most High, and remain eternally yours in all righteousness,

JOHN REEVE.

P. S. My wife's kind love to you all.

(John Reeve's Letters from)

A

STREAM FROM THE TREE OF LIFE:

OR, THE

THIRD RECORD VINDICATED.

BEING THE

COPIES OF SEVERAL LETTERS AND EPISTLES

Wrote by the two last Witnesses of Jesus Christ.

WHERIN

TRUTH RIDES TRIUMPHANT AND IMAGINATION IS CONFOUNDED.

These were not included in the Volume of Spiritual Epistles because of the great expense.

Printed from the original Manuscript in the year of our Lord

M.DCC.LVIII.

A DISCOURSE between John Reeve and Richard Leader, Merchant; recited by Lodowick Muggleton, one of the two last Witnesses and Prophets of the most high God, the Man Christ Jesus in Glory.

THIS Richard Leader, not withstanding he was well satisfied in spiritual Things, as to his eternal Happiness, yet there was some Things as to temporal Matters, which we had declared, that he could not as yet consent unto, because it was contrary to the Rule and Art of Astrology and Philosophy; for I asked him what it was; he said, you declare the Sun is not much bigger than it seemeth to be, and our Art saith it is threescore Times bigger than the Earth: Also, said he, you say the Moon doth not borrow any Light of, nor from the Sun: Likewise you say, that the Heavens is not much above six Miles high from the Earth; and we by our Art do say, the Heavens are Thousands of Miles high from the Earth; these Things, saith he, seemeth something strange.

Then I answered, and said unto him, You are a Man, that have travelled through many Parts of the World, and you have been in that Place, called the equinoctial Line, where the Sun is nearest to the Earth of any other Place, where the Heat is so great, that no Creature can scarce live, the Sun is so hot; did the Sun seem any bigger to your Sight, when it was near to the Earth, than at other Times, when you were at a Distance? You saw the full Proportion of it, did you not? He answered, and said, he did. Then said I, did the Sun seem any bigger to your Eye-sight, where it was near to the Earth, than at other Times? He answered, no not any bigger, as he could discern. Why then, said I, will you believe your lying Figure, before you will believe your own Eye-sight? You must either say, the Sight of your Eye is false, or the traditional Figure you depend upon is false; now hath not God appointed the Sight of the Eye to be Judge of that it sees? But Men hath chose rather to believe their lying Imagination, which they never saw, nor never can see, nor knows not what it is; therefore it hath erected a Figure, that Man might be led into Darkness, imagine Things that are not; and make People believe, that the natural Sight, that God hath given Men in their Creation, to be Judge of what it sees, to be a false Sight, and a false Judge; and your dark Imagination and Figure to be a true Light, and a true Judge of the Bigness of the Sun. For consider,

That the Imagination of Reason in Man, doth always judge God to be bigger than he is, or lesser than he is; likewise Imagination being blind, it judgeth God's Power to be greater than it is, or lesser than it is; and so it doth in the Works of Creation: As for Example; the Imagination of Man judgeth, that God made this vast Earth and Waters of Nothing; which is more than God could do, for he never made any Thing of Substance of Nothing, for of Nothing comes Nothing; for what Thing or Creature, that God made of Nothing, God will turn it to Nothing again. Then would it be well for all wicked Men, if the Earth was made of Nothing, and Men made of the Dust of the Earth; then, when this Earth is turned to Nothing, its Original also; but this Earth was an eternal dark Chaos, and shall return at the last Day into Darkness again, and wicked reprobate Man shall live upon this Earth in eternal Torments, in utter Darkness, for ever and ever.

So that neither the Earth, nor wicked Man, the Seed of the Serpent, shall neither of them both be turned to Nothing, but shall be in utter Darkness to Eternity. Again, the Imagination judgeth the Sun, Moon, and Stars, to be of vast greater Bigness, though they seem to be small Bodies to us; so that the Imagination of Man, being blind, judgeth every Thing bigger than it is, or lets than it is; though God hath made the Sun, Moon, and Stars, little Bodies, to give Light unto the Earth and Waters, and in their Light, the Creatures here on Earth do see Light; and God hath made these Lights, Bodies in Heaven, to answer to that Light that is in little Bodies here on Earth. And shall a Man say, the Light of his Eyes is no true Light, but the Imagination, that seeth not at all, is called true Light; thus it is with Astrology, and Philosophy, that judgeth God to be bigger than he is, or lesser than he is, and his Power to be greater than it is, to create this vast Earth and Waters of Nothing; and the Sun, Moon, and Stars, of such a vast Bigness, all out of Nothing: So that the lying Imagination hath created to itself a bigger God than the true God, and this God hath a greater Power, and hath created Things of a more bigger Magnitude, than the true God ever did, and could do, as to make this Earth of Nothing, and the Sun, Moon, and Stars, of such a vast Bigness, far bigger than ever the true God made them. But to tell the Imagination of Man of the true God, that created Man in his own Image, he became Flesh, and became a little Child, and grew to a Man, and suffered Death by his own Creatures. O! no, faith the Reason in Man, God could not die, it is impossible for God to die; here God's Power is looked upon, by the Imagination of Men's Hearts, to be less than it is.

Objection 1. Said he, The Sun may seem to be but a little Body, because of the great Distance from us: As for Example, let a Man upon the Top of Paul's, and at a Distance he will shew as little as a Crow. To this he answered and said, Indeed a dark Body at a Distance doth shew less than it is. But, said I, let a light Body, as a Torch, or Candle, be but a Mile above the Earth, if it were possible, and it shall shew bigger a hundred Miles Distance from it. As for Example:

When a Beacon is let on Fire, it seemeth a greater Blaze forty Miles Distance, than it doth near at Hand, for it is but a little Thing of itself; yet nevertheless, it is the Nature of all light Bodies, to shew rather bigger at a Distance, than they are of themselves; and it is the Nature of all dark Bodies, to seem less at a Distance, than they are in themselves. When he heard this, he was convinced; and did acknowledge, that it must needs be so in Nature, that light Bodies did show bigger at a Distance, and dark Bodies less; so that the Sun being a bright Fire, light Body, and running so swift in its Course, it could not be much bigger than it seemeth to be, notwithstanding he had long imagined the contrary.

Objection 2. Saith he, We by our Art doth judge, that the Moon doth borrow her Light of the Sun, because; saith he, In far as the Sun is right against the Moon, so far the Moon is light, and when the Moon is at the Full, the Face of the Sun is right over it; so that sometimes the Moon seems to have a dark Body, only a little Piece of it forked, why is it then, said he? Because the Sun is right against no more of the Moon, and so much of it as the Sun is against it, it receiveth Light from the Sun, and the rest of the Body of the Moon seemeth dark: To this I answered and said,

If this should be so, then that Saying of Scripture, Gen, i, v. 16, must be laid aside, where it is said, God made two great Lights, the greater Light to rule the Day, and the lesser Light to rule the Night. Certainly the Moon hath Light in itself to rule the Night, else those Words cannot be true; for if God made the Moon a dark Body, and that it hath no Light in itself, but what it receiveth from the Sun, then God made but one great Light, and one dark Body, and not two great Lights; for if the Moon hath not Light in herself, but doth borrow of the Sun, then the Moon had no Light in her Creation: A Man may as well say, That a Man is a living Man, that hath no Life in him; for if a Man hath not Life in himself, he cannot move no farther, than a Man that hath Life doth carry him; so likewise if the Moon were a dark Body, and had no Light in itself, how could it move to rule the Night? The Sun, that hath always Light in itself, must carry the Body of the dark Moon, and move it about the Firmament of Heaven, to rule the Night, which would be a great Trouble to the Sun to do two Bodies Works; for God hath set every Thing in order, and every particular Thing shall do it's own Work; the Sun shall rule the Day, and the Moon shall rule the Night, and the Stars shall give their Light; so that every Thing that God hath made, shall do their own Works, according to the Law God hath placed in their Natures. If the Moon must rule the Night according to God's Command, certainly he gave the Moon a Light in itself to rule with, else it could not rule; for borrowed Lights never ruleth well. A Man that is Stone-blind, may as well say to another Man that can see, I would borrow your Eye-sight, that I may see the Light of the Sun, as you do: This cannot be done, for in Light we see Light; for there must be two Lights, else a Man cannot tell that there is any Light at all.

For that Man that was born blind, could not tell that there was any Sun or Light at all in the Day-time, but as he heard others say; but when Christ opened his Eyes, then he law Light, because he saw Light in himself; and when he received his Light, was not this Light of his Eyes in himself? Was it any borrowed Light, or Light for Christ? I trow not, for God hath made every Creature, that hath Light in itself, to see another Light that is out of itself; so that in Light we see Light; there must be two Lights, else Things cannot be distinguished; for dark Bodies, that hath not Life and Light in itself, cannot borrow Life and Light of any other; neither can the Moon borrow any Light of the Sun at all, for it hath an inherent Light in itself in it's Creation, as the Sun hath in it's Creation; so that the Words of Moses are true, that God made two great Lights, the Sun to rule the Day, and the Moon to rule the Night; only the Moon hath a lesser, but both hath a Light in themselves, and doth not borrow one Light of the other; else how could the Moon fight with the Sun in the Eclipse sometimes; if the Moon were a dark Body, and had no Light in itself, could it oppose the Sun as it doth, that the Moon even darkens the Sun in the Fight? Can a dark Body fight with the Light of the Sun? You may as well say, that a dark Body may fight with a living Man: But these Fictions of Men's Imaginations, hath deceived the whole World, and keepeth the People in Darkness, and putteth out their own Light of their Eyes, and calleth Darkness Light, and Light Darkness, even in Things that are visibly seen.

Objection 3. Then said he, How comes it to pass, that there is so many new Moons, and sometimes we see but a Piece of the new Moon, and do discern the rest of the Body to be dark, and so the Moon doth intrace the dark Bodies filled up with Light; so that in a Matter of fifteen Days, the Moons full and all Light, and in a little Time, it is quite gone, and seen no more in our Horizon. To this I answered, and said,

Were you ever up in the Firmament of Heaven? Do you know by your Imagination how God hath framed it, and how many Chambers he hath made in it? And how many Planets, Stars, and Lights, he hath put in every Chamber, in the Firmament of Heaven? You Astrologers yourselves say there is twelve Houses and four Housons, are you sure there is no more Houses in the Firmament of Heaven, but twelve? And do you know how many Lights there is in every House, and when these Lights do remove out of one House into another? Or do you know whether one Star doth take its Light from another Star? Or hath every Star Light in itself? Or doth the Light of the Stars and Planets remain in their own Bodies, and neither increase nor decrease their Light, since they were made and fit in the Firmament of Heaven? Is there any of those Stars or Lights in the Firmament of Heaven missing, that were made at first? Or hath any of them lost their Light God put in them at first, when God created the Heavens and the Earth?

If you can tell this, then you can say something, as the Moon borroweth Light of the Sun; but to give you a little further satisfaction; God hath placed the Sun, Moon, and Stars in the Firmament of Heaven, and every one of these, Houses of their own, that is, the Place where they first began to give Light, and to shine upon the Earth, that is, the House of the Sun, Moon, and Stars; now God that made them, knoweth the House and the Place of the Firmament of Heaven, where they first began to give Light; because he had measured out the Firmament of Heaven, because he made it; but Man doth not know, nor cannot know by his Imagination, Art, and Figure; also God hath given these Lights Power to go out of their own House, into any of the Chambers of Heaven, even as a Man doth out of his own Dwelling House, into more remote Parts, yet the Man retaineth his own Wisdom and Knowledge, when he is remote from his own Dwelling House, as at Home; so it is with the Sun, Moon, and Stars, though they go out of their own House, yet they retain the same Light in themselves, wherever they go. And if God hath made the Sun so swift and bright, to run through all the Houses of the Firmament of Heaven, in twenty-four Hours, yet that is the Sun's own House, where it went first from, and it is the Work God hath appointed the Sun to do every Day and Night; and when the Sun is absent, in its Place, the Moon supplieth her Light, and the Moon not being so swift as the Sun, it cometh not so soon into our Horizon as the Sun doth; betides, it passeth throughout the same Region as the Sun doth, but in a Region of a lower Degree in the Firmament of Heaven, than the Sun doth; and the Cause why the Moon sheweth the Light, but a little Piece of her, when the is but a Quarter old, so by Degrees she increaseth, till she is at the Full, so that the Full Face and Light of her, may be seen by the Light of the Eye. The Cause why we see her by a little and a little, is, the cometh out of one Chamber or House of Heaven into another, and as the Houses and the Firmament of Heaven be at such a Distance one from another, so we see her Light the more, and we see her sometimes half light and half dark; now the Piece that seemeth dark, it is because she is not come out of that House or Region; but when she is come to that Horizon, where the was at the Full, then she is all Light and no Darkness at all; not but that she was all light in herself before at all Times, but she was in some Chamber of Heaven, which shadowed her so, that we could not see her whole Light of her whole Face. As for Example: Suppose a Man stand in a Bottom, and there be two high Hills before him, at a Distance one from the other, the Man standing in the Bottom, discerneth a Man upon the Top of the farther Hill, so seeing him come down the Hill a pretty Way, but a little lower he loseth the Sight of the Man, until such Time as the Man cometh up that Hill nigh to him, and when he cometh to the Top of this Hill before me, I do discern first his Head, then after his Face, then after his Body, so that I see it is a perfect Man which I law at first, but this Hill before me hindred the Sight of him till he came to the Top of it: So it is with the Moon, a Man cannot discern the full Face of her, till she hath passed in her Journey thro' all those Houses of the Heavens, which lieth lower in that Region where she is, so that the Hill and Mountain of the Earth doth hinder the Sight of her, until she cometh to the Top of the Hill of our Horizon, then can we see her whole Face; for the Earth is as a Ball, standing upon and in the Air; that is, the Power of God's Word hath made the Air a Foundation for the Earth to stand upon; therefore it is, that the Earth standeth upon Nothing as a Man can see; and this is the Foundation God hath laid this vast Earth upon: And who could lay the Foundation of this Earth upon such a Foundation as the Air? None but God only, whose Power is infinite and unspeakable. Likewise the Earth about with the Element, then the Earth must needs interpose and shadow the Light of the Moon, so that she cannot be seen in her perfect Light, until she stands upon the Top of the Ball; but those that are on every Side and underneath the Ball cannot see her. for she is always at the Full in herself, tho' a Man cannot see her so perfectly, but when she is at the Full; yet the Moon is the same Light in herself always, as when she is at the Full, tho' those on the Sides and underneath cannot see her; neither is there any Newness in her, but she is the same Today, Yesterday, and same for ever, as long as the World lasteth; ever the great Light, which God created and appointed to rule the Night in one Place or other of this World continually: This is Truth, and Moses's Words are Truth, whatever Man by their Imaginations do say to the contrary.

Objection 4. Well, said he, how will you make it appear, that the Heavens are not above six Miles high from the Earth?

I answered and said, that I will make it appear by Scripture and Reason. That will do well, (said he.) Then said I, see that Scripture, Gen. xi. 4. And they said, Go to, let us build us a City, and a tower, whose Top may reach unto Heaven: And in the 5th Verse, And the Lord came down to see the City and the tower which the Children of Men builded: And the 6th Verse, And the Lord said, behold the People is One, and they have all one Language, and this they begin to do, and now nothing will be restrained from them, which they have imagined to do. Here, said I, it is plain, that there was a Possibility for the Sons of Men to build a tower up to Heaven; now if Heaven had been Thousands of Miles high, as the lying Art of Astrology saith, there could have been no Possibility to build up to Heaven, and that these Men's Reason know well enough, neither could they have laid a Foundation to build Thousands of Miles high; now the Imagination of Reason in these Men were more right, which went by no Figure, nor Rule of Art, but by the Sight of the Eye, and their Reason and Sense; and they did imagine by the Sight of the Eye, that it could not be above three Miles to the Clouds, which the Philosophers grant by their Art, the Clouds to be but three Miles high from the Earth; so they imagined that the Firmament could not be above three Miles higher; and we do imagine, said they, in themselves, that they might lay a Foundation to build six Miles, and thought they, when we come up to the Clouds in Building, we shall see then how far it is to the Firmament, and so build up unto it. Now, the Lord himself said, it was possible for them to do what they had imagined, for (saith he,) Nothing will restrain them for what they have imagined to do. So that God knew there was a Possibility to build up to Heaven, else he would never come down from Heaven himself, to prevent them, in confounding their Language, if the Heavens had been Thousands of Miles high: Besides, said I, do you think, when Christ ascended up to Heaven, after he was risen from the Dead, that he ascended with that Body thousands of Miles high, from where he ascended up to Heaven? It is said Acts i 9. While the Men beheld, a Cloud received him out of their Sight. That is, they saw him ascend up as far as the Clouds, which is half Way to the Firmament of Heaven; for the Clouds opened for him to pass through, and closed together again, out of their Sight; for they could not see no farther than the Clouds: Likewise, when the Prophet Elijah went up to Heaven in a fiery Chariot with Horses of Fire, Do you believe that he had thousands of Miles to Heaven? He said, No: Besides, there is a Possibility to build up to Heaven now, as there was then, only it is forbidden of God: But this I say, if it were lawful, and that a Man was fore to live 7 or 800 Years upon this Earth, as they did then, then a Man might as easily build up to Heaven now, as then; were it lawful, as I said before.

So that God hath not made the Heavens so high, as the lying Imagination of Reason hath; for Reason imagineth the Heavens to be higher than they are; and Reason imagines Hell to be lower than it is; so that Heaven is so high, that Reason can never ascend up to it, and Hell so deep, that Reason can find no Bottom; therefore called, A Bottomless Pit, when indeed Hell is but six Miles Distance from Heaven to this Earth, where Men acted all their Wickedness, shall be that Place of Hell for all the Damned, and the Place where the Devil and his Angels, which are wicked Men and Women, shall be tormented to Eternity.

But the Seed of Faith knoweth the Heighth of the Heavens, and but a few Miles high, and can easily ascend up to it; and Faith knoweth the Bottom of Hell, and knoweth it is upon this Earth, and no deeper than this Earth, and that the Bottomless Pit, so much feared by Man, it is in a Man, and not without a Man: Therefore, said I unto him, your Figure, Rule and Art, must be laid down; but Arithmetick and Numbers is necessary only for Things on this Earth, to measure Land, and other Accounts between Man and Man here on Earth; your Arithmetick and Figures is not to measure the Heighth of the Heavens, nor the Depths of Hell, that belongeth only to the Seed of Faith, being God's own Nature.

Faith measureth the Height of Heaven, and the Deepness of Hell: Therefore, in these Things, you are to lay aside your Figure Art, and depend wholly upon Belief of what we have said in there Things, because your Reason, Skill and Art, let it be never so great, cannot disprove a stedfast Faith.

When he heard this Discourse, with much more than is here written, he was very well satisfied in there Things, and many others, and he grew very mighty in Wisdom and Knowledge, both in natural Wisdom and heavenly; so that every great Man of his Acquaintance did submit to his Wisdom, and loved him for his Knowledge; so he continued in it all his Life: But about a Year or two after John Reeve died, he died at Barbados.

An EPISTLE To A QUAKER

Dear and loving Friend,

I Shall not salute thee about perishing Natures, or empty Observations, for the exalting of an Idol; but the Desire of my Soul is, that we may be found real in the Things of the Spirit, that we may be impowered to perform our Christian Duties to each other, in the Things of Flesh; which is that which girts the Spirit, or strengthens the Soul with lasting Peace.

Is it not a real Comprehension of him that made us, by Virtue of his heavenly Light or Love abiding in us? If this be true, as I am certain it is, how is it possible then, that we should be one in Spirit, or in the Flesh either, until the true God be made manifest to us, or in us? Indeed Time was when I was strongly deceived with an Imagination of the eternal Salvation of all Mankind, though they lived and died under Power of all Manner of Unrighteousness whatsoever. And this Error arose in me through a lying Doctrine, founding in my Ears, of a pretended universal Love to the whole Creation, from those People called Ranters, which gilded Love I found at length to be nothing else but carnal Lust, in the Bottom of it; why, because it had no spiritual Foundation to build his Faith and Hope upon, but within itself only.

Peradventure, thou at this present mayst imagine, that thy Society, called Quakers, are endued with more excellent Light than all others whatsoever; but if I should condescend to such an Imagination, I must belye the Light of all Things, which, through his eternal free Love, hath lately shined into my dark Soul; but it hath not so shined into it as to persuade me to mind no other God or Christ, present Light, or future Glory, but what is within me only, as formerly I did, when I was deluded to idolize my own lying Imagination with Titles of divine Glory, by worshipping of it with the holy Name of eternal Jehovah, or Jesus, and calling of it the high and lofty One, or holy One of Israel, the only begotten Son of God, the everlasting Father, the Daughter of Sion, the Glory of all Perfections, with many other such like heavenly Expressions, which indeed belongs only to a glorious personal God, eternally living without me, and not to any spiritual God or Christ, Light or Glory, that is, or may be within me, in the least.

For whilst I groped after Light and Life, only within myself, behold I met with nothing but thick Darkness, and a secret Fear of an everlasting Vengeance; but since I came really to understand that all the spiritual Godhead is wholly abiding, remaining, or dwelling in the glorified Body of the Man Christ Jesus, and that by the Light or Virtue of his Spirit only, he lives by his redeemed Ones, I have enjoyed much sweet Peace, and pure Hopes of spiritual Glories, in that Life to come, which are eternal.

Moreover, though the Variety of spiritual, or temporal Joy and Glory, be of none Effect to the Creature, without an inward Manifestation of it, yet, when I feel a Want of new and heavenly Consolations, to satisfy my hungry Soul, thro' the manifold Temptations of the Flesh, behold I seek not for it from any spiritual Light or Life that is within me, or within Men or Angels, because, by woful Experience, I certainly know it is not there to be found; but the Light in me ascends up on high without me, even into the glorious Body of the everlasting God-Man Christ Jesus, the Lord both of Quick and Dead, whose spiritual Godhead wholly died with its Manhood, and lived again alone by his own Power, and from thence, from whence alone all spiritual Excellencies proceed, received I divine Satisfaction in this Life, according to my present Necessity, with a full Assurance of a transcendent bodily Glory in that Life to come, at the Resurrection of all the Souls and Bodies of Mankind that are dead, asleep in the Dust of the Earth, when Time shall be no more.

I say again, as aforesaid, that all the true Peace, Joy, or Glory, which the Creature doth or shall enjoy in this Lifer or the Life that is to come, proceeds not from any spiritual God or Christ, Light, or Life, or Glory, that is within the Spirits of Men or Angels, in the least; but it flows only from an infinite Fountain of spiritual Glories, which are wholly dwelling in the Man Christ Jesus, that is without them, the personal Majesty, in the Sight of many true Witnesses, visible ascended far above all imaginary bodiless Gods, Heavens, Angels, or Men.

Furthermore, notwithstanding all this, if thou shouldst still imagine, that both our Lights may or will produce eternal Life in us at the last, though we should be at Variance about the Knowledge of the true God and his divine Worship, to our Lives End, I am not of thy Mind. Why? because as there is but only one true God, so likewise I certainly know there is but only one true Light or Worship, appertaining to his glorious Person, which Worship of his is now only spiritual and invisible, suitable to an invisible Glory.

Now thou mayst suppose thou art guided by an inward pure Light, yet certainly know, that instead of spiritual teaching, grounded upon a firm Foundation, thou art in Bondage to outward Forms and empty Declarations, proceeding from Man's carnal Spirit, who, through fleshly Guilt and Loftiness of Spirit, with a pretended pure Language and Practice above all other, Pope-like, are violently hurried about, to proselyte the whole World to themselves, which cunningly they endeavour to bring to pass by the Sword of the Tongue, for Want of a Sword of Steel in their Hand, deluding their own Souls, and many of their Hearers, vainly to imagine, that all Men and Women have so much true Light in them, which will make them eternally happy, if they will.

But the Light in me witnesses the contrary; for by it I am really informed, that there are select Numbers of Mankind, who, in the free Love of the Creator, were set apart for the Enjoyment of the Light of Life eternal, even before the Foundation of the World was laid.

So likewise, on the contrary, I am fully satisfied against all Gainsayers, that there is a Generality of Men and Women, who, in the Foreknowledge or Purpose of the living God, were ordained to an Estate of Unbelief in his glorious Person, and the spiritual Mysteries of his heavenly Kingdom, that they might everlastingly perish, even for Want of the Light of Life eternally shining in them: So that it is clear to a spiritual Eye, that it is not in him that willeth, nor in him that runneth, but in God alone that sheweth Mercy unto eternal Salvation, or withholds his divine Light or Love to himself, unto everlasting Condemnation, as aforesaid.

And who shall be able, in the great Day of Accompt, to look on his Face, and to say unto him, Why haft thou made one all glorious, and another altogether miserable? Woe be unto them that contend with their Maker, by speaking Evil of him and his secret Councils, which they know not, which he hath not revealed to the dark Multitude, nor never will, no, nor to any Speaker that hath handled a Sword of Steel to slay Mankind, or hath defiled his Marriage Bed, under what Pretence whatsoever.

Again, I say unto thee, that the Light in me disowns those Men to be spiritual Commissioners, or Witnesses unto the true God, that say they are guided by an infallible Spirit, through which they speak against all deceivable Preaching or Writings to the People, and yet do the very same Thing.

Moreover, the Light in me bears Witness against all Kind of publick or private Meetings in the World, in a ministerial Way of Worship, as not by a Commission from the Holy One of Israel, Why? Because of the great Ignorance I find in them of the one spiritual God, and personal Glory, prepared for his Elect, and bodily Misery ordained for the Reprobate, at the last Day; therefore, as before, I certainly know, that such Men have no Authority from the living God, to prophecy, preach, or speak of heavenly Things to the People, but only from their own lying Imaginations.

Furthermore, I say again, the Light in me bears Witness against those Men that own no other spiritual God or Christ, but what is within the Creature, or within this Creation only, to be for the present in the deepest Darkness of all Mankind, concerning heavenly Things, or that worship the literal Word Light, instead of Jesus Christ, the eternal Word, who alone is both God and Man in one single Person, glorified as aforesaid, whole ever-blessed Body is a fiery glorious Substance, distinct from all Things and Places, that he alone is worthy, may have the Pre eminency over all, and in all, who above all is worthy, having purchased it from himself, by Virtue of the pouring forth of his Godhead-Life, Blood unto Death, and quickening that divine Life again, in the very same Body that died, into transcendent ravishing Glories, even out of silent Death, or Darkness itself.

Now I am compell'd from undeceivable Experience, to let thee know, that thou haft never heard such a Language of seeming glorious Enjoyment, from any imaginary God or Christ abiding within the Creature only, as I have done; therefore it is not the Words of Men or Angels that can now convince me in the least, that they are in the Truth, unless they are able plainly to declare who or what that God or Christ is, both in his Nature, Form, and Essence, from whence they suppose they enjoy such spiritual Consolation above all others, that are not endued with the same Light.

For as Men's painted Words will not fill the Belly, nor cloath the Back, without Food and Raiment; so likewise an imaginary God of goodly Words, only living within the Creatures, will not satisfy my hungry Soul, without the real Knowledge of a glorious Substance to feed upon.

But peradventure, thou mayst reply and say unto me, that every rational Man and Woman, hath so much true Light in them, that will lead them to the real Knowledge of the true spiritual God, whereby they may attain everlasting Happiness if they will, by hearkening unto it with a diligent and obedient mind; Many are called, but few are chosen, for all Men have not Faith: Wherefore to this I answer, if this thy supposing of all Men possessing spiritual Light in them, were as true as it is false, indeed then there would be no need of any other spiritual God to instruct Mankind but what is within them only.

Again, if every rational Soul were possest with never so little of Salvation Light in it, how is it possible that it should live and die in Wrath with God or Man, as commonly it doth? What, is Man principally guided in spiritual Things, is it the Light of his own Spirit or another Spirit? Now if you acknowledge it to be the Light of Gods Spirit that bears Rule in the Creatures, what is it then that purifies the whole Man from all Filthiness of Flesh and Spirit, and leads it into Righteousness? is it the Light or Will of his own Spirit, or of the Spirit of God, as aforefaid? Now if it be the Light of another Man's Spirit, that opens Man's dark Understanding, enabling them, in some Measure, to comprehend the glorious and wonderful Things of Eternity, and not the Light of their own Spirit, as I am certain it is; it is not then in the Power of any Man's Will, at his Pleasure to obey or disobey the Light that is in him, as many Men vainly imagine. But it is the Power of God's Will only by his most blessed Spirit, to perswade

Man's Spirit to be willing to yeild Obedience to the Light that he hath freely given him, or sometimes it is his Pleasure to leave him to his own Strength, through which he rebels against the Light that is in him, to the wounding of his own Soul, That he may learn to know, that the Power by the Virtue of which he is perswaded from Eternal Ruin, is not in himself but in the living God that made him, who freely gives the Light of Life eternal, to whom it pleaseth him, but neither can nor will give his Glory to Men or Angels, or to the Light that is in them; why, because the Tree of eternal Life and Glory is not within them, but the Fruit of that heavenly Tree only, as, abundantly aforesaid.

Wherefore, whither Spiritual Obedience, Praise or Glory belongs to the Fruit or the Tree, judge ye.

Now thou mayest know there is a twofold Light in Mankind, a natural and a spiritual, the natural Light comprehends natural Things or Notions only, but the spiritual Light comprehends heavenly Things that are past, present, and to come, and is not ignorant of natural Things neither; for the natural Light enthralls the Soul with fleshly Whimsies, literal Observations, censorious Madness, and what not.

But the spiritual Light lets the Soul at perfect Liberty, from inward Wrath and outward Rage, carnal Whimsies, or invented Formalities, leading the Soul into all spiritual Loveliness and Peace, to the utmost of its Power, with all Mankind even all its Days, not that it can have any heavenly Communion, with any but those which enjoy its own Light. What Communion hath Light with Darkness, or Life with Death; Now in that personal God and his Light declared in this Epistle, I am thy loving Brother in the Flesh and in the Spirit for ever. I do fully expert thy Answer to this Writing, and shall with Patience wait for it, that the true and saving, Light may distinguish between the Spirits that set Pen to Paper.

JOHN REEVE, One of the Lord's two last Witnesses unto the Foundations of all Truth, and Pen-Man to this Epistle.

AN EPISTLE of JOHN REEVE to his loving Friend Christopher Hill.

Brother Hill, in the Eternal Truth,

MY Love to you and the Rest of our Friends. This is a spiritual Love Letter that I am moved to write unto you, wherefore by Virtue of my Commission I pronounce thee Tho. Martin, William Young, and Eliz. Wyles, the Blessed of the, Lord to Eternity; the Remembrance of this the Lord's Blessing, will do you no harm when I am in my Grave; in the mean Season, our good God cause you to love one another more than your temporal Enjoyments, and that will become a Heaven upon

Earth in your innocent Souls; Faith fetcheth spiritual Comfort, the Fountain to each particular Soul; but Love fulfilleth all Righteousness both to God and Mans Oh! the transcendent Excellency of the Love of Christ in his new born People, it is not to express'd by the Tongues of Men or Angels.

JOHN REEVE.

A copy of a LETTER wrote by the Prophet JOHN REEVE to Mrs. Alice Webb, containing her Blessing, and the Six Principles, on August 15, 1656.

Loving Friend,

DESIRING your Eternal Happiness in that Place of Glory above the Stars, I am moved from the Spirit of the Lord to write these Lines unto your serious Consideration.

This I know as sure as God knows himself, that Jesus Christ from his Throne of Glory spake to me by Voice of Words three Mornings together, which Speaking of his hath opened my dark Understanding to declare such spiritual. Light to the Chosen of God, as never was so clearly manifested before, especially in, these six Foundations.

First, What the Person of the true God is, and his Divine Nature.

Secondly, What the Persons of the holy Angels are, and their Nature.

Thirdly, What the Persons of the. Devils are and their Natures, and what the Person of the Devil was before he became a Devil, and begot Millions of dark Angels or Devils,   it being all one.

Fourthly, In what condition the Man Adam was created, in and by what Means he lost his first Estate and the Effects of it.

Fifthly, What Heaven and Glory is, and the eternal Residence of it.

Sixthly. What Hell and eternal Death is, and the Place where it shall be to Eternity.

This I know certainly, That before the Lord sent me to declare his Pleasure unto his People, no Man upon this Earth did clearly understand any one of these fix fundamental Truths, which to Understand is Life eternal, and to be ignorant of them is Death eternal. Now the Lord hath sent his two Messengers to declare them, I mean, to all those that may be informed in these spiritual Things, and do reject us (that are the Lord's Messengers of these Things of Salvation) through the Love of carnal Things, they must all perish to Eternity.

Again we know from the Lord by that infallible Spirit that he hath given us, of divers Persons that shall be eternally blessed with us: and all that we pronounce Cursed to Eternity are eternally Cursed, as sure as Jesus Christ the Lord of Life is Blessed, because it is his Curse and not ours.

Again, if the Lord Jesus do not bear Witness unto our Testimony, and make it evident that he hath sent us in a few months, than you may conclude, that there never was any true Prophets nor Christ, nor Apostles, nor Scripture spoken from the Mouth of God to Men. But there is nothing but the Wisdom of Men and Nature their God. But we know, that those that are joined with us, are Partakers of the Truths, and shall be blessed for evermore, and shall in the mean Time patiently wait the fulfilling of our Prophecy, and shall have Power over their Thoughts, Words, and Deeds, purifying their Hearts by Faith in the Person of God even as he is pure, trampling all the Riches and Honour of this World, under the Feet of their Souls as Dung, because they have tasted of that Glory to come, that no Tongue of Men or Angels can express, and this makes them not only love one another in carnal Things, but for the Truth's sake they are ready if (need require) to forsake all Relations, and Life itself for one another, and is that Power of that one only Faith and Truth, declared from the Spirit of God, the Man Jesus by us, which none enjoys but those of this Faith.

Much more might I write, but speaking Face to Face; (if it may be) is far more profitable: Farewell.

JOHN REEVE, the true Prophet, of the only true Personal God, the Lord Jesus Christ upon the Throne of immortal Glory in the highest Heavens.

An EPISTLE of JOHN REEVE to a Friend, written in May, 1657.

Shewing,

THAT Elect Angels are distinct from him who visibly beheld him Face to Face; and what that reprobate Serpent-Angel was in his Creation, which by the secret Council and unsearchable Wisdom of God, fell from his created Glory like Lightning from the invisible Heaven above, to this visible Earth beneath; and through his super-seeming God like Counsel, he overcame innocent Eve; and the yielding unto him, he wholly entred into her Womb, and naturally changed himself into her Seed, and so became the first-born Son of the Devil, and afterwards a cursed Cain, and the Father of all those Cananitish Reprobate Angels, spoken of in the visible Records of the Scriptures; Not as Cain, who was of that wicked one, and slew his Brother; the

1st of John, the 3d Chapter, and 18th Verse. And the Tares are the Children of the wicked one, Math. 13th Chapter, and the 18th Verse. Also in what Condition Adam was created in, and how he came to fall from his created Estate, and what that Sin was that Eve and he were guilty of, and how Sin came first in their pure created Natures.

Again, what that heavenly Glory is and where it is, that God's Elect Wheat, which are the Seed of Adam, and not of Cain shall possess when time shall be no more, and what that shameful Eternal Death is, and where it is reserved for the Seed of Cain, and not of Adam, who are either a Spirit given up to persecution of Men's Consciences, or else they are left in Darkness to condemn the Things of Eternity, because they cannot comprehend them for want of a true distinguishing Spirit, which is a Gift of the Holy Ghost, unto him which is immediately sent by the Lord of Glory, that he may be distinguished by the new born of God, from all those counterfeit or deceived Preachers or Speakers in the World, who are apt and ready to judge Men in Darkness, if they soberly ask them needful Questions concerning things of Eternity; the understanding of those glorious Excellencies, which is the Saints inheritance, being utterly hid from them, because they went before they were sent.

Friend and Brother in the Eternal Truth,

By this infallible Demonstration, you may know a Man that hath not a Commission from the true God, to preach and speak unto the People.

If a searching Speaker or Writer, deliver any thing unto those People that joyn with him, then for fear of his Weakness or Ignorance being discovered, he will counsel the Hearers to stick close to the Ordinances in the Word of God, or to hearken to them, or to that in their Consciences, and to beware of false Christ's and false Prophets, and such like borrowing Scriptures Languages, to prevent the People of ever hearing the Glorious and dreadful Things of Eternity from the ever-living God, revealed both by Voice of Words without, and Inspiration within, unto his two last despised true Messengers.

Thus it is clear, they have not the true Spirit of Paul in them, who gave the true Saints Liberty to try all Things or Opinions of Men, (for that was his Meaning) but to hold fast to that which was good.

Again, that Speaker or Preacher to People, whether publick or private, that declares against all Appearances that are contrary to his Way, discovers himself to a discerning Spirit not to be of the Lord, unless he can demonstrate a Spiritual Commission received by Voice from Heaven, from the Mouth of the Lord Jesus Christ, so that no Man can disprove him, though few from a true Understanding received him.

Again, he that preaches or teaches only of a God or Christ in Men's Consciences, doth he not question the Scripture Records concerning the Resurrection and Ascension of the glorious Body of the Lord Jesus

Christ, who through Faith in his invaluable Bloodshedding, the Consciences of the Elect being sprinkled, are purified from the Power of all Unrighteousness of Flesh and Spirit, and so doth he not question the Resurrection of Mankind after Death.

Again, if after Death there be no bodily Resurrection for the Spirit to possess an immortal God like Glory, or to suffer an eternal Devil-like Shame, according to their Deeds done in their Bodies; is it not one of the vainest Babblings under Heaven, for Men to talk of a God or Christ, or of Righteousness, or Purity, or Mercy, or pure Love without Envy, or of any Spiritual Excellency whatsoever, unless it be for Gain or Glory amongst Men.

The eternal Spirit and alone everlasting Father, which essentially reigneth in the glorified body of our Lord Jesus Christ his eternal Son, and spiritually, and motionally, or virtually liveth or reigneth in elect Men and Angels, bear Record between me and you for Everlasting, or World without end, whether this Witnessing be not sent unto you, and all the Elect that shall view it principally for the re-establishing of your tender Spirit, upon that spiritual Rock of all Ages, the Lord Jesus God and Man, in one distinct Person Glorified and everlastingly Honoured, with all Variety of Spiritual new Songs and Praises, from his Redeemed or Elect Men or Angels, when all Time or Times is swallowed up into Eternity or Eternities.

JOHN REEVE.

Another EPISTLE of JOHN REEVE's

SIR,

YOUR Replication to mine doth but still harp upon the same Matter as your former, and yet you suppose you have given such Arguments as may quite silence my former Assertions, were that there are no Spirits without Bodies, but such as mere Shadows and that God is not a bodiless Spirit, but hath and ever had Form, Substance, and Shape, and that is no other but the Form of a Man.

This is Contradicted by you, and so you affirm these Particulars following.

1st, You take at those my Words which said, that if a Spirit have no Body or Shape, then it is no more then a meer Shadow: This you deny, by saying, that a Shadow is only privative, but a Spirit, say you, is possitive.

2dly, You further say, that there is such immaterial Substances, which have a separate Existence from such gross Bodies which we have about us; witness say you the Soul of Man, which is immaterial, and lives after the Body is dead, which is, say you, confirmed by Paul, 2 Tim. i. 10. which saith, that the Gospel brings Life and Immortality to Light.

3dly, This Doctrine, say you, was known by the Light of Nature to the Heathen Philosophers, and hath since been confirmed by Scripture of the New Testament to us, and so conclude it no ways repugnant to right Reason.

4thly, You charge me with quoting the Scripture falsly, when I said, that Christ reply'd to the young Man, saying, That no Man was good but one, which was God; therefore say you it is false that the Scripture saith, that God is a Man.

To each of these take this particular Answer, 1. If your Spirit have neither Shape nor Substance, it is but a Shadow and no more than what the Egyptians Sorcerers produced before Pharaoh, what Moses brought up were real Substances, but their's no other but Shadows, but therefore a Spirit without Substance is not positive; for that which is privative can have no Being without a positive, because that which is positive hath a Being or Substance: Now he that will not admit God to have a distinct Being of himself, his God that he worships is nothing but a Shadow.

2dly, Where you speak of Spirits being immaterial Substances if they be immaterial, how are they Substances, and what Existence can they have, and how can a Soul be immortal in a mortal Body; it is said, the Soul that Sins, it shall die; yet you, it is immortal and cannot die, and would prove it in Tim. i. 10. when as that Place shews plainly, that it was Christ's Death and Resurrection which brought Life and Immortality to Light; so that if there be not a Resurrection, then can there be no immortal Life.

Therefore it is, that the Scriptures doth affirm, that there can be no Salvation without a Resurrection, so that if the Dead should not rise, then were all Faith vain, and God the God of the Dead (seeing Death is not abolish'd) and not of the Living; so that there is no Spirit that can subsist or have any Existence without a Body, either Spiritual or Natural.

Again, doth not the Gospel bring Life and Immortality to Light, and is this Life and Immortality brought to Light without a Body, but it will have a Spiritual Body suitable to that mortal Spirit made immortal. And doth not the Scripture affirm, that it shall have a Body like unto God's own glorious Body, and yet you say, God hath no Body, and a Soul hath no Body.

Do you not read also, that Christ had a Body, and that it was after the express image of his Father's Person: Would you trace substantial Truth into an Allegory, and say Righteousness, Knowledge, and Holiness is the Image of God, and yet must have no Body to act forth itself in. When God said, be ye holy, as I am holy, must we turn our Souls out of our Bodies, to make them like your bodiless God.

When we are said to worship God in Spirit and Truth, is this spiritual Worship performed without a Body, although there is a Mental, Privy, and Praise without a vocal Expression, yet it muff arise from a Heart, and that Heart mutt be placed in a Body.

There is no Light without a Sun, no Stream without a Fountain, and no Spirit without a Body.

3dly, As to your third Particular, this I must tell you, that no Light of Nature can discover Spiritual and Evangelical Truths, and it is very gross for any Man to subject the Spiritual Truths of the Gospel, to the heathenish Principles of Philosophers, making the New Testament no other but for the, Confirmation of the Principles of Nature, which Nature you call right Reason, which say, you never repugns the Gospel, nor the Gospel it.

By this your Discourse I find, that you own that Christ came, but to confirm the heathenish Principles of Nature, as, that God, and Spirits, and Angels, were all without Bodies, being immaterial Beings, and you know not what.

Now give me leave to be plain with you, and to tell you, that I could never read that the Gospel of Christ was ever sent to enlighten Nature, Nature or Reason hath no Interest in it at all. In the moral Law it hath, and therefore it is written, the Law came by Moses; and what to do, but only to enlighten Reason unto whom the Law was given: But as to the Gospel, it came by Jesus Christ, and particularly belonged to another Seed; namely, to the lost Sheep of the House of Israel; so that you can no more distinguish between the Law and the Gospel than between the two Natures of Faith and Reason it is all a Mystery to you. Do you know what right Reason is, if you do, you must ascend up into the Kingdom of Heaven, and view it in the holy Angels; for you will not find neither pure, nor right, nor uncorrupted Reason any where in this Orb below the Stars; For it is evident that Reason's Notion can never be capable to comprehend Spiritual Truths, as from the Power of its own Nature, it only serves to comprehend natural and temporal Things, it being but natural itself; but Gospel Truths are comprehended by another. Light, according as it is written by David saying, in thy Light shall we see Light, &c.

So that from what is said, we need not fear (as the World have) of the Heathens rising up in Judgment against us, for maintaining Gospel Truths against their Darkness of Reason.

4thly, As to your fourth Point, where you charge me of fathering upon the Scripture those things that are not, and you make a

Wonderment of it, that I should say, that God was a Man, and to quote Christ's Words for it, telling the young Man, that there was no Man good but one, which was God, this you tell me was false, for you say, the Text saith that none is good but one, which is God. Here your ignorance appears very great, and may be wonder'd at considering your great Learning and continual Study; but it appears, it is but in those heathenish Philosophers; for observe for better instruction, did not that young Man call Christ Master, and own him to be a Man and no more: Now to this you may find that Christ's Answer did tacitly imply, that if he was but a Man, he was not perfectly good, and that no Man could be perfectly good.

And furthermore for a more full Answer in the Old Translation, attending to mark it, is render'd thus Word for Word that there is no Man good but one, which is God.

This is plain Scripture, and yet you are ignorant of it; I perceive you are not very conservant in Scripture, your Philosophy turns you out of all Scripture knowledge. But to proceed farther, cannot you find by Scripture that God was ever called a Man, did not you ever read that Scripture that faith, God was a Man of War.

Much more might be said of this and several positive Proofs from Scripture might be produced to confirm it withal, but because it is not the general received Opinion, therefore it must be quarrelled with; for the Honour of this World must be both fought after and submitted to.

And whereas you farther say, that the Apostles of Christ did ever teach after they had received their Commission, that Spirits were immaterial and could subsist without Bodies, now answer to this:

It is most certainly evident, that the Apostles never taught, that any Spirit could subsist without a Body, but the contrary altogether; for their Doctrine was, that as the Soul and Body lives together, so it dies together, and at the Last Day rises together, and is ever without Separation.

When the Apostles said, That many Spirits were generate into the World, which denied that Christ was come in the Flesh, did he mean Spirits without Bodies: And when Paul said, that the Spirit speaketh expresly, that some shall depart from the Faith Now what Spirit was that, but Paul's own Spirit of Faith, in his own mortal Body; for without a Tongue it could not be expressed.

And where the Apostles tells of the Doctrine of Devils were those Devils bodiless, and teached damnable Doctrine?

So that the Apostles never taught that there was any Spirits without Bodies, but always Spirit and Body went together, and so makes Longitude and Latitude profoundly, as your Philosophical Notions teacheth, although you cannot apply it to any sublime or spiritual Thing, you knowing nothing of it but all is nothing and of no Substance; and so in that your Darkness I leave you, seeing you are no Friend to the Lights and rest yours in all civil Respects,

JOHN REEVE the only true Witness unto the very true God, amongst many pretended Spiritual Messengers in this confused Age.

An Epistle wrote by the Prophet JOHN REEVE to ISAAC PENNINGTON, Esq; dated 1658. concerning an Answer to a Book of his, with several Mysteries and Divine and Spiritual Revelations declared by the Prophet, concerning God's visible appearing in the Flesh.

IN your Self-return, you seem to mourn over the sunk Spirit of both Creations, so termed by you. Also you write as though many from a satanical Spirit write most accurately, both of the Works of Creation and Mystery of Redemption by an immediate Gift of God from our Lord Jesus Christ. To this I answer, a little Season will produce Mourning enough in you, when you shall see your angelical Motions like Lightning, cast down with Confusion of Fear, from their former Perfection of imaginary Glory, rational Dreams and Visions, Revelations, Inspirations, Experiences, or Voices proceeding from an incomprehensible Spirit.

Again; I have both read and heard a Voice to say, that the Secrets of the Lord are his choice Treasures, reserved only for Redeemed ones; but I never read or heard from any spiritual wise Man before now, that any satanical Spirit was able to intellect deceived Persons, exactly to write of the hidden Mysteries of the Everlasting God. Again, you pretend unto no such Revelations as I proceed upon, but say you, there is another Way more certain than Reason or Revelation, which whether as I presume you were led into, the Lord will one Day make manifest, from the true Light of Life Eternal. To this I answer, your Light as terming of the true Inspirations of the Lord Jesus Christ, written by me to you, is because as yet his Holy Spirit viels them from your Eyes; but as for your new Sound of teaching them from your God, more certain than Reason or Revelation, from the Divine Voice spoken in the Ear, through the glorious Mouth of my Lord. I declare that in all Ages the Elect loft Sheep of Israel, did never read or heard of any more than two original Ways either natural or spiritual in Mankind, whether you call them Creature or Creator, Light or Darkness, Truth or Error, Revelation and Reason, Inspiration and Imagination, Truth and Unbelief, Flesh and Spirit, and such like.

'Tis confessed, that visible Appearances of God or any else unto Mortals is teaching of all, but he that expects that kind of Teaching any more until Men are immortalized, lieth under at present as great an imaginary Deceit, as ever yet appeared in this Land. It is also granted that the most holy God speaketh to his Chosen Messengers by Voice of Words, even to the hearing of the Ear unto which Truth for Ends belt known unto himself, by his gracious Power only, can bear Record in this present Generation, unto the Grief only of all angelical

Wise, envious, proud, inglorious, hypocritical Reprobates that hear of it.

Moreover if your more sure Way of teaching from God were Vision itself, yet it is impossible for you to enjoy any true and lasting Peace, unless it swallows up all your former Writings produced from your own Spirit, without an immediate Commission from God, and in the Room thereof, perswade your Soul to pour in your Oil, into the natural Wounds of oppressed Persons, under what Opinions or Appearances whatsoever.

Again, you say, O Lord God, pity the Captivity of Man, yea, pity the Captivity of thy own poor Seed, hear the Prayers of that Spirit that interceedeth with thee for every Thing, not according to any fleshly Imaginations, but according to Truth and Righteousness of thine own Ballance. From the God of Truth, to this I answer, concerning that spiritual Captivity of the Elect, in Reference of a right Understanding of the Creator, you need not trouble yourself about that, unless you think through much importuning the unchangeable God, may be perswaded to loose their Bonds before the decreed Time thereof; but if you think that Glory of God's eternal Love towards them, will provoke to their spiritual Darkness through the invisible Appearances of his own pure Light, then you may know, until his own glorious Season, that all the Desires of Men or Angels are of no Effect, no nor of the Son himself, if you imagine a Father besides. 'Tis confessed, when the Time draweth near of some great Deliverance of the Chosen of God, usually the Lord provokes his People to cry unto him with Sighs and Groans, which cannot be uttered but from the innocent Spirit of his spiritual redeemed Ones, as his Due, he may receive all. Honour, Praise and Glory for their Deliverance out of their natural Darknesses, unto his marvellous Light.

Again, I declare from the true Light of the true aft that the Spirit which interceedeth with the Creator for all Mankind, upon the Account of his eternal Happiness, was never principled upon a spiritual Foundation of Truth, whatever subtile Expressions of God's righteous Ballance procedeth from him. Moreover, is it not the new heavenly Glances of Christ Jesus in Man's dark Soul, which upon an immortal Account, becomes all Light, Life, or ravishing Glory in him; and of the contrary, is it not the absenting Voice or Virtue of the uncreated Spirit of the Lord Christ Jesus, that occasions Men's Spirits to be full of satanical aspiring Wisdom about the Creator; and whence think you cometh this to pass, or possible could be of the Spirit, if the Creator were, and Angels were essentially living in one another there.

Again if your literal Request unto the Lord God, as in Reference unto the miserable Captivity of poor Mankind, lying under the miserable Yoak of unmerciful rich Tyrants, especially over his own innocent Seed or chosen People, then this will most necessarily follow; nay, you cannot deny it, if there be any Light in you, that all your conceived Spiritual Speakings, or Writings, or Prayers, in the great

Day of the Lord Jesus Christ, will became but fiery burning Death in you of utter Darkness, according to the true Saying If that Light in you be Darkness, how great is that Darkness? Unless as before said, answerable to your Profession of Love unto God, and Pity unto Man, you ate a bountiful Reliever of his oppressed Ones, according to his Bountifulness towards you, then mind the Virtues of Christ Jesus thus shining in you, will occasion from the refreshed Bowels of his own Seed new spiritual Acknowledgments, and a loving Return in the Lord for you, Why? because it is rare to find a merciful rich Man.

Friend, I certainly know that if you are one of God's Elect, you cannot be offended with me for writing the Truth, though at present, I be contrary to you in Spirit. Again, you write that you would beg unto the Lord for me, both with Tears and Blood, and you would speak somewhat concerning me, but you are afraid to open the Spirit before the Season thereof. Friend, As to that if ever the Lord of Life and Glory manifest himself to your Soul, then you will see clearly the Vanity of those Words.

Moreover, if I should tell you, that in the pure Eyes of the Lord Christ Jesus, that one handful of your Silver Tears, are of more Value than a Horse Load of your Tears and Blood, you might account it a very strange Paying from me; truly I unfeignedly believe it will be found a principal Truth, when our Lord Jesus Christ shall say in the day of Judgment, Come ye blessed of my Father; inherit the Kingdom prepared for you, for when I was hungry, you fed me; Go ye Cursed into everlasting Fire, when I was hungry ye fed me not: So that without Controversy, there is nothing in Man comparable to Love, Mercy and Forgiveness, even to his greatest Enemies.

Again, it is a marvellous Thing, if you or any other Man, should have a Spiritual Gift to distinguish between divine and diabolical Appearances, and yet defer the Examination thereof to another Season, or did the most wise God ever commission any Man or Angel to make a Discovery of any spiritual Counterfeits, and yet that Messenger remaineth dark in his own Understanding, concerning the Creator that sent him. I remember such a like Scripture Saying as this, him "whom you ignorantly worship, declare I unto you. Moreover, if the most wise Creator, either visible or invisible by himself or Angel, hath appeared in your Spirit, whereby unto your thinking, I was clearly discovered as a deceived Person among the rest, is it not a strange Thing that you should have Power over that Light above Men or Angels before you, for the Producing of it at another Season, the Creator himself will visible make it manifest, even so come Lord Jesus Christ, for thy glorious Name-sake, come quickly, and in the visible Sight of Men and, Angels bear Record whether thy Holy Spirit sent me (as I have declared almost these three Years) or no. Again, when the Lord made Choise of such a simple poor Man as I was, as many can witness in the City of London, that have known me about these twenty Years, that I might

instrumentally discover the two principal Heads of mischievous
Darkness in the Land; as namely John Robins past, and John Tawney
almost spent, truly I had no Power in me to put by his Message until
another Time; why because (whether you can believe it or no) his
Voice was so glorious in me, that it shone as the Sun, and it was of
Motion swifter than Thought, and so pleasant to be declared by
Tongue; yet for all that Godlike Glory piercing in me, and through me
there arose a Desire in me to be eased of that Burden of the Lord committed to my Charge, because of that sharp Sentence that I was to
declare against any Man that should despise it; then the Lord spake
again unto my Soul, Words of burning Death, of sensible unutterable
Darkness, answerable to that Jonas-like Rebellion in me, against so
great convincing Glory; and truly I was compelled immediately to cry
unto him for Deliverance from the Wounds or Anguish of my Soul,
that I might presently obey his Word that shined in me with such
Light, and Majesty, and Glory in whatsoever it should command me.

Wherefore, Friend happy are you if preserved from slighting an
Appearance, that is contrary unto your Light, though it strike at the
Foundation   on   which   is   built   all   your   Spiritual
Enjoyments; for alas, you know in the End, all false Lights will be
made manifest unto those that possess the true Light of Eternal Life
in them; blessed therefore are those, that in Obedience unto the
Creator from a purified Spirit are compassionate to all Men, but
especially to those innocent Appearances, in the Name of the Lord,
though they all differ in their Declaration for them. If there be but one
true Messenger from the Lord amongst the rest, they shall as
formerly, receive an Angel of God unawares, and with him be
Partakers of the glorious Secrets of the everliving God, to their eternal
Consolation: for this I know, from the Spirit of Truth, that those that
are left under a Spirit of rejecting and despising of false Appearances,
coming forth in the Name of the Lord, they not clearly knowing them
to be so, they will as readily despise a true Messenge of the Lord to
their eternal Hurt; wherefore are all those, that neither Honour nor
Life itself is dear unto them, but upon an Account of Spiritual Wisdom
amongst wise Man, when the Glorious Things of Eternity, though in
base Appearance presented unto them, from that Spiritual Rock of all
Ages, which is our Lord Jesus Christ, God and Man, is one district
Body or Person glorified; for whatsoever Men dream from their
imaginary Gods, of two or three Persons, or a vast incomprehensible
Spirit, essentially living in all Things and Places; from an immediate
Voice from the highest Heavens, I positively affirm against Men or
Angels, that there neither is, nor ever was any other God or Creator,
but that God-man Christ Jesus, which was nailed to the Cross, the
which Glorious God will one Day visibly appear with his mighty
Angels, to the everlasting Terror of those that reject his Person, as to
love a Thing for an infinite God to dwell in or to be; yea this very true
God in Opposition to all other Gods, Men or Angels, is already come

with his invisible pure piercing Light, to make an everlasting Distinction between the imaginary notional Misteries of Men in rational Darkness, and the spiritual Misteries of his everlasting Kingdom, by true Inspirations from an holy and unerring Spirit. Even so come Lord Jesus Christ, visibly also according to thine own Word, come quickly. Amen.

Yours with all the Elect, in that only wise very true God, which in the Sight of Men and Angels visibly appeared in Flesh, and in that very Body of Flesh and Bone, is ascended far above all Gods, Heavens, Angels, or Men, and there to remain until the Resurrection of all elect Things, or the Judgment-Day, whose uncreated Spirit of fiery Love, is all Variety of immortal Crowns of new ravishing Glories, prepared for all those that long for his visible appearing, to make an everlasting Separation, between the merciful Elea, and unmerciful Reprobate.

JOHN REEVE, the only true Witness unto the very true God, amongst many pretended Spiritual Messengers in this confused Age.

An EPISTLE of the Prophet REEVE. Written in the Year, 1656.

BLESSED are all those that shall read, or hear this Epistle with a meek Soul, and are kept from judging Things that seem strange at first Appearance, but by sober searching of the Scriptures, compare spiritual Things with spiritual, as those noble born did in the Apostles Time, being made patient to wait the Lord's Leisure, who reveals his Secrets to such only who with a pure Conscience hearken to his Spirit; He that believeth maketh not Haste.

In the 6th Chapter of St. John 36th Verse, are these Words, The Words that I speak unto you are Spirit and Life; and in the 10th, 17th, and 18th Verses, it is thus written, I lay down my Life that I may take it again: No Man taketh it from me, but I lay it down of myself I have Power to lay it down, and Power to take it again. Therefore, that you may increase in your most holy Faith unto your eternal Glory, which are appointed to believe in that distinct glorified Body of the Lord Jesus Christ, the only God and everlasting Father, from the Holy Spirit, I shall shew you wherein that Power did consist of Christ dying and living again.

This his Power was secretly hid in the Truth of his Word speaking. Why? Because the Nature of Christ's Soul within his blessed Body was only one Voice of spiritual Faith and Truth. Therefore, you may understand, whatever he spoke in that Word speaking, was all Power to effect the Thing spoken of. The Words that I speak unto you are Spirit and Life, that is, as if Christ should have said, "My Words tend not to Joy in carnal Things that perish, but in the rejoicing in spiritual Things which are eternal; or, as if the Lord should have said, "My Word is all spiritual Light and Love, Meekness, "Patience, with all

Variety of immortal glorious Joys beyond " the Comprehension of the Spirit of Men and Angels.

Again, Christ's Words are said to be Spirit and Life, because all Spirits in the Creation were made by his Word speaking only: Furthermore, because his Word only, is the original Cause of all Light, Life and Glory in Heaven and Earth, and in Men and Angels; I have Power, said Christ, to lay down my Life, and Power to take it again. I declare from the Holy Spirit, none in Heaven and Earth could ever truly speak those Words, but that Man Christ only.

Again, it is as if Christ should have said, "I only have all Power within my Soul, by a Word speaking, to die and live again".

Moreover, Christ Jesus being Lord of Life and Death, did believe without any Motion of doubting in him, that whatsoever he spoke should come to pass, and that gave a Being to the Thing spoken of, and that made him to say in the 24th of St. Matthew, ver. 25. Heaven and Earth shall pass away, but my Word shall not pass away.

So that Christ being the only God of all Truth, you may underhand that it was his Faith in that living Truth, or Virtue of his Word speaking, which gave him Power to lay down that divine Soul, or spiritual Godhead Life in the Hell of the Grave, and to quicken his spiritual Life again from Death, to reign in immortal Glory to Eternity, in that very Body of Flesh wherein he suffered Death. For I declare, from the Holy Spirit, from that everliving Virtue continually flowing from the former Suffering of God on this Earth, in the Body of Christ, the Tongue of Men nor Angels can never express the Variety of new glorious Joys, the eternal Spirit of God the Father hath in that glorious Garment of Flesh he hath clothed himself withal.

Again that divine Faith of Christ in that living Truth and Virtue of his Word speaking gave him Power over Life and Death, that by his precious Blood shedding, he might purchase from himself the Lordship of the Dead and Quick.

Again, If God had not been able to have made his Soul to die in his Body, and by the living Virtue of that almighty Word of Truth, spoken through his holy Mouth, to quicken a new and glorious Life again, O then would it be impossible for him at the last Day, by the Power of his Word to quicken and make alive, all the Souls and Bodies of Mankind that are dead asleep, and buried in the Grave.

You may understand, that living Virtue of his divine Word of Truth, spoken before he died, was that God, which raised the everliving God from Death to Life again.

Therefore, because the Lord your God liveth, ye which are to live eternally with him with astonishing Wonder and Admiration behold your God, that was absolutely dead and alive at one and the same Time.

Therefore Christ spoke those Words to his Apostles of the Power of Faith, Matt. xxi. 21. and Jesus answered and laid unto them, Verily I said unto you, if ye have Faith, and doubt not, ye shall not only do what I have done to the Fig-tree, but also if you say to this Mountain, take thyself away, and cast thyself into the Sea, it shall be done; and in Matt. xix. and 26. But with God all Things are possible, and in Gen. xiv. Is any Thing hard to the Lord.

Woe, Woe, Woe therefore, to all that are left under the Power of carnal Reason, that they may ever war against that incomprehensible Power of spiritual Faith and Truth essentially reigning in the glorious Body of the only wise God, your alone Redeemer, which long for his Appearance, which by the almighty Power of his Word speaking of that Substance of Earth and Water, created both Worlds, and all living Forms that in them are, into that Order they appear now to be, whether for a Time; or for Eternity, which also twice changed the Condition of his glorious Form by the almighty Power of the Spirit of Faith and Truth speaking thro' his heavenly Mouth.

Moreover, his divine Godhead died in the Flesh and quickned in the Spirit, not only to redeem his elect loft Sheep of the House of Israel, from the bitter Cup of eternal Death, but also to prove his infinite Power and Wisdom of Truth speaking, and for the disproving of all lying Reprobates, which always either in Heart or in Tongue, speak against that glorious Power of their Creator.

You know, that it is a common Thing for them to say, that it is Blasphemy for any Man to say, that God could possibly die, with many such like cursed Speeches against incomprehensible Power. And why do atheistical Hypocrites say, that God could not die? Because of their lying Imagination they cannot comprehend by what Means God should possibly live again if he were dead.

Thus they measure that incomprehensible Power of divine Faith or heavenly Truth, by the narrow Compass of their blind Reason, and bottomless Pit of lying Imagination, which understand nothing of that spiritual Power of true Faith.

And because they are not able to comprehend the spiritual Ways of the Lord Jesus Christ, they hate both him and his Elect, and call him a Liar to his Face, both in his Person and in his Word, and in his Prophet, and in his People.

Moreover, because they see no Power in themselves, neither to live nor to die, presumptuously they take upon them to judge the God of all Power over Life and Death, by their no Power at all.

Again, if that God that said, I have Power to lay down my Life, and Power to take it again, did not die, and was buried both Soul and Body in the Grave, and after the decreed Time of three Days and three Nights, by a quickening Spirit revive a new and glorious Life again in Despite of Death's Power, then (angelical Reprobate) the following Scriptures were Words of Truth, spoken from the Spiritual Mouth of the everlasting God, that sent me to declare this Secret, who did die, but cannot possibly lie; for lying is of a mortal Man, like unto thyself. In the Words of Isa. lv and the last Verse, Because he poured out his Soul unto Death. In Psal. 16. ver. 11. For thou wilt not leave my Soul in Hell, neither wilt thou suffer thine holy One to see Corruption. In Acts ii. 27, 31. Because thou wilt not leave my Soul in the Grave, neither wilt thou suffer thine holy One to see Corruption; he knowing that he before spoke of the Resurrection, of Christ, that his Soul should not be left in the Grave, neither should his Flesh see Corruption. Rom. xiv. 9, For Christ- therefore died and rose again, and revived, that he might be Lord both of the Dead and and Quick. In Rev. i. 17, 18. Saying unto me, Fear not, I am the first and last I am he that liveth, and was dead, and behold I am alive for evermore, Amen; and have the Keys of Hell and Death. And Rev. ii. 8. These Things saith the first, and the last, which was dead and is alive.

If this Truth be not sufficiently cleared by the Letter of the Scriptures concerning Christ's Soul and Body being both dead and buried in the Grave, and living again by his own Power, I would it were. This I am certain of, that they that deny this Truth, are not only naturally blind, but wilfully also do shut their Eyes, and flop their Ears, and call the Scriptures Lies, because of the Cross of Christ, without which there is no Crown of Glory.

Again, if the everlasting God for a Moment could not have, died, and left himself void of all Light, or Life, spiritual or natural (as the Condition of all Mankind is, which are dead asleep in the Dust of the Earth) then he could not possibly have experimentally known the State of the Dead, whether elect or reprobate. Moreover, neither could he possibly, in his Creatureship Condition, be capable of entering into the immortal Glory of his Creatorship again, but by his entering into Death, that he might live again, and upon his glorious Head, instead of a Crown of Thorns, wear a double Crown of eternal Glory.

Again, that he might also shew unto his elect Men and Angels, his almighty Power and unsearchable Wisdom, by quickening an immortal, transcendent, glorious Life, out of Death itself.

Thus the Lord of Life and Death, by suffering all Conditions in his innocent Soul and Body, did purchase, at a dear Rate, from himself, a prerogative Power of being Lord and King over all Conditions whatsoever; and from hence he experimentally knows what immortal Crowns and Glory are most suitable for all suffering Conditions his blessed ones undergo; and, by Virtue of his unspeakable Sufferings at the Hands of Jewish, Canaanitish Devils, he knoweth what Measure of eternal Death in utter Darkness is most meet for the Souls and Bodies of all the Sons and Daughters, proceeding from the Bowels of cursed, bloody Cain, that reprobate, angelical, old wise Serpent-Devil, and Father of all the Damned; who through the Decree of God, was call out of Heaven into this World, that he might bring forth his generation of proud, envious, scoffing, persecuting wise Serpent-Devils; not only to war against the Lord of Life and the Truth of Holy Scriptures, but also against his Holy Spirit of divine Faith or Truth, in all the elect lost Sons and Daughters proceeding from the Loins of *Adam:* So that their eternal perishing by the secret Decree of God, being hid from them by his Wisdom, they might justly be damned in themselves from the everlasting Remembrance not only of all their Actions of vainglorious Hypocrisy, but unmerciful Cruelties.

This will be that gnawing Worm of Conscience which never dieth, and that fiery Curse of the Law, of the Wrath of God in Mens Souls, that never goeth out.

And so much concerning that everlasting Word of Truth that was spoken by the glorious Mouth of the everlasting God, that Man Christ Jesus, upon the Throne of all immortal Crowns of Glory and Majesty, far above all Heavens, Angels, and Men.

Yours, who love the Lord Jesus, more than this perishing World.

JOHN REEVE.

(John Reeve's Letters from)

SUPPLEMENT
TO
THE BOOK OF LETTERS,
WRITTEN BY
JOHN REEVE AND LODOWICKE MUGGLETON,
THE TWO
Last Prophets of the only true God,
OUR
LORD JESUS CHRIST.

BELOVED BRETHREN,

WITH the authority of the Church we have made diligent search through the Manuscript Records of the Church, and have found the following Letters, not in print in the "Book of Letters." The following Letters may be considered the conclusion of all the Writings of the Prophets REEVE and MUGGLETON, both of spiritual matter and temporal advice, as far as the Church is in possession of.

JOSEPH & ISAAC FROST.

LONDON:
PRINTED BY R. BROWN, 26, ST. JOHN STREET, CLERKENWELL.
1831.

SUPPLEMENT
TO
THE BOOK OF LETTERS,
&c. &c.

An Epistle of JOHN REEVE to CHRIS. HILL.

Dear Friend in the eternal Truth, my love to you and the rest of our spiritual friends remembered.

Brother Hill,

IT seems very strange to me, that you with the test of former friends, make no enquiry after me whether I am dead or alive. What, have the unnecessary things and cares of this world swallowed up your former love to the truth? Though I am moved in this manner to write unto you, I trust you have not so learned Christ.

Friend, the reason of my not sending unto you this long season is this, because my wife and I were both very sick and weak, of which sickness the 29th of March last my wife died.

Immediately after I had buried my wife, the Lord our God called me to visit some of his people living near the City of Cambridge, as he once called me to visit you; yea, it was in the very same manner, for one of the chief speakers of the Ranters being convinced by this truth, who formerly had deceived them, took a parcel of my books and presented them to them, upon which they greatly desired me as you formerly did; I hope there is about half a score of them that have received the truth in sincerity of heart; they are husbandmen and tradesmen that labour for their bread as you do; they rejoice in those that really possess this truth though by face unknown.

Christopher Hill,

You seem to forget your engagement to your father-in-law, you know the time is expired concerning your payment of the money which was lent to you, and not to him; wherefore as you love the truth, I desire you to send me the fifteen shillings remaining behind speedily, that I may restore it to the right owner.

Now concerning my own condition, it is thus; on May Day last, I was senseless two or three times, insomuch, that if a faithful friend had not been by me to relieve me with a little cordial, I had immediately died. I still continue very sick and weak, so that of necessity I must either mend or end in a little space. As for relief now I have most need of it, it hath been very small of late; I wish it may not be a burthen to the conscience of some when I am gone; the widow's mite will be a witness against all carnal excuses in those that own this truth. It may be you may think I have no need of your charity now, because the merchant for a little season allowed me five shillings a week; but if you think so you are much mistaken, for I have had none from him a pretty while, neither do I know whether I shall have any more from him at all, for when he took ship for Barbadoes, he had not wherewithall to leave for his wife and children, through the unjust dealings of unreasonable men. Brother Hill you may remember you sent me word, that if the London Christians would contribute weekly or monthly to my necessity, you would do the like, you will do well to keep your covenant.

And so I commit you to the most High, and remain yours in all righteousness,

JOHN REEVE.

My dwelling is in Bishopsgate Street, near Hog Lane End, with three sisters that keep a sempstris shop.

Direct your letters, to our brother MUGGLETON, to he conveyed to me, and the fifteen shillings to him for me, you know where he dwells; it is in Trinity Lane, over against a Brown Baker's

London, June 11th, 1656.

Another Epistle of JOHN REEVE'S to the same person.

For his loving friend CHRISTOPHER HILL, Heel Maker, in Stone Street, in Maidstone, in Kent. These

Brother Hill,

I HAVE received your letter and your kind token, for which I acknowledge your kindness to truth.

As for my neglect in writing to you, my great troubles of sickness and mortality hath hindered it, I hope whilst I am able to write for time to come you shall not charge me with any such neglect; in the mean season I do not desire your charity unless you can spare it. Remember my kind love to your mother Wyles, to Thomas Martin, and Goodman Young, and I rejoice in the Lord for you that the truth abides in you. As for the fifteen shillings I am glad of your care for the truth's sake, because it was lent to me upon that account.

No more at present, but desiring my God abundantly to establish you in all spiritual excellencies, unto whose infinite grace I commend you all, and remain yours in all righteousness,

JOHN REEVE

London, June 30th, 1656.

A
GENERAL EPISTLE
TO
MINISTERS,
WITH EXTRACTS FROM "SACRED REMAINS;"
COMPRISING
A GENERAL TREATISE ON THE THREE RECORDS,
WHAT WAS FROM ETERNITY,
THE ONE PERSONAL UNCREATED GLORY,
AND
A CLOUD OF UNERRING WITNESSES,
BY JOHN REEVE AND LODOWICK MUGGLETON,

THE TWO LAST SPIRITUAL WITNESSES, AND ALONE TRUE PROPHETS OF THE HOLY SPIRIT, BY COMMISSION FROM THE TRUE GOD, THAT EVER SHALL WRITE OR SPEAK UNTO UNBELIEVING MAGISTRATES, MINISTERS, AND PEOPLE, UNTIL THE ONLY LORD OF LIFE AND GLORY, THE MAN JESUS, PERSONALLY APPEARETH, IN THE AIR, WITH HIS MIGHTY ANGELS, TO BEAR WITNESS TO THIS TESTIMONY: EVEN SO, COME, LORD JESUS.

FIRST PRINTED FOR THE AUTHORS IN THE YEAR OF OUR LORD 1652, THEN RESIDING IN LONDON.

FOURTH EDITION.

LONDON:

PRINTED FOR JOSEPH FROST, 17, HALF MOON STREET, BISHOPSGATE STREET,

BY LUKE JAMES HANSARD, 5, PEMBERTON ROW, GOUGH

SQUARE, FLEET STREET,

1854

A GENERAL TREATISE OF THE THREE RECORDS OR DISPENSATIONS FROM HEAVEN.

WRITTEN IN THE YEAR OF MY COMMISSION, RECEIVED BY VOICE OF THE LORD JESUS FROM HEAVEN, 1651, AND IN THE 27th OF JULY, 1652, BY REVELATION FROM THE MAN JESUS, MY GOD ALONE; UNTO ALL THE ELECT THAT LOOK FOR THE APPEARING OF THE ONE ONLY, IMMORTAL, INVISIBLE, WISE GOD, AND ALONE ETERNAL FATHER, THE LORD JESUS CHRIST; GOD, BLESSED FOR EVER OF ALL THE ELECT, MEN AND ANGELS. BY JOHN REEVE, AND THE HOLY SPIRIT'S TRUE MINISTER OF THE THIRD AND LAST DISPENSATION OF THE LORD JESUS, UNTO ALL THE ELECT WORLD.

CHAPTER I.

1. Three Dispensations of the Lord unto the elect World: (1.) Of Moses and the Prophets; (2.) Of Jesus and the Apostles; and (3.) Of the Two Witnesses, Rev. xi. 2. The Dispensation of Moses, moral and ceremonial, belonged to the Jews only. 3. The Manner of Divine Worship under the second Dispensation was not revealed to Moses. 4. Every true Commissioner had charge of the several Manners of Divine Worship. 5. Thus Moses and the Prophets were faithful until the end of their Commission, all suffering persecution, and some death, for their message' sake. 6. The Jews, by violence, got into Moses' chair, and sat as Scripture Interpreters; and then, 7. Slew the Prophets.

THERE are three dispensations, or commissions of the Lord, unto the elect world, and but three. The first, of Moses and the prophets. The second, of Jesus and the apostles. The third and last are the two witnesses in the eleventh of the Revelations; who are the true ministers of the Holy Spirit, revealing or declaring the mind of God, the man Jesus, unto all the elect world; who are the seed of the woman, the children of faith, which is the divine nature of God.

2. Again, I declare, by revelation from the Lord Jesus, that all the Lord's commissioners have power given them to bless or to curse, and it is so: therefore it had been good for them that are left to despise them that they had never been born.

3. Again, the three commissioners, and they only, are Christ's witnesses, because they have the gift of the Holy Ghost, or spirit of revelation, to interpret the scriptures: therefore all that are saved shall bow unto the revelations of God in them.

4. Again, I declare, from the Lord Jesus, that all the prophets and priests that were in the time

of Moses were liars, except they that were called of the Lord, as Moses and Aaron were, or were called by succession from them: therefore it is a most dangerous thing for a man to take upon him the place of a prophet, a priest, or Levite, or minister, without a commission from the Lord.

5. What do they, but offer strange fire unto the Lord, as Corah, Dathan, and Abiram did, before they were called to the office by God's commissioners, and bring a curse upon their souls?

6. Remember Jezebel's prophets. Were they not cut in pieces for drawing the princes' hearts from the true worship of the living God?

7. And this their ignorance of God was, because they went before they were sent.

8. Therefore lying prophets, for silver, are in a perishing condition, with all the scripture-merchants in the world.

9. Again, I declare, from the Lord, that Moses was the first prophet that wrote scriptures by commission from the Lord. Note.—By inspiration from the spirit of revelation, God witnessing from heaven, by signs and wonders, that his commission was from the Lord.

10. Now the commission of Moses was full of ceremonies, ordinances, and shadows, concerning things to come, very tedious unto the people.

11. So long as the commission of Moses and the prophets continued, there was no nation under heaven had anything of the true worship of God, but the Jews only, and those that joined with the Jews, because the oracles of God were committed to the Jews only. "Salvation is of the Jews," as it is written.

12. Again, I declare, from the Lord Jesus, that the law of Moses, both moral and ceremonial, with all the Jewish observances, or worship whatsoever, did belong to the Jews only; and this their worship continued until Christ, and no longer, who was the giver of the law, and the fulfiller of that law only, and the putting down that worship, and observing of the law of Moses for ever.

13. Therefore accursed be that man that sets up the worship which God pulls down, or pulls down that worship which God sets up, until God remands it himself; for that is adding or diminishing of the word of God in the book of scriptures.

14. Again, I declare, from the Lord, that the sword of steel did belong in Moses' commission to the nation of the Jews, and was never to be used in the two commissions following by any that professed the faith of Jesus, being utterly unlawful by the command of God, the man Jesus, in his second commission.

15. Again, I declare from the Lord, that God never revealed to Moses, nor any of his prophets, in what manner his worship should be in the second dispensation, by Jesus and the apostles, because he will have all the honour; therefore, by his own wisdom his counsels are

unsearchable, and his ways past finding out.

16. Again, I declare from the Lord, that every true commissioner hath the several manners of the worship of God committed unto his charge, to declare unto men; and that when the second commissioner declares his message of worship from the Lord, then the worship of the first messenger is ended, never to be more.

17. So, likewise, when the third and last commissioner declares his message of the manner of worship of God, then is the second commission ended likewise for evermore.

18. Thus every commissioner is to mind his own charge only, and to be faithful in his trust, having nothing to do with one another's commission, concerning the worship of God, but to be faithful unto God, in all things committed to their charge, that they may give up the account of their stewardship with joy, receiving that reward, or crown of glory, with the Lord Jesus, in his everlasting kingdom.

19. Thus Moses was faithful in all his house with the prophets, in the time of the law, unto the end of their commission, all of them suffering persecution for their message' sake, and some of them death itself.

20. Again, I declare, from the Lord, that the Jews, long before the commission of Jesus appeared, persecuted and put to death the true commissioners and interpreters of the law of Moses; and, when they had so done, they got up into Moses' chair, not being sent, but by violence, and so they became the scripture-interpreters, which was given to Moses and the prophets only;

21. And, finding that being the lords of the letter of scripture, and skilfully merchandizing them, great honour and wealth came thereby, making them equal with the princes; they took counsel together, and made a decree, that none but the learned only should meddle with the interpretation of scripture.

22. Thus the Jews put the true prophets to death who declared the message of God freely; and then their children painted the sepulchres of the prophets, and set up their writings by a law, because of the glory that came thereby.

23. Thus these scripture-usurpers sat like kings in Moses' chair, uncontrollable, as if they were the Lord's commissioners, until the coming of Jesus and the apostles.

24. Again, I declare, from the Lord, if the Jews that sat in Moses' chair had been interpreters of the law by commission from the Lord, then would they have known the law-giver, the Lord Jesus, and have yielded obedience to him, as John the Baptist did, he being the true messenger of the Lord: but quite contrary, devil-like, being of their father, the devil Cain, who slew the first Abel;

25. So the children of Cain—the learned scribes and pharisees—slew the Lord of life and glory, the heir of all truth,

that the inheritance of the interpretation of the letter of the scripture might remain in the possession and power of the learned for ever.

26. But Jesus, whom they slew, did often confound them, out of the mouths of unlearned babes and sucklings, by the power of his Spirit.

27. As it is very hard for a rich man to enter into life, and that very few of the rich will be saved, because riches blind the eyes of the understanding; so will it be as hard for a learned man to be saved, because learning draws forth the pride of the spirit of man, making it uncapable of the voice of God's Spirit, charm it never so wisely.

28. Woe unto all learned men, especially if they be rich! for learning and riches are the snares of God, to draw men into eternal perdition.

CHAPTER II.

1. When the second Dispensation was given by Jesus, the first was abrogated for ever. 2. The Jewish Sabbath was a ceremonial Observance. 3. Every day is a Sabbath to the true Christian; but, 4. The Sabbath of the Reprobate is a visible day. 5. The second Dispensation terminated with the Ten Persecutions, which continued about three centuries after the death of Christ; since which period there has been no true Interpreter of the Scriptures, but, 6. The ministry has been grounded on Magistracy, and is not of the Lord.

AGAIN, I declare, from the Lord Jesus, the man of glory, and my alone God and eternal Father, that, when this Jesus gave the second commission of the preaching of the gospel, then all observances of the law of Moses were of no use for ever; whether circumcision, or the Jewish sabbath, or new-moons, or tythes, or any sacrifices under the law whatsoever;

2. Because all worship of the law of Moses were but types and shadows of the worship in the gospel of Jesus, therefore all that are gone back to the law of Moses are under the curse; as it is written, "Cursed be every one that continueth not in the law to do it perfectly."

3. Again, in the commission of the gospel of Jesus, given unto the apostles of Jesus, there were ordinances also for baptism, breaking of bread, preaching the gospel in season and out of season, meeting together the first day of the week, not observing it as a moral sabbath, but as wisdom directed them for conveniency, once a week, for the consolation of one another.

4. They met upon the first day of the week, which is called the Lord's-day, because God upon that day rose from the dead.

5. Not but every day is a sabbath, or Lord's-day, unto true Christians; for he that is entered into faith is entered into his sabbath, having rested from the works of the law, from all ceremonial observing of a sabbath-day, or any other ceremony of the law of Moses whatsoever.

6. As God entered into his

eternal sabbath's rest on the seventh day (as it is written), when he had finished the six days' work of creation, by the power of his word-speaking;

7. So that faith is the true sabbath of all the elect, who walk not after the fleshly worship of men, in observing a sabbathday, or the like, but are led by the Spirit of God, the man Jesus, to offer a spiritual sabbath of faith and love to God all the days of their life, which is a full testimony to their souls of their keeping a spiritual sabbath with their God, the man Jesus, eternally in the heavens.

8. But the sabbath of the reprobate hypocrite is a visible day—as Sunday or the like—sometimes doubting whether Sunday is the right, or Saturday.

9. Thus they are to seek of the sabbath concerning the day, and so of their God; for they that are ignorant of the true sabbath must needs be ignorant of the true God.

10. Thus all the worship of the several formal hypocrites is all outwardly, to the vainglorious fleshly eye, and in bondage to sin, therefore under the curse and wrath of God for ever; because God hath not revealed unto them that spiritual sabbath of faith, to purify their hearts from all unrighteousness, making them to understand that obedience is the sabbath that God requires, and net sacrifice.

11. God's sabbath is obedience, and the visible sabbath is sacrifice. Woe unto all that despise this truth! It had been better they had never been born.

12. Again, I declare, by revelation from the Lord Jesus Christ, that his second dispensation or commission of God given to the apostles, with all the ordinances contained in that dispensation, continued no longer than the putting to death and banishing of the commissioners in the ten persecutions, which continued about 300 years.

13. Since that time, it being about 1350 years, I declare, from the Lord Jesus, there hath not been one true interpreter of the mind of God in the scriptures, to preach the everlasting gospel of Jesus Christ, by commission from heaven unto the seed of his own body, the elect; but they have all climbed up the wrong way; idle shepherds, that the Lord never sent, therefore few of them will be saved in the day of the Lord.

14. What are they but spiritual witches, blind leaders of the blind? therefore both must needs fall into the ditch; children of Cain, and merchants of the word of life, almost all of them despisers of the spirit of revelation, which is the only testimony of a true messenger of the Lord.

15. Woe unto them that have gone the way of Balaam, loving the wages of iniquity! for any man to preach or prophesy, without a commission from the Lord, is but a work of iniquity.

16. For how can he preach unless he be sent; for the Lord is one with those that he sends, giving them power to bless all those that receive their message,

and to curse all those that shall despise it.

17. This is the power of every true commissioner or messenger of the Lord Jesus Christ; and whosoever hath not this power in his commission was never sent of the Lord No earthly king giveth a commission to his servants, but this commission is powerful to all them it concerns.

18. Again, the apostles' commission and ordinances being finished in the ten persecutions, then the children of those that put them to death took possession of the apostles' chair, as the children of the Jews took possession of Moses' chair, when their fathers had put the prophets to death; and, when the apostles were put to death, their children that put them to death painted their sepulchres, setting up their writings by a law, that none but the learned only should be the scripture interpreters;

19: And so it hath continued, wherever the scripture came, almost to this day; the magistrates and ministers joining together to maintain the power of the scriptures in the hands of the minister by a law from the magistrate, which minister is to the magistrate a false prophet.

20. When these scripture-merchants had purchased to become the scripture-interpreters, by the blood of the apostles, then did they piece the old cloth to the new, and so made the rent worse.

21. They have so mixed the writings of Moses and the apostles together, both in books, chapters, lines, and words, throughout the two Testaments, that no man can find the truth, but by the same Spirit that spake them, by the mouths of the prophets and the apostles.

22. Again, I declare, that all the ministry that was or is grounded upon magistracy, since the coming of Christ Jesus in the flesh, and since the commission of Jesus to the apostles, is not of the Lord: the Lord sent them not, it was the magistrate, their lord, sent them; therefore their reward is from him, which is the penny of this world only.

23. Again, I declare from the Lord, that no magistrate did ever own any of the ministers or prophets of the Lord, as to establish their ministry in their dominions, but those commissioner-magistrates under the law, in the time of Moses.

24. Therefore, the magistrates, in the time of the apostles, not being commissioner-magistrates of the Lord's, instead of owning the true apostles of the Lord, they persecuted them to the death; like unto those Gentile, heathen, non-commissionate-magistrates, in the time of the law, as Pharaoh, and such as he was.

25. Neither did the apostles own the magistrates for the defence of their ministry, knowing that the Lord had not sent them, nor appointed them to receive it, but had left them to persecute it, to their own destruction, for ever.

26. Neither will any magistrate own any ministry, so long as the world endureth, but a ministry of his own setting up;

for the Lord hath left them in darkness, lest they should be converted, and he should heal them; as it is written, "Which of the rulers have believed on him?"

27. Again, "The kings and the rulers take counsel together against the Lord and his anointed;" and the apostle Paul saith, "The princes of the world have nought in him."

28. The apostle speaks as though there would hardly one prince or ruler be saved (since the coming of Jesus) in the day of the Lord, because, instead of yielding unto Christ's cross, that he may reign over them, they themselves reign like gods and kings over their poor brethren.

29. Therefore, in that day my God, the man Jesus, will say, "And those mine enemies, whether great or small, that would not that I should reign over them, bring them and slay them before my face."

CHAPTER III.

1. The third or last Dispensation is that of the Two Witnesses, Rev. xi. 2. This Dispensation is all spiritual; therefore, 3. All visible Forms of Worship are inventions of Man's imagination from the letter of the Scripture's. 4. The visible Worship now in the world is the chief occasion of Wars, and many other wickednesses. 5. False Shepherds are over the flock of Christ. 6. True Worship is to hear and obey the Holy Spirit. 7. The Elect have power to show Mercy to their Enemies, and, 8. To love one another. 9. They only have the spirit of Revelation.

AGAIN, I declare by revelation from the Lord Jesus, that the two witnesses spoken of in the eleventh chapter of the Revelations, is the third or last dispensation, or commission of God, unto the elect world; and that JOHN REEVE, and LODOWICK MUGGLETON are those two witnesses or ministers of the last commission of the Holy Spirit, unto the end of the world.

2. Again, I declare from the Lord, that this dispensation of the Holy Spirit hath no ordinances or observances annexed unto it, but is all spiritual; neither are there any visible natural signs tied unto it, nor wonders to satisfy devils that this commission is from the Lord; this commission being only spiritual, as it is written, "And if any man will hurt them, fire proceedeth out of their mouths, and devoureth their enemies."

3. For God hath put the two-edged sword of his Spirit into their mouths, that, upon their pronouncing God's curse upon their enemies, the fire of God's wrath seizeth upon their spirits to all eternity; because they that despise them have sinned against the Holy Ghost; because we only are the ministers of the Holy Spirit, to declare unto man what is the worship indeed that God requires of his elect, until the coming of Jesus Christ.

4, Again, God hath honoured them with the spirit of discerning his elect, that, upon their pronouncing them blessed, they increase in understanding of the scriptures from the Holy Spirit, and are blessed to all eternity.

5. Again, I declare from the Lord Jesus, that all visible forms of worship that are now extant in the world, are not by command from the Lord, but are the invention of man's imagination, from the letter of the Scripture; therefore as acceptable unto God as the cutting off of a dog's neck.

6. I declare again, from the Lord, that the visible worship now in the world, set up by magistrates and ministers, whether public or private, is so far from being by commission from the Lord, that it is the chief occasion of all wars, and many other secret wickednesses, committed under heaven.

7. Thus all that are not quite blind, through the long custom of the false prophets or priests, set up or countenanced by the magistrate, may clearly see that none of them are by commission from the Lord, but false shepherds, that went before they were sent; therefore, but few of them will escape the vengeance of eternal fire in the day of the Lord.

8. Again, I declare from the Lord Jesus Christ, God alone, blessed for ever, that the worship that now is, and shall be to the end of the world,—Note, it is to hearken what the Holy Spirit saith unto the soul, and to yield unto it; and in so doing thou shalt never want peace.

9. Thou shalt hear a voice behind thee, saying, "This is the way, walk in it;" hearken unto that voice and yield obedience unto it; and thou shalt see eternal life abiding in thee.

10. This is the voice of God from heaven, called the Spirit of faith or revelation, filling the soul with pure spiritual love, patience, meekness, and all other virtues of the Holy Spirit; which Holy Spirit is the only minister or teacher of all the elect, unto life eternal, even to the end of the world.

11. They that are led by this Spirit, they are kept from the committing of sin: I do not say they have no temptations or motions of sin from their own spirits; but I say the Spirit of faith purifies their hearts, giving them power against those motions or temptations of the flesh; and so, their bodies and spirits, being kept pure, are fit temples for the in-dwelling of the Holy Spirit.

12. For all that are born of God know the voice of his Spirit, and have this power over sin, as I have declared; for the Spirit of Jesus is one and the same in all his elect, only in a greater measure of understanding the word of God in the scriptures to some than to others, especially to the commissioners, who are sent to declare his mind unto the elect; as it is written of Peter, "When thou art converted, strengthen the brethren."

13. Thus God's commissioners have a greater measure of his Spirit than private Christians, because they are made public, and appointed to greater sufferings than those that are private believers.

14. Again, it is written: "My sheep hear my voice, and they

follow me:" that is, the newborn elect know the voice of God's Spirit, and so are made obedient to his voice; and "a stranger they will not follow."

15. The stranger is the voice of reason, which is the voice of the devil, that would draw the soul from the voice of faith, which is the voice of the Spirit of God, in all the sheep of Christ.

16. Again, this blessed Spirit gives power unto the elect to show mercy unto their greatest enemies; yea, and to forgive them, although they should kill them; and gives a man power to leave all vengeance unto God, unto whom only it doth belong.

17. Again, I declare, from the Lord, all that are of this faith are of one spirit, and have power given them to love one another as their own soul; yea, they have all of them power given them to lay down their lives for this their faith, because it is the faith of the holy prophets and apostles, the true faith of Jesus, the power of God unto salvation.

18. This is that faith that keeps the soul spotless, from lying unto his neighbour, and from all other unrighteousness whatsoever; the which no other churches nor opinions in the world do, but will lie unto one another for gain, but this church of Christ.

19. Once again, from the Lord, I declare that this church of Christ only being the elect, they only have the Spirit of revelation of the mind of God, always increasing in the Spirit of the scriptures, and are God's only lights in this world, and

those that are appointed of God as his judges over all their enemies, both great and small, in the world; that despise the Spirit of revelation.

20. Note.—Again, I declare, from the Lord, that none can understand what God is, nor what the devil is, nor what is after death, nor whether ever their bodies ever appear any more, nor any invisible thing, but by the Spirit of revelation, which is the voice of God, leading his own elect sheep and lambs into all spiritual pastures; whilst unbelieving lions,—Note, —that despise this Spirit, are hunger-bit; yea, and sent away empty of all spiritual consolations.

21. Again, I declare, from the Lord, that all that have this Spirit of revelation or faith in the man Jesus, they know that there is no other God but the man Jesus, that in his person only the eternal Father always lived, and that there was never any other God, or eternal Spirit, or Father, but this Jesus only, that man of glory, whose goings out have been from everlasting;

22. And that all the names or titles in the letter of the scriptures, of "Father," or "Jehovah," or "Melchizedek," or "I am," or "Eternal God," or "Eternal Father," or "Wonderful Counsellor," or "Prince of Peace," or "Alpha and Omega;" yea, and all other names or titles spoken of in the law and gospel by the prophets and the apostles and the two witnesses in the Revelation, they are all attributed unto this Jesus, the

eternal God, and man of glory, who is a distinct God, in the person of a man, from all creatures in heaven and on earth, from all eternity to all eternity.

23. Therefore, they that have this Spirit of faith, cannot take the sword of steel to slay their brother, because they know that man is the image of God; neither can they go to law with their neighbour, whatever loss may come thereby; neither can they take upon them any place of honour from the lords of this world, because their kingdom is no more of this world than it was to the Lord Jesus, who came on purpose to show unto his elect himself of his spiritual kingdom of glory.

24. And when they had tasted a little of the spiritual kingdom, from that moment, instead of yielding to the customs of nations, to make them honourable, they were made willing to deny themselves, and to suffer reproach with the Lord Jesus Christ, because they know there is no way to the crown of glory with their God, but to drink the same cup of persecution and afflictions as their Lord did before them.

25. "The servant is not greater than his Lord." And this only is the way of all the elect, until the coming of our Lord Jesus Christ, the man of glory, God alone, blessed for evermore.

CHAPTER IV.

1. The Three that bear record in Heaven. 2. The Three that bear record on Earth. 3. The Spiritual Person of God converted itself into a natural Body.

AGAIN, it is written, "there are three that bear record in heaven, the Father, the Word, and the Spirit, and these three are one."

2. Note further. —There are three that bear witness on earth, "water," "blood," and "spirit," and these three agree in one.

3. Now these three witnesses on earth, "water," "blood," and "spirit," are the three commissions or dispensations of the Lord aforesaid, which the Spirit of God hath written unto you that are his elect, for your information and eternal consolation.

4. The water, that is Moses' commission; the blood, that is the commission of Jesus; the spirit, that is the commission of the two witnesses, spoken of in Revelations chap. xi., whose commission, or message from the Lord, is all spiritual.

5. Again, as for the three that bear record in heaven, the mind of God in that saying is this; that God, in the name of " Father," "Word," and " Spirit," did in or from heaven, his throne of glory, three times bear witness unto those commissions on earth aforesaid, by signs and wonders, that these three only were the Lord's commissioners.

6. According unto their several dispensations did the Lord witness from heaven, in the

hearts of his elect only, that they were indeed the prophets of the Lord. As for the reprobate, because the Lord reveals it not to him inwardly by his blessed Spirit, therefore he always tempts his God, devil-like as he is, for an outward visible sign, to make him believe an invisible God.

7. But the elect believer is kept from tempting his God, being always made to wait for an invisible sign or testimony from the Spirit of God, whether the commissioner or prophet be from the Lord or no.

8. He that believes makes not haste, he is made to wait: he only knows that, by entertaining of some strangers, he has received angels; unto him only it is revealed what that blessing is, unto those that are made to receive a prophet or disciple of the Lord, in the name of a prophet or disciple of the Lord, Jesus Christ.

9. Unto him alone it is revealed, that he, with the prophets, shall inherit together a crown of glory in those persons they now enjoy, being made like unto their God, the man Jesus, at his visible appearing in the clouds, in his everlasting kingdom of glory.

10. Again, unto him only it is revealed what that curse is that shall be upon the souls and bodies of all the despisers of the message of the prophets of the Lord to all eternity.

11. Again, I declare from the Lord, that it is revealed unto us only, that have received this faith of Jesus, what things shall be after death; we only are capable to know, that God, the man Jesus, was in the person of a man before he became flesh and bone, from all eternity.

12. Note.—Unto us it is known, that there never was any spirit without a body or person, because the body or person is the form of the invisible spirit, that can never be seen or known, but through a visible body or person, which is the house or tabernacle of every invisible spirit, in heaven and on earth.

13. So that a spirit is an invisible substance, yet nothing at all without its form of body or person; neither is the body or person anything at all without the invisible spirit, which is the God, spirit, or life of the created or untreated formable body or person.

14. As the soul and body of man is both one person, and that one is nothing without the other, being both of one nature, begot together, and so living together, neither of them living one without the other; and so dying or falling asleep together (being both one creature) until the resurrection of their death of sleep from their dust; and so being raised, as they lived together before death, being both one creature, so shall they now after death remain together in glory or in shame, to all eternity.

15. So I declare, from the Lord, that the eternal spiritual God the Father—Note,—always liveth in a spiritual form of body or person; the which body, or spiritual person, was the eternal Son of the eternal Father; the

which eternal Son is the holy city, or tabernacle of glory, wherein the Father, which is the eternal Spirit, hath his glorious delight, from eternity to eternity.

16. Again, I declare, from the Lord Jesus, that this spiritual person, or body of God, that was from all eternity, did convert itself into a natural body of flesh, blood, and bone, and so became subject unto death; and when it became a natural body, the Father, which is the Spirit eternal, and Godhead of the body, which was the eternal Son, lived only in that person.

17. "For in him lived the fulness of the Godhead bodily;" that is, in his body lived the eternal Spirit, God the Father, bodily; because this natural body was the eternal son of God, which formerly was the eternal spiritual body of God, Note, the eternal spirit from all eternity; therefore it is written, "the word became flesh," God became flesh, "and dwelt amongst us."

18. The word was the eternal spiritual body, or person, or Son of God, the eternal Father or Spirit, which, by its own power, became flesh, or a pure natural body, wherein the eternal Father only lived.

19. And there was no other eternal Father in heaven, or on earth, but only in the body of the man Jesus, that died, and rose again by his own power, God blessed for evermore.

20. This is that God, the man of glory, who descended by his own power, from his throne of glory, into a pure natural body; and after he had died, and rose again alone by his own power, then did he ascend up in that pure spiritual body, which was natural before he died, but now spiritual, by his rising from the dead; and did glorify himself, with that same glory that he formerly possessed with his Father, the eternal Spirit, to all eternity.

CHAPTER V.

1. The Glory that the Elect shall enjoy to all eternity. 2. The Sorrows that the Reprobate shall endure to all eternity.

AGAIN, I declare, from the Lord, what the Spirit hath revealed unto us, concerning the glory that the elect shall enjoy to all eternity, and the sorrows of the reprobate to all eternity.

2. As to the elect, the very same bodies, or persons, with their memory, and senses of flesh and bone, wherein they lived or died, in that truth of faith (of the Lord Jesus, to be the only God), I say from the Lord, those very bodies of theirs shall be made spiritual, and glorious; brighter than the sun, like unto the person of their glorious God, the man Jesus.

3. And with their eyes shall they see their God, face to face, and body to body, for ever; yea, we shall see him, and know him, as far as we possibly can be made capable of his spiritual glory, as we see and know one another in this mortality.

4. Then shall their thoughts, words, and deeds, be Godlike for

ever. And as the person of God is an overflowing fountain continually, of new infinite pleasures, of glorious delights, of unspeakable joy, to all his elect; so shall the souls and bodies of the elect, as a fountain, overflow with variety of new songs and praises everlasting, world without end, unto the glorious and alone God, the man Jesus, blessed to all eternity.

5. Again, it is written, "there shall be a new heaven, and a new earth, wherein dwelleth righteousness;" that is, the glorious person of God, with the persons of elect men and angels made glorious.

6. This new heaven, and new earth, are both spiritual, suitable to the persons of God, angels, and men, that are therein.

7. Again, it is called a new heaven and a new earth, because the bodies of the elect, that ascended into that glory at the last day, were never there before.

8. Again, the natural bodies and souls of the elect are become a new heaven and a new earth, because their persons are glorious, both within and without, like unto the glorious person of God, whose blessed presence maketh all persons or places, things or beings, to become new and glorious, like unto himself, to all eternity.

9. Again, it is called a new heaven and a new earth, because all things in this world wax older and older as a garment, unto an eternal dissolution.

10. So that the persons of God, elect men, and angels, in that new heaven and new earth, become newer and newer, younger and younger, in all unspeakable, new, and glorious heavenly delights, for evermore.

11. Again, I declare, from the Lord, that as a natural body is never in its proper centre, but when it is fixed upon the earth; and if the earth or place give way, the natural or earthly body sinketh down also, let it fall never so deep: so the spiritual body, when it is glorified in its own nature, is its own centre.

12. And the nature of man is to stand upon nothing, and to be as swift as thought, and to ascend higher and higher, be it never so high.

13. Also the nature of it is to see and know one another perfectly, if we be never so far asunder, as if we were near at hand.

14. Again, the glorious life and liberty of a spiritual person is this, that the spirit is not shut up, nor barred within the body, from motioning forth, which motioning is the life of it; and is at perfect liberty, to all eternity, to motion forth upon the persons of God, elect men, and angels, for its variety of new and glorious pleasures everlastingly.

15. Again, from the Lord, I declare what the condition of the reprobate is, and where it is.

16. Thus it shall be to all eternity: this whole creation—as, namely, the visible heavens, above the firmament, with the sun, moon, and stars—shall vanish, and be put out as the snuff of a candle, never giving light

more, because the decreed time of their being is finished, they only being appointed for lights of this creation, or mortal world.

17. The earth also shall be burnt up: that is, all the nature or sap, which is the heart of the earth, shall be burnt up, with all natural food remaining upon the earth, and in the sea, and in the air;

18. The sea, and all rivers and water-springs, being dried up for ever, because their decreed time is fully ended.

19. Then this world, or whole creation, will become as a barren wilderness, that is burnt up with heat, and a chaos of everlasting confusion, of utter darkness, for ever: yea, as dark as the darkness of Egypt, both for spiritual darkness and natural darkness; not three days and three nights, but even to all eternity.

20. Then shall all reprobates, men and women, appear in the same natures, souls and bodies, that they lived and died in, or fell asleep; and they shall have the same senses and reason they had before.

21. And they shall perfectly remember all their former glory, with all their former cruelty; and, according to their deeds, they shall receive their everlasting punishment, in the same bodies they delighted in sin.

22. Their own bodies must be their prison of hell, and their own unclean spirit of reason, the devil, that shall be barred close prisoner within their bodies, that they cannot have one motion, or thought, of any spiritual or natural comfort, because they are both departed for evermore.

23. Then shall the spirit of man be a more terrible fire than any natural fire or brimstone whatsoever; the body being all on fire, the which flesh and bone is the fuel of hell; the spirit which is the devil, now an eternal prisoner within the body, causing unspeakable lamentations, and gnashings of teeth.

24. And the chief ground of their sorrows is this, because their body, which was formerly their only heaven, is now become their only hell; and their proud spirit, which formerly was their only God, is now become their only devil; being both prisoners together in hellish darkness, being barred from the presence of God, elect men, and angels, to all eternity.

25. Again, I declare, from the Lord, that in the same place where the bodies of men and women do appear at the resurrection, there shall they remain, naked as they were born, never stirring from that place; either standing, sitting, or lying along; bearing one another's lamentations, but never seeing one another's faces, to all eternity.

26. And, instead of singing new songs and praises unto God, they shall, because of their unspeakable misery, blaspheme the name of God continually with new curses, because their miseries are everlastingly increasing anew, according as the songs of the elect are newly increasing, causing new songs of

joy to all eternity.

CHAPTER VI.

1. God the Creator was, from all eternity, an immortal distinct Person, of Spirit and Body, even as Man. 2. Earth and Water were eternally in the Presence of this Personal God; 3. Who, from them, created all things that were made; and, 4. First, the angels; 5. Then, all variety of creatures. 6. Further remarks upon the Creation.

AGAIN, I declare, from the Lord, by revelation from the Holy Spirit of the Lord Jesus Christ, that God the Creator, from all eternity, was an immortal distinct person, of spirit and body, even as man, who is the image of God, is a distinct mortal person, of soul and body.

2. Again, I declare, from the Holy Spirit of the Lord Jesus, that in the world above, or beyond the stars, where the person of God is resident, from all eternity, there was in the presence of this eternal God, whose eternal Spirit was the Father, and whose eternal spiritual body was the Son, being but one distinct personal God; I say, from all eternity there was earth and water with him.

3. So that there is nothing that this personal God hath created in the upper world, or heaven, or in the lower world, or earth beneath, but that he had matter or substance, whereof he created all things that were made.

4. So that when this personal God saw good, for the setting forth of his glory, he spake the word to the eternal earth, and immediately there came forth of this earth an innumerable company of spiritual persons, like unto the person of God, which were named holy angels.

5. Now, the natures or spirits of these personal angels are pure reason; but the nature of the personal God is faith, which is all power, dwelling in his own person, or overflowing from itself only; or increasing within itself, in power, wisdom, joy, and glory, continually like an overflowing fountain, from all eternity.

6. Now, the nature of pure reason is very unlike unto God; therefore it desires to know the person or Spirit of God that made it.

7. Wherefore, to keep the holy angels' nature pure from disobedience in his presence, the Lord reveals some of the overflowings of his glorious nature, or Spirit of faith, unto them: so that all the wisdom, joy, glory, and power, that is in the persons of the holy angels, doth not proceed from their own natures or spirits, which are pure reason, but from the glorious nature or Spirit of the person of God, which is pure faith, distinct from the nature of pure reason, that God alone may have all the glory, both in heaven, and on earth.

8. Again, the Lord spake the word unto the earth, out of which the angels were made, and from the same eternal earth presently appeared all variety of creatures, for a further

manifestation of his glory, to remain in the world, to all eternity; as there is all variety of mortal creatures, made out of this mortal earth, by the word of this personal God, to endure for a season, for the glory of his name.

9. Again, I declare, from this personal God, that he spoke the word into those eternal waters, and all variety of creatures appeared in those waters, for a further manifestation of his glory, there to remain to all eternity: even as he created, out of these lower waters, all variety of creatures by a word-speaking, to endure for a sea- son, for the manifestation of his glory.

10. Now you must understand, that the creation that is to all eternity, in the presence of God, that their natures and they are all pure, not desiring generation; but all of them have, in the room thereof, a more transcendent joy, in their several natures or spirits; all of them, according to their kind, giving praise and glory to a spiritual personal God, their Creator, to all eternity.

11. That is, the kingdom where the lion and the lamb lie down together in peace? World without end; in this upper world, of eternal heavens, eternal earth, and eternal waters; wherein the first creature of the eternal personal God first appeared, visible in his presence.

12. Again, I declare, from the Lord Jesus, that in that kingdom of glory only, the whole creation is visible, and of perfect love, and pure peace, unto all eternity.

13. Again, I declare? From the Lord Jesus, that this lower world or mortal creation, from the stars unto the depths of the earth, or waters, were all made out of the creation in the presence of the Lord Jesus, which only is to endure to eternity; where the elect are to remain and enjoy it personally, not only invisibly, but visibly also, to all eternity.

14. Now, that you may understand something of this mortal creation, I declare, by revelation from the Holy Spirit of the Lord Jesus, that the waters that are in this creation were divided from those eternal waters that are in the world above, or beyond the stars: and, further, the earth that is here beneath was created or made out of that eternal earth, which is above or beyond the stars.

15. I declare further, from the Lord, that the firmament, or lower visible heaven, the Lord hath created, is made of the water, or substance of water; and that this firmament of the lower heaven, being made of the water, it was but a dark body of water, until light was created, to make this darkness a body of light.

16. Therefore the Lord speaks unto this dark body of water, saying, "Let there be light;" and it was so.

17. Now, the light that the Lord made, and set in the firmament of the heavens,—as, namely, the sun, moon, and stars,—he made them of the water, or substance of water, and fixed them in the firmament

of heaven, to give light above in the firmament of heaven, which was a dark body before, but now a heaven, because the Lord hath set or fixed lights in it, not only to make the dark firmament a heaven above, but to give light unto the dark waters and dark earth beneath.

18. For your further information, I declare, from the Lord Jesus, that the bodies of the sun, moon, and stars, which the Lord hath created of water, and hath set or fixed in the firmament of heaven, he hath made of waters also, which are the chief natural lights of this mortal creation, or lower world, to continue for a season.

19. I say again, from the Lord, that they are not much bigger in their bulk or bodies, than they appear to be in the firmament of heaven, where they are until time shall be no more.

20. Wherefore, concerning that old lying imagination of wise men (so accounted), concerning the great bulk or bodies of the sun, moon, and stars; I declare, from the Lord Jesus, the ground or cause of this gross darkness in them, concerning the knowledge of creation of creatures, is this; because they are utterly ignorant of the knowledge of the Creator, who revealeth himself, and this creation of the two worlds, unto him whom he hath chosen for a witness, against all despisers in this last age, even to all eternity.

21. Now, to you that have faith, I declare, from the Lord, this is the infinite power of an infinite personal God, for his glorious person to be only resident in one place at once.

22. Yet, by the power of his word-speaking, both men and angels are filled with his glorious wisdom; and the two worlds, standing by his decree alone, the one unto all eternity, for the glory of his immortal person in the heavens above; and the other for a season, for the glory of his person also, when he had laid down his immortal glory in the heavens above, and brought forth himself a pure natural person on the earth beneath.

23. And then, by the power of his word or decree, all creatures in this lower world bring forth according to their kind: and yet this glorious infinite personal God preserveth his person and nature distinct from all creatures, both in heaven and on earth; except men and angels, unto whom he imparts or reveals a little of the Overflowings of his divine nature, or Spirit, to keep them in obedience.

24. And (as I said before) I declare, from the Lord Jesus, that the bodies of the sun, moon, and stars, are but a very little bigger than they appear to be; whereby the infinite power and glory of an infinite personal God, doth much more appear; that through such little bodies there should shine forth so great a light, through the whole creation; for the things of my God are but little or small, yea, of little value or of no account unto the wisdom of reason; through which his infinite power, wisdom, or glory, is seen only to elect men and angels; as it is

written, "With God all things are possible."

25. So I declare, by revelation from the Holy Spirit of the Lord Jesus, that the Lord made the man, Adam, of the dust of the ground, or earth, of this lower creation.

26. Now this word of this personal God, spoken unto the dust, immediately brought forth a living soul; that is, a personal man, of a pure nature, or divine Spirit; the which divine Spirit, or pure nature, was the Spirit of faith, which was the very nature of the Spirit of God, by one voice only speaking in him all obedience unto his Creator, from whom did flow continually nothing but joy and peace, unspeakable and glorious.

27. Now, you must understand, the body, or outward form, was the image of God; because the pure image of the invisible Spirit of the person of God, angels, or men, cannot

truly be known or described by the tongue of men or angels.

28. Therefore Christ said unto the Jews, when they tempted him, "Whose image or superscription is this?" The answer was, "Caesar's." Then it is clear that the image of God, men, or angels, is the outward form only, and not the inward spirit, whose form cannot be described.

29. One thing more I declare from the Lord: that neither the holy angels, spirits, nor any other creature's spirits, in heaven or in earth, were of the nature of the Spirit of the personal God, but man only; but they are all several distinct spirits or natures, differing from the spirit or nature of God their Creator; that his infinite wisdom, power, and glory might manifest itself through all his creatures in heaven and on earth, according to the pleasure of his good will.

WHAT WAS FROM ETERNITY.

AN EPISTLE CONCERNING THE ONLY TRUE GOD, OF HIS GLORIOUS THRONE, AND THE PURE CREATION, FROM THAT WHICH IS FALSE.

CHAPTER I.

1. Introductory Remarks. 2. Of the Sun. 3. Analogy between that Luminary and the Son of God. 4. Summary of the Contents of this Epistle. 5. There is another Created World besides this, a place of Glory, where God, Elect Men, and Angels, shall be to all Eternity. 6. This World of Glory is of immeasurable vastness.

MY spiritual friends, and beloved brethren, in things of eternity, being inspired in some small measure with the original of all divine delight, it being my principal work, designed from the Most High; what I receive from the Lord Jesus Christ, who is the eternal Being, that I freely declare unto you.

2. Now, I know you that are spiritual indeed cannot possibly despise the letter called the book of the scriptures, or visible records of invisible eternities.

3. Why? Because you know that without words it is impossible to demonstrate things to one another: therefore I shall nominate the letter before I speak the mind of the Spirit.

4. This epistle is to you, who are made capable to comprehend all opinions or high notions that are or shall appear to be, because your spirits are made virtually one with eternity itself; but not essentially one, for then there would be no distinction between the Former and the formed.

5. For this I would have you to understand, that the creature, sun, in the firmament, is a distinct body or circumference, about the bigness of a square chamber, whatsoever lying sophisters, by their imaginations, tell you to the contrary: from the Lord I know it to be truth.

6. Now, you know that the body or essence of the sun always hath its abode where it is fixed, ever running its course round the firmament called heaven, where it remains in its essence till time is no more. Also you know that virtually it giveth forth its light, heat, and strength, into natural things that seem to be absolutely dead, which natural virtue occasioneth life and joy, from the essential body of the sun to all sensible or rational living creatures.

7. So, likewise, it is with the invisible Son of God, the eternal Creator; for he is a distinct glorious being, by virtue of his word, fixed, as it were, in respect of his bodily or personal presence, in the invisible heavenly glory, where elect angels remain until time be swallowed up in eternity.

8. And, virtually, motionally, or spiritually, from his glorious body shineth all glorious light and heavenly life into the spirits of elect men and angels, ever retaining his essential infinite glory in himself to himself, that the uncreated Being of beings may remain in his distinct decreed form or centre to eternity; that uncreated glory may glory in its own eternal glory, and the created glory may glory, not in itself, or any light or life within itself, but in the glory of its Creator, who is the fountain of all light, life, and glory, visible and invisible.

9. That which is to be treated upon in this epistle is, What there was from Eternity; Whether there is any other World, or created Being, or Place, besides this; also, What the true Creation of God is, from the lying imagination, which is the devil, in man.

10. In Hebrews xi. 3, it is thus written: "Through faith we understand that the worlds were ordained by the word of God, so that things which are seen are not made of things which did appear."

11. And in the 13th, 14th, 15th, and 16th verses of the same chapter are these words: "And they confessed that they were strangers and pilgrims on the earth; for they that say such things declare plainly that they seek a country; and, if they had been mindful of the country from whence they came out, they had leisure to have returned but now they desire a better, that is, a heavenly one: wherefore God is not ashamed to be called their God; for he hath prepared for them a city."

12. Compare these sayings with John xiv., 1st, 2nd, and 3rd verses, and there you may see, that have the single eye of the heavenly glory within you, who this God is that hath prepared that heavenly city, place, or kingdom of eternal glory, chiefly for you which own no other God, nor Father, nor eternal Spirit, nor Creator, nor Being of beings, but the Lord Jesus Christ alone;

13. That man of all immortal crowns, of eternal glory, infinitely transcending all heavens, angels, and men, who, in the days of his creaturely condition, said unto his chosen ones, "Let not your hearts be troubled: ye believe in God; believe also in me. In my Father's house are many mansions: if it were not so, I would have told you. I go to prepare a place for you: I will come again, and receive you to myself, that where I am, there ye may be also."

14. And in the last chapter of the prophet Isaiah, the first verse, "Thus saith the Lord, the heaven is my throne, and the earth is my foot-stool."

15. And in the first of the Acts, and the 11th verse, it is thus written: "Ye men of Galilee, why stand ye gazing into heaven? This Jesus which is taken up from you into heaven, shall come as ye have seen him go into heaven."

16. And in St. Matthew xxii. 22, "He that sweareth by heaven sweareth by the throne of God, and him that sitteth thereon."

17. I might mention many other records in scripture to this purpose, but I have spoken too many already to those dark lights which disown any God, or scripture, or glory to come, or immortality, after the dissolving of this mortality; but glory of an immortality of eternity, which is in them already; and yet after death they are utterly ignorant whether they shall have any being at all, mortal or immortal, but blindly suppose an eternal swallowing up into an unknown glorious being, or else an eternal ceasing to be.

18. I know unto you that have received the spiritual oil of divine faith, in the truth of holy writ, which is quoted from the visible record of scriptures, it is sufficient to prove that there is another created world, or residential place of glory, besides this, where the glorious persons of God, elect men, and angels, shall solace themselves together, to all eternity.

19. Again, you may understand the throne of God's residence in immortality is no ways like this foot-stool of his Majesty; for we know that this global

world is enclosed all with a firmament, as with a brazen wall.

20. And why think you is it so? Truly and chiefly to keep within its own kingdom the dark imagination of angelical serpents, that they may only pry into the secrets of all things within this orb.

21. But as for the new heaven and new earth, above the stars, it is a place of glory, suit able to a God of glory: I mean, in respect of its height, length, breadth, or compass, it is of an infinite unmeasurable vastness.

22. For it must needs be so. Why? Because in the place of the eternal Being's glory there is no sun, moon, nor stars, nor firmament; and where there is no firmament there is no bounds: for you acknowledge the Creator to be boundless, and so is the kingdom of glory, where the residence of his immortal Person is eternal.

23. In Revelations xxi. 23, it is thus written: "And their city hath no need of the light of the sun, neither of the moon, to shine in it; for the glory of God did lighten it, and the Lamb is the light of it."

24. And in the last chapter, and the 5th verse, "And there shall be no night there, and they need no candle, neither the light of the sun; for the Lord giveth them light, and they shall reign for evermore."

25. And this by the way: there is not anything can reign eternally, but that which is a distinct glory in itself; and there is no glory or excellency whatsoever, whether mortal or immortal, can possibly have any sensible being, without a distinct form, to possess its glory in.

26. Moreover, the residence of glory of necessity must be a throne of infinite circumference.

27. Why? Because, if it were enclosed as this world is, then, instead of spiritual liberty, it would be a place of bondage, like unto this.

28. Because the glorious persons of God, elect men, and angels, which of motion are swifter than thought, would be prevented from ascending or descending in it, for variety of spiritual glories, according to their divine natures.

29. For you know that, if our bodies, within this lower world, were as swift of motion as our thoughts, our spirits would then be in more bondage than now they are, for want of room to pass to and fro, according to their spiritual motions; because, if the world were ten thousand millions of miles in height, length, breadth, or compass, and no more, you know that a spiritual body would ascend as swift as thought, as if it were but one mile or furlong only.

30. So that now you cannot be ignorant, but that a glorified body must have a kingdom and throne of glory, of an infinite vastness, according to its nature, to display its glory in, or upon, for its unutterable satisfaction.

31. Again, you know that it is the nature of the spirit of reason in mortal men to desire to know the height, breadth, length, or compass of the world it resideth

in; and, because it cannot attain to its desire, therefore it is unsatisfied.

32. So, likewise, you may understand, on the contrary, that it is all spiritual satisfaction to the nature of divine faith, or truth, in the spiritual bodies of men, in the world to come, not only because they have no desire in them to know the infinite vastness of that kingdom of glory they eternally are to remain in, but also because it is incomprehensibly beyond all desire in the creature of the knowledge of it.

CHAPTER II.

1. The Substance of Earth and Water was from Eternity. 2. The untreated Essence of God was alone, until His creative Power manifested itself. 3. The Divine Form was an immortal bright Glory, like unto a Man. 4. An error corrected. 5. The Creator formed all things out of some eternal Substance.

AGAIN, some may say, if there be such a place of infinite glory, for the persons of God, elect Men, and angels, eternally to inhabit in (the which cannot be denied, according to your scripture-arguments), our desire (if known unto you) is to know, Whether the infinite place of heavenly glory was in that condition it is now in from eternity; or, whether the Creator, by the almighty power of his word-speaking, formed it of nothing, or made it from or by a word-speaking only?

2. To this great query, from the gift of the infallible Spirit of divine glory, I answer: In respect of the infinite vastness of the place of glory itself, it was eternally so; but, in respect of its created form, it had a beginning to itself.

3. My meaning is plain and easy unto you, which are strong in the true divine faith of the true God.

4. The substance of earth and water, or a place and being for its residence, must needs he from eternity, in the presence of the eternal God; so that I would have you clearly to understand that it cannot possibly be otherwise, but that that infinite place, which is the throne of God, and this finite being or place, which is the foot-stool of his Majesty, was from eternity, in respect of their substances and residences, only they were in themselves matter both dark and senseless, and so without form, and void:

5. But, on the contrary, you may understand, that the un-; created or glorious power, or essence, of God was alone, in respect of any creature's visible living to themselves in his presence, for his heavenly society; for the manifestation of his infinite wisdom, power, and glory, for those angelical creatures that should be formed by him, of that dark substance, or senseless earth, aforesaid.

6. Again, but you may also understand, that the, divine form, or person of the Creator, in its own nature, was of an immortal, bright, burning glory, both within and without; and in

respect of his divine virtues; the Holy Spirit of fiery faith, and, burning love, and all other spiritual excellences, did essentially reign in his heavenly form, infinitely over-flowing like unto a crystal clear fountain, with all variety of new heavenly wisdom, and transcendent glorious delights, to solace himself

7. I hope in time that all the chosen ones of the Most High shall clearly understand that it is impossible for God, man, or angels, to possess any joy or glory at all, unless they have a form or body of their own distinct from all other forms, sensibly to enjoy that glory unto themselves.

8. I do not deny, but through union of spirits; also, there is unutterable joy and glory in one another; but I utterly deny that any spirits are essentially one, or that there are any sensible living spirits without forms, to display their life in, or ever shall be, whether mortal or immortal, visible or invisible.

9. Thus, ye blessed ones of the Most High, by the single eye of your most holy faith, you are made to see that your God, from eternity, was a glorious distinct form or person, in form like unto a man, before he became a man, or took on him the form of a servant, or a man:

10. As it is written in the second of the Philippians, "Who being in the form of God, thought it no robbery to be equal with God, but he made himself of no reputation, and took on him the form of a servant, and was found in the shape of a man."

11. Thus you may see that the only wise God, the Lord Jesus Christ, was an immortal form, before he became a mortal form of flesh, blood, and bone: and although the immortality of his divine God-head, with the brightness of his glorious form, was wholly transmuted or mortalized into the condition of a spotless man, or creature; yet the visible form of his former invisible form, with the purity of his divine nature, was never changed, nor possibly could be.

12. But to go forwards to the point. Wherefore this serves for the reproof and condemnation of that grand error, naturally flowing from that lying imagination of men, which is as old as the evil imaginary angel himself, concerning creation: that is to say, that to create a form or thing is to make it by a word-speaking, without any matter or substance at all.

13. Further, and if they were convinced to acknowledge, according to the truth or scripture records, that God formed men and angels, and all other creatures that he had made, of material earth and water, or anything else; yet they suppose that those substances of earth and water were not in the eternal presence of God; but they say, that God, by the power of his word-speaking, made them of nothing.

14. Behold, this is contrary to faith, yea, and reason itself.

15. Why? Because then this will follow, that earth and water must needs be the Creator or divine Being itself; and so, by the

sequel, there is no God at all, but nature; and so all things that appear to be were from eternity, and will so remain to eternity. There is no avoiding these absurdities.

16. Again, if men were ashamed of this their error, and shall confess, that from eternity there was a Creator of a spiritual substance, then, without all contradiction, from eternity, there must of necessity be a residential place or being for the God of glory to display his essential life or glory in or upon.

17. Therefore earth and water, and its place of residence, must of necessity, from eternity, be in the presence of God, they being distinct in their substances, from his glorious essence or divine person.

18. So that now, by the divine speakings of God in you, according to holy records, you may easily understand, that the Creator formed all things or creatures, in both worlds, of some matter or substance; and that without materials of earth and water he created nothing that is made, neither possibly could.

19. Again, you may understand, also, that it is the very nature of that unclean spirit, the devil in man, to imagine a Creator and a creation, quite contrary to the truth of divine records, utterly abhorring that God and his creations in the least measure can be made manifest to his creature.

20. But the imaginary devil in man loves to hear and speak of a Creator, and of a creation, and of a heavenly glory, and of a hellish misery, that no man can possibly be capable of in this mortality to comprehend the truth of any such things; or at least, if anything to this effect may be known, they affirm it only makes a man happy in this life, but whether there is any certain knowledge of anything that shall be after death, this they utterly deny.

21. Why? Because as yet the true divine light of the true God hath not shined into their understandings, as to the assurance of eternal life; for I assure you, from the ever-living God, that in what soul soever the eternal Being shineth in life unto life eternal, in some measure the things of eternity that shall be after death, or when time is no more are manifested unto that soul.

22. But, indeed, for the most part, the cause why men remain dark in this great secret of things of eternity is, because they are under the power of some secret lust or other, which they love as their lives, not heeding that the wages of sin is death eternal, and the fruit of righteousness is life eternal, both manifesting their effects in due time.

23. I could speak more of the folly of this error in men, of their imagining of God's creating the two worlds of nothing; but it being so ridiculous, it is not worth the while, and I know a few words are sufficient to the wise.

24. Again, You which have received the divine faith and pure love of the glorious Spirit of

the Lord Jesus Christ, unto life eternal, may know that this is the true meaning or mind of the Spirit of the eternal Being, in the word "creating."

25. That is to say, that the glorious God, by the power of his word only, speaking into or unto those senseless substances of earth and water, immediately from thence to produce what several natures he thinks fit, and forms suitable to their spirits or natures, and yet to retain his own divine nature and form to himself, distinct from all those natures and forms that he hath made; and yet all those created spirits are pure also in their kinds, though they are of variety of natures to each other.

CHAPTER III.

1. The Powers of Creation or Transmutation consist in either new creating, or changing the condition of things already created. 2. The wonders of Creation that will be manifest at the last day. 3. The Creation of some for eternal Glory, of others for everlasting Darkness. 4. The presumption of human Conceit.

AGAIN, the power of creation, or transmutation, lieth in the new creating, or changing the condition of things already created.

2. As for example, God,—for his prerogative, will, or pleasure, to manifest the glory of his infinite power, either by eternal condemnation, or salvation,—to transmute the most glorious angel in heaven, to become the chiefest devil in hell, or in flesh and to convert one of the greatest devils by nature on earth, to become one of the most glorious saints in heaven. Cain and Mary Magdalen shall bear witness to what I have written, in due time, of this particular.

3. Again, if you understand the infinite power of a Creator making all things new, by the power of his word or decree, and his turning the bodies and souls of mankind into dust again, from whence they were taken, is it not a wonderful new creation, in the last day or end of time, for the Creator, by the mighty power of his decreed word-speaking only, though there be ten hundred times ten hundred thousand several spirits mixed together in the dust of the earth, yet to make every seed or spirit to bring forth its own body or form, that he lived and died in?

4. That is to say, he that had the divine seed of God remaining in him, shall appear with a glorious body, like unto his God, to eternity; and he that hath the unclean seed of cursed imagination remaining in him, shall appear with a body of nothing but spiritual darkness, of unspeakable misery, for everlasting. "As the tree falleth, so it lieth."

5. Again, is it not a wonderful thing, for the God of glory, of the same lump, to create one man, to be of his own divine nature and form, and in due time to make him eternally glorious like unto himself; and to create and form another man, to be of a

contrary nature, nothing but darkness of shame, and confusion of face or spirit, for everlasting?

6. So much concerning the true creation of God.

7. Again, notwithstanding the dark imaginary spirit of man, by taking thought never so long, cannot possibly make one hair either white or black, to cover his head if it were bald; yet he can teach his Creator a creation beyond the wisdom of God himself, a creation which cannot possibly be.

8. For he is so wise in his own conceit, that lie imagines, if he had been the Creator, he could have made materials of earth and water of nothing at all, even by the power of his own word-speaking only, as well as have formed what he pleased of those materials afterwards; or that he could have formed it only by his word-speaking, without any material substance at all.

9. Thus, being shut up in utter darkness, he calls his very reason the divine nature of God, when God knows he nor no mortal man else hath any pure reason at all; but his understanding is all confusion in respect of knowing anything of the matter or manner of the true creation of God, or any eternal spiritual things, which as yet are invisible to mortals, but visible only to Moses, Elijah, Enoch, and the elect angels, in the personal presence of the Lord Jesus Christ, God-Man or Man-God, blessed for ever and ever.

10. Again, for want of the true discerning of the divine voice of the Holy Spirit of the true faith to distinguish between the voice of God's Spirit, and the voice of their own unclean spirit, the devil in them, they call God the devil, and the devil God; and so they, being left, willingly are ignorant of any other world, or God, or angels, or glory to come, but what is within this world only,

11. The which orb is but the foot-stool of our God, it being but as a mole-hill to a mighty mountain in comparison of that eternal kingdom of glory which is above the stars, without the glory of this perishing world.

12. Wherefore, because they are reserved under the guards of eternal darkness, from this their utter darkness, they judge themselves only in the eternal light, and blasphemously call themselves, who are mortal dust, "Eternity," "Everlasting love," or "I am," and "There is none besides me," or "One pure being," with the "Creator," wholly taking all the glorious titles of the eternal Majesty upon them, who by no means will give his glory to men or angels, either of his nature or his names.

13. Again, if a man talks with these high-flown atheistical no-tionists, concerning knowledge of any God at all, or of a life to come, they abhor it, because it is hid from them,

14. But they love to speak or hear of an unknown God, which they call an infinite, invisible, incomprehensible Spirit, which (as they say) is essential in all places and all things at once; and seeth all things, heareth all

things, and understandeth all things, particularly; and yet hath no eyes to see, nor ears to hear, nor spirit to understand anything at all, through any distinct form or person of his own.

15. This is the blind reprobates' worldly or imaginary God, only of bare words, who are left under eternal perishing darkness.

16. And so much concerning what was from eternity, with a true spiritual distinction between the true creation and the false, and the true God and the false God.

OF THE ONE PERSONAL UNCREATED GLORY.

CHAPTER I.

1. The Man, Jesus Christ, and his Father, were from eternity only one personal Majesty in both worlds. 2. The Creator could not appear in the condition of a creature without first leaving the representative spiritual office, of God the Father, in the glorified Persons of Moses and Elijah. 3. The Creator appeared in the condition of a Man, (1.) To manifest his eternal Love for his redeemed ones; and, (2.) To enhance his own Glory. 4. By virtue of their Divine Commission, Moses and Elijah filled the Lord Jesus with inspirations of his former Glory when on the Throne of the Father; and, 5. Testified from Heaven that he was the only true God. 6. Further remarks on their Divine Office.

IF it should be granted that the man Christ Jesus, and his Father, were from eternity, in time, and to eternity, only one distinct personal Majesty in both worlds; yet because of those literal sayings, "My Father is greater than I;" "My God, my God, why hast thou forsaken me?" "Father, into thy hands I commend my spirit;" "I ascend to my Father, and to your Father; to my God, and to your God;" with many such like throughout the New Testament:

2. Therefore many elect ones, whose souls have been filled with glorious experiences, not being clear in these scriptures, they may say unto me, What was that God and Father that Christ prayed or cried unto, in his greatest extremity upon the earth?

3. This query being of high concernment, before I make answer thereunto, give me leave to cite a scripture or two.

4. In Psalm xci. 11, 12, and St. Matthew iv., it is thus written: For he shall give his angels charge over thee, to keep thee in all thy ways: they shall bear thee in their hands; they shall lift thee up, lest at any time thou shouldest dash thy foot against a

stone."

5. Thus you that are spiritually quick in discerning hidden secrets may clearly see, in the very letter of the scriptures, that, when Christ Jesus was in the glory of the Father, he gave a wonderful commission to his angels, in reference to the protection of his own person, in that time of his creaturely condition.

6. Why? Because you may know, when untreated infiniteness was wholly transmuted into a creature-like finiteness, it must needs be disenabled of its former glorious power to protect itself, under all temptations and unutterable sufferings, unto death itself, it was to bear at the hands of unbelieving reprobates.

7. Thus you may see it was utterly impossible for the Creator to become or appear in the condition of a spotless creature, without first leaving the representative spiritual office of God, the everlasting Father, in the glorified persons of Moses and Elijah: for they were those angelical men that were entrusted with that glorious power aforesaid.

8. But you may say, if the Creator did appear in the condition of a perfect man, and commit the representative power of his eternal God-head to his angelical creatures, to what end did he thus abase himself?

9. To this I answer, You may know that his unsearchable wisdom moved him unto it for two respects: first, in reference to the manifestation of his eternal love to his redeemed ones; secondly, in relation to his own personal glory:

10. For, as he knew no other way to restore the fallen estate of his elect Israelites, so, likewise, he foresaw that in the lowest abasing himself lay secretly hid a twofold infinite glory that would redound to himself in his exaltation; because from hence originally arise, in elect men and angels, all those glorious new songs or ravishing admirations of the Creator's wisdom, love, and humility, to eternity, the which would not possibly be attained by the Creator, if he had not thus humbled himself.

11. Again, this angelical charge in Moses and Elijah of spiritual protectorship, in reference to God, elect men, and angels, may be thus understood: that is to say, by virtue of this their commission, even as a spiritual God and Father, they filled the Lord Jesus with inspirations of his former glory, which he possessed when lie was on the throne of the Father.

12. For you that have received Jesus Christ alone to be your God, may know, when he was in a creature-like condition, he neither was, nor possibly could be, capable to comprehend all that infinite glory which he enjoyed when he was in the condition of a Creator.

13. Wherefore, as aforesaid, for the protection of his blessed body, they were not only set apart, to fill him with a perfect assurance of possessing a more transcendent glory, through sufferings, than he formerly enjoyed in his heavenly kingdom; but they were appointed also to

bear record from heaven, in the sight of elect men and angels, unto Jesus Christ, upon this earth, to be the only very true God, everlasting Father, and alone Creator of both worlds, angels, and men, and all other creatures, as they did unto Peter, James, and John, at the transfiguration of Christ, the Lord of all light and life.

14. Moreover, their spiritual charge was to supply the saints with an inspiring light, as a guide to direct them to that fountain of all infinite glory; God manifested in a body of flesh, as they did to Joseph, and John the Baptist.

15. Furthermore, their divine office was also to uphold the holy angels, with their appointed food of new revelations, concerning that wonderful salvation-mystery, that God was bringing forth in the man Christ Jesus, for his elect' sake.

16. That the angels, which were in great power and glory, might be kept in obedience to their God, then appearing in weakness and shame, until that his body of flesh and bone was ascended into the throne of the Father; that from his own personal majesty he might fill elect men and angels with glorious inspirations, concerning a new thing, that he alone had done upon the earth.

17. Again, if it should be granted, that the Creator did thus humble himself in a body of flesh, because when his glory moves to a thing, what can hinder it? "Is anything hard or impossible to God," in such a case as this is or was?

18. Yet, there being such an innumerable company of angels, that never were defiled, it may be thought strange by some that he should pass them all by, and exalt two men to so high a dignity, who had been sinners.

19. To this I answer, You may know therein did appear a nearer union between God and elect men than between God and elect angels.

20. For God himself, in the body of his flesh, became a little lower than angels, in respect of death, that as before-said, through sufferings, with more infinite advantage, he might exalt himself on his throne again, above men or angels.

21. So, likewise, you know it is written: "If we suffer with him" (or for him), "we shall also reign with him."

22. Moses and Elijah wanted no sufferings for Christ's sake, when he was in the condition of the Father. Wherefore, they being kept faithful to their Oust on this earth, in due time their persons were rewarded with God-like glorification in the high heavens, that they might be fit representatives of an infinite Majesty, and so with God himself be exalted in dignity, above the holy angels.

23. It is written, "He took not on him the nature of angels, but the seed of Abraham."

24. Thus in the Creator's abasement, he was clothed with the seed wherein his own divine nature, of spiritual faith, was capable of suffering, and entering into his glory again; and

not with that angelical nature of pure reason, that is no way capable of any kind of suffering in the least, but if it were not continually preserved with the incomes of divine faith, it would trample such God-like humility under foot, as foolishness itself.

25. Wherefore, the bodies of angels being spiritual, and their natures only rational, and so unfit to suffer for their God, as Abraham's children are, or were; therefore they were uncapable to represent the person of God, the everlasting Father, or to sit upon thrones of God-like glory, with the apostles, spiritually to judge the twelve tribes of Israel.

26. But of the contrary, the nature of the glorified bodies of Moses and Elijah, being all inspiration of heavenly new wisdom, and like unto the Creator himself; though formerly they were inferior to angels, in reference to natural pain, and soul-mortality; yet, being possessed with that nature by which angels were created, they only, and not angels, were fit representatives of an everlasting Father unto Christ Jesus, their Creator, And glorious redeemer, in the days of his humiliation.

27. Moreover, though Moses and Elijah for a season, by divine wisdom, were so highly exalted; yet you may know this Godlike power or charge possessed by them was in measure only; because none was capable of Spirit above measure but God only, which is Christ Jesus our Lord.

28. Furthermore, when the Creator was wholly transmuted into a creature-like state, though the nature of his Spirit was all divine satisfaction in itself, yet, because that divine soul was one divine essence with the body, subject to man's infirmities, of hunger, thirst, sleep, and such like; was it not therefore of absolute necessity, that Elijah, or some other, should not only be in a God or Father-like condition, as a glorious object for Christ Jesus to fix his faith upon, but also to protect him both sleeping and waking, in all conditions, that he might become a perfect pattern of child-like obedience in all things unto death, to his redeemed ones?

29. That from thence they might learn to know unto whom all spiritual obedience was meritoriously due, when that ever blessed body of Christ's flesh and bone was risen from the dead, and ascended into the glory of the Father again, from whence he descended.

CHAPTER II.

1 The Scriptures mention a visible as well as invisible manifestation of God the Father to Moses and Abraham; but, 2. There is no record of any such manifestation to Christ Jesus. 3. The glory of Christ's transfiguration was from the appearance of Moses and Elijah in glory. 4. Of the Divine Power in Christ's Resurrection.

AGAIN, the scriptures clearly make mention of a visible, as well as invisible, appearance of

God the Father unto Moses and. Abraham, and familiarly talking with them, as a man talks with his friend.

2. But of the contrary, though the scripture makes mention of a voice that came from heaven, saying, "This is my well-beloved Son, in whom I am well pleased;" yet you have no other record to prove, that ever any other God and Father appeared, either visible or invisible, unto Christ Jesus, familiarly talking with him, but Moses and Elijah, two men in white raiment, angels, or such like.

3. Now I humbly beseech you, if there had been any other God, or Father of our Lord Jesus Christ, in the invisible high heavens, but those glorious representatives before-said, can you possibly believe, imagine, or think, that that everlasting Father would, in such a loving manner, have appeared to his sinful servants, and neglect his only Son and Heir of heavens, earth, angels, and men, and all things else, unto whom alone all divine honour, and praise, or glory, is ascribed from all capable creatures, for everlasting?

4. Which you know will not be accepted of by saints or angels, in scripture records, but alone by the everlasting Jesus, that everlasting Father, who always accepted of divine honour, from them that he knew to have faith in his person, unto life eternal; but seemed to reject it from those that knew him not.

5. Also you know it is written, "God will not give his glory to another." Therefore, it is impossible that there should be any other God, Father, or Creator, but the glorified person of Christ Jesus our Lord; because, as beforesaid, no man can prove throughout the scriptures, nor any other ways, that there was ever any other personal Majesty, but him only.

6. Moreover, as the skin of Moses' face, through the appearance of God talking with him upon the mount, shone so bright, that the Israelites were compelled to face him through a veil: so likewise you know, when Christ was transfigured upon the mount, his face shone like the sun, to the great amazement of his apostles; it was only through the appearance of Moses and Elijah in glory talking with him.

7. Behold a spiritual wonder! Christ Jesus the eternal Creator, having transmuted his in finite glory into flesh, was fain to seek, or wait for, the appearance of a glimpse of that glory again, from his angelical creatures.

8. Thus you in whom is rooted the light and life of One Personal Glory, may see somewhat clearer into the hidden mystery, of God manifesting himself in the Man Christ Jesus our Lord; and of a more spiritual oneness between him and elect mankind, than between those holy angels which visibly see him face to face.

9. Here you may know also, that the man Cain, and his angelical generation, of merciless gilded-tongued hypocrites, are designed for eternal sufferings, of a sensible dying life or living

death; because, as aforesaid, the Lord Jesus took not on him the nature of angels, but the seed of Abraham.

10. Much more might be spoken upon this account, but I suppose I have written sufficient for the satisfaction of that soul, that is really redeemed from the bewitching love of things that perish, through the divine appearance of glorious things which have no end.

11. In St. John, vi. and x., it is thus written: "The words that I speak unto you are spirit and life." "I lay down my life, that I might take it again. No man taketh it from me, but I lay it down of myself. I have power to lay it down, and power to take it again."

12. Some tender-hearted soul, being well satisfied of the soul and body's essential oneness, and so of their wholly dying as well as living together, may say unto me, If the soul of Christ died in or with his body, what was that which raised it from death to life again?

13. From a divine gift, to this I answer, That spiritual power of Christ's totally dying, and living again, consisted only in the wonderful virtue or truth of his word speaking.

14. Why? Because you may know, that the nature of Christ's soul did consist only of one divine voice, or echo of all variety of glorious truth, through which he could not possibly err in his sayings. Wherefore, as aforesaid, whatever he spake in that very word, was all power to effect the thing spoken of.

15. Moreover, you may know, that word proceeding through Christ's mouth, was the very voice of the divine God-head itself, reconciling the elect lost Israelites, in the Man Christ Jesus, to himself through death.

16. Furthermore, when Lazarus, according to Christ's words, was dead and buried, four days in the grave (as it is written), if his soul was alive, in paradisaical or heavenly places of divine glory, surely that glory was in the grave; and from thence was Lazarus raised from death to life. "My words," saith the Lord Jesus Christ, "are spirit and life." And he was "the resurrection and the life," as he said unto Martha.

17. Wherefore, you may know, that man's body and soul, being but one living substance, they are essentially one in death also: and it was that everlasting virtue of Christ's word only, which was that God that raised the soul and body of Lazarus out of the grave or sleep of death unto life again.

18. "The words that I speak unto you," saith Christ, "are spirit and life." That is as if he should have said, My words alone are all spiritual life, love, peace, with variety of glorious new joys, beyond all comprehension, in the spirits of men and angels; or, as if he should have said, My words principally tend to the satisfying of the soul, with all divine excellencies; which are eternal.

19. "I have power," saith Christ, "to lay down my life, and have power to take it again."

That is as if he should have said, I only have all the Godhead power, in my own person, to die, and to command life out of death itself.

20. Again, moreover, if there be but only one personal Majesty, or glorious power, over heavens, earth, angels, and men who then besides the Lord Jesus could speak these words? For, alas! you may know, it is impossible for any creature, Whether men or angels, to have power in themselves in the least, either to live or die.

21. Furthermore, the Lord Jesus, being the only God over all life and death, did verily believe, or undoubtedly know, that whatever he said should come to pass; that rather than he would or could be prevented in his words, not only heaven and earth, but all things else, may sooner pass away, and be no more seen.

22. That moved him to say, "Heaven and earth shall pass away, but my words shall not pass away." And to say, "But after that I am risen, I will go into Galilee before you."

23. Hence you may understand, if the God-man Christ Jesus be your living life, that, as aforesaid, it was his faith, in the ever-living virtue of his word-speaking, which empowered him to lay down his divine soul, or God-head life, in the hell of the grave, for a moment, with his blessed body; and from thence, as the most pure grain, even naturally to quicken and revive that life again out of death itself, that it might live, in a new and

glorious manner, in immortality to eternity, even in that body that died, and no other.

24. For now I may boldly say, with unshaken confidence, that the variety of all unutterable joy or ravishing glory, that God himself eternally possesses, naturally floweth in him, only from the virtue of his manifold deaths, of deadly sufferings, formerly endured in that very body of flesh and bone now glorified.

CHAPTER III.

1. Christ Jesus, by his Death and Resurrection, became Lord of the Living and the Dead. 2. He, who out of Chaos created both Worlds, also twice changed the condition of his own glorious Person. 3. His Death not only proved Divine Truth, but confounded Carnal Reason. 4. Unless the Divinity of Christ had died with his Humanity, God could not have experimentally known the condition of the Dead. 5. The Godhead's Suffering gave him prerogative power over all conditions. 6. Conclusion.

AGAIN, Christ Jesus being the only God, the everlasting virtue of his word-speaking gave him all power over life and death, by his most precious life poured forth in his blood unto death, that he alone might purchase from his divine self, in a new way, to become the only Lord both of the dead and quick.

2. It is not the natural life, or half-dying, of a God or of his Son, if they were distinct; but it must be the blood or whole life of

an infinite power itself, that can cleanse the conscience from dead works, to enable a man spiritually to obey the ever-living God;

3. According to that in Acts xx., where it is thus written; "For I have kept nothing back, but have showed you all the counsel of God." And in the twenty-eighth verse are these words: "To feed the church of God, which he hath purchased with his own blood."

4. With astonishing admiration, behold a divine wonder! God himself was absolutely dead and buried out of the sight of all men and angels, and yet was virtually living everywhere at one and the same time, but was not sensible of it in his own person until he was risen from the grave: but this spiritual food is for strong men in Christ, and not for babes.

5. Moreover, by virtue of his word of truth's speaking only, he created, out of a confused chaos, both worlds, and all in them which were created, whether for a time or for eternity: who, by the same power also, twice changed the condition of his own glorious person.

6. Furthermore, his divine soul died in the flesh, and quickened in the spirit, not only to prove the infinite power of truth, speaking through his spiritual mouth, but also for the confounding that carnal reason in man, which upon all occasions contends against his divine wisdom, and all other his unsearchable counsels.

7. It being a common saying among men, that it is blasphemy for any man to say that God could possibly die, notwithstanding the scripture says, "Is anything too hard for God?" and "With God," said Christ, "nothing shall be impossible."

8. And why, think you, do men say, the Godhead neither did nor possibly could die? Truly, because they by no means can imagine which way the Creator should live again, if once dead.

9. Thus they measure the Almighty power of an infinite Majesty by the narrow compass of blind reason, proceeding out of the bottomless pit of their own lying imagination, which neither doth nor possibly can understand anything of the spiritual power of truth's speaking.

10. And because the Lord Jesus Christ's wonderful power, divine faith, or truth, is hid from them, therefore they are at enmity with him and his elect, unto whom alone his secrets are revealed; and so they always call the divine Majesty a liar to his face, both in his person and people.

11. And, because they see no power in themselves to live or die, from this their no spiritual power at all, impudently or ignorantly they take upon them to judge the God of all divine power over life and death, who is blessed for ever.

12. And, because he could not possibly lie, therefore by the word of his power he did die, and live again; or else what mean the scripture-sayings, "Because he poured forth his soul unto

death." "For Christ therefore rose again and revived, that he might be Lord both of the dead and of the quick."

13. "I am that first and that last, and I am alive, but was dead; and behold, I am alive for evermore." "These things saith he which is first and last, that was dead, and is alive."

14. "Thou wilt not leave my soul in the grave, neither wilt thou suffer thy Holy One to see corruption." "He, knowing that, before spake of the resurrection of Christ, that his soul should not be left in the grave, nor should his flesh see corruption."

15. More scriptures might be mentioned to this purpose; but if this saving truth, concerning the whole Godhead and manhood dying, and living together again, by its own quickening power, be not sufficiently cleared from the true record itself, I would it were.

16. Sure I am, those that shall vilify this glorious truth, after the perusal of this epistle (according as it is written), "they have eyes and see not, ears and hear not, hearts and understand not;" and account the scriptures but mere fancies, and human natural wisdom, whatsoever they shall pretend to the contrary.

17. Again, unless the divinity had died with the humanity, how could the glorious God experimentally, in his own person, have known what condition the dead are in, whether they be the elect or reprobate?

18. How could he, being in a creaturely condition, be capable of entering into the glory of the Creatorship again Any other way

but through death, that from thence he might live again, and, in the room of a crown of thorns, wear upon his head a double crown of immortal and eternal glory, in the visible sight of elect men and angels, which could not possibly be attained unto any other way but through death?

19. Is it therefore anything else but the devil in man, that wars against this divine secret? If it be not so, when Peter said, Master, spare thyself," why did Christ so sharply reprove him, saying, "Get thee behind me, Satan; thou savourest not the things that be of God, but the things that be of men?"

20. Moreover, that elect men and angels might more admire the Creator's wisdom, power, and glory, in raising such transcendent eternal excellencies out of death itself, than all other things!

21. Furthermore, you may know it was the Godhead's suffering, under all conditions, which gave him his prerogative power over all conditions, and from thence the Lord did experimentally know what crowns of immortal glory were most suitable for all suffering conditions, that his chosen ones are to undergo in this vale of tears, for truth's sake;

22. Also, what measure of eternal death, in utter darkness, was most meet for cursed Cain, and his generation of angelical merciless men and women, whose serpentine wisdom is that wicked one that is no way able to endure these salvation-mysteries, because they discover

their hypocritical gloryings in gilded words only, that perish, instead of glorious things, which are eternal.

23. This will be that gnawing worm of conscience that never dies, and fiery curse of the law that will never be quenched in men's souls, when the Lord Jesus Christ shall appear with his saints and angels to eternal judgment.

24. And so much at present concerning the spirituality of words speaking through the heavenly mouth of the only and ever-living God-man, Christ Jesus our Lord, who sits in the midst of the throne of crowns, of all varieties of immortal glory and majesty, in the highest heavens, and lowest hearts, even to all eternity.

Yours, in all Spiritual
And Natural Righteousness,

JOHN REEVE.

A CLOUD OF UNERRING WITNESSES.

PLAINLY PROVING THAT THERE NEITHER IS, NOR EVER WAS, ANY OTHER GOD BUT JESUS CHRIST THE LORD.

CHAPTER I.

I. Subject of this Epistle. 2. The Creator, though styled in Scripture by the threefold Name of Father, Son, and Holy Ghost, is but one Essence, even as Man is but one Person, though spoken of in Scripture by the threefold Name of Body, Soul, and Spirit.

A CATALOGUE of scripture records, of undeniable truths, bearing testimony unto the only wise God, immortal, invisible, yet visible, distinct personal God; Creator, Redeemer, and alone Everlasting Father.

2. The righteous spiritual God-man from eternity, who came down from his glorious throne, and, in fulness of time, became of the seed of the Virgin a child of unspotted flesh, blood, and bone, in the appearance of mortal man; yea, and in due time became an absolute man, in all things like unto us (sinful reason or lying imagination, only excepted); that he might make himself capable, both soul and body, of entering into death;

3. And by virtue of his everlasting spiritual word, or almighty decree, in or through death, to quicken and revive that

same pure spirit and body again, into a far more transcendent spiritual condition, than it was in before it died, or capable of before he became a body of flesh; that he alone might be Lord of quick and load, and in the same body of flesh and bone he died in, and no other, as fire naturally ascended, even visibly, into his immortal throne, of his eternal glory, from whence he came, the invisible heaven and earth, above or beyond the stars:

4. Which place of blessedness is an infinite habitation, throne, or kingdom of unutterable glories; suitable to an infinite Majesty, and spiritual glorious bodies, which are there to remain world without end; and essentially distinct from this global, perishing world, when all time is past, trampling it under foot, as an habitation or hell for all reprobates, there to remain in utter darkness.

5. Thus, by the single eye of your most holy faith, you may see the eternal uncreated divinity, or Godhead fulness, now united with flesh and bone, God and man, being but one personal essence, or glorified substance, even essentially distinct from heaven, earth, angels, and men, from eternity to eternity; and from this glorious city made without hands, much like unto the little body of the sun in the firmament, virtually he displayeth the splendour of his heavenly light, life, and glory, into the spirits and bodies of elect men and angels; eternally retaining his infinite bright burning glory within his own divine person:

6. Because no created beings, whether they be angels or men, are capable of the essential in-dwelling of the eternal Spirit of God, but that man Jesus only; who was from eternity essentially one with it.

7. Wherefore (whatever men may imagine), it is as impossible for any man, from scripture records, or any way else, to prove the only Creator to be two or three distinct essences, because of his three-fold name of Father, Son, and Holy Ghost, or Lord Jesus Christ; as it is to prove a man's body may live without a soul, or that a man is two or three distinct essences, because he is styled in scripture records by a three-fold name, of body, soul, and spirit.

8. When our Lord was personally upon this earth, it was written that lie said, " No man can serve two masters:" wherefore he that hath received in his understanding the records of holy writ, which were spoken by the Holy Spirit of Jehovah, or Jesus, through the mouths of his true prophets and apostles, to be the very truth of God; when, with his most serious consideration, he hath meekly perused this writing, the desire of my soul is this:

9. If the scriptures in the exact letter of them be the rule of all truth, unto his Spirit, that from those testimonies he would show me any God, Creator, or Father, out of Christ at all, or essentially distinct from Christ, when he was upon this earth, or before the man-child Jesus;

10. Whether it be a spiritual personal God to his comprehension or apprehension, or an incomprehensible infinite eternal Spirit, without a distinct bodily form (as most men blindly imagine), or whatever he understands him to be, I will submit to the scripture records.

11. But if plainly from them he cannot prove any other God at all, but what was in Christ essentially from eternity, in time, and to eternity: then, in the name of the Lord Jesus, I require him to submit to the truth of the scriptures.

12. Also, that he would, for time to come, dispute no more of any God at all, but of Christ only, if by Christ he expects the eternal salvation of his person, in his second last visible appearance in the clouds or air, with his mighty angels, to make an everlasting separation between those that would have none to reign over them but him only, by his blessed Spirit, and them that walk even contrary to true faith, scriptures, or sober reason itself, and have another God besides Christ, above Christ, or before Christ,

13. Take special notice of this saying of our Lord Jesus, you that own the true scriptures of the Old Testament, as well as the New: "And he said unto them, These are the words which I spake unto you while I was yet with you, that all must be fulfilled which are written of me in the law of Moses, and in the Prophets, and in the Psalms," Luke xxiv. 44.

14. But I never read or heard that Job, or Solomon, were any prophets of the Lord at all, though they spake many excellent truths: yet neither by Christ, the only God of all true scriptures, nor by the holy apostles, are they mentioned to be penmen of holy writ.

15. I do not thus write, to undervalue them in the least; but the truth is the truth, though all men should speak against it.

SCRIPTURES PROVING THAT CHRIST JESUS IS THE ONLY GOD.

"For unto us a child is born, unto us a Son is given, and the government shall be upon his shoulder; and his name shall be called Wonderful, Counsellor, the Mighty God, the everlasting Father, the Prince of Peace."—Isaiah ix. 6.

"Behold a Virgin shall be with child, and shall bear a Son, and they shall call his name IMMANUEL; which is, by interpretation, God with us."—Matt. i. 23.

"But whilst he thought on these things, behold the angel of the Lord appeared to him in a dream, saying, Joseph, the son of David, fear not to take Mary thy wife, for that which is conceived in her is of the Holy Ghost, and she shall bring forth a Son, and thou shalt call his name Jesus: for he shall save his people from their sins."—Matt. i. 20, 21.

"Then said Mary to the angel, How shall this be, seeing I know not man? And the angel said unto her, The Holy Ghost shall come upon thee, and the power of the Highest shall overshadow thee. Therefore, also, that holy thing which shall be born of thee, shall be called the Son of God."—Luke i. 34, 35.

"And she cried with a loud voice, and said, Blessed art thou among women, because the fruit of thy womb is blessed. And whence cometh this to me, that the Mother of my Lord should come to me? And thou, babe, shalt be called the prophet of the Most High: for thou shalt go before the face of the Lord, to prepare his ways."—Luke i. 42, 43, and 76.

"In the beginning was the word, and the word was with God, and the word was God; the same was in the beginning with God. All things were made by him; and without him was nothing made that was made. He was in the world, and the world was made by him, and the world knew him not. And the word was made flesh, and dwelt among us (and we saw the glory thereof, as the glory of the only-begotten Son of the Father), full of grace and truth."—John i. 1, 2, 3, 10, and 14.

"Let the same mind be in you that was even in Christ Jesus, who, being in the form of God, thought it no robbery to be equal with God; but he made himself of no reputation, and took on him the form of a servant, and was made like unto man, and was found in shape as a man."—

Phill. ii. 5, 6, 7.

"In whom we have redemption through his blood; that is, the forgiveness of sins, who is the image of the invisible God, the first-begotten of every creature. For by him were all things created which are in heaven, and which are on earth, things visible and invisible, whether they be thrones, or dominions, or principalities, or powers; all things were created by him, and for him, and he is before all things, and in him all things consist." — Coloss. i. 14-17.

"For it pleased the Father that in him should all fulness dwell."—Verse 19.

"In whom are hid all the treasures of wisdom and knowledge."— Coloss. ii. 3.

"For in him dwelleth all the fulness of the Godhead bodily." —Coloss. ii. 9.

"And of his fulness have we all received grace for grace."— John i. 16.

"All things are given to me of the Father, and no man knoweth the Son but the Father; neither knoweth any man the Father but the Son, and he to whom the Son will reveal him."—Matt. xi. 27.

"No man hath seen God at any time; the only-begotten Son, which is in the bosom of the Father, he hath declared him."— John i. 18.

"Not that any man hath seen the Father, save be which is of God, he hath seen the Father. This is that bread which came down from heaven, that he which eateth of it should not die. I am that living bread which came down from heaven; if any man eat of this bread he shall live for ever. What, then, if ye shall see the Son of Man ascend up where he was before?" —John vi. 46, 50, 51, 58, 62.

"And whither I go ye know, and the way ye know. Thomas said unto him, Lord, we know not whither thou goest; how can we know the way? Jesus said unto him, I am the way, the truth, and the life; no man cometh to the Father but by me. If ye had known me, ye should have known the Father also: and from henceforth ye know him, and have seen him. Philip said unto him, Lord, show us the Father, and it sufficeth us. Jesus said unto him, I have been so long time with you, and hast thou not known me, Philip? He that hath seen me hath seen my Father: how, then sayest thou, show us the Father? Believest thou not that I am in the Father, and the Father in me? The words that I speak unto you I speak not of myself, but my Father, that dwelleth in me, he doth the work. Believe me, that I am in the Father, and the Father in me; at least, believe me for the work's sake."—John xiv. 4-11.

"But Thomas, one of the twelve, called Didymus, was not with them when Jesus came; the other disciples therefore said unto him, We have seen the Lord. But he said unto them) Except I see in his hands the print of the nails, and put my finger in the print of the nails, and put my hand into his side, I will not believe. And eight days after, again his disciples were within, and Thomas was with them: then came Jesus, when the doors were shut, and stood in the midst, and said) Peace be unto you. After said he to Thomas, Put thy finger here, and see my hands, and put forth thy hand, and put it into my side; and be not faithless, but faithful. Then Thomas answered, and said unto him, Thou art my Lord and my God." —John xx. 24-28.

"And he that seeth me seeth hint that sent me."—John xii.45.

"As the Father knoweth me, so know I the Father. I and my Father are one."—John x. 15-30.

"And if I also judge, my judgment is true; for he that sent me is with me. The Father hath not left me alone, because I do always those things that please him. Then said they unto him, Where is thy Father? Jesus answered, Ye neither know me nor my Father. If ye had known me, ye should have known my Father also."—John viii. 16, 19.

"He must increase, but I must decrease. He that is come from on high is above all. He that is of the earth is of the earth, and speaketh of the earth; he that is come from heaven is above all; for no man ascendeth up to heaven but he that hath descended from heaven, the Son of Man, which is in heaven." — John iii. 13, 30, 31.

"The first man is of the earth, earthly; the second man is the Lord from heaven."—1 Cor. xv. 47.

"And all things are of God, which hath reconciled us unto himself by Jesus Christ; for God was in Christ, and reconciled the world to himself." 2 Cor. v., part of the 18th and 19th verses.

"And when he had spoken these things, while they beheld he was taken up, for a cloud took him out of their sight; and while they looked stedfastly towards heaven, as he went, be hold, two men stood by them, in white apparel, which also said, Ye men of Galilee, why stand ye gazing into heaven? This Jesus, which is taken up from you into heaven, shall so come, as ye have seen him go into heaven."—Acts i. 9, 10, 11.

"What concord hath Christ with Belial? Or what part hath the believer with the infidel? And what agreement hath the temple of God with idols? For ye are the temple of the living God; as God hath said, I will dwell among them, and walk there; and I will be their God, and they shall be my people; and I will be a Father to you, and ye shall be my sons and daughters, saith the Lord Almighty." —2 Cor. vi., the latter end.

"There is one Lord, one faith, one baptism, one God and Father of all, which is above all, and through all, and in you all; but to every one of us is given grace, according to the measure of the gift of Christ. Wherefore he said, When lie ascended on high, he led captivity captive, and gave gifts unto men. Now in that he ascended, what is it, but that he had also descended first into the lowest parts of the earth? He that descended is even the same that ascended far above all heavens, that he might fill all things."—Ephes. iv. 5-9.

"Of whom are the fathers, and of whom concerning the flesh Christ came, who is God over all, blessed for ever. Amen."—Rom. ix. 5.

"Kiss the son, lest he be angry, and ye perish from the right way. When his wrath is kindled but a little, blessed are all they that put their trust in him."—Psalm ii., the last verse.

"The Lord said unto my Lord, Sit thou on my right hand, until I make thine enemies thy footstool."— Psalm cx. 1.

"And be fell to the earth, and heard a voice, saying unto him, Saul, Saul, why persecutest thou me? And he said, Who art thou, Lord? And the Lord said, I am Jesus, whom thou persecutest; it is hard for thee to kick against the pricks." —Acts ix. 4, 5.

"Now the same Jesus Christ, our Lord and our God, even the Father, which hath loved us, and hath given us everlasting salvation, and good hope through grace, stablish you in every good work."—2 Thess. the two last verses.

"And did all eat the same spiritual meat, and did all drink the same spiritual drink; for they drank of that spiritual rock that followed them, and that rock was Christ. Neither let us tempt Christ, as some of them tempted him, and were destroyed of serpents."—1 Cor. x. 3, 4, 9.

"We know that an idol is nothing in the world, and that there is no other God but one; for though there be that are called Gods, whether in heaven or in earth, as there be many Gods and many Lords, yet unto us there is but one God, which is the Father, of whom are all things, and we in him, and one Lord Jesus Christ, and we by him." —1 Cor. viii. 4, 5, 6.

"For we preach not ourselves, but Christ Jesus the Lord, and ourselves your servants, for Jesus' sake; for God, that commanded the light to shine out of darkness, is he which hath shined into our hearts, to give the light of the knowledge of the glory of God, in the face of Jesus Christ." —2 Cor. iv. 5, 6, 7.

"For ye know the grace of our Lord Jesus Christ, that he, being rich, for your sakes became poor; that ye, through his poverty, might be made rich." —2 Cor. viii. 9.

" But our conversation is in heaven, from whence also we look for the Saviour, even the Lord Jesus Christ, who shall change our vile bodies, that they may be fashioned like unto his glorious body, according to the working whereby he is able even to subdue all things unto himself."—Phil. iii., the two last verses.

"For ye are dead, and your life is hid with Christ in God; when Christ, who is our life, shall appear, then shall ye also appear with him in glory."—Coloss. iii. 3, 4.

"I would not (brethren) have you ignorant concerning them which are asleep, that you sorrow not, even as others, that have no hope; for if we believe that Jesus is dead, and is risen, even so you which sleep in Jesus will God bring with him; for this say we unto you, by the word of the Lord, that we which live, and are remaining at the coming of the Lord, shall not prevent them which sleep; for the Lord shall descend from heaven with a shout, and with the voice of the archangel, and with the trumpet of God, and the dead in Christ shall rise first; then shall we which live, and remain, be caught up with them also in the clouds, and so shall we be ever with the Lord. Therefore comfort yourselves one another with these words." —1 Thess. iv., the last verse.

"Now the very God of peace sanctify you throughout, and I pray God that your whole spirit, and soul, and body, may be kept blameless, unto the coming of our Lord Jesus Christ. The grace of our Lord Jesus Christ be with you. Amen." —1 Thess. v. 23, 28.

"For it is a righteous thing with God to recompense tribulation to them that trouble you, and to you which are troubled, rest with us; when the Lord Jesus shall show himself from heaven with his mighty angels, in flaming fire, rendering vengeance unto them which do not know God, and which obey not unto the gospel of our Lord Jesus Christ, which shall be punished with everlasting perdition from the presence of the Lord, and from the glory of his power."—2 Thess. i. 6-9.

"I have fought a good fight, and have finished my course; I have kept the faith; from henceforth is laid up for me the crown of righteousness, which the Lord, the righteous Judge, shall give me at that day; and not to me only, but unto all them that love his appearing."—2 Tim. iv. 7, 8.

"And if there be any other thing that is not contrary to wholesome doctrine, which is according to the glorious gospel of the blessed God, which is committed unto me. Therefore I thank him, which hath made me strong; that is, Christ Jesus our Lord; for he counted me faithful, and put me in his service. Nevertheless, for this cause was I received to mercy, that Christ should first skew me all long suffering, unto the example of them which should in time to come believe him, unto eternal life. Now unto the King everlasting, immortal, invisible, to God only wise, be honour and glory, for ever and ever. Amen."— 1 Tim. i., part of verses 10, 11, 12, 16, and 17.

"For bodily exercise profiteth little, but godliness is profitable unto all things, which hath the promise of the life present, and of that which is to come. This is a true saying, and by all means worthy to be received; for therefore we labour, and are rebuked, because we trust in the living God, which is the Saviour of all men, especially of those that believe."—1 Tim. iv. 8, 9, 10.

"And without controversy, great is the mystery of godliness, which is God manifested in the flesh, justified in the Spirit, seen of angels, preached unto the Gentiles, believed on in the world, received up into glory."—2 Tim. iii., the last verse.

"At sundry times, and in divers manners, God spake in the old time unto our fathers by the prophets. In these last days he hath spoken unto us by his Son, whom he hath made heir of all things; by whom also he made the world; who, being the brightness of his glory, and the engraven form of his person, and bearing up all things by his mighty word, hath by himself purged our sins, and sitteth at the right-hand of the Majesty on high, in the highest places; and is made so much the more excellent than the angels, inasmuch as he hath obtained a more excellent name than they. For unto which of the angels said he, at any time, Thou art my Son, this day begot I thee? And again, I will be his Father, and be shall be my Son. Again, When he bringeth in his first-begotten Son into the world, he saith, Let all the angels of God worship him. And of the angels he saith, He makes the spirits his messengers, and his ministers a flame of fire; but unto the Son he saith, O God, thy throne is for ever and ever; the sceptre of thy kingdom is a sceptre of righteousness; thou hast loved righteousness, and hated iniquity; therefore God, even thy God, hath anointed thee with the oil of gladness above thy fellows. And thou, Lord, in the beginning, hast established the earth, and the heavens are the works of thy hands."—Hebrews i. 1-10.

"But we see Jesus crowned with glory and honour, which was made a little inferior to the angels, through the sufferings of death, that, by God's grace, he might taste death for all men. It became him, for whom are all things, and by whom are all things, seeing that he brought many children unto glory, that he should consecrate the Prince of their salvation through afflictions."—Heb. 9, 10.

"And he shall divide the spoil with the strong, because he hath poured out his soul unto death."—Isaiah liii., part of the 12th verse.

"For whether we live, we live unto the Lord; or whether we die, we die unto the Lord; whether we live, therefore, or die, we are the Lord's; for Christ therefore died, and rose again, that he might be Lord both of the dead and quick."—Rom. xiv. 8, 9.

"And all flesh shall know, that I, the Lord, am thy Saviour and thy Redeemer, the mighty one of Jacob."—Isaiah xlix., the last verse.

"Looking unto Jesus, the author and finisher of our faith, who, for the joy that was set before him, endured the cross, despised the shame, and is set at the right hand of the throne of God."—Heb. xii. 2.

"Wherefore, seeing we receive a kingdom which cannot be shaken, let us have grace, whereby we may so serve God, that we may please him with reverence and fear; for our God is a consuming fire, and a jealous God."— Heb. xii. 28, 29.

"And we know that the Son of God is come, and hath given us a mind to know him who is true, and we are in him which is true;

that is, in that his Son Jesus Christ, the same is the very God, and eternal life."— 1 John v. 20.

"Now unto him that is able to keep you, that you fall not, and to present you faultless, before the presence of his glory, with joy; that is, to God only wise, our Saviour, be glory and majesty, and dominion and power, both now and for ever. Amen."—Jude, the last verse.

"Lift up your heads, O ye gates! be ye lift up, ye everlasting doors! and the King of Glory shall come in. Who is this King of Glory? It is the Lord, strong in battle; even the Lord, mighty in battle. Lift up your heads, O ye gates! and be ye lift up yourselves, ye everlasting doors! and the King of Glory shall come in. Who is the King of Glory? Even the Lord of Hosts, he is the King of Glory."—Psalm xxiv. 7, 8, 9.

"I beheld till the thrones were set up, and the Ancient of Days did sit, whose garment was white as snow, and the hair of his head like pure wool; his throne was like fiery flame, and his wheels as burning fire; a stream issued, and came forth from before him; thousand thousands ministered unto him, and ten thousand thousands stood before him. The judgment was set, and the books were opened: I beheld, and the same horn made battle against the saints, yea, and prevailed against them, until the Ancient of Days came, and judgment was given to the saints of the Most High, and the time approached that the saints possessed the kingdom."—Daniel

vii. 9, 10, 21, 22.

"Behold he cometh with clouds, and every eye shall see him, even they which pierced him through; and all kindreds of the earth shall wail before him: even so. Amen. I am ALPHA and OMEGA, the beginning and the ending, saith the Lord; which is, and which was, and which is to come, even the Almighty. And I was even ravished in spirit on the Lord's day, and heard behind me a great voice, as it had been of a trumpet, saying, I am Alpha and Omega, the first and the last. Then I turned back to see the voice that spake with me; and when I was turned I saw seven golden candlesticks, one like unto the Son of Man, clothed with a garment down to the feet, and girded about the paps with a golden girdle; his head and hair were as white wool, and as snow, and his eyes were as a flame of fire; his feet like unto fine brass, burning in a furnace; and his voice as the sound of many waters. And he had in his right hand seven stars, and out of his mouth went a sharp two-edged sword; and his face shone as the sun shineth in his strength. And when I saw him, I fell at his feet as dead. Then he laid his right hand upon me, saying unto me, Fear not; I am the first and the last; and I am alive, I was dead; and, behold I am alive for evermore. Amen. And I have the keys of hell and death."—Rev. i., last part.

"And they were full of eyes within; and they ceased not, day nor night, saying, HOLY! HOLY! HOLY! Lord God Almighty, which was, and which is, and which is to come. And when those beasts gave glory, and honour, and thanks, to him that sat on the throne, which liveth for ever and ever, the twenty-four elders sat down before him that sat on the throne, and worshipped him that liveth for evermore; and cast their crowns before the throne, saying, Thou art worthy, O Lord, to receive glory, and honour, and power; for thou hast created all things, and for thy will's sake they are and have been created." —Rev. viii. 9, 10, 11.

"Then I beheld, and heard the voice of many angels round about the throne, and about the beast, and the elders, saying, Worthy is the Lamb that was killed to receive power, and riches, and wisdom, and strength, and honour, and glory, and praise; and all creatures which are in heaven, and on the earth, and under the earth, and in the sea, and all that are in them, heard I, saying, Praise, and honour, and glory, and power, be unto him that sitteth on the throne, and unto the Lamb, for evermore. And the four beasts said, Amen. And the twenty-four elders fell down, and worshipped him that liveth for evermore." Rev. v. 11-14.

"After these things I beheld, and lo, a great multitude, which no man could number, of all nations, and kindreds, and people, and tongues, stood before the throne, and before the Lamb, clothed with long white robes, and palms in their hands; and they cried with a loud voice, saying, Salvation cometh of our

God, that sitteth upon the throne, and of the Lamb. And all the angels stood round about the throne, and about the elders, and the four beasts; and they fell before the throne on their faces, and worshipped God, saying, Amen; praise, and glory, and wisdom, and thanks, and honour, and power, and might, be unto our God, for evermore, Amen. And one of the elders spake, saying unto me, What are these which are arrayed in long white robes? And whence came they? And I said unto him, Lord, thou knowest. And he said unto me, These are they which came out of great tribulation, and have washed their long robes, and have made their long robes white, in the blood of the Lamb; therefore are they in the presence of the throne of God, and serve him day and night in his temple. And he that sitteth upon the throne will dwell among them, they shall hunger no more, neither thirst any more, neither shall the sun light on them, nor any heat; for the Lamb, which is in the middle of the throne, shall govern them, and shall lead them unto the lively fountains of water; and God shall wipe away all tears from their eyes." —Rev. vii., from the 9th to the last verse.

"And the seventh angel blew the trumpet, and there were great voices in heaven, saying, The kingdoms of the world are our Lord's, and his Christ's, and he shall reign for evermore. Then the twenty-four elders, which sat before God on their seats, fell upon their faces, and worshipped God, saying, We give thee thanks, Lord God Almighty," (mark with a single eye,) "which art, and which wast, and which art to come; for thou hast received thy great might, and hast obtained thy kingdom. And the Gentiles were angry, and thy wrath is come, and the time of the dead, that they should be judged, and that thou shouldest give reward to thy servants the prophets, and to the saints, and to them that fear thy name, to small and great; and shouldest destroy them which destroy the earth."—Rev. xi. 15-18.

"And I saw heaven opened, and behold a white horse, and he that sat upon him was called FAITHFUL AND TRUE; and he judgeth and fighteth righteously. And his eyes were as a flame of fire, and on his head were many crowns. And he had a name written that no man knew but himself, and he was clothed with a garment dipped in blood, and his name was called THE WORD OF GOD; and out of his mouth went a sharp sword, that with it he should smite the heathen; for he shall rule them with a rod of iron; for he it is that treadeth the winepress of the fierceness and wrath of Almighty God. And he hath upon his garments, and upon his thigh, a name written, THE KING OF KINGS, AND LORD OF LORDS." —Rev. xvi. 11-16.

"And I saw a great white throne, and one that sat upon it, from whose face flew away both the earth and heavens, and their place was no more found."—Rev.

xx. 11.

"And he that sat upon the throne said, I make all things new. And he said unto me, Write, for these things are faithful and true. And he said unto me, It is done: I am Alpha and Omega, the beginning and the ending; he that overcomes shall inherit all things, and I will be his God, and he shall be my Son."—Rev. xxi. 5, 6, 7.

"I am Alpha and Omega, the beginning and the end, the first and the last. I, Jesus, have sent my angel, to testify these things in the churches. I am the root, and the generation of David, and the bright morning star. He which testifieth these things saith surely, I come quickly. Amen. Even so, come Lord Jesus."—Rev. xxii. 13, 16, 20.

CHAPTER II.

1. On the Divine Names, (1.) In the Time of the Law; (2.) After Christ Jesus became Flesh; and, (3.) After his Ascension to Glory. 2. Conclusion.

IN the spiritual bowels of the Lord Jesus Christ, I humbly beseech those that shall take the pains to peruse this writing, that, with an upright conscience, as in the presence of God, they would compare scripture with scripture; and then they may clearly see that the same Jehovah, in the time of the law, was the very same Jesus in the time of the gospel.

2. And that which made the seeming difference between the Father, and the Son, and the Holy Ghost or Spirit, as though they were two or three distinct essences or persons, it is nothing else but the appearance of the only High and Mighty God, in a twofold or threefold manner or condition, unto the sons of men, at two or three several times; and so altering his names or titles, according to his several appearances;

3. As, namely, under the law, before his spiritual body became flesh, you know he went under these and such like titles: "Jehovah," the "High and Lofty One of Israel," the "Lord of Hosts," the "Most High God," the "Mighty God of Jacob;" but, when the glorious Jehovah or "I am" became Jesus in the flesh, then you may know, according to the transmuting of his condition for his elect's sake, so, likewise, he changed his names or titles, as to call himself the "Only-Begotten Son of God," or "Son of Man," or "Mediator," or "Brother," or "Servant," or "Redeemer of his People."

4. Thus, when the High and Mighty God had abased himself in the form of a servant, in the lowest manner, you see be altered his titles or names according to his condition.

5. Again, in the third place, when the most glorious God, alone in flesh, had wrought our redemption by the shedding his most precious blood, and pouring out his soul unto death, and being ascended upon the throne of his eternal, immortal personal glory again:

6. Now, at the last, since he

alone is become the Teacher of his people, by the inspiration of his most blessed Spirit, he is pleased to title himself by the name of Holy Ghost, or Spirit, or such like; so that, by the single eye of your most holy faith, you may see and know that Christ, and the Father, and the Spirit, were and are and can be no other but one undivided glorious essence, or spiritual personal substance, from all eternity; and

now are become a Person of flesh and bone, glorified to all eternity.

7. The Lord, from his glorious throne, and infinite free grace, open your understandings, that are his tender-hearted chosen ones, that you may know and love that personal, only-wise God, our Saviour, the Lord Jesus Christ, above your lives, who is the everlasting Father, unto your eternal glory: even so. Amen, Amen, Amen. So be it. Amen.

The Servant of the
Most High and Mighty Jehovah or Jesus,
And True Messenger of his Eternal Spirit,

JOHN REEVE.
THE END.

LUKE JAMES HANSARD, PRINTER, 5, PEMBERTON ROW, GOUGH SQUARE, FLEET STREET.

SACRED REMAINS,
OR, A
DIVINE APPENDIX;
BEING A
COLLECTION
OF
FIVE SPIRITUAL EPISTLES,

ORIGINALLY WRITTEN ABOUT THE YEAR 1654:
ALSO
WILLIAM SEDGWICK'S
REPLIES TO SEVERAL QUERIES SENT TO HIM,
BY THE LORD'S LAST IMMEDIATE MESSENGER

JOHN REEVE,

THEN RESIDING IN LONDON.

THIRD EDITION.

AND NOW, AFTER CAREFUL EXAMINATION BY THE MOST
CORRECT
COPIES, COMMUNICATED FOR THE CONSOLATION AND
ESTABLISHMENT OF THE CHURCH OF CHRIST BY
THEIR BRETHREN, WHOSE FAITH IN THESE
AND ALL OTHER HIS IRREMANDABLE
DECLARATIONS,
DOTH (AND BY DIVINE PROTECTION WILL) REMAIN UNSHAKEN
TO ETERNITY.

LONDON

REPRINTED FOR JOSEPH FROST, 17, HALF MOON STREET,
BISHOPSGATE STREET;
BY ANDREW T. ROBERTS, 2, HACKNEY ROAD, OPPOSITE SHOREDITCH CHURCH.
1856.

THE SACRED REMAINS

CONTAIN ONLY FIVE LETTERS AND WILLIAM SEDGWICK'S REPLIES,
SINCE THE TREATISE ON THE THREE RECORDS;
ON WHAT WAS FROM ETERNITY, OR,
A ONE PERSONAL GLORY;
WITH THE SCRIPTURES PROVING CHRIST TO BE THE ONLY GOD:
THESE TREATISES BEING GENERAL, THEY HAVE BEEN
PUT INTO CHAPTER AND VERSE, AND WERE ADDED TO
THE GENERAL EPISTLE TO MINISTERS, IN THE YEAR 1854.

CONTENTS:—

The Prophet Reeve's Queries sent to William Sedgwick
William Sedgwick's Replies
The Prophet Reeve's Answer to William Sedgwick's Replies
The Prophet Reeve's Answer to Isaac Pennington, Esquire
The Prophet Reeve's Epistle to the Earl of Pembrooke
The Prophet Reeve's Epistle to His Kinsman

This Third Edition of Letters have been reprinted with great care from the Second Edition of the above, and uniform with the following books:—

REPRINTED.

2nd Edition of the Book of 168 Letters   1820
3rd Edition of Sacred Remains, 5 Letters   1856

FIRST PRINTED.

1st   Edition of Stream from the Tree of Life, 17 Letters   1758
1st   Edition of Supplement and Conclusion of the Book of
        Letters,—23 Letters   1831

And are intended to form the Third Volume of the
THIRD TESTAMENT OF OUR LORD JESUS CHRIST.
Hoping at the next reprint they will be arranged into the same order of
Chapter and Verse as the Bible and Testament.

JOSEPH FROST.

QUERIES SENT TO WILLIAM SEDGWICK,
BY THE
PROPHET JOHN REEVE.
JUNE the 11th, 1654.
See Acts of the Witnesses, 3rd part, Chap. IV.

COURTEOUS FRIEND,

I SUPPOSE my temporal condition in some measure to you hath been made known and manifest, through which the Most High already hath moved you these five years past, to supply my quarterly necessity: and though you want no objects of mercy, yet I shall be constrained to visit you upon this account, until the Creator hath opened some other way. Therefore if our God see it good, my desire is, that your spirit may freely and cheerfully act your charity towards me, that you may have consolation in the deed, and I joy in the Lord Jesus from whom alone all good proceeds. But passing by the perishing comforts, suffer me to write unto you about things of more concernment, which I am moved to in a querying way.

Dear Friend, Countryman, and Brother in the flesh, O that I could knowingly say so in the deep things of the Spirit also; then should I be fully assured, that these following queries by Divine operation, would rather satisfy you, and move you silently to sit down in peace, than offend you in the least.

1. My first query is this, whether you do knowingly believe Jesus Christ alone to be both Father, Son, and Spirit, in only one distinct person glorified?

2. Whether any man can truly demonstrate who or what the living God is against all gainayers, without an immediate commission from his eternal Spirit?

3. Whether it be not spiritual treason against our Lord Jesus Christ, for a man to execute the office of a prophet or a minister of the gospel, without an immediate command from His own Majesty?

4. Whether any man that prophesieth or preacheth can have any real knowledge of his own salvation abiding in him, without an unquestionable assurance of his own soul, that the Most High hath anointed him?

5. Whether the Lord's former Ambassadors were not all empowered to pronounce a temporal or eternal glory or misery to come, according to the obedience or disobedience of those they were sent unto?

6. Whether any man in this age can be an experimental speaker of the counsels of God, without an infallible knowledge of divine mysteries above all other men in the world?

7. Whether a non-commissionated or unsent ambassador, or speaker to the people upon a spiritual account, may not be in as much danger of an eternal vengeance as a counterfeit ambassador upon a natural account is of a temporal vengeance?

8. Whether you are fully satisfied against all gain-sayings, that it was the Spirit of Christ alone that formerly, or at this time, moved you to preach or speak in a ministerial way to the people?

9. Whether, as your own faith or judgment you do not hold forth to the people, that God alone is the teacher of his chosen ones, by the inspiration of His most Holy and Blessed Spirit?

10. And lastly, if the Lord Jesus Christ alone be the only teacher of His beloved ones, by the continual incomings or enlightenings of His most glorious Spirit; what then are those that acknowledge God alone to be the teacher of His saints, and yet in a ministerial way gather the people together under pretence of preaching Christ, or speaking the experimental movings of His Spirit to them, but mockers of God, deceivers of the people, and deadly enemies to their own true peace; unless from on high, God bears witness by infallible testimonies in the spirits of His new-born ones, that He hath sent them by an immediate speaking to them from His glorious throne, as abundantly before said?

Now, in obedience to that commission which I once received by voice of words from The One Personal Glory itself even to the hearing of the outward ear as well as the inward soul, never having had the least sound of the truth of it, in all love, meekness, and humility of soul, present I these few queries to your private meditations, and shall, I trust, with patience wait the Lord's leisure for His loving answer in you to these things,

Yours in the Lord's

Eternal Majesty,

JOHN REEVE.

June the 11th, 1654.

William Sedgwick's Replies to John Reeve.

MR. REEVE,

I AM not wholly against Queries; they are much used by that cavilling and disputing spirit that is in all sects, and may be better used by humble minds who are inquiring after truth; but I think they least of all agree with that infallible Spirit which you profess to have.

1. To the first query I answer, I may say I do believe what you there express, but it may be not in your sense; but I choose rather to say, I desire my faith may not stand in a form of words, but in the power of God.

2. To the second I answer, I know none that do demonstrate who or what God is perfectly or with power: in, weakness and in part many do show who and what He is. Secondly, if you mean by "against all gain-sayers" a confident cleaving to what they affirm without being removed, that is very common: if you mean a silencing or convincing gainsayers, it is not yet done by you nor any man that I know. Thirdly, the commission of the Spirit which you would seem to appropriate is larger than you imagine; for "no man can say Jesus is the Lord but by the Holy Spirit," and "There are diversities of gifts, but the same Spirit," 1 Cor. xii., 3, 4.

3. To the third I answer, In the general it is true, it is treason only I except against the word "immediate" used in this and the second query, being jealous that you do, in it and in your ministry, either deny or veil the mediator betwixt God and man, for immediate is without a mediator; for by virtue of Christ, who is mediator betwixt God and man, and who is the light of the world, and enlighteneth every man that cometh into the world, "every man may minister according to the gift that is given him," Rom. xii. "If he have faith he may speak according to the measure of his faith," Psalm cxvi. 10. "I have believed, therefore have I spoken;" or if he have experience he may speak according to his experience, Acts iv. 20: "For we cannot but speak the things we have heard and seen." Nay, they not only may, but ought, 1 Cor. xii. 7: "For every gift is given to profit with, of what kind soever it be;" and I fear it is the enemy in you that denies it.

4. To the fourth I answer, First, a man may have salvation abiding in him, and yet he not know it. Secondly a man may have a real knowledge of salvation abiding in him, and yet come to lose it. Thirdly, a man may think himself saved when he is lost, and lost when he is saved. There are that have their lives but shall lose them, and there are that lose their lives and yet save them. Fourthly, he is not sure that knows, but he is sure that God knows that he shall be saved. Fifthly, that is not the best assurance which you call unquestionable, but that which is joined with fear and trembling, especially at this time. Sixthly, a man may be anointed to the work of prophesying, and yet not have salvation abiding in him. The Spirit of God came upon Saul and upon Balaam, and they did prophesy by it.

5. To the fifth I answer, I do suppose they were so empowered, and that every man, according to the proportion of faith in him hath the same power; First, If he speak truth temporally, a temporal punishment or reward attends that truth as men obey or disobey it. And if any man speak truth eternal, the punishment or reward is eternal according as it is obeyed or disobeyed, there is matter of eternal condemnation in it; but the absolute eternal condemnation which you

declare is not justified in my heart, neither do I see it at all justified of any.

6. To the sixth I answer, I do own myself an experimental preacher, though in very great weakness and manifold infirmities. What I do feel or have felt evil, I warn others of; but cannot own an infallible knowledge of divine mysteries above all other men in the world. If I should it would be great pride of spirit in me; and I judge it so in any that assume such things to themselves. And let me speak my experience, and desire you to reflect, if you can upon your own words and see what a narrow lofty spirit runneth in them. High swelling words none must speak but he that hath an infallible knowledge of divine mysteries above all other men in the world: and who hath this infallible knowledge but yourself and your companion? I can experimentally warn you of that which saith, "I am, and there is none else beside me: I shall not sit as a widow," Isai. xlvii. 8. Another experience I have observed, that you and your friend have allowed preaching by experience without any such lofty qualification which you now express, and therefore you yourselves are not true to what you declare.

7. To the seventh I answer, Every one that goes without a commission, or that goes beyond his commission, is in danger of eternal vengeance: therefore it concerns you and me very much to stand in awe, to tremble at the word, lest we fall under the curse for adding to and taking from His word. I believe some will suffer for running before they are sent, and some for running beyond what they are sent about. But concerning speaking, I desire you to consider how large a commission the Scriptures give: "The heavens declare day unto day, and night unto night uttereth speech; their sound is gone through the earth, and their words to the end of the world," Psalm xix., cxlviii.; and cl. 6: "Let every thing that hath breath praise the Lord." All believers seem to be commissionated. Rom. xix. 9 and 10: "The word is nigh thee, even in thy heart and in thy mouth; that is, the word of faith which we preach." Ver. 10: "With the heart man believeth unto righteousness, and with the tongue confession is made unto salvation:" Therefore the apostolical ministry is to continue in the church in all ages, and Christ promiseth His presence with them and that ministry to the end of the world, Matthew xxviii. 20. And there will be found in the midst of the great apostacy, when the church comes out of captivity, "apostles and prophets," Rev. xviii. 20.

8. To the eighth I answer, that when I did speak formerly, I was as fully satisfied, as you are now satisfied in your ministry; neither do I now wholly condemn my former speaking, but have seen an evil spirit which got into it; and it was not, the least evil of that spirit that I did undertake to judge all others.

9 and 10. To the two last queries answer, I am of this faith, that God alone doth teach His chosen ones; yet Christ himself taught, and the apostles taught, and the prophets taught. You likewise hold the

same faith, and yet you teach. God teacheth by His Son, by His servants, by His word, by afflictions, and in all by His Spirit. For that charge of mockers, deceivers, &c., I shall bear it from you and others, till the Lord plead my cause. For your commission received by voice of words, I judge it not, but leave it to the Lord. I am exceeding weak, I fear and tremble every time I preach; I rather think that my mouth may be stopped, than that I should hold out preaching: my ears and my heart are open to rebukes. But this I may say, I charge my ministry more strongly and deeply than you do, and yet it stands staggering for aught I know; if you can knock it down, you will do me a kindness.

WILLIAM SEDGWICK.

The Prophet John Reeve's Answer to William Sedgwick's Replies.

July 30th, 1654.

SIR,

IT is confessed that subtile serpents accustom themselves to propound carnal curious queries, to ensnare the innocent: but it doth not therefore follow, that sober queries of the highest moment should offend that man which hath any true light in him. Why? Because all such queries are sent forth by the Spirit of Christ, either for the trial of men's faith and love to the truth, or for a witness against them, when the secrets of all hearts shall be opened, for their ministerial meddling with divine mysteries, without an infallible light of an immediate commission from the Lord.

1. In your first reply you write, you may say you do believe what I there express, but it may be not in my sense. To this I answer, What I there express is none of your faith, unless you believe it in my sense; for there is but one spiritual sense to every truth that is declared, and what I there exactly wrote in the letter is my very faith in the spirit, to wit: that there is no other spiritual God, Creator, or Father, but only within the blessed body of Christ Jesus glorified. "For in Him dwelleth all the fulness of the Godhead bodily." His invisible Spirit is the ever-lasting Father; His visible glorious body residing in the heavens above the stars is the eternal Son; His heavenly enlightening in His new-born people is the Holy Ghost. If this be not your understanding concerning God, as yet my faith is not your faith, neither is my God your God. In the latter part of your reply, your words are these: But you choose rather to say, you desire your faith may not stand in a form of words, but in the power of God. To this I answer, It is the power of God only that enables a man to speak or write a form of

wholesome words concerning Himself and the mysteries of His ever-lasting kingdom: but the reason of men's words being so full of confusion or formless contradiction about spiritual things, is because the true understanding of His divine power is hid from them. For that man who enjoys a real comprehension of the divine power, being moved to treat of salvation and condemnation to his brethren, is not guided by the fallibility of supposings or imagination, but by an infallible assurance of the truth of what he speaks or writes in his own soul; neither doth this man want a manifestation of the power of them in his life and conversation.

2. In your second reply, you say: you know none that do demonstrate who or what God is perfectly, and with power; but in weakness and in part, you say, many do show who and what He is. To this I answer, Though at present it be hid from your eyes, yet we truly and boldly affirm, without any doubt or fear of after shame, that God hath manifested Himself with as much perfection or power upon some spirits, by His truth spoken through our mouths, as ever He did by any true prophet or apostle since the world began: but to name or present the particulars to you as witnesses to this truth, it will be of no value until you see it or feel it in your own soul. I mean, a glorious manifestation of salvation, through a powerful believing our declarations, and an unmoveable seal of everlasting damnation upon those who despise them, both in life and death. If you mean God doth manifest Himself in men's weak bodies through natural infirmities, that is common to all mortals: but if you mean He doth manifest Himself through the weakness or uncertainty of the mind, that is utterly denied by us. For we affirm, that such men were neither sent nor moved by the true Spirit to demonstrate who or what God is, neither in part nor perfection, in power nor in weakness. For no man is meet to speak or write concerning things which are eternal, without an infallible testimony of the truth of them dwelling in his own soul. Moreover you say, if I mean a silencing or convincing gain-sayers, it is not yet done by me, nor any other that you know. To this I answer, that ministry that neither silenceth nor convinceth gain-sayers, is not of God; but that gainsayers have been both silenced and convinced by our ministry, not only God, but several spirits in other nations do bear witness to it at this day; wherefore if it neither silence nor convince you, the great day shall make it manifest. And further you say: the commission of the Spirit, which I would seem to appropriate, is larger than I imagine. To this I answer, I am so far from what you seem to accuse me concerning appropriating to myself, that God and His light in me are my witnesses, that when it was put upon me I would have given the whole world, if I had it, to have been eased of its burthen: as for the largeness of the commission, it is only known to Him that gave it. But let me tell you without offence, the letter gives you not, nor no man else, one jot or tittle of right to the commission of the Spirit. Indeed, a spiritual commission gives a man a great measure of

infallible knowledge of the truth of the letter; but a literal commission gives no man a certain understanding of the truth of the Spirit in the least. For if it should, then all literal acutants would be the only spiritual men in the world. Sir, I would gladly have you convinced of that general deceit of pleading a ministerial commission from the Scriptures to maintain your preaching.

3. In your third reply, you say: In the general you grant it to be treason, only you except against the word "immediate," being jealous, that in it and in our ministry, we do either deny or veil the mediator betwixt God and man; for immediate, you say, is without a mediator. To this I answer, In your excepting against the word "immediate" you except against the teachings of the Spirit; for God in all ages ever taught His chosen prophets and apostles by an immediate voice or invisible movings of His Holy Spirit. Holy men of old spake as they were moved by the Spirit; and the Spirit moving in them was not mediate, but immediate: therefore their records have power over the conscience to the end of the world, because they were immediate words of truth. Indeed, the teachings of men are all mediate, but the teachings of God are all immediate, especially to His commissionated prophets and apostles; to wit, that they might become the mediate true teachers of all salvation secrets to their elect brethren that heard them, and witnesses of condemnation in the consciences of all gain-saying and despising reprobates. If you mean we seem to deny or veil the mediator betwixt God and man, because we own no other God at all, but our Lord Jesus Christ only; in that sense we shall always seem to deny or veil the mediator, to all those that ignorantly worship a divided God: for we can own but only one undivided personal glorious God, and no more, even the man Christ Jesus, blessed for ever and ever as aforesaid. But if you own another God besides Him, before Him, or distinct from Him, it is you that seem to deny or veil the mediator, by giving that glory, which is only due to Him, to an idol of your own lying imagination. "He that honoureth the Son honoureth the Father;" but he that giveth the honour due unto the Son to any God, infinite Spirit, or Father, but what is wholly abiding in His person, that man through his ignorance denieth both the Father and Son. That man doth not truly understand who or what God is, who worships Him under the notion of two or three distinct persons or spirits. But he that truly understands that the Father and the Son are but one divine bosom, to wit, that from all eternity they were but only one spiritual person in form like a man; that man, indeed, in a good measure knows the Lord, as he is known of Him. In the latter part of this reply, you repeat the Scriptures which were spoken by the Lord's immediate commissioners; and from thence you seem to maintain your present ministry. But let me tell you, if I had not a more sure witness than the literal sayings of my brethren, the holy prophets and apostles, I were the most miserable man that ever appeared in the name of the Lord. Moreover, though it be lawful for saints to converse

one with another about their faith, or experience in spiritual things, for the provoking of each other to love and good works; it doth not therefore follow, that it is lawful for the most eminent saint in the world to gather the people together in a ministerial way, to exercise Scripture ordinances, without an immediate commission from the Spirit of Christ, or a mediate commission from an immediate commissioner, as the saints had that preached in the apostles' time. Faith comes by hearing, and hearing by the word of God preached; and how shall they preach except they be sent?" Because there, is not a man of you immediately or mediately sent by the Lord, how is it possible therefore that you should preach the true faith concerning God, or devil, heaven, or hell, or any of His counsels concerning the world to come? And though you seem to fear it is the enemy that would hinder you from exercising your ministerial gift; if my God make you obedient to it, you shall find it was the best friend that ever spake to you in all your life. " Obedience " as well as mercy, "is far more excellent than sacrifice; therefore whether you hear or forbear, you shall one day know to your weal or woe, that it was the light of Christ in me, warning you not to embassy yourself about things of eternal concernment, without a commission from the glorious mouth of God Himself. The literal commission killeth, but the spiritual commission giveth life and peace.

4. In your fourth reply, you say, a man may have salvation abiding in him, and he not know it. Further you say, a man may have a real knowledge of salvation abiding in him, and yet come to lose it. To this I answer, salvation in men is the grace of the Spirit, and the fruits of the Spirit are all light and life, and the nature of the light is to discover darkness, and it is given unto men for that very end: how then a man should have salvation abiding in him, and he not know it, to me seemeth ridiculous; it is all one as if you should say, a man may be abiding with me in my chamber, and yet I neither see it nor know it.

It is the abiding of the light of Christ, before the comprehension of the mind, that makes a man really to know his own salvation; and whilst that crystal light abides in the memory of that man, the nature of it is to present nothing else unto him, but life and salvation. It is true a man may be elected unto salvation and he not know it: but it is impossible for him to have the seal of salvation abiding in him, and he not know it. For when a man is ignorant of it, it cannot properly be said to be abiding in him, though it should be in him. Why? Because the abiding of it in him is that which makes the man sensibly to know it, as aforesaid. Therefore if salvation sensibly abides in man's memory, as long as he lives he can be no more ignorant of it than a man that lives all his life-time in one house can be ignorant of it, enjoying his right mind.

Moreover, if you mean a, man may totally come to lose it after he hath had salvation knowingly abiding in him, that is utterly denied by us. Why? Because we certainly know that there was never any reprobate possessed with the grace of salvation knowingly abiding in him. Therefore in the parable of the sower you shall find, though the seed of grace did seem to scatter itself in every ground, yet it rooted itself but in one only; which "good ground, where it took root, brought forth fruit unto everlasting life, in some thirty, in some sixty, and in some an hundred-fold." So that it is clear, where salvation makes its abode, that man is safe from an eternal vengeance. But if you mean, through the committing some gross evils, a man may come to lose the sensible enjoyment of salvation abiding in him as formerly; and in its room, be often subjected with fears of condemnation, even all his days; I consent to it. For I am persuaded this was the prophet David's very condition. For in such cases I am apt to believe, that either God takes back the assurance of salvation to Himself, or else suffers the creature's light almost continually to be veiled with the darkness of his guilt, that when He sees good, He may glorify Himself anew, with a ministration of salvation to His afflicted creature. Furthermore you say, he is not sure that knows, but he is sure that God knows that he shall be saved. Also you say, that is not the best assurance which I call unquestionable, but that which is joined with fear and trembling, especially at this time. To this I answer: The happiness of man's salvation in this life consists, not in God's knowing of it, but in his own assurance of it. For if I want the sensible knowledge of my own salvation, I may be full of fears of condemnation all my days, notwithstanding the Creator's knowing of it. Therefore till I am possessed with an assured seal of my own salvation, what profit is it to me that God knows it? Wherefore' whatever you mean by fear and trembling, there is no creaturely assurance comparable to that which is always unquestionable; for that is freed from all faithless fear, or sinful trembling. "If you believe and doubt not, all things shall be possible," saith Christ. "If our hearts condemn us not, then have we boldness to the throne of grace." Sir, I have some experience of this, besides a spiritual fear and trembling before the infinite Majesty. But a carnal fear and a trembling before men, O Lord, preserve me from, for ever! You say also, the Spirit of the Lord came upon Saul, and upon Balaam, and they did prophesy by it. To this I answer, Moses, David, Samuel, Elijah, and many others, were anointed with the grace of spiritual prophecy, through which they became penmen of divine secrets and ministrators of holy things, even all their days. Wherefore though Saul was once among the prophets, and Balaam was compelled to declare good things concerning Israel, it doth not therefore follow, that they were the Lord's anointed prophets, to declare His salvation secrets to His redeemed ones. No, that could not be for none can truly declare such things, unless they enjoy them in their own souls. The secrets of God are with those that are possessed with the love and fear of His Majesty, through which they are not only delivered from the language of high swelling words, but also from the power of every proud imagination, that would exalt itself against the Lord, and His heavenly light within them. But this grace and favour of God abides not in them, in whom wickedness reigns all their days, as it did in king Saul, and in Balaam. Therefore salvation must needs be far from abiding in such men. But it appears to them only as a witness against them in the great day, for all their unrighteousness committed against the Lord and His anointed ones. Sir, if through inconsiderateness you imagine our condition of prophecy to be like Saul's or Balaam's, I hope you will bear with us for retorting them back again, among those that prophesy or preach without a spiritual commission from the Lord Jesus. Indeed, the Scriptures make mention of the fallacy and wickedness of divers prophets and priests that were rich: but, you shall never find it charge any poor prophet with falsehood, or cruelty to his neighbour.

5. In your fifth reply you say you do suppose they were so empowered and that every man; according to the proportion of faith in him, hath the same power. To this I answer, If you do but suppose it, you occasion a doubt in me whether you do really believe it; all speaking by way of supposition, to me seems doubtful; therefore you have left me wholly unsatisfied, in your answer to this part of my query. So that I have no groundwork of replication. You say also, there is matter of eternal condemnation in all; but the absolute eternal condemnation which we declare is not justified in your heart, neither do you see it justified upon any. To this I answer, If you mean there is sinful darkness in all which will suffer eternal condemnation, but all souls shall be saved at the last; I am not of that mind. Why? Because I certainly know, there is no sin or evil capable of the least suffering, unless it hath its being in a sensible spirit. Nay, moreover, an evil spirit and its darkness are essentially one: therefore they are undivided in their eternal sufferings. But if you mean, there is that in all that would naturally produce their eternal condemnation, if the elective love of God did not prevent it; I am of the same belief. For we certainly know, that the original cause of eternal salvation or condemnation lieth not in the power or will of the creature, but in the will and pleasure of the Creator only, whatever may be imagined to the contrary: for His is the kingdom, the power, and the glory." But if it lay in any excellence in the creature, it could not possibly then be avoided, but it would share with the Creator's power and glory in His everlasting kingdom. For as spiritual righteousness reigning in men to their death is not the primary cause of their eternal salvation, but the seal of it only; so spiritual wickedness reigning in men to their lives' end is not the absolute cause of their eternal vengeance, but the witness only. This truth is a stumbling-block to almost all men that own a Creator. Sir, the true prophets and apostles were absolute in their declarations, which they received from the Lord: so that, in your disowning the absolute pronunciation committed to our charge, you do through ignorance deny all that spiritual and temporal power that

was committed to the former commissioners, both in the law and in the gospel; and though at present you neither see it justified in yourself nor in any other, it doth not therefore follow that it is not justified, nowhere at all. Yea, for God knows, and by His light we know, also some of His elect know with us, that in this great city, His ministry in us hath occasioned the seals of eternal life and death to manifest themselves upon divers persons. If we had never seen any convincing effects in our ministry, because you have not seen it, truly we might have sunk long before now in the depth of despair. Yea, it would have been enough to have made us question the light of the sun, though it shone never so bright. If ever you come to see it, our God grant, if it be His good pleasure, that you may feel the eternal blessing of it in your own soul, and not the curse!

6. In your sixth reply you say, you do own yourself an experimental preacher, but cannot own an infallible knowledge of divine mysteries, above all other men in the world: if you should, it would be great pride of spirit; and you judge it so, in any that assume such things to themselves. To this I answer, It is granted, if you or I, or any man else, should assume such things to themselves, it savours of the greatest luciferian pride as possibly can be, and an extraordinary vengeance would undoubtedly attend such a presumption. But it doth not therefore follow that either you, or any other man in the world, can or ever shall prove us guilty of any such assumption. Sir, have you an infallible judgment concerning spirituals? If you have not, how can you be a competent judge in this thing? Is it possible, think you, for a man to be endued with the knowledge of divine mysteries above all other men in the world? I trow not; for I am apt to believe, it was the apostle Paul's very condition, from his own words concerning revelations above his brethren. But whether it was or no, it matters not: my business is to make my defence against your uncharitable or unadvised judgment concerning me in this particular. Sir, why are you angry with our God? Do you not know He will do what He will? Hear, O my friend William Sedgwick, I beseech thee hearken to what I shall say without offence. God, even the Lord Jesus that made us all, did, in plain words from the throne of His eternal glory, say unto me, that He had given me understanding of His mind in the Scriptures above all the men in the world: even to the hearing of the visible ear, as well as the invisible soul, were these His words spoken. Who then, think you, can in the least cause me to question my commission, or my condition, whilst the presence of these glorious and gracious words remains in my memory? No, the light of life shines too clear in me, for darkness to predominate over it, or any man's words to daunt it. All praise and glory to Him alone that gave it me. Wherefore, Sir, though you seem experimentally to warn me of a narrow lofty spirit that runs in us, and of high swelling words; in answer to this, from an infallible judgment, we boldly yet humbly affirm, that this your experience concerning us neither proceeded from the Spirit nor light

or Christ in you, but only from your own angry imagination. Because, by virtue of our commission, we declare that no man can truly preach Christ, without an infallible Spirit. The things of the Spirit are all infallible, and eternal: how then, think you, can they be declared by an uncertain, fallible, or imaginary light? O that our good God would once convince you of the danger of preaching from the letter, without a commission from the Spirit, by voice of words from above. And further you say, another experience you observe in me, that I and my friend have allowed preaching by experience, without any such lofty qualification which we now express, and therefore we ourselves are not true to what we declare. To this I answer, We did never allow any of our own faith, in a ministerial way, to preach to the people; nay, knowing the danger, they durst not do it without a commission from the Lord Jesus Christ. Moreover, after we had declared the contrary, did we ever allow any man, under pretence of speaking his experience, to pray and preach, and then conclude praying, in the priestly way of the nation in their satanical synagogues or anywhere else, in their vain-glorious hypocritical forms? I trow not. For then you might truly charge us with folly in this particular. If men, therefore, have been convinced with the deceitfulness of the national ministry, to wit, that their preaching is by way of art and trade, and not by the immediate teachings of the Spirit, as I suppose you and divers others have been, and yet shall walk in the same form of preaching; how can such men but be full of fears and doubts concerning the truth or authority of their ministry, whatever they pretend of speaking their experience to the people?

7. In your seventh reply you say, "Every one that goes without a commission is in danger of eternal vengeance. Therefore it concerns you and me very much to stand in awe, to tremble at the word, lest we fall under the curse for adding to or taking from His word." Also you say, you believe some will suffer for running before they are sent, and some for running beyond that which they are sent about. But concerning speaking, you desire me to consider how large a commission the Scriptures give. To this I answer, It is a work of the highest concernment that possibly can be, for a man to execute the office of a prophet or minister of Christ. Wherefore we unquestionably affirm, that all those that go into the ministry of the letter, without a spiritual commission, they are not only in danger of an eternal vengeance, but very few of them will escape it, that have been warned of it by commissionated messengers of the Lord's own sending. Therefore know, that neither your experience, nor the effects of your ministry, no, nor the Scriptures themselves, will bear you out in the day of trial, for want of that sure word abiding in you: "I the Lord have chosen thee to be a minister to my people." But as concerning a spiritual commissioner being in danger of eternal vengeance for falling short or going beyond his commission, that is denied by us. A temporal vengeance, indeed, attends them in such a case, as namely,

a whale's belly, or slaying by a lion, as Jonas and another prophet were. But if you mean he may have some secret fears of eternal vengeance in him for rebelling against the commission, that is not denied by us; but that he shall be in danger of it in reference to God's purpose, that we utterly deny. Why? Because we know that God anoints none with the spirit of heavenly prophecy but those that were elected to salvation before the foundation of the world was laid. For as men formerly, that were anointed with oil, had a cheerful countenance, so likewise all those that are anointed with the grace of spiritual prophesying or preaching, enjoy a cheerful and settled mind. Kings commit their secrets to none but favourites only; so likewise the God or King of Glory commits His secret counsel, by way of dispensation, to none but His beloved commissioners only. It is granted that all those that believe in the true Jesus are acquainted with a measure of God's secrets, according to the proportion of their faith: but the public declarations of them, as aforesaid, are committed to none in a prophetical or ministerial way, but those that are immediately sent forth by the eternal Spirit. "To you it is given to know the mysteries of the kingdom, but to them it is not given, or in parable only." To whom is it given? To chosen prophets or apostles only, that they might demonstrate them to their elect brethren. "When thou art converted," saith Christ to Peter, "strengthen thy brethren." It is true, the secrets of the Lord are with all those that serve Him with an upright heart, as before; but it doth not therefore follow that they are capable to manage them in a prophetical or ministerial way, for the convincing or converting their elect brethren into a real comprehension of them to their everlasting establishment. No; I say again, from an unerring light, none can do that but spiritual commissioners only. O that you, and all preachers that are of a merciful spirit, were convinced of this saving truth!

Moreover, you say, "David called upon all creatures and all men, kings and all people, and upon everything that had breath, to praise the Lord, " To this I answer, Did he call upon them all, or any of them at all, to praise the Lord in a prophetical or ministerial way, as he himself often did? I trow not; that was none of his intent when he uttered these words; for he knew that none but selected ones could do that. But it was an extraordinary comprehension of the love and goodness of God to his soul and body, which caused him with such zeal to call upon all breathing things to praise the Lord for His goodness towards them according to their kind or light, as he did according to his light. Also you say: "And therefore the apostolical ministry is to continue in the church in all ages; and Christ promises His presence with them and that ministry to the end of the world." To this I answer, If you mean an exact form according to the letter, as namely, visible praying, preaching, baptizing, breaking of bread, laying on of hands, anointing with oil, and such like; I know none capable to administer those apostolical ordinances for want of the gift of tongues and miracles. Whoever, therefore, imitates the apostles' ministry from the letter, are but scripturian usurpers and deceivers of their own souls and the people, for want of a commission from the Spirit, as aforesaid. But if you mean, Christ will own the invisible spiritual ministry of the apostles with His presence in His elect church or people, in all ages to the end of the world, we join with you. For whensoever the Spirit of Christ convinces a soul to believe the truth of the Scriptures, and to yield a spiritual obedience to them to the utmost of his power, it may properly be said, that He owns the apostles' ministry with His presence in the creature. Why? Because they were the penmen of those records of truth. Again, if a man, through the hearing of a national preacher, should be convinced of the truth of the Scriptures as aforesaid, what doth he do in such a case? Truly he justifies the ministry of the true prophets and apostles, and sits down in peace in his own soul, and becomes wiser than his teacher, by seeing him in the dark in spiritual things; and so hears him no more, but pities him. This is the condition of all those that are taught by the Spirit.

Now this I shall commend unto you, If any minister in the nation or world, mediately or immediately, were moved or sent by the Spirit of God to preach unto the people, no man would be capable to become his teacher. Why? Because the oracles of God are committed to such men only, upon the account of ministerial declarations. If David's teachers had been all Nathans, he would hardly have said he was become wiser than all his teachers. For I dare boldly say, there was never any of the apostles' hearers did attain to an equality of spiritual understanding with them. Why? Because the power and glory of God would be obscured and His messengers put to open shame, and the truth delivered by them subject to be questioned by all, if the hearers should become wiser than or equal with their commissionated teachers in things of eternal concernment. Sir, I would not have you guilty of calling the following truth out of its proper name, to wit: from an infallible light we declare, that God has chosen us two only, in this age, to bear witness unto Himself, and His invisible true teachings in His people by His Spirit, in opposition of all visible teachings in the world in a ministerial way, as false, vain, and of none effect to the preachers thereof, but rather a dreadful witness against them in the great day, for their ministerial meddling with holy things without a spiritual command. What answer doth the glorious Commissioner say He will make unto them, when they shall think to plead their ministry before him? "I never knew you. Depart from me, ye that work iniquity." That is, I never knew you as ministers of my sending; you have had the reward of your ministry already; you have had your souls' chiefest desire of riches, pleasure, or honour among the earthly honourable ones; whilst my poor messengers were afflicted with many necessities, persecuted and despised as dross, and deadly enemies against your ministerial happiness; you have had your reward already. Go, therefore, into everlasting shame with them that set you to work, whilst my poor messengers receive a crown of eternal glory in my kingdom, with myself and my holy angels, as a recompence of all their faithful sufferings for my name's sake. Be faithful unto the death, and I will give thee a crown of life.

8. In your eighth reply you say, when you did speak formerly, you were as fully satisfied as we are now satisfied in our ministry, neither do you now wholly condemn your former speaking, but you have seen an evil spirit that got into it; and you say it was not the least evil of that spirit that you did undertake to judge all others. To this I answer, If your satisfaction had been the same as ours is, it would have remained with you to this day, neither could an evil spirit have got into it if you have been kept unspotted of the world; for so long as a man is preserved from outward pollutions, the evil one in him hath no power over him nor his ministry, nor an evil spirit without him 'could have any power over him (if you think there is any). Moreover, if your satisfying ministry had been from the Lord, as you suppose it was, we verily believe an evil spirit could not have had power over it one day, no, nor yet one hour. For let me tell you, if your ministry had been of God, the higher the light had appeared, the lower would your soul have been humbled in the sight of your brethren. For though the true prophets and apostles had their natural failings through the manifold infirmities attending them in their ministry, yet an evil spirit of lofty exaltation above their brethren, because of their great light and favour with God, did never predominate over them. Indeed, a seeming glorious light proceeding from men's own imagination, is that which will not only exalt a man above his brethren, but also above all that is called God. Nay, it is so highly conceited with its own rational wisdom, that it would rather it had never had a being, if it may not bear rule over all inferiority or equality; it is an abomination to such a spirit. Therefore, if you now find an evil spirit captivated your former ministry, either with lofty conceits of an essential oneness with God Himself, or a triumphing over men with your empty notions and such like; what good thoughts soever you may have of that ministry in reference to the joy and glory you then possessed, yet we dare boldly say, from that God that sent us, that the head of that ministry was an angel of darkness. Furthermore, if that ministry of yours had been from the Spirit of God, though it had given judgment against all gain-saying opinions in the world, yet the Lord would have justified you in it. Why? Because the sentence proceeded from Himself. "We know," saith the apostolical commissioner, "that we are of God, and the whole world lieth in wickedness." In this saying the intent of the apostle was, not that they knew that all men in the world were in bondage to their own sinful lusts, except themselves. No; but the meaning was, that they certainly knew that their ministry was spiritual and of God, and that all the contrary ministry in the world was carnal and of the devil. Wherefore, Sir, whatever you think of your present ministry, the same

spirit remains in it as formerly. If you are moved, therefore, to acknowledge an evil spirit in your former ministry, that we might apply it to ourselves; truly, Sir, you have lost your labour in this particular. Why? Because we have the seal of everlasting satisfaction abiding in us, that our commission and declarations are of the Lord, whether they be unto eternal salvation or condemnation. If any man therefore can truly convince us of wrong done unto him since we received our commission, we are both ready and willing to acknowledge it and bear our shame. But as concerning our inward or outward failings towards God, in reference to our ministerial commission, the acknowledgment of such things belongs only unto Him, because none can cure it or pass it by but Himself only. For because we say the Lord only hath made us two His spiritual commissioners in this age, therefore we know that all men are subject to lie in wait to catch us, though they be taken in their own net.

9 and 10. In your reply to the two last queries, you say you are of this faith, "that God alone doth teach His chosen ones," but you omitted that clause, "by the inspiration of His most holy Spirit." And you say, "Yet Christ Himself taught, and His apostles taught, and the prophets taught." To this I answer, If you mean there is another spiritual God to teach men besides Christ, we disown that; for God is our Christ and Christ is our only God, who is a spiritual God-man, in one distinct person glorified. As for two or three distinct persons and but one essence, or an infinite formless Spirit, we own no such imaginary confusions. Yet we hold forth a three-fold spiritual trinity in unity and unity in trinity; under a threefold title of Father, Son, and Spirit. But this glorious mystery is operated only in the singular person of our Lord Jesus Christ, as aforesaid. Moreover, you say we likewise hold the same faith, and yet we teach. To this I answer, We have a commission from the Lord for our ministry; but we know that you have none, because you cannot own those words of "immediate" or "infallibility." And besides this, we deny that ever we used the national form of teaching at all. Indeed, when we first appeared there came divers unto us to prove our commission by way of queries; to whom we gave answers endeavouring their satisfaction. And this was and is, with our declarations by writing, our manner of teaching, adding this further; for the discovery of the ignorance and fallacy of all the ministry in the world and their formal worship, we are moved in a discoursive way, to treat of the foundation of spiritual things; which things were so opposite to some of the hearers, and did so enrage them, that they did not only condemn them as blasphemy and delusions of the devil, but would also willingly have torn us in pieces, and (some of them falling under the Lord's eternal sentence for their despising) with a warrant apprehended us. The Lord knoweth what we have suffered and are to suffer at the hands of merciless men, for His name's sake. Our joy and glory is, that our sufferings principally are for yielding obedience to His blessed command. Again you say, "God

teaches by His son, by His servants, by His word, by afflictions, and in all by His Spirit." To this I answer, as afore, God never did nor never will own any man as a teacher to his people, but him only that he commissionates. It is confessed, God teaches by his Son, which Son is Himself; or rather teaches in His Son, for that is most proper. For God was in Christ, reconciling the world to Himself; and God did teach by His commissionated servants, the prophets and apostles; but it doth not therefore follow that any shall be truly taught by you or me, or by any man else, unless we have a spiritual commission, as those his servants had. If we have, then we may be confident of a blessing in our ministry; otherwise our expectations will certainly come to nought. Sir, if you mean, all mankind are or may be capable of spiritual teachings; that is denied by us. But if you mean, all God's elect through the whole world are immediately taught by His Spirit only, in the things of salvation, where his commissioners are not; we join with you. Moreover, you say, for our commission received by voice of words you judge it not, but leave it to the Lord. To this I answer, though here you say you judge it not but leave it to the Lord; yet in your sixth reply, appears to me as harsh a judgment almost as possibly could be given. But seeing you have here disowned it, our God will pass it by. Sir, I now humbly beseech you seriously to consider what I shall write unto you, in relation to your true and lasting peace. In the holy name and power of our God, we advise you to cease from your ministerial way of preaching; not minding your honour in the thing, for you will never find any true peace in it, but the contrary altogether, after so clear a discovery of the fallacy of it, as this is. Christ Jesus our God never committed the ministry of His gospel to the rich, but He hath chosen the poor and contemptible things of this world for the confounding the mighty and honourable things thereof. If you should think that Paul was rich and honourable, I believe he enjoyed it but a very little season after his conversion. "I will have mercy and not sacrifice," saith our God. Sir, we have not looked upon you as one of the tithe-mongering ministers of the nation. Therefore in Christ's stead we desire you never to imitate them more in their hypocritical forms. For we are persuaded that God hath made you a steward of great possession, principally for a covering to many of His afflicted ones, in this hard-hearted time. Therefore go on, not in your ministry, but in your mercy, and prosper. For (whatever you may think to the contrary) all the peace you enjoy springs only out of the bowels of your compassion to helpless souls. "Love covereth a multitude of sins." "There is none can stand in judgment, but the merciful." "Blessed are the merciful, for they shall obtain mercy," saith our God. O the manifold real praises that ascend up to the Lord of Glory, through the charity of the merciful No man, nor angel, can ever speak forth the excellency of charity. Why are the most of our rich men uncharitable? Truly, because there is no spiritual light or love in them. "Howl, ye rich men," saith St. James. For what? Because you had no compassion to your poor afflicted brother, notwithstanding your bags of gold and silver. That rich man only that hath found mercy unto eternal life, is made very tender of men's natural lives, hot to give away a whole estate, from an imaginary call thereunto; that is none of our intent, the Lord knows, but to refresh the bowels and backs of the oppressed, with the overflowings of his possessions; that was the very intent of this exhortation. To conclude, In the peat day, the Lord Jesus seems to take notice of nothing else in the rich but their charity, or their want of charity, in that saying, "Come, ye blessed of my Father; when I was hungry ye gave me meat." "Go ye cursed; when I was hungry, ye gave me no meat." Thus you may see, it is not a rich man's ministry, but his mercy that will stand in stead in the great day. Sir, if you are not satisfied, I shall wait for your return. That no flesh may glory in His presence, the Lord Himself satisfy you in this, and all things else, that may further your eternal happiness.

This return was delivered into Mr. William Sedgwick's own hand, July the 30th, 1654.

The Prophet John Reeve's Answer to a Letter sent to him by Isaac Pennington, Esquire.

IN THE YEAR 1654.
See Acts of the Witnesses, 3rd Part, Chap. IV.

HAVING soberly perused thy last writing, and with much deliberation weighed it in the balance of divine truth, I doubt not but the Most High will move thy ponderous spirit to do the like without just offence at me.

Therefore, most acute penman, I confess, that in reference to my real understanding of the Holy Spirit, its wonderful commission,. and revelation, with the nature of my own spirit, I cannot but confess thy counsel is much like that of Jethro's unto Moses. Wherefore undeceiving truth being the only searcher of all spirits, by it I am first moved to write a little of man's unutterable deceits.

Friend, It is kindly confessed that man's carnal imaginary reason is an angel of such satanical depths, that the most high God-like men that ever were, have oftentimes been snared therewith. And why so? That they might not put confidence in any received light in them whatsoever, but with trembling spirits be abased before that infinite Personal Glory without them, from whence it proceeded.

Again, from the aforesaid darkness, a man may mightily counterfeit lying visions, signs, and wonders, concerning God, angels, and men, to the utter deceiving himself, yea, and the blessed ones also (if it were possible), for everlasting.

Moreover, I am filled with confidence, that a man by mere supposition may imagine to discern much weakness in the declarations of truth, from a man sent by the Creator; and to know the true God's various operations in his own soul, notwithstanding he owns no God or Creator at all, but an imaginary God only, which he calls an infinite, or vast Spirit, which is without form and void.

Furthermore, I am not ignorant now, that from natural parts and education only, a man may be endued with such sharp comprehensions, profound languages, divine sentences, and seeming self-denial, that neither man nor angel can possibly discover him, till the Lord Jesus makes him manifest by his fruits.

Again, I suppose it possible, that, from a meritorious conceit only, a man may have power to distribute all he hath to the poor, and give his body to the fire, and yet be but a cast-away, for want of acting mercy, in obedience from a divine light or love in him, to an infinite Personal God or Glory without him.

Moreover, because the serpent-angel, or devil in man's flesh, naturally winds itself into every good desire, thought, word and deed, oftentimes predominating over men's spiritual peace; therefore a son, full of God-like compassion, is subject to question his eternal inheritance, when an uncompassionate child, possessed with goodly words only, is under deep damnation and knows it not, until his light descend into sensible darkness of a fiery life or everlasting burning death.

In the next place, having manifested thy suspicion of the truth of my commission, or inspiration, as proceeding from the Spirit of all truth; or if true, of a thorough renewing of my spirit by it, or of walking Contrary to it; somewhat shall be declared in answer thereunto.

Friend, if thy light informs thee, that the most high and Holy One may empower a man in this age to declare divine secrets to the heirs of immortal crowns; is it not wisdom's way, rather to magnify himself in a contemptible vessel, than in that which is with riches and honour among men?

Again, be it known unto thee, that as a man speaks privately with his friend, so did the Creator Himself speak eight times distinct words unto my spirit, even to the hearing of the outward ear; by virtue of which powerfully I was sent forth to demonstrate the substantial things of eternity, prepared only for those spirits that proceeded out of the nature of the glorious Spirit of all variety of infinite excellences.

Therefore, though many angel-like men may be under their seasons of light and darkness, doth it therefore of necessity follow, that the commissioners of the unerring Spirit should be in the same condition?

Is it not more meet they should be preserved from the power of visible or invisible temptations, above all other men; seeing Paul-like, they have been and are to be abundantly tried, by serpentine spirits, in another manner, in relation to Him that sent him, concerning His wonderful secrets of eternal life and death upon the spirits and bodies of all mankind very suddenly?

Moreover, their persons being prevented from the honour or dishonour of riches, or any Worldly incumbrances, above many of their brethren; may they not, in all stillness of mind, have more communion with the Holy Spirit, concerning unutterable glories to come, than other men?

Moreover, being set apart to be more than ordinarily enlightened with a real understanding of the Personal Glory of an infinite Majesty itself; as soon as ever they feel the carnal serpent begin to sting, before it becomes a fiery serpent or dragon, to torment the whole man; may they not, by the light in them, look upon the Son of Man in His glory, and be immediately healed?

Again, it is written, "There remaineth therefore a rest to the people of God: for he that is entered into his rest is also ceased from his own works, as God did from His." What thinkest thou then of the restlessness often arising in wise men's spirits? May it not be for want of the power of love in them unto their poor brethren, from their mixing divine notions and carnal notions together, and building them upon an imaginary God, instead of the spiritual Rock of all Ages?

Moreover, if men, whose tongues and faces appear like angels in comparison of others, shall often be subjected with eternal snares; is God's eternal rest indeed manifest to such men?

Furthermore, though angelical subtile serpents, and simple doves, or childish saints, may be subjected to many sad soul-distempers, through ignorance of the spiritual foundation of glorious peace; yet may not those men, unto whom the living light hath manifested itself in power, be entered into their royal rest for ever, unless they are left to commit some known rebellion against the Lord, and His heavenly light within them?

Again, may not those men which enjoy the aforesaid divine rest, certainly know that the principal cause of many wise men's sorrows, whether rich or poor, is through want of a clear comprehension of the glorious Person of the high and mighty God? For if men's spirits were really acquainted with the Lord of all light and life, how could their souls frequently want spiritual rest, being virtually one with salvation itself? And how can those men but be as springs of settled light of life eternal, unto whose spirits an incomprehensible God of Glory hath appeared as the sun in his brightness? But, on the contrary, thinkest thou those men can possibly be freed from many agonies of deep darkness, who idolize a false God, or vainly imagine that no man is capable to know the true God, because He is infinite?

Moreover, though the Spirit of our Personal God, by virtue of its glorious Brightness, comprehends all spirits at once, yet, except men are enabled by the light of life in some measure to comprehend His infinite glory also, for what I know they may everlastingly perish.

Furthermore, though men or angels have no divine light of life in them, but from the influences of an infinite Majesty; yet thou mayest know, that His all comprehensiveness consists not in its spiritual Quantity, but glorious Quality only. If I should say to thee, that the Essence of an infinite Glory, in its quantity, is but as a spark of fire, canst thou or any creature disprove me? And if so, doth not His transcendent excellence so much the more appear to those which shall in some measure be enabled to comprehend so wonderful secrets?

Again, If thou art really convinced in thy conscience that there is a Creator, and dost truly understand Him to be a distinct Personal Glory from thee, and all things and places, as He is; then with us (which live in this light) thou must needs know, that the Spirit of our Lord Jesus Christ, God and man, in one person glorified, is called infinite, incomprehensible, vast, or boundless, upon the account aforesaid. O! would it not be a divine rarity, if but the honourable wise men should own this our God in power, and His glorious truths revealed by us His poor despised messengers? Why? Because they clearly discover the sandy foundation of all those who, through darkness, slight a Personal Glory, and adore an incomprehensible formless spirit, otherwise an infinite Nothing, but glittering words only.

Again, says he, "If the spirit of satan cannot utter great mysterious things, both concerning the creation and redemption, whence did those arise that John Robbins, and his prophets, did wonderfully utter in this kind?"

To this, from the light, may be answered, if the Spirit of an infinite Majesty had discovered John Robbins to thee as it did in love to me, about eight months before his recantation to Oliver Cromwell, thou couldst not then have possibly yoked us together; but the light of life in me imputes it only to thy not knowing of John Robbins' cursed tenets and carnal designs, when his own hellish darkness appeared in its power upon him, and those that were under the same deceit, by thee called prophets.

Moreover, notwithstanding thy carnal confidence, that divine mysteries may be truly declared by a satanical spirit: as to that, from a glorious light I am emboldened to affirm, that neither men nor angels from a false spirit acre capable to demonstrate the wonderful mysteries of creation and redemption. Why? Because thou mayest know, that the right understanding of all spiritual excellences is inclosed only in these two secrets. As it is written, "Why speakest thou to them in parables? He answered, and said unto them, Because to you it is given to know the mysteries of the kingdom, but to them it is not given."

Furthermore, are any secrets comparable with those of Christ's everlasting kingdom? Again, seeing all is not gold that glitters, was it the Spirit of God that moved thee to write, that His salvation secrets may be truly laid open by a lying spirit?

Moreover, suppose a man, by a natural instinct, be able to comprehend all men's ordinary experiences, yet this man hath not heard the voice of God at any time, neither certainly knoweth whether ever the Creator did speak to man or no; was it the Spirit of God moved that man to judge his writings, who hath not only heard the Lord's voice, but hath also inwardly both seen and felt the exceeding Brightness of His Glory, yea, and the dreadful horror of his own natural darkness, even as that man did who cried out, he was undone, when the glory of the Lord appeared in him? But who can attain to heavenly wisdom, till it be given him from on high? And can that man wait for a spiritual distinction between the things of eternal life and death, who already is possessed with great confidence that the choicest secrets of the Most High may be truly demonstrated by a diabolical spirit, notwithstanding himself hath no immediate commission or revelation from a known God or glory to build his understanding upon? But what shall I say to such an angel-like man as thou art, concerning the glorious and dreadful things of eternity, seeing thou art exalted in the midst of such notional and natural heavens already? Only this: The secrets of the Lord are with them that fear Him, and love Him, and His beloved ones, with His own pure love rooted in them, from a real understanding of His Personal Glory, in the wonderful mysteries of creation and redemption. But unto glittering worldlings, this light appears as weakness or foolishness; because it discovers the vanity of their perishing gods of gold, silver, precious stones, fleshly honour, good language, and such like. And how can they bear it, till a more excellent Glory powerfully presents itself unto them?

Again, thou advisest me seriously to consider, whether I was immediately moved by the Spirit of the Lord, to present that writing unto thee. As to that, if the love of God or man so shines in thy soul, that thou art not concerned in that epistle, blessed art thou above thousands. Nevertheless, it is unquestionably known unto me, and some others also, that the Creator will one day own the substance of that epistle as from His own Spirit, to the utter confounding of all gain-sayings for everlasting. Moreover, though natural wise men's God is health, wealth, honour, long life, and goodly words only, and who take the Creator's name in vain all their life long; yet I cannot forbear much mentioning of His Glorious Person, because He spake unto me from the third heaven, as He did unto Paul.

Furthermore, If the everlasting true God, in variety of spiritual discerning, hath appeared in thy soul, thou canst not then be a stranger to almost all that is here written: but on the contrary, if a spiritual majesty, with the Personal Glory, the glory of the elect and shame of the reprobates, at the great day is as yet veiled from thine eyes; then indeed what is here related may appear unto thee but as brain-fancies only. Nevertheless, except these substantial truths be written in thee, I aver, from that God from whom thou hadst thy being, that all thy former writings or speakings to thy brethren, as upon a spiritual account, were but as the language of a parrot.

Again, thou sayest, that I harp much concerning thy distributing thy outward possessions, in which thy spirit doth not at all answer mine. As to that, if thy spirit had been clear as to that glorious Spirit or God of real love or pity, through whose appearance my soul is preserved from those inward snares of eternal burning death in utter darkness; my epistle could not have been slighted by thee upon that account, except thy light persuades thee, that to improve thy talent for the exaltation of thy own relations only, is the greatest pitch of charity, and to feed thy helpless brethren only with goodly words.

Moreover, if, upon a spiritual account, thy soul hath travailed under the condition of eternal life and death; and upon a natural account, thou art acquainted with a condition of straitness as well as fulness: findest thou more inward satisfaction in bowels of enlargement, or when thou wast chained up from all brotherly pity whatsoever?

Furthermore, Though it be not in the power of any creature to think a good thought, or prevent an evil thought; yet if any man shall pretend experimentally to own a glorious God or Spirit of all variety of infinite love itself, and tender compassion to the sons of men, and shall neglect the spiritual duty, of doing as he would be done unto, from a conceit of waiting a divine motion thereunto, his heart may become as adamant to all God-like pity for evermore.

Again, thy language is like unto him that certainly knows that there is no hiding of men's serpentine wiles from the All-seeing glorious Eye. If thou speakest from thy own possessed light, thou knowest it to be impossible for any man to enjoy true and lasting peace, but from love increasing to an infinite Majesty, manifesting itself unto men, representing His glorious image. Nevertheless, blessed thou art above all temporal inheritors, if thou art guided to know when and how to act thy charity for divine enjoyment, according to the Spirit of the Lord.

Again, thou sayest, revelations are of great danger, and do lift up the flesh, making way for a greater fall, unless the spirit be sufficiently poised beforehand, by the natural growth and power of life, that maketh thee undesiring of any such thing, though thou acknowledgest it to be of esteem and worth.

To this I answer, doth not true wisdom teach men to speak or write in their own line, and not in another man's? Wherefore, seeing thou art so far unacquainted with the nature of divine revelation, that thou never didst desire it, how canst thou know thy affirmation to be true? Moreover, dost thou think it possible for any man really to know the nature of spiritual or temporal secrets, if his soul hath never tasted them? But who can blame thee for not desiring the knowledge of eternal excellences, if thou supposest it dangerous to enjoy them? Furthermore, if (according to thy declaration) thy soul is unacquainted with the operation of divine revelation, how canst thou then know the effects of it, upon my account, in another man? When Saul was travelling to Damascus, with a bloody intent to all that published the name of Jesus, was he fore-qualified to receive a commission, vision, or revelation from the Lord Jesus in glory? Wherefore, seeing the glorious power of divine revelation as yet veils itself from thy understanding, what moved thy pen to determine of it? Was it not the same spirit or light in thee aforesaid, which gave judgment concerning the mysteries of creation and redemption?

Again, may not the greatest appearance of light that ever was in men or angels become the deepest darkness in the end, except it be preserved with the holy inspirations of an infinite purity? It is confessed, there are degrees of this purifying light; but what thinkest thou, would it not have been better for all sorts of angelical speakers, or spiritual nonconformists, that they had never been born, if they enjoy not a measure of it before their death?

Moreover, though this everlasting light have not clearly manifested itself in thy soul at present; yet because thou mayest enjoy it in due time, when the Holy Spirit presents the superexcellency of it into thy spirit, therefore suffer me to write a little of the effects of it in my own soul.

From the truth itself, be it known unto thee, before I was possessed with this light, I wanted power to bear an angry word from any one living; but since this light became my guide, for bearing witness to my God's commission and revelation to our brethren in the flesh, I have been enabled patiently to bear many bitter words, blows, shame, and scorn, even before the powers, among brutish men, besides seven months' close imprisonment, and often in danger of life itself; yet for all this I was made willing to return good for evil to my sharpest per-secutors; wherefore (as most due is) all honour, praise, and glory be rendered' from elect men and angels to the God of all inspiration, for ever, lasting Also, the higher the vision appeared, the lower was and is my dark spirit humbled before its incomprehensible brightness; yet because I find doubting in thy spirit of a real discovery of my inward carnalities, therefore I confess to thee, that this light hath broken the head of an aspiring serpent in my flesh, that, John Robbins-like, would have exalted itself above all that is called God, and trampled His infinite glorious wisdom and heavenly love, in all His redeemed ones, under foot, if it had not been prevented by His divine appearance. Wherefore, that words may provoke thee to thirst after these unknown excellences, I say, that this light doth not only discover and destroy men's carnal rebellions against the Creator's Person, and show men the beauty of those inward virtues of eternal life through which their souls are delivered from judging things unrevealed, but it doth also enable them, in some measure, to comprehend an infinite Majesty itself, and His vast glorious throne, with the variety of transcendent excellences fitted for elect men and angels; and everlasting sensible burning death or wrath in utter darkness, which is stored up for all those that are left to exalt their own wisdom of words, above this inspiring light of the things of life eternal.

Again, thou sayest, thou shouldst have concluded with a solemn prayer for me, but that thou perceivest it so great an offence to me. As to that, who could have known thy formality by thy language, if thou couldst have contained thy light to thyself? Suppose thou art under literal, natural, or notional prayers, what virtue is there in them to cure my infirmities? Indeed, they may pacify thy own spirit if it be void of charity, for a moment, as David's harp quieted the merciless spirit of Saul.

Moreover, if thy light be spiritual, thou knowest then that an heir of immortal glory sounds a trumpet no more in his prayers, than his alms. Furthermore, if the light of God hath appeared in thy soul, then His love in thee undoubtedly beareth witness of the excellency of mercy above all sacrifice. Nevertheless, if, Cornelius-like, thy private prayers and alms are entered into the glorious ears of the Lord of Hosts, as the effects of His divine love abiding in thee, then what is aforesaid, concerning compassion to thy poor brethren, can be no offence to thee, it being but a repetition of thy own enjoyment.

Again, if in very deed, from a divine fulness, thou art not only bountiful to men's natural wants, but art often also compelled to pray for eternal blessedness upon a spiritual account; if thou hadst really known my condition, it would have appeared unto thee, that my soul was then, and now is, almost always in a frame of spiritual prayer and praises unto the Personal Majesty of our Lord Jesus Christ in the throne of eternity. Moreover, if thou art a praying man, thou mayest know, that that spirit which hath been filled with inspiration from a known God is so qualified, that it is ever hearkening to His divine motions, or full of heavenly desires for His elect brethren as his own soul, or spiritual liftings up for all conditions to the throne of divine excellences, or in continual expectation, not only of the invisible but visible appearing also of the divine Majesty, with His mighty angels, to make an everlasting separation between compassionate Israelites, and bowel-less Canaanites.

O Lord God, if through many fiery temptations, and almost unutterable afflictions, thy own beloved ones scarcely be saved, where shall merciless gilded-tongued hypocrites show their faces, which, for truth's sake, were never acquainted with any spiritual or temporal sufferings in their own persons in the least?

Furthermore, if thou approve of prayer to an infinite Majesty, I humbly beseech thee, are not the inward speakings of the spirit, in all stillness of soul, the only prayer? That is, to all those that are under the teachings of the Spirit. Note, I do not in the least deny the use of the tongue in prayer, and praises also, so that a man be undoubtedly moved thereto by the true light of the righteous Judge of quick and dead; but glittering words, flowing from natural parts only in merciless men, are abomination to our God, and His tender love in His new-born people.

I say again, blessed art thou above millions of mankind, if thou art one of this number; then for the most part thou knowest, that, earthly possessions are men's only God, therefore grievous to part with any of them in private upon the account of charity. Wherefore, to stop the mouth of an accusing conscience, instead of seeming mercies, thou knowest they offer up many blind sacrifices to an unknown infinite Nothing, but goodly words only; and so, for want of an enjoyment of pure love to an infinite known God, powerfully manifested to poor innocent men, representing His glorious person, through the excessive love and deceit of uncertain riches they everlastingly perish.

JOHN REEVE.

An Epistle from the Eternal Jehovah, or Jesus, unto that noble christian gentleman, styled by the name of the Earl of Pembrooke, wherein is recited an Answer to a public assertion of Isaac Pennington, Esquire, by the last true Messenger and spiritual Prophet of the Lord Jesus Christ, God and man in one distinct Person, blessed for evermore.

WRITTEN IN THE YEAR 1654.

See Acts of the Witnesses, 3rd Part, Chap. IV.

———————

Loving Friend and Brother in the only Lord of all truth, when you have perused this writing, if you shall count it worthy of the press, my desire is, for the truth's sake, that you would be pleased to further the publishing of it, because of my inability.

MOST COURTEOUS AND CHRISTIAN GENTLEMAN,

THAT good report of God-like compassion in you, especially unto the innocent lambs of, Jesus Christ, hath made me to present this epistle unto your spiritual consideration.

In the first chapter to the Corinthians, the 26th, 27th, 28th, and 29th verses, it is thus written: "After the flesh not many mighty, not many noble are called; but God hath chosen the foolish things of this world to confound the mighty things, and vile things of the world and things which are despised hath God chosen, and things which are not, to bring to nought things that are, that no flesh should rejoice in his presence."

Sir, It was my lot to peruse a printed book, written by Esquire Pennington, son of Alderman Pennington, of this city of London, which book is styled by the name of " Divine Essays: or, Considerations about several things in Religion." And among several expressions, in the fourth page of that writing are these lines, viz. "Now who knoweth whether those things which have been so contrary in all dispensations hitherto, shall not here meet? Life and death, heaven and hell, which everywhere else are at such a distance, may here touch one another, and agree sweetly together, and so fully that both their names and natures, whereby they did appear and were so various in their dispensations, may here be drowned and vanish; yet it is not, by either's real loss of anything whereby or wherein they differed, they become thus harmoniously united, but by their entering into a more perfect fulness; and he to whom this seemeth strange, and is so much offended at it, let him fairly answer me this following question:

"Were not heaven and hell in union in their root? Before they were brought forth, were they not at rest and peace in the power of God, from whence they were produced? Without controversy, whatever lay there lay in rest. Now did the Lord bring forth anything that He cannot bring back again? And who can say He will not? Surely everything most naturally breatheth after that condition of rest and fulness which it can enjoy in His bosom. Most certain it is, the vast Spirit of the Lord taketh in all things, howsoever it disposeth of them; whence they came, whither they return, there they are; and doubtless there they may be found in union and agreement by him whose spirit is quick and piercing enough. Happy is he that can read this truth in the Spirit of the Lord; but wretchedly miserable is he who frameth false imaginations is his own spirit, by the vanity of his own mind concerning it."

Sir, As the esquire, by his high imagination, was moved to propound, a hard question, so likewise the Spirit of God moved me to return him a soft answer, which is as followeth: Sir, by your writing I perceive that all experiences have passed through you concerning religion, or opinion among men, but you should not therefore have concluded your affirmation infallible, for the Lord shall fairly answer you by the hand of his poor despised messenger. And as with moderation you would have men to peruse your labour, the like is required of you; and as you count them happy, which are not guided by their own imaginations, so likewise happy are you, if you are preserved from judging the inspirations of the eternal Spirit of the Lord Jesus Christ by your high imaginary reason, which is utterly incapable to comprehend invisible things that are eternal, unless it be inspired into you from on high.

Sir, I confess, that if the Lord of Glory Himself had not spoken to me from His immortal throne by distinct words, voice to voice, as one man speaks to another, I could not possibly have set pen to paper to so high a query. Your question is this, were not heaven and hell at union in their root before they were brought forth?

From the true Spirit of the Lord Jesus Christ I answer you, that from all eternity, hell was a distinct being in itself, there was no harmonious union between it and the Creator; but light and darkness, life and death, heaven and hell, in the sight of God, eternally were distinct from one mother, both in their root and in their fruit.

But it will be said to me, how can I make this appear to any man's understanding? First, I shall speak something of the Creator Himself kand then, in order to the clearing this truth, unto those whose faith is strong in the true God, by inspiration from the Holy Spirit of the only true God, I declare that the Creator neither is, nor never wasp, an infinite or vast Spirit without any bodily form, as men blindly imagine, for want of a spiritual distinction in them. But from all eternity, that uncreated Creator of all sensible, spiritual, natural, and rational creatures, was a distinct, immortal, bodily substance, in the form and likeness of a man; only His divine form, or person, was an unutterable bright burning, fiery glory, in motion swifter than thought; and His divine excellence, as a crystal fountain or sea, infinitely overflowing in Him, as namely, pure faith, His almighty power, or heavenly love, His ravishing glory, or any spiritual glory or virtue that can be named.

Thus you may see, if the Lord will, that before any creature was formed to live in His sight, the eternal Majesty possessed His glorious joys by Himself alone. Now the original ground of all infinite variety of new spiritual wisdom, joy, and glory, that the Creator did enjoy, or foresee He should possess to all eternity, naturally sprang in Him, from His- incomprehensible knowledge of His own endless infiniteness, or from His perfect understanding of an eternal increase in himself of all manner of heavenly excellences to solace Himself withal, or men or angels that should be created by Him.

So much, as a brief description concerning the immortal person of the true God, His divine nature, and heavenly glory, that from eternity He enjoyed, before any living creature was formed in His sight.

Sir, If this demonstration of the only blessed Creator seem as a low thing, or as a paradox unto you, from the eternal Spirit of the Lord Jesus Christ, my counsel unto you shall be this, that you beware of the imaginary devil of unclean reason within you, because, since it possessed mankind, the nature of it is to exalt itself and its own earthly wisdom above the heavenly wisdom of its Creator, and by it to condemn the things of its God, because it cannot comprehend them. For since the fall of Adam, the devil and his angels, so frequently spoken of in Scripture, both great and small, are all clothed with flesh, blood, and bone; but men, for want of the knowledge of the true God, are utterly ignorant of the right devil also.

Again, when it is the good pleasure of the Most High to reveal Himself to you, as from His eternal free love He hath unveiled a glimpse of immortal glory unto me, then shall you know indeed and in truth, that the eternal God, and alone Creator of heaven, earth, angels, and men, and all living creatures, is now clothed with flesh and bone upon His glorious throne, even the man Christ Jesus, who inseparably is both Father, Son, and Holy Ghost or Spirit, in only one distinct glorified body, or person, to all eternity.

Again, if you acknowledge there is a Creator, and that this Creator is a distinct spiritual substance; and that there is but only one wise God and Creator, and no more; then without controversy the man Christ Jesus, that all true Scripture bears record unto, must of necessity be that unknown Creator and Redeemer of His elect, God alone, blessed for evermore, which men so much discourse about, as if the immortal, Personal essence or glory of this mighty God were all within them, and yet they remain utterly ignorant of Him; many of them glorying in this their darkness, as if it were the only light of eternal life in them not to know the Creator at all, and forsaking the truth of the visible record of the invisible spiritual God, the man Christ Jesus, by their imaginary blind reasonings they have converted the eternal spiritual truths of the only everlasting God into vain, empty, notional fancies, which they call the mystery of the history, when the Lord knoweth it is the Babylonish mystery of iniquity of men in darkness, in opposition to the true mystery of God, the everlasting Father, clothing Himself with flesh and bone as with a garment, and in that glorious body displaying the splendour of His spiritual beams into the spirits and bodies of elect men and angels to all eternity.

Sir, I would not willingly wear out your patience with a superfluity of words. Oh! bear with me a little, I humbly beseech you, and conceive it to be from the love of the divine voice of God Himself, our Lord Jesus Christ, in me unto you, and all of your sweet and tender spirit.

Again, in the next place, by inspiration from the Lord Jesus, I declare, that from all eternity, those elements of earth and water were uncreated substances, distinct from the ever-living Spirit, person, nature, or glory of the uncreated eternal God, or Creator of all living forms.

Wherefore, if you grant there was a time in which all things that have life had a beginning, then of necessity the Creater must from eternity reign alone, before anything was formed to live in His sight. Wherefore if you imagine the Creator to be an infinite or vast Spirit, without any bodily form; yet you cannot possibly deny, but that He must have a place to display His glorious life in or upon; so that (without controversy) earth and water, in respect of their matters and substances, must needs be eternal with God, or in His presence. Indeed it cannot be denied, that if the Creator should be an infinite or vast bodiless Spirit, as you have declared Him to be, but earth and water, and all things else, from eternity must needs be harmoniously one with Him. But as the Lord liveth, and all creatures that He hath made and formed into life, either for a time or to eternity, it is no such thing. For there is no such God, or vast bodiless Spirit, nor never was at all; but death, hell, or utter darkness were eternally secretly hid in those dark, dead, or senseless elementary substances of earth and water, only of themselves they could not appear to be, but must be produced by the powerful word of a sensible living Creator.

Thus it is clear, the glorious eternal God being all light and no darkness, all life and no death, all heaven and no hell; He could not possibly be essentially one with any living creature he had formed, as men vainly imagine. "For God is light, and in Him is no darkness at all;" as in John.

Again, but you will say unto me, I have not clearly answered you to the question. Why? Because if it be granted, that from all eternity the Creator was a distinct glorious person or form, whose spiritual nature was nothing else but light and life; and that the elements of earth and water were distinct substances from Him, and that death, hell, and darkness were secretly hid in them, yet they could not possibly produce any living life or living death of themselves, but were all brought forth by the ever-living Spirit of the Creator; then what was that spirit or life that entered into elementary earth or waters, but the divine nature of God Himself?

By inspiration, from the Holy Spirit of the Lord Jesus, to this I answer (the man Adam only excepted), that neither the elect invisible angels, who are spiritual bodies in the forms of men, whose natures are pure reason, nor any other living creatures, were of the same nature of His Spirit that formed them; but they were all variety of natures to one another, and to their Creator also. And in their kind, their natures or spirits were all pure in their creation, and in a sweet communion one with another, and with their Creator also, so long as, and no longer than, they continued in their created state.

Again, this secret I would gladly have the chosen of the Most High to understand, that herein lay hid the unsearchable wisdom of the Creator, by the almighty power of His word speaking into those substances of earth and water, from thence to produce as many several spirits or natures as seemed good in His sight; and yet wholly to retain the divine nature or essence of His own glorious Spirit in Himself, distinct from all those living forms created by Him, even as if they were not of Him, or created by Him at all.

Again, from the unerring Spirit of the Lord Jesus Christ, I declare, that it was impossible for the Creator to form both angels and men to be of His own divine nature. The ground of which impossibility is this, because His prerogative royal glory was the eternal wheel that moved Him to create any living creature in His sight; and if they had been formed of His own divine nature, I pray you what distinction of the variety of His power and wisdom could ever have been seen or known by men or angels? Nay, moreover, would not men and angels rather have been gods, or all creators, than creatures, in their creation, if they had been both in spirit and body of His own divine nature or

Spirit; and so were not capable to be changed from their created state, either to a more transcendent ascending God-like glory, or to an unutterable descending devil-like shame?

Again, in the Spirit of truth, and God of order and not of confusion, I humbly beseech you seriously to consider this truth, wherein all the eternal glory of God's creating of men or angels consists. Are there any bowels of love, mercy, or compassion in the Holy Spirit of the Creator? Is there any life, light, or ravishing glory in Him? Or hath He any power in Himself to do His own pleasure with His own glorious excellences? Or to do His pleasure with any creatures formed by Him? If thou shalt grant Him this His royal prerogative, then, without all controversy, this will follow, that unless He had created two vessels, of variety of natures or spirits, for a time to remain in their created purities; and in His appointed time and season did withhold the inspiration of His glorious light from them both by which they stood, that they might fall from their created state by their unlawful uniting of spirits or natures together, to produce two worlds, or two generations of people, for the manifestation of fixing His eternal love, light, life, and immortal God-like glory upon the one, and retaining the splendour of all this glorious excellences to Himself from the other; all His variety of new and glorious wisdom and power must have been veiled from men and angels, and they must have remained in their creation, like unto senseless stocks or stones, to all eternity, in respect of any spiritual or natural understanding of their Creator's infinite power, wisdom, or glory. It is written, "He made all things for His own glory, and the wicked for the day of wrath;" and "the carcasses of the rebels shall be cast out, where the worm never dieth, nor the fire ever goeth out." When you shall see visibly an increasing glory in God, and elect men and angels, then you shall know indeed the truth of what is written.

Again, I humbly beseech you, can there be any distinction between God, angels, or men, unless there be a variety of natures, or names, to manifest a difference between them? Can there now be any God at all, and no devil or devils? Can there be any heaven at all, and no hell? Or any light, and no darkness? Or any life, and no death? Or any eternal life and glory for some of the children of men, and no eternal death, darkness, or shame for other some of the children of men? Can you possibly think, either from true faith or sober reason itself, that one of these can be without the other? Doth not the one give a being to the other? Can you therefore possibly destroy the being of the one, and preserve the being of the other?

Now, by the true inspiration of God, you may see, in due time, that there is no possibility of an harmonious uniting of heaven and hell together, by their entering into a more perfect fulness, according to your description. But heaven must needs be distinct from hell, or else there can be no perfect heaven; and hell must be distinct from heaven, or else there can be no certain hell. Thee Lord my God, if it be

His good pleasure, preserve you from exalting your natural wisdom of earthly reason above the spiritual wisdom of true faith, which is the heavenly nature of the only wise God, the man Jesus in glory!

Again, I humbly beseech you meekly to consider what I shall write unto you, concerning your charitable thoughts of heaven and hell's uniting together at the last:

By inspiration from the God of all truth, I declare, that since the fall of man, Christ and His angelical believers, who are the lost seed of Adam; and Cain, and his reprobate, unbelieving, unmerciful generation, who are the seed of the angelical serpent;—thus, hell and heaven, or light and darkness;—were never in a spiritual union or communion together since they had a being, nor can possibly be reconciled, whatever men dream of, unity with the whole creation. These natures and names, conditions and places, whether of eternal life, light, and glory, or eternal death, darkness, and shame, are to be distinct and utterly opposite to one another, to all eternity as aforesaid, for the manifestation of His royal prerogative, of the variety of His heavenly glories unto some, whereby they become persons full of ravishing excellences, when time is no more, like unto Himself; and withholding the brightness of His love from other some, through which they become utterly darkness, eternally tormenting themselves with their former filthy rebellions, or the vain-glorious pleasures they lived in. Hence ariseth continually all variety of heavenly songs, from elect men and angels, unto the Brightness of His uncreated Majesty, because they are not also cast out of His heavenly presence with him.

Again, concerning those words of yours, "Most certain it is that the vast Spirit of the Lord taketh in all things, and doubtless they may be found in union and agreement by Him whose Spirit is quick and piercing enough;" from the Holy Spirit I declare, he that can prove this your assertion to be certainly true, as you have declared it, he hath or is endued with a spirit more spiritually quick and piercing, more wise and loving, or merciful, than God Himself, elect men, or angels, and may prove them all liars, both in the spirit and in the letter.

Wherefore, in opposition to this your opinion, from the Lord Jesus I affirm, that there is no spirit that over was created that returns into the Creator again; but they are to be distinct from Him in their essence for everlasting, that the Creator, to the visible sight of the creature, may remain to be the Creator, and the creature continue to be a creature, unto the glorious praise of His transcendent brightness, even face to face, World without end.

Moreover, when man dies, and turns to his dust again from whence he was taken, his soul or spirit doth not return into the Spirit of the Creator, as men, from Solomon's words, blindly imagine, who was no prophetical penman of the Holy Spirit of the Scripture records; but the soul, and all created life or motion, dieth within the body of man, and turneth to dust. Even as fire goeth out and turneth to ashes in an oven that is closed, for want of aerial motion, even so man's mortal fiery spirit goeth out like the snuff of a candle within his body, because he is shut up by the Most High from all airy or fiery motion, until the visible appearing of the mighty God and our Saviour in all His glory, with His mighty angels, to judge both the quick and the dead. Then, and not till then, shall every seed and spirit of mankind, that was sown in the heart of the earth by the almighty word or powerful decree of God, bring forth its own body in glory or in shame, and shall remain so to all eternity.

Again, by inspiration from the Holy Spirit of the Lord Jesus Christ I declare, that no spirit hath any sensible being distinct from its body; no, nor never had, nor possibly can have, neither of the Creator Himself, nor men, nor angels, nor any other created living form.

Wherefore the Creator is no such vast bodiless Spirit as you have described Him to be; no, nor ever was; but as from all eternity He was an immortal substance or body, distinct from elementary earth and water, so likewise He is now become a glorified body of flesh and bone, in the likeness of a man, and is essentially distinct from men and angels to all eternity; and the compass or substance of His glorious Person is no bigger than a man is, and the essence of it is but in one place at once. Only take notice of this, that His little eyes are so transcendently bright and glorious, that at one look or view they pierce through heaven and earth, angels and men, and at once, or one word speaking, through His heavenly mouth, it entereth (if it be His pleasure) into all the spirits of men or angels, or into one man's or angers spirit only; so that all things in heaven or earth, or under the earth, continue acting His pleasure, by the almighty power of His word that He hath spoken, or shall speak, notwithstanding the essential being of His bright burning glorious Person is distinct from them all, as one man's person is distinct from another. This is the only very true God and eternal life to believe, or eternal death not to believe, or rather to despise it.

And now, in the last place, I shall write a little of eternity itself. That which is essentially everywhere is not infinite, but finite, or rather no living thing at all.

Wherefore, that God or Creator that is so essentially vast, that all places and things become as it were a God, that can be no God nor Creator, nor being of beings at all, but mere senseless earth or water, stocks or stones.

But, as aforesaid, He is an ever-living true God, Creator, or pure spiritual substance, which is but of small circumference, and whose glorious essence or personal substance is resident but in one place only at once; and yet, by the power of a word speaking, through His heavenly mouth, all variety of spiritual or natural wisdom floweth into the spirits of men or angels, like rivers of living waters, and naturally returns back again all honour and glory unto the uncreated Fountain of all eternal excellences.

Thus desiring the Lord, the Most High, to reveal the true

understanding of Himself unto you and all His chosen ones, I remain yours, in the eternal Spirit of love itself, and witness unto the only very true God, the man Jesus, aforesaid,

JOHN REEVE,

A pilgrim and stranger unto the blind vain-glorious age of confusion in religion, or notional opinion.

The Prophet Reeve's Epistle to his Kinsman.
WRITTEN IN THE YEAR 1654.

KINSMAN, unknown in the flesh, but well known in the spirit, by the divine seed or voice of love speaking in me, and the Holy Spirit of the glorified body or Person of the Lord Jesus and everlasting Father, present I these lines unto your spiritual understanding.

Loving friend in Jesus Christ, you long professing a desire of knowing the very true God, that you might, by His power in you, render all glory to His eternal Majesty, which is not hid from me: likewise it is made known unto me (you being of an inquiring spirit after truth), that there hath come to the view of your understanding almost all seeming spiritual appearances since the delusions thereof; and that that one, eternal, true, and only wise God, the Lord Jesus Christ, my Creator and alone Redeemer, within whose blessed body essentially abide all immortal crowns of eternal glory, would reveal Himself unto you, and to all those meek and patient souls that are so united to the love of such spiritual things which are eternal, that they are made to trample upon all the perishable vanity of honour among men, as dung, and snares of eternal death, appointed for all men and women, which with their tongues seem to love the Lord Jesus and His innocent people above all others, but in their hearts and souls this world, and the glory thereof, is their only heaven. You may know that they are those glittering Pharisees, which take upon them, by the letter of the Scriptures, to judge the inspirations of God in His chosen ones, because they are contrary to their quaint formalities.

Again, there is another generation deceived, called "Ranters," which are looked upon as the elect of God, that are spiritually weak, as the only inward lights in this land.

These are those that glory of a union with a God or Christ within them, calling themselves eternity, or everlasting love, and one pure being with the Creator; and when they are sifted, they call themselves the very Creator, utterly denying the Lord Jesus Christ and the Scriptures, and the resurrection of mankind after death, either to glory or shame. These are those (or the generality of them) which act all uncleanness, and cursedly call it the appearances of God in them.

There are many of the tender-spirited elect of God among them which are of their lying opinion, but are kept from their abominable practices because of the Lord's eternal love towards them; who, in due time, will call them back again.

There are many other seeming strange appearances, both in city and country, which pretend to be called or sent forth by the power of God coming upon them at certain seasons, deceiving their own souls, many being deceived also.

Friend, the Lord of Glory hath been pleased to make choice of me, the weakest of ten thousand, for the discovery of all appearances or opinions in the world, that are not by inspiration from the Holy Spirit of the Lord Jesus Christ; for there is not any seeming spiritual appearance in this land of any account that hath not, by the hand of the Lord, been weighed by the gift of the Holy Ghost or Spirit in me; and by this I find them too light in the spiritual balance of the living God, in that they know no God at all but what is within them, nor that either.

Loving kinsman, I am not ashamed to tell you, that the Lord Jesus Christ counted me worthy, for His name's sake, in the city of London, to have such a trial with the chief magistrates thereof as never was in this land, nor I am sure ever shall upon any account again. Seven months was I, and one more with me upon the same account, close prisoners, chiefly for our declaring Jesus Christ in glory to be the only wise God and man, in one distinct Person, and the Creator of all things, and the alone everlasting Father.

And now, being utterly released from bonds, I was moved to see my own native country, and not only that, but also to see your city of Bristol, because in it are some that have received the everlasting gospel,—I mean, the man Jesus in glory, to be the very true God, and none besides Him; for which spiritual power in them, in love to that glorious God, from that eternal love of His glory they are made willing, not only to act all righteousness to all men, but to suffer all kind of wrong also, returning good for evil, in full expectation of the sudden visible appearing of the Lord of life and glory in the air, with all His mighty elect angels, to judge both the dead and the quick; I mean, to make an eternal separation between the persons of the elect and the persons of the reprobate. For this I would have you to understand (if it be His good pleasure who is both Father, Son, and Spirit in one distinct glorious Person), that, except Moses, Enoch, and Elias, whose persons were translated into the highest heavens in glory, all mankind, elect and reprobate, both souls and bodies, are dead asleep in the dust of the earth, until Christ cometh in His glory.

Then shall the elect, by the decree or voice of Jesus Christ the Archangel, first appear out of the graves, and in the twinkling of an eye, with all the elect that are then living, as one man, with a glorious shout, shall, with distinct immortal bodies, like unto their God, ascend to meet the Lord in the air, and with Him and His mighty angels, as swift as thought, enter into that infinite vast new heaven and new earth above the stars, where actual sin was never committed against Him, there visibly beholding His glorious Person face to face; and the persons of elect men and angels naturally singing new songs and glorious praises, in eternity to eternity, unto their blessed Redeemer.

Then immediately also shall the reprobates appear out of the dust, with bodies of a descending nature, according to their former earthly-mindedness. My meaning is this: their bodies spiritually shall be as dark as pitch, and naturally as heavy as lead; and their own spirits shall be the devil, and their own bodies shall be their prison of hell; which, through the absence of the voice or motions of the Spirit of God in them as formerly, and the presence of all their former glory and filthy thoughts, imaginations, actions, and their desires, their spirits shall burn with an envious living death and dying life, beyond all natural fire whatsoever; and their flesh shall burn above all natural brimstone, never seeing one another's dreadful faces, nor stirring their bodies from the place they appear in to all eternity. And the reason of this their utter darkness, both within and without also, will be this: because the sun, moon, and stars, with all their natural lights within this world, through the absence of the Lord Jesus, will go out like the snuff of a candle; and all the glory of this whole world, from the firmanent of heaven to the earth, will be burnt up and vanish like smoke, and come to nothing; the seas and rivers or springs shall be dried up as if they had never been, and the earth that we now tread upon shall be like unto the fiery burning sands, suitable for those hellish firebrands who, at this time, in the days of their mortality, despised to yield obedience to the spiritual Person of the Lord Jesus Christ, and scoff at all purity in His angelical saints.

You are my beloved kinsman in the spirit, if you are made one with what I have written; for as sure as the Lord liveth, and as certain as you are a man of flesh, blood, and bone, what I have written is as true as truth itself, and will suddenly come to pass. Oh! blessed are all those which long for the second and last appearing of Almighty God, who alone, by His own precious blood-shedding, hath redeemed elect mankind from the wrath of eternal death, before mentioned in this epistle.

Your kinsman, in the only eternal pure Being, and glorious Fountain of all streams in elect men and angels, the Lord Jesus Christ, infinitely transcending all heavens, angels, or men,

JOHN REEVE,

The Son of Walter Reeve, deceased, commissionated Messenger of the Lord Jesus Christ, by voice of words from on high.

Lightning Source UK Ltd.
Milton Keynes UK
UKOW032127300513

211529UK00004B/48/P